Trading and Exchanges

FINANCIAL MANAGEMENT ASSOCIATION
Survey and Synthesis Series

The Search for Value: Measuring the Company's Cost of Capital
Michael C. Ehrhardt

Managing Pension Plans: A Comprehensive Guide to Improving Plan Performance
Dennis E. Logue and Jack S. Rader

Efficient Asset Management: A Practical Guide to Stock Portfolio Optimization and Asset Allocation
Richard O. Michaud

Real Options: Managing Strategic Investment in an Uncertain World
Martha Amram and Nalin Kulatilaka

Beyond Greed and Fear: Understanding Behavioral Finance and the Psychology of Investing
Hersh Shefrin

Dividend Policy: Its Impact on Firm Value
Ronald C. Lease, Kose John, Avner Kalay, Uri Loewenstein, and Oded H. Sarig

Value Based Management: The Corporate Response to Shareholder Revolution
John D. Martin and J. William Petty

Debt Management: A Practitioner's Guide
John D. Finnerty and Douglas R. Emery

Real Estate Investment Trusts: Structure, Performance, and Investment Opportunities
Su Han Chan, John Erickson, and Ko Wang

Trading and Exchanges: Market Microstructure for Practitioners
Larry Harris

Trading and Exchanges

Market Microstructure for Practitioners

LARRY HARRIS

UNIVERSITY PRESS

2003

OXFORD
UNIVERSITY PRESS

Oxford   New York
Auckland   Bangkok   Buenos Aires   Cape Town   Chennai
Dar es Salaam   Delhi   Hong Kong   Istanbul   Karachi   Kolkata
Kuala Lumpur   Madrid   Melbourne   Mexico City   Mumbai   Nairobi
São Paulo   Shanghai   Singapore   Taipei   Tokyo   Toronto

Copyright © 2003 by Oxford University Press, Inc.

Published by Oxford University Press, Inc.
198 Madison Avenue, New York, New York, 10016
www.oup.com

Oxford is a registered trademark of Oxford University Press

Library of Congress Cataloging-in-Publication Data
Harris, Larry, 1956–
    Trading and exchanges : market microstructure for practitioners /
Larry Harris
        p. cm.—(Financial Management Association survey and synthesis
series)
Includes bibliographical references and index.
    ISBN 978-0-19-514470-3
    1. Markets.   2. Exchange.   3. Commerce.   I. Title.   II. Series.
    HF5470 .H37 2002
    332.64—dc21

                                                                2002004622

28 27

Printed in the United States of America
on acid-free paper

This book is dedicated to the memory of the victims
of the September 11, 2001, terrorist acts
in New York, Virginia, and Pennsylvania
and to the honor of those people
whose heroic actions on that day saved so many lives.

Acknowledgments

Many people contributed to the success of this project with their encouragement, advice, knowledge, and expertise. I would not have started this project without their interest, and I would not have completed it without their support. The book is much better for their contributions.

I received my first encouragement as a graduate student at the University of Chicago, long before I knew anything about market microstructure. Professor Arnold Zellner advised me to publish a book based on lectures I would give when I became a professor. Although it seemed unimaginable to me at the time, I never forgot his advice or his confidence in me. I look forward to the time when I will read a book written by one of my students.

Several publishers suggested that I write this book. I particularly appreciate the interest shown by editors Mike Junior, Randall Adams, Maureen Riopelle, Kenneth MacLeod, and Paul Donnelly. I have no doubt that they all would have been very helpful in the development of this book. I regret that I could not work with them all. Their encouragement, enthusiasm, and vision helped kindle and sustain my interest.

This book would not have been possible without the many insights that I learned from my academic colleagues. I especially appreciate the lessons that they taught me, and the strong expressions of interest and valuable constructive criticism that they have given me. I wish to acknowledge the following colleagues by name:

Anat Admati	Doug Foster	Eugene Kandel
Yacob Amihud	Jennie France	Jon Karpoff
Jim Angel	Bill Freund	Don Keim
Gail Belonsky	Mendy Fygenson	Laura Kodres
Hank Bessembinder	Stuart Gabriel	Pete Kyle
Bruno Biais	Ann Gillette	Josef Lakonishok
Bernie Black	Tom Gilligan	Charles Lee
Fischer Black	Larry Glosten	Ruben Lee
Marshall Blume	Charles Goodhart	Bruce Lehmann
Michael Brennan	Sandy Grossman	Ken Lehn
Corinne Bronfman	Joe Grundfest	Marc Lipson
Mark Carhart	Eitan Gurel	Andy Lo
Henry Cheeseman	Yasushi Hamao	Francis Longstaff
Kal Cohen	Puneet Handa	Bob Lucas
Harry DeAngelo	Joel Hasbrouck	Craig MacKinlay
Linda DeAngelo	Kaj Hedvall	Ananth Madhavan
Ian Domowitz	Pierre Hillion	Steve Manaster
Rob Engle	Craig Holden	Terry Marsh
Wayne Ferson	Kose John	Tom McInish
Steve Figlewski	Charles Jones	Haim Mendelson
Margaret Forster	Avner Kalay	Morris Mendelson

Bob Miller

Mert Miller

David Modest

Dale Morse

Belinda Mucklow

Harold Mulherin

Rob Neal

Anthony Neuberger

Maureen O'Hara

Daniel Orr

J. Peake

André Perold

Mitch Petersen

Paul Pfleiderer

Avri Ravid

Mark Ready

Jay Ritter

Kevin Rock

Ailsa Roell

Tavy Ronen

Ehud Ronn

Mark Rubinstein

Tony Saunders

Myron Scholes

Bob Schwartz

Eduardo Schwartz

Bill Schwert

Duane Seppi

Kuldeep Shastri

Alan Shapiro

Eric Sirri

Sy Smidt

Vernon Smith

Chester Spatt

Sanjay Srivastava

Jim Stancill

Laura Starks

Dave Stewart

Hans Stoll

René Stulz

Avanidhar
  Subrahmanyam

Sheridan Titman

Walt Torous

Anand Vijh

S. Viswanathan

Dan Weaver

Mark Weinstein

Ivo Welch

Ingrid Werner

Randy Westerfield

Bob Whaley

David Whitcomb

Joe Williams

Bob Wood

This book would not have been creditable were it not for the many practitioners and regulators who have shared their time with me to explain what they do. I particularly appreciate the generosity and encouragement that the following individuals have extended to me:

Stanley Abel

Howard Baker

Frank Baxter

Brandon Becker

Gil Beebower

Jeff Benton

Dale Berman

Charles Black

David Booth

Harold Bradley

Kurt Bradshaw

Pearce Bunting

Richard Cangelosi

Jim Cochrane

David Colker

Cromwell Coulson

Larry Cuneo

David Cushing

Harry Davidow

Pina DeSantis

Mike Edleson

Jim Farrell

Tom Fay

Gene Finn

Ed Fleischman

Russ Fogler

Gifford Fong

Stuart Fraser

Dean Furbush

Jim Gallagher

Gary Gastineau

Brian Geary

Steven Giacoma

Jim Gilmore

Phil Ginsberg

Gary Ginter

Keith Goggin

Wendy Gramm

Dick Grasso

Bob Greber

Leo Guzman

Spence Hilton

Dave Hirschfeld

Blair Hull

Billy Johnston

Rick Ketchum

Rick Kilcollin

Ray Killian

Howard Kramer

Ken Kramer

Arthur Leavitt

Charlie Lebens

Marty Leibowitz

Dave Leinweber

Rich Lindsey

Evelyn Liszka

Bob Litterman

Bill Lupien

Bernie Madoff

Peter Madoff

Steven Malin

David Malmquist

Tim McCormick

Dick McDonald

Seth Merrin

Dick Michaud

Mark Minister

Nate Most

Annette Nazareth

Gene Noser

Bill Pratt

Eddie Rabin

Murali Ramaswami

Bill Ryan

Henry Sasser

Evan Schulman

Andy Schwarz

Christina Sciotto

Jim Scott	Eric Sorensen	Genie Williams
Jim Shapiro	Olof Stenhammar	Steve Wallman
David Shaw	Rob Tesar	Steve Wunsch
Katy Sherrerd	Artie Tolendini	Steve Youngren
Fred Siesel	Jack Treynor	Dorit Zeevi
Deborah Soesbee	Wayne Wagner	
George Sofianos	Jeffery Wecker	

Four people particularly influenced the development of this book. Wayne Wagner thoroughly reviewed an early draft of the manuscript. His suggestions greatly improved every part of the book. Craig Holden used early drafts of the text in his trading course at Indiana University. I am especially indebted to him for the confidence and vision he expressed to various publishers. Ananth Madhavan commented on early drafts of the book and supplied many bibliographic references. I have greatly appreciated having him as a colleague at USC. Finally, Jack Treynor was instrumental in helping me appreciate the importance of the zero-sum game in trading. Most principles of market microstructure somehow involve properties of zero-sum games.

Several generous sponsors provided financial support for this project. I received "angel financing" from the New York Stock Exchange (Dick Grasso, Billy Johnston, Jim Cochrane, and George Sofianos), the Jefferies Group (Frank Baxter), Mellon Capital Management Corporation (Bill Fouse and Tom Loeb), Bernard L. Madoff Investment Securities (Bernie and Peter Madoff), First Canada Securities International (Jim Medlock), Cantor Fitzgerald (Stuart Fraser and Phil Ginsberg), and First Quadrant (Rob Arnott). Their early support allowed me to take time off from my teaching to start this project. I am also grateful to Oxford University Press, which provided a developmental grant with which I was able to pay research assistants.

I appreciate the support provided to me by the USC Marshall School of Business through the Fred V. Keenan Chair in Finance. The generosity of our donors has been instrumental to the remarkable development of our faculty, school, and university over the last ten years under the leadership of Marshall School deans Jack Borsting and Randolph Westerfield, and USC president Steven B. Sample. Our most important accomplishments appear in the largely unseen influences that we have upon our students, and upon the policy makers and business executives who rely upon our research when making significant decisions. Our work rarely provides us with suitable opportunities to thank everyone who makes it possible. I am grateful for this opportunity to thank our donors for their confidence, vision, and support. I am especially pleased to recognize Fred Keenan, whose loyalty and generous support to the university have been an inspiration to us all.

Many people at USC helped me with the preparation of the manuscript. I am grateful both for their contributions to this book and for teaching me to write better. I gratefully thank my research assistants—Namrata Aggarwal, Chris Bandouveris, Claire Yu Cui, Shane Enete, Cynthia Lee, Jeff Lin, Jennifer Ly, Anna Nguyen, Venky Panchapagesan, and Jia Ye—and my departmental assistants—Deborah Jacobs, Marilyn Johnson, Terry Lichvar, and Helen Pitts. I am particularly pleased to recognize Cynthia Lee for her very extensive assistance with grammar, style, and proofreading.

Several people were notably helpful with proofreading early drafts. I thank Jennifer Chang, Abby Harris, Naftali Harris, Naomi Harris, Hai Lu, and especially Joey Engelberg for the careful attention that they paid to the manuscript.

My family and friends also contributed to the successful completion of this book in more ways that would be appropriate to list here. I particularly appreciate the support given to me by Alex Baskin, Jack Birns, Brian Greene, Bernard Harris, Devera Harris, Sam Jason, and Alissa Rimon. My wife, Abby, and my children were especially supportive. Without their support, I would not have attempted or completed this project.

My editors at Oxford University Press were extremely helpful with the development of this book. Copyeditor Beth Wilson and Managing Editor Lisa Stallings are skilled professionals whose contributions regrettably are rarely well recognized. They did an excellent job and were a pleasure to work with. I particularly appreciate the contributions of Executive Editor Paul Donnelly. Paul's vision brought this project to Oxford; his guidance greatly improved the book; and his promotion ensured that others would appreciate it.

Finally, I am indebted to the many students at USC who studied with me in my Trading and Exchanges course. Their interest in trading encouraged me to first offer the course in 1991. This book grew out of the lectures that developed to present the course to them. The lessons that I learned from my students while teaching Trading and Exchanges greatly influenced the organization and presentation of the topics that appear in this book. I believe that I have learned more from my students than from anyone else.

I have inevitably failed to acknowledge many people who richly deserve it. Regrettably, the ability to remember names easily is not one of the many gifts that I enjoy. Please forgive me for my oversight.

Thank you to everyone who has helped make this project successful.

Contents

Trading and Exchanges

Introduction

Markets are fascinating. They change constantly as prices adjust to new information, as winning traders replace losing traders, and as new technologies evolve.

Highly skilled professional traders employ clever strategies in their search for trading profits. They ultimately profit from investors, gamblers, and foolish traders.

The stakes in some markets are very high. Traders may arrange multimillion-dollar trades in seconds. They sometimes make or lose fortunes overnight.

The prices that traders negotiate ultimately determine how market-based economies allocate their scarce resources. Free economies owe much of their wealth to their well functioning markets.

1.1 SCOPE OF THE BOOK

This book is about trading, the people who trade securities and contracts, the marketplaces where they trade, and the rules that govern trading. You will learn about investors, brokers, dealers, arbitrageurs, retail traders, day traders, rogue traders, and gamblers; exchanges, boards of trade, dealer networks, ECNs (electronic communications networks), crossing markets, and pink sheets; single price auctions, open outcry auctions, and brokered markets; limit orders, market orders, and stop orders; program trades, block trades, and short trades; price priority, time precedence, public order precedence, and display precedence; insider trading, scalping, and bluffing; and investing, speculating, and gambling. This book will teach you the origins of liquidity, transaction costs, volatility, informative prices, and trader profits.

This book is not about the securities and contracts that people trade. We will not consider how to value them, who should trade them, how to design them, or how to issue them. Books about investments and corporate finance examine these questions.

Market microstructure is the branch of financial economics that investigates trading and the organization of markets. This field of study has substantially grown in size and importance since the October 1987 stock market crash.

This book presents the economics of market microstructure in simple English prose. Although some simple mathematics and graphics appear in a few supplementary examples, I fully explain all essential concepts in the main text.

1.2 OBJECTIVES

This book will help you understand how markets work, and how governments and exchanges regulate them. You will learn how prices come to reflect information about fundamental values, who makes markets liquid, and why some traders consistently profit from trading while others lose. You will be able to predict how various trading rules affect price efficiency, liquidity, and trading profits. Finally, you will understand the forces that govern regulatory processes.

With this knowledge, you can improve your trading strategies, and you can better manage the brokers who work for you. If you are—or aspire to be—a regulator or an exchange official, this knowledge will help you design better markets.

The primary objectives of this book are to understand the origins of the following characteristics of market quality:

- *Liquidity* Traders and regulators often talk about liquidity, but they are rarely careful about what they mean. This book explains what liquidity is, and where it comes from. If you intend to offer or take liquidity, you must understand it well.

- *Transaction costs* Traders must effectively manage their transaction costs to trade successfully. This book explains how to measure and manage transaction costs. If you trade actively, you must understand transaction costs.

- *Informative prices* Speculators must understand how and when prices become informative in order to trade successfully. Informative prices are essential to the wealth of our economy. This book explains the processes by which prices become informative. If you intend to speculate, you must understand price efficiency.

- *Volatility* Traders care about volatility because it can have a significant impact on their wealth. This book explains how prices become volatile, and how regulators try to control volatility. If risk scares you, you must understand volatility.

- *Trading profits* Trading is a zero-sum game in which some traders win and others lose. Traders who do not expect to win should refrain from trading. This book explains why some traders consistently win while other traders consistently lose. If trading profits interest you— whether you manage your trading yourself or have someone manage it for you—you must understand what determines trading profits.

The secondary objective of this book is to understand how market structure—trading rules and information systems—affect each of these five market characteristics.

1.3 INSTRUMENTS AND MARKETS

Market microstructure examines organized trading in instruments. *Instruments* include common stocks, preferred stocks, bonds, convertible bonds, warrants, options, futures contracts, forward contracts, foreign exchange contracts, swaps, reinsurance contracts, commodities, pollution credits, water rights, and even many betting contracts. Most ideas discussed in this book apply equally well to trading in all these instruments.

Legislatures and judges have created numerous legal definitions of the term "security." These definitions often distinguish between instruments that represent ownership of assets like stocks and bonds (usually called securities) and instruments that derive their values from commodities or from other security values (derivative contracts). They also universally exclude betting contracts. We will pay attention to these distinctions only when they affect the markets through the regulatory process.

A *market* is the place where traders gather to trade instruments. That place may be a physical trading floor, or it may be an electronic system in which traders can easily communicate with each other. The New York Stock Exchange, the Chicago Mercantile Exchange, and the EuroNext Amsterdam Options Exchange are examples of markets where traders meet on trading floors. Nasdaq, the Euronext, the Hong Kong Futures Exchange, and the interbank foreign exchange market are examples of electronically linked markets. This book considers how trading markets are organized and how their rules affect traders.

1.4 A BRIEF OVERVIEW OF TRADING AND EXCHANGES

This section gives a brief overview of some main points introduced in this book. It provides you with an outline of what you can expect to learn from this book. Do not be alarmed if you do not understand it all now. The remainder of the book explains everything in detail.

Trading is a search problem. Buyers must find sellers, and sellers must find buyers. Every trader wants to trade at a good price. Sellers seek buyers willing to pay high prices. Buyers seek sellers willing to sell at low prices. Traders also must find traders who are willing to trade the *quantities*, or *sizes*, they desire. Traders who want to trade large quantities may have to find many willing traders to complete their trades.

Dealers and brokers help people trade. *Dealers* trade with their clients when their clients want to trade. The prices at which a dealer will buy and sell are the dealer's *bid* and *ask* prices. After they trade with their clients, dealers then try to trade out at a profit by selling what they have bought or by buying back what they have sold. In effect, clients pay dealers to take their trading problems. The dealers then try to solve them at a profit. Dealers profit by buying low and selling high. Successful dealers must be excellent traders.

Brokers are agents who arrange trades for their clients. They help their clients find traders who are willing to trade with them. They profit by charging commissions.

Patient traders obtain better prices than impatient traders do because they are willing to search longer and harder to arrange their trades at favorable terms. Impatient traders pay for the privilege of trading when they want to trade.

Traders who offer to trade give other people options to trade. These options sometimes are quite valuable. Traders who expose their offers can lose to clever traders who use various front-running trading strategies to extract these option values. Traders therefore must expose their offers very carefully. They should expose only to traders who are most likely to trade with them.

Traders who trade only to accommodate other traders risk trading with, and losing to, well-informed speculators. *Speculators* are traders who trade to profit from information they have about future prices. *Well-informed speculators* can predict futures prices better than other traders can. They then choose to buy or sell based upon which side they expect will be profitable.

Dealers lose to well-informed speculators because they end up being on the wrong side of the trade. Prices tend to move against their positions before they can trade out of them. All traders try to avoid trading with well-informed speculators.

Dealers recover their losses to informed speculators by widening the spread between the bid and ask prices at which they will buy and sell. Uninformed traders therefore pay more for their trades when dealers lose a lot to informed traders. In effect, uninformed traders lose to well-informed traders through the intermediation of dealers.

Traders who can estimate fundamental values cause prices to reflect their value estimates. They buy when price is below their value estimates and sell when price is above. Their buying pushes prices up, and their selling pulls prices down. They do not trade if they believe that prices reflect values. Well-informed traders make prices informative.

Bluffers can sometimes fool uninformed traders into trading unwisely. In general, they can profit if the price impacts of their buying and selling are not exactly opposite to each other. Since dealers may trade when bluffers want them to trade, dealers must be highly disciplined to avoid losing to bluffers.

Trading is a zero-sum game when gains and losses are measured relative to the market average. In a *zero-sum game*, someone can win only if somebody else loses. On average, well-informed speculators and bluffers win, and poorly informed traders and foolish traders lose. Informed traders can profit only to the extent that less informed traders are willing to lose to them.

Poorly informed traders trade for many reasons. *Investors* use the markets to move money from the present to the future. *Borrowers* do the opposite. *Hedgers* trade to manage financial risks they face. *Asset exchangers* trade one asset for another they value more. *Gamblers* trade to entertain themselves.

Exchanges and brokerages design markets to minimize the search costs of trading. They usually organize markets so that everyone who wants to trade gathers at the same place. A common gathering place helps traders find those traders who will offer the best prices.

Exchanges and brokerages once organized their markets exclusively on physical trading floors. Now they can do so within computerized communications networks that allow buyers and sellers to arrange their trades remotely. Electronic marketplaces have rapidly expanded as the costs of electronic communications technologies have dropped.

Most traders want to trade in well-established markets because other traders trade there. When many traders trade in the same place, arranging trades is very easy. The attraction of traders to other traders makes it hard to start new markets.

Entrepreneurs create new markets when old markets do not adequately meet the needs of a significant set of traders. Since traders face a diversity of trading problems, no single market can best meet every trader's needs. Many diverse markets may form when exchanges and brokerages compete to attract traders.

Arbitrageurs ensure that prices do not vary much across markets. When prices diverge, they buy in cheaper markets and sell in more expensive markets. The effect of their trading is to connect sellers in cheaper markets to buyers in more expensive markets.

An exchange's trading rules affect the quality of its markets. They determine the balance of power between informed traders and uninformed traders, between public traders and professional traders, and between large traders and small traders. Trading rules are very important.

Markets work best when they trade fungible instruments. An instrument is *fungible* if one unit (a share, a bond, a contract, etc.) of the instrument is economically indistinguishable from all other units. If that is so, buyers do not care which units they receive. Since all sellers offer identical units, buyers can buy from any seller who offers an attractive price. Sellers likewise can sell to any buyer. Fungible instruments therefore are easier to trade than instruments that have idiosyncratic characteristics. In derivative markets, the benefits of fungible instruments cause trading to concentrate in just a few standardized contracts.

1.5 KEY RECURRENT THEMES

A number of important issues appear repeatedly throughout this book. This section identifies these issues. Watch for them as you read this book.

Information asymmetries   Traders who know more about values and traders who know more about what other traders intend to do have a great advantage over those who do not. Well-informed traders profit at the expense of less-informed traders. Less-informed traders therefore try to avoid well-informed traders. Pay attention to who is well-informed and to how traders learn about values.

Options   The option to trade is valuable. People who write limit orders give free trading options to other traders. Clever traders can extract the value of these options. Pay attention to when traders create trading options and to how they prevent other traders from extracting their values.

Externalities   People create *positive externalities* when they do something that benefits other people without compensation. People create *negative externalities* when they do something that harms other people without penalty. The most important externality in market microstructure is the *order flow externality* Traders who offer to trade give other traders valuable options to trade for which the offerers are not compensated. The order flow externality attracts and binds traders to markets because they want to benefit from free trading options. Pay close attention to when, why, and how traders offer to trade. Also pay attention to how markets, brokerages, and dealers benefit from the order flow externality.

Market structure   *Market structure* consists of the trading rules, the physical layout, the information presentation systems, and the information communication systems of a market. Market structure determines what traders can do and what they can know. It therefore affects trader strategies, the power relationships among different types of traders, and ultimately trader profitability. Always consider what effects market structures have on trading strategies and on the balance of power between various types of traders.

Competition with free entry and exit   Traders compete in markets to make profits. Trading strategies that generate large profits attract traders who want to participate in those profits. Their entry lowers the profits that everyone makes, on average. Conversely, traders quit using trading strategies that are not profitable, which allows remaining traders to make more profits, on average. Free entry and exit ensures that alternative trading strategies produce equal net profits, on average, after accounting for all costs. Wherever you see people competing, consider how the costs of entry and exit affect their ability to maintain profits or avoid losses. This principle will help you understand the determinants of bid/ask spreads, dealer profits, informed-trader profits, and order submission strategies.

Communications and computing technologies Markets are essentially information-processing mechanisms. They process information about who wants to trade, how much, and at what prices. The resulting prices aggregate information about fundamental values. The growth in information technologies has changed, and will continue to change, how people trade. Pay attention to the role of information-processing technologies in the markets.

Price correlations Markets for similar instruments are closely related. They tend to have similar conditions, and they often compete fiercely with each other for order flow. The order flow externality generally ensures that one market among a set of closely related markets will eventually dominate the others. Pay attention to markets that trade similar instruments and to the differences among them that make them unique. These issues affect how markets compete with each other.

Principal–agent problems Principal–agent problems arise when agents do what they want to do rather than what their principals want them to do. The most important principal–agent problem in market microstructure involves brokers and their clients. Brokers do not always do what you want them to do, and they may not work as hard on your behalf as you would. Pay close attention to how traders control their brokers.

Trustworthiness and creditworthiness People are *trustworthy* if they try to do what they say they will do. People are *creditworthy* if they can do what they say they will do. Since people often will not or cannot do what they promise, market institutions must be designed to effectively and inexpensively enforce contracts. Pay close attention to the mechanisms which ensure that traders will settle their trades. Attempts to solve trustworthiness and creditworthiness problems explain much of the structure of market institutions.

The zero-sum game All trades involve two or more parties. The accounting gains made by one side must equal the accounting losses suffered by the other side. Understanding the origins of trading profits therefore requires that we understand both sides of a trade. We must understand why traders on one side expect to profit, and why traders on the other side either are willing to lose or do not understand that they should expect to lose.

1.6 OUTLINE OF THE BOOK

The book is organized into seven parts. Part I examines the structure of trading. Several chapters describe how markets are organized and regulated, and how traders trade in them. Although much of the information is descriptive, the text also analyzes how various market structures affect trading strategies.

Part II considers what benefits markets produce for traders and for the wider economy. We must address these questions in order to judge whether the markets are working well. The first of the two chapters in this part of the book considers why people trade. The other chapter explains how markets benefit the whole economy. This chapter concludes with my opinion about what markets should do and for whom they should do it. Your opinion may differ from mine.

To understand how trading rules affect traders, you must first understand how traders behave. The book therefore next devotes many chapters to understanding what various traders do. These chapters should be especially interesting to readers who want to become traders and to traders who want to improve their trading skills. Part III includes chapters that consider various speculative trading strategies. Part IV examines the traders who offer liquidity.

Part V contains two chapters that will help you to better understand the origins of liquidity and volatility. Both concepts are described in relation to the various trading strategies introduced in parts III and IV.

We consider the problems of evaluating trader performance in part VI. You must understand these issues if you intend to manage brokers, or if you want to know why index markets are so popular. These chapters lay the foundation for understanding who profits, and who loses, from trading. If you intend to trade for profit or invest your money with a money manager, the chapter on performance evaluation and prediction will be of great interest to you.

Finally, part VII concludes with several chapters that consider the economics of various market structures. These chapters examine how markets are organized, how they compete with each other, and how they respond to extreme volatility. These chapters will obviously interest regulators and exchange officials. They should also interest farsighted traders: Being able to predict how changes in rules, technologies, and competitive relationships affect markets distinguishes winning traders from losers.

Numerous sidebars appear throughout the book. These sidebars contain examples, stories, and historical explanations that illustrate and illuminate points made in the text. They are useful as mnemonic devices for remembering jargon and concepts. I beg your indulgence for the puns, wordplay, lighthearted jabs, and unsolicited opinions that appear in them.

I took the examples that appear throughout the book from all types of markets and from many different countries. A disproportionate number, however, involve equity trading in the United States because these markets are the best-known markets in the world. As noted above, most principles that apply to these markets also apply to all other markets.

1.7 AN IMPORTANT DISCLAIMER

Traders often encounter significant legal and tax issues. Some types of trades are illegal, many trades create significant tax liabilities, and many commercial relationships in trading create important legal liabilities. If you trade, you must know the legal consequences of your actions.

The purpose of this book is to examine economic issues in trading, not legal issues. The text addresses many legal issues because legal issues often have significant economic implications for the markets, and because economic issues often are the basis for legal regulation. This book will help you to better understand the economic implications of laws that regulate securities, contracts, traders, and exchanges. It will also help you understand the economic bases for many regulations. It is not an authority for what the law is or for which laws you should pay attention to.

▶ Bulls and Bears

Traders call rising markets *bull markets* and falling markets *bear markets*. According to legend, these terms originated from morbid contests that promoters once staged between bulls and bears. Bulls fight by thrusting upward with their horns. In contrast, bears fight by striking downward with their claws. This image has generated a small cottage industry of artisans who create bull-fighting-bear sculptures that traders buy to adorn their offices and living rooms. ◀

Do not rely upon this book for guidance on any legal issues. I am not a qualified legal adviser. Consult a qualified attorney when you must address legal questions.

1.8 SUMMARY

This book will help you understand the theory and practice of trading in exchange markets and dealer networks. When you master this subject, you will be able to trade more effectively, you will better appreciate the organization of our markets, and you will be able to form well-reasoned opinions about how the markets should be organized.

Markets have changed substantially during the last 100 years, and they will continue to change in the next 100 years. The current pace of change is fast, and is accelerating. By the time you read this, some specific descriptive information in this book will undoubtedly be dated. The economic principles governing markets and the traders in them, however, will remain the same. These concepts will help you understand all markets—past, present, and future.

This chapter presents stories about how traders arrange routine trades in
stocks, bonds, futures contracts, and currencies. If you are new to trading, you should read this chapter to help you appreciate the trading problems that people solve. If you are already quite familiar with trading, you
also may want to read this chapter. Although these stories describe routine
trades, they highlight difficult issues that traders confront when trading.

This chapter is full of institutional details. Do not worry if you do not
understand all of them on your first reading. After you have finished reading this book, you will be able to understand these stories completely. For
now, just read them to get a feel for what trading is about. The impressions
that you form will help you appreciate the practical importance of the analyses that this book presents.

2.1 A RETAIL TRADE IN
AN NYSE-LISTED STOCK

Jennifer wants to buy 200 shares of AT&T. She calls her retail broker, with
whom she has already established an account. (Jennifer could also have used
her broker's Internet-based order entry system.) Jennifer's broker might work
for a full-service broker/dealer, such as Merrill Lynch; a national discount
brokerage, such as Charles Schwab; or perhaps a local deep-discount brokerage, such as Brown & Company.

Jennifer provides the broker with her account number and identifies herself. She then asks for the current quotes for AT&T common stock. The
broker looks at a screen on his desk that is similar to the Bridge Information Systems quotation display in figure 2-1. On the screen are the best bids
and offers for AT&T that traders display in the Consolidated Quotation
System. The quotes come from dealers at the New York Stock Exchange
(NYSE), from dealers at several regional exchanges, from some independent NASD (National Association of Securities Dealers) members, and from
some electronic communications networks (ECNs) that display limit orders
that their clients have placed with them. The broker responds by quoting
the best current prices at which traders can immediately buy or sell AT&T
(ticker symbol "T") shares. Given the information in figure 2-1, the broker
reports that the best (highest) bid for AT&T is for 19.83 dollars and the
best (lowest) offer is at 19.85. The broker also tells Jennifer that the last
trade in AT&T was at 19.84 dollars, which is down 0.10 from the previous day's close. Jennifer considers the quote. She then instructs her broker
to buy the shares.

To convey her intentions, Jennifer will use either a market order or a
limit order. A *market order* instructs the broker to buy at the best price available. A *limit order* instructs the broker to buy at the best price possible, but
in no event to pay more than a *limit price* that Jennifer specifies. If Jennifer

```
us;T              AT and T Corp *#                                 Common Stock
+      19.84 DN        0.10  (N)  14.06  H      20    L     19.51 V 8,341,400

E/MM    TIME     -BID-      SIZE(H)     E/MM    TIME     -ASK-      SIZE(H)
(N)   14.06 +      19.83      6 dq      MADF   14.06       19.85      50
CAES  14.06        19.83      1         CAES   14.06       19.85      50
(T)   14.06 +      19.83      1         (T)    14.06       19.85      50
TRIM  14.06        19.83      1         (C)    14.06       19.85      1
(B)   14.04 +      19.80      30        (N)    14.06       19.86      33 dq
(M)   14.06 +      19.73      1         ARCA   14.06       19.89      5
(P)   14.01 +      19.72      20        (B)    14.04       19.94      30
MADF  14.06        19.70      5         (M)    14.06       19.96      1
(C)   14.06 -      19.70      1         (P)    14.01       19.98      20
SBSH  14.00        19.69      1         TRIM   14.06       19.99      2
(X)   14.06 +      19.58      1         NYD    12.24       20         500
NYD   12.24        19.50      500       (X)    14.06       20.11      1
SWST   9.42        9          1         SBSH   14.00       20.14      1
ARCA  14.06        0.01       1         SWST    9.42       24.99      1

OI BUY  :   LEHM    FBCO   GSCO   NATW   MLCO   SBSH   MONT
OI SELL :   PRUS    UBSS   NATW   DLJP   SALB   RSSF   MONT

T/q    04-Oct-01 14:06 NYC                                      (c) BRIDGE
```

FIGURE 2-1.

A Bridge Information Systems Quotation Montage for NYSE-listed AT&T Common Stock

AT&T common stock (US ticker symbol T) last traded at 19.84, down 0.10 from the previous day's closing price. The trade occurred at the NYSE (N) at 14:06 Eastern Time when the high and low prices of the day were respectively 20 and 19.51, and 8,341,400 shares had already traded. The quotation montage consists of two sets of four columns each for bid and ask quotes. The first column identifies the quote maker. Exchanges have one or three letter symbols; dealer-brokers and electronic communications networks have four letter symbols. The quotation sizes are expressed as hundred-share lots. The rows are sorted so that the bids with the highest prices and asks with the lowest prices appear at the top of their respective columns. The first line of the montage shows that buyers at the NYSE were willing to buy at least a total of 600 shares for 19.83 while a dealer working for Madoff Investment Securities (MADF) was willing to sell at least 5,000 shares at 19.85. The two rows near the bottom present order indications (OI) that brokers and dealers have asked Bridge to display for Bridge clients. Bridge subscribers can query these firms to learn more about their orders.

Source: Reuters

uses a limit order, she will also specify when she wants the order to expire. For example, a *day order* will expire when the trading session ends.

Jennifer decides to submit a day limit order to buy 200 shares of AT&T, ticker symbol "T," for no more than 19.80 dollars per share. The broker enters Jennifer's order into his computerized order entry system. The system then confirms that Jennifer is authorized to make the trade. Next, the broker reads back the order to ensure that it is exactly what Jennifer intended. (The brokerage firm records telephone calls in case a dispute arises about what was said.) After Jennifer confirms the order, the broker releases it, and the order entry system sends it to an exchange or to a dealer.

Although AT&T trades primarily at the New York Stock Exchange, Jennifer's brokerage house might not send her order there. As figure 2-1 demonstrates, many other exchanges and dealers trade AT&T. The brokerage might send the order to a regional exchange or to a NASD dealer. Where the brokerage order system sends the order may depend on the prices the various markets quote. It may also depend on cash payments and other nonmonetary inducements that dealers offer brokerages to obtain their order flow.

The brokerage's order entry system sends Jennifer's order to the NYSE by transferring it to the NYSE's SuperDot order-routing system. SuperDot then presents the order to the specialist who manages AT&T trading on the floor of the Exchange. The specialist will act as the floor broker for Jennifer's order. Jennifer's order appears on a workstation screen that the specialist rents from the Exchange.

The AT&T specialist is a trader who works for a member firm of the NYSE. He sometimes trades as a dealer for his firm's account and sometimes as a broker for his clients. The Exchange gives the specialist some special privileges and special responsibilities. The specialist receives all of the SuperDot order flow in AT&T. He organizes the AT&T trading to ensure that it is orderly, and he represents all orders entrusted to him. In return, the Exchange requires that he trade for his own account to fill customer market orders if no one else is willing to do so.

Since Jennifer's order is a limit order, the specialist first sees if anyone is interested in filling it immediately. No sellers are presently interested because other traders are bidding higher prices. The specialist then places her order in his electronic limit order book. Jennifer's order will stand in the book until the specialist can match it with someone who wants to sell at or below its limit price, until the order expires, or until Jennifer tells her broker to cancel it.

(If Jennifer submitted a market order instead of a limit order, the specialist would conduct an auction to find the trader willing to sell at the lowest price. A trader on the floor, a standing limit order in the order book, or the specialist himself might offer that price. If no one wants to fill the market order, the specialist will fill it himself by selling some of his own shares in AT&T to Jennifer.)

A few minutes after Jennifer enters her order, a large seller sends a market order through SuperDot. The specialist uses his computer to match this order with several orders including Jennifer's. The orders all trade at 19.80 dollars. The Exchange trading systems then report the trade to the Consolidated Trade Reporting System, which reports trade prices and sizes to various data vendors. These vendors immediately distribute trade reports throughout the world.

SuperDot also reports the trade to Jennifer's broker in a process called confirming the trade. The broker then reports the confirmation to Jennifer. If the order had been a market order, the time between the order entry and the final confirmation might have been less than half a minute. Jennifer might have received her trade confirmation during the same telephone call in which she placed her order. Since Jennifer's limit order took a while to trade, the broker phones Jennifer with the confirmation.

Jennifer now has to pay for her purchase. That day, the brokerage house mails her a written confirmation of the trade. The confirmation instructs her to pay the purchase price times 200 shares purchased plus the brokerage commission. If Jennifer trades through a deep discount brokerage, the commission may be as low as 15 dollars. It could have been even lower had she entered her order through the Internet.

Three business days later, the trade settles. Jennifer's brokerage pays for the stock, and the seller delivers it to her brokerage. If Jennifer has not yet paid for the stock, her brokerage will collect the money from any cash she holds in her account. If no cash is available and if Jennifer has executed a margin agreement, the brokerage will lend her the money and charge her interest on the amount due. The brokerage will use Jennifer's newly acquired AT&T stock and other securities in her account as collateral for the loan. If Jennifer does not pay, if she had no margin agreement with her brokerage, or if she does not have adequate collateral to support a new loan, the brokerage will eventually sell the stock and charge her for the commissions and for any losses incurred.

After Jennifer pays for her stock, the brokerage places the shares in her account. If she asks to have a stock certificate issued, her brokerage will instruct AT&T's transfer agent to issue the certificate and mail it to her. In that case, Jennifer should place the certificate in a safety deposit box for safekeeping.

2.2 A RETAIL TRADE IN A NASDAQ STOCK

Jennifer now wants to sell 100 shares that she holds in Microsoft. Unlike AT&T, Microsoft does not trade at traditional stock exchanges like the NYSE. Instead, about 40 independent dealers who publish their quotes in the Nasdaq National Market System trade Microsoft. The dealers sit at their desks throughout the country and enter their quotes into Nasdaq workstations that are linked through a private network.

When Jennifer asks her broker for a quote, the broker pulls up a screen on his desk that is similar to the Bridge Information System display in figure 2-2. This display ranks the bids and offers of the 39 Nasdaq market makers and electronic communications networks that were providing quotes in Microsoft on October 5, 2001, at 11:26 Eastern Time. The bids are ranked from highest to lowest, and the offers (asks) are ranked from lowest to highest. Looking at this screen, the broker reports that Microsoft (MSFT) last traded at 55.97, down 0.47 from the previous close; the market is currently 55.97 bid; 55.98 offered.

With this information, Jennifer instructs her broker to sell 100 shares of Microsoft at the market. This instruction tells the broker that she wants the order filled quickly, at the best price available.

The broker then asks Jennifer whether she owns the shares of Microsoft that she intends to sell. He needs to know where the shares will come from in order to settle the trade. Jennifer tells the broker that she owns the shares. If Jennifer did not own the shares, she would be selling the stock short. To settle the trade, Jennifer would have to borrow 100 shares from someone. Since borrowing shares is sometimes difficult or impossible, the broker would have to arrange to borrow the shares before Jennifer could sell them.

The broker enters Jennifer's order into his order entry system and reads it back to her. When Jennifer confirms the order, he releases it. If the brokerage firm does not deal in Microsoft, its order entry system will send the order to the Nasdaq Small Order Execution System (SuperSoes). If the brokerage has a trader who is a Nasdaq dealer in Microsoft, the broker will probably send the order to that trader.

```
us;MSFT        Microsoft Corp *#                               Common Stock
  -    55.9700 DN    0.4700  (Q)   11.25  H     56.6400 L   54.9400 V 15,130,100

  E/MM    TIME     -BID-     SIZE(H)     E/MM    TIME    -ASK-      SIZE(H)
   (Q)   11.25 +   55.9700      9         (Q)   11.25   55.9800      19
  INCA   11.25     55.9700      9        ISLD   11.25   55.9800      19
  ISLD   11.25     55.9600      6        REDI   11.25   55.9800       2
  BTRD   11.25     55.9500      6        INCA   11.25   55.9900      54
  FCAP   11.24     55.9400      1        GSCO   11.25   55.9900      10
  ARCA   11.25     55.9100      4        BRUT   11.25   55.9900       2
  SBSH   11.25     55.8900      1        ARCA   11.25   55.9900       1
  NITE   11.24     55.8800     29        SCHB   11.25   56           20
  SCHB   11.25     55.8800      1        PERT   11.24   56           11
  GSCO   11.25     55.8700     10        BEST   11.24   56           10
  MLCO   11.23     55.8500     10        NITE   11.24   56            6
  MSCO   11.25     55.8500     10        JEFF   11.10   56            1
  REDI   11.25     55.8300     10        RAJA   11.18   56            1
  MKXT   11.25     55.8100      5        ABNA   11.03   56.0300       1
  MONT   11.19     55.8000     10        FBCO   11.24   56.0300       1


  OI BUY  :  GSCO   MLCO   BEST
  OI SELL :  FBCO   GSCO   CANT

MSFT/q/Pg2     05-Oct-01 11:26 NYC                         (c)BRIDGE
```

FIGURE 2-2.
Page 1 of a Nasdaq Level II Quotation Montage for
Microsoft Common Stock
Source: Reuters

SuperSoes routes the order to one of the Nasdaq dealers. Jennifer's brokerage, like most other retail brokerages, specifies the dealer to which SuperSoes sends her order. If the brokerage did not specify a dealer, Super-Soes would have sent the sell order to one of the dealers displaying the best (highest) bid. Her brokerage specifies a particular dealer because that dealer has arranged to give the brokerage a cash payment or some nonmonetary inducement to obtain her order.

The dealer who receives Jennifer's order executes it by buying the stock for his own account. Many dealers have computer systems that automatically execute small market orders when they arrive. The trade price will be at least 55.97 dollars (assuming that the best bid has not changed). Even if the dealer is not presently quoting a bid of 55.97, he will match that price.

After the dealer fills the order, he reports the trade to Jennifer's broker and to Nasdaq. The broker then confirms the trade to Jennifer by phone and by mail. If the brokerage does not already hold Jennifer's shares, the broker will ask Jennifer to deposit her certificates in her brokerage account. Nasdaq forwards the trade report to various data vendors, who report it to the public.

The trade settles three business days later. At that time, the brokerage delivers the 100 shares of Microsoft to the dealer, and the dealer pays for them. The brokerage credits Jennifer's account with the proceeds of the sale, less any commission charged and a small fee that the Securities and Exchange Commission collects from sellers of securities.

2.3 AN INSTITUTIONAL TRADE IN A NYSE STOCK

Bob is a trader who works for Rocket Science Investment Management (RSIM), a (fictitious) investment management firm that manages money for several corporate pension funds. These pension funds have each given RSIM authority to trade on their behalf. RSIM manages a total of 2 billion dollars, invested primarily in U.S. equities.

At 12:30 P.M., Eastern Time, an RSIM portfolio manager asks Bob to buy 400,000 shares of Exxon Mobil Corporation for their clients. Since the price of Exxon Mobil is near 40 dollars, the principal value of the trade is about 16 million dollars. This makes it a large trade, but not especially so. On October 4, 2001, this trade would have represented only 0.006 percent of the total number of shares outstanding in Exxon Mobil (6.87 billion), 0.8 percent of the firm's portfolio, and 5 percent of the average daily volume (about 9 million shares) in Exxon Mobil. Bob's job is to get this order filled at the lowest possible cost.

Bob first asks the portfolio manager why he wants to buy the stock. If the manager wants the stock because he suspects that Exxon Mobil will very soon announce the discovery of new reserves, Bob must trade quickly. The price will rise as others come to the same opinion, and it will surely rise when Exxon Mobil makes its announcement. In contrast, if the manager wants to buy the stock because he believes that it is fundamentally undervalued, Bob can be more patient. The prices of such stocks usually do not rise so quickly that Bob needs to hurry to trade. The portfolio manager says that he wants to buy Exxon Mobil because he believes it is fundamentally undervalued.

Bob then uses an electronic information retrieval system to examine the recent price and trade history for Exxon Mobil. He looks to see whether other traders are trying to fill large orders. If a large seller is pushing prices down, Bob might be able to fill his order quickly at a good price. If Bob must compete with another large buyer, the order may be hard to execute at a good price. Falling prices often indicate that large buys will be easier to fill than large sells. Rising prices may indicate the opposite. Since movements in the price of Exxon Mobil closely correlate with movements in the market as a whole, Bob also compares Exxon Mobil's recent price history against movements in the S&P 500, which is a broad market index. If Exxon Mobil is unchanged, but the market is down, Bob's purchase may be easier to arrange on good terms than if the market is up. Bob finds that Exxon Mobil is down slightly while the market is largely unchanged.

Bob next tries to discover whether there is any large trader interest in Exxon Mobil. He consults one or more of the electronic information systems that collect information about trader interests. Bridge, Liquidnet, Autex, and Instinet are among the more important systems. These systems show that several traders have indicated interest in Exxon Mobil. Bob cannot tell from the screen how serious they are, or whether they have already filled their orders. One of the traders is a Morgan Stanley broker.

Bob calls one of the many brokers with whom RSIM does business. He chooses a floor broker whom he trusts to keep quiet, since he does not yet want to reveal that he is in the market. Without stating his intentions, he asks the broker, who happens to work for Merrill Lynch, what market conditions are like in Exxon Mobil. The Merrill floor broker goes to the post where Exxon Mobil trades on the NYSE floor and tries to collect some useful information. He may stand around watching the trading, or he may ask the specialist and other nearby traders who has been interested in trading. They may or may not tell him what he wants to know, and they may not answer with complete honesty. Traders generally will not reveal their interest without some indication that they are revealing to someone who is able and willing to trade with them on the spot. The Merrill Lynch broker reports to Bob that no large trader interest is currently visible in the stock. He also says that the Morgan Stanley broker was actively selling earlier in the day.

At 12:50 P.M., Bob sends an order to buy 400,000 shares in Exxon Mobil to POSIT. POSIT (POrtfolio System for Institutional Trading) is an electronic trading system run by Investment Technology Group. POSIT collects buy and sell orders from large, primarily institutional traders and attempts to match them. The service is completely confidential. It does not reveal any information about orders to anyone. Bob sends his order directly to POSIT, using software it provides.

Eight times daily—at 9:40 A.M., 10 A.M., 10:30 A.M. and hourly from 11 A.M. to 3 P.M. Eastern Time, POSIT conducts crosses to match buyers with sellers. If the total POSIT buy order volume exceeds the total POSIT sell order volume, the sell orders are all filled completely, and the buy orders are partially filled. The fraction filled depends on the extent to which buy order volume exceeds sell order volume. If buy order volume is twice the sell order volume, POSIT will fill half the total volume of all buy orders. The actual fill rate for any given order depends on a complex set of rules that POSIT uses to best serve the needs of its clients. A similar set of matching rules applies if sell order volume exceeds buy order volume.

POSIT assigns the trade price by choosing a time at random within the seven minutes that immediately follow the cross. At that time, POSIT computes the average of the bid and ask in the primary market for the stock. POSIT uses that average as the trade price for all crossed orders. As soon as the cross is completed, POSIT reports the trades to its clients and to the NASD.

At 1:10 P.M., Bob learns that 48,000 shares of his 400,000-share order filled at a price of 39.84 dollars. From this information, Bob knows only that POSIT buy order volume exceeded POSIT sell order volume. He can roughly infer the size of the unfilled POSIT buy order volume from the total size of the cross, which he can read off the Consolidated Tape. (The POSIT report appears on the tape with an exchange marker of "O," which indicates third market trades.) If the cross were for 48,000 shares, Bob would know that he was the only buyer. If the cross was for 100,000 shares, he could roughly infer that the total POSIT buy order volume was a bit more than 800,000 shares because the 48,000-share partial fill on his 400,000-share order represented about half of trade volume. The estimate is rough because POSIT does not use a strict pro rata rationing algorithm to match the orders. After consulting trade records reported to the electronic Consolidated Trade Reporting System, Bob concludes that his order was probably the only large buy order in POSIT.

Bob then calls a sales trader at Morgan Stanley, with which his firm has an account, to inquire about the posted indication he had seen earlier. This broker sits at Morgan Stanley's equity trading desk on the trading floor at Morgan Stanley's headquarters in midtown Manhattan. The broker says that he has already filled his client's sell order and apologizes for failing to remove the indication. The broker then suggests that his client may be willing to sell more. Bob expresses some interest, and the broker calls his other client while putting Bob on hold. A negotiation takes place through the broker's intermediation. In the end, the broker arranges a trade for 200,000 shares at 39.87.

The sales trader then telephones a Morgan Stanley floor broker at the NYSE and asks him to print the trade. The floor trader goes to the Exxon Mobil post and tells the specialist that he would like to cross a block of 200,000 shares at 39.87. The specialist is currently quoting a market of 38.86 bid and 39.88 asked, and the last trade was at 39.86. The specialist gives his approval. (If the proposed trade price were higher than 39.88, the specialist would have required the floor broker to allow the sell orders standing in the limit order book below that price to participate in the trade.) The specialist reports the trade to an Exchange computer that forwards it to the Consolidated Trade Reporting System.

At the same time, other traders standing at the post ask the Morgan Stanley floor broker whether there is more interest on either side of the trade. The broker says that he will call to find out. He calls his trading desk, and the sales trader calls Bob.

Just before Bob gets this call, he receives a call from the Merrill Lynch floor broker with whom he had earlier spoken. The broker reports that Morgan Stanley just crossed 200,000 shares. Bob tells him that he was the buyer. Bob then gives the Merrill Lynch broker a market-not-held buy order for 80,000 shares. The market-not-held instruction tells the floor broker to buy shares at his discretion. When Bob gets the call from the Morgan Stanley sales trader, he says that he is no longer actively interested in the stock.

The Merrill broker now stands in the crowd and waits to see what happens. In the next hour, he buys 20,000 shares at 39.88, 32,000 shares at 39.90, and 28,000 shares at 39.95. He calls Bob back with the confirmations.

Bob then gives the Merrill broker a market-not-held order to buy the remaining 72,000 shares. The specialist's quote is now 39.95 bid, good for 240 round lots of 100 shares (24,000 shares) and 40.00 offered, good for 500 round lots. Before the floor broker arranges any more trades, the broad market starts to rise. The Merrill broker looks at the S&P 500 futures contract price and sees that it has risen faster than the S&P 500 Index, so that the spread between the future price and the index has widened. This evidence suggests that the stock market may continue rising. It also suggests that index arbitrageurs may soon start buying Exxon Mobil, which is the largest stock in the S&P 500 Index. The Merrill broker turns to the specialist and immediately asks to buy 72,000 shares for 40.00. The specialist, acting as broker for several traders whose sell limit orders are on the book at 40.00, sells him the shares and reports the trades. The specialist then raises his bid and offer, and the Merrill broker calls Bob to report his trades.

Bob has now completely filled his 400,000-share order. The average cost of his trades was 39.898 dollars per share, not counting commissions. Bob reports the trades to his firm's back office, which will arrange settlement. He also reports the trades to the portfolio manager. A summary of these trades appears in table 2-1.

Bob's firm, RSIM, will not actually purchase the shares that Bob bought. Instead, RSIM's pension fund clients will purchase and hold the shares. The back office must now tell the custodians of these funds that RSIM made purchases on their behalf. RSIM divides the 400,000 shares among the various pension funds in proportion to the money that they have placed under

TABLE 2-1.
Summary of Bob's Trades

SHARES	PRICE	NOTES
48,000	39.84	POSIT
200,000	39.87	Morgan Stanley block trade
20,000	39.88	Merrill Lynch floor trades
32,000	39.90	Merrill Lynch floor trades
28,000	39.95	Merrill Lynch floor trades
72,000	40.00	Merrill Lynch trades with book
400,000		

management at RSIM. Three days later, the various pension fund custodians will pay for and receive their Exxon Mobil shares. Each will pay the same price per share.

2.4 AN INSTITUTIONAL TRADE
IN A NASDAQ STOCK

Bob's portfolio manager now asks him to sell 10,000 shares in United States Lime & Minerals (USLM), a Texas-based producer of pulverized limestone, quicklime, and hydrated lime products. USLM trades at about 4.85 dollars per share, so the principal value of this transaction is 48,500 dollars. Although the order represents only 0.17 percent of the total shares outstanding (about 6 million), it is about ten times bigger than the average daily volume in USLM. Bob expects that his order will be difficult to fill.

Bob calls up the USLM Nasdaq quote montage using Bridge Information Systems (figure 2-3). Only three dealers are actively making a market in USLM. The best bid is 4.85 and the best offer is 4.90, so that the bid/ask spread is 1 percent of price, which is quite wide. Moreover, the total displayed size on the bid side of the market is only 500 shares. As of 11:32 Eastern Time, the stock has not yet traded. The fact that the stock has not yet traded, the wide spread, and the small displayed size all suggest that the order will be expensive to fill.

Bob picks up the phone and calls Spear, Leeds, Kellogg and Co. (SLKC). SLKC is a very large dealer that is making a market in USLM. He chooses SLKC because the firm has provided him good service in the past. SLKC is not bidding the most aggressive price, but it is not far from the market. He also notes that SLKC's offer is way behind the market, which suggests that SLKC has no interest in being a seller. Bob generally assumes that the dealers bidding the most in Nasdaq are the most eager to buy, although he knows that this is not always the case.

When the SLKC dealer answers the phone, Bob asks him for quotes to buy or sell 10,000 shares of USLM. He asks for both sides because he does not yet want to reveal that he is a seller. If Bob had said that he wants to sell, the dealer might have been tempted to lower his quote. Since the dealer does not know whether Bob is a buyer or seller, he is more likely to quote prices that fairly reflect his best estimate of value of the stock.

```
us;USLM       United States Lime and Minerals Inc            Common Stock
-    4.9000 UNCH   (Q)  1 DNT  H      0    L    0    V 0

E/MM   TIME     -BID-     SIZE(H)    E/MM   TIME    -ASK-     SIZE(H)
(Q)  10.36 +    4.8500      3        (Q)  10.36     4.9000     12
HRZG  9.31      4.8500      3        LEGG 10.36     4.9000     12
SLKC  8.35      4.7800      1        HRZG  9.31     5.5000      1
LEGG 10.36      4.4000      1        SLKC  8.35     6.6200      1




OI BUY  :
OI SELL :

USLM/Q    05-Oct-01  11:32 NYC                          (c) BRIDGE
```

FIGURE 2-3.
Nasdaq Level II Quotation Montage for United States Lime
and Minerals
Source: Reuters

Before quoting, the dealer looks at the Nasdaq market and confirms that no recent news stories have appeared about USLM. The dealer wants to make sure that Bob does not know something important about the stock that he does not.

Although SLKC's Nasdaq quote is 4.78 bid, 6.62 offered for 100 shares, he gives Bob a quote of 4.70 bid, 5.05 offered for 10,000 shares. Bob then asks whether the dealer will pay 4.75 for 10,000. The dealer accepts the offer and buys 10,000 shares from Bob. The dealer must report the trade to Nasdaq within 90 seconds. Bob reports the trade to his back office, which notifies the custodians of the various pension plans for which RSIM provides investment management.

2.5 A VERY LARGE BLOCK STOCK TRADE

Until the day of his death last year, John Smithson was the chairman and principal stockholder in Smithsonian Industries, a (fictitious) firm that trades at the NYSE. Smithson founded the firm 55 years earlier with two friends whom he subsequently bought out. He was its CEO until five years ago, when he decided to go into semiretirement.

Over the years, Smithsonian Industries financed its extraordinary growth through a series of secondary stock offerings and convertible debt offerings. The firm also made some acquisitions that it financed by swapping stock. Although these transactions substantially reduced the fraction of shares that Smithson owned, upon his death he still owned 4 percent of the common stock. Various institutions owned another 54 percent of the stock. Management owned less than 2 percent. Private shareholders held the remaining 40 percent. The firm currently has 40 million shares outstanding. At the current price of 80 dollars a share, the firm has a total capitalization of 3.2 billion dollars.

Smithson was always disappointed that his children never showed any interest in the business. He therefore left all of his 1.6 million shares in Smithsonian to Edna Wilkerson, his only grandchild and the darling of his golden years. He also appointed her executrix of his estate.

Edna hired a financial adviser, who told her that she would have to borrow money or sell shares in Smithsonian to pay inheritance taxes. He also suggested that she should sell shares in Smithsonian to diversify her port-

folio. Edna then spoke to the Smithsonian CEO and explained her problem. The CEO, who was now also the newly appointed chairman, suggested
that Edna contact Goldman Sachs. Goldman had managed the last two secondary offerings made by the firm.

Edna spoke to brokers in the private client services group at Goldman
Sachs and arranged for them to sell 900,000 shares of Smithsonian Industries. The brokers suggested that she sell all 1.6 million shares. Edna was
reluctant, however, because of a sense of loyalty to her grandfather and because she felt her grandfather had picked an excellent successor.

The private client services brokers then passed the order to brokers on
Goldman's block brokerage desk. These brokers now have to find buyers for
900,000 shares of stock. Since daily trading volume in the stock is averaging only 60,000 shares, they are unlikely to find the buyers on the floor of
the exchange. They will have to find them elsewhere.

Goldman's block brokers face the following predicament. If nobody
knows that they have stock to sell, they will not be able to sell it. However,
if too many people know that a large block of stock is hanging over the
market, speculators will push the price down. The Goldman brokers thus
must be selective when approaching potential buyers.

Before contacting anyone, the brokers do some research to determine
who will most likely be interested in buying the stock. They first draw up
a list of their clients who have shown recent interest in Smithsonian Industries. They then examine the CDA/Spectrum database to see what institutions currently own Smithsonian and which ones have been increasing
their positions in that stock. Various classes of investors have to make quarterly reports of their positions to the Securities and Exchange Commission.
CDA/Spectrum collects these publicly available 13F Holdings Reports, sorts
the positions by stock, and publishes the information in an electronic database. The brokers access this information through computers on their desks.
The brokers also try to identify large funds for which an investment in
Smithsonian Industries would make strategic sense. When their research is
complete, the brokers rank potential buyers by their likely interest in the
trade and by the likelihood that they will trade on the information revealed
to them.

The Goldman block brokers then start contacting potential buyers and
try to sell the stock. The current NYSE quote for Smithsonian Industries
is 81.00 bid, 81.15 offered.

Traders who show interest in the block all ask the same questions. They
want to know who the seller is, and why he or she is selling. In particular,
they want to know that Edna is not selling the stock because she believes
that it is overvalued. The brokers explain that Edna must sell the stock to
raise money to pay inheritance taxes. They add that Edna has no other assets that she could sell to raise the money. Traders also want to know the
discount at which the brokers will price the block to sell it. The brokers
must offer a discount to encourage the buyers to participate. The brokers
estimate that the discount will be 1.50 dollars. Finally, the potential buyers
want to know whether Edna is selling her entire holdings of Smithsonian
Industries. In particular, they want to know whether Edna will offer more
stock after she sells this block. If she does, the next block probably will further depress prices. The traders who purchase the first block will see an immediate loss on their investment. The brokers explain that Edna is not

offering all her stock, despite their encouragement to do so. Although they cannot guarantee that she will not offer more stock later, they do not expect her to do it soon. In an effort to put a positive spin on this information, they argue that her reluctance to sell more of the stock suggests that she thinks it is undervalued.

The brokers continue contacting potential buyers until they have identified sufficient commitments to complete the transaction at a reasonable price. After contacting 10 potential buyers in 15 minutes, the Goldman Sachs brokers obtain firm commitments from three buyers who are willing to buy a total of 850,000 shares at 80 dollars per share. The brokers then call one of their floor brokers and ask him to print the trade.

The Goldman Sachs floor broker approaches the post and observes that the current quote has dropped to 80.75 bid, 81.00 offered, even though the broad market has risen slightly. He then asks the traders there whether anybody wants to buy Smithsonian Industries. A First Boston floor broker indicates that she is interested. The Goldman broker asks how much she wants to buy. She says 10,000 shares. He then asks whether that will fill her order. She answers yes. The Goldman floor broker then tells the specialist that he wants to print a block of 900,000 shares at 80. The specialist consults his limit order book and says that there are buy limit orders totaling 20,000 shares on his book at prices between 80.00 and 80.75. He also indicates that he is interested in buying 5,000 shares for his own account. The limit orders and the First Boston buy order have precedence over the three primary buyers of the block. They must be filled if the price drops to 80. The Goldman trader agrees to allow the limit orders, the First Boston order, and the specialist to participate in the block trade at 80. Goldman Sachs purchases the remaining 15,000 shares for its own account.

Everybody involved starts making reports. The specialist reports the trade to the exchange information systems. The Goldman broker calls his block trading desk and tells them that he had to include 35,000 shares from the floor in the trade. The block desk calls Edna and the three primary purchasers with their confirmations. The First Boston broker calls her client with her report. The specialist has SuperDot report confirmations for the limit orders that brokers entered into the book through SuperDot. He asks his assistant to page two floor brokers who gave him limit orders to hold in his book. When they call in, the assistant gives them their confirmations. Within a few minutes, a market commentator on CNBC reports that Smithsonian Industries is down a dollar and 25 cents for the day following a 900,000-share block that just crossed the tape.

2.6 SOME CASH COMMODITY AND ASSOCIATED FUTURES MARKET TRADES

Moline Meal (MM) is a (fictitious) soybean processor located on the Mississippi River in Moline, Illinois. Moline is on the Iowa-Illinois border about 150 miles west of Chicago, in the heart of soybean country at the junction of interstate highways 75 and 80. Several railroads pass through the city.

MM buys soybeans from farmers up and down the river and from both sides of the river. It crushes most of the beans to separate the oil from the meal. MM sells the oil to food processors and the meal to feedlot operators.

Low margins, high volumes, and volatile prices characterize the business. Prices are volatile because weather conditions make harvests unpredictable and because the demand for meat (and hence for soy meal for feed) fluctuates with the business cycle. To manage the risk in its business, MM hedges extensively in the Chicago soybean futures markets.

The Chicago Board of Trade (CBOT) has three soybean contracts: a bean contract, an oil contract, and a meal contract. The bean contract calls for the delivery of 5,000 bushels of beans, or slightly more than 1.5 standard railroad carloads (each of which holds approximately 3,300 bushels). The oil contract calls for the delivery of 60,000 pounds of oil, and the meal contract calls for the delivery of 100 tons of meal. These quantities are approximately the amount of oil and meal that millers produce when they crush 5,000 bushels of beans.

Sellers must deliver the beans in Chicago when the contracts expire. Contracts for eight delivery months are traded. The delivery months are November, January, March, May, July, August, and September. Trading in each contract starts about a year before it expires.

On the morning of October 12, an MM trader speaks by phone with the representative of a local farmers cooperative. He negotiates a purchase of 150 carloads of beans from the cooperative. The farmers will deliver the beans in December, following the harvest, and MM then will pay for them. After specifying grade, quality, and delivery terms (most of which are standardized), the traders turn their attention to the price.

By custom, they express cash soybean prices relative to the price of the Chicago futures contract nearest to expiration. The negotiators therefore discuss only the local price differential, which traders call the basis. After a few offers and counteroffers, the traders agree to a basis of −5 cents. When the farmers deliver their beans, the price they will receive will be 5 cents less than the then current January futures contract price.

MM does not yet have buyers for the beans or for the meal and oil that they will probably press from them. If the price of beans drops after MM pays for them, but before MM sells the beans or their pressed products, MM will lose money. If the price rises, MM will make money. Although on average MM will probably break even, MM management is uncomfortable with the price risk and does not want the firm to pay the costs of financing large, unpredictable cash flows.

Management also is concerned that its traders may inadvertently place the firm into speculative positions in soybeans. To reduce these risks, MM has a risk management program. Unless specifically exempted, MM requires that all its traders must always hedge their exposed positions.

Until MM takes delivery on the beans and pays for them, it is not exposed to price risk. If the price of beans rises, it will pay more for more valuable beans. If it falls, it will pay less for less valuable beans. After MM takes delivery, MM will be very exposed to price risk.

To hedge this risk, the MM risk manager will hold an offsetting short futures position in the January soybean futures contract. The risk manager needs 99 futures contracts (150 carloads × 3,300 bushels per carload ÷ 5,000 bushels per contract) to hedge the price risk. To minimize the exposure of the firm to price risk, the risk manager must construct this position when MM takes delivery of the beans.

Immediately following the trade, the MM trader calls the MM risk manager and reports that he just arranged to buy 150 carloads of December soybeans. The trader also reports that the cooperative will exchange a January short position of only 50 contracts with the beans in a transaction known as an *exchange for physical* in the futures markets and as a *cash exchange* in the grain trade. (This transaction is unusual because the cooperative normally would exchange a 99-contract short position rather than just a 50-contract position.) The risk manager therefore will have to sell 49 additional contracts upon delivery.

When MM takes delivery in December, the risk management officer calls a broker who works for Iowa-Illinois Investor Services (IIIS), a (fictitious) futures commission merchant. IIIS is one of many futures brokerages with which MM maintains an account. The risk manager identifies himself and instructs the broker to sell 49 January soybean futures contracts at the market. The broker enters the order into a computer, repeats it, and obtains his client's confirmation. The risk manager also instructs the broker to do an exchange of 50 contracts with the cooperative's broker.

The broker sends the market sell order to the CBOT trading floor, where it prints on an "Electronic Clerk" printer in the soybean pit. A IIIS clerk immediately picks up the order and gives it to the IIIS floor trader.

The pit is a structure on the floor of the exchange in which the traders stand. The inside looks like a miniature football stadium. The bottom is flat. The sides are terraced with steps that go all the way around the pit. The traders stand shoulder to shoulder on the bottom and on the steps. This design makes it easier for everyone to see everyone else. Above and to the side of the pit is a podium on which exchange price reporters stand. They watch the trading in the pit and immediately report trade prices as traders make them. Surrounding the pit are large screens that display the most recent trade prices to the trading crowd. About 200 traders fill the soybean futures pit. The CBOT has about 20 different trading pits on its main trading floor.

The traders are a diverse set of people. Each trader has a seat on the exchange. Some own their seat; some lease it; some use a seat provided by their employer. Most traders are locals, and most locals are scalpers and day traders. Locals are typically one-person operations. Scalpers are dealers who buy and sell for their own account. They try not to hold large positions for more than a few minutes. They are continuously acquiring and unwinding their positions. Day traders are speculators who may be willing to hold positions through the trading session but rarely overnight. Some scalpers and day traders also act as brokers for other traders. The remaining traders are brokers who work either for themselves or for large national firms.

The traders all wear large identification badges that can be seen from across the pit. Most also wear distinctive jackets, often with wild color schemes, to make them easier to find. The jackets have large outside pockets for holding papers. The traders all have a pencil in one hand and a trade card in the other hand. Increasingly, some traders carry handheld trade reporting devices that transmit trades as they record them.

The IIIS clerk finds her floor trader, Jack, by looking for his yellow jacket with two-inch pink polka dots in the place where he normally stands. She gives Jack MM's sell order. Jack reads it with a well-practiced poker face and then sticks it into a pocket.

Traders communicate in the pit by shouting and using hand signals. They shout out their bids and offers so that everyone can hear what they say. The noise can be so great that few traders actually hear what they say, though many can read lips well. Traders therefore also use hand signals to make their bids and offers. They use fingers to indicate prices and sizes. The orientation of the hand (up or sideways) shows whether they are expressing prices or quantities. Hand orientation also shows whether the trader wants to buy or sell: Palm out indicates an offer to sell; palm in indicates a bid from a buyer. By using both voice and hand signals, the traders reduce the chance that they will misunderstand each other.

Traders arrange trades by accepting another trader's bid or offer. Traders yell "sold" to accept a trader's bid or offer. The acceptor also points at the other trader to get his or her attention and to make eye contact. The traders then negotiate the size of the trade.

The IIIS trader thus has two ways that he can arrange to sell soybeans for MM. Jack can offer the beans for sale and hope that a buyer will accept the price. Alternatively, he can wait until a buyer bids and then accept the buyer's price.

When Jack receives the order, the last reported trade price was $678^3/_4$. Some traders are bidding $678^3/_4$ cents and others are offering at 679 cents. Jack's trader accepts the bids from two traders at $678^3/_4$ cents and negotiates to sell three contracts with one and four contracts with another. He quickly writes the terms of the two trades and the two trader IDs on his trade card. The two traders do likewise. Jack then shouts an offer for $678^1/_2$ cents, but no one takes it. After about five seconds, he lowers his offer to $678^1/_4$ cents, and still receives no interest. Some traders bid for $677^3/_4$. He lowers his offer to 678, and three traders take his offer. Jack negotiates to sell the remaining 42 contracts at 678, and the four traders record their trades.

Jack then reports the trades to his clerk. The clerk calls the Moline office with the confirmation, and the broker there then calls MM's risk manager. After reporting the trade, the broker tells the risk manager that MM must post 198,000 dollars in margin to guarantee its performance should the price of soybeans rise. The risk manager posts the margin by transferring Treasury bills worth 200,000 dollars to this account.

Shortly after the 1:15 P.M. (Central Time) close of trading, the final settlement price for the December soybean contract is set at the closing price of $684^1/_4$ cents. Since MM is short 99 soybean contracts sold at an average price of 678.25 cents, MM has lost 6 cents per bushel on its new position. The total dollar loss is 6 cents per bushel times 5,000 bushels per contract times 99 contracts, or 29,700 dollars. MM transfers this amount to IIIS that afternoon.

None of the traders with whom Jack traded knows Jack's order came from MM. Jack likewise does not know whether the traders with whom he traded were trading for their own accounts or for others.

At the end of the trading session, Jack submits a list of all his trades to the Board of Trade Clearing Corporation (BOTCC). The BOTCC takes Jack's trade reports and those of all other traders, and attempts to match the buys with the sells. A trade clears when two traders both report that they traded the same quantity with each other at the same price. About 95 percent of all trade reports clear without problem. The remaining reports are called out-trades. The BOTCC returns these reports to the traders, who must resolve the discrepancies among themselves. Transcription errors generally cause most out-trades. Occasionally they result from misunderstandings. On very rare occasions, out-trades are due to fraudulent reports. The traders must resolve their out-trades before trading starts the next day.

The BOTCC guarantees all trades. Although traders negotiate their contracts with each other, their contracts are actually commitments to the BOTCC. BOTCC thus acts as the buyer for each seller and the seller for each buyer. This arrangement ensures that traders do not need to decide whether another trader is creditworthy before they trade. The clearing members of the CBOT and the MidAmerica Commodity Exchange own the BOTCC. If one of the members defaults, the others bear the resulting losses. To reduce the potential losses, the BOTCC requires that its members post and maintain margin (performance bonds) for each contract they clear.

2.7 AN OPTIONS MARKET TRADE

Lisa holds 2,000 shares of Microsoft stock, which is currently trading for 55 dollars per share. The stock has risen greatly in value since she bought it in 1993 for the split-adjusted equivalent of 5 dollars per share. If she sold it today, she would realize a capital gain of 50 dollars per share and would have to pay a substantial capital gains tax. Lisa now thinks that Microsoft is overvalued, but she is not certain. If it drops in value, she would like to sell her position at today's prices and, if possible, defer the capital gain for a few months to move it into the next tax year. If the price rises, she would like to keep the stock and continue deferring her substantial tax liability.

To achieve her investment goals, Lisa decides to buy 20 Microsoft January 55 put option contracts. Each of these contracts gives her the option to sell 100 shares of Microsoft at 55 dollars per share any time before or on the third Friday in January. If the price of Microsoft rises before then, she will make money on her Microsoft stocks. The options will lose their value, however, and she will not exercise them. If the price of Microsoft falls, the options will become quite valuable, and her loss in her Microsoft stock will be offset, almost one for one, by her gains on the options. In that case, Lisa will decide in January to realize the gains on the options by selling them or by exercising them. If she sells the options, she will pay the capital gains tax on their increase in value at her short-term combined federal and state rate of 44 percent. If she exercises them and sells her Microsoft stock for 55 dollars per share, she will pay the tax on her capital gain at the long-term rate of 26 percent. Although the capital gain will be larger in the stock than in the options, she may exercise the options rather than sell them because of the higher short-term capital gains rate of 44 percent. In either case, she will have deferred the capital gain into the next year.

Lisa calls her securities brokerage, with which she has set up an account with options trading privileges. To obtain these privileges, Lisa had to convince a senior registered options principal at the brokerage that she understands how options work and the risks to which they can expose her. She also had to demonstrate to the principal's satisfaction that she is financially able to withstand the potential losses that can be associated with options trading. The Securities and Exchange Commission, the Options Clearing Corporation (OCC), and the brokerage impose these suitability requirements upon options customers to prevent people from taking risks that they do not understand or cannot afford.

After reaching her broker and giving him her account number, Lisa asks for a quote for the Microsoft January 55 put option contract. To obtain the quote for this option, the broker must first find its ticker symbol. After consulting an electronic list of available trading vehicles for MSFT (the stock ticker symbol for Microsoft), the broker confirms that the ticker symbol for the January Microsoft 55 put contract is MSQMK. The first three letters refer to Microsoft. The last two letters refer to the January 55 put contract. He enters this information into his quotation system to obtain the quote that Lisa requested. The quote for the contract is 4.20 bid, 4.50 offered, last sale at 4.30. The broker also reports that Microsoft stock last traded at 55.44.

Upon hearing the quote, Lisa decides to issue a limit order. She instructs her broker to buy 20 Microsoft January 55 put option contracts, limit price 4.40. The broker enters the order into his electronic order entry system, and then reads it back to Lisa for her confirmation. After listening carefully to the broker, Lisa confirms that the order is correct. The broker then releases the order.

The brokerage's order-routing system sends the order electronically to the Pacific Exchange's order-routing system. This system, called POETS (Pacific Options Exchange Trading System), can forward the order to any of several destinations on the Exchange options floor in San Francisco. For this order, the brokerage's system instructs POETS to route the order to the exchange order book, which an exchange order book official (OBO) manages. The OBO is an employee of the Pacific Exchange who will act as the broker for the order.

The Exchange shows its order book overhead on large computer displays to a crowd of about 20 traders standing in front of the post where Microsoft options trade. Some of these traders are brokers who represent their clients, and some are dealers called market makers, who trade for their own account. When Lisa's order arrives, all the traders notice it. Several traders try to sell at 4.40 by immediately shouting, "Sell that book." The OBO trades a total of 20 contracts with three traders. The OBO then enters information about the trade into POETS, and POETS sends a report of the trade to Lisa's broker.

The broker confirms the trade with Lisa. Although Lisa is initially quite pleased with the trade price, it occurs to her to ask where Microsoft stock is now trading. The broker reports that the last trade in Microsoft was 55.84, 40 cents higher than before. Since the price of Microsoft has risen, the put contract price has dropped. Although the price she obtained was good, it was not as good as it initially seemed. Lisa asks for the current quote in the January 55 put option. The broker reports that the quote is now 4.00 bid, 4.30 offered.

The brokerage, the exchange, and the other traders arrange for settlement of the contract through the Options Clearing Corporation. The OCC clears all exchange-traded option contracts in the United States. It also guarantees performance on all contracts, using mechanisms similar to those described above for the futures markets.

2.8 A BOND MARKET TRADE

Sam works for Sheltered Life, a large (fictitious) insurance company, where he helps manage the bond operations. The firm, like many other insurance companies, invests a substantial fraction of its reserves in long-term corporate bonds. Periodically, the firm must buy new bonds to replace those which have matured and to invest additional funds that its clients give it to manage.

Every day, throughout the day, Sam receives phone calls from sales traders at various investment banks who would like to sell him bonds. The sales traders sometimes offer newly issued bonds that their banks have underwritten. Other times, they offer seasoned bonds that their banks have in inventory. Because Sam is a very big client, the traders all try to please him. Sam talks to them to keep abreast of market conditions.

This morning, Sam has determined that he needs to buy 50 million dollars of long-term corporate investment-grade bonds. After examining his portfolio, and after studying general conditions in the credit markets, Sam has decided that he would like to buy bonds issued by a high-tech firm.

From many years of experience, Sam believes that he will most likely obtain the type of bond he wants today at the best price from Salomon Brothers. He calls up the sales trader who manages his account there and asks him to fax over a list of the long-term, investment-grade high-tech bonds that they have in inventory.

After receiving the list, Sam sees that it contains the IBM $7\frac{1}{2}$ s13 bond. This bond pays a coupon of $7\frac{1}{2}$ percent and matures in 2013. Sam is already familiar with the bond covenant (the terms of the bond) and with IBM's general creditworthiness. He decides that if he can get a good price, he would like to buy this bond. Sam now turns to his Bloomberg terminal to examine prices in the credit markets to get some idea of the price the bond should trade for.

Sam then calls the Salomon Brothers sales trader and asks him to quote a price for the bond. The sales trader quotes him an offering price of 112, which corresponds to 112 percent of the face value of the bond. Sam explains that this price is too high, given current market conditions and the various options that appear in the covenants for that bond. He instead proposes to buy the bond for 70 basis points over the rate of return implied by the on-the-run 10-year Treasury bond. This bond trades in a very active market organized by Cantor Fitzgerald, which is the world's largest U.S. government bond brokerage. After performing some quick calculations, the sales trader determines that the equivalent price is $111\frac{1}{8}$, which is too low for him. The two traders continue negotiating until they agree to a price of $111\frac{5}{8}$.

They both write up trade tickets and give them to their respective operations clerks to settle the trade. The clerks arrange for settlement through a clearinghouse called the National Securities Clearing Corporation (NSCC), a division of the Depository Trust and Clearing Corporation (DTCC). NSCC is by far the largest clearinghouse in the United States. It will act as an escrow agent in a process known as delivery versus payment. NSCC uses a book entry settlement system in which it transfers securities electronically from one account to another.

Sam's clerk reports the trade to Sheltered Life's custodial bank, Chase Manhattan, which will settle the trade. A custodial bank is a firm that holds securities and money on behalf of its clients. A clerk at Chase reports the trade to NSCC, and ensures that enough money is available in Chase's account at NSCC to cover the transaction.

Salomon Brothers acts as its own custodian. The Salomon operations clerk reports the trade directly to NSCC and arranges to transfer the bond to its account there.

On the day of the trade, NSCC should receive both reports of the trade. Overnight, NSCC will match the reports. If the two reports match perfectly, NSCC will confirm the trade to both sides on the next day. If the two reports do not match, or if one trader does not report a trade, NSCC will send DK (Don't Know) notices to both sides to report the discrepancies. The traders then will attempt to reconcile the reports.

On the third day after the trade, known as T+3, NSCC will simultaneously transfer the bond from Salomon's account to Chase's account, and the money from Chase's account to Salomon's account. These transfers will settle Salomon's side of the trade. The bank then will transfer the bond from its account to Sheltered Life's account and the money from Sheltered Life's account to the bank's account to complete the settlement for Sheltered Life.

2.9 A FOREIGN EXCHANGE TRADE

BINC is a medium-sized U.S.-domiciled manufacturer of electric parts used in extreme pressure and chemical environments. It has decided to open a manufacturing subsidiary in Scotland to gain a toehold in the European Community. Until the new operation starts to generate its own revenue, BINC will need to convert dollars to British pounds to pay its rent and salaries.

Olive, BINC's CFO, needs to buy 5 million pounds and transfer them to its account at a Scottish commercial bank. She first consults an Internet page created by Yahoo! that reports current exchange-rate indications. There she sees that the approximate exchange rate is 1.447 dollars per pound. She then calls her banker, Bill, and asks him to quote a price for the purchase and transfer of 5 million pounds to BINC's Scottish commercial bank. After verifying that BINC has sufficient dollars on deposit to buy the pounds, Bill asks Olive to hold while he calls the foreign exchange desk of his bank.

Although BINC's bank is a large regional commercial bank, it does not make a market in British pounds. Instead, it will buy the pounds from a dealer and then sell them to BINC.

Fred, the bank's FX (foreign exchange) trader, takes the call and immediately consults an FX page on his desktop Reuters Dealing 3000 terminal to see some representative dealer quotes. While keeping Bill on the line, Fred picks up another line and calls Norm, a dealer at a large New York bank, to ask him for his quote. Fred calls Norm because he believes he generally receives good service from him, and perhaps also because Norm occasionally takes Fred to NBA basketball games. Norm bids 1.4473 dollars per pound for pounds and offers pounds at 1.4475 dollars per pound. Fred then tells Bill that the bank will sell BINC 5 million pounds at the rate of 1.4477 dollars per pound. Bill tells Olive, who agrees to the transaction. Bill then tells Fred, who immediately arranges to buy pounds from Norm. By convention, both Fred and Norm understand that the quotes are good only for 1 million dollars. Fred asks to sell 7 million dollars, and Norm agrees.

Fred therefore purchases 4.835 million pounds from Norm (7 million dollars ÷ 1.4475 dollars per pound). Fred and Norm then report the trade to their clerks, who will arrange a wire transfer between their two banks. Meanwhile, Sam arranges with Olive to debit BINC's dollar account by 7,238,500 dollars (5 million pounds × 1.4477 dollars per pound) and to wire 5 million pounds to BINC's Scottish bank. The regional bank takes the remaining 154 thousand pounds from its pound accounts. Since the 5 million pounds cost the bank 0.002 dollar per pound less than it paid for them, the bank makes 1,000 dollars on the transaction.

The chapters in this part describe how traders arrange their trades. We start in chapter 3 with a quick introduction to the trading industry. This chapter provides some background information about who trades, what they trade, where they trade, and how their trading is regulated. You can safely skip reading this chapter if you are already familiar with the industry.

Chapter 4 describes how traders communicate their orders to the brokers, dealers, and exchanges that arrange their trades. We describe the orders that traders use and examine the properties of those orders. We also establish important concepts about the origins of liquidity in this chapter.

In chapter 5, we consider how market structures vary. The differences in how markets organize their trading are important because they affect the profitability of different types of traders. We start to consider the relative advantages of various trading systems in this chapter.

Chapter 6 describes how exchanges use order-driven market mechanisms to arrange trades. The discussion introduces important issues that affect how traders formulate optimal order submission strategies.

Chapter 7 discusses how brokers serve their clients. We carefully describe their roles as trade negotiators and as clearing and settlement agents. You may find this chapter most interesting for its discussions about how markets prevent traders from engaging in various types of fraudulent activities.

Part I
▷
The Structure of Trading

3

▷

The
Trading
Industry

This chapter provides a brief survey of the trading industry. If you are already familiar with the industry, you can safely skip this chapter. If you are new to trading, the discussions here will provide you with the "big picture" that will allow you to better understand the rest of this book. In particular, you will be better able to discriminate between issues of primary and secondary importance if you know the context in which traders solve their trading problems.

This chapter is full of financial jargon and institutional detail. Most of it is not necessary for understanding the remainder of this book. If you are interested only in understanding market structure, you need not master the details.

We first consider who trades. Then we characterize trading instruments and the markets where they trade. Finally, we examine how regulators oversee trading.

3.1 WHO ARE THE PLAYERS?

Traders are people who trade. They may arrange their own trades, they may have others arrange trades for them, or they may arrange trades for others. *Proprietary traders* trade for their own accounts, and *brokers* arrange trades as agents for their clients. Brokers are also called *agency traders*, *commission traders*, or *commission merchants*. Proprietary traders engage in *proprietary trading*, and brokers engage in *agency trading*.

Traders have *long positions* when they own something. Traders with long positions profit when prices rise. They try to buy low and sell high.

Traders have *short positions* when they have sold something that they do not own. Traders with short positions hope that prices will fall so they can repurchase at a lower price. When they repurchase, they *cover their positions*. *Short sellers* profit when they sell high and buy low.

The trading industry has a buy side and a sell side. The *buy side* consists of traders who buy exchange services. Liquidity is the most important of these services. *Liquidity* is the ability to trade when you want to trade. Traders on the *sell side* sell liquidity to the buy side. A substantial fraction of this book considers how interactions between buy-side and sell-side traders determine the price of liquidity.

(The buy and sell sides of the trading industry have nothing to do with whether a trader is a buyer or a seller of an instrument. Traders on both sides of the trading industry regularly buy and sell securities and contracts. The terms "buy side" and "sell side" refer to buyers and sellers of exchange services.)

3.1.1 The Buy Side

The buy side of the trading industry includes individuals, funds, firms, and governments that use the markets to help solve various problems they face.

TABLE 3-1.
The Buy Side of the Trading Industry

TRADER TYPE	GENERIC EXAMPLES	WHY THEY TRADE	TYPICAL INSTRUMENTS
Investors	Individuals Corporate pension funds Insurance funds Charitable and legal trusts Endowments Mutual funds Money managers	To move wealth from the present to the future for themselves or for their clients	Stocks Bonds
Borrowers	Homeowners Students Corporations	To move wealth from the future to the present	Mortgages Bonds Notes
Hedgers	Farmers Manufacturers Miners Shippers Financial institutions	To reduce business operating risk	Futures contracts Forward contracts Swaps
Asset exchangers	International corporations Manufacturers Travelers	To acquire an asset that they value more than the asset that they tender	Currencies Commodities
Gamblers	Individuals	To entertain themselves	Various

These problems typically originate outside of trading markets. For example, investors use securities markets to solve intertemporal cash flow problems: They have income today that they would like to have available in the future. They use the markets to buy stocks and bonds to move their income from the present to the future. We discuss this problem and other buy-side trading problems in chapter 8.

Many buy-side institutions are pension funds, mutual funds, trusts, endowments, and foundations that invest money. These institutions are known collectively as *investment sponsors*. Investment sponsors frequently employ *investment advisers* to manage their funds. Investment advisers are also called *investment counselors*, *investment managers*, or *portfolio managers*. Investment advisers often employ traders to implement their trading decisions. These traders are *buy-side traders*. The people and institutions who will ultimately benefit from the funds that *investment sponsors* hold are *beneficiaries*. A summary of buy-side traders appears in table 3-1.

3.1.2 The Sell Side

The *sell side* of the trading industry includes dealers and brokers who provide exchange services to the buy side. Both types of traders help buy-side traders trade when they want to trade.

Dealers accommodate trades that their clients want to make by trading with them when their clients want to trade. Dealers profit when they buy low and sell high. We discuss dealers in chapter 13.

▶ The Wire in Wirehouse

Traders often call large broker-dealers *wirehouses*. The word "wire" in wirehouse once referred to the telegraph. Following its invention, broker-dealers used the telegraph to collect orders from branch offices in distant cities. Those who quickly adopted it were able to expand their businesses substantially and thereby greatly increase their profits. The ability to communicate quickly was—and remains—very important in the trading industry. ◀

In contrast, *brokers* trade on behalf of their clients. Brokers arrange trades that their clients want to make by finding other traders who will trade with their clients. Brokers profit when their clients pay them commissions for arranging trades with other traders. We discuss brokers in chapter 7.

Many sell-side firms employ traders who both deal and broker trades. These firms therefore are known as *broker-dealers* or *dual traders*.

The sell side exists only because the buy side will pay for its services. We therefore must understand why the buy side trades before we can understand when the sell side is profitable. We consider how and why both sides trade in subsequent chapters. Table 3-2 provides a summary of the sell side of the trading industry.

3.2 TRADE FACILITATORS

Many institutions help traders trade. We introduce exchanges, clearing and settlement agents, depositories, and custodians in this section.

3.2.1 Exchanges

Exchanges provide forums where traders meet to arrange trades. Exchange traders may include dealers, brokers, and buy-side traders. Only members can trade at most exchanges. Nonmembers trade by asking member-brokers to trade for them. Historically, traders met on exchange floors. Now, at many exchanges, traders meet only via electronic communications networks.

Some exchanges only provide a forum where traders meet to arrange their trades as they see fit. Other exchanges have *order-driven trading systems* that arrange trades by matching buy and sell orders according to a set

TABLE 3-2.
The Sell Side of the Trading Industry

TRADER TYPE	GENERIC EXAMPLES	WELL-KNOWN U.S. EXAMPLES	WHY THEY TRADE
Dealers	Market makers Specialists Floor traders Locals Day traders Scalpers	Spear Leads & Kellogg LaBranche & Co. Bernard L. Madoff Investment Securities Knight Trading Group TimberHill LLC	To earn trading profits by supplying liquidity
Brokers	Retail brokers Discount brokers Full-service brokers Institutional brokers Block brokers Futures commission merchants	Charles Schwab & Co. E*Trade Dreyfus Brokerage Services Abel/Noser Corp. XpressTrade Cargill Financial Markets Group	To earn commissions by arranging trades for clients
Broker-dealers	Wirehouses	Goldman Sachs Merrill Lynch Salomon Smith Barney Morgan Stanley Dean Witter Credit Suisse First Boston	To earn trading profits and trading commissions

of rules. These exchanges may use computers, clerks, or their member-traders to process orders. Order-driven exchanges are essentially brokerages because they arrange trades for their clients. Exchanges and brokerages therefore often compete with each other.

Some U.S. equity trading systems are known as *electronic communications networks* (ECNs). These are order-driven trading systems that are not regulated as exchanges. Brokerages, dealers, or other entities may own them. The most important ECNs are Island ECN, Instinet, REDIBook, Archipelago, and Bloomberg Tradebook. Many ECNs are in the process of registering to become exchanges.

Exchanges once were owned and controlled by their members. Membership organizations, however, tend not to be nimble competitors. Conflicts among members and cumbersome governance mechanisms often ensure that membership organizations cannot innovate quickly. To compete more effectively with ECNs, brokerages, and other exchanges, many exchanges have converted, or are in the process of converting, to corporate ownership. With corporate ownership, they hope to obtain highly motivated, empowered, entrepreneurial management. The Nasdaq Stock Market, the Chicago Mercantile Exchange, the Stockholm Stock Exchange, the Toronto Stock Exchange, and the Deutsche Börse are examples of exchanges that have recently demutualized.

Not all trading takes place at exchanges. In many markets, dealers and brokers arrange trades *over the counter*. The corporate bond market is an example of a large market in which almost no trading takes place at organized exchanges.

3.2.2 Clearing and Settlement Agents, Depositories, and Custodians

Several agencies facilitate trading by helping traders settle the trades they have arranged. They also prevent problems that can arise when some traders are not trustworthy or creditworthy.

3.2.2.1 Clearing Agents

When traders arrange trades on exchange floors or over the telephone, the buyers and sellers both make a record of their trades. They record the terms of their trades and the identities of the traders with whom they traded. To settle their trades, buyers and sellers must compare their records. In most markets, traders submit their records to a common clearing agent to facilitate these comparisons. The *clearing agent* matches the buyer and seller records and confirms that both traders agreed to the same terms. Once trades are cleared, traders then settle their trades. The largest securities clearing agency in the United States is the *National Securities Clearing Corporation* (NSCC).

A trade *clears* if the buyer and seller both report that they traded with each other, and their reported terms of trade are identical. If the records do not match exactly, the clearing agent reports the discrepancies to the traders, who then try to resolve them. In the futures markets, such trades are called *out-trades*. In the securities markets, they are called *DK*s (for *Don't Know*).

Clearing is a trivial exercise when automated order-matching systems arrange all trades. Since these systems know everything about the trades they arrange, they always report matched trades.

▶ T+5 and Counting Down

Brokers and regulators would like to settle security trades as quickly as possible in order to minimize trader exposure to credit risks. During the time between the negotiation of a trade and the time it settles, prices can change substantially. The side that is hurt by the price change then may be unable or unwilling to settle the trade. Such failures can be quite painful to the other side. Traders minimize failure risk by settling their trades quickly. Until June 1995, the U.S. securities industry settled stock and bond trades on T+5. It now settles trades on T+3. Starting in June 2005, the industry intends to settle on T+1. T+1 settlement will require most traders to deposit money and certificates with their brokers before they trade, to ensure that they can settle the next day. ◀

3.2.2.2 Settlement Agents

Settlement agents help traders settle their trades. They receive cash from buyers and securities from sellers. When both sides have performed, the settlement agent gives the cash to the seller and the securities to the buyer.

Traders use settlement agents because the agents are very efficient at settling trades, and because they can help them avoid the losses that can arise if they trade with an untrustworthy or uncreditworthy trader. In the real estate markets, settlement agents are called *escrow agents*. Since clearing and settlement are closely related, the National Securities Clearing Corporation is also, not surprisingly, the largest U.S. securities settlement agency.

Much of the efficiency in the settlement process is due to net settlement. Under *net settlement*, for each client, the settlement agent nets the buys and sells in each security to a single net security position. The settlement agent also nets all money credits and debits into a single net money position for each client. The agent then settles only the net positions. Through netting, the settlement agency can vastly reduce the number of transactions necessary to settle trades. Net settlement works best when all traders use the same settlement agent.

In U.S. securities markets, *normal-way settlement* occurs three business days after trades are arranged. Such settlement is called *T+3* settlement. Almost all transactions settle on T+3. Traders can also arrange special settlement on other days. The most common special settlement instruction is *cash settlement*, which occurs on the day of the trade.

3.2.2.3 Clearinghouses

Many futures, options, and swaps markets have clearinghouses associated with them. The *clearinghouses* clear and settle all trades in these derivative contracts. They also usually guarantee that both parties will perform on their contracts. They do this by acting as buyer for every seller and as seller for every buyer. They therefore are the issuers and guarantors of their contracts.

Clearinghouses generally are owned by *clearing members*, who are jointly responsible for settling all trades. Traders who are not clearing members must have a clearing member guarantee the settlement of their trades. If a trader fails to settle a trade, his clearing member must do so. If a clearing member fails to settle a trade—usually due to bankruptcy—the clearinghouse can tax its other members to settle the trade. The clearinghouse is therefore like a mutual insurance company.

Since losses can be quite significant, clearinghouses pay very close attention to the credit quality of their members and to the potential settlement risks that they can impose upon other traders. To control these risks, clearinghouses require that their members post collateral called *margins* to secure their obligations, provide timely information about their financial conditions and their trading activities, and not exceed positions limits that the clearinghouse establishes for them. The exchanges do not allow members to trade without approval from the clearinghouse.

In futures markets, final settlement takes place when the contracts mature. After every trading day, traders also make an intermediate settlement of their accounts in which they transfer profits earned that day from losers to winners. Brokers make these transfers to and from their customers' margin accounts through the intermediation of the exchange clearinghouse. These *variation margin* adjustments ensure that the incentives to default on a contract do not grow as prices move against a losing position.

The Brazilian Straddle

A trader has a *straddle* when he holds positions in two different types of instruments. The risks in the two instruments often offset each other so that the combined position is less risky than either position held alone. In the options markets, a straddle consists of a position in a put and an offsetting position in a call.

Technically bankrupt traders present a special problem to the firms that guarantee their trades. Traders are *technically bankrupt* when they no longer have enough wealth to settle their trades. If prices do not change in their favor, they soon will be forced into actual bankruptcy.

When traders know that they are technically bankrupt, they have nothing to lose by massively increasing their positions. If prices change so that their positions make money, they may escape their financial problems. If prices change against them so that they lose even more, those who guarantee their trades will suffer the losses.

A trader who uses this strategy is said to hold a Brazilian straddle. A *Brazilian straddle* consists of a large market position held against a one-way airline ticket to Brazil in the breast pocket. If the market position proves profitable, the trader sells the ticket and comes back to trade tomorrow. If the trader continues to lose, he runs off to Brazil and leaves his clearing member to clean up the resulting mess.

Clearing members must carefully monitor the traders who clear through them to ensure that their customers do not try to play the Brazilian straddle. To avoid the problem, they require that their customers report their positions frequently during the day. They also require that their customers make margin payments within the day when prices move substantially against their positions. Finally, when they determine that their customers cannot settle their trades, they prohibit them from trading.

Clearing firms also execute contracts with their customers that allocate any profits earned by technically bankrupt customers to the clearing firm if the customer did not report the problem. This provision takes the profit out of the successful Brazilian straddle. It works, however, only if the clearing firm detects the bankruptcy. ◀

A Typical Set of Relationships

A large state pension fund receives money from the state treasury to hold and invest for its beneficiaries. The pension fund deposits the money in its account at its custodian bank. It also notifies its investment adviser that it has money available for investment.

A portfolio manager who works for the investment adviser considers how to best invest the funds. The manager considers the portfolio that the sponsor presently holds, the expected pension liabilities that the fund must satisfy, and the investment opportunities that the adviser believes it can identify. The manager decides to buy 30,000 shares of Cisco Systems.

The portfolio manager contacts his firm's buy-side trader—a fellow employee—and instructs her to buy 30,000 shares of Cisco Systems. She then issues an order to the state pension fund's broker to buy the shares. For political reasons, the state pension fund may direct its investment adviser to use brokers domiciled in the state when trading on its behalf.

The broker calls a dealer and arranges the trade. The dealer sells the shares to the pension fund out of its inventory. The dealer and the broker both report the trade to the National Securities Clearing Corporation (NSCC). The broker also reports the trade to the pension fund and to the investment adviser. Three days later, on instructions from the dealer and the pension fund, NSCC settles the trade. The custodian bank sends money to the pension fund's account at the Depository Trust Company (DTC). The DTC then provides the money to settle on behalf of the pension fund, and it receives the 30,000 shares on behalf of the pension fund. ◀

Straight-Through Processing

Trading systems that fully automate the clearing and settlement process provide *straight-through processing* (STP) to their clients. Traders like STP because it is cheap and minimizes the potential for errors. ◀

3.2.2.4 Depositories and Custodians

Depositories and custodians hold cash and securities on behalf of their clients. They help settle trades by quickly delivering cash and security certificates—when properly instructed—to settlement agents. Depositories and custodians also help ensure the security of their clients' assets.

The largest depository in the world is the *Depository Trust Company* (DTC). DTC holds nearly 20 trillion dollars in assets for its participants and their clients. It is a subsidiary of the Depository Trust and Clearing Corporation (DTCC). The other major subsidiary of DTCC is the National Securities Clearing Corporation (NSCC).

3.3 TRADING INSTRUMENTS

The securities, contracts, commodities, and currencies that traders trade are collectively known as *trading instruments*. Trading instruments vary by type. They include real assets, financial assets, derivative contracts, insurance contracts, and gambling contracts. *Financial instruments* include financial assets, derivative contracts, and insurance contracts.

This section describes various classes of trading instruments and special aspects of the markets in which they trade. It also defines some common trading instruments. A summary of the various classes of instruments appears in table 3-3.

TABLE 3-3.
Trading Instrument Summary

CLASS	INSTRUMENT	CREATORS
Real assets	Spot commodities	Farmers, miners, manufacturers
	Intellectual properties	Inventors and artists
	Real estate	Builders
	Pollution emission rights	Governments
Financial assets	Stocks and warrants	Corporate issuers
	Bonds	Corporate issuers, governments
	Trust units	Trusts
	Currencies	Governments, banks
Derivative contracts	Futures contracts	Sellers
	Forward contracts	Sellers
	Options	Sellers
	Swaps	Sellers
Insurance contracts	Insurance policies	Corporations
	Reinsurance contracts	Corporations
Hybrid instruments	Warrants	Corporate issuers
	Index linked bonds	Corporate issuers
	Convertible bonds	Corporate issuers
Gambling contracts	Numerous types	Individuals
		Bookies
		Casinos
		Racetracks

3.3.1 Real Assets

Real assets include physical commodities, real estate, machines, patents, and other intellectual properties. Real assets also include *pollution credits*, which are rights to emit a specified quantity of a given type of pollution. Real assets are instruments that would appear only on the asset side of a balance sheet.

The real assets that trade in the most liquid markets are industrial and precious metals, agricultural commodities, fuels, and pollution credits. These instruments generally are quite fungible: One unit is very similar, if not identical, to all other units. Traders in these commodities generally are more concerned about price than about quality variations. They usually can easily adjust prices for any quality variations.

3.3.2 Financial Assets

Financial assets are instruments that represent ownership of real assets and the cash flows that they produce. Stocks and bonds are financial assets because they represent ownership of the assets of a corporation. Stockholders own the assets of a corporation after all creditors have been paid off. Bondholders own the assets of a corporation if the corporation defaults on its creditors and becomes bankrupt. Other financial assets include currencies, warehouse receipts that represent ownership of physical commodities, and trust units that represent ownership of the assets of a trust.

Issuers create all financial assets. Corporations issue stocks, bonds, and warrants. Governments issue currencies and bonds. Warehouses issue commodity receipts. Trusts issue trust units. Many securities are called *issues* because issuers issue them.

Financial assets appear on both sides of a balance sheet. A financial asset appears as a liability on the issuer's balance sheet and as an asset on the holders' balance sheet.

Issues trade in *primary markets* when issuers first create and sell them. Subsequent trading occurs in *secondary markets*. *New issues* become *seasoned securities* after they are issued. Traders therefore trade new issues in primary markets and seasoned issues in secondary markets. Traders say that primary trading in new equity issues takes place in the *initial public offering* (IPO) *market*.

Issuers often use the services of *underwriters* to help them sell their securities. *Underwriters* are broker-dealers at investment banks who find buyers for the securities. In a *best efforts offering*, the underwriter acts strictly as a broker. In an *underwritten offering*, the underwriter guarantees the issuer an offering price. If the underwriter cannot find buyers for the securities at the offering price, the underwriter buys them for its own account. In a *fixed-price open offering*, the underwriter sets a price and buyers subscribe to the offering. If the offering is oversubscribed, the underwriter conducts a lottery to allocate the shares. Underwriters generally charge issuers fees for their services.

Commodities and currencies trade for immediate delivery in *spot markets*. They trade for future delivery in *forward markets* or *futures markets*. Farmers, miners, and manufacturers create most physical commodities, and national central banks create most currencies.

3.3.2.1 Definitions of Some Common Financial Assets

Equities

Stocks represent ownership of corporate assets, net of corporate liabilities. Stock values depend on corporate assets, liabilities, and income. They also

Stripping Bonds

When traders want more zero-coupon bonds than are available, zero-coupon bonds become expensive relative to straight bonds. *Fixed-income arbitrageurs* then buy straight bonds and *clip* the coupons. They bundle the coupons by their interest payment dates and sell the bundles and the remaining final principal payments as zero coupon bonds.

Traders call this process *stripping a bond*. The term comes from a time when all bonds were bearer bonds. The owners of *bearer bonds* are not registered with bond issuers. Since issuers cannot keep track of who owns their bearer bonds, they make interest payments only when the bondholders present them with interest coupons clipped from the side of the paper upon which the bonds are printed. The coupons are dated so that each one corresponds to an interest payment date. The final principal repayments occur when the bondholders present the now fully stripped bonds to the issuers. ◄

depend critically on how well traders expect corporate managers will use corporate assets in the future.

Preferred stocks are stocks that pay dividends at contractually specified rates. Corporations must pay all accrued dividends on preferred stocks before they can pay any dividends on common stock.

American depository receipts (ADRs) are trust units that traders use to trade foreign stocks in U.S. markets. Each trust holds only the stock of a single foreign company. ADRs are popular because they allow traders to avoid international settlement problems.

Exchange-traded funds (ETFs) are mutual funds that trade at exchanges. They have become extremely popular in recent years. Most ETFs are *index funds* that try to mimic the returns of a market or industry index.

Real estate investment trusts (REITs) are trusts that own real estate. By *securitizing* real estate, they allow investors and speculators to trade real estate interests like common stock shares.

Debt Instruments

Bonds are debt securities issued by corporations, governments, and occasionally individuals. Debtors create bonds when they borrow money. Bond values depend on interest rates, issuer creditworthiness, assets pledged as collateral, and attached options. Traders usually quote bond prices as a percentage of their *par value*. For example, the price of a million-dollar Treasury bond quoted at 97 is 970,000 dollars.

A *straight bond* is a bond that pays interest periodically until it matures. At maturity, the issuer redeems the bond for its *principal* or *face value*. Straight bonds usually do not have attached options.

Credit quality, the probability that a bond issuer will make all bond payments when they are due, greatly concerns bond investors. Investors expect that the issuers of *investment grade bonds* will make all interest and principal payments on time. The interest and principal payments on *junk bonds* are less certain. The latter are also called *high yield bonds* because investors require high yields to compensate for the probability that the issuers will default on their payments. The credit quality of a bond depends on the financial strength of its issuer and upon that collateral and bond covenants that the issuer uses to secure the bond.

Treasury bills, *Treasury notes*, and *Treasury bonds* are debt securities issued by a country. Bills normally mature in one year or less. Notes normally mature two to five years after they are issued, and bonds normally mature ten or more years after they are issued. Bills do not pay interest. Instead, they sell at a discount from their *face value*.

Zero coupon bonds pay no interest. They simply return their principal value at maturity. Since they pay no interest, buyers will buy them only at a discount from their face value. *Zero coupon bonds* therefore are also known as *pure discount bonds*. The greater the time to maturity, the greater the discount. A straight bond is equivalent to a bundle of zero coupon bonds consisting of one zero-coupon bond due on each interest payment date plus a zero-coupon bond due when the straight bond matures. The principal values of the various bonds correspond to the various payments due on the straight bond.

Commercial paper is a short-term debt security issued by a corporation. Commercial paper usually matures in nine months or less from the date it is issued.

Mortgage-backed securities are bondlike instruments which receive the mortgage payments that borrowers make on their mortgages. The securities are backed by a specified set of mortgages called a *mortgage pool*. Since they receive the mortgage payments as they are paid, they are examples of *pass-through securities*.

Collateralized mortgage obligations (CMOs) are mortgage-backed securities that divide rights to the cash flows from the mortgage pool into several different *tranches*. Each tranche has different rights to the payments that the mortgage borrowers make. Issuers generally structure the CMO tranches to look like various types of bonds. The first tranche has the highest claim on the mortgage payments and therefore is the least risky. When its claims are satisfied, the next tranche is paid, and so on until the available funds are exhausted. The last tranche, which is usually called the Z tranche, gets whatever is left over. It is obviously the most risky tranche. CMOs are also called *real estate mortgage investment conduits* (REMICs). Companies issue CMOs to distribute mortgage prepayment risk and interest rate risk among investors with varying degrees of risk tolerance.

All debt instruments are collectively known as *fixed-income products*.

3.3.3 Derivative Contracts

Derivative contracts are instruments that derive their values from the values of the *underlying instruments* upon which they are based. They are contractual agreements between buyers and sellers that specify the exchange of certain privileges and liabilities. Derivative contracts include forward contracts, futures contracts, options, and swaps.

Sellers create derivative contracts when they first sell them. Derivative contracts therefore are in *zero net supply*. The sum of all long positions minus the sum of all short positions is always zero.

All derivative contracts have an element of *futurity*: Their values depend on future events. For example, the prices of futures, options, and forwards all depend on future prices of their underlying instruments.

Almost all derivative contracts have an *expiration date*. On that date, traders make final settlement and the contract expires. European traders refer to this date as the *expiry* of the contract. Contracts that do not expire are *infinitely lived*. Exchanges and investment banks have proposed many infinitely lived derivative contracts, but none have been notably successful.

Derivative contracts may be physically settled or cash settled. A *physically settled contract* requires that the seller deliver the underlying instrument to the buyer when obligated to do so. At that time, the buyer pays cash for the instrument at the agreed price. A *cash-settled contract* requires that the seller deliver the cash value of the underlying instrument to the buyer when obligated to do so. At the same time, the buyer pays the agreed-upon purchase price. In practice, the traders transfer only the difference between the value and the price. If the contract is a futures contract, the difference might be negative. In that case, the seller pays the buyer the difference. If the contract is an option contract, the difference will never be negative because contract holders will not exercise their options when doing so would require that they make additional payments.

Derivative contracts always have a *notional size* or *notional value*. For physically delivered contracts, the *notional size* is simply the amount that

▶ **Toxic Waste**

The riskiest CMO tranches are called *toxic waste* because no one wants to hold them. They typically sell at highly discounted prices. Foolish people often pay too much for them because these tranches will realize very high rates of return if very few mortgage borrowers default on their obligations. Toxic waste is worthless, however, if too many borrowers default. The inability of various organizations to fully appreciate the default risks in toxic waste has led to some spectacular trading losses. ◀

▶ **A Tomato Forward**

A tomato forward contract is an agreement between a buyer and a seller in which the buyer agrees to pay a fixed price for tomatoes that the seller will deliver in the future. The seller may not own the tomatoes when they negotiate the contract.

Tomato farmers generally execute forward contracts with food processors. The farmers obtain fixed prices for their harvests, and the food processors obtain fixed prices for the tomatoes they must buy to produce their products. ◀

The Eurex ODAX Contract

Eurex trades a cash-settled option contract based on the German Deutscher Aktienindex (DAX) equity index. The notional value of this ODAX contract is five euros per index point, or 29,500 euros, given the 5,900 level of the DAX at the end of June 2001.

If you buy an ODAX call option with a strike price of 6,200 for 26.00 euros, you will pay 130 euros for the contract. If the DAX on the expiration date closes at 6,500, you will make five times the difference between the closing price and the strike price, or 1,500 euros. If the DAX remains below 6,200, you will not exercise the option, and it will expire worthless. ◀

Variation Margin Example

Brad buys a 5,000-troy-ounce silver futures contract for 4.50 an ounce from Sharon at the COMEX division of the New York Mercantile Exchange (NYMEX). The NYMEX Clearing House guarantees that both traders will perform on the contract. On the next day, the price of silver rises by 5 cents. The NYMEX Clearing House requires that Sharon pay it 250 dollars (5,000 ounces times 0.05 dollar per ounce) in variation margin. Simultaneously, the Clearing House pays Brad 250 dollars in variation margin. If the price of silver is the same when the contract expires, Brad will pay 4.55 an ounce for the silver, and Sharon will receive 4.55 an ounce. ◀

the seller must deliver. For cash-settled contracts, a formula specifies the *notional value* that determines the final cash settlement.

Many derivative contracts require that buyers and sellers make variational margin payments on a regular basis. *Variational margin payments* transfer money from buyers to sellers or from sellers to buyers to adjust the prices of their contracts to reflect current market conditions. This procedure ensures that contract values do not change as market conditions change. Variation margin payments therefore reduce the chance that traders will default when their contracts expire.

3.3.3.1 Some Derivative Contract Definitions

Forward contracts are contracts for the future sale of some commodity. The commodity may be a physical commodity, like pork bellies, or a financial commodity, like a currency. Since these contracts derive their values from the values of the underlying commodities, they are derivative contracts.

Standardized futures contracts are forward contracts that an exchange clearinghouse guarantees. Futures traders therefore do not care whether their counterparts are creditworthy. They only need to consider whether the clearinghouse is creditworthy. Moreover, since buyers and sellers trade the same contracts, and since the clearinghouse is a buyer to every seller and a seller to every buyer, traders can open a position by buying a contract from one trader and close the position by selling it to someone else. They do not need to buy and sell with the same trader to offset their positions.

An *option* represents the right—but not the obligation—to do something. *Option contracts* give their holders the option to buy or sell an underlying instrument (or, in the case of a cash-settled option, the cash value of an underlying instrument) at a fixed price. The *writer* of the option is the trader who sold the contract. The option is *written upon* the *underlying instrument*. A *call option* is an option to buy at a fixed *strike price*. A *put option* is an option to sell at a fixed strike price. If the option holder can exercise the option any time before the *expiration date*, it is an *American-style option*. If the holder can exercise only on the expiration date, it is a *European-style option*. Since option contracts depend on underlying security values, they are *derivative contracts*.

A *futures option contract* is an option contract written on a futures contract. The holder of a call option on a futures contract has the right to purchase a futures contract at a specified strike price. Likewise, the holder of a futures put option has the right to sell a futures contract at a specified strike price. Futures option contracts trade at the exchange where the underlying futures contracts trade.

Swaps are contracts for the exchange of two future cash flows. A *cash flow* is a series of payments. An *interest rate swap* provides for the exchange of a future series of fixed-rate interest payments for a future series of variable floating-rate interest payments. When they enter the contract, the traders negotiate the fixed-rate payments and agree upon a formula for computing the future variable-rate payments. A *currency swap* provides for the exchange of a future series of fixed payments in one currency for a future series of payments in another currency. Since the values of these contracts depend on the values of the cash flows that the traders swap, swaps are *derivative contracts*.

▶ The Third Order Derivative of LIFFE

The London International Financial Futures and Options Exchange (LIFFE) trades a euro interest rate swap futures contract called the Swapnote. This is a cash-settled futures contract that prices the expiration day value of a standard bond-pricing formula for a hypothetical fixed-rate bond. The hypothetical bond consists of a series of notional fixed 6 percent interest payments followed by the return of the notional principal at the maturity of the hypothetical bond. The pricing formula uses discount rates that are derived from the *swaps yield curve*, which is computed from ISDA Benchmark Euribor Swap Rate fixings. The Swapnote futures contracts thus derive their values from prices in the swaps market.

LIFFE also trades options on Swapnote futures. The Swapnote futures option is a derivative on a derivative on a derivative. (It is an option contract on a futures contract based on swaps contract prices.) ◀

Source: www.liffe.com

Swaptions are options on a swap contract. A trader who owns a swaption call has the right to buy a swap at the specified strike price.

3.3.4 Insurance Contracts and Gambling Contracts

Insurance contracts and *gambling contracts* are instruments that derive their values from the outcomes of future events. For example, the value of a fire insurance contract on a building depends on whether the building burns down. The value of a point spread bet on the Lakers depends on whether they win their basketball game by more than the specified point spread.

The distinction between an insurance contract and a gambling contract depends on the reasons why people buy them. People who are concerned about the loss that they would experience if some future event takes place buy insurance contracts. Such traders are called *hedgers*. Gambling contracts are arranged by people who have no other financial stake in the underlying event. People arrange gambling contracts for entertainment, whereas they arrange financial contracts to raise capital and reallocate risk.

Like derivative contracts, insurance contracts and gambling contracts have an element of futurity. They are also in zero net supply.

Whether the future price of an instrument is equal to some specified value is itself a future event. Derivative contracts therefore are contracts whose values depend on future events. We therefore can classify derivative contracts as insurance contracts or gambling contracts. In fact, many hedgers use derivative contracts to insure against risks that they face, and many traders use derivative contracts to gamble on future events in which they have no financial interest.

3.3.5 Hybrid Contracts

Some trading instruments defy easy classification because they embody elements of more than one type of instrument. For example, some oil companies issue oil-linked bonds. The interest that they pay depends on the price of oil. These bonds are financial assets because they represent ownership of the assets of the firm in the event of bankruptcy. They also are

▶ Why Discuss Gambling Contracts?

Although we do not normally consider gambling contracts to be securities, the same economics that govern traditional securities markets also govern gambling markets. The close analogy between the two markets is both useful and harmful. It can be a source of powerful economic intuition, but it also has been the source of many important public policy problems. We will consider the role of gamblers in the markets throughout this book. ◀

▶ Shall We Quibble?

The distinctions between real assets, financial assets, derivative contracts, insurance contracts, and gambling contracts are somewhat arbitrary:

- Any instrument that defines a relation between a buyer and a seller is a contract. For example, a bond is a contract between bondholders (the buyers) and an issuer (the seller). We reserve the term "contract" for agreements that define a continuing relation between generally unrelated buyers and sellers.
- We could consider anyone who sells a contract an issuer. We reserve the term "issuer" for instruments that only one seller—typically a corporation—can create.
- All issues are in zero net supply if we count short positions of issuers. We reserve the term "zero net supply" only for contracts that public traders can create by selling.
- Virtually all instruments have an element of futurity because the value of anything that is not immediately perishable depends in large part on future events. For example, the value of cattle sold on the spot market depends on the future prices of meat, leather, and milk, and on the future prices of alfalfa, energy, and veterinarian services. We apply the term "futurity" only to contracts that settle in the future.
- All instrument values are correlated to some extent. For example, stock values are correlated with bond values because the discount rates that analysts use to value stocks depend on interest rates. These observations suggest, then, that we could classify stocks as derivative instruments. We reserve the term, however, for instruments whose values depend directly on other instrument values through some contractual mechanism rather than indirectly through common valuation factors.
- Precious metals like gold and silver are such close substitutes for money that many people consider them financial assets as well as real assets. Let's not quibble over this one. ◀

derivative contracts because they derive at least part of their value from the price of oil.

An *equity warrant* issued by a corporation is another example of a hybrid contract. *Warrants* are options that allow the holder to purchase stock at a specified price from the issuing corporation at some time in the future. Since a corporation issues them, and since they represent ownership of the assets of the corporation under certain circumstances, they are financial assets. Since their value depends on the value of the underlying stock, they are like derivative contracts.

Convertible bonds are also hybrid contracts. The holder of a *convertible bond* can exchange it for stock under some circumstances. A convertible therefore is the combination of a straight bond plus an option to exchange the bond for stock. The straight bond is a financial asset. The option gives the convertible bond derivative properties because its value depends on the values of the straight bond and of the stock.

3.4 WHERE ARE THE TRADING MARKETS?

We briefly survey trading markets in this section. The main points to identify are the following:

- Stocks represent less wealth than the widespread attention given to them by the media would suggest.
- Trading volume depends in part on the number of available instruments. Markets with a great number of different instruments are often quite illiquid.
- Exchanges everywhere have been consolidating.

We first characterize trading in various instrument classes. Then we discuss where trading occurs in each instrument class.

3.4.1 The Magnitude of Trading

Organized markets appear throughout the economy. Table 3-4 characterizes the relative importance of the various types of traded instruments in the United States. Despite the tremendous attention given to the stock market in the media, stocks represent only about 20 percent of the capital wealth of the country. Most of the wealth is in real estate, which rarely trades, and in various types of bonds. Derivative contracts represent no wealth because they are all in zero net supply and do not represent ownership of real assets.

The major national exchanges in the United States list about 8,250 stocks, of which only a fraction trade actively. At the NYSE, the 250 most active stocks accounted for 62 percent of the total reported trading volume, and a larger percentage of the total dollar volume, in 2000. When trading the most active stocks, public traders often trade with other public traders. Otherwise, public traders often trade with sell-side dealers. Most trades are small retail trades; large institutional traders account for most share volume.

Although listed option contracts do not trade for most stocks, the number of listed option contracts far exceeds the number of stocks. For each option-eligible stock, options exchanges list many put and call options for various expiration months and for various strike prices. Very few option contracts trade frequently, however. The most frequently traded options are current month calls on actively traded stocks for which the strike price is close

TABLE 3-4.

U.S. Markets by Instrument Class

CLASS	CAPITAL WEALTH	TOTAL INSTRUMENTS	ACTIVELY TRADED INSTRUMENTS	TRADE FREQUENCY	NOMINAL TRADING VOLUME
Common stocks	20%	15,000	1,000	High	Low
Equity option contracts	0%	160,000	500	Moderate	Very low
Corporate bonds	15%	100,000	50	Low	Low
Municipal bonds	10%	1,000,000	0	Low	Low
Government bonds	10%	50	3	Moderate	Moderate
Futures contracts	0%	100	20	High	Moderate
Swap contracts	0%	20	2	Moderate	Moderate
Currencies	<1%	200	10	High	High
Spot commodities	<1%	Millions	25	High	Moderate
Real estate	50%	100,000,000	0	Very low	Low

Source: Author's estimates.

Note: The percentages add up to more than 100 percent primarily because corporations own real estate.

▶ The New York Stock Exchange's Quantitative Listing Standards for Domestic Companies

Domestic companies that wish to list with the New York Stock Exchange must meet all of the following quantitative listing standards:

1. The company must have at least 2,000 U.S. shareholders that each hold at least one round lot, or it must have at least 2,200 shareholders and monthly average trading volume of at least 100,000 shares over the last six months, or it must have at least 500 shareholders and average monthly trading volume of at least 1 million shares over the last 12 months and at least 1.1 million publicly held shares.

2. The publicly held shares of the company must have an aggregate market value of at least 100 million dollars, or 60 million dollars if the company is listing at the time of its initial public offering.

3. The company must meet at least one of four alternative financial standards. These standards are quite detailed. We therefore consider only the first one: Pretax earnings must total at least 2.5 million dollars in the latest fiscal year, together with 2 million dollars in each of the preceding two years; or 6.5 million dollars in the aggregate for the last three fiscal years, together with a minimum of 4.5 million dollars in the most recent fiscal year, and positive amounts for each of the preceding two years. ◀

Source: NYSE Listed Company Manual *at www.nyse.com/listed/listed.html, quoted on June 6, 2001.*

---

to the stock price (at-the-money options). Public traders sometimes trade these contracts with each other, but they typically trade with dealers when they buy or sell options.

The large number of corporate and municipal bond issues ensures that most issues hardly ever trade. Highly secure bonds are very good substitutes for each other when the bonds have similar financial terms. Managers of portfolios that hold high-quality investment grade bonds therefore are less concerned about the specific bonds they buy than about their financial terms. Since many fixed-income portfolios hold their bonds until maturity, some bond issues never trade again after they are first issued. The buy side trades bonds almost exclusively with dealers because the public buyers and sellers rarely simultaneously want to trade the same bond issue. When they do, they rarely know of each other's interest.

Government bond issues are far less numerous than corporate and municipal bond issues. They are also far larger. The tremendous size of these issues and the widespread interest in these securities make these markets extremely liquid. Although the public often trades government bonds with dealers, buy-side traders increasingly trade directly with other buy-side traders in new electronic trading systems.

Some of the world's most liquid instruments trade in futures markets. Contracts on major agricultural, industrial, and financial commodities are extremely useful to hedgers throughout the economy. The contracts also interest many speculators. Trading by hedgers and speculators, and trading among the dealers who serve them, generate very large volumes in many futures markets.

▶ Some Regional Exchange Trivia

The Cincinnati Stock Exchange was founded in Cincinnati in 1885.
Following adoption of the 1975 amendments to the Securities Exchange
Act of 1934, it became the first U.S. electronic stock exchange. Its members
now trade exclusively from their offices. The Exchange's computers reside
in Chicago in the same building occupied by the Chicago Stock Exchange.

The Chicago Stock Exchange (CHX) was founded in 1882. It merged
with exchanges in St. Louis, Cleveland, and Minneapolis/St. Paul to form
the Midwest Stock Exchange in 1949. This name explains why its market
quotation symbol is M. The Midwest Stock Exchange changed its name
back to Chicago Stock Exchange in 1993. Measured by dollar trading
volume, the CHX is the third largest stock exchange in the United States
after the NYSE and Nasdaq. The CHX has aggressively used its unlisted
trading privileges to trade Nasdaq stocks.

The merger of the San Francisco Stock and Bond Exchange (founded in
1882) and the Los Angeles Stock and Oil Exchange (founded in 1899)
formed the Pacific Stock Exchange in 1957. It later changed its name to the
Pacific Exchange (PCX). Following the merger, PCX maintained separate
trading floors in Los Angeles and San Francisco where competing specialists
traded the same stocks. To save money, the PCX closed its equity floors in
2001 and 2002, and allowed its traders to trade from their offices. In
2000, PCX entered a joint venture agreement with the Archipelago ECN to
form a fully electronic exchange called Archipelago Exchange. After the
SEC approved its application for exchange status in October 2001, the
PCX moved its equity trading to the Archipelago Exchange in 2002. ◀

The most important world currencies trade in extremely liquid markets.
Volumes are high because international trade and cross-border capital transactions generally require currency conversions. The structure of currency
markets also ensures that dealers trade several times with each other for
every trade that they make with a client.

Real estate trades in brokered markets because every parcel is unique.
The difficulties that buyers and sellers have finding each other make the
real estate market the least liquid of the markets we have discussed. Electronic multiple listing services have lowered trader search costs, but these
costs are still very high. Clearing and settlement in real estate markets is
also quite expensive because the trades usually are large, complex, and among
traders who do not have standing credit relationships.

3.4.2 Stock Markets

Corporations apply to exchanges to *list* their stocks. Exchanges generally
list all companies that meet their listing standards and that pay their *listing
fees*. All but the smallest publicly traded stocks are listed for trading at one
or more markets.

The *listing standards* of an exchange generally require that its listed companies meet specified minimum standards for capital value, numbers of
shareholders, and financial strength. Most exchanges also require listed companies to report their accounts regularly according to *generally accepted
accounting practices* (GAAP). Some exchanges also regulate the control structures of their listed companies. *Control structure* refers to how the shareholders elect the board of directors who appoint the managers and set

▶ Double- and Triple-counting Volumes

The volume figures that markets report often are not directly comparable. Trading systems that match public buyers directly to public sellers generally report lower volumes than do trading systems in which dealers act as intermediaries between public traders. For example, a 100-share trade between a public buyer and a public seller creates 100 shares of volume at the NYSE. If the same trade took place in Nasdaq with the intermediation of a single dealer, the total volume would be 200 shares: 100 shares when the dealer bought from the public seller and 100 more shares when the dealer sold to the public buyer. Even greater volume results when more than one dealer is involved. If Dealer A buys from the public seller, Dealer B sells to the public buyer, and Dealer B buys from Dealer A, the market will report 300 shares.

Although both markets will accurately report their volumes, the reported figures will have different meanings. In markets that exclusively match public buyers directly to public sellers, volume measures only the trading activity of public traders. In dealer markets, volume measures the total trading activity of public traders and dealers. In such markets, volume provides only indirect—and sometimes highly inflated—information about the activity of public traders.

Some markets also count volume that other markets report. For example, Nasdaq reports all volume that Nasdaq broker-dealers report. Some Nasdaq broker-dealers, however, run trading systems that separately match buyers to sellers. Their reported trading volume thus overstates total trading volume because they count the same trades twice.

The *World Federation of Exchanges* (WFE) classifies markets by how they count their volumes. *Trading System View* (TSV) markets count only transactions that pass through their trading systems or that occur on their trading floors. *Regulated Environment View* (REV) markets count all transactions that are subject to their regulatory supervision. The WFE classifies the NYSE as a TSV market and the Nasdaq Stock Market as an REV market. ◀

company policy. The NYSE, for example, devotes considerable resources to regulating corporate control structures.

3.4.2.1 The U.S. Stock Markets

The exchange where a corporate stock issue is primarily listed is its *primary listing market*. The main primary listing markets in the United States are the New York Stock Exchange, the American Stock Exchange, and the Nasdaq Stock Market. Stocks listed at the New York Stock Exchange and the American Stock Exchange are known as *listed stocks*. Nasdaq stocks were once known as *over-the-counter* stocks, but now they are simply called Nasdaq stocks.

The New York and American stock exchanges have floor-based trading systems. Floor brokers arrange trades for their clients on the floor of the exchange, often with the assistance of dealers who are known as *specialists*. The Nasdaq Stock Market is an electronic communications network that allows brokers and dealers to meet each other in a screen-based environment managed by computers.

Most listed stocks in the United States also trade in one or more regional stock markets. The *regional exchanges* presently include the Boston

Stock Exchange, the Chicago Stock Exchange, the Cincinnati Stock Exchange, the Archipelago Exchange, and the Philadelphia Stock Exchange. Many more regional exchanges once existed, but after many mergers and failures, only these five remain. In addition to listed companies, the regional exchanges trade some Nasdaq stocks under *unlisted trading privileges* granted to them by the U.S. Securities and Exchange Commission.

U.S. exchange-listed stocks also trade in the *third market*. The third market includes dealers and brokers who arrange trades in exchange-listed stocks away from an exchange. These dealers typically display their quotes on the Nasdaq Intermarket.

Finally, U.S. stocks also trade in various electronic trading systems known as *alternative trading systems* (ATSs). Registered broker-dealers sponsor most of these systems. *Electronic communications networks* (ECNs) are the best-known alternative trading systems. Many alternative trading systems are essentially electronic exchanges. The term *fourth market* refers to trading in exchange-listed stocks within these systems. A summary of the U.S. equity markets appears in table 3-5.

TABLE 3-5.
Some U.S. Equity Markets with 2000 Total Dollar Volumes (billions)

MARKET TYPE	EXAMPLES	DOLLAR VOLUME	QUOTATION SYMBOL
Primary listing markets	New York Stock Exchange	11,060	N
	American Stock Exchange	945	A
	The Nasdaq National Market	20,274	Q
	The Nasdaq SmallCap Market	122	S
	OTC Bulletin Board Service	101	U
	National Quotation Service Pink Sheets	20	
Regional markets	Boston Stock Exchange	258	B
	Chicago Stock Exchange	1,190	M
	Cincinnati Stock Exchange	173	C
	Pacific Exchange	157	P
	Philadelphia Stock Exchange	80	X
Third market dealers	Madoff Investment Securities	1,000+	MADF
	Knight Trading Group	1,000+	TRIM
Third market brokers	Jefferies Group	NA	JEFF
	ITG	NA	ITGI
Electronic communications networks (ECNs)	Archipelago	777	ARCH
	BRUT ECN	NA	BRUT
	Instinet	3,336	INCA
	Island	3,449	ISLD
	REDIBook	NA	REDI
Other alternative trading systems	POSIT	335	
	Global Instinet Crossing	NA	
	Arizona Stock Exchange	0.2	

Sources: Exchange fact books and personal correspondence. Some data are not available for proprietary reasons.

3.4.2.2 International Stock Markets

In the late twentieth century, stock markets throughout the world grew substantially as firms increasingly sought public equity financing instead of bank loan financing and as governments privatized various enterprises. Many exchanges consolidated to take advantage of economies of scale.

Almost all the former Communist countries have established stock exchanges. They often created these exchanges before they had stocks to trade, property and bankruptcy laws to define who owns what, and securities laws to regulate issuers and traders. Despite these deficiencies, these countries established stock exchanges because they are symbols of free market economies. Not surprisingly, the most successful of these markets are in countries that carefully defined property rights, privatized most of their government-run enterprises, adopted good securities laws, and diligently enforced those laws.

Table 3-6 presents a summary of trading activity in the larger national stock markets. Not surprisingly, trading is most active in countries with strong market-based economies.

3.4.3 Equity Options Markets

3.4.3.1 U.S. Markets

Five exchanges in the United States presently trade standardized equity and index option contracts. The Options Clearing Corporation (OCC) is the clearinghouse for all contracts that trade at these exchanges. Buyers therefore can buy contracts at one exchange and sell them at other exchanges to offset their positions. The most actively traded option contracts trade at all of the exchanges. A list of these exchanges appears in table 3-7.

Four of the five options exchanges employ floor-based trading systems. Each of these exchanges also employs automated systems to support their dealers and floor brokers. The International Securities Exchange, formed in 1997, started trading in 2000 with a completely automated trading system. Its market share has grown very quickly.

Investment banks also trade specialized option contracts *over the counter* (OTC) with their clients. These contracts usually have strike prices, maturity dates, settlement terms, or other features that are different from the standardized options available at the exchanges. This business is part of the *synthetic derivatives business*. Synthetic derivatives also include other *structured products*—primarily swaps—that investment banks create for their clients.

3.4.3.2 International Equity Derivatives Markets

Exchange-traded equity derivatives include stock option contracts, equity index option contracts, equity index futures contracts, options on equity index futures contracts, and futures on individual stocks. Table 3-8 provides a characterization of organized trading in equity derivatives throughout the world.

Outside of the United States, most organized trading in standardized stock option contracts takes place at the same exchange at which the underlying stocks trade. In the United States, the SEC has not permitted equities and their associated options to trade side by side. When they trade at the same exchange, they generally trade in different rooms.

Most organized trading in equity index futures outside of the United States also takes place at the same exchange at which the underlying stocks trade. In the United States, these contracts trade on futures exchanges.

TABLE 3-6.
Trading Activity in Some International Stock Markets (2001)

TIME ZONE	EXCHANGE	VOLUME REPORT TYPE	DOLLAR VOLUME (BILLIONS)	NUMBER OF LISTED FIRMS	YEAR-END TOTAL CAPITALIZATION (BILLION DOLLARS)	ANNUAL TURNOVER RATE
North	Amex	TSV	817	605	60	NA
America	Mexico	REV	70	172	126	34%
	Nasdaq	REV	10,935	4,128	2,897	388
	NYSE	TSV	10,489	2,400	11,027	88
	Toronto	TSV	460	1,316	615	72
South	Buenos Aires	TSV	8	119	33	16
America	Santiago	TSV	4	250	56	9
	São Paulo	TSV	65	429	186	36
Europe,	Athens	TSV	38	314	85	48
Africa,	Copenhagen	REV	72	217	85	80
&	Deutsche Börse	TSV	1,440	984	1,072	120
Middle	Euronext	REV	3,180	1,345	1,844	165
East	Helsinki	TSV	182	155	190	84
	Irish	TSV	23	87	75	28
	Istanbul	TSV	78	310	47	174
	Italy	TSV	710	294	527	113
	Johannesburg	TSV	70	519	147	33
	Lisbon	TSV	28	99	46	63
	London	REV	4,551	2,891	2,150	76
	Madrid	REV	842	1,482	468	187
	Oslo	REV	62	214	69	88
	Stockholm	REV	387	305	237	111
	Switzerland	REV	594	412	527	86
	Tel-Aviv	TSV	16	649	58	30
	Valencia	TSV	41	508	NA	12
	Vienna	TSV	8	113	25	31
	Warsaw	TSV	10	230	26	53
Asia &	Australian	TSV	244	1,410	375	61
Pacific	Hong Kong	TSV	241	867	506	47
	Jakarta	TSV	10	315	23	35
	Korea	TSV	381	688	194	218
	Kuala Lumpur	TSV	21	807	119	19
	New Zealand	TSV	10	195	18	51
	Osaka	TSV	175	1,335	NA	9
	Philippine	TSV	3	232	21	16
	Singapore	TSV	72	386	116	56
	Taiwan	TSV	545	586	293	212
	Thailand	TSV	31	382	36	74
	Tokyo	TSV	1,661	2,141	2,265	57

Source: World Federation of Exchanges website at www.world-exchanges.org.
Note: Trading System View (TSV) markets count only transactions that pass through their trading systems or that occur on their trading floors. Regulated Environment View (REV) markets count all transactions that are subject to their regulatory supervision. Dollar volumes include investment funds. The number of listed firms includes both domestic and foreign listings and excludes investment funds. Total capitalization includes only domestic companies and excludes investment funds.

▶ Some International Stock Market Trivia

Teléfonos de México, S.A. de C.V. (Telmex) is the largest Mexican stock issue. The New York Stock Exchange, however, has a greater share of its worldwide trading volume than does the Bolsa Mexicana de Valores.

By capitalization and trading volume, the largest Israeli stock market is the U.S. Nasdaq Stock Market. Many high-tech Israeli companies do not list their shares at the Tel Aviv Stock Exchange.

The Stock Exchange of Hong Kong uses an electronic trading system to match buyers to sellers. However, until recently, the Exchange required its members to sit in the Trading Hall of the Exchange to trade. The Trading Hall is a large room filled with members and their clerks, seated at desks upon which sit computer screens and telephones. Members now also can trade through off-floor trading devices in their offices.

Chinese law requires that all trading in securities listed at the Shanghai Stock Exchange take place at the Exchange, and all shares held by domestic traders (A class shares) remain on deposit at the Exchange's depository. Domestic traders who wish to trade at the Exchange must deposit funds with their brokers before trading. Since all money and securities are on deposit before the Exchange arranges any trade, the broker can refuse to accept orders that would produce trades which traders cannot settle immediately. Although the Exchange once settled its A share trades on the day of the trade, it now settles them on the next day (T+1). The Shenzhen Stock Exchange uses similar procedures. ◀

▶ Some Options Market Trivia

The Chicago Board Options Exchange (CBOE) began trading in 1973 as the first organized equity options exchange. Although it is a Chicago Board of Trade subsidiary, it is independently governed, operated, and regulated.

The New York Stock Exchange, the Midwestern Stock Exchange (now called the Chicago Stock Exchange), and Nasdaq also created organized options markets. These markets were not notably successful. The NYSE sold its options market to the CBOE in 1997. The Midwestern Stock Exchange and Nasdaq simply closed their options markets.

The Securities and Exchange Commission has not approved *side-by-side trading* of stocks and their associated options at the same exchange. Exchanges that trade stocks and their associated options must physically separate the stock trading from the options trading. ◀

▶ FLEX Options

To capture institutional business in specialized options, the options markets developed *FLEX Options* (FLexible EXchange) for indexes and E-FLEX Options for equities. Using a special *request for quote* (RFQ) procedure, institutional traders specify the option type (call or put), strike price, maturity date (up to three years distant), and exercise style (American or European) for the option contract in which they are interested. Exchange market makers then quote the option in a competitive environment. The Options Clearing Corporation is the issuer and guarantor of all FLEX and E-FLEX contracts, as it is for all other options traded at U.S. exchanges. ◀

TABLE 3-7.

U.S. Equity Options Exchanges and 2001 Total Contract Volumes (millions)

		CONTRACT VOLUME		
EXCHANGE	NICKNAME	EQUITIES	INDEXES	QUOTATION SYMBOL
Chicago Board Options Exchange	CBOE	254	52	CO
American Stock Exchange	Amex	204	1	A
Pacific Exchange	P-Coast	103	—	P
Philadelphia Stock Exchange	Philly	96	5	X
International Securities Exchange	ISE	65	—	I

Source: The Options Clearing Corporation 2001 Annual Report, *p. 3, at www.optionsclearing.com/about/ann_rep/ann_rep_pdf/annual_rep_01.pdf.*

TABLE 3-8.

Contract Volumes in Some World Equity Derivatives Markets in 2000 (thousands)

TIME ZONE	EXCHANGE	STOCK OPTIONS	INDEX OPTIONS	INDEX FUTURES	STOCK FUTURES
North	AMEX (USA)	205,716	1,998	NT	NT
America	CBOE (USA)	281,182	47,387	NT	NT
	CBOT (USA)	NT	200	3,572	NT
	CME (USA)	NT	5,089	59,957	NT
	ISE (USA)	7,716	NT	NT	NT
	Montreal SE (Canada)	4,753	89	1,272	NT
	PHLX (USA)	73,021	2,607	NT	NT
	PSX (USA)	108,990	1	NT	NT
South	BOVESPA (Brazil)	30,295	414	NT	NT
America	MMD (Mexico)	NT	NT	49	17
Europe, Africa &	Athens (Greece)	NT	NT	913	NT
Middle East	EUREX (Germany)	89,238	44,200	NT	31,595
	Euronext Amsterdam	47,107	4,531	2,479	349
	Euronext Brussels	589	1,693	29,519	NA
	FUTOP (Denmark)	4	11	989	NT
	MEFF (Spain)	16,586	766	4,183	NT
	OM (Sweden)	30,692	4,167	11,477	2,145
	Wiener Börse (Austria)	839	205	431	
	TASE (Israel)	NT	26,974	122	NT
Asia &	ASXD (Australia)	9,508	NT	NT	437
Pacific	HKFE (Hong Kong)	4,189	550	4,178	3
	KLOFFE (Malaysia)	NT	349	367	NT
	Korea SE (S Korea)	NT	193,829	19,667	NT
	NZFOE (New Zealand)	65	NT	1	NT
	Osaka (Japan)	104	5,717	8,708	NT
	SFE (Australia)	NT	1,099	3,825	9
	Singapore Exchange	NT	710	8,461	NT
	Taiwan Futures Exchange	NT	NT	1,927	NT

Source: World Federation of Exchanges website at www.world-exchanges.org

Notes: NT = not traded; NA = not available

Since contract sizes vary substantially both within and among exchanges, the contract volume data do not permit fine comparisons among exchanges.

Until December 2001, it was illegal to trade futures on individual stocks in the United States. The Commodity Futures Modernization Act of 2000 now permits trading in these contracts.

3.4.4 Futures Markets

Most futures exchanges have their own clearinghouses. Exchanges therefore do not compete to trade the same contracts. Instead, each exchange and its associated clearinghouse try to create contracts that will attract traders. Most exchanges have large research and marketing departments that design contracts they hope will attract traders. Chapter 8 identifies some of the factors that make contracts successful.

Futures exchanges generally trade several contracts that vary by expiration date for each commodity that they trade. Most commodities have at least four *delivery months*. The contract that will expire next is called the *front contract* or *front month contract*. The other contracts are called the *back contracts*.

In financial and industrial commodities, traders mostly trade only the front month contract. When it expires, they roll their positions into the next contract.

The most actively traded agricultural contracts are the front month contracts and the first harvest contracts. The *first harvest contract* is the first contract on which traders can deliver the currently growing crop. Hedgers and speculators usually have great interest in this contract.

3.4.4.1 U.S. Futures Markets

Four major and several smaller exchanges trade standardized futures contracts in the United States. These exchanges are often called *boards of trade*. Futures exchanges have experienced substantial consolidation over the years, as have other markets. Table 3-9 provides a brief summary of the currently active U.S. futures exchanges.

3.4.4.2 International Futures Markets

Table 3-10 lists global futures exchanges with the greatest contract volumes in 2001. Unlike U.S. futures exchanges, many of the exchanges on this list also trade common equities.

3.4.5 Corporate and Municipal Bond Markets

Throughout the world, most corporate and municipal bonds trade *over the counter* in investment banks or commercial banks. Some stock exchanges list corporate bonds, but exchange bond trading volumes are generally trivial compared to over-the-counter volumes. Less than 0.1 percent of all corporate bond trading volume occurs in the New York Stock Exchange and American Stock Exchange bond markets. The exchange bond price tables that appear in many daily newspapers therefore present less reliable information than you might imagine.

3.4.6 Treasury Markets

Most national treasuries conduct public auctions at which they issue their bills, notes, and bonds. Some smaller nations, however, use underwriters to issue their securities. Generally, anyone may participate in Treasury auctions. The auction rules vary by country.

TABLE 3-9.
Active U.S. Futures Exchanges with 2001 Contract Volumes (millions)

EXCHANGE	CLEARINGHOUSE	MAJOR CONTRACTS	CONTRACT VOLUME	REMARKS
Chicago Mercantile Exchange (CME)	CME Clearing House	Livestock, dairy products, stock indexes, Eurodollars and other interest rates, currencies	208.5	The CME was formed in 1898 as the Chicago Butter and Egg Board. It became the CME in 1919. It trades futures on a variety of agricultural products.
Chicago Board of Trade (CBOT)	Board of Trade Clearing Corporation (BOTCC)	Grains, U.S. Treasury notes and bonds, other interest rates, stock indexes	197.8	The CBOT, founded in 1848, was the first organized commodity exchange. Futures trading started in 1865 in agricultural commodities including wheat, corn, and oats.
New York Mercantile Exchange (NYMEX)	NYMEX Clearing House	Precious and industrial metals, energy products	84.7	NYMEX was founded in 1872 as the Butter and Cheese Exchange of New York. COMEX merged into NYMEX in 1994. COMEX was founded in 1933 from the merger of the New York Metal Exchange, the Rubber Exchange, the National Raw Silk Exchange, and the New York Hide Exchange.
New York Board of Trade (NYBOT)	New York Clearing Corporation (NYCC)	Sugar, coffee, cocoa, cotton, orange juice concentrate, currencies, stock indexes	14.0	The NYBOT is the parent of the Coffee, Sugar & Cocoa Exchange (CSCE) founded in 1882, the New York Cotton Exchange (NYCE) founded in 1870, and the New York Futures Exchange (NYFE) founded in 1979. NYBOT was formed in 1998 when the CSCE and the NYCE merged. FINEX and Citrus Associates are divisions of NYCE.
Kansas City Board of Trade (KCBT)	Kansas City Board of Trade, Clearing Corporation	Wheat, natural gas, stock indexes	2.4	Kansas City merchants established the KCBT in 1856 to trade grain. Grain futures trading began in 1876.

(continued)

TABLE 3-9.
Active U.S. Futures Exchanges with 2001 Contract Volumes (millions) *(continued)*

EXCHANGE	CLEARINGHOUSE	MAJOR CONTRACTS	CONTRACT VOLUME	REMARKS
Minneapolis Grain Exchange (MGE)	MGE Clearing House	Spring wheat	1.0	The MGE was established in 1881 to promote trade in grains. In 1947, it became the MGE.
MidAmerica Exchange (MIDAM)	Board of Trade Clearing Corporation (BOTCC)	Soybeans, wheat, corn, U.S. T-bonds	0.7	The MIDAM is a subsidiary of the CBOT. It trades many CBOT contracts with smaller contract sizes.
Cantor Financial Futures Exchange (CX)	New York Clearing Corporation (NYCC)	U.S. Treasury and agency notes	0.4	Founded in 1998, the CX is a joint venture of the NYBOT and Cantor Fitzgerald & Co. CX provides a proprietary electronic trading platform.
Merchants' Exchange of St. Louis (MESL)	Board of Trade Clearing Corporation (BOTCC)	Barge freight	0.0	The MESL was established in 1836 as a cash commodity market. In 2000, it was approved as a contract market. It operates as an electronic exchange offering contracts in barge freight service futures.

Sources: Commodity Futures Trading Commission. The "Remarks" column is an edited version of a similar column at www.cftc.gov/dea/deadms_table.htm. The volume data come from the Commodity Futures Trading Commission FY 2001 Annual Report at http://www.cftc.gov/files/anr/anr2001.pdf.

Note: This table lists all U.S. boards of trade that are designated as contract markets under the Commodity Exchange Act and that traded futures contracts in 2001. The volume data are for the fiscal year ending September 30, 2001. Since contract sizes vary, the exchange rankings would differ if they were based on nominal dollar volumes.

TABLE 3-10.
Top 40 Global Futures Exchanges by Contract Volume in 2001 (millions)

REGION	EXCHANGE	VOLUME	RANK
North America	Chicago Mercantile Exchange, USA	316.0	2
	Chicago Board of Trade, USA	210.0	3
	New York Mercantile Exchange, USA	85.0	6
	New York Board of Trade, USA	14.0	17
	Bourse de Montreal, Canada	7.3	24
	Winnipeg Commodity Exchange, Canada	2.9	33
	Kansas City Board of Trade, USA	2.4	36
Europe	Eurex, Germany and Switzerland	435.1	1
	LIFFE, UK	161.5	4
	London Metal Exchange, UK	56.2	8
	Paris Bourse SA, France	42.0	9
	International Petroleum Exchange, UK	26.1	14
	OM Stockholm, Sweden	23.4	15
	MEFF Renta Variable, Spain	13.1	18
	Italian Derivatives Market of the Italian Stock Exchange, Italy	6.0	26
	Euronext Brussels Derivatives Market, Belgium	3.4	30
	Amsterdam Exchanges, Netherlands	3.3	32
	Budapest Commodity Exchange, Hungary	2.6	35
	Budapest Stock Exchange, Hungary	2.3	37
	Helsinki Exchanges, Finland	1.0	40
Asia	Tokyo Commodity Exchange, Japan	56.5	7
	Korea Stock Exchange, Korea	31.5	11
	Singapore Exchange, Singapore	30.6	12
	Central Japan Commodity Exchange, Japan	27.8	13
	Tokyo Grain Exchange, Japan	22.7	16
	Tokyo Stock Exchange, Japan	12.5	19
	Korea Futures Exchange, Korea	11.5	21
	Osaka Securities Exchange, Japan	10.5	22
	Tokyo International Financial Futures Exchange, Japan	7.6	23
	Fukuoka Futures Exchange, Japan	6.4	25
	Hong Kong Exchanges and Clearing—Derivatives Unit, China	5.8	27
	Shanghai Futures Exchange, China	5.6	28
	Taiwan Futures Exchange, Taiwan	4.3	29
	Osaka Mercantile Exchange, Japan	3.4	31
	Kansai Commodities Exchange, Japan	2.9	34
	Yokohama Commodity Exchange, Japan	1.3	38
Southern Hemisphere	BM&F, Brazil	94.2	5
	Sydney Futures Exchange, Australia	34.1	10
	South African Futures Exchange, South Africa	11.9	20
	New Zealand Futures Exchange, New Zealand	1.0	39

Source: Futures Industry Association, *at http://www.futuresindustry.org/fimagazi-1929.asp?a=756. Reprinted by permission.*
Note: Since contract sizes vary, the rankings would be different if they were based on nominal dollar volumes.

▶ **They Trade Enormous Volume but Receive No Year-end Bonuses**

The Federal Reserve conducts U.S. monetary policy primarily through its *Open Market Operations Desk*. Traders who work at the Federal Reserve Bank of New York implement the policy. When the Fed wants to add monetary reserves to the banking system, it buys seasoned U.S. Treasury bills and bonds, and simply creates the money to pay for them. When it wants to decrease the reserves, it sells bills and bonds, and simply destroys the money it receives in payment. Since the reserves have grown over time, the Federal Reserve is the largest holder of U.S. Treasury instruments. On June 20, 2001, the Fed held 533 billion dollars of government debt instruments in its System Open Market Account (SOMA). The Desk rarely sells securities because bills mature in the SOMA account every week. When the Fed wants to slow the growth of the money supply, it merely does not buy as many securities as it otherwise would.

The Federal Reserve trades only with a small set of large institutional broker-dealers called *primary government securities dealers*. In exchange for the privilege of dealing with the Fed, these primary dealers must quote firm prices for large sizes whenever the Fed wants to trade. In addition, they must participate meaningfully in Treasury auctions, and they must supply information about market conditions to the Federal Reserve. As of October 31, 2001, there were only 24 primary dealers. Most of these were investment and commercial banks.

In 2000, the Fed traders purchased 44 billion dollars of debt on behalf of the government in unmatched transactions and an additional 4.4 trillion dollars in matched Treasury bill transactions (repurchase agreements and matched sale-and-purchases). They arrange their trades by computer from their offices on the ninth floor at the Federal Reserve Bank of New York.

Since the Federal Reserve banks are not government agencies, their traders are not civil servants. However, they work under a similar pay schedule. The Fed traders make only a small fraction of what large private buy-side traders make. They also do not receive year-end bonuses.

This salary comparison is not fair, however. The Fed traders are more like exchange officials than like buy-side traders because they generally do not negotiate trades and they do not trade throughout the day. Instead, they merely request bids and offers to fill the Fed's daily requirements. They then arrange trades with the dealers who offer the best prices. The Fed traders occasionally also act as brokers for foreign governments, central banks, and official international organizations. ◀

Secondary trading of Treasury securities occurs primarily over the counter in investment and commercial banks. Several brokers, however, organize markets in which government bond dealers and some larger buy-side traders trade with each other. These *interdealer brokers* permit their clients to trade on an anonymous basis. Dealers generally do not want other dealers to know what trades they are doing. The largest such interdealer government bond broker is Cantor Fitzgerald. Their government bond markets are among the world's most liquid markets in any instrument.

3.4.7 Swaps and Spot Currency Markets

Swaps and spot currencies mostly trade over the counter in investment and commercial banks. Some brokers and some data providers organize markets in these instruments. Traders use their services to lower the costs of searching for counterparts.

▶ Some Wholesale OTC Brokers

Reuters is the world's leading foreign exchange broker. Its Dealing 3000 trading system is an anonymous electronic brokerage service that many foreign exchange traders use. As of August 2001, traders using 7,500 workstations could use the system to trade 38 spot currency pairs and 22 forward currency swaps.

Garban-Intercapital is the world's leading swap broker. The firm specializes in brokering wholesale trades between dealers and between dealers and large customers. Its securities, derivatives, and money brokerage businesses have daily transaction volumes in excess of 200 billion dollars.

Cantor Fitzgerald is the world's leading U.S. government bond broker. In addition to its fixed-income businesses, it has significant presence in the equity, foreign exchange, energy, bandwidth, and environmental markets throughout the world. Before the September 11, 2001, terrorist attacks destroyed its offices at the World Trade Center, its various businesses had daily volumes in excess of 160 billion dollars. ◀

Sources: about.reuters.com/transactions/d3_intro.htm; www.garban.com; www.cantor.com.

▶ The Retail Currency Markets

If you have traveled abroad, you may be an experienced foreign exchange trader. You probably did not negotiate the terms of your trades, however, unless you traded in a *black market* in an alley.

Retail foreign exchange markets in airports and tourist areas are notoriously expensive. Currency dealers usually charge a significant fee for their transactions. They also profit from the wide spread between the prices at which they are willing to buy and sell currencies.

The high transaction costs in the retail foreign exchange market are due to the high rents dealers must pay for their shops at airports and near tourist sites, to the costly security precautions that ensure they are not robbed while tending their shops and delivering and collecting currencies, and to the salaries they must pay clerks, who are often idle.

Transaction costs in retail currencies dropped significantly with the introduction of international withdrawals from automatic teller machines. When you withdraw currency from ATMs, you pay a small access fee. The exchange rates that you receive are far better than those you can obtain yourself. Your bank gives you a better rate because it can consolidate your transaction with many others, and because it has much more negotiating clout than you do. ◀

3.5 MARKET REGULATION

Regulators create and enforce rules that facilitate trading. Most traders believe that securities markets work best when they are well regulated but not excessively regulated. Good regulations help ensure that traders communicate effectively with each other, that people do not defraud others, and that all things generally are as they appear.

Regulators sometimes create and enforce rules that promote other objectives. Such regulations may give privileges—usually protections from competition—to favored traders, brokers, or exchanges. For example, regulators often try to protect domestic markets from foreign competition. They may also try to protect incumbent traders and incumbent markets from new domestic competition. Ideologically motivated regulators also may impose restrictive regulations because they do not like the markets, or because they want to redistribute wealth. For example, governments sometimes tax trading to raise money for the national treasury. Regulations that make it difficult or expensive for traders to arrange mutually beneficial trades generally harm the markets and the wider economy.

The stated purpose of a regulation often is not its true objective. Since most people agree that regulation should be in the best interests of the markets or, at a minimum, in the national interest, regulators generally justify their regulations with explanations about how they promote the common good. Through ignorance, self-interest, or malice, however, regulators often adopt regulations that do not promote the common good. The knowledge you gain from reading this book will help you judge the true effects of regulatory policies.

Since regulators set the rules of the game, and since rules help determine who will be successful, people devote tremendous efforts to lobbying for rules that they favor. They naturally argue in favor of high principles, even though they often are actually arguing for their personal gain. Regulatory debates therefore are often very controversial.

The controversies that surround regulatory efforts make regulation an exciting and often frustrating area in which to work. Regulators who truly want to promote the common good take great satisfaction in the good regulations that they write and enforce. They suffer great frustration when they lose regulatory battles to other interests.

3.5.1 Regulators

Most countries divide the responsibility for regulating markets among many agencies. Legislatures enact laws that directly regulate markets. They generally delegate enforcement of these laws to various public and private regulatory agencies. Legislatures also enact laws that delegate their legislative powers to these agencies. These laws authorize agencies to write regulations that have the force of law. The agencies then enforce their regulations through judicial proceedings.

Governments usually require that regulatory agencies regulate in the public interest when they delegate their state powers. The definition of what is in the public interest, however, may be vague. Regulators therefore often have significant power to promote their personal agendas.

3.5.1.1 Governmental Regulatory Agencies

Most countries have created governmental regulatory agencies to oversee traders and trading practices. These agencies generally are independent commissions. Table 3-11 shows that some countries delegate regulatory powers over the markets to ministries of the executive branch of the government, or to their national central banks.

U.S. Regulatory Agencies

The main U.S. governmental agencies that regulate trading are the *Securities and Exchange Commission* (SEC) and the *Commodity Futures Trading Commission* (CFTC). The SEC regulates securities markets (stocks, bonds, warrants, investment company shares, and trust units), equity options markets, and cash-settled equity index options markets. The CFTC regulates commodity spot, forward, and futures markets. Most countries consolidate

▶ The SEC Mission

The *Securities Exchange Act of 1934* created the U.S. Securities and
Exchange Commission. Section 3f of the Act charges the Commission as
follows:

> *Whenever pursuant to this title the Commission is engaged in
> rulemaking, or the review of a rule of a self-regulatory organization, and
> is required to consider or determine whether an action is necessary or
> appropriate in the public interest, the Commission shall also consider, in
> addition to the protection of investors, whether the action will promote
> efficiency, competition, and capital formation.*

Nearly identical text also appears in Section 2b of the Securities Act of
1933 and in Section 2c of the Investment Company Act of 1940. These
three acts together form the legislative foundation for securities regulation in
the United States.

Although this directive seems quite explicit, it provides no guidance to
regulators confronted with issues that require trade-offs among the named
objectives. For example, rules that prohibit insider trading protect investors
while simultaneously making markets less efficient in the sense that they
produce less informative prices. This directive also provides no guidance
about issues that require trade-offs within the named objectives. For
example, rules that protect the interests of small investors often hurt large
investors. In these cases, regulators generally freely decide what they
believe is in the public interest. ◀

these regulatory functions into a single agency. Concerns over the inefficiencies of having two agencies perform similar functions have caused many
people to propose merging the two agencies.

The SEC and the CFTC write regulations to interpret and implement
the laws that fall within their jurisdictions. The law also allows them to enforce their regulations through administrative hearings. These agencies can
also ask that the Department of Justice prosecute violators in the federal
courts. Most national regulatory agencies throughout the world have similar powers.

In addition to their regulatory functions, the SEC and CFTC collect
and disseminate information useful to traders, investors, speculators, and
legislators. The SEC collects various financial reports from issuers and position reports from large traders. Investors who are interested in estimating
security values can access these reports over the Internet via the SEC's *Edgar*
information retrieval system. The CFTC likewise collects and publishes information about commodity market supply and demand conditions and large
trader positions. Traders use this information to value commodities and to
forecast what other traders might do in the future. Both organizations also
provide information to Congress through their regular annual reports, their
special reports on specific issues, their testimony at congressional hearings,
and their responses to requests for information from members of Congress
and their staffs.

Several other governmental organizations also regulate securities trading
in the United States. The Federal Reserve Board sets speculative margins.
Speculative margins specify the minimum amount of capital that traders must
have to buy or sell securities and to hold long or short positions. Traders
call these margins *Regulation T margins*, or simply *Reg T margins* because
the Federal Reserve Board specifies them in its Regulation T. The various

TABLE 3-11.

Selected National Trading and Securities Regulators

COUNTRY	AGENCY
Argentina	Comisión Nacional de Valores
Australia	Australian Securities and Investments Commission
Brazil	Comissão de Valores Mobiliários
Canada (British Columbia)	British Columbia Securities Commission
(Ontario)	Ontario Securities Commission
(Quebec)	Commission des Valeurs Mobilières du Québec
Chile	Superintendencia de Valores y Seguros
China (People's Republic)	China Securities Regulatory Commission
Chinese Taipei	Securities and Futures Commission
Denmark	Finanstilsynet
Finland	Financial Supervision Authority
France	Commission des Opérations de Bourse
Germany	Bundesaufsichtsamt für den Wertpapierhandel (BAWE)
Greece	Capital Market Commission
Hong Kong	Securities and Futures Commission
India	Securities and Exchange Board of India (Sebi)
Indonesia	Indonesian Capital Market Supervisory Agency
Ireland	Central Bank of Ireland
Israel	Israel Securities Authority
Italy	Commissione Nazionale per le Società e la Borsa
Japan	Financial Services Agency
	Ministry of Agriculture, Forestry, and Fisheries
	Ministry of International Trade and Industry (MITI)
	Securities and Exchange Surveillance Commission
Korea	Financial Supervisory Commission/Financial Supervisory Service
Malaysia	Securities Commission
Mexico	Comisión Nacional Bancaria y de Valores
Netherlands	Stichting Toezicht Effectenverkeer
Norway	Kredittilsynet
Poland	Polish Securities and Exchange Commission
Portugal	Comissão do Mercado de Valores Mobiliários
Russia	Federal Commission for the Securities Market of the Russian Federation
Singapore	Monetary Authority of Singapore
South Africa	Financial Services Board
Spain	Comisión Nacional del Mercado de Valores
Sweden	Finansinspektionen
Switzerland	Commission Fédérale des Banques
Turkey	Capital Markets Board
United Kingdom	Financial Services Authority
United States of America	United States Securities and Exchange Commission
	Commodity Futures Trading Commission

Source: Agencies selected by the author from lists of ordinary and associate members of the International Organization of Securities Commissions that appear at www.iosco.org/iosco.html.

▶ Regulatory Competition

The division of regulatory oversight between the SEC and CFTC has created numerous conflicts over jurisdiction between these agencies. These "turf wars" generally occur when markets or issuers create new trading products that have characteristics of both securities and commodity contracts. For example, oil-linked bonds are like securities because corporations issue them to obtain financing. They are like commodity contracts because they derive their value primarily from the price of oil.

Before 1982, the *Commodity Exchange Act* gave the CFTC authority to regulate any exchange contract that has an element of futurity. Although the Securities and Exchange Commission had authorized trading in stock option contracts, the federal courts were then considering whether the CFTC was the proper regulator of these contracts.

At the same time, the futures markets wanted to create futures on equity indexes. The SEC argued that it had regulatory authority over these contracts because it regulated the underlying instruments.

Chairmen John Shad of the SEC and Phillip McBride Johnson of the CFTC reached an accord in 1982 to divide regulatory responsibilities between the two agencies. Their agreement, which Congress enacted into law, gave the CFTC jurisdiction over futures trading in broad equity indexes and options on those futures contracts. The SEC obtained exclusive jurisdiction over options on individual stocks and cash-settled options on indexes. The chairmen agreed that no futures on individual stocks or on narrow indexes would trade anywhere. The Commodity Futures Modernization Act of 2000 amended the law to permit trading in these previously prohibited futures contracts.

Perhaps the most interesting aspect of the Shad-Johnson accord concerns the regulation of equity index options. As noted above, the SEC regulates cash-settled equity index options while the CFTC regulates futures options on equity index futures contracts. The risks inherent in these two types of contracts are nearly identical when they are based on the same underlying index. Two regulatory agencies thus separately regulate instruments that have essentially identical risk characteristics.

Some people believe that this redundancy is foolish. Others believe that the competition between regulators has made both of them more reasonable. Still others believe that this competition has made both regulators too lax. ◀

states also have securities commissions. These commissions primarily enforce state antifraud statutes.

3.5.1.2 Self-regulatory Organizations

Private regulatory agencies include exchanges, clearinghouses, and trader associations. These organizations regulate their members to lower their costs of doing business together, to improve their business prospects, to ensure that no member hurts another member, and to provide quality assurances to their members' clients. Organizations that regulate their members are called *self-regulatory organizations*, or SROs.

Exchanges primarily regulate their members' trading practices. Their rules specify how their members arrange trades and how they should relate to their clients. We discuss the implications of exchange rules throughout this book.

Many securities exchanges also regulate their listed firms. For example, their listing standards generally require a minimum level of financial reporting.

▶ The Buttonwood Tree Agreement

The New York Stock Exchange traces its beginnings to an agreement traders made in 1792 to regulate their commissions and to trade with each other. According to legend, the traders met under a buttonwood tree, near what is now Wall Street in lower Manhattan. Their written agreement— which entered the NYSE archives in 1840—indicates that they all would charge their clients no less than 0.25 percent commission for their brokerage services. The full text of their agreement, signed by 24 brokers and merchants, is as follows:

> We the Subscribers, Brokers for the Purchase and Sale of Public Stock, do hereby solemnly promise and pledge ourselves to each other, that we will not buy or sell from this day for any person whatsoever, any kind of Public Stock, at a less rate than one quarter per cent Commission on the Specie value and that we will give a preference to each other in our Negotiations. In Testimony whereof we have set our hands this 17th day of May at New York. 1792.

The New York Stock Exchange stopped regulating brokerage commissions 183 years later, in 1975.

For much of its life, the NYSE prohibited its members from trading shares in its listed companies away from the Exchange. In response to pressure from its members and from the SEC, the Exchange gradually relaxed these restrictions. It repealed Rule 390, its last restriction on off-exchange trading, in December 1999. ◀

Sources: New York Stock Exchange Archives; Securities and Exchange Commission Release no. 34-42758 at www.sec.gov/rules/sro/ny99480.htm.

Clearinghouses primarily establish capital adequacy standards and trade-reporting practices for their members. They design their regulations to ensure that their members and their members' clients will honor their trading contracts. Their regulations also minimize the losses that occur when traders fail to settle their contracts.

Trader associations regulate how traders relate to each other and to their clients. The primary SROs that regulate brokers and dealers in the United States are the *National Association of Securities Dealers* (NASD) and the *National Futures Association* (NFA). The law requires all U.S. futures brokers and dealers to belong to the NFA and to submit themselves to its regulations. Although the law does not require that all security brokers belong to the NASD, it is essentially impossible to do business in the United States without being a member. The NASD and the NFA both administer a series of exams that traders take to certify their competence.

SROs enforce their regulations by threatening to expel members who do not comply. They also enter into contracts with their members that allow them to sue their members in civil court if they fail to comply with their regulations. These enforcement mechanisms are most effective when the costs of compliance are small and the benefits are large. They can be ineffective, however, when dishonest members can profit greatly from violating the rules.

To prevent such problems, some governments give SROs the power to write regulations that have the force of law. The SROs then can rely upon the criminal justice system to help enforce their regulations. Since regulators can abuse the power to write regulations, and since constitutional gov-

▶ Crying Over Onion Futures

Commodity markets can be especially volatile when the traded commodity is perishable. When commodity supplies will soon spoil, their prices dive if they are in excess supply, and they rocket upward if they are in short supply.

Onions are quite perishable. They can be stored from harvest to harvest, but nobody wants an old onion when the new harvest arrives. Prices of onions for delivery before the new harvest therefore are quite volatile.

In the 1950s, onion futures markets suffered several extreme price fluctuations that hurt farmers and local dealers. The farmers and dealers attributed the volatility to speculative trading in the onion futures market. They complained to their senators, who prevailed upon their colleagues to solve the problem. In 1958, they complied by prohibiting all exchange trading in onion futures. It is still illegal to trade onion futures contracts on, or subject to, the rules of any board of trade in the United States.

Consequently, the natural beneficiaries of onion futures markets—the farmers who produce onions and the food processors who use onions—cannot use futures contracts to cheaply exchange onion price risk. Instead, they now use forward contracts. ◀

Source: U.S. Public Law 85-839 (7 U.S.C. 13-1).

ernments generally cannot delegate their legislative and judicial powers to private agencies, SROs must have their rules approved by the government. In the United States, the various SROs apply to the SEC or CFTC for approval of their rules. These agencies approve proposed rules if they find that they are in the public interest.

The delegation of regulatory powers from national legislatures to regulatory nongovernmental agencies allows experts who are most familiar with the markets and their problems to regulate them. This system helps avoid the unintended consequences that often result when poorly informed legislators try to micromanage regulatory policies. It also protects markets from capricious actions that legislatures occasionally take. When the system works well, the legislature provides a broad framework for regulatory oversight, and the regulatory agencies implement this framework in the public interest.

3.5.1.3 Other Private Regulators

Several private agencies regulate traders, issuers, and investment managers in the United States. The *Financial Accounting Standards Board* (FASB) sets accounting standards by which firms must report their accounts. The SEC, which has ultimate authority for specifying reporting standards for public firms, has recognized the FASB standards as authoritative since 1973.

The *Association for Investment Management and Research* (AIMR) sets performance reporting standards that many investment managers use to report their results. Although the standards are voluntary, many firms choose to comply in order to satisfy their clients.

Brokers commonly purchase insurance policies on behalf of their clients to ensure that their clients will not lose if the brokerage goes bankrupt. The insurance companies that write these policies regulate the brokers who purchase these policies in order to minimize the probability that the brokers will fail, and thus impose costs on their funds.

▶ Unintended Consequences

In 1997, the Brazilian government imposed a 0.38 percent tax on all financial transactions in order to raise revenue. The unintended consequence of this tax was to cause institutional traders to trade Brazilian stocks as American depository receipts (ADRs) in New York to avoid the tax. The tax therefore raised less revenue than expected, and the Brazilian equity markets lost liquidity. Daily trading volume at the São Paulo Bovespa dropped from 1.2 billion reais (1.08 billion dollars) a day in 1997 to 350 million reais (136 million dollars) a day in 2001. Although some of the drop-off undoubtedly was due to the Brazilian financial crisis of 2001, many of the 32 Brazilian ADRs trade more volume in New York than in São Paulo. The Brazilian government announced in September 2001 that stock transactions would be exempt from the tax in late 2001. ◀

Source: Jennifer L. Rich, "Brazil to Exempt Stock Trades from a Tax," New York Times, September 7, 2001, p. W1.

▶ Chartered Financial Analysts

The Association for Investment Management and Research charters financial analysts. Financial analysts who wish to become a *chartered financial analyst* (CFA) must pass rigorous examinations that the AIMR administers over a three-year period. The AIMR bases its examinations on a curriculum that covers all aspects of financial analysis, investment management, and corporate finance. The AIMR requires its CFAs to engage in a continuing education program to maintain their charters. It also requires that its CFAs uphold ethical standards of behavior. CFAs who violate those standards risk losing their charters. The AIMR charter makes CFAs very attractive to employers because it certifies that they are highly knowledgeable financial professionals. ◀

For more information, see www.aimr.org.

3.5.2 International Regulatory Organizations

Several international organizations try to coordinate market regulation across national boundaries. Although they cannot easily impose standards upon their members, they provide useful forums for sharing information about market structure and for exploring solutions to common regulatory and operational problems. The most important of these organizations are the *International Organization of Securities Commissions* (IOSCO), the *World Federation of Exchanges* (WFE), and the *International Councils of Securities Associations* (ICSA). These organizations of government regulatory agencies, exchanges, and dealer associations meet regularly to discuss issues of interest to their members.

3.6 SUMMARY

The trading industry consists of traders who trade instruments in regulated markets. This short introduction has identified the traders, instruments, markets, and regulators who operate in this industry.

Although our discussions describe how the trading industry is organized, we have hardly considered why it is organized as it is. In subsequent chapters, we will increasingly examine why things are as they are. This introduction to the trading industry should provide you with the background for more interesting discussions to come.

3.7 SOME POINTS TO REMEMBER

- The buy side buys liquidity services. The sell side provides them.
- Dealers trade for their own account. Brokers trade for others.
- Stocks get more attention than their values would indicate.
- Many markets compete for order flow.
- Exchanges often compete with brokerages to arrange trades.
- Legislatures, regulatory agencies, and SROs regulate the markets. Legislatures provide the regulatory framework, the SROs provide the details, and governmental regulatory agencies provide oversight.
- Private regulators try to create respected standards.

3.8 QUESTIONS FOR THOUGHT

1. What do sell-side and buy-side traders have in common? How do they differ? Do you expect much labor mobility between these two types of traders?

2. How do brokerages and exchanges differ? How are they alike?

3. On what basis would you regulate brokerages and exchanges differently?

4. Suppose that a single organization offered the functions of an exchange, a clearinghouse, a depository, and a brokerage under one roof. What advantages and disadvantages would such an integrated organization have? Should regulators create—or encourage the creation of—such organizations?

5. Should the government require that all trading in a particular instrument take place in the same market?

6. Why are markets for precious stones generally not very liquid? How could they be made more liquid?

7. How are the common stock, preferred stock, and bond issues of a corporation like the tranches of a collateralized mortgage obligation?

8. *Index participations* (IPs) were instruments that several U.S. options exchanges traded in 1989–1990. ("Index participation" is also a generic name for Canadian exchange-traded index funds.) The index participation was an instrument cleared by the Options Clearing Corporation that was created when a trader with no position sold it to a buyer. At the option of the buyer or seller, traders could periodically redeem the IP for a specified multiple of its specified underlying equity index. Otherwise, the IP had an infinite life. Traders with short IP positions were required to pay periodic dividends to traders with long IP positions at a rate determined by the dividend payout rate of the underlying index. IP positions were subject to Regulation T margins. The futures exchanges and the CFTC argued in court that the index participation was a futures contract. The securities exchanges and the SEC claimed that it was a security. A federal court in Chicago ruled that the IP was a futures contract. Was it correct?

9. What is the difference between a gambling contract and a futures contract?

10. What advantages and disadvantages do cash-settled futures contracts have, compared to physically settled futures contracts?

11. Why are markets with many instruments less liquid than markets with few instruments?

12. How might competition among regulatory agencies benefit the economy? What effect do you expect it would have on innovation in trading products and trading procedures?

13. Should Congress consolidate the SEC and the CFTC into a single regulatory agency?

14. Why do traders, brokers, and exchanges generally welcome regulation? When do they oppose it?

15. How should regulators decide issues?

16. Who should appoint regulators?

4

▷

Orders
and
Order
Properties

*O*rders are trade instructions. They specify what traders want to trade, whether to buy or sell, how much, when and how to trade, and, most important, on what terms. Traders issue orders when they cannot personally negotiate their trades.

Orders are the fundamental building blocks of trading strategies. To trade effectively, you must specify exactly what you want. Your order submission strategy is the most important determinant of your success as a trader. The proper order used at the right time can make the difference between a good trade, a costly trade, and no trade at all.

Many markets arrange all their trades by using a set of rules to match buy and sell orders that traders submit to them. To understand how these markets work and to use them effectively, you must understand how traders specify their orders.

Understanding orders will also allow you to see where liquidity comes from. *Liquidity* is the ability to trade when you want to trade. Some orders *offer liquidity* by presenting other traders with trading opportunities. Other orders *take liquidity* by seizing those opportunities. Trader decisions to offer or take liquidity therefore affect market quality. To understand liquidity, you must understand how traders form their order submission strategies.

This chapter will show you what orders are, how traders specify them, and, most important, what properties they have. Traders choose orders with properties that allow them to best solve their trading problems.

Familiarize yourself with the many trading terms introduced in this chapter. We will use them throughout the book. Traders use specialized words and phrases to communicate quickly and accurately with each other. Whether you intend to trade or simply want to learn about trading, you need to be familiar with market nomenclature.

Although order instructions have the same meanings in all markets, their properties differ according to the type of market to which traders submit them. In this chapter, we will assume that traders submit their orders to a *continuous trading market* that arranges trades as orders arrive. Identical orders have slightly different properties in *call markets* that collect and process all orders at the same time. We examine call markets and the properties of orders submitted to them in chapter 6.

4.1 WHAT ARE ORDERS, AND WHY DO PEOPLE USE THEM?

Orders are instructions that traders give to the brokers and exchanges which arrange their trades. The instructions explain how they want their trades to be arranged.

An *order* always specifies which instrument (or instruments) to trade, how much to trade, and whether to buy or sell. An order may also include conditions that a trade must satisfy. The most common conditions limit the prices that the trader will accept. Other conditions may specify for how long the order is valid, when the order can be executed, whether it is okay to partially fill the order, where to present the order, and how to search for the other side. Some orders even specify the traders with whom the trader is willing to trade.

Orders are necessary because most traders do not personally arrange their trades. Traders who arrange their own trades—typically dealers—do not use orders. They decide on the spot what they want to do and how to do it. All other traders must carefully express their intentions ahead of time.

For many small traders, it is not economical to continuously monitor the market. These traders use orders to represent their interests when they are not paying close attention to the market.

Traders who arrange their own trades have an advantage over traders who use orders to express their intentions. The former can respond to market conditions as they change. The latter must anticipate such changes and write contingencies into their orders to deal with them. Carefully written orders will adequately represent traders' interests even when conditions change. When orders do not do so, traders must cancel them and submit new instructions. During the time it takes to cancel and resubmit orders, traders can lose because their old orders trade before they can cancel them, or because they cannot submit new orders in time to take advantage of the changing market conditions. Traders therefore must carefully specify their intentions when they use orders to trade.

In general, traders who can respond most quickly to changes in market conditions have an advantage over slower traders. Traders who submit and cancel orders manually are slower than traders who use computers to monitor and adjust their orders. Where speed is of the essence, floor traders and computerized traders are the most successful traders.

Clear and efficient communication is essential when trading in fast markets. Brokers must understand exactly what traders want. Otherwise, extremely costly errors may occur. To avoid mistakes, most traders use standard orders to decrease the probability that they will misunderstand each other when communicating quickly. All traders recognize and understand these orders.

This chapter introduces the standard orders and describes their properties. We must define some basic terms first.

4.2 SOME IMPORTANT TERMS

Traders indicate that they are willing to buy or sell by making *bids* and *offers*. Traders *quote* their bids and offers when they arrange their own trades. Otherwise, they use orders to convey their bids and offers to the brokers or automated trading systems that arrange their trades. Bids and offers usually include information about the prices and quantities that traders will accept. Traders call these prices *bid* and *offer prices*. They also use the terms *bidding price*, *offering price*, *asking price*, or simply *bid* and *ask*. They refer to the quantities as *sizes*.

Prices are *firm* when traders can demand to trade at those prices. Prices are *soft* if the traders who offer them can revise them before trading. Orders generally have firm prices.

The highest bid price in a market is the *best bid*. The lowest offer price is the *best offer* (or, equivalently, the *best ask*). Traders also call them the *market bid* and the *market offer* (or *market ask*) because they are the best prices available in the market. A *market quotation* reports the best bid and best offer in a market. A market quotation is often called the *BBO*, which is the acronym for *Best Bid and Offer*. Many markets continuously publicize their *market quotations*. The best bid and offer anywhere in the United States is the *NBBO—National Best Bid and Offer*.

The difference between the best ask and the best bid is the *bid/ask spread*. Traders sometimes call it the *inside spread* because the space between the highest bid price and the lowest ask price is *inside the market*. The English often refer to the spread as the *touch*. In sports betting markets, bettors and bookies call it the *vigorish*.

An order *offers liquidity*—or equivalently *supplies liquidity*—if it gives other traders an opportunity to trade. For example, suppose Joe issues an order to buy 100 shares of IBM for no more than 100 dollars per share from the first person to contact him before trading closes today. Joe's bid offers liquidity because other traders now have the opportunity to sell IBM for 100 dollars per share. Joe's bid is a *day limit order* because it is valid only for the day, and because Joe limits the price that he will pay.

Both buyers and sellers can offer liquidity. Buyers offer liquidity when their bids give other traders opportunities to sell. Sellers offer liquidity when their offers give other traders opportunities to buy.

The dual use of the word "offer" may seem confusing. It may refer to an offer of an item for sale or to an offer of liquidity. If you think of liquidity—the ability to trade when you want to trade—as a service that you can buy or sell, the use of the word "offer" makes sense. This perspective leads to many useful insights. For example, dealers make money by selling liquidity to their clients.

Standing orders are open offers to trade. Joe's order will stand until someone sells to Joe at 100 dollars or less, the order expires at the end of the day, or Joe cancels it. Standing orders are also called *open orders*. Since standing orders allow other traders to trade when they want to trade, traders offer liquidity when they have orders outstanding.

Traders who want to trade quickly *demand liquidity*. Traders *take liquidity* when they accept offers—standing limit orders or quotes—that other traders have made. If Sue is willing to sell 100 shares of IBM at 100 dollars, she can initiate a trade by taking Joe's offer.

Traders who demand to trade immediately demand *immediacy*. We show in chapter 19 (Liquidity) that immediacy is one of several dimensions of liquidity.

A market is *liquid* when traders can trade without significant adverse effect on price. Markets with many standing limit orders and small bid/ask spreads are usually quite liquid.

The prices at which orders fill are *trade prices*. Buy orders that trade at high prices and sell orders that trade at low prices trade at *inferior prices*.

Markets and traders sometimes treat orders differently, depending on whether they are agency orders or proprietary orders. *Agency orders* are orders that brokers represent as agents for their clients. *Proprietary orders* are orders that traders represent for their own accounts. In many organized markets, agency orders have precedence over proprietary orders at the same price.

After traders submit their orders to their brokers, but before their brokers agree to accept them, the order is *pending*. Brokers often hold orders pending confirmation that the account is authorized to trade. They also hold short sale orders pending confirmation that securities can be borrowed to settle the trade. After a broker accepts an order, but before it is filled or canceled, the order is *working*.

4.3 MARKET ORDERS

A *market order* is an instruction to trade at the best price currently available in the market. Market orders usually fill quickly, but sometimes at inferior prices. Impatient traders and traders who want to be certain that they will trade use market orders to demand liquidity. The execution of a market order depends on its size and on the liquidity currently available in the market.

Small market orders usually fill immediately with little or no effect on prices. A small market buy order will typically trade at the best (lowest) asking price, and a small market sell order will typically trade at the best (highest) bid price.

4.3.1 Market Orders Pay the Spread

Market order traders *pay the bid/ask spread*. To see why, imagine that Amy uses a market buy order, followed by a market sell order, to complete a quick round-trip bond trade. Her market buy order buys the bond for 102, when the best bid is 100 and the best offer is 102. Her market sell order sells the bond for 100, assuming that the best bid did not change. The total loss for her two trades is the bid/ask spread. Since Amy pays the bid/ask spread for two opportunities to trade immediately, her *transaction cost* per trade (exclusive of commissions) is half of the spread. The spread—actually half of the spread—is the price traders pay for immediacy when using market orders.

You can also see that market order traders pay the bid/ask spread by considering how Amy's trade prices differ from our best estimate of the value of the bond. If we assume that Amy is an uninformed trader (her erratic behavior seems to bear this out), the only information available to us about the value of the bond is that a trader is willing to buy it for 100 and another trader (perhaps the same trader) is willing to sell it at 102. With no further information, our best estimate of value is the average of these two prices, or 101. Using this estimate of value, we can see that Amy paid 102 for a bond worth 101. The difference of 1—which is half the bid/ask spread—is what she paid for liquidity. When she sold it, she also paid half the spread for liquidity because she received only 100 for a bond worth 101.

4.3.2 Price Improvement

In markets where traders negotiate prices, market orders may sometimes trade at better prices than the market bid and offer. Such orders receive *price improvement*. Price improvement takes place when a trader is willing to step in front of the current best price to offer a better price to the incoming market order. This often happens when the spread is wide and the incoming market order is small. Price improvement lowers the cost of liquidity.

▶ **Market Order Example**

AstroPower (APWR) trades in the Nasdaq market. Nasdaq dealers are bidding 36.80 for APWR and offering it at 36.85. These quotes are good for 500 shares on the bid side and 400 shares on the ask side. Bill submits a market order to buy 200 shares of APWR. He buys all 200 shares for 36.85. ◀

▶ Price Improvement Example

The market for AnnTaylor (ANN) at the New York Stock Exchange is 23.35 bid, offered at 23.45. At these prices, buyers are willing to purchase 500 shares and sellers are willing to sell 1,000 shares. Tom submits a market order to sell 300 shares of ANN. The ANN specialist (a dealer who trades for his own account on the floor of the exchange) may choose to fill the order at 23.38. If he does, Tom would receive a price 3 cents better than the 23.35 bid price at which his market sell order would otherwise have traded.

The specialist, of course, would prefer to buy ANN at 23.35. Exchange regulations, however, prevent him from buying at the same price at which public traders are willing to buy. The specialist therefore must improve the price to buy ANN. ◀

4.3.3 Market Impact

Large market orders are more difficult to execute than small ones. Traders willing to take the other side of a very large trade are often hard to find. They may not be interested in the instrument, or they may be afraid to trade with someone who may be well informed about the value of the instrument.

To attract traders, large impatient traders often must move prices. Large buyers bid prices up to encourage sellers to sell to them. Large sellers offer prices down to encourage buyers to buy from them. The premiums that large buyers pay, and the discounts that large sellers offer, are *price concessions*. When traders move prices to fill their orders, they have *market impact*. (Market impact is also known as *price impact*.) Since market impact increases with order size, it generally is the most significant cost of trading large orders. Traders who submit large market orders often pay more than half the bid/ask spread for liquidity.

The price impact of a market order depends on the liquidity available in the market. In small, illiquid markets with few participants, small orders may be difficult to execute without significant price impacts, and large orders may be impossible to execute. Conversely, in large, liquid markets with many active traders, traders may routinely execute very large orders involving millions of dollars without much price impact.

▶ Market Impact Example

Martha wants to buy 400 March orange juice concentrate futures contracts. The contracts trade at the Citrus Associates division of the New York Cotton Exchange, which is a subsidiary of the New York Board of Trade. Traders there are currently bidding 84.20 cents per pound and offering 84.25 cents per pound. Yesterday 6,505 contracts traded for all delivery months.

Martha breaks her order into two equal market orders. She gives the order to one broker who immediately buys 20 contracts for 84.25 cents, then another 30 for 84.40 cents, and an additional 150 for 84.70 cents. Later in the day, Martha gives a different broker a market order for the remaining contracts. At that time, the market is 84.55 bid, offered at 84.60. The second broker buys 5 contracts for 84.60 cents, 75 contracts for 84.80, another 45 contracts for 85.00, and the remaining 75 contracts for 85.15. To complete her trades, Martha's brokers had to raise the price by 0.90 cents. ◀

4.3.4 Execution Price Uncertainty

The prices at which market orders trade depend on current market conditions. Since market conditions can change quickly, traders who use market orders risk trading at worse prices than they expect. Economists call this risk *execution price uncertainty*. Execution price uncertainty is due to quote changes that may occur between the submission of an order and its execution, and to the unpredictable price concessions that may be required to fill large orders. Traders who are concerned about this risk may prefer to submit limit orders.

4.4 LIMIT ORDERS

A *limit order* is an instruction to trade at the best price available, but only if it is no worse than the *limit price* specified by the trader. For buy orders, the trade price must be at or below the limit price. For sell orders, the price must be at or above the limit price.

In continuously trading markets, a broker (or an exchange) will attempt to trade a newly submitted limit order as soon as it arrives. If no trader is immediately willing to take the opposite side at an acceptable price, the order will not trade. Instead, it will stand as an offer to trade until someone is willing to trade at its limit price, until it expires, or until the trader who submitted it cancels it.

Standing limit orders are placed in a file called a *limit order book*. Depending on the market, a broker, an exchange, or even a dealer will maintain the limit order book. Figure 4-1 presents an example of a limit order book from Island ECN.

The probability that a limit order will trade depends on its limit price. If the limit price of a buy order is too low, the order will not trade. Likewise, if a sell limit price is too high, the order will not trade. Buy limit orders with high prices and sell limit orders with low prices are *aggressively priced*. Aggressively priced limit orders are the easiest limit orders to fill.

4.4.1 Limit Price Placement

Traders classify limit orders by where they place their limit prices relative to the market. *The market* is the range of prices bounded above by the best offer (lowest price) and below by the best bid (highest price).

A *marketable limit order* is an order that the broker (or exchange) can execute immediately when a trader submits it. The limit price of a marketable limit buy order is at or above the best offer. The broker therefore can arrange to buy immediately from the seller quoting the best offer. For a sell order, the limit price is at or below the best bid, and the broker can arrange to sell immediately to the trader quoting the best bid.

Marketable limit orders are like market orders, except that they limit the price concessions that brokers can make to fill them. Marketable limit orders with very high limit buy prices or very low limit sell prices are essentially market orders. Traders use marketable limit orders instead of market orders to limit execution price uncertainty and to limit what they will pay for liquidity.

Limit buy orders that stand at the best bid, and limit sell orders that stand at the best offer, are *at the market*. The traders who submit these

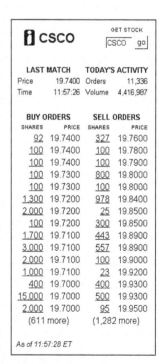

FIGURE 4-1.
The Top of the Island ECN Limit Order Book for Cisco Systems at 11:57:28 ET on January 28, 2002
Source: www.island.com.
Copyright 1998–2002 The Island ECN, Inc.—Member NASD/ CSE/SPIC, The book appears in color on the Island website.

TABLE 4-1.
Terms Traders Use to Describe Limit Price Placement

LIMIT PRICE PLACEMENT	BUY ORDERS	SELL ORDERS
Above the best offer	"Marketable"	"Behind the market"
At the best offer	"Marketable"	"At the market"
Between the current best bid and best offer	"In the market"	"In the market"
At the best bid	"At the market"	"Marketable"
Below the best bid	"Behind the market"	"Marketable"

orders *make the market.* Traders *make a new market* when they submit orders that improve the current best bid or offer. Buyers make a new market when they raise the best bid, and sellers make a new market when they lower the best offer. Whenever traders place their limit orders *in the market* (between the current best bid and best offer), they make a new market.

Limit orders that stand behind the best bid or offer are *behind the market.* Such orders are *away from the market.* A buy order is behind the market if its limit price is less than the best bid. A sell order is behind the market if its limit price is above the best offer. These orders are "behind the market" because traders who maintain manual order books place tickets for these orders behind those of more aggressively priced orders. A summary of this nomenclature appears in table 4-1.

To summarize, marketable limit orders are the most aggressively priced limit orders. The next most aggressive orders are those which make a new market, followed by orders that match the market at the best bid or offer. The least aggressive limit orders stand behind the market. Figure 4-2 illustrates these relations.

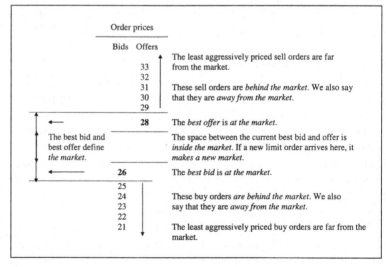

FIGURE 4-2.
Terms Traders Use to Describe Standing Limit Orders
Note: This figure presents a simplified limit order book for a hypothetical market. The market is "26 bid, offered at 28" because the best bid is 26 and the best offer is 28.

4.4.2 Standing Limit Orders Are Trading Options That Offer Liquidity

Traders who submit standing limit orders offer liquidity to other traders. Their limit orders give others the ability to trade when they want to trade.

Since traders can choose whether they want to trade with a standing limit order, standing limit orders are options to trade. In particular, sell limit orders are call options that give other traders opportunities to buy when they want to buy. Buy limit orders likewise are put options that give other traders opportunities to sell when they want to sell. The option strike prices are the limit prices.

Knowing that standing limit orders are options is very useful. This observation will help you understand what liquidity is, why brokers are essential in many markets, why markets consolidate (why traders like to trade in the same place), how traders choose their order submission strategies, what the minimum price change (tick) should be, and why fast traders have an advantage over slower traders. Since this concept is very important, we need to understand the option characteristics of limit orders thoroughly. We will first consider how limit orders differ from option contracts, and then what factors determine the value of a limit order option.

Standing limit orders are options, but not option contracts. An *option contract* is an option to trade an instrument at a specified price that a *writer* sells to another trader. The buyer of the contract pays a *premium* to the writer regardless of whether the buyer ultimately exercises the option. In contrast, traders who write standing limit orders do not sell them to other traders. Instead, they freely grant their options to the market. Unlike with option contracts, traders do not own the trading options that limit orders represent. Any trader who wants to exercise a limit order option may do so by submitting a market order or a marketable limit order.

The *option value* of a limit order is the value of the order to other traders. Limit order option values depend on the limit price, how long the orders will stand, and price volatility.

The most important variable is the limit price. If the limit price is far behind the market, the option to trade has little value because traders prefer to trade first with orders that offer better prices. Conversely, if the limit price is at the market, traders who want to trade immediately will value the option to trade. If the order offers an exceptionally good price, traders will jump to take its price, and the order will fill quickly.

Limit order option values also depend upon how long traders expect the orders will stand. Orders that will remain available for a long time allow traders to defer their trading decisions. When presented with such options, traders like to wait and see what happens before committing to trade. If values rise, traders will try to buy from limit sell orders, and they will ignore limit buy orders. Conversely, if values fall, they will try to sell to limit buy orders, and they will ignore limit sell orders. When prices change substantially, these trades will be most profitable. Because values change more in long intervals than in short intervals, limit order trading options are more valuable when traders expect that they will remain available for a long time rather than for a short time.

Traders cannot wait too long to trade with valuable limit orders, however. Valuable limit orders often disappear quickly because other traders take them, or because the traders who write them cancel them. Limit orders that

▶ Option Contracts Are Sold Limit Orders

Traders who are willing to honor their limit orders until some future date can sell their orders to other traders by writing option contracts. The traders to whom they sell their orders pay them for the liquidity that they offer.

To sell limit orders, traders must give up their right to cancel them at any time. No one would buy an order that the seller could cancel at any time.

Traders sell limit orders when they write option contracts. Option contracts give the holder the right to exercise the limit order at any time before the contract expires. Traders are willing to buy option contracts because the exclusive right to exercise a limit order at any time before its expiration date can be quite valuable.

Some traders who issue standing limit orders would be better off if they sold option contracts instead. For example, suppose that you want to offer to sell shares in Allied Arctic Authentic Apparel (AAAA) at 100 dollars while you are away exploring the Arctic ice pack. Rather than submit a limit order to sell at 100, you should consider selling (writing) a call option with a strike price of 100. In both cases, you will probably sell at 100 if the price of AAAA rises above 100 before you return. If you submit the limit order, you will receive only 100. If you sell the option, you will receive 100 dollars plus the option premium.

The choice is not as simple as it seems, however. Suppose that the price of AAAA rises above 100 and then falls below 100 while you are away. If you submitted a sell limit order, you probably would have sold at 100 when the price went above 100. If you sold a call option, however, the buyer might not have exercised the option when the price went above 100. The buyer certainly would not have executed the option after the stock fell below 100. If the buyer does not exercise the option, you will still own the stock, plus, of course, the option premium. ◀

are close to the market therefore are valuable to traders who want to trade immediately, but have little value to traders who want to wait and see what happens before deciding to trade.

Price volatility, which refers to how fast prices change, also affects limit order option values. Limit order options are valuable in volatile markets because volatility increases the probability of executing a profitable trade with a limit order. In volatile markets, values may change substantially before traders can cancel their orders. Traders who can execute limit orders quickly, before traders cancel them, value limit orders more in volatile markets than in stable markets.

Since traders do not like to give away option values, they often place their limit orders far from the market when the market is volatile in order to reduce their option values. Bid/ask spreads consequently tend to be wide in volatile markets.

4.4.3 The Expected Compensation for Offering Liquidity

The compensation that limit order traders hope to receive for giving away free trading options is a better price. Buyers who submit standing limit orders hope to buy at the bid. If they had submitted market orders instead, they would pay the higher asking price. Sellers likewise hope to receive the ask instead of the lower bid.

They do not always realize their hopes. Limit order traders receive better prices only if their orders trade. If the market moves away from their orders, they may never trade. If they still want to trade, they will have to *chase the price* by raising their bid or lowering their offer. Thus, the trade prices that they ultimately obtain may be worse than the prices they would have obtained had they used market orders.

In chapter 14, we show that spreads adjust so that traders expect to obtain better average prices by using limit order strategies than by using market order strategies. The average difference in prices is their compensation for offering liquidity. If there were no compensation for offering liquidity, traders would not offer it.

4.4.4 The Risks of Using Standing Limit Orders

Traders face two risks when using standing limit orders. The first is *execution uncertainty*. When prices move away from their orders, limit order traders fail to trade and wish that they had. Traders who are certain that they want to trade are very concerned about this risk.

Limit order traders can minimize execution uncertainty by aggressively pricing their limit orders to increase the probability that they will trade. Traders who want to be very sure that they trade should submit market orders. These strategies reduce execution uncertainty, but they increase the cost of trading.

The second risk that traders face when using standing limit orders is that they may trade and subsequently regret it. This happens when prices move toward and through their limit prices (i.e., down for a buy order and up for a sell order). Their orders fill, and then the market moves against their newly established positions so that they lose money. Economists call this risk *ex post regret*. All traders face ex post regret regardless of how and why they trade.

Ex post regret particularly concerns dealers who trade only to profit from offering liquidity to impatient traders. Dealers do not like to trade with traders who know more about future values than they do. When they do, more often than not the dealers will be on the wrong side of the market. If prices change before they can restore their original positions, they will lose money. Economists call this risk *adverse selection risk*. Adverse selection risk is the most important cause of ex post regret.

Limit order traders can minimize the risk of ex post regret by placing their orders far from the market. This strategy gives them better prices, should their orders execute, but it decreases the probability that they will trade. Alternatively, they may place their orders close to the market to increase the probability that they trade quickly. This strategy reduces the time that they are exposed to adverse selection risk, but it worsens the price they receive if their orders trade.

In later chapters, we will discuss ex post regret in several different contexts. It arises when traders employ clever strategies to extract limit order option values (chapter 11), when bluffers try to persuade other traders to offer liquidity foolishly (chapter 12), when dealers trade with better-informed traders (chapter 13), and when large traders pose as small traders (chapter 15).

4.4.5 Limit Orders Represent Absent Traders

Many traders use limit orders to tell their brokers the conditions under which they would be willing to trade. Their brokers then monitor the market on their behalf to determine when these conditions are met. By ex-

> ▶ **Chasing the Price with a Limit Order**
>
> Jill wants to buy 500 shares of General Motors. The market for GM at the New York Stock Exchange is currently 48.05 bid, offered at 48.11. Jill submits a limit order to buy 500 shares of GM for no more than 48.05 dollars per share. The price of GM, however, rises, and her order does not execute. After the market moves to 48.15 bid, 48.20 asked, Jill cancels her limit order and replaces it with a market order that immediately trades for 48.20 dollars per share. Had her original limit order traded at 48.05, Jill would have paid 6 cents less than she would have if she had initially submitted a market order. As it happened, she ended up paying 9 cents more. ◀

▶ Ex Post Regret Example

Andy is a dealer who trades S&P 500 index futures contracts overnight in the GLOBEX electronic trading system. He typically submits limit orders to buy at the bid and to sell at the ask. He makes money when he is able to buy at the lower bid price and sell at the higher ask price.

At 2:30 A.M. Chicago time, Andy submits a limit buy order for 20 contracts at the best bid of 901.05. The market is 901.05 bid, offered at 901.20. Including Andy's order, the total quantity at the best bid is 30 contracts.

Five minutes later, a market sell order for 50 contracts arrives. The GLOBEX computer immediately matches this order with the orders totaling 30 contracts at 901.05. It then fills the rest of the order with 12 contracts bid at 901.00 and with 8 more contracts at 900.90. Following these transactions, the market is 900.90 bid, offered at 901.20. In the next minute, traders submit new buy and sell limit orders so that the market spread closes to 900.95 bid, 901.00 offered.

Andy lost money. He bought 20 contracts at 901.05. If he needed to sell them immediately, he would receive only 900.95 for them. Since the nominal value of the S&P 500 contract is 250 times the index value, Andy has lost 500 dollars (250 × 0.10 dollar per contract × 20 contracts). He places a limit sell order at 901.00 and hopes the market does not fall further. ◀

▶ Limit Order Example

Sandy wants to buy five July sugar futures contracts if their price drops below 10 cents per pound. The contract trades at the New York Coffee, Sugar and Cocoa Exchange. Rather than watch the sugar market herself, she gives her broker a limit buy order with a 10-cent limit price. Her broker then watches the sugar market for her while she attends to other business. ◀

pressing their orders, traders can participate in the markets while they attend to business elsewhere.

4.5 STOP ORDERS

A *stop instruction* stops an order from executing until price reaches a *stop price* specified by the trader. Traders attach stop instructions to their orders when they want to buy only after price rises to the stop price or sell only after price falls to the stop price. Orders with stop instructions are called *stop orders.*

Traders can attach stop instructions to any type of order. They most often attach them to market orders. Once they are activated, brokers and exchanges treat stop orders like all other orders. In particular, a stop order remains valid even if price crosses back over the stop price.

Traders most commonly use stop orders to stop their losses when prices move against their positions. For example, suppose that Stan buys 10 cotton futures contracts at 80 cents a pound. To limit the potential loss on this position, Stan may issue a market sell order for 10 contracts with a stop price of 70 cents. If cotton drops to or below 70 cents, Stan's broker will immediately try to sell 10 contracts at the best price then available in the market. Traders often call such orders *stop loss orders.*

The price at which a stop order executes may not be the stop price. In the above example, if cotton prices fall quickly, the market order may trade at a price substantially below the 70-cent stop price. For example, if the price of cotton drops from 72 cents to 67 cents on news that the harvest will be greater than expected, Stan's broker may be able to sell the 10 contracts for only 66.90 cents.

To guarantee a trade at a particular price, a trader must purchase an option contract. In our example, if Stan wants to guarantee that he can sell for 70 cents, he must buy a put option contract with a strike price of 70 cents. This contract transfers the risk of selling for less then 70 cents from Stan to the writer (seller) of the put contract. The transfer makes good economic sense if the writer is a better trader than Stan is, or if the writer has some reason for wanting to be short a put.

4.5.1 Stop Orders and Limit Orders

Novices often confuse stop orders with limit orders because both specify price conditions. The difference lies in the purpose of the specified price. A stop instruction provides for the activation of an order when the market price reaches or passes a specified stop price. In contrast, a limit order can be executed only at a price equal to or better than a specified limit price. To clarify the distinction, consider how a market sell order with a stop set at 5 euros differs from a limit sell order with a limit price of 5 euros. A trader would typically submit the stop sell order when price is above 5 euros. It will activate only when the market price drops to the 5-euro stop price. At that time, it becomes a standard market order, and it should trade at the best price then available. In contrast, a trader would typically submit a limit sell order when price is below 5 euros. It can be filled only if price rises to 5 euros or more.

When traders attach a stop instruction to a limit order, they must specify two prices. The stop price indicates when the limit order becomes active, and the limit price indicates the terms upon which a trade may be arranged. The combined order is a *stop limit order.*

Stop orders are like limit orders in one respect. Both order instructions allow traders to tell their brokers conditions under which they are willing to trade in the future. As noted earlier, traders who specify such instructions do not need to monitor the market, and thus are free to attend to other business.

4.5.2 Stop Orders and Liquidity

Stop orders accelerate price changes. Prices often change because traders on one side of the market demand more liquidity than is available. When these price changes activate stop orders, the stop orders unfortunately contribute to the one-sided demands for liquidity. Stop orders accelerate price changes by adding buying pressure when prices are rising and selling pressure when prices are falling. They demand liquidity when it is least available. Traders say that stop orders *add momentum* to the market.

Traders who pursue *momentum trading strategies* buy when prices are rising and sell when prices are falling. Momentum trading therefore destabilizes prices. Momentum traders often implement their strategies by giving stop orders to their brokers, who then monitor the market on their behalf. Alternatively, they may monitor the market themselves and submit standard orders when they want to trade.

Contrarian traders employ the opposite trading strategy. They buy when prices are falling and sell when prices are rising. They therefore stabilize prices when they trade. Contrarians can implement their trading strategies by using standard limit orders.

The destabilizing effects that stop orders and momentum strategies have on the market concern many regulators, traders, and exchanges. We also

> ### ▶ Stop Limit Order Example
>
> Suppose that you would like to buy Ashton Technology Group only if its price rises to 10 dollars, and then only if you can buy it for less than 10.37. You would submit a limit buy order with a limit price of 10.37 and a stop price of 10: "Buy 100 ASTN, 10 stop, 10.37 limit." ◀

consider this issue when we discuss front runners in chapter 11, market manipulation in chapter 12, and extreme volatility in chapter 28.

4.6 MARKET-IF-TOUCHED ORDERS

A *market-if-touched order* (MIT) is a market order that is activated when price reaches (touches) some preset *touch price*. In contrast to stop orders, traders submit market-if-touched orders to buy when prices fall to their touch prices or to sell when prices rise to their touch prices.

Market-if-touched orders are like standing limit orders because traders can use both order types to buy when prices drop and to sell when prices increase. They differ from limit orders because, upon activation, market-if-touched orders become market orders that will fill at the best available price. In contrast, limit orders must trade at their limit price or better. Otherwise, they will not trade. Traders use market-if-touched orders instead of limit orders when they want to be sure that they will trade if prices reach their touch prices. Table 4-2 summarizes differences among orders with various price contingencies.

Market-if-touched-orders are quite uncommon. Most traders use limit orders rather than market-if-touched orders when they want to wait for prices to move in their favor.

Market-if-touched orders demand liquidity in a narrow sense and supply liquidity in a broader sense. When they are triggered, they become standard market orders that demand immediacy. However, they supply liquidity in a broader sense because they offer liquidity to traders who push prices to their touch prices. They thus decrease the price impacts of other traders.

Traders who issue market-if-touched orders stabilize the market because they trade against the motion of the market. They buy when the market is falling and sell when it is rising.

TABLE 4-2.
Differences Among Sell Orders with Various Price Contingencies Set at £5

ORDER TYPE	USAGE	MARKET PRICE ON SUBMISSION	WHEN THE ORDER CAN TRADE	TRADE PRICE
Standing limit sell order with a £5 limit price	Common	Below £5	After price rises to or above the limit price	At or above the limit price
Market stop sell order with a £5 stop price	Occasional	Above £5	After price falls to the stop price	Whatever the market will bear after the order is activated
Limit-stop sell order with a £5 limit price and a £5 stop price	Rare	Above £5	After price falls to the stop price and then when price is at or above the limit price	At or above the limit price
Market-if-touched sell order with a £5 touch price	Very rare	Below £5	After price rises to or above the touch price	Whatever the market will bear after the order is activated

4.7 TICK-SENSITIVE ORDERS

Traders classify prices by their relation to previous prices. Price is on an *uptick* if the current price is higher than the last price, a *downtick* if lower, and a *zero tick* if the same. They further classify zero tick prices by the last different price. A zero tick price is on a *zero downtick* if the last different price was higher and a *zero uptick* if it was lower.

Traders who want to condition their orders on the last price change submit *tick-sensitive orders*. A *buy downtick order* can be filled only on a downtick or zero downtick price. The trade price must be lower than the last different price. Likewise, a *sell uptick order* can be filled only on an uptick or zero uptick. The trade price must be higher than the last different price.

When brokers receive tick-sensitive orders, they immediately check to see whether they can match them with other orders without violating their tick conditions. If this is not possible, they hold these orders until an opportunity to fill them arises.

4.7.1 Tick-Sensitive Order Properties

The tick condition ensures that tick-sensitive orders have no market impact. A broker holding a buy downtick order cannot bid up prices to encourage sellers. Instead, the broker must wait until someone is willing to trade at a price lower than the last different price. Likewise, a broker cannot fill a sell uptick order by offering the market down. Since tick orders cannot have market impact, traders cannot use them to demand liquidity. Since they allow other traders to trade when they want to trade, tick-sensitive orders supply liquidity.

Tick-sensitive orders are essentially limit orders with dynamically adjusting limit prices. A buy downtick order implements the following equivalent limit order strategy: Submit a buy limit order just below the last different price. If price rises, raise the limit price to a price just below the new price. If price falls, leave the limit price alone. This strategy is attractive to traders who want to keep their limit orders close to the market when prices move away from them.

Dynamic limit order submission strategies are almost impossible to implement effectively in fast markets. Traders must continuously monitor the market and immediately cancel and resubmit their limit orders whenever prices change. Most traders cannot cancel and resubmit quickly enough to trade these strategies effectively. Traders therefore use tick-sensitive orders when they want to use dynamic limit order strategies.

Tick-sensitive orders are most attractive when the minimum price increment is large. The *minimum price increment*—also called the *tick* or the *minimum price variation*—is the smallest amount by which two prices can differ. It is usually set by exchange regulations. Traders who use tick-sensitive orders forgo taking liquidity in exchange for a price that typically is just one tick better. The strategy therefore is more attractive when the tick is large.

The decimalization of the U.S. stock markets in 2000 decreased the minimum price increment for most stocks from one-sixteenth dollar (6.25 cents) to 1 cent. This change made tick-sensitive orders much less attractive than they used to be.

▶ **Tick Examples**

The last trade price for Coca-Cola (KO) is 56.05 dollars. The previous trade price is 56.08. KO is on a downtick because 56.05 is less than 56.08. KO now trades three times, all at 56.05. KO is now on a zero downtick. You now try to sell KO for 56.07. If you succeed, you will sell on an uptick. ◀

▶ **Tick-Sensitive Order Example**

You want to buy American Skiing (SKI) at less than the ask price, but you are not available to cancel and resubmit your orders if prices rise. To achieve your objectives, you submit a buy downtick order to your broker.

When your broker receives your order, SKI is on a zero uptick at 1.02. Your broker cannot buy SKI for you until price drops to or below 1.01. Unfortunately, price rises to 1.03. Now the maximum price your broker can pay is 1.02. Your broker continues to watch the market. When a market sell order arrives, you buy for 1.02. ◀

4.8 MARKET-NOT-HELD ORDERS

Market-not-held orders are orders that brokers do not need to fill immediately. Traders use this order instruction to tell their brokers to use their discretion when filling their orders. The brokers then can offer liquidity or take liquidity according to current market conditions.

Traders give their brokers market-not-held orders when they want their brokers to make order strategy decisions on their behalf. Brokers are often better traders than their clients are because they have more experience, and because they generally know more about current market conditions.

When brokers decide to wait to obtain better prices, they risk trading at worse prices if prices move away from them. Since prices often move away from even the best of brokers, traders who give their brokers discretion over order submission strategy cannot reasonably hold their brokers accountable when they fail to trade at prices that subsequently look attractive. Traders submit market-not-held orders to indicate that they will not hold their brokers accountable for failing to trade.

Traders who submit standard market orders can hold their brokers accountable for failing to trade if suitable opportunities were available. Market order traders often can use legal remedies to compel their brokers to provide them with the executions that they would have received had their brokers not been negligent. Traders who submit market-not-held orders do not have these rights. Their only recourse is to withhold future orders from brokers who do not provide them with consistently good service.

Traders most often use market-not-held orders when they give their brokers large orders to fill. Large orders, if exposed all at once, can have very large market impacts. To minimize these price impacts, brokers carefully control the exposure of large orders by revealing only small portions and only to traders they deem likely and able to trade the other side. Market-not-held orders ensure that brokers will not be held accountable for failing to trade if prices move away while they are waiting for better prices or for more size.

Traders most commonly give market-not-held orders to brokers who work on the floor of an exchange. Floor traders generally know more about market conditions than do any other traders. Some traders also give market-not-held orders to brokers who operate *electronic order desks* that use complex econometric models to formulate optimal order submission strategies.

4.9 VALIDITY AND EXPIRATION INSTRUCTIONS

Traders specify *validity and expiration instructions* to indicate when their orders are valid and when their orders expire. Although traders may specify these instructions for all order types, they are especially important for standing limit orders and stop orders. These orders generally do not trade immediately upon submission. Some may never trade. Traders therefore need to tell their brokers what to do with their unfilled orders.

Open orders are orders that have not yet been executed or canceled. A *good order* is an order that can be executed. Traders generally do not distinguish between open orders and good orders because all good orders are open orders. Although most open orders are also good orders, some are not. For example, an order to buy stock after some specified date is an open order, but before that date it is not a good order.

Day orders are valid for the trading day on which traders submit them. They expire when the market closes if they have not been filled. The day order instruction is the most common validity instruction. If it is not specified, most brokers assume that an order is a day order.

Good-till-cancel (GTC) *orders* are valid until the trader expressly cancels them. To ensure that traders do not forget about their GTC orders, many brokers provide their clients with a list of their unfilled GTC orders at the end of every month. They also often mail written confirmations of these orders on the day that traders submit them. Some brokers cancel GTC orders after a month or two in order to avoid the costs of keeping track of stale orders. Traders should be careful not to forget their good-till-cancel orders. They may trade as long as they remain open.

Good-until orders are good until a date specified by the trader. Not all brokers accept this order instruction because it requires that they keep track of the expiration date. *Good-this-week* (GTW) and *good-this-month* (GTM) are special cases of good-until orders.

Immediate-or-cancel orders (IOC) orders are orders that are valid only when they are presented to the market. Whatever portion of the order that cannot be filled immediately is canceled. Traders use immediate-or-cancel orders when they do not want to give trading options to the market. In some markets, immediate-or-cancel orders are called *fill-or-kill orders* (FOK) or *good-on-sight orders*.

Good-after orders are good only after some specified date. These orders are quite rare. Most brokers will not accept them unless you are a very important customer.

Market-on-open orders are market orders that a broker can fill only at the beginning of the trading session. Traders use these orders primarily in markets that open with a single price auction. In such markets, a market-on-open order usually guarantees that the trader will receive the opening price. Since these orders are usually easy to execute, brokers sometimes charge lower commissions than they would for a regular market order.

Market-on-close orders are market orders that a broker can fill only at the close of the trading session. Traders who submit these orders often do so because they hope to trade at the closing price. Closing prices are particularly attractive to mutual funds because they value their funds for deposits and redemptions by using net asset values computed from closing prices. Brokers will not guarantee that market-on-close orders will fill at the closing price, however. Traders who want such guarantees can buy them from their dealer-brokers by paying higher commissions. (See table 4-3.)

4.10 QUANTITY INSTRUCTIONS

Traders specify quantity instructions to indicate whether their brokers can arrange multiple trades to fill their large orders. They usually do so to minimize the costs that they pay to clear and settle their trades.

The most common quantity instructions are all-or-none instructions and minimum-or-none (minimum acceptable quantity) instructions. Brokers must fill *all-or-none* (AON) orders all at once. They can arrange multiple trades to fill *minimum-or-none orders*, but each trade must be larger than a

TABLE 4-3.
Order Validity and Expiration Instructions

INSTRUCTION	USAGE	GOOD	EXPIRES
Immediate-or-cancel (IOC); Good-on-sight; Fill-or-kill (FOK)	Occasional	When submitted	Immediately following submission
Day order	Common	When submitted	End of day
Good-this-week (GTW)	Rare	When submitted	End of week
Good-this-month (GTM)	Rare	When submitted	End of month
Good-until	Rare	When submitted	On specified date
Good-till-cancel (GTC)	Common	When submitted	Never
Good-after	Rare	After specified date	Not specified
Market-on-open	Occasional	At open	After open
Market-on-close	Occasional	At close	After close

▶ **Rolling a Futures Position with a Spread Order**

In early June, Fulvio wants to roll a long S&P 500 Index futures position from the expiring June contract into the September contract. He issues a spread order to sell the June contract and to buy the September contract. The last trade prices for the June and September contracts were respectively 1276 and 1289, which implies a spread of 13. As is usual, the back month trades at a premium to the current month.

Fulvio places a limit of 10, premium to the buy side, on the spread order. The spread, however, never drops to his limit, and the order does not execute. Fulvio subsequently replaces his limit spread order with a market spread order. The order then executes at a spread of 12. ◀

minimum size that the trader specifies. In some markets, these two instructions are also known as *all-or-nothing* and *minimum acceptable quantity* (MAQ) instructions.

4.11 OTHER ORDER INSTRUCTIONS

4.11.1 Spread Orders

Traders issue *spread orders* when they want to buy one instrument and simultaneously sell another instrument. The two instruments usually are closely related. For example, they may be futures contracts for different delivery months of the same commodity. Spread orders can be market orders or limit orders.

When the spread order is a limit order, the trader specifies a limit for the difference between the two prices that he or she is willing to accept. Traders always specify the limit as a premium to the buy side or to the sell side. If you want to sell one instrument at a higher price than you want to pay to buy the other instrument, the premium is to the sell side. The order can be filled only if the difference between the sales and purchase prices is greater than or equal to the limit. If the instrument you want to buy is priced above the instrument that you want to sell, the premium is to the buy side. In that case, the order can be filled only if the difference between the purchase and sales prices is less than or equal to the limit.

4.11.2 Display Instructions

Traders give *display instructions* when they want to specify how their brokers should display unfilled portions of their standing limit orders. These instructions typically tell brokers to show no more than some maximum quantity. Traders restrict the display of their orders when they fear that showing their full sizes would cause the market to move away from them. Or-

▶ Undisclosed Order Example

Michael wants to sell 90,000 shares of Alcatel Cable at the Euronext Paris Bourse. He is willing to display only 10,000 shares at a time because he is afraid that revealing his full size might move the market down. He places an undisclosed limit order to sell 90,000 shares at 408 francs, with instructions to display only 10,000 shares. His order makes a new market.

Liza sees the offer to sell 10,000 shares at 408 francs. She is willing to buy 60,000 shares, but she does not want to reveal this information. She knows that more shares may be hidden behind the 10,000 displayed shares. Liza submits a fill-or-kill limit order to buy 60,000 shares for 408 francs. She can be sure of trading at least 10,000 shares. If she does not trade the full 60,000 shares, the remainder of her order will be canceled.

When the Bourse's automated trading system receives Liza's order, it immediately fills the entire order. Liza and Michael both will receive reports that they have traded 60,000 shares. The 30,000-share remainder of Michael's sell order will stay in the system with 10,000 shares displayed at 408 francs and another 20,000 undisclosed shares behind it. ◀

ders that are not fully displayed are called *undisclosed orders*. Traders also call them *hidden orders*, or *reserve orders* (because they hold some size in reserve), or *iceberg orders* (because other traders can see only the top of the order).

To fill an undisclosed order, a broker must fill the exposed portion first. As the order fills, the broker can then expose more size up to the maximum display quantity. This process continues until the broker fills the entire order.

Some electronic exchanges, such as the Euronext, permit traders to issue undisclosed limit orders. Traders who want to trade with these orders can discover their full sizes only by submitting large marketable orders with fill-or-kill instructions attached. If the size is present, they trade. If it is not, their orders cancel.

4.11.3 Substitution Orders

Traders give *substitution orders* to their brokers when they want to invest or divest a specified amount of money by trading any of several securities. The brokers then use their discretion to choose which securities to trade, based on which ones appear to provide the best prices.

4.11.4 Special Settlement Instructions

Traders attach *special settlement instructions* to their orders when they want nonstandard settlement. In U.S. equity markets, *regular-way settlement* occurs three days after the trade (T+3). Traders who want to settle on a different date attach special settlement instructions to their orders.

The most common nonstandard settlement is *cash settlement*. Cash settlement trades settle that day. Traders typically specify cash settlement when they decide at the last moment that they want to be a shareholder of record before a vote or before some distribution.

Traders also use special settlement instructions when they pursue dividend capture strategies. We describe these strategies in chapter 8.

Orders with special settlement instructions are more difficult to trade than are regular orders. Traders who want special settlement cannot simply

▶ Substitution Order Example

Steve wants the stock portfolio he manages to have more automobile industry exposure. He does not care whether he buys Ford, General Motors, or Chrysler, as long as he gets a good price for his purchase. Steve instructs his broker to buy 35 million dollars of Ford, General Motors, or Chrysler. The broker examines the trading in these stocks. He learns that a large buyer is accumulating GM and pushing prices up. He therefore buys Ford and Chrysler to fill the order. ◀

▶ Cash Settlement Example

Today is Thursday. In two weeks, ABC will spin off its XYZ division to its shareholders. All shareholders of record tomorrow will receive one share of XYZ for every share of ABC that they own. You would like to own both companies, but presently you hold no shares in ABC. If you buy ABC today with normal three-day settlement, your trade will settle on Tuesday, and you will not receive the XYZ shares. If you buy ABC today with cash settlement, you will be a shareholder of record tomorrow, and you will own both companies.

With regular-way settlement, the last day that you could have bought ABC and still have been entitled to receive the distribution was two days ago (Tuesday). On that day, the price reflected the values of both companies. On Wednesday, the price of ABC fell because buyers were no longer entitled to receive XYZ. The price you pay for your cash purchase on Thursday will therefore be substantially higher than the normal-way price because you will receive two companies instead of one. ◀

demand it. Instead, they must negotiate for it. If no one wants to provide special settlement, these orders will not fill. Some brokers charge higher fees for special settlement because of the greater costs of arranging and settling these trades.

4.12 SUMMARY

Traders use orders to communicate their intentions to the brokers and exchanges that arrange their trades. The most important and most common order types are market orders and limit orders. Traders use market orders when they want to trade immediately at the best price the market will bear. They use limit orders when they want to place limits on the prices at which they are willing to trade.

Orders differ by their associated uncertainties. Traders who use market orders are uncertain about the prices at which they will trade. Conversely, traders who use limit orders are uncertain about whether they will trade.

Orders also differ by whether traders use them to supply or demand liquidity. Traders who use limit orders grant trading options to the market because they allow other traders to trade when they want to. Limit order traders therefore supply liquidity to the market. Traders who exercise these options take liquidity. Traders generally use market orders when they want to take liquidity. Table 4-4 provides a summary of the properties of the various orders considered in this chapter.

Since limit orders typically supply liquidity and market orders typically demand liquidity, we must understand how traders make their order submission decisions in order to understand the origins of market liquidity. In future chapters, we will carefully consider how traders make these decisions.

4.13 SOME POINTS TO REMEMBER

- Traders use stylized order instructions to reduce communication errors.
- Market order traders demand immediacy.
- The bid/ask spread is the cost of immediacy for small market orders.

TABLE 4-4.
Order Properties

ORDER TYPE	USAGE	EFFECT ON LIQUIDITY	PRICE CONTINGENCIES	ADVANTAGES	DISADVANTAGES
Market order	Common	Demands immediacy	None	Fast execution	Uncertain price impact
Standing limit order	Common	Supplies liquidity	Trade price must be at or better than the limit price	Limited price with no price impact	May never execute
Marketable limit order	Common	Demands immediacy	Trade price must be at or better than the limit price	Limited price impact	Some price impact possible
Tick sensitive order	Occasional	Supplies liquidity	Must sell on an uptick or buy on a downtick	No price impact; adjusts with the market	Uncertain execution price
Stop market order	Occasional	Demands liquidity when it is least available	Triggered when price touches or moves through the stop price	Often used to stop losses when the trader is not present	Price impact can be large
Stop limit order	Rare	Triggered when liquidity is least available; offers liquidity on the side not needed	Triggered when price touches or moves through the stop price; trade price must be at or better than the limit price	Limits price impact	May not execute
Market-if-touched order	Very rare	Demands immediacy and supplies resiliency	Triggered when price touches or moves through the touch price	Fast execution following trigger	Uncertain price impact
Market-not-held order	Common among institutions	Broker decides whether to offer or take liquidity.	Whatever the broker decides	Expert brokers may make better trading decisions with better information	Trader loses control over the broker

- Large market orders can have substantial and unpredictable price impacts.
- Limit order traders supply liquidity by granting trading options to other traders.
- Limit order traders who must fill their orders can lose substantially if their orders do not fill when the market moves away from them.
- Some traders use limit orders to participate in the market when they are not present.
- Stop orders are not limit orders.
- Stop orders tend to destabilize prices.

4.14 QUESTIONS FOR THOUGHT

1. When should a trader use a limit order as opposed to a market order?
2. Under what circumstances would a trader use a stop buy order?
3. Under what circumstances should you be unwilling to expose a trading option?
4. How would you expect order instructions to change with the invention of new electronic communications technologies?
5. Since limit orders and quotes provide trading options to the market as a whole, what effect would an increase in volatility have on bid/ask spreads?
6. Should limit order traders place their orders close to or far from the market when they cannot adjust their limit prices quickly?
7. Some electronic systems allow traders to issue indexed limit orders. *Indexed limit orders* have limit prices that are linked to an index so that the limit price adjusts as the index changes. Why might traders prefer such orders?
8. Do contrarian traders offer or take liquidity when they trade using market orders?
9. Why are there no buy uptick and sell downtick orders?

The trading rules and the trading systems used by a market define its *market structure*. They determine who can trade; what they can trade; and when, where, and how they can trade. They also determine what information traders can see about orders, quotations, and trades; when they can see it; and who can see it.

Market structure is extremely important because it determines what people can know and do in a market. Since power comes from knowledge and the ability to act on it, market structure helps determine power relations among various types of traders. These relationships greatly affect who will trade profitably.

To trade effectively, you need to know the structure of every market in which you trade. The trading strategies that are successful in one market often do not work well in markets with different structures. The best order submission strategy for a given trading problem generally depends on the structure of the market where the trader intends to solve the problem. Traders therefore behave differently in different markets.

You must understand market structure, and how it affects trader behavior, in order to understand the origins of market liquidity, price efficiency, volatility, and trading profits. These variables all depend on trader behavior. Since market structure affects trader behavior, it helps to determine whether markets will be liquid, whether prices will be informative, and which traders will trade profitably.

We will introduce and describe a framework for classifying market structures. This classification scheme will help you recognize how markets are similar and dissimilar. Being able to classify market structures will be useful to you because trading problems have similar solutions in similar markets. If you understand how to trade in one market, you should be able to apply your knowledge and experience to similar markets. We will use this classification system throughout the rest of this book.

We will start by discussing the different types of trading sessions that exchanges, brokerages, and dealers organize. We then will discuss the various execution systems that traders use to arrange their trades. Finally, we will describe the information-processing systems that transmit orders into and out of markets, present market information to traders and to the public, and store open orders.

5.1 OVERVIEW

Trading takes place in *trading sessions*. The two types of trading sessions are continuous trading sessions and call market sessions. In *continuous trading*, traders can attempt to arrange their trades whenever the market is open. In *call markets*, all trades take place only when the market is called.

▶ Physically Convened Screen-based Markets

Although screen-based trading systems are ideally suited for distributed access markets, many Asian exchanges with screen-based trading systems once required their traders to be on their trading floors to use their electronic systems. This arrangement made it easier for exchanges to regulate their traders. It also allowed them to construct reliable communications networks, which was once an important issue in countries with poor telecommunications infrastructures.

Many traders like to trade in physically convened markets because they enjoy the society of other traders. Though exchange regulations no longer require them to be there, many traders have stayed on the exchange floor. ◀

Trading forums are the places where traders arrange their trades. In *physically convened markets*, traders must be on a *trading floor* to negotiate their trades. Physically convened futures markets trade in *trading pits*. Physically convened stock markets trade at *posts*. In *distributed access markets*, traders use telephones or screen-based trading systems to arrange their trades from their offices.

Some countries require that traders arrange all trades in a given instrument at a particular exchange. For example, with few exceptions, it is illegal to arrange trades in a Chicago Board of Trade corn futures contract outside of the corn futures trading pit on the CBOT floor. These restrictions are common in many futures markets and in the equities markets of some Asian and Eastern European countries.

Traders and exchanges use various *execution systems* to arrange trades. In *quote-driven systems*, dealers arrange most trades when they trade with their customers. In *order-driven systems*, all trades are arranged by using *order precedence rules* to match buyers to sellers and *trade pricing rules* to determine the prices of the resulting trades. In *brokered trading systems*, brokers arrange trades by helping buyers and sellers find each other.

Various systems move information in and out of the market, present it, and store it. *Order-routing systems* send orders from customers to brokers, from brokers to dealers, from brokers to markets, and from markets to markets. These systems also send reports of filled orders back to customers. *Order presentation systems* present orders to traders so that they can act upon them. The systems may use *screen-based*, *open-outcry*, or *hand-signaling* technologies. *Order books* store open orders. *Market data systems* report trades and quotes to the public.

In most markets, traders can use only prices that are an integer multiple of a specified *minimum price increment*. The size of the increment, measured as a fraction of price, varies considerably across markets. In chapter 11, we show that the increment is an extremely important determinant of market quality in many markets.

5.2 TRADING SESSIONS

Markets have *trading sessions* during which trades are arranged. The two types of trading sessions are continuous market sessions and call market sessions.

5.2.1 Continuous Markets

In *continuous markets*, traders may trade anytime the market is open. Trading is continuous in the sense that traders may continuously attempt to arrange their trades. In practice, they usually trade only when a trader demands liquidity.

Continuous trading markets are very common. Almost all major stock, bond, futures, options, and foreign exchange markets have continuous trading sessions.

5.2.2 Call Markets

In *call markets*, all traders trade at the same time when the market is called. The market may call all securities simultaneously, or it may call the securities one at a time, in a *rotation*. Markets that call in rotation may complete only one rotation per trading session or as many rotations as their trading

▶ Price Clustering

Traders do not use all possible prices equally. Instead, their usage clusters on round numbers. In markets with fractional prices, they use whole numbers more often than halves, halves more often than odd quarters, quarters more often than odd eighths, and eighths more often than odd sixteenths. In markets with decimal prices, prices that are integer multiples of 1.00, 0.50, 0.25, 0.20, 0.10, and 0.05 are most common. The clustering of prices is most pronounced when the minimum price increment is a small fraction of price, the market is highly volatile, and the instrument is thinly traded.

Clever traders often consider the clustering of limit order prices when they place limit orders. They frequently place their orders just above or just below a round number to take advantage of the fact that many other traders may place their prices at the round number. ◀

---

hours permit. Markets that call in rotation were once very common. Now only the stock markets of a few small countries call in rotation.

Many continuous order-driven exchanges open their trading sessions with call market auctions and then switch over to continuous trading. These markets also use calls to restart their trading after trading halts. Open-outcry futures exchanges, however, start continuous trading immediately when they open.

Call markets are used as the exclusive market mechanism for many instruments. Most governments sell their bonds, notes, and bills in call market auctions. Some stock markets use calls to trade their least active securities. The Deutsche Börse and Euronext Paris Bourse are examples of such markets.

Call markets usually arrange their trades using order-driven execution systems. They most commonly use batch execution systems, but a few call markets allow bilateral trading. Markets with *batch execution systems* arrange all trades at the same time by matching orders with order precedence rules. These rules usually arrange *multilateral trades* that involve more than one buyer and more than one seller. In markets that allow *bilateral trading*, traders arrange their trades among themselves.

5.2.3 Call Versus Continuous Trading Sessions

The main advantage of call markets is that they focus the attention of all traders interested in a given instrument at the same time and place. When buyers and sellers search for liquidity at the same time and place, they can easily find each other.

The main advantage of continuous trading is that it allows traders to attempt to arrange their trades whenever they want. This flexibility can be very important to impatient traders who do not want to wait for the next market call.

Recent developments in the equities markets suggest that traders prefer continuous markets with opening calls to exclusive call markets. Many national equity exchanges have switched from call market rotations to continuous trading with opening calls, but none has changed from continuous trading to exclusive call markets.

▶ Call Market Betting at the Horse Races

U.S. horse racetracks offer *pari-mutuel betting* to their betting clients. In pari-mutuel betting, bettors receive a share of the total money bet on all horses—less a fixed percentage for the track and the state—if their horse wins. Bettors can place their bets anytime until betting closes a few moments after the start of the race. The track *totalizator* system displays the projected winnings for each bet while the bettors place their bets.

Pari-mutuel betting is a call market auction in which the totalizator simultaneously prices all bets on a race. (The price of each bet is the amount bettors must bet to receive a dollar if their horse wins.) The call occurs when betting closes. Since the system allows only market orders, many traders wait until the last moment to bet so that they can see what the prices will be. ◀

► Market Sonar

Like the deep sea, markets are often quite opaque. In continuous markets, traders can *ping* the market to obtain information about the prices at which other traders will trade. Traders ping by submitting orders to see what happens to them. ◄

► Lunchtime Recess

Some continuous markets stop trading for lunch. They divide their trading days into a *morning session* and an *afternoon session*. The Tokyo Stock Exchange is the largest exchange to stop for lunch. At exchanges that trade through lunch, traders either skip lunch or eat it on the trading floor (or at their desks) so that they do not miss anything.

Intraday trading activity at the NYSE and in Nasdaq generally is lowest at lunchtime. Low lunchtime volumes may simply reflect the fact that lunchtime is midway between the market open and the market close, both of which are very active for a variety of reasons. Alternatively, at lunchtime people may be more interested in lunch than in trading. ◄

5.2.4 Trading Hours

A market's *trading hours* specify when the market accepts orders and arranges trades. Continuously trading markets schedule their regular trading sessions during normal business hours. They often open an hour or two after the start of the business day and close an hour or two before the end of the business day. The New York Stock Exchange and the Nasdaq Stock Market, for example, open at 9:30 A.M. and close at 4 P.M. Eastern Time. Traders use the hours before the open to collect and submit orders. They use the hours after the close to settle trades and to report the results to clients.

Some markets trade at odd hours within their time zone so that they can be open during normal hours in another time zone. The Pacific Exchange opens trading at 6:30 A.M. Pacific Time and the Chicago Stock Exchange opens trading at 8:30 A.M. Central Time to coincide with the New York Stock Exchange opening at 9:30 A.M. Eastern Time. Since many currency markets trade around the clock, foreign exchange traders often keep very unusual hours.

Some markets permit trading after normal hours in special *after-hours trading sessions*. Exchanges provide these sessions to appeal to clients in other time zones or to permit traders to *clean up* (adjust) their positions after the regular trading session. For example, the Chicago Board of Trade, the Chicago Mercantile Exchange, and the FINEX division of the New York Cotton Exchange all run nighttime trading sessions in many of their contracts. Many electronic trading networks provide *extended trading hours* for their clients.

5.3 EXECUTION SYSTEMS

Every market has procedures for matching buyers to sellers. These procedures define the *execution system* of the market. Since the execution system is the defining characteristic of a market, analysts frequently classify markets by their execution systems. The three main types of markets are quote-driven markets, order-driven markets, and brokered markets. *Hybrid markets* use some combination of these three systems.

5.3.1 Quote-driven Dealer Markets

In pure *quote-driven markets*, dealers participate in every trade. Anyone who wants to trade must trade with a dealer. Either traders negotiate with the dealers themselves, or their brokers, acting as their agents, negotiate with the dealers. The dealers frequently trade among themselves, but public traders cannot trade with each other. For example, if Barbara wants to buy a security, she must find a dealer who will sell it to her from his or her *inventory*. Likewise, if Saul wants to sell a security, he must find a dealer who will buy it from him to add to his or her inventory. Although Barbara might be willing to buy the security directly from Saul, in a pure quote-driven market they generally cannot arrange such trades. Instead, they trade indirectly with each other through the intermediation of one or more dealers. Such markets are called *quote-driven markets* because the dealers quote the prices at which they will buy and sell. They are also known as *dealer markets* because dealers supply all the liquidity.

▶ **Bookies Are Dealers**

Most sport betting markets are quote-driven dealer markets in which bookies are dealers. The bookies try to maintain a balanced book with equal volumes bet on both sides. They profit from small differences in the payoffs that they offer each side. The difference between these payoffs is the *vigorish* or *juice*. It is essentially a bid/ask spread. The vigorish for a typical football point spread bet is 1 dollar for a 10-dollar bet. A perfectly balanced book ensures that bookies earn 1 dollar for every 20 dollars bet.

Bookies work hard to balance their books. Interest in a game is rarely balanced, and point spreads and odds change in response to new information about the contest. Bookies with lopsided books will often lay off some of their risk by placing offsetting bets with other bookies. The bets are costly because they have to pay the vigorish.

When bookies have balanced books, their only risk is that their losing clients will not pay up. Dealers minimize their credit risks by carefully screening their clients. They limit the credit that they extend to clients, and they require that their least creditworthy clients post substantial sums to cover their potential losses. Ruthless bookies also minimize their credit losses by threatening the kneecaps of their deadbeat clients. ◀

In some dealer markets, traders can trade with each other without the direct intervention of a dealer. Although these are not pure quote-driven markets, they are still known as quote-driven dealer markets because dealers supply most of the liquidity and arrange all the trades. The Nasdaq Stock Market is an example of a quote-driven market in which dealers often broker trades among public traders.

In most dealer markets, dealers and their customers choose each other when they want to trade. The customers—or their brokers acting as their agents—choose dealers who offer good prices and good service. The dealers trade only with traders they believe are trustworthy and creditworthy. Traders who do not have credit relationships with dealers trade through brokers who guarantee that they will settle their trades. Many dealers specialize in serving clienteles such as small retail traders or large institutional traders. Such dealers may refuse to trade with customers who are not among their preferred clientele. Most dealers also try to avoid trading with customers they believe are well informed about future prices, because they often lose to well-informed traders.

In some dealer markets, *interdealer brokers* help dealers arrange trades among themselves. Many dealers do not like their rivals to know about their trades. By allowing dealers to trade with each other anonymously, interdealer brokers protect dealers and their clients from predatory actions by rivals.

Quote-driven dealer markets are very common. Almost all bond and currency markets, and many stock markets, are quote-driven markets. Most dealer markets are informal networks of dealers who communicate with their clients and among themselves by telephone. More structured dealer markets usually have proprietary electronic data systems to facilitate communications with and among dealers. The Nasdaq Stock Market, the London Stock Exchange, the eSpeed government bond trading system, and the Reuters 3000 foreign exchange trading system are examples of quote-driven markets organized, respectively, by a dealer association, an exchange, a broker, and an electronic data vendor.

▶ You Can't Tell the Players Without a Scorecard

Brokers and dealers established the first exchanges as membership organizations. These exchanges provided them with a common place to do their business and with rules to regulate it. The members arranged all the trades, either for themselves or for their clients.

Many exchanges eventually adopted rule-based order-matching systems that arrange trades between buyers and sellers. Initially, exchange members or clerks operated these systems. Now many exchanges use computers to arrange trades. When exchanges adopted rule-based order-matching systems, they became more than just a place to do business under regulatory supervision. They essentially became brokerages.

Many brokerages have created similar rule-based order-matching systems to provide low-cost service to their customers. These brokerages therefore look very much like many exchanges. They grant their clients trading privileges instead of memberships.

Recently, entrepreneurs have created many for-profit companies that offer rule-based order-matching systems. These *electronic communications networks* (ECNs) look like exchanges and operate like brokers. Many of these firms also develop software and provide network communications.

Many exchanges are converting from membership organizations to for-profit companies. They want the flexibility to compete with for-profit organizations that have streamlined control structures.

Most government regulations distinguish between brokers and exchanges. The practical differences between these organizations, however, are increasingly unclear, and therefore are often a subject of regulatory debate. Although exchanges invaded the brokerage business before brokers invaded the exchange business, this chronology provides little guidance for deciding how best to regulate these organizations. ◀

5.3.2 Order-driven Markets

In *order-driven markets*, buyers and sellers regularly trade with each other without the intermediation of dealers. These markets have *trading rules* that specify how they arrange their trades. Their *order precedence rules* determine which buyers trade with which sellers, and their *trade pricing rules* determine the trade prices.

Most order-driven markets are *auction markets*. In an auction market, the trading rules formalize the process by which buyers seek the lowest available prices and sellers seek the highest available prices. Economists call this the *price discovery process* because it reveals the prices that best match buyers to sellers.

In order-driven markets, traders can offer or take liquidity. Traders who offer liquidity indicate the terms at which they will trade. Traders who take liquidity accept those terms.

Dealers can—and often do—trade in order-driven markets. In pure order-driven markets, they trade on an equal basis with all other traders. In some order-driven markets, dealers provide most of the liquidity. These markets are still known as order-driven markets because the dealers cannot choose their clients. Instead, the exchange rules require that they trade with anyone who accepts their offers.

Order-driven market structures vary considerably. Some markets conduct *single-price auctions* in which they arrange all trades at the same price following a market call. Other markets conduct *continuous two-sided auctions*, in which buyers and sellers can continuously attempt to arrange their trades at prices that typically vary through time. Still others conduct *crossing networks*, in which they match orders at prices taken from other markets.

Order-driven markets vary considerably in how they implement their trading rules. In markets that conduct *oral auctions*, traders negotiate their trades face-to-face on an exchange floor. The trading rules in these markets determine who can negotiate and when they can negotiate. These auctions are also known as *open-outcry auctions* because the traders cry out their bids and offers. In markets that have *rule-based order-matching systems*, the markets use rules to match orders that traders submit to them. Most order-matching markets use electronic systems to match buy and sell orders automatically. Their trading rules are coded in their order-processing software. Order-matching markets that still have manual operations use clerks to match their orders.

The rules used by order-driven markets are extremely important because they affect market liquidity. Some trading rules encourage traders to offer liquidity while others discourage them. In chapter 6, we will consider how rules affect trading strategies in order-driven markets.

Since order-driven markets use order precedence rules to arrange trades, traders cannot choose with whom they trade. They therefore often trade with traders with whom they have no credit relationships. To prevent settlement failures, order-driven markets have elaborate mechanisms to ensure that all their traders are trustworthy and creditworthy. We consider these mechanisms in chapter 7.

Order-driven markets are quite common. All markets that conduct electronic auctions or open-outcry auctions are order-driven markets. These include all major futures exchanges, most stock and options exchanges, and many trading systems created by brokerages and ECNs to organize trading in stocks, bonds, swaps, currencies, and pollution rights. Governments commonly issue their new debt securities in order-driven market calls.

5.3.3 Brokered Markets

Brokers actively search to match buyers and sellers in *brokered markets*. Most searches start when their clients ask them to fill their orders. Brokers, however, also initiate many searches when they suggest trades to their clients.

The distinguishing characteristic of a brokered market is the broker's role in finding liquidity. In markets where traders usually do not make public offers to trade, brokers must search for traders who will make those offers. These markets are typically illiquid markets in which dealers will not normally trade.

Two types of traders offer liquidity in brokered markets. *Concealed traders* know that they want to trade but, for reasons that we discuss in chapters 11 and 15, they will not expose orders to the public. They offer their liquidity when brokers present them with suitable trading opportunities. *Latent traders* do not know that they want to trade until brokers present them with attractive trading opportunities. They thereby avoid the costs of deciding whether they want to trade until they have the opportunity to trade. Latent traders are common when trading decisions are costly and the opportunities to trade on those decisions are rare. Good brokers can find concealed traders and latent traders.

> ### The World's Most Prolific Market Organizer
>
> eBay has created more markets than any other market organizer. At any given moment, eBay is conducting pure order-driven auctions for millions of items. In 2001, more than 30 million traders were registered to participate in its markets.
>
> Most of eBay's auctions are call market auctions to which buyers can submit only limit orders. When the auction closes, the highest bidder wins. The "buy it now" feature of some eBay markets allows buyers to take a seller's offer before the auction closes.
>
> eBay does not guarantee settlement among its traders. Traders therefore must be careful when they send money to sellers they do not know and trust. Although many frauds have occurred, the settlement failure rate is very small. To help traders check credit, eBay provides a rating service that allows traders to rate each other and to see those ratings. Traders who are especially concerned about settlement can hire escrow services.

Brokered markets are very common throughout the economy. They usually arise when the item traded is unique and when dealers will not hold inventories. The most important brokered securities markets are those for large blocks of stocks and bonds. Although these securities may trade in very liquid markets for small sizes, brokers must find suitable counterparts for most large blocks. Real estate markets and markets for going business concerns are additional examples of brokered markets. In all three types of markets, dealers generally will not take positions because the items are too large and trade too infrequently, and order-driven markets are not viable because traders will not issue standing orders. We consider how block trading markets operate in chapter 15.

5.3.4 Hybrid Markets

Hybrid markets mix characteristics of quote-driven, order-driven, and brokered markets. For example, although the New York Stock Exchange is essentially an order-driven market, it requires its specialist dealers to offer liquidity if no one else will do so. The NYSE therefore has elements of a quote-driven market. The Nasdaq Stock Market is also a hybrid. Although essentially a quote-driven market, it requires its dealers to display, and in many circumstances to execute, public limit orders. Nasdaq therefore has some elements of an order-driven market. Since brokers sometimes arrange large block trades in both of these markets, they also have some characteristics of brokered markets.

5.3.5 Summary

The execution system that a market uses to arrange its trades is the most important characteristic of its market structure. Table 5-1 summarizes the differences among the primary execution systems.

TABLE 5-1.
Execution System Summary

MARKET TYPE	CLASSIFICATION	WHO OFFERS LIQUIDITY?	WHO ARRANGES TRADES?	HOW ARE BUYERS AND SELLERS MATCHED?	COMMON EXAMPLES
Dealer markets	Quote-driven	Dealers	Dealers	Clients (or their brokers) choose dealers	OTC markets in currencies, bonds, and stocks
Oral auctions	Order-driven	Dealers and public limit order traders	Traders	Trading rules regulate negotiations	Floor-based stock, futures, and options auctions
Order-matching systems	Order-driven	Traders who issue limit orders	Brokerages or exchanges	Trading rules match orders	Electronic exchanges and automated brokerage systems
Brokered markets	Brokered	Public traders	Brokers	Brokers match traders	Block trading

5.4 MARKET INFORMATION SYSTEMS

Markets employ many systems to transmit, organize, present, and store information about orders, quotes, and trades. These systems are important because they determine what traders see and when they see it. We will briefly examine these systems and consider how new communications technologies are changing the markets.

5.4.1 Information Collection Systems

Markets produce information about instrument values, transactions, who has traded, who wants to trade, and the terms on which they are willing to trade. This information is very valuable. Traders use it to predict where prices are going and how much trading will cost. Who has access to market information, when they can access it, and the form in which they can access it greatly influence who will trade profitably and who will pay high transaction costs.

Most markets collect information from their trading systems. They present some information to their traders, they sell some to data vendors, and they save most for regulatory purposes.

Market data sales are often very lucrative. At many major exchanges, data revenues account for more than 20 percent of total exchange revenues.

Markets with electronic trading systems can easily collect any market information they want because all information is already in electronic form. In contrast, floor-based markets, telephonic markets, and other manually operated markets must create special systems to collect information. Since information is valuable and manual collection is quite expensive, electronic systems have a strong cost advantage over other systems.

Many floor-based exchanges employ clerks called *market reporters* to observe and report on trading activity. The reporters enter trade prices into electronic data systems. They may also report quotes and trade sizes. The exchange trading rules usually require traders to ensure that the market reporters know what they are doing. In large futures markets, the reporters sit on podiums above the trading pit so they can see all the traders. Some reporters may stand in the crowd and use hand signals to pass information to the reporters on the podium. In many markets, reporters use handheld wireless devices to report information.

Some telephonic markets and some floor-based markets require traders to report their trades to their electronic trade reporting systems. Traders usually must report within a fixed time. For example, in the Nasdaq Stock Market, dealers must report within 90 seconds of trading when they arrange trades by telephone.

Many over-the-counter dealer markets have no formal organization. Market data vendors often try to collect market information from the dealers in these markets. Either the dealers provide the information for a fee, or they provide their information on the condition that they can access the information the other dealers provide. These arrangements appear in some bond markets.

In dealer markets where interdealer brokers help dealers arrange trades among themselves, the brokers collect much information about market conditions. If the dealers object to how a broker distributes that information, they may refuse to trade through that broker.

▶ **Archipelago's Integrated Book**

The Archipelago ECN distributes its entire limit order book, integrated with those of several other ECNs, via the Internet, free of charge. The system uses a Java applet to display the book in real time. ◀

Source: www.tradearca.com/ automm/arca_book.asp.

> ## Securities Information Processors (SIPs)

In the U.S. equity markets, almost all markets, dealers, and trading systems must send their trades and quotes to a *securities information processor* (SIP), which then distributes the consolidated information to data vendors. The *Securities Industry Automation Corporation* (SIAC) is the SIP for exchange-listed stocks, and the NASD is the SIP for Nasdaq and OTC stocks. ◀

5.4.2 Information Distribution Systems

Markets distribute the information they collect to their members and to the public. In most markets, members can access more information than can unaffiliated traders. They also may obtain it faster.

Market data systems report trades and quotes to the public. Markets sell this information to various *data vendors*, who repackage it for distribution to the public. Customers may buy real-time services or time-delayed services. Customers who subscribe to *real-time services* can receive data as it is generated, but they must pay additional fees to the exchanges for these services. Customers who subscribe to *time-delayed services* receive the data with a constant 5-, 10-, 15-, or 20-minute delay. Exchanges offer both services in order to price discriminate among those who require immediate information and those who are less time sensitive. Table 5-2 lists the monthly fees that some exchanges charge for providing real-time data to nonprofessional subscribers.

Data vendors offer broadcast services and query services. *Broadcast services* provide continuous streams of information. *Price and sale feeds* and *ticker tapes* broadcast trade prices and sizes. *Quotation feeds* broadcast quotations. *Query services* provide information on demand. Users submit requests for information to the vendor's data server. The server then looks up the information and reports it. To fill these requests, the data servers receive and archive broadcast information from market feeds. Some data vendors sell software programs that allow users to run their own data servers. Traders use these programs when their electronic proprietary trading systems require extremely fast query services.

Data vendors such as Bloomberg, Bridge Information Systems, PC Quote, and Reuters reformat market information to make it more useful to their customers. Traders, for example, do not have time to watch a ticker tape when they want to see the latest prices and quotes for various instruments. Instead, they subscribe to broadcast systems that present and continuously update this information on specially designed *pages*. Customers can customize their pages to show only the information that interests them.

TABLE 5-2.
Monthly Exchange Fees for Real-time Data for Nonprofessional Subscribers

EXCHANGE	FEE
American Last Sale & Bid/Ask	1.00
Canadian Consolidated Equities (Alberta, Montreal, Toronto, and Vancouver)	9.50
Chicago Board of Trade and MidAmerica Commodity Exchange	30.00
Chicago Mercantile Exchange	60.00
COMEX, Inc.	60.00
Commodity Exchange Center (Coffee, Sugar, & Cocoa Exchange, New York Cotton Exchange, and New York Futures Exchange)	94.00
MidAmerica Commodity Exchange (only)	7.50
Nasdaq Last Sale NMS & Bid/Ask (Level I)	1.00
Nasdaq Level II	10.00
New York Consolidated Last Sale & Bid/Ask	1.00
New York Mercantile Exchange	60.00
Options Price Reporting Authority (all U.S. options)	1.00

Note: Professional subscribers generally pay higher fees.

Most systems allow both graphic and numeric presentations. Data vendors compete to provide easy-to-use information systems that deliver data in useful formats at low cost.

In the U.S. equity markets, data vendors are subject to the Vendor Display Rule. This rule requires vendors to construct consolidated quotes from all trading venues. Without this rule, many data vendors would not include quotes from small markets, which would make it very difficult for innovative trading systems to compete for order flow.

Floor-based exchanges post information on electronic screens and boards so that all floor traders can see the current state of the market. The exchanges place these displays in, around, and often above the trading pit or post. The information that they publish on the floor is usually the same information that they provide to the public. Indeed, the same data vendors often provide both services.

In screen-based trading systems, participants often can access more information than can the public. For example, the Toronto Stock Exchange allows its members to see the complete composition of the system limit order book. Public traders get to see only aggregate order sizes at the best five prices on either side of the market.

5.4.3 Ticker Symbols

Exchanges and data vendors use *ticker symbols* to identify trading instruments. The naming conventions vary by exchange, country, instrument class, and data vendor. Generally, each exchange assigns ticker symbols to its instruments. The data vendors occasionally add their own suffixes or prefixes to these symbols to make them more useful for their clients.

In the United States, listed common stocks have ticker symbols consisting of one to three letters. The one-letter symbols are rare, and therefore coveted for the special status they convey. Exchanges usually reserve them for their largest firms. Nasdaq National Market System stocks all have four-character ticker symbols, and Nasdaq SmallCap stocks have five-character ticker symbols. U.S. open-end mutual funds have five-character ticker symbols, the last character of which is always X.

Ticker symbols for U.S. futures contracts generally consist of a one- or two-character code that indicates the commodity followed by a number that indicates the expiration year and a letter that indicates the delivery month. (Some systems place the month code before the year number.) For example, LC2Z refers to the Chicago Mercantile Exchange December 2002 live cattle futures contract. The second character of the commodity code can be a number. For example, E7 is the contract code for the CME E-Mini EuroFX contract; thus E72H refers to the March 2002 E-Mini Euro contract. A list of futures contract delivery month symbol codes appears in table 5-3.

TABLE 5-3.
Futures Contract Delivery Month Symbol Codes

MONTH	CODE	MONTH	CODE	MONTH	CODE
January	F	May	K	September	U
February	G	June	M	October	V
March	H	July	N	November	X
April	J	August	Q	December	Z

TABLE 5-4.
Equity Option Contract Expiration Month Designators

MONTH	CALLS	PUTS	MONTH	CALLS	PUTS
January	A	M	July	G	S
February	B	N	August	H	T
March	C	O	September	I	U
April	D	P	October	J	V
May	E	Q	November	K	W
June	F	R	December	L	X

The *Option Price Reporting Authority* (OPRA) assigns ticker symbols for exchange-traded U.S. equity and equity index option contracts. These ticker symbols have three to five characters. The first one to three characters form the options root. They refer to the underlying instrument. The options root is often the ticker symbol of the underlying instrument, or it may include some portion of it. Securities with options having many strike prices often have several options roots. Each root designates a different set of strike prices. The second-to-last character indicates the option type and expiration month. The final character indicates the option contract strike price. The same character can indicate different strike prices. If an options class includes contracts with strike prices that have the same option contract strike price code, the security will have multiple option roots, and the option root will distinguish between the contracts. Lists of equity option contract expiration month designators and equity option contract strike price codes appear in tables 5-4 and 5-5, respectively.

Many equity index option contracts like the Nasdaq 100 Cube (QQQ) have many closely spaced strike prices. They therefore use several different option root symbols, and they use a different set of strike price codes.

The symbol naming conventions that futures exchanges use for their options on futures contracts vary. Generally, the first two characters represent

TABLE 5-5.
Equity Option Contract Strike Price Codes

CODE	STRIKE PRICES			CODE	STRIKE PRICES		
A	5	105	205	N	70	170	270
B	10	110	210	O	75	175	275
C	15	115	215	P	80	180	280
D	20	120	220	Q	85	185	285
E	25	125	225	R	90	190	290
F	30	130	230	S	95	195	295
G	35	135	235	T	100	200	300
H	40	140	240	U	7.5	37.5	
I	45	145	245	V	12.5	42.5	
J	50	150	250	W	17.5	47.5	
K	55	155	255	X	22.5	52.5	
L	60	160	260	Y	27.5	57.5	
M	65	165	265	Z	32.5	37.5	

TABLE 5-6.

Expiration Month Codes for Options on Futures

MONTH	CALLS	PUTS	MONTH	CALLS	PUTS
January	F	A	July	N	L
February	G	B	August	Q	O
March	H	C	September	U	P
April	J	D	October	V	R
May	K	E	November	X	S
June	M	I	December	Z	T

the commodity, the third character represents the month and type of option, and the final two or three characters are numbers that represent the strike price. The month codes for options on futures differ from the month codes for equity options. (The call codes are the same as the futures delivery month codes for the futures contracts.) A list of these codes appears in table 5-6.

5.4.4 Transparency

The data that markets release to the public are quite valuable. The public uses these data to predict future price changes, to predict when their orders will execute, and to evaluate their brokers' performance. Without this information, public traders would not have much confidence in the markets. Markets vary in the degree to which they report information to the public.

Transparent markets quickly report complete information to the public. Markets that quickly report quotes and orders are *ex ante transparent*. Those which quickly report trades are *ex post transparent*. The terms *ex ante* and *ex post* refer to the time of the trade. The terms *pre-trade transparency* and *post-trade transparency* are also used. *Opaque markets* are not transparent.

Markets that report only the best bid and offer show the *top of the book*. Markets that report bids and offers at multiple prices show the *market by price*. These markets have *open limit order books*.

The degree of transparency varies across markets. Table 5-7 shows that U.S. equity and equity options markets are quite transparent. U.S. futures markets are ex post transparent, but not ex ante transparent. In these oral auctions, quotes generally do not stand long enough to be reported. Over-the-counter corporate and municipal bond markets are generally quite opaque. The U.S. government bond markets are more transparent. In these markets, interdealer bond brokerages such as Cantor Fitzgerald provide information to the public.

Traders are often ambivalent about transparency. They favor transparency when it allows them to see more of what other traders are doing, but they oppose it when it requires that they reveal more of what they are doing. Generally, those who know the least about market conditions most favor transparency. Those who know the most oppose transparency because they do not want to give up their informational advantages.

Markets produce an enormous volume of information, much of which is redundant. Traders say that the first half of that information is much more important than the second half. Being able to see just a little of what is

▶ **Transparency and Dealer Profitability**

Large U.S. investment banks generally make more money trading bonds than stocks. The greater transparency of the U.S. stock markets may help explain this result. When customers know current market conditions well, they negotiate better prices with their dealers. ◀

TABLE 5-7.
Market Transparency in Some U.S. and International Markets

MARKET	CURRENT QUOTES	TRADE REPORTS
U.S. equity and equity options exchanges	The best bid and offer immediately No other prices or quantities	All trades immediately and in no event later than 90 seconds
Nasdaq	All dealer quotes immediately	All trades immediately and in no event later than 90 seconds
U.S. futures markets	Reported only by your broker's representative on the floor	All price changes immediately
U.S. OTC corporate and municipal bond markets	Generally not reported	Only through some bond brokers
U.S. government bond markets	Provided by various interdealer bond brokers	Provided by various interdealer bond brokers
Foreign exchange markets	Provided by various data vendors	None
Toronto Stock Exchange	Aggregate quantities of all orders at the five best prices on both sides of the market	All trades immediately
Deutsche Börse	All displayed order size, aggregated by price for continuous markets, less information for single price auctions	All Xetra trades immediately; very large privately negotiated trades may never be reported
Euronext Paris Bourse	All orders	All trades immediately
London Stock Exchange	All dealer quotes in SEAQ (dealer market) stocks, the best bid and offer in SETS (electronic order book) stocks	All small trades immediately; larger trade reports are delayed

going on is extremely important to traders who would otherwise be in the dark.

5.4.5 Order Routing Systems

Order-routing systems transmit orders. Customers use them to send orders to their brokers and dealers, brokers use them to send customer orders to dealers and to exchanges, dealers use them to send orders to other dealers, and exchanges use them to send orders to other exchanges. Traders also use order-routing systems to transmit cancellation instructions, and exchanges and dealers use them to report trades to their customers.

Good order-routing systems are fast and accurate. Traders demand fast systems because they do not want to miss trading opportunities and because they value their time. They need accurate systems because mistakes obviously can be very costly.

The strategies that traders can profitably undertake depend on the order-routing systems available to them. Short-term traders who implement

▶ QuantEX

ITG is a U.S. equity brokerage and a supplier of electronic trading software. The premier trading platform that it offers to its clients is QuantEX. The QuantEX system runs on a dedicated Sun workstation. It receives real-time trade and quotation feeds and has a high-speed electronic link to ITG's order-routing system.

QuantEX includes a programming language that traders use to analyze, present, and respond to real-time market data. QuantEX users program their systems to process and display real-time data in any format that they want, to manually or automatically generate and submit orders based on rules that they specify, and to keep track of orders and the prices at which they trade.

Traders most commonly use QuantEX to manage large trading programs. Some traders also use it to implement high-frequency proprietary trading strategies. ◀

Source: www.itginc.com/products/clientsite/index.html.

high-frequency trading strategies must submit and cancel orders quickly and reliably in order to trade profitably. Either they must trade on the floor of an exchange, or they must use fast order-routing systems, preferably with good computer interfaces.

Traders use many technologies to transmit orders. They now send most orders by electronic data transmission systems or by telephone. In some places, however, traders still carry, shout, or hand-signal orders across rooms.

Electronic order-routing systems are usually faster, more accurate, and cheaper to operate than other routing systems. Although they are often expensive to build, they are rapidly replacing other systems. All major markets, brokerages, and dealers now use electronic order-routing systems. The main disadvantage of these systems is that they can handle only the standardized orders and instructions that they are programmed to recognize. When traders want to issue special instructions, they typically use the telephone. Traders also use the telephone when they want to talk to their brokers about current market conditions before they submit their orders.

Which order-routing systems traders use depends on how often they trade, on how large their trades are, and on whether they can physically access an electronic communications network. Infrequent traders usually do not use electronic systems because the fixed costs of building them and learning to use them are large relative to their needs. Large traders often use the telephone because they want more access to market information. Their size gives them the power to demand attention from their brokers. Floor brokers often receive their orders from *runners* who physically deliver them or from order clerks who transmit them by hand signals. With the invention of cellular telephones, wireless electronic data networks, and mobile terminals, these floor brokers are also receiving electronic order flow.

Most retail traders send orders to their brokers by telephone. Increasingly, many also use the Internet. Retail brokerages generally offer lower commissions for orders entered through the Internet because they are less costly to handle than telephone orders. Brokerages that take Internet orders do not need to employ telephone order clerks, and they avoid mistakes that occasionally occur when a telephone order clerk hears or records something different from what a customer intends.

▶ Lattice Trading

State Street offers an electronic order management system called Lattice. The system allows traders to route orders to the best market as conditions dictate. Among its many other features, it enables traders to create strategies to dynamically adjust limit orders as market conditions change. ◀

Source: www.statestreet.com.

▶ **Floor Trader Advantages**

Floor traders have an advantage over off-floor traders because they can see and react to market developments well before off-floor traders can. Off-floor traders must obtain their information through market data systems, and they must respond through order-routing systems. The best market data systems report information in less than three seconds. The best order-routing systems pass orders from the client to a broker in less than five seconds. If the routing system requires a runner, the delay can be substantially longer. These delays allow floor traders to take advantage of opportunities before off-floor traders can.

Floor traders also can observe all market information revealed on an exchange floor, and not just what the market data systems report. In particular, they observe who is trading. Knowing who is trading can be valuable if you can guess why they want to trade or whom they represent. Floor traders and off-floor traders whose brokers can give them access to this information therefore have a significant advantage over other traders. ◀

▶ **The Telegraph and Hand Signaling at the American Stock Exchange**

The American Stock Exchange is the only U.S. stock exchange that permits its traders to use hand signals to transmit orders on the exchange floor. The practice originated when the Exchange literally used to trade on Broad Street in lower Manhattan. It was then known as the New York Curb Exchange because its members worked on the street curbs.

After the introduction of the telegraph, brokerages could quickly receive orders from distant branch offices and send back trade reports. Brokerages that had access to the telegraph had a competitive advantage over those which did not.

Brokerages could not install their telegraph lines on the curb, however. Instead, they installed them in offices that they rented above Broad Street. Telegraph operators would give incoming orders to clerks who stood at the windows. The clerks then used hand signals to transmit the orders down to their brokers on the street, and brokers sent trade reports back through the same system.

The Exchange moved indoors to its present site at 86 Trinity Place in 1921. Its trading floor was constructed with galleries on both sides in an attempt to replicate the street. The brokers' clerks—now telephone operators—sat in the galleries and hand-signaled orders down to the floor. With the introduction of telephones on the floor of the Exchange, hand signaling became less common. A few traders, however, still use it occasionally. ◀

Source: Robert Sharp, The Lore and Legends of Wall Street (Dow Jones-Irwin, 1989), ch. 46.

Institutional traders most commonly send orders to their brokers and dealers by telephone. Large institutional traders often have several dedicated telephone lines that connect them to the brokers and dealers with whom they do the most business. These brokers and dealers often provide these lines at no charge to attract more business from their large clients. Institutional traders also increasingly use electronic systems to deliver their orders. These systems may operate over the Internet or over private proprietary networks provided by data vendors like Bloomberg, Reuters, and Bridge

▶ Telegraphs, Ticker Tapes, Telephones, and Electronic Data Networks

Innovations in telecommunications have substantially transformed trading. Before the telegraph, all information coming into or going out of an exchange moved no quicker than express riders could travel on horseback. Consequently, every major city had its own exchange, and prices for the same instruments would differ substantially across geographic regions.

The telegraph and subsequent inventions allowed traders to learn about market conditions in other cities and to send orders to wherever the best prices were. Although the first users were arbitrageurs, other traders soon started routing their orders to the best markets. Markets that acquired a reputation for being liquid attracted more orders and thereby became even more liquid. Smaller markets then started to fail. They either quit trading or combined to form larger markets.

This process continues today. Every innovation in telecommunications has increased competition among traders and has led to market consolidation. ◀

Information Systems. In some cases, they also send electronic orders over leased lines directly to their brokers and dealers.

Brokers, dealers, and exchanges communicate with each other by telephone and by proprietary data networks. Almost all exchanges and organized dealer networks have electronic order-routing systems. These systems bring orders in for processing and send out trade reports. At floor-based exchanges and in dealer networks, these systems deliver orders directly to the traders who process them. At electronic exchanges, they deliver the orders to the computerized order-matching system. Exchanges and dealers compete with each other to provide low-cost order-routing systems that are easy to use, fast, and reliable. Table 5-8 lists the primary electronic order-routing systems used by U.S. equity, options, and futures exchanges.

From a regulatory viewpoint, the most interesting order-routing system in the U.S. equity markets is the *Intermarket Trading System* (ITS). ITS is an electronic system that allows traders in one market to send orders to another market. It therefore plays an important role in keeping the U.S. equity markets integrated and competitive. We discuss ITS further when we consider how exchanges compete with each other in chapter 26.

5.4.6 Order Presentation Systems

Order presentation systems reveal information about orders and quotes to the traders who arrange trades. Markets use several technologies to present this information.

Markets with *screen-based trading systems* present the orders on computer screens. These systems are becoming more common as electronic communications technologies become cheaper. Traders like screen-based systems because they can use them anywhere and can update them easily.

Some screen-based trading systems broadcast all information presented to all participants. Screen-based markets commonly use these systems. Others systems, called *messaging systems*, allow traders to send private messages to specific traders or classes of traders. Traders in dealer markets often use these systems to negotiate their trades.

▶ Nasdaq Level I, II, and III Services

Nasdaq provides three levels of quotation services through various data vendors:

- Level I service consists of real-time inside bid/ask quotations for Nasdaq Stock Market securities and for OTC Bulletin Board securities.

- Level II service provides real-time access to all dealer quotations in these securities.

- Level III service is available only to registered Nasdaq market makers. It consists of all Level II service information plus the ability to enter quotations, route orders, execute orders, and send messages. ◀

TABLE 5-8.
U.S. Exchange Order Routing Systems

MARKET	ACRONYM	FULL NAME	INSTRUMENTS
New York Stock Exchange	SuperDOT	Super Designated Order Turnaround	Equities
Nasdaq Stock Market	SuperSoes	Super Small Order Execution System	Equities
	SelectNet	Select Net Order Entry	Equities
American Stock Exchange	PER	Post Execution Reporting System	Equities
	AMOS	American Options Switching System	Options
Pacific Exchange	PCOAST	Pacific Computer Order Access System	Equities
	POETS	Pacific Options Exchange Trading System	Options
Philadelphia Stock Exchange	PACE	Philadelphia Automated Communications and Execution System	Equities
	AUTOM	Automated Options Market System	Options
Chicago Stock Exchange	MAX	Midwest Automated Execution	Equities
Boston Stock Exchange	BEACON	Boston Exchange Automated Communications and Order-routing Network	Equities
Cincinnati Stock Exchange	NSTS	National Securities Trading System	Equities
All exchanges for U.S. listed equities	ITS	Intermarket Trading System	Equities
Chicago Board Options Exchange	ORS	Order Routing System	Options and equities
	CSTS	CBOE Stock Trading System	Options and equities
Chicago Board of Trade	ORS	Order Routing System	Futures and options on futures
Chicago Mercantile Exchange	TOPS	Trade Order Processing System	Futures and options on futures

Screen-based systems are the technological successors to board-based trading systems. In *board-based* trading systems, traders or exchange clerks write orders on a big board for all to see. In some markets, orders for infrequently traded stocks are still presented on boards. Most boards, however, are now published electronically.

Bulletin boards are information systems upon which people post indications of interest. An *indication of interest* (IOI)—also known as an *order indication*—is an expression of interest in trading. Indications usually show the name of a broker-dealer, the name of the security, and whether the broker represents a buyer or a seller. Indications may also show prices, but they are rarely firm. Traders use indications to show other traders that they are interested in trading. They also sometimes use them to discover who is interested in trading.

The U.S. equities markets have several popular bulletin boards. For listed stocks, institutional traders primarily use AutEx or Bridge Information Systems to post electronic order indications. For thinly traded, over-the-counter stocks, traders use the Nasdaq OTC Bulletin Board. For the smallest and least frequently traded stocks, traders post their indications in the *Pink Sheets* published by the National Quotation Bureau.

Data vendors also offer electronic systems that present indications in pop-up windows on a trader's workstation. These systems try to anticipate what trades will interest traders' clients and direct only those indications to them.

Traders in oral auctions present their orders by yelling out bids and offers on a trading floor. Floor traders like oral auctions because they are very quick. Their communications are prone to error, however, because traders often do not say what they intend to say and because traders often do not hear what other traders have said.

Traders in many dealer markets also negotiate their trades orally. Since they usually use the telephone, they cannot see the visual clues that help us understand speech. They therefore must be careful to avoid misunderstanding each other.

5.4.6.1 Accuracy in Oral Communications

All traders who negotiate trades orally must communicate very accurately. They must understand exactly what other traders say, and they must be sure that other traders understand exactly what they say. Otherwise, very serious and costly errors may result.

Effective communication can be very difficult when traders are in a noisy environment, when significant distractions compete for their attention, and when they hurry. On trading floors, traders may be yelling or pushing, several phones may be ringing, one or more televisions may be on, ticker tapes and news wires will be running, and clerks may be requesting or reporting information. When the market moves quickly and everything happens all at once, error-free communication can be quite a challenge.

Communications errors in some oral markets are quite common. In open-outcry trading in large futures pits, the out-trade rate is often as high as 4 percent. An *out-trade* results when one trader reports a trade that does not exactly match a report from another trader. In equity markets, unmatched trade reports are called *DKs* (*Don't Know*).

Traders use various systems to avoid misunderstandings. The most effective systems allow both traders to show each other what they intend on

▶ **The Big Board**

The New York Stock Exchange once presented orders on boards hung on the walls above its trading floor. As a reflection of its importance, the NYSE became known as the "Big Board." Although the Exchange long ago replaced these boards with electronic systems, its nickname endures. ◀

▶ **Early Video Display Systems**

The first video market information systems were closed-circuit video systems that distributed real-time images of exchange boards. Digital systems replaced these analog systems when computing systems matured, and when off-floor traders wanted to use their computers to manipulate market information. ◀

▶ See What You Say

In 1992, Lehman Brothers' bond traders in New York experimented with a particularly innovative error correction system. An automatic voice recognition system listened to their telephone calls. As they spoke, it wrote their words and those of their counterparts onto screens on their desks so that they could see exactly what they said. This system allowed them to recognize and correct errors as they occurred. It also forced them to enunciate clearly.

Lehman Brothers abandoned the system because the speech recognition technology then available was too primitive to transcribe speech accurately. With recent advances in this technology, attempts to use this system should be more successful. ◀

electronic screens. Instinet, Nasdaq, and Liquidnet, among others, provide messaging systems that equity traders can use for this purpose. Cantor Fitzgerald's eSpeed government bond trading system allows traders to see what they have said to their Cantor broker.

In face-to-face oral negotiations, traders sometimes use hand signs to convey their intentions. These signals are especially common in futures pits. Traders indicate that they are sellers by holding their palm away from them. In effect, they push the item away. Buyers hold their palms inward, to pull in the item. Traders convey prices and quantities by extending fingers, by holding the hand upright or sideways, and by touching their faces in various places.

Traders commonly express their bids and offers in fixed formats to avoid confusion. When bidding, they express the price followed by the preposition "for" and then the quantity. A trader who shouts out "6 for 20" is a buyer willing to pay 6 for 20 contracts. When offering, traders express the quantity first followed by the preposition "at" and then the price. A trader who shouts "40 at a quarter" is a seller willing to sell 40 contracts at the price of a quarter.

To further reduce confusion, traders usually express only the last digit or fractional portion of the price. Since the rest of the price is common knowledge, they do not need to express it. This practice speeds up their communications, and it reduces the amount of noise that traders might mistake for significant information.

Traders who trade over the telephone often repeat what they hear and then ask for confirmation. Brokers commonly use this protocol to avoid errors when receiving instructions from their clients. Most record their telephone calls to help resolve any disputes that may arise from misunderstandings.

When errors do occur, the involved traders attempt to determine who was mistaken. Usually, one trader will recognize his error and correct it. If

▶ The Pink Sheets, Nasdaq, and Technological Evolution

The National Quotation Bureau (NQB) started publishing weekly editions of the *Pink Sheets* in 1913 and daily editions five years later. They are called pink sheets because NQB prints them on pink paper. NQB now publishes a weekly edition on paper and a daily electronic edition. Traders post their indications by calling or faxing them to NQB.

Until the National Association of Securities Dealers organized the original NASD Automated Quotation (NASDAQ) trading system, the *Pink Sheets* were the primary source of market information about over-the-counter stocks. Since the NASDAQ system allowed traders to present, access, and exchange information faster, it largely replaced the *Pink Sheets*. The NASDAQ system grew into the Nasdaq Stock Market and the Nasdaq OTC Electronic Bulletin Board. The Nasdaq Stock Market now trades some of the largest stocks in the world. The Nasdaq OTC Electronic Bulletin Board reports indications for smaller stocks sponsored by NASD dealers. The *Pink Sheets* now report order indications only for the smallest publicly traded U.S. stocks.

NQB now offers a real-time interactive version of the *Pink Sheets*. The new electronic bulletin board allows traders to post and revise their indications at any time, and to send electronic messages to each other to facilitate their negotiations. ◀

▶ **Microwaving Traders at the Hong Kong Futures Exchange**

When brokers first brought cellular telephones onto the floor of the Hong Kong Futures Exchange, they inadvertently circumvented the audio tape system that the Exchange used to record their negotiations. To obtain better reception for their cell phones, the brokers would stand near the windows on the sides of the trading room. Trading moved away from the center of the pit to the windows, where the microphones could not properly pick up their negotiations. The Exchange solved the problem by installing a low-powered cellular phone transceiver station inside the trading room.

The Exchange later switched to an electronic trading system called HKATS (Hong Kong Automatic Trading System) in 1995. Traders now trade from their respective offices, and HKATS produces a complete record of their activities. ◀

they cannot assign responsibility, the traders often resolve the disputed trade by splitting the difference. However, traders quickly shun traders who make many mistakes.

5.4.7 Order Books

All brokers, exchanges, and dealers that represent orders maintain *order books* to hold open orders that they cannot yet fill. The order books may be electronic databases, files, boxes of paper order tickets, or simply desktop piles of order tickets. Order books mostly contain standing limit orders. They may also include stop orders and market-if-touched orders with price contingencies that have not yet been met.

Order books hold extremely valuable information. They reveal the conditions under which traders will trade. We show in chapter 11 that clever traders who know what other traders intend to do often can make money by trading ahead of them. Access to the order book therefore is an important determinant of trader profitability.

Open book markets fully display their order books to all traders. *Closed book markets* do not show their orders.

Traders generally want to see the order book. Many traders, however, do not want other traders to see their orders. When trading in open book markets, these traders do not submit standing orders. They, or their brokers, instead hold them until suitable trading opportunities arise.

Rule-based order-matching systems work best when traders place standing limit orders in their system order books. To protect limit order traders, some markets either restrict access to the book or allow traders to specify that their standing orders not be displayed in the book. Euronext, for example, allows traders to submit undisclosed limit orders.

Brokers are responsible for representing the unfilled orders of their clients. Since they usually cannot closely monitor all markets in which their customers have placed orders, they may give their clients' orders to others to manage. In markets with rule-based order-matching systems, they usually will submit the order to the system order book. In other markets, they may give orders to brokers or dealers who specialize in the specified securities.

Many dealers maintain order books as a service to the brokers who send them order flow. By encouraging brokers to send them limit orders, the dealers hope that brokers will also send them market orders. Moreover, some dealers like to hold limit orders because they provide them with free trading options that they often can use to trade more profitably. Dealers usually do not charge for the brokerage services that they provide to brokers.

5.5 SUMMARY

Market structures differ widely across markets. The differences determine how the markets operate, who can supply liquidity, who knows current market conditions best, and who can act first. Market structure therefore affects market liquidity, transaction costs, and price efficiency. These factors help determine who will trade profitably.

Markets differ most in how they arrange trades. In quote-driven markets, dealers arrange all trades and provide all liquidity. In order-driven markets, traders or electronic trading systems arrange trades by matching public orders. In brokered markets, brokers arrange trades by finding traders who are willing to trade.

Markets differ significantly in when and where they trade. Call markets trade only when the market is called. Continuous markets trade whenever the market is open. Physically convened markets trade on exchange floors. In distributed access markets, traders trade from their offices.

Markets also differ in how traders negotiate with each other. In screen-based markets, traders communicate through electronic data systems. In oral auctions, traders negotiate their trades by yelling to each other on an exchange floor. In other markets, traders negotiate over the telephone.

Finally, markets differ in their transparency. Transparent markets allow traders to see all orders, quotes, and trades as they occur. In opaque markets, many traders never see this information.

Traders, regulators, and academics often passionately debate which structure is best for a market. The great diversity in existing market structures suggests that good answers to this question may be complex. The best structure for a given market undoubtedly depends on the instrument, on why people want to trade it, and on the communications and computing technologies that traders can use to trade it.

To form a reasoned opinion about the best structure for a market, you must thoroughly understand how markets operate, why people use them, and what traders do in them. These are the main objectives of this book. In the last part of this book, we will return to the question of which market structures are best.

5.6 SOME POINTS TO REMEMBER

- Call markets convene all traders at the same time and place.
- Continuous markets arrange trades when willing buyers arrive and find waiting sellers, or when willing sellers arrive and find waiting buyers.
- Dealers supply all liquidity in pure quote-driven markets. Public traders and dealers supply liquidity in order-driven markets. Public traders supply liquidity in brokered markets.
- Order-driven markets arrange trades by applying a set of rules to a set of orders.
- Brokers arrange trades by searching for willing traders in brokered markets.

- Access to information about orders and trades is extremely valuable to traders.
- Public traders generally favor transparent markets.

5.7 QUESTIONS FOR THOUGHT

1. Should markets be open around the clock?
2. What are the arguments for and against lunch recesses?
3. The NYSE last changed its trading hours in 1985, when the open was moved from 10 A.M. to 9:30 A.M. Why did the Exchange make this change? Should it change its trading hours again?
4. What are the benefits of requiring that traders arrange all trades in the same market? What are the disadvantages of such requirements?
5. How would you trade off the advantages of focused liquidity in a call market against the availability of a continuous market?
6. When markets call in rotation, in what order should they call the securities? What special problems confront arbitrageurs who trade in markets that are called in rotation?
7. Many regulators say, "Sunshine is the best disinfectant." What do they mean, and what implications does this have for market transparency? If you were a large buy-side trader, how would you feel about ex ante market transparency?
8. Which traders favor dealer quote-driven markets? Which traders favor public order-driven markets?
9. Which instruments are best traded in quote-driven markets? In order-driven markets? In brokered markets?
10. Why would dealers not want other dealers to know about their trades?
11. Do you think that someday all markets will be fully automated electronic markets?
12. What factors determine whether traders favor order and trade price transparency?
13. Brokers who are exchange members often compete with their exchange for business. If such brokers have power over the management of the exchange, the exchange may not be able to compete effectively with them. What advice would you give an exchange that faces this problem?
14. If an exchange has regulatory power over its brokers, the brokers may not be able to compete effectively with the exchange. What advice would you give a brokerage that faces this problem?
15. Market data are quite valuable. Exchanges, brokerages, dealers, public traders, and data vendors all fight over who owns information. Who owns market data? Should the prices at which market data are sold be regulated? If so, who should regulate these prices?
16. Why is trade price transparency more common in exchange markets than in labor markets?

6

▷

Order-driven
Markets

Order-driven markets use trading rules to arrange their trades. These markets include oral auctions, single price auctions, continuous electronic auctions, and crossing networks. You will learn how these markets work and how trading strategies depend on market structure.

Order-driven markets are quite common. Almost all of the most important exchanges in the world are order-driven markets. Most newly organized trading systems choose an electronic order-driven market structure.

Despite the great variation in how order-driven markets operate, their trading rules are quite similar. All order-driven markets use *order precedence rules* to match buyers to sellers and *trade pricing rules* to price the resulting trades.

Variations in trading rules distinguish order-driven markets from each other. The trading strategies that work best in one market may work poorly in markets with different rules. Traders therefore need to know how trading rules affect optimal trading strategies.

If you trade in order-driven markets, the principles introduced in this chapter will be of immediate and obvious value to you. They will also help you understand front-running and block trading strategies that we will consider in later chapters.

The topics in this chapter should interest you if you are concerned with market structures. Most recent innovations in trading technologies involve order-driven market structures. To evaluate new trading technologies, you must thoroughly understand how they work.

We will first discuss how oral auctions work. In these order-driven markets, traders arrange trades by negotiating on a trading floor. Since many readers may already be acquainted with these markets, they provide us with a familiar context for introducing various trading rules. We then will turn our attention to rule-based order-matching systems. These systems include single price auctions, continuous order book auctions, and crossing networks.

6.1 ORAL AUCTIONS

Many futures, options, and stock exchanges use continuous bilateral oral auctions to trade their contracts and securities. The largest oral auction market is the U.S. government long treasury bond futures market. This market, which the Chicago Board of Trade organizes, regularly attracts 500 floor traders. It may be the most liquid market in the world. The smallest oral auctions may include only two traders.

In an *oral auction*, traders arrange their trades face-to-face on an exchange trading floor. Some traders cry out their bids and offers to attract other traders. Other traders listen for bids and offers that they are willing to accept. Most traders do both. Trades occur when a buyer accepts a seller's offer, or when a seller accepts a buyer's bid. In the former case, the buyer will call out "take it" to accept the offer. In the latter case, the seller will call out "sold" to accept the bid. Buyers and sellers often take turns bidding and offering until they agree on a price and quantity to trade. Traders *offer liquidity* when they make bids or offers to trade. They *take liquidity* when they accept bids or offers.

The traders must obey the market trading rules. These rules organize trading to ensure fairness for all traders and to provide for the efficient exchange of information necessary to arrange trades. The trading rules also help protect brokerage customers from dishonest brokers.

The first rule of an oral auction is the *open-outcry rule*. Traders must publicly express all bids and offers so that all traders can act on them. This requirement ensures that all traders can participate fairly in the market. In most oral auctions, any trader can accept another trader's bid or offer, even if he or she is not actively negotiating with that trader. The first trader to accept a bid or offer generally gets to trade. The open-outcry rule also requires traders to express their acceptances publicly, so that all traders are aware of the trades they arrange. This information helps traders evaluate market conditions. It also protects customers from dishonest brokers who might try to arrange trades privately to benefit their friends instead of their clients.

6.1.1 Order Precedence Rules

The *order precedence rules* of an oral auction determine who can bid or offer, and whose bids and offers traders can accept. In oral auctions, the primary order precedence rule is always *price priority*. The secondary precedence rules depend on the market. Futures markets use *time precedence*. U.S. stock exchanges use *public order precedence* and then time precedence.

6.1.1.1 Price Priority

The *price priority rule* gives precedence to the traders who bid and offer the best prices. Traders cannot accept bids or offers at any inferior price. Buyers can accept only the lowest offers and sellers can accept only the highest bids.

Price priority is a *self-enforcing rule* because honest traders naturally search for the best prices. Exchanges therefore do not have to adopt special procedures to enforce it. They keep the rule on their books so that they can prosecute dishonest brokers.

Most oral auctions do not allow traders to bid below the best bid or offer above the best offer. Since only the best bid and best offer interest traders, bids and offers behind the market only create confusion and noise.

Traders acquire price priority by bidding or offering prices that improve the current best bid or offer. Any trader may improve the best bid or offer at any time.

6.1.1.2 Time Precedence

The *time precedence rule* used in most oral auctions gives precedence to the traders whose bid or offer first improves the current best bid or offer. While they have time precedence, no other traders may bid or offer at the new best bid or offer.

Traders retain their time precedence as long as they maintain their bid or offer, or until another trader accepts it. Afterward, anyone may bid or offer at the new price, and all traders at that price will have equal standing.

In oral auction markets, bids and offers generally are good only for a moment. Traders say, "A quote is good only as long as the breath is warm." In practice, traders who do not honor their quotes for a reasonable period find that nobody wants to trade with them. Traders maintain their precedence by repeating their quotes as often as is necessary to show that they remain interested in trading. Traders may repeat their quotes continuously in large, very active markets.

The time precedence rule encourages traders to improve prices aggressively. Traders who want to trade ahead of a trader who has time precedence must improve the price. Time precedence rewards aggressive traders by giving them the exclusive right to trade first at the improved price. The time precedence rule thus encourages price competition among traders.

Time precedence is meaningful only when the minimum price increment is not trivially small. The *minimum price increment*, or *tick*, is the smallest amount by which a trader may improve a price. It is the incremental price that traders must pay to acquire precedence, through price priority, when they do not have time precedence. If it is very small, the time precedence rule gives little privilege to the traders who improve price.

The effect of the tick on price competition varies by tick size. If the tick is too small, it decreases price competition by weakening the time precedence rule. If the tick is too large, traders are reluctant to improve prices because of the expense. Since the minimum price increment significantly affects market quality, exchanges and regulators pay close attention to it.

Unlike price priority, time precedence is not a self-enforcing rule. Most traders do not care whose bid or offer they accept as long as they get the same price. Traders who have time precedence must therefore defend it when someone improperly attempts to bid or offer at the same price. When this happens in futures markets, they usually yell out, "That's my bid," or "That's my offer," or "It's my market."

▶ Leapfrog

The orange juice concentrate futures market is currently 103.10 cents bid, offered at 103.25 cents. (Traders quote prices per pound for 15,000-pound contracts.) Guy is the bidder at 103.10. He has time precedence at that price, and he is defending it. If you want to buy at 103.10, you must wait until Guy trades. If you want precedence, you must improve the bid to 103.15. You then would have price priority over his bid and time precedence over all subsequent bids at 103.15. If Guy wants to reclaim his precedence, he would have to improve the market again by bidding 103.20. Time precedence encourages traders to play leapfrog by jumping over each other's prices with improved prices.

Good traders carefully consider their leapfrog strategies. For example, if you are willing to bid 103.20 and you are confident that Guy will bid 103.20 if you bid 103.15, you may want to skip over 103.15 and bid first at 103.20. If you bid 103.20 and Guy still wants to trade first, he will take the offer at 103.25. In that case, he will trade immediately and you will still have time precedence at 103.20. Of course, if you are quite impatient to trade, your best strategy may be to take the offer at 103.25 immediately. ◀

▶ The Common Cents Stock Pricing Act of 1997

In March 1997, Republican Representative Mike Oxley and others introduced a bill to require that U.S. stock markets trade on dollars and cents rather than on dollars and fractions of a dollar. The bill had wide popular support because most people find decimal pricing simpler to understand than fractional pricing. The bill never passed. Instead, the exchanges decided to switch to decimals on their own.

The bill was remarkable because it represented an attempt by the U.S. Congress to micromanage trading rules in the stock markets. The exchanges probably decimalized at least in part to prevent the passage of this bill.

The U.S. equity markets completed their decimalization in 2001. The minimum price increment decreased from one-sixteenth (6.25 cents) to 1 cent. Not surprisingly, the switch to a much smaller tick profoundly changed the equity markets. Most notably, the decrease in tick size reduced the value of time precedence and thereby greatly reduced displayed order sizes. Many analysts believe that it would have been much better had the markets adopted a 5-cent minimum price increment.

The most remarkable aspect of the bill may be that a conservative Republican, with a reputation for fighting government intervention in the economy, introduced it. Several representatives from both parties recognized and commented upon this incongruity during hearings on the bill. Perhaps Rep. Oxley's interest in the bill had something to do with the pun in its title. Several of his legislative initiatives have titles that incorporate the words "common sense." ◀

6.1.1.3 Public Order Precedence

Some equity exchanges prohibit their members from trading ahead of a public trader who is willing to trade at the same price. Exchanges adopt this *public order precedence rule* to give public traders more access to their markets and to weaken the informational advantages that floor traders have. Without this rule, exchange members usually can acquire time precedence at a new price before public traders can, because members see prices change first and can quote faster than public traders can submit orders. The public order precedence rule allows public traders to take precedence over a member even when the member has time precedence.

The public order precedence rule also increases investor confidence in the exchange markets by assuring them that exchange members cannot step in front of their orders. The decrease in tick size that accompanied the decimalization of the U.S. markets greatly weakened this rule. Not surprisingly, the incomes of member dealers at the NYSE rose substantially.

6.1.2 The Trade Pricing Rule

The *trade pricing rule* used in oral auctions is quite simple. Every trade takes place at the price proposed by the trader whose bid or offer is accepted.

Economists call this rule the *discriminatory pricing rule*. It derives its name from a strategy that large, aggressive traders use to lower their trading costs. Large traders often break their orders into several pieces to trade one at a time. The first pieces trade at the best prices initially available in the market. The remaining pieces trade at progressively inferior prices as the traders exhaust the available liquidity and as the market discovers the true order

▶ Price Discrimination

Sally has 100 soybean futures contracts to sell at the market. She does not tell anyone about her order.

Colin and Martin both want to buy soybeans. Colin is willing to bid as much as 602½ cents per bushel for 40 contracts. He is currently bidding 602 and he is the best bidder. Martin is willing to bid as much as 601½ for 75 contracts, but he has not revealed this to anyone.

Sally immediately accepts Colin's offer and negotiates to sell 40 at 602. Martin then bids 601½. Sally accepts his offer and negotiates to sell 60 at 601½. Her average sales price is 601.7. Although Colin purchased at a price he was willing to pay, he could have bought at 601½ if he had known about Sally's order. By discriminating between Colin and Martin, Sally obtained a better average price for her sale. Since the bean contract is for 50,000 bushels, her total savings are 10,000 dollars. ◀

sizes. Large traders thus discriminate among the traders who are most willing to trade and those who are willing to trade only at inferior prices. They obtain their best prices from the former and their worst prices from the latter. This strategy lowers their trading costs because the traders most willing to trade would not offer such good prices if they knew the full order sizes.

6.1.3 Trading Floors

Futures markets that conduct oral auctions trade in trading pits. A *trading pit* is a place on an exchange floor designated for trading a particular contract or set of related contracts. For actively traded contracts, the trading pits are depressions in the floor that have steps all around the sides. The traders stand on the steps and on the bottom of the pit. This design allows all traders to see all other traders clearly. The pits in smaller markets are often round tables or round rails at which the traders sit or stand.

Stock, options, and bond markets that conduct oral auctions trade at trading posts. Like a trading pit, a *trading post* is a place on the floor of an exchange designated for trading specific securities. The term probably first came into usage when markets traded outdoors. The original posts may have been light posts or hitching posts. Now, posts are simply counters around which traders and clerks congregate.

Exchanges that run oral auctions require that traders conduct all trading in each security or contract at its assigned post or in its assigned pit. This rule makes it easier for buyers and sellers to find each other. It also helps the exchange enforce its trading rules.

6.2 RULE-BASED ORDER-MATCHING SYSTEMS

Most exchanges, some brokerages, and almost all electronic communications networks use rule-based order-matching systems to arrange their trades. *Rule-based order-matching systems* use trading rules to arrange trades from the orders that traders submit to them. Traders negotiate with each other only by submitting and canceling orders. Most systems accept only limit orders. Systems that accept market orders treat them as very aggressively priced limit orders. All orders specify the maximum quantities that traders will accept. Rule-based order-matching systems process this price and quantity information to arrange their trades. Almost all rule-based systems now use electronic trading systems to process their orders.

If the market is a call market, the market collects the orders before the call. Immediately following the call, its trading system makes one attempt to arrange trades. If the market is a continuous trading market, its trading system attempts to arrange trades whenever new orders arrive.

Every rule-based order-matching system uses the same sequence of procedures when attempting to arrange trades. They first match orders using their order precedence rules. They then determine which matches can trade. Trades will occur only if at least one buy order offers terms acceptable to at least one seller. Finally, they price the resulting trades using their trade pricing rules. Although the trading rules vary considerably across order-driven markets, all markets apply them the same way.

6.2.1 Order Precedence Rules

To arrange trades, markets with order-matching systems use their *order precedence rules* to separately rank all buy and sell orders in order of increasing precedence. They match the orders with the highest precedence first.

The order precedence rules are hierarchical. Markets first rank orders using their *primary order precedence rules*. If two or more orders have the same primary precedence, markets then apply their *secondary precedence rules* to rank them. They apply these rules one at a time until they rank all orders by their precedence.

All order-matching markets use *price priority* as their *primary order precedence rule*. Under price priority, buy orders that bid the highest prices and sell orders that offer the lowest prices rank highest on their respective sides. Market orders always rank highest because the prices at which they may trade are not limited.

Markets use various secondary precedence rules to rank orders that have the same price. The most commonly used rules rank orders based on their time of submission, on their display status, and on their size. All rule-based order-matching systems must have at least one secondary precedence rule. Some use more than one.

Time precedence gives orders precedence according to their time of submission. *Floor time precedence* gives the first order to arrive at a given price precedence over all other orders at that price. The remaining orders are *at parity* with each other and must be ranked by another secondary precedence rule. This version of time precedence is called *floor time precedence* because it is the same as the time precedence rule used in oral auctions. *Strict time precedence* ranks all orders at the same price according to their submission time. Systems that rank orders based only on price priority and strict time precedence are *pure price-time precedence systems*.

Display precedence gives displayed orders precedence over undisclosed orders at the same price. Markets give precedence to displayed orders in order to encourage traders to expose their orders. If an order is partly displayed and partly undisclosed, the market usually treats the two parts separately.

Size precedence varies by market. In some markets, large orders have precedence over small orders, while in other markets, the opposite holds. When two or more orders are at parity, and they cannot all be fully filled, some markets allocate available size on a pro rata basis. In a *pro rata allocation*, orders fill in proportion to their size. Such orders *participate* in the trade.

Most exchanges allow traders to issue orders with size restrictions. Traders may specify that their entire order must be filled all at once, or they may specify a minimum size for a partial execution. Orders with size restrictions usually have lower precedence than unrestricted orders because they are harder to fill. Large traders use these restrictions to avoid paying fixed costs for settling numerous small trades. These costs include exchange fees, settlement fees, and the costs of accounting for each trade.

6.2.1.1 Order Precedence Ranking Example

Suppose that traders submit the orders in table 6-1 to an auction that uses the pure price-time precedence hierarchy. An order book that arranges these orders by pure price-time precedence appears in table 6-2, where the orders with the highest precedence appear at the top on the sell side and at the

▶ **Pro Rata Allocation Example**

Two standing buy orders for 10 contracts and 20 contracts are at parity with each other. A sell order for 18 contracts arrives that can trade with both orders. In a pro rata allocation, the two buy orders will fill the same fraction (18/30) of their total size. The first buy order will fill 6 contracts, and the second order will fill 12 contracts. ◀

TABLE 6-1.
Example Orders

TIME	TRADER	ORDER SIDE	SIZE	PRICE
10:01	Bea	Buy	3	20.0
10:05	Sam	Sell	2	20.1
10:08	Ben	Buy	2	20.0
10:09	Sol	Sell	1	19.8
10:10	Stu	Sell	5	20.2
10:15	Bif	Buy	4	market
10:18	Bob	Buy	2	20.1
10:20	Sue	Sell	6	20.0
10:29	Bud	Buy	7	19.8

bottom on the buy side. These positions would be reversed if the prices in the center column were arranged in decreasing instead of increasing order. Sol's sell order has highest precedence on the sell side because it offers the lowest price. Bif's buy order has highest precedence on the buy side because it is a market order. Bea's order and Ben's order have the same price priority, but Bea's order has time precedence over Ben's order because it arrived first.

6.2.2 The Matching Procedure

Order matching proceeds after the market ranks its orders. In a call market, this happens immediately following the market call. In a continuous market, it happens whenever a new order arrives.

The market first matches the highest-ranking buy and sell orders to each other. If the buyer will pay at least as much as the seller demands, the match will result in a trade. The price of the trade will depend on the trade pricing rules of the market, which we discuss below. If one order is smaller than the other, the smaller order will fill completely. The market then will match the remainder of the larger order with the next highest-ranking order on the opposite side of the market. If the first two orders are the same size, both will fill completely. The market then will match the next highest-ranking buy and sell orders. This process continues until the market arranges

TABLE 6-2.
Example Order Book

SELLERS		BUYERS		
TRADER	SIZE	ORDER PRICE	SIZE	TRADER
Sol	1	19.8	7	Bud
Sue	6	20.0		
		20.0	2	Ben
		20.0	3	Bea
Sam	2	20.1	2	Bob
Stu	5	20.2		
		market buy	4	Bif

all possible trades. Since the market processes orders ranked by decreasing price priority, the last match that results in a trade often involves two orders that bid and offer the same price. The next match does not result in a trade because the buyer's bid price is below the seller's offer price.

6.2.2.1 Order-matching Example

Suppose that the traders in the previous example submit their orders to a call market auction that calls at 10:30. At 10:30, the market will arrange trades as follows:

1. The market first matches Sol's order to sell 1 at 19.8 with Bif's order to buy 4 at the market. This match fills Sol's order and leaves Bif with a remainder of 3 to buy at the market. Sol can trade with Bif because Bif's market order has no price restriction.

2. The market then matches Bif's remainder of 3 with Sue's order to sell 6 at 20.0. Sue's order goes next because it has the highest precedence on the sell side now that Sol's order is filled. This match fills the remainder of Bif's order and leaves Sue with a remainder of 3 to sell at 20.0. Bif can trade with Sue because Bif's market order has no price restrictions.

3. The market then matches Sue's remainder of 3 with Bob's order to buy 2 for 20.1. This match fills Bob's order and leaves Sue with a remainder of 1 to sell at 20.0. Sue can trade with Bob because Bob is willing to pay more than Sue demands.

4. The market then matches Sue's remainder of 1 with Bea's order to buy 3 for 20.0. This match fills the remainder of Sue's order and leaves Bea with a remainder of 2 to buy for 20.0. Sue can trade with Bea because Sue is offering 20.0 and Bea is bidding 20.0. The only price at which they can trade is 20.0.

The next match does not result in a trade. Bea's remainder of 2 to buy for 20.0 cannot trade with Sam's order to sell 2 at 20.1 because Bea will not pay as much as Sam demands. No further trades are possible. Table 6-3 summarizes the trades.

The order book with the remaining unfilled orders appears in table 6-4. Note that the buy and sell orders no longer overlap. If this market now started continuous trading, the market quote would be 20.0 bid for 4, 2 offered at 20.1. Continuous markets always have a spread between the best bid and the best offer. If they did not, a trade would result.

TABLE 6-3.
Call Market Trades

MATCH	SELLER	BUYER	QUANTITY
1	Sol	Bif	1
2	Sue	Bif	3
3	Sue	Bob	2
4	Sue	Bea	1
		Total:	7

TABLE 6-4.

Order Book After the Market Call

SELLERS			BUYERS	
TRADER	SIZE	ORDER PRICE	SIZE	TRADER
		19.8	7	Bud
		20.0		
		20.0	2	Ben
		20.0	2	Bea
Sam	2	20.1		
Stu	5	20.2		

6.2.3 Trade Pricing Rules

The trade pricing rules depend on the type of market. Single price auctions use the *uniform pricing rule*. Continuous two-sided auctions and a few call markets use the *discriminatory pricing rule*. Crossing networks use the *derivative pricing rule*. The following three sections introduce these three rules and the markets associated with them.

6.3 THE UNIFORM PRICING RULE AND SINGLE PRICE AUCTIONS

Single price auctions are quite common. Most continuous order-driven stock markets and most electronic futures markets open their trading sessions with a single price call market auction. These markets also use single price auctions to restart trading following a halt. Some call markets also trade using single price auctions exclusively. Various national treasuries use them to sell their bills, and the Arizona Stock Exchange offers them for trading U.S. equities.

In a single price auction, all trades take place at the same *market-clearing price*. The last match that leads to a feasible trade determines the clearing price. If the buy and sell orders in this match specify the same trade price, that price must be the market-clearing price. Any other price would be either too high to satisfy the buy order or too low to satisfy the sell order. Matching by price priority ensures that this market-clearing price is also feasible for all previously matched orders. These matches involve buy and sell orders with higher (or at least equal) price priority. Since all buyers with higher price priority are willing to trade at higher prices than the market-clearing price, and all sellers with higher price priority are willing to trade at lower prices than the market-clearing price, all matches can trade at the market-clearing price.

If the buy and sell orders in the last feasible trade specify different prices, the buy order will bid a higher price than the sell order offers. The market can clear at either of these two prices or at any price between them. The market rules will specify the clearing price in this unusual event.

6.3.1 Single Price Auction Example

Suppose that the auction of the previous example is a single price auction. The last feasible trade is between Bea and Sue. The market-clearing price

▶ The Arizona Stock Exchange and Arizona

The Arizona Stock Exchange (AZX) is an alternative trading system that arranges single price auctions in listed and Nasdaq securities. Unlike the single price auctions conducted at the NYSE open, the AZX auctions provide users with continuous price and volume indications up to the time of each auction.

The AZX has not been particularly successful, but its markets have excited many traders. Recent changes in the timing of its auctions and additions to the securities that it trades may substantially increase its popularity.

R. Steven Wunsch founded the AZX as Wunsch Auction Systems. The firm conducted its first auctions in 1991. Trading volumes did not grow quickly, however, and the firm soon needed new financing.

In the early 1990s, the Commerce Department of the State of Arizona was looking for ways to attract and finance high-tech industries. To improve the state's image, Arizona provided a 2.9 million-dollar nonrecourse loan to Wunsch Auction Systems. In exchange for this loan, the firm changed its name to Arizona Stock Exchange, opened a small office in Phoenix, and moved its computer there. Funding for the loan came from Arizona's security registration fees. ◀

Source: Author's interview with R. Steven Wunsch.

---

therefore must be 20.0. Bea is unwilling to buy at any higher price, and Sue is unwilling to sell at any lower price. Sol is happy with the market-clearing price because he is a willing seller at 19.8. Bob is happy with the price because he is a willing buyer at 20.1. We presume that Bif is happy with the price because he submitted a market buy order. If the price is more than he is willing to pay, he should have submitted a limit order instead of a market order.

6.3.2 Supply and Demand

The single price auction clears at the price where supply equals demand. The orders in the limit book determine the supply and demand schedules. The *supply schedule* lists the total volume that sellers offer at each price. It slopes upward because sellers will sell more at higher prices than at lower prices. The *demand schedule* likewise lists the total volume that buyers want at each price. It slopes downward because buyers will buy less at higher prices than at lower prices.

These schedules allow us to determine how much the market can trade at any given price. Since the market cannot force buyers and sellers to trade, the total trading volume at a given price is the minimum of supply and demand at that price. At prices below the clearing price, there is *excess demand*: Buyers want to buy more than sellers offer. The supply schedule then determines the total quantity traded. Since the supply curve slopes upward, the market could trade more volume at a higher price. Likewise, at prices above the clearing price, there is *excess supply*: Sellers offer more than buyers want. The demand schedule then determines the total quantity traded. Since the demand curve slopes downward, the market could trade more volume at a lower price.

Single price auctions maximize the volume of trade by setting the clearing price at the price where supply equals demand. At prices above the clearing price, volume would decrease along the demand curve. At prices below the clearing price, volume would decrease along the supply curve.

Because prices and quantities are discrete, single price auctions often have excess supply or demand at the market-clearing price. If there is excess supply, all buyers at that price have their orders filled, and the secondary precedence rules determine which sell orders fill. If there is excess demand, all sellers have their orders filled, and the secondary precedence rules determine which buy orders fill. Of course, ranking by price priority ensures that all buy orders placed above the market-clearing price and all sell orders placed below the market-clearing price also fill.

6.3.2.1 Supply and Demand Schedules

The supply and demand schedules for the orders in our example appear in table 6-5 and figure 6-1. To construct these schedules, first sum the total size bid or offered at each price. In our example, the only sum that must be computed is on the buy side at 20.0 dollars, where Ben's bid and Bea's bid total 5. Next, sum these quantities across prices in order of decreasing price priority. Sum the supply schedule from lowest price to highest price and sum the demand schedule in the opposite direction. To compute excess demand schedule, subtract the supply schedule from the demand schedule at every price.

Supply does not exactly equal demand at any price in this example. The two schedules are closest at 20.0 and 20.1. The market-clearing price is 20.0 because more volume can trade at 20.0 than at 20.1. At 20.0, where there is excess demand, the supply schedule indicates that 7 will trade. At 20.1, where there is excess supply, the demand schedule indicates that only 6 will trade.

The market-clearing price is easy to find in the following plot of the supply and demand schedules. The two schedules cross at the market-clearing price of 20.0. The schedules are not smooth because the order prices and quantities are discrete. (See figure 6-1.)

Table 6-6 and figure 6-2 show that the supply and demand schedules no longer cross following the auction. No further trades are possible.

6.3.3 Trader Surpluses

The single price auction also maximizes the benefits that traders derive from participating in the auction. To explain why, we must first discuss how to measure the benefits that traders obtain from trading.

TABLE 6-5.
Single Price Auction Example Supply and Demand Schedules

SELLERS			BUYERS		
SUPPLY SCHEDULE	TOTAL SIZE AT PRICE	PRICE	TOTAL SIZE AT PRICE	DEMAND SCHEDULE	EXCESS DEMAND SCHEDULE
1	1	19.8	7	18	17
7	6	20.0	5	11	4
9	2	20.1	2	6	−3
14	5	20.2		4	−10
14		Any higher price	4	4	−10

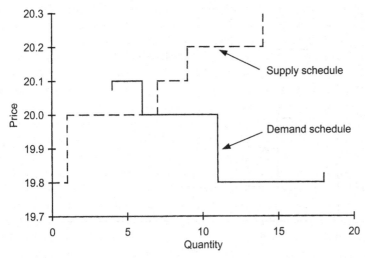

FIGURE 6-1.
Single Price Auction Example Supply and Demand Schedule Plot

Economists measure trader benefits by computing their surpluses. For a seller, the *trader surplus* is the difference between the trade price and the seller's valuation of the item. For a buyer, it is the difference between the buyer's valuation and the trade price. Since sellers should never offer to sell at prices below their valuations and since buyers should never bid at prices above their valuations, trader surpluses should always be positive. Trader surplus measures the *gains from trading*. All traders would like to maximize their surpluses.

When a buyer and a seller trade, the sum of their surpluses does not depend on the trade price. It depends only on the difference in their valuations. The buyer's surplus is the buyer's valuation minus the trade price. The seller's surplus is the trade price minus the seller's valuation. Their combined surplus therefore is the buyer's valuation minus the seller's valuation. Auctions maximize total surplus by matching the buyers who most value the item with the sellers who least value it.

The distribution of the surplus does depend on the trade price. The seller naturally wants to receive a high price, and the buyer wants to pay a low price.

▶ **Trader Surplus Example**

A confectioner is willing to pay 28 cents per pound for two carloads of refined domestic sugar, each of which holds 112,000 pounds of sugar. If he can buy sugar for 23 cents per pound, his total trader surplus will be $(0.28 - 0.23) \times 112,000 \times 2 = 11,200$ dollars. ◀

TABLE 6-6.
Supply and Demand Schedules Following the Single Price Auction

SELLERS			BUYERS		
SUPPLY SCHEDULE	TOTAL SIZE AT PRICE	PRICE	TOTAL SIZE AT PRICE	DEMAND SCHEDULE	EXCESS DEMAND SCHEDULE
0		19.8	7	11	11
0		20.0	4	4	4
2	2	20.1		0	−2
7	5	20.2		0	−7

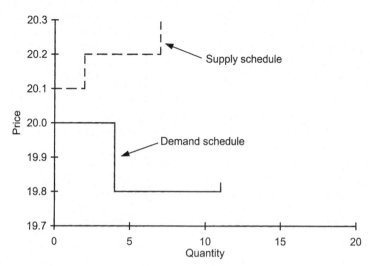

FIGURE 6-2.
Supply and Demand Schedules Following the Single Price Auction

Measuring trader surpluses is difficult because we never know the values that traders place on the items they trade. Traders reveal some information about their valuations through their orders. Rational buyers should never set a limit price above their valuations. Buyer valuations therefore should be greater than or equal to their limit prices. Seller valuations likewise should be less than or equal to their limit prices. Traders who submit market orders presumably expect to trade at prices they would accept. Market order buyers therefore should have valuations above the clearing price, and market order sellers should have valuations below the clearing price.

The single price auction maximizes total trader surplus if the outcome of the auction satisfies all traders. The outcome will satisfy all traders if no trader regrets trading, and if no potential trader regrets not trading. No trader will regret trading if he or she bids and offers rationally. In particular, no buyer should bid more than his valuation, and no seller should offer less than her valuation. Traders regret not trading when they fail to trade and wish that they had. This can happen when they do not price their orders aggressively enough to participate in the auction. They then may fail to trade at a price that would have satisfied them. If traders set their limit prices equal to their valuations, the auction outcome will always satisfy all traders.

The single price auction maximizes total trader surplus (if the outcome of the auction satisfies all traders) because it uses price priority to determine who trades. Matching by price priority matches the buyers who value the item most with the sellers who value it least. To maximize the total surplus, these traders must trade because their surpluses are greatest.

The clearing price is the dividing line between buyers who value the item highly and potential buyers who value it less. It also divides sellers who do not value the item much from potential sellers who value it dearly. The resulting trades include every buyer who values the item by more than the clearing price and every seller who values the item by less than the clearing

▶ An Inexperienced Bidder

John wants to buy a 1-million-dollar, two-year U.S. Treasury note that pays 5⅜ percent interest. The U.S. Treasury will sell the note in a single price auction. The Treasury will offer 6 billion dollars of these notes. Buyers must express their bids in yield percentages. The Treasury computes the actual dollar price for the note from the market-clearing yield. A high yield implies a low price, and vice versa.

John will accept a yield of 5.400 percent. John mistakenly believes that his bid may affect his purchase price. He therefore bids 5.500 percent in the hope of obtaining a lower purchase price. The auction-clearing price turns out to be 5.495 percent, which corresponds to a price of 99.776 dollars per 100-dollar face value. John does not buy because his bid was too low. (His quoted yield was too high.) Since he was willing to pay the clearing price, he will regret not trading.

Had John bid his 5.400 valuation, he would have bought the note and received a yield of 5.495 percent. His small order probably would have had little or no effect on the clearing price. If John thinks carefully about what happened, he probably will not make the same mistake again. ◀

price. They exclude every potential buyer who values the item by less than the clearing price and every potential seller who values the item by more than the clearing price. Because the same clearing price divides both the successful buyers from the potential buyers and the successful sellers from the potential sellers, no successful buyer will have a lower valuation than will any successful seller.

Any other trading arrangement will reduce the total trader surplus. For example, in markets that arrange trades at multiple prices, a successful buyer in one trade might value the item less than does a successful seller in another trade. In that case, the buyer would have bought the item at a lower price than the seller would have sold it. Having this buyer sell the item back to this seller at an intermediate price would increase the total surplus.

6.3.3.1 Trader Surpluses in the Single Price Auction Example

The trader surpluses for the single price auction example appear in table 6-7. The analysis assumes that the limit order trader valuations are equal to their limit order prices and that the market order buyer's valuation is arbitrarily equal to 20.3.

TABLE 6-7.
Trader Surpluses in the Single Price Auction Example

TRADER	ORDER	FILLED SALES	FILLED BUYS	TRADE PRICE	ASSUMED VALUE	TRADER SURPLUSES
Sol	Sell 1 limit 19.8	1		20.0	19.8	$(20.0 - 19.8) \times 1 = 0.2$
Sue	Sell 6 limit 20.0	6		20.0	20.0	$(20.0 - 20.0) \times 6 = 0.0$
Bea	Buy 3 limit 20.0		1	20.0	20.0	$(20.0 - 20.0) \times 1 = 0.0$
Bif	Buy 4 at market		4	20.0	20.3	$(20.3 - 20.0) \times 4 = 1.2$
Bob	Buy 2 limit 20.1		2	20.0	20.1	$(20.1 - 20.0) \times 2 = 0.2$
Totals		7	7			1.6

6.4 THE DISCRIMINATORY PRICING RULE AND CONTINUOUS TWO-SIDED AUCTIONS

Continuous rule-based order matching systems use the *discriminatory pricing rule* to price their trades. The rule is the same discriminatory pricing rule that oral auctions use. (Both are examples of two-sided auctions.) To see how continuous order-matching auction markets apply the rule, consider first how they operate.

Continuous auction markets maintain an *order book* to keep track of standing orders that are waiting to fill. The buy and sell orders are separately sorted by their precedence. The highest-priced bid and the lowest-priced offer are the best bid and the best offer.

When a new order arrives, the matching system attempts to arrange a trade between the new order and the order on the opposite side with the highest precedence. A trade is possible only if the new order offers terms acceptable to that order. If the new order is a buy order, the order must indicate that the trader will pay at least the best offer price. If it is a sell order, the order must indicate that the trader will sell at or below the best bid. If a trade is possible, the new order is *marketable*. Market orders and aggressively priced limit orders are marketable orders.

If the new order is not marketable, the market places it in the order book—according to its precedence—to wait for orders to arrive on the opposite side. Traders who do not want their unfilled orders to stand in the book must attach a fill-or-kill or an immediate-or-cancel instruction to their orders.

If the new order is marketable, the matching system arranges a trade by matching the new order with the highest-ranking order on the other side of the market. If this trade does not completely fill the new order, the market then matches the remainder of the new order with the next highest-ranking order on the other side. This process continues until the new order fills completely or until no further trades are feasible. The market places any remaining size in the order book unless the trader instructs otherwise.

Under the *discriminatory pricing rule*, the limit price of the standing order determines the price for each trade. If the market matches a large incoming order with several standing limit orders placed at different prices, trades will take place at the various limit order prices.

6.4.1 Continuous Trading Example

Suppose that traders submit the same set of orders used in the single price auction example to a continuous two-sided auction market. These orders appear in table 6-1. This section explains what would have happened. We assume that the limit order book was empty at the start of trading.

1. At 10:01, Bea submits the first order. The market cannot match it with any other order because no standing orders are in the book. The market places Bea's order to buy 3 limit 20.0 in the book. The market quote is now 20.0 bid for 3, no offer.

2. At 10:05, Sam submits the second order, to sell 2 limit 20.1. Sam cannot trade with Bea because Bea will not pay what Sam demands. The market places Sam's order in the book. The market quote is now 20.0 bid for 3, 2 offered at 20.1. In some electronic screens, the quote

would appear as "20.0–20.1 3 × 2." Traders read this as "20 to a dime, 3 by 2," or "20 bid for 3, 2 offered at a dime."

3. At 10:08, Ben submits the next order, to buy 2 limit 20.0. This order is at the same price as Bea's buy order. The market places it in the book behind Bea's order because Bea has time precedence. The market quote is now 20.0 bid for 5, 2 offered at 20.1.

Order Book After First Three Orders

SELLERS			BUYERS	
TRADER	SIZE	ORDER PRICE	SIZE	TRADER
		20.0	2	Ben
		20.0	3	Bea
Sam	2	20.1		

The market is 20.0–20.1 5 × 2.

4. At 10:09, Sol submits the next order, to sell 1 at 19.8. Sol's order is marketable because it can trade immediately upon submission. The market matches Sol's order with Bea's buy order, which has highest precedence on the buy side. Sol's order fills, and Bea's order leaves a remainder of 2. The trade price will be 20.0, the price of Bea's standing limit order. Note that Sol sells for 20.0, although he would have been willing to accept as little as 19.8. The market quote is now 20.0 bid for 4, 2 offered at 20.1.

Order Book After Four Orders

SELLERS			BUYERS	
TRADER	SIZE	ORDER PRICE	SIZE	TRADER
		20.0	2	Ben
		20.0	2	Bea
Sam	2	20.1		

The market is 20.0–20.1 4 × 2.

5. At 10:10, Stu submits the next order, to sell 5 limit 20.2. Stu's order is less aggressively priced than Sam's sell order. The market places it in the book behind Sam's order. The market quote is still 20.0 bid for 4, 2 offered at 20.1.

Order Book After Five Orders

SELLERS			BUYERS	
TRADER	SIZE	ORDER PRICE	SIZE	TRADER
		20.0	2	Ben
		20.0	2	Bea
Sam	2	20.1		
Stu	5	20.2		

The market is 20.0–20.1 4 × 2.

6. At 10:15, Bif submits the next order, to buy 4 at the market. The market first matches the order with Sam's sell order. This match fills Sam's order and leaves Bif with a remainder of 2. The trade price will be 20.1, the price of Sam's standing limit order. The market then matches the remainder of Bif's order with Stu, leaving Stu with a remainder of 3. The price of this second trade will be 20.2, the price of Stu's standing limit order. The market quote is now 20.0 bid for 4, 3 offered at 20.2.

Bif benefits from discriminatory pricing. The average price of the two trades is 20.15. Had the market used the uniform pricing rule, Bif would have had to pay the higher price of 20.2 for both trades.

Order Book After Six Orders

SELLERS			BUYERS	
TRADER	SIZE	ORDER PRICE	SIZE	TRADER
		20.0	2	Ben
		20.0	2	Bea
Stu	3	20.2		

The market is 20.0–20.2 4 × 3.

7. At 10:18, Bob submits the next order to buy, 2 for 20.1. The order cannot trade, but it does improve the buy side of the market. The market quote is now 20.1 bid for 2, 3 offered at 20.2.

Order Book After Seven Orders

SELLERS			BUYERS	
TRADER	SIZE	ORDER PRICE	SIZE	TRADER
		20.0	2	Ben
		20.0	2	Bea
		20.1	2	Bob
Stu	3	20.2		

The market is 20.1–20.2 2 × 3.

8. At 10:20, Sue submits the next order, to sell 6 at 20.0. The order trades 2 with Bob at 20.1, 2 with Bea at 20.0, and 2 with Ben at 20.0. Sue benefits from the discriminatory pricing rule because her average sale price of 20.033 is slightly higher than the sale price of 20 implied by the uniform pricing rule. The market now has no bid and has 3 offered at 20.2.

Order Book After Eight Orders

SELLERS			BUYERS	
TRADER	SIZE	ORDER PRICE	SIZE	TRADER
Stu	3	20.2		

The market is 0–20.2 0 × 3.

9. At 10:29, Bud submits the last order, to buy 7 for 19.8. It cannot be filled, so the market places it in the book. The market is now 19.8 bid for 7, 3 offered at 20.2.

Order Book After Nine Orders

SELLERS			BUYERS	
TRADER	SIZE	ORDER PRICE	SIZE	TRADER
		19.8	7	Bud
Stu	3	20.2		

The market is 19.8–20.2 7 × 3.

The market has now processed all the example orders from table 6-1. Table 6-8 summarizes the trades arranged in this continuous auction.

6.4.2 Discriminatory Versus Uniform Pricing Rules

For a given set of standing orders, large impatient traders prefer the discriminatory pricing rule to the uniform pricing rule. The discriminatory pricing rule allows them to trade the first parts of their orders at better prices than the last parts. Under the uniform pricing rule, their entire orders would trade at the same price. That price would be the worst price they would receive under the discriminatory rule. Large impatient traders therefore trade at more favorable terms when they can discriminate among the traders who offer them liquidity.

Not surprisingly, for a given set of orders, standing limit order traders prefer the uniform pricing rule. They do not want large traders to discriminate among them. They would rather that all traders receive the same price when filling a large order.

These conclusions assume that traders would issue the same orders whether they traded under the discriminatory pricing rule or the uniform pricing rule, hence the qualification "for a given set of orders." In practice, traders issue different orders when trading in different market structures.

Limit order traders tend to issue more aggressively priced orders when trading under the uniform pricing rule than under the discriminatory pricing rule. When choosing a limit price, traders consider both the probability that their orders will trade and the prices they will receive if their orders

TABLE 6-8.
Trades in the Continuous Auction Example

TIME	SELLER	BUYER	PRICE	QUANTITY
10:09	Sol	Bea	20.0	1
10:15	Sam	Bif	20.1	2
10:15	Stu	Bif	20.2	2
10:20	Sue	Bob	20.1	2
10:20	Sue	Bea	20.0	2
10:20	Sue	Ben	20.0	2
			Total:	11

trade. Under both pricing rules, the order limit price determines its precedence, and therefore its probability of trading. The two rules have different effects on the trade price, however. Under the discriminatory pricing rule, the limit price determines the trade price. Under the uniform pricing rule, the limit price rarely determines the trade price unless the order is very large relative to the other orders in the auction. Limit orders often trade at better prices, especially when they trade with large orders. Traders therefore are more aggressive when trading under the uniform pricing rule than under the discriminatory pricing rule. The benefits from price discrimination that large traders actually obtain relative to uniform pricing therefore are smaller than they would be if traders issued the same orders under either rule. The effects of price discrimination on limit order traders likewise are overstated.

Since markets want to encourage traders to bid and offer aggressively, continuous trading markets might consider adopting the uniform pricing rule instead of the discriminatory pricing rule. Continuous markets cannot enforce uniform pricing, however. Large traders who want to price-discriminate can circumvent the uniform rule by breaking up their orders and submitting them as a sequence of smaller orders. The first parts will receive the best prices and the last parts will receive inferior prices. They will thus obtain discriminatory pricing for their full orders, even though the trade pricing rule calls for uniform pricing. Under the discriminatory pricing rule, the market splits large orders. Under the uniform pricing rule, traders would split their orders before submitting them.

To effectively switch to a uniform pricing rule, continuous trading markets must stop trading. Some continuous markets have *trading halt rules* to achieve this purpose. These markets halt trading if a large order imbalance would cause the price to move too far or too quickly. (Their rules specify the conditions that stop trading.) They resume trading after some time with a single price auction. The trading halt therefore represents a transition from the discriminatory pricing rule to the uniform pricing rule. Large traders can still break up their orders, but doing so delays the execution of their trades. If the delays are sufficiently long, they may discourage large traders from splitting their orders.

Trading halts may also decrease volatility by alerting traders to unusual demands for liquidity. If traders step in to supply liquidity, prices may not change as much as they would have changed if the market immediately processed the orders that caused the imbalance.

6.4.3 Continuous Markets Versus Call Markets

In chapter 5, we argued that the main advantage of call markets is that they focus the attention of all traders on the same instrument at the same time. The common focus makes it easier for buyers and sellers to find each other. When traders can easily find each other, the total trader surplus should be high.

We previously proved that the single price auction maximizes the gains from trading. For a given order flow, no other method of arranging trades can produce a higher total trader surplus than that produced in a single price auction.

A comparison of the results from the single price auction example with those from the continuous two-sided auction example confirms that the continuous auction produces a smaller trader surplus when processing the

TABLE 6-9.

Trader Surpluses in the Continuous Auction Example

TRADER	ORDER	FILLED SALES	FILLED BUYS	AVERAGE TRADE PRICE	ASSUMED VALUE	TRADER SURPLUS
Sol	Sell 1 limit 19.8	1		20.00	19.8	$(20.00 - 19.80) \times 1 = 0.2$
Bea	Buy 3 limit 20.0		3	20.00	20.0	$(20.00 - 20.00) \times 3 = 0.0$
Sam	Sell 2 limit 20.1	2		20.10	20.1	$(20.10 - 20.10) \times 2 = 0.0$
Bif	Buy 4 at market		4	20.15	20.3	$(20.30 - 20.15) \times 4 = 0.6$
Stu	Sell 5 limit 20.2	2		20.20	20.2	$(20.20 - 20.20) \times 2 = 0.0$
Sue	Sell 6 limit 20.0	6		20.03	20.0	$(20.03 - 20.00) \times 6 = 0.2$
Bob	Buy 2 limit 20.1		2	20.10	20.1	$(20.10 - 20.10) \times 2 = 0.0$
Ben	Buy 2 limit 20.0		2	20.00	20.0	$(20.00 - 20.00) \times 2 = 0.0$
Totals		11	11			1.0

same order flow. The trader surpluses for the continuous auction example appear in table 6-9. The total surplus is 1.0, which is smaller than the 1.6 total surplus of the single price auction.

The continuous auction has a lower surplus because Sam and Stu both sold, even though they have relatively high assumed valuations of 20.1 and 20.2. Since they both sold at their assumed valuations, they did not contribute to the total surplus. However, Bif, who bought from them, obtained a lower surplus than he would have in the single price auction because of the higher prices.

If Sam and Stu do indeed value the item at 20.1 and 20.2, they presumably would want to be buyers at 20.0. These valuations are higher than the 20.0 valuation that Bea and Ben both have. After Sam and Stu sold to Bif, Bea and Ben bought from Sue at 20.0 when Sue's sell order arrived. More surplus would have been created had Sam and Stu been the buyers instead of Bea and Ben. Had Sam and Stu repurchased their shares at 20.0, their surpluses for these trades would have totaled $(20.1 - 20.0) \times 2 + (20.2 - 20.0) \times 2 = 0.6$. With these trades, the total surplus for the continuous auction would have matched that of the single price auction.

Sam and Stu would essentially have been trading as dealers had they repurchased from Sue. In effect, their trades would have allowed Bif to trade with Sue, even though Bif and Sue arrived at different times. Sam and Stu's total trader surplus would have been their round-trip trading profits. These profits are the benefits that dealers obtain from the markets in order to facilitate efficient allocations among traders.

Although the continuous auction produces less trader surplus, it does allow traders to trade when they want to trade. Bif paid a higher price because he wanted to buy at 10:15. Had he known that Sue would arrive at 10:20, willing to sell at 20.0, he might have been willing to wait for the better price. Instead, he paid Sam and Stu for the ability to trade when he wanted to trade. Being able to trade when you want to trade is valuable, but the trader surplus does not measure this benefit.

Assuming that both auctions received the same order flow, this analysis of trader surplus demonstrates how the concentration of order flow increases total trader surplus. In practice, traders will not send the same orders to both market structures. Most obviously, dealers will trade differently in continuous markets than in call markets. Although they extract profits from the markets, they help the markets efficiently allocate the item traded between the buyers and the sellers.

For a given order flow, the single price auction will trade a lower volume than the continuous auction. Volume therefore is a poor measure of the ability of a market to produce trader surpluses. The clearing price of a single price auction maximizes the total volume of trade possible at a uniform price. Continuous markets can trade more than single price auctions because they may trade at more than one price. Exchanges could maximize their trading volumes by matching buyers with sellers in order to minimize the difference between the buyer's valuation and the seller's valuation for each trade. This strategy, however, minimizes the total trader surplus.

6.5 THE DERIVATIVE PRICING RULE AND CROSSING NETWORKS

Crossing networks are the only order-driven markets that are not auction markets. In a crossing network, all trades take place at prices determined elsewhere. Crossing networks obtain their *crossing prices* from other markets that trade the same instruments. Since the prices are derived elsewhere, crossing networks use *derivative pricing rules*.

Crossing networks do not discover prices as auction markets do. In auction markets, prices adjust to match buyers to sellers. In crossing networks, prices are completely independent of the orders that traders submit. Crossing networks only discover whether traders are willing to buy or sell at the crossing prices.

The most important crossing networks trade U.S. equities. These include ITG's POSIT, Instinet's Global Instinet Crossing, and the New York Stock Exchange's After-hours Trading Session I. Table 6-10 lists the major U.S. crossing markets.

These crossing networks are all call markets. Traders submit buy and sell orders to them before the call. After the call, the crossing networks use their order precedence rules to match the buy orders with the sell orders. All matches that can trade at the crossing price become trades.

Instinet's Global Instinet Crossing and the NYSE's After-hours Trading Session I both cross stocks after-hours, using 4 P.M. closing prices for their crossing prices. Many traders use these systems because they provide a second chance to trade at closing prices.

POSIT crosses stock eight times daily during regular trading hours. It assigns crossing prices for its crosses by choosing a time at random within the seven minutes that immediately follow each call. At that time, POSIT computes the average of the bid and ask in each stock's primary market and uses that price as the clearing price. Traders use POSIT because it gives them an opportunity to fill their orders at the midpoint of the spread without any price impact.

Since crossing networks do not choose market-clearing prices, they invariably have excess demand or supply at their crossing prices. If buyers want to buy more than the sellers offer, all sell orders fill completely. If sellers want to sell more than the buyers offer, all buy orders fill completely. Crossing networks allocate the fully filled side to the oversubscribed side according to their order precedence rules.

TABLE 6-10.
Major U.S. Crossing Networks

CROSSING NETWORK	SPONSOR	CUSTOMERS	INSTRUMENTS	AVERAGE DAILY SHARE VOLUME (2000)	CROSSING TIMES	ALLOCATION RULES	CROSSING PRICES
POSIT	ITG, a brokerage	POSIT customers and their clients	U.S. equities	31 million	9:40, 10:00, 10:30, 11:00, 12:00, 13:00, 14:00, 15:00	Pro rata	The average of the primary market bid and ask prices sampled at a random time within seven minutes after the call
Global Instinet Crossing	Instinet, a brokerage	Instinet customers and their clients	U.S. equities	15 million	18:30	Minimum quantity to all orders, remainders allocated on a pro rata basis	Closing primary market price for exchange-listed stocks; average of the closing bid and ask for Nasdaq stocks
After-Hours Trading Session I	NYSE, an exchange	NYSE members and their clients	NYSE listed-stocks	1 million	17:00	Precedence hierarchy based on order type and time precedence	NYSE closing prices
Barclays Internal Crossing Network	Barclays Global Investors, an investment manager	Funds managed by Barclays Global Investors	U.S. equities	N/A but probably largest in the world	End of day	Pro rata	Closing primary market price
E-Crossnet (EXN)	Barclays Global Investors, Merrill Lynch Investment Managers, and other investment managers	Registered participants	European equities	N/A	8:30, 10:00, 11:30, 14:00, 14:30, 15:30	Pro rata	The average of the primary market bid and ask prices sampled at a random time within five minutes after the call; closing prices for after-hours crosses

▶ Pro Rata Allocation of Excess Demand in POSIT

Traders submit one sell order and two buy orders in Stewart Information Services Corp. to the 1 P.M. POSIT cross. The sell order is for 3,000 shares. The two buy orders are for 5,000 and 10,000 shares.

POSIT uses pro rata allocation to allocate excess supplies and demands. Since the total sell volume is 20 percent of the total buy order volume, the entire sell order will fill and 20 percent of each buy order will fill. The first buy order will trade 1,000 shares, and the second order will trade 2,000 shares. ◀

Crossing networks fill only a small fraction of the total order volume that traders submit to them. Traders frequently find that no one is on the other side of the market. Less than 10 percent of their order volume ever crosses. Traders whose orders do not fill in crossing networks often submit their orders elsewhere.

Traders use crossing networks because they allow buyers and sellers to find each other without having any impact on prices. Although most order volume does not fill, traders still attempt to cross orders because crossing commissions are only 1 to 2 cents per share and because crossing has no immediate market impact.

All three major crossing networks are completely confidential and anonymous systems. They do not display trader orders, and they do not display order imbalances following their crosses. Traders want this confidentiality because most will submit the unfilled remainders of their orders to other markets. They do not want other traders to know what they intend to do. If the crossing networks displayed their orders, traders would submit only a portion of their orders so as to avoid displaying their full sizes. Since these networks profit only from filled orders, they want traders to submit their full order sizes.

Some crossing networks operate continuously. These networks attempt to arrange trades whenever orders arrive. Orders that cannot immediately trade either wait in the system order book or are forwarded to other markets. Many brokerages try to cross their customer orders before they forward them to exchanges.

6.5.1 Price Ownership

Crossing networks work well only if traders will trade at their crossing prices. If traders do not trust the crossing prices, they will not trade. Successful crossing networks therefore must take their prices from markets that produce credible prices.

The primary markets from which crossing networks obtain their crossing prices believe that crossing networks unfairly compete with them. The crossing networks take many orders that otherwise might go to them. Since the orders that lead to crosses are the easiest orders to fill, the primary markets complain that crossing networks skim the cream of their order flow without properly compensating them for using their prices. They argue that they should receive the crossing orders because they produce the prices that crossing networks require to operate successfully.

Crossing network customers rebut this argument by asserting that they should not have to pay for price discovery when they do not participate in it. Crossing market traders who also submit orders to primary markets further argue that primary market prices should belong to them because their orders produce the prices.

6.5.2 Problems with Derivative Pricing

Traders who trade at derivative prices must be aware of two problems with such prices. They must be sure that these prices are not stale, and they must be sure that other traders do not manipulate these prices. A *stale price* is an old price that no longer accurately reflects the value of an instrument. A

▶ Informed Trading in Crossing Networks

Stock values continue to change following the 4 P.M. close of equity trading in the primary U.S. listing markets (the NYSE, AMEX, and Nasdaq). After the close, corporations may release news; governments may release reports; many significant events may take place; and people may change their opinions about values as they reflect on the day just ended.

We observe direct evidence of these changes in value by watching the prices of listed stocks that continue to trade at the regional exchanges until 4:30 P.M., and Nasdaq stocks that continue to trade after-hours in various ECNs. We also see changes in index futures contracts and index option contracts that trade in Chicago until 4:15 Eastern Time.

Well-informed traders consider this information when submitting orders to the crossing market and the NYSE After-hours Trading Session I. Both systems cross in the early evening, using 4 P.M. closing prices. These crossing networks generally receive more buy order volume than sell order volume when prices have risen in after-hours trading, when there is good news about security values, or when the closing price occurred at the bid instead of the offer. Similar results hold when values decrease.

To partially address the adverse selection problem, both crossing networks do not conduct crosses for stocks that have significant after-hours news events. ◀

manipulated price is a price that a trader has deliberately changed in order to obtain some advantage.

6.5.2.1 Stale Prices and Well-informed Traders

The stale price problem arises when traders arrange trades at predetermined prices. A price that was fair when it was determined may not still be fair when the trade takes place. Instrument values may change in the interval. Traders who assume that the price is still fair will find that if they can easily arrange their trades, they will often regret doing so. In addition, when they cannot arrange their trades, they will often wish that they had. This happens because traders who know that values have changed will eagerly trade at stale prices if they can benefit from the change in value, and they will refuse to trade otherwise. If values have risen, well-informed traders will eagerly buy at the low stale price, and they will refuse to sell at that price. If values have fallen, they will eagerly sell and refuse to buy.

The stale price problem is an *adverse selection* problem. The well-informed traders select the side of the market on which to trade to the disadvantage of their uninformed counterparts. Adverse selection is one of the most important forces that affect trading. As the accompanying box illustrates, it explains some empirical regularities found in after-hours crossing markets.

6.5.2.2 Price Manipulation

The potential for price manipulation exists whenever traders agree to trade at a price to be determined elsewhere in the future. The buyer and seller both may be tempted to manipulate the price they will use for their trade. The buyer would like a lower price, and the seller would like a higher price. If their trade is large, one or both of the traders may spend considerable

▶ Price Manipulation and Derivative Pricing

Suppose that Bob has a contract to buy 500,000 shares of IBM from Sally at the last NYSE trade before 1:30 P.M. Bob would like that price to be low, and Sally would like it to be high. If Bob submits a 1,000-share market sell order at 1:29:30 P.M. that depresses IBM's price by 3 cents, he will save 15,000 dollars on his 500,000 share purchase at a cost of only 30 dollars. ◀

▶ Jesse Livermore's Manipulation of Some Bucketeers

Jesse Livermore was a famous turn-of-the-century speculator. He collaborated with Edwin Lefèvre to write an autobiography titled *Reminiscences of a Stock Operator*. The book is a classic about trading.

The book describes a number of manipulations in which Livermore participated, as either victim or perpetrator. One such manipulation occurred while he was trading in some illegal bucketeering shops.

A *bucketeer* is essentially a bookie who allows his customers to bet on stocks. His business operates like a regular brokerage where traders buy and sell stocks. The bucketeer fills the orders from his account, however, rather than sending them to an exchange. Since the trade prices in the bucketeer's shop are derived from the next trade prices that come over the ticker tape, traders can manipulate them.

To profit from the bucketeers, Livermore simultaneously submitted orders to five different bucketeers to buy 100 shares each of a somewhat illiquid stock. At the same time, he submitted an urgent order to sell 100 shares of the same stock to a legitimate broker. The legitimate broker wired the sell order to the New York floor, where it filled at a low price. This low price allowed Livermore to buy from the five bucketeers at a low price. Later, he conducted the same operation in reverse. Although he lost money on the 100-share New York trades, he more than made it up on the 500 total shares that he traded in the bucketeering shops. ◀

resources to manipulate the price. If both attempt to do so, however, their efforts probably will cancel out, and both will lose.

Price manipulation is illegal in the United States and in most other countries. However, it may be more common than is widely acknowledged because it usually is hard to detect.

Since POSIT traders submit their orders before the crossing prices are determined, a potential for price manipulation exists in the primary markets. Traders who believe that they will buy in POSIT have an incentive to place sell orders in the primary market to lower prices there, and thereby lower the POSIT crossing price. POSIT sellers likewise would like to raise the primary market prices. If the crossing trade is large and if traders can move the primary market with a small order, this strategy can be profitable.

To discourage price manipulation, POSIT picks its crossing prices at random times within seven minutes following the call. Potential manipulators must therefore depress prices for a seven-minute period rather than at a single point in time. This procedure increases the costs of manipulation by increasing the number of orders that manipulators would have to submit. The greater number of orders also makes it easier to detect and prosecute manipulators.

POSIT also frustrates potential manipulators by keeping all orders confidential and by reporting crosses only after it prices them. POSIT traders therefore cannot know before the cross whether they will trade and how much they will trade. To protect themselves from market manipulators, POSIT traders likewise should not allow other traders to know about their orders.

The final settlement prices for cash-settled futures and option contracts are derived from the cash prices of their underlying instruments. Consequently, these prices are sometimes subject to manipulation when these contracts expire. To prevent manipulations, some cash-settled contracts specify that the exchange may choose final settlement prices to represent fair values when market values appear to be wrong.

6.6 SUMMARY

Order-driven markets include oral auctions, single price auctions, continuous rule-based auctions, and crossing networks. These markets use order precedence rules to match buyers to sellers, and trade pricing rules to price the resulting trades.

The trading rules are very important. They affect how traders behave, and they determine who has power and privilege in the market. Since these rules affect how traders form their order submission strategies, they greatly influence whether traders decide to supply or take liquidity.

The first precedence rule at all markets is the price priority rule. This rule encourages traders to bid high and offer low. Various secondary precedence rules then follow. Time precedence rules encourage traders to submit their orders early. In conjunction with price priority, time precedence rules also encourage traders to bid high and offer low. Display precedence rules encourage traders to display their orders. Public order precedence rules give power to public traders over exchange members. Depending on the market, size precedence rules may give precedence to large traders or to small traders.

Trade pricing rules vary by market type. Continuous trading auction markets use the discriminatory pricing rule. This rule favors large liquidity-demanding traders over small liquidity suppliers. Single price auctions use the uniform pricing rule. This rule gives power to small liquidity suppliers at the expense of large traders. Crossing networks use the derivative pricing rule. This rule favors well-informed traders over uninformed traders, and market manipulators over weak and honest traders.

Many current issues in market structure involve order-driven markets. Should oral auctions convert to automated auctions? Should crossing networks exist, and if so, should they be better integrated with the markets from which they derive their prices? Should markets organize more single price auctions and should they encourage traders to participate in them? How large should the minimum price increment be? In general, which market structure is best?

Each market structure has its advantages and disadvantages. This chapter identifies only some of the issues. To fairly compare market structures, you need to know more about why people trade, how they trade, and what brokers do. We will return to discussing the pros and cons of various market structures in the last part of the book.

6.7 SOME POINTS TO REMEMBER

- Limit order traders favor the uniform trade pricing rule.
- Large market order traders prefer the discriminatory trade pricing rule.
- Price priority is self-enforcing, but secondary precedence rules are not.
- Secondary precedence rules require a large minimum price increment to be economically significant.
- Single price auctions maximize trader surplus.
- Continuous auctions generate more volume for a given order flow.
- Markets that use the derivative trade pricing rule are subject to price manipulation.

6.8 QUESTIONS FOR THOUGHT

1. Should exchanges make the minimum price increment very small and get rid of secondary precedence rules?

2. Continuous trading markets that want to enforce a uniform pricing rule must either prevent traders from splitting their orders or somehow reprice earlier trades when traders do split their orders. Can you imagine mechanisms that continuous order-driven exchanges can implement in electronic environments in order to effectively enforce uniform pricing? What considerations suggest that markets will not adopt such mechanisms?

3. Computerized traders in electronic trading systems have some of the same informational advantages that floor traders have in oral auctions. Some oral auctions have public order precedence rules to give public traders more power in their markets. Should electronic trading systems have a similar rule to give human traders precedence over computerized traders?

4. Should crossing networks pay for the right to use prices determined in other markets to price their crosses? Who should own the prices produced at exchanges?

5. How does informed trading hurt uninformed traders who use crossing networks to arrange trades at closing prices?

6. Should automated trading replace floor-based trading?

7. Suppose that a continuous auction starts the day with an empty book. Only one buy and one sell order arrive during the day. The buy limit price is 20 and the sell limit price is 19. If the buy order arrives first, the trade price will be 20. If the sell order arrives first, the trade price will be 19. The trader who first offers liquidity thus receives the worst price. Is this sensible? What makes this example unusual? What are the implications of this example for trading strategies in very inactive markets?

7
▷
Brokers

*B*rokers are agents who arrange trades for their clients. Unlike dealers, who trade with their clients, brokers trade their clients' orders. Clients usually pay brokers *commissions* for their services.

Many brokers are also *financial advisers* who advise their clients about their investments or their financial plans. They may also provide their clients with investment information. In these capacities, they often influence the trading decisions that their clients make.

Unless you arrange your own trades, you will use the services of a broker when you implement your trading strategies. You therefore must understand what brokers can do for you—and to you—in order to trade effectively. This chapter describes what brokers do and the problems that traders may have with lazy or dishonest brokers.

You also need to know what brokers do if you want to be a broker yourself. The discussions in this chapter will allow you to better understand how brokers compete with each other for business, and how the best brokers win these competitions.

You must understand what brokers do in order to predict when electronic order-matching systems will be successful. Automated order-driven execution systems are essentially electronic brokers. Since traditional brokers and electronic order-matching systems both match buyers to sellers, they compete with each other. To fully understand either system, you must understand the economics of both trading systems.

Finally, you must understand what brokers do if you are interested in the distinctions that regulators make between automated order-driven execution systems and traditional brokers. Some automated order-driven execution systems are regulated as exchanges, whereas other nearly identical systems are regulated as brokers. If you are interested in these distinctions, you must ask how the order matching done by traditional brokers differs from the order matching done by automated systems.

We begin this chapter by considering how brokers serve their clients, how they organize their operations, and what determines their profits. We then discuss how the most important management problem—the principal–agent problem—affects brokers and their clients. The chapter closes with a discussion of problems that traders can have with dishonest brokers, and how traders can prevent these problems.

7.1 WHAT BROKERS DO

Brokers arrange trades for their clients. They search for traders who are willing to trade with their clients; they represent their clients at exchanges; they arrange for dealers to fill their clients' orders; they introduce their clients to electronic trading systems; and they match their clients' buy and sell orders.

TABLE 7-1.

Types of Brokered Transactions

MARKET TYPE	TRADES	MARKET STRUCTURE	BROKERAGE ROLE
Order flow	Small to medium sizes in seasoned securities and contracts	Order-driven or quote-driven	Brokers receive orders and match them with orders and quotes made by other traders.
Block	Large sizes in seasoned securities and contracts	Brokered	Brokers receive an order on one side and must search for traders who will take the other side. Brokers occasionally identify both sides.
New and seasoned offerings	Large size offered by an issuer or one or more large holders	Brokered	Brokers sell securities to buyers on behalf of issuers and large holders.
Mergers and acquisitions	Company to company	Brokered	Brokers find one or both parties.

Brokers conduct these activities in various types of markets. In *order flow markets*, brokers take orders that their clients give them and match them with orders and quotes made by other traders. Exchanges, dealers, or the brokers themselves may operate these markets. Brokers generally search for the best price only among traders who are willing to display their limit orders and quotes in these markets. In *block markets*, brokers take large client orders and try to find other traders to fill them. Brokers often must search among traders who have not expressed interest in trading to discover those traders who are willing to trade. In *offering markets*, brokers distribute new issues and seasoned issues to traders. Brokers often must market these securities to generate buyer interest. Finally, in *merger and acquisition markets*, brokers help firms buy other firms. Brokerage firms that engage in large capital transactions are called *investment banks*. Table 7-1 summarizes the different types of brokered transactions.

Only the largest investment banks operate in all types of markets. Most brokerage firms specialize in only one or two of these markets.

In all markets, brokers are their clients' agents. Their clients tell them what trades they want to make, and under what terms they will trade. The brokers then try to arrange the best trades that they can, subject to the constraints imposed upon them. Generally, clients expect that brokers will seek the lowest possible prices when buying and the highest possible prices when selling.

Clients use brokers to arrange their trades because brokers usually can arrange trades at a much lower cost than their clients can. The following reasons explain why brokers are low-cost traders:

- Brokers can solve clearing and settlement problems at a lower cost than their clients can.
- Brokers can access exchanges and dealers that their clients cannot access.
- Brokers generally know better than their clients who might be willing to trade.

- Brokers are often better negotiators than their clients are.
- Brokers can represent orders for their clients when their clients are unavailable to represent them themselves.

We examine these points in the remainder of this section.

7.1.1 Clearing and Settlement Among Traders

The most important, but perhaps least appreciated, reason why traders use brokers to arrange their trades involves clearing and settlement. Clearing and settlement problems can arise whenever traders do not settle their trades immediately after they negotiate them. During the time between arrangement and final settlement, traders risk that their counterparts may not acknowledge their trades, may refuse to settle their trades, or may be financially unable to settle their trades. Traders therefore are reluctant to trade with people they do not know are trustworthy and creditworthy.

Without the assistance of brokers, traders would have to check the credit of every trader with whom they trade. Brokers assist traders by helping them avoid this expensive problem.

Brokers solve clearance problems by clearing their clients' trades. If a client fails to acknowledge a trade, the broker must resolve the problem with the client. The broker thus protects the trader on the other side of the trade.

Brokers solve the settlement problem either by guaranteeing that their clients will settle their trades, or by staking their business reputations on whether their clients will settle their trades. When brokers guarantee their clients' trades, the brokers settle trades that their clients will not. When the brokers simply vouch for their clients, they risk losing future business if they acquire a reputation for representing clients who do not settle their trades. In both cases, brokers must ensure that they represent only trustworthy and creditworthy clients. Otherwise, undesirable clients will impose significant costs upon them. The credit function that brokers provide is especially important in order-driven markets, since such markets generally arrange trades among total strangers.

Brokers are especially good at solving settlement credit problems because they know their clients. Brokers will not accept orders to buy more than they believe their clients can afford, or to sell more than they believe their clients have. To form these opinions, brokers consider what securities and money their clients have on deposit with them, and they consider their clients' past behavior. Brokers may also consider other information that they obtain from their clients or from credit agencies. Most brokers use electronic systems to manage this information.

Brokers also can efficiently solve settlement credit problems because they control assets that their clients deposit with them. When a broker settles a trade on behalf of a client, but the client fails to settle with the broker, the broker can liquidate assets in the client's account to cover the trade. For example, if a client does not pay for a stock that he bought, the broker can sell the stock and use the proceeds to settle the trade. The broker can then charge any loss on the round-trip to the client's account and, if necessary, liquidate assets in the account to settle the debt. Likewise, if a client does not deliver a security that she has sold, the broker can buy or borrow the security from another trader and use it to settle the trader's sale. The broker can then liquidate assets in the account to settle the debt.

▶ Multiplying Credit Checks

When traders arrange trades that they intend to settle in the future, they must be confident that their counterparts can and will perform. Traders routinely perform *credit checks* to determine whether their counterparts are creditworthy.

In a market with no brokers, each trader must be prepared to check the credit of every other trader. If exactly 1 million traders trade in such a market, the total number of potential credit relationships is 999,999,000,000, or slightly less than one trillion. In such markets, traders will check the credit only of traders with whom they intend to trade. They will naturally prefer to arrange trades only with traders whose credit they have already checked.

Now suppose that this market has brokers who guarantee their clients' trades. Three types of credit relationships are present in this economy:

1. Brokers must check the credit of their clients to protect themselves.
2. The clients must check the credit of their brokers to ensure that they can trust them. These credit checks may be perfunctory if everyone knows that a broker is creditworthy.
3. Each broker must check the credit of every other broker with whom he or she arranges trades.

If the market has 100 brokers, each of whom serves 10,000 different clients, the total number of potential credit relationships is only 2,009,900. This sum is 500,000 times smaller than the total number of potential credit relationships in the economy without brokers! ◀

▶ Membership Has Its Benefits

Some large traders become exchange members so that they do not have to trade through brokers. By employing their own traders, they obtain greater control over their trades, and they avoid exposing their orders to brokers they may not trust. ◀

7.1.2 Brokers Provide Access to Exchanges

Traders also use brokers because brokers can provide access to exchanges that they cannot access themselves. Exchanges generally allow only their members to trade. Nonmembers who want to trade must have members arrange trades for them. The most important reasons why exchanges exclude nonmember traders involve clearing and settlement issues and the need to regulate traders on exchange floors.

7.1.2.1 Clearing and Settlement at Exchanges

Since order-driven exchanges often arrange trades among strangers, they generally do not allow anyone to trade who does not have an approved credit relationship with the exchange clearinghouse or with a clearing member who will guarantee settlement of their trades. Since most traders do not have these relationships, they must trade through brokers who do.

Some brokers neither clear nor execute their own trades. Instead, these *introducing brokers* pass their order flow to another broker who is a clearing member. The clearing member is then responsible for execution, clearing, and settlement. Introducing brokers are so called because they introduce their clients to other brokers. Introducing brokers usually establish the commission rates that their clients pay, even though their clients' accounts are carried *on account* of a clearing member. Clearing members charge their introducing brokers for transaction services.

Many brokers allow their clients *direct access* to the electronic order-routing systems that exchanges, dealers, ECNs, and other brokers maintain. When these systems connect to automated order execution systems, the

▶ What's Happening Here?

Most first-time visitors to the floor of an exchange—especially a futures exchange—are overwhelmed by sensory overload. Although the activity on exchange floors is highly organized, it appears very chaotic to infrequent visitors. Traders and clerks wearing multicolored jackets run everywhere, carrying papers. People yell loudly, gesture wildly, and pass hand signals among themselves. Brokers talk on their telephones and enter information into their handheld computers. Discarded paper litters the floor. Bells occasionally sound, personal pagers beep, and telephones ring constantly. Overhead monitors display constantly changing information, television screens present network talking heads pointing at lines and numbers, and electronic ticker tapes scroll continuously.

After visitors overcome their sense of awe, their next emotion is usually frustration. They generally cannot follow what is happening. They get confused about who is buying, who is selling, and what they are trading. They cannot distinguish between prices and quantities, and the prices they hear often do not make sense.

Trading is hard for novices to understand because traders use jargon, abbreviations, body language, and hand signals to save time and reduce trading errors. For example, most traders yell only the last digits when quoting a price. When they bid 10, they assume that everyone knows that they mean 147.10. They do not say 147.10 because it takes too long and because they do not want to confuse anyone with unnecessary digits. When they name an instrument, they often use nicknames or ticker symbols that a novice does not recognize. They may not even name the instrument when other traders know what they are talking about from the context. Trader jargon like "I'll take 30 at the figure" is hard to understand without knowing that *take* implies that I am a buyer, and *the figure* means the closest integer price.

No new trader walks in off the street and starts to trade in such markets. Instead, most traders start as clerks working for other traders or for the exchange. If they pay close attention and are reasonably sharp, they get the hang of things in a few weeks, and they master the language in a few months. At that point, they may not be able to trade well, but they will know what is going on, and they should not be a liability to other traders. ◀

clients effectively become the traders. The brokers, however, usually remain responsible for guaranteeing settlement.

Clients who have direct access to trading systems are often called *subscribers*. Public subscribers to a trading system must have a broker sponsor and authorize their trades. To help brokers manage credit relations with their sponsored subscribers, many electronic trading systems allow brokers to set real-time credit limits on their subscriber accounts.

7.1.2.2 Floor-based Trading Skills

Floor-based exchanges exclude nonmember traders from their floors because orderly trading on floor-based exchanges requires skilled traders who know the trading rules, the trading protocols, the specialized jargon, and the sign languages that traders use to negotiate their trades. Traders use these skills to increase the speed and accuracy of their trading.

Most markets do not allow their members to trade until they pass an examination which demonstrates that they have mastered basic trading skills.

The examination protects traders from unskilled traders who might slow the markets, confuse others, and generate mistakes.

7.1.3 Brokers Provide Access to Dealers

Many traders use brokers to access dealers that they cannot access themselves. Brokers provide this service primarily to retail clients. Retail traders rarely trade directly with dealers because credit, clearance, and settlement relationships are expensive to establish. Neither retail traders nor dealers want to pay for creating relationships they will not use often. Retail clients also use brokers to trade with dealers because brokers usually have better information about which dealers are offering the best prices or will likely offer the best prices than do their clients.

Institutional clients often trade directly with dealers. Their large and frequent trades make the costs of establishing direct access relationships relatively small compared to the benefits of direct access. Institutional traders usually employ *buy-side traders* to negotiate trades with dealers. These traders typically have information systems that allow them to see all dealer quotes, and they can rely upon their experience to determine which dealers will most likely offer them the best prices. Buy-side traders generally do not pay commissions to dealers when they arrange their trades. Instead, they trade on a *net price basis*. The dealers price the trades to recover any expenses that commissions would otherwise fund. In the U.S. equity markets, this practice is changing as bid/ask spreads have narrowed in response to the 2001 decimalization.

7.1.4 Brokers Are Expert Traders

Many traders use brokers because brokers are experts at trading. Brokers generally know more about who wants to trade than do their clients, they are better negotiators than are their clients, and they are better able to manage order exposure than their clients can. In this subsection, we consider each of these areas of expertise.

7.1.4.1 Block Brokers

The most successful block brokers know who wants to trade, and who would want to trade if they were presented with suitable trading opportunities. They can predict what securities will interest their clients and at what prices their clients will be interested. They use this information to arrange trades.

Brokers learn about their clients by paying close attention to them. They talk with them frequently, and they study their portfolios to determine what interests them. If their clients manage money for others, brokers will also consider the interests of their clients' clients.

7.1.4.2 Better Negotiators

Traders use brokers to negotiate transactions—especially very large ones—on their behalf. Good negotiators must be careful about the information they reveal when negotiating. Depending on their negotiating strategy, they may want to hide information or they may want to bluff credibly. In either event, they must represent their positions clearly and convincingly. Good negotiators also must create relationships in which their counterparts are willing to compromise and accommodate.

Not everyone negotiates effectively. Many of us cannot adequately control our emotions when discussing issues about which we care deeply. We

▶ How to Break into the Major Leagues

Block brokers must know their clients well in order to serve them well. New brokers often have trouble establishing relationships because clients generally do not like to waste their time talking with brokers who are not *players*. A *player* can offer valuable services to his or her clients. Since new brokers usually do not know much about who would want to take the other side of a trade, they have little to offer their clients.

The problem that new brokers face involves a circularity. If they do not know their clients well, they cannot serve them well. If they cannot serve their clients well, their clients will not talk to them. If their clients will not talk to them, they will not know them well.

Established brokers benefit from the opposite side of this circularity. Since they know their clients well, they know who will trade what and at what price. They therefore can provide them with good service. Clients will talk with established brokers because they obtain good service from them. Established brokers thereby get to know their clients well.

This circularity is an example of a *network externality*. Brokers who have large networks of contacts can provide more service to their clients than can brokers with few contacts. The more service that brokers can provide to their clients, the more clients they will have, and the bigger will be their networks of contacts. The network externality allows the strong to get stronger, and it ensures that the weak have trouble competing.

To become players, new brokers must attract clients with something other than information about who wants to trade. They most often offer investment research. If their clients value their research, they will form relationships that will allow the brokers to learn more about their clients' trading interests.

New brokers also try to meet with their clients by entertaining them. They often take them to fancy dinners, to the Super Bowl, to the NBA finals, or to the theater. These contracts have a twofold purpose. The brokers want to learn more about their clients so that they can serve them better. They also want to generate goodwill so that their clients feel obliged to use them.

Since well-established brokers compete with new brokers, they also provide investment research and entertainment services to remain competitive. They do not need to provide as much to stay in business as they did to get established. Established brokers have an advantage simply because they know more about who will trade, what they will trade, and at what prices they will trade than do new brokers.

The economics of brokerage markets implies that the best brokers are those who work hardest to learn about their clients. The network externality ensures that their productivity per hour worked increases as the time they work increases. Accordingly, brokers often work long hours without much vacation. When they do vacation, they often do so at conferences where they can meet their clients. Brokers therefore host many client conferences at which they entertain them, educate them, generate goodwill, and, most important, learn about what trades might interest them. The need to continuously relate to their clients also explains why most brokers vacation during the same months that their clients do. ◀

may be nervous about losing a valuable opportunity, desperate to avoid further loss, mad about our circumstances, too eager to please, too proud, too modest, or unable to control our egos. Our emotions often cloud our judgment and cause us to reveal information that does not further our goals. Many of us cannot convincingly represent our true positions or maintain a poker face when bluffing. Finally, and unfortunately, many of us do not have adequate social skills to develop productive relationships with people whose interests differ from our own.

Traders who recognize their shortcomings as negotiators often employ brokers to negotiate on their behalf. Since brokers usually do not have a stake in their negotiations other than in obtaining commissions for closing successful deals, they are often much less emotionally involved than their clients are. In addition, since brokers are merely agents, they often do not know their clients' final positions. Clients therefore can use their brokers to misrepresent their positions. If they later need to back down, the brokers can save face by claiming that they misunderstood their clients' instructions. If negotiations break down, clients often blame their brokers, assert a misunderstanding, and then start negotiations with new brokers. Although their adversaries may recognize these tactics, if enough credible doubt exists about what happened, productive negotiations may be renewed.

7.1.4.3 Brokers Provide Order Exposure Management

Traders whose orders are likely to move the market significantly do not want to widely expose their orders. Traders either will stand out of the way until the order has its impact on the market price, or they will trade ahead of the order to profit from its expected price impact. Both strategies increase the costs of filling large orders.

The traders who are most concerned about these issues are those who are widely known to be well informed and are known to trade in large size. These traders would rather trade anonymously so that no one knows with whom they are trading. If their orders are large, they typically expose only parts of their orders so that no one knows their full sizes.

These traders employ brokers to represent them so that they can avoid showing who they are and how large their orders are. Their brokers display only to traders whom the brokers expect will be willing to fill the orders. They take special care to avoid traders who will front-run them. In markets where traders see all exposed orders, brokers break up their orders so that other traders cannot determine their full sizes. Large traders sometimes distribute their orders among several brokers so that nobody knows the full extent of their interests.

Brokers add value to the trade process by knowing how best to expose their clients' orders. Good brokers fill their large orders without moving the market much. Poor brokers allow information about the order to leak out so that its execution suffers.

7.1.5 Brokers Represent Limit Orders

Many traders employ brokers to represent orders that they cannot, or do not want, to represent themselves. Clients who have other things to do besides monitoring the market often give limit orders and stop orders to their brokers to tell them what they want to do if market conditions change. The brokers then monitor the market for them. This brokerage function is more important for retail clients who do not spend much time trading than for institutional buy-side traders whose jobs require that they continuously pay attention to the markets.

7.1.6 Summary

Brokers provide many services to their clients. They help them identify suitable counterparts, they help them negotiate their trades, they represent their interests when they are unable or unwilling to represent them themselves, and they help them clear and settle trades. Traders use brokers because brokers generally can trade more effectively and at a lower cost than they can.

7.2 THE STRUCTURE OF A BROKERAGE FIRM

We now consider how brokerage firms structure their operations to provide transaction services to their clients. Since each brokerage organizes its operations differently, the discussion in this section cannot adequately represent all brokerage firms. The primary purposes of the discussion are to introduce you to the complexity of brokerage operations and to expose you to the jargon that brokers use to describe their operations.

The activities of a brokerage firm consist of *front office* operations, *back office* operations, and *proprietary* operations. All activities that involve client contact occur in the *front office*. These activities primarily involve soliciting and taking orders, executing trades, and advising clients. *Back office* operations include all activities that support the front office operations. Back office departments clear and settle trades; maintain accounts; produce investment research; and create and operate various information systems. *Proprietary* operations include the cash and risk management activities of the firm and any speculative trading that the firm conducts for its own accounts. These classifications are somewhat arbitrary. We will use them to organize our discussion of how brokers structure their firms.

7.2.1 Front Office Operations

Brokers solicit order flow by advertising and by contacting prospective clients. They also often give their clients extensive investment information and investment research to encourage them to use their brokerage services. To further develop their business, they may entertain their clients.

Sales brokers primarily interact with clients. They work in the *Sales and Trading Department* of the firm. *Floor brokers* arrange trades at exchanges and on their firm's trading floors. Their division of the firm is often called *Floor Operations*.

Brokers who help distribute large stock and bond offerings generally work in the *Corporate Finance Department* of the brokerage firm. They work closely with sales brokers to distribute the issues.

Many brokerage firms employ *financial analysts* to produce investment reports for their clients. The sales brokers use this information to develop relations with their clients. These analysts usually specialize in an industry or a commodity. Their primary responsibilities include forecasting future prices and earnings. At investment banks, equity analysts sometimes suggest mergers and acquisitions to brokers who work in the Corporate Finance Department. Financial analysts also help clients understand how they can use new trading instruments and techniques to achieve their objectives. The financial analysts usually work in the *Research Department* of the firm.

Most brokerages have *customer service agents* who help their clients manage their accounts. These agents establish, transfer, and close accounts; they take deposits and arrange withdrawals and transfers to and from accounts; and they help their customers interpret their account statements. They usually work in the *Customer Service Department*.

▶ **Why Does the Archer Daniels Midland Company Broker Agency Orders?**

The Archer Daniels Midland Company (ADM) is a large agricultural dealer, shipper, and food processor. The company frequently trades in the futures markets to hedge risks inherent in its businesses. It also sometimes speculates in these markets, using information that it obtains about market conditions from its extensive operations.

ADM is a member of many futures exchanges. It employs many floor traders at these exchanges. The ADM traders trade proprietary ADM orders. They also trade agency orders introduced to them through a subsidiary, ADM Investor Services, that sells execution, clearing, and settlement services to introducing brokers.

ADM undoubtedly hopes to profit from the fees it obtains from its agency brokerage business. The subsidiary also provides ADM with an important secondary benefit: The agency order flow makes it difficult for other traders to determine when ADM is trading for its own accounts and when it is trading for other traders. Consequently, ADM probably obtains better execution for its proprietary orders. ◀

▶ The Wednesday Trading Halts of 1968

By 1968, volumes in U.S. equity markets had grown to the point that brokerage firms could not keep up with their paperwork. Accounting, clearing, and settlement then still involved substantial manual efforts. From June through December 1968, exchanges closed on Wednesdays to give the back offices a chance to catch up. They also closed two hours early on the other weekdays. Firms ultimately solved the "paperwork crisis" by automating their accounts. ◀

7.2.2 Back Office Operations

The back office of a brokerage is responsible for supporting the trading activities of the firm and its clients. The primary responsibilities of the back office include the following activities:

- Maintaining accounts.
- Clearing and settling trades.
- Providing the information systems that the firm uses to transmit market data, quotes, orders, and confirmations to employees, clients, dealers, exchanges, other brokers, clearing agents, settlement agents, and custodians.
- Ensuring that the firm extends credit only to good credit risks.
- Ensuring that the firm and its clients comply with all regulations to which they are subject.

Brokerage firms often place these activities under the supervision of a *chief information officer* (CIO) who oversees all information systems.

7.2.2.1 Accounting Systems

Brokerage firms now universally use computerized accounting systems to keep track of their accounts and to clear and settle their trades. The benefits of such systems are obvious and need no further comment.

Small brokerage firms and many large firms buy their accounting systems "off the shelf" from system vendors. Some large brokers use their own systems, in part because they designed them to meet their special needs, but mostly because they built them before they could buy them cheaply.

7.2.2.2 Corporate Reorganizations

Clients hold their securities in *street name* when they allow their brokers or their depositories to hold them on their behalf. Traders often hold their securities in street name to avoid losing them, to use them as collateral for margin loans, and to ensure that they are available for settlement when they want to sell them. When brokers hold securities on behalf of their clients, they legally own them. Their clients hold only corresponding interests in their accounts.

Brokers who hold securities in street name assume many responsibilities. They must collect dividends and interest payments, and properly assign them to the appropriate client accounts. They must keep track of and properly handle corporate name changes, stock splits, mergers, acquisitions, and liquidations. Finally, they must ensure that issuers can communicate with their clients, the *beneficial owners*. The *Corporate Reorganizations Department* of a brokerage firm generally handles these activities.

7.2.2.3 Market Data and Order-routing Systems

Brokerage firms invest very heavily in data and voice systems that allow their brokers to communicate with their clients, with markets, with dealers, and with each other. Third party vendors now mostly provide these systems.

The simultaneous use of market data systems written by different vendors can create significant coordination problems when the systems need to exchange information. For example, clearing and settlement systems need to report trades to accounting systems, and accounting systems need to report positions to clearing and settlement systems.

Data systems are very hard to integrate when they use different protocols for sharing information. The trading software industry therefore developed several communications protocols that make it easier for systems developed by different vendors to exchange information with each other. The most important of these protocols are the *Financial Information eXchange* (FIX) protocol and the Open Financial Exchange (OFE) protocol. FIX primarily serves institutional traders, and OFE primarily serves Internet-based retail traders. These systems allow traders to route orders and other market information in standard formats that all FIX- or OFE-capable systems can interpret.

7.2.2.4 Credit Management

Brokerage firms often extend credit to their clients, to other brokers, and to dealers. They extend credit to clients when they allow clients who have insufficient money in their account to buy securities, when clients sell securities that they do not have in their accounts, when they lend money to clients on margin, and when they guarantee that their clients will settle their contracts. Brokerage firms extend credit to other brokerage firms and to dealers when they settle their trades, and when they loan securities and money to them.

To ensure that they do not extend credit to poor credit risks, brokers must carefully evaluate all credit relationships in which they are exposed to potential loss. The *credit manager* of the firm is responsible for checking credit and for managing credit risks.

7.2.2.5 Compliance

The *compliance officers* of a brokerage firm ensure that the firm and its clients comply with all applicable regulations. The regulations may concern margins, trading practices, and *client suitability*. The compliance officers of a brokerage firm usually reside in the *Compliance Department* or the *Margin Department* of the firm.

Many regulators do not permit brokers to arrange trades that are not suitable for their clients. A trade creates an unsuitable position if the client cannot afford the potential loss of the position or cannot reasonably appreciate the risk in the position. Brokers who allow their clients to make such trades risk civil lawsuits or criminal prosecution. To protect themselves from this risk, brokers must *know their customers*. To this end, brokers often require that their clients tell them about their finances and their trading experience. Questions about these issues usually appear on account applications. Brokers occasionally interview their clients when they become concerned about the suitability of their trades or positions. Most brokers have electronic systems that monitor their clients' accounts to ensure that their trades are suitable for them.

7.2.3 Proprietary Operations

The *proprietary trading operations* of a brokerage firm include all trading activities that the firm conducts for its *house account*. For pure brokers, these activities primarily include cash management and the borrowing and lending of securities. If the firm also engages in *principal trading* as a dealer, speculator, or arbitrageur, the proprietary trading operations of the firm include these activities.

▶ **Squawk Boxes**

In many brokerages, traders need to talk with colleagues who may sit on the other side of the trading room, or in another trading room that may be thousands of miles away. To facilitate such communications, many brokerage firms place *squawk boxes* at each trader workstation. Squawk boxes are two-way intercoms that are always open. ◀

▶ **How to FIX Babble**

The FIX protocol grew out of a desire by Fidelity Investments and Salomon Brothers to link their information systems and thereby reduce their traders' dependence on telephone calls and handwritten records. Following their initial specification of the standard in 1992, they invited other firms to participate in its further development.

FIX is now a public-domain specification owned and maintained by FIX Protocol. The mission of the organization is "to improve the global trading process by defining, managing, and promoting an open protocol for real-time, electronic communication between industry participants, while complementing industry standards." ◀

Source: www.fixprotocol.org.

▶ Graduated College and Thought You'd Never Have to Take an Exam Again?

Some brokerage firms give their clients a written examination to prove that they understand the risks inherent in their trades. Clients who do not pass the examination cannot trade.

These examinations will become more common as brokers and their clients increasingly relate to each other only through the Internet. The examinations allow the compliance officers to certify the competency of their clients. ◀

7.2.3.1 Cash Management and Stock Lending and Borrowing

Brokerage firms that hold client assets generally invest the cash and often lend the securities. The cash managers of the firm try to keep all cash balances fully invested. Brokers usually house their cash management operations in the *Cashier's Department* under the supervision of the firm's *cashier*. The employees responsible for security lending operations are often those responsible for borrowing securities for short selling. They are often housed in the *Margin Department* or in the *Stock Loan Department*.

7.2.3.2 Risk Management

The *risk manager* of the firm monitors all activities of the firm to ensure that the firm does not lose control over the risks it assumes. The risk manager must ensure that large losses never surprise the firm's managers. In particular, the risk manager must make certain of the following:

- The firm's management is aware of all significant financial and legal risks to which the firm is exposed.
- Adequate controls are in place to prevent rogue traders from creating unauthorized positions.
- The financial implications of all its proprietary positions are well recognized and understood.
- The firm adequately understands the creditworthiness of those to whom it extends credit.
- The firm does not extend too much credit to poor credit risks.

The risk manager's job is not to prevent losses. Firms often lose money because they undertake risky activities that do not work out as they hope. Firms engage in these activities because they expect that the possible rewards are sufficiently large and sufficiently probable to more than compensate for the possible losses. The risk manager's job is to ensure that the managers of the firm adequately understand all possible losses and their probabilities of occurrence.

The risk manager often reports directly to the CEO of the firm. The firm usually gives the risk manager authority and power to investigate any potential source of risk within the firm. These arrangements are necessary to ensure that the risk manager has the independence and power to discover any serious problems.

In smaller brokerage firms, the risk manager and the compliance officer are often the same person. In larger firms, the compliance officer may work for the risk manager, or the two officers may work separately.

7.3 BROKER PROFITABILITY

Like all firms, brokerages profit when their revenues exceed their expenses. Their revenues come primarily from commissions, while their expenses are primarily due to labor costs. Most brokerage firms have many other significant sources of revenue and cost. Their other income lines often explain why some brokers can charge low or no commissions and still stay in business. Their other costs help explain why large brokers often have significant competitive advantages over smaller brokers.

In this section, we will examine the determinants of profitability. Our discussion will help you understand how brokers compete with each other and what factors determine the sizes of their firms.

7.3.1 Revenues

Most brokers obtain their primary revenue from commissions. Important secondary sources of revenue include payments for orders, interest on cash balances, margin interest on loans, underwriting fees, merger and acquisition consulting fees, and security lending fees.

7.3.1.1 Commissions

Brokerage commissions are negotiable in most countries. A few countries have government or exchange regulations that specify *fixed commission rates* that brokers must charge. For example, the minimum stock brokerage commission in Hong Kong is 0.25 percent. Such regulations are becoming quite rare. Stock commissions were deregulated in 1975 in the United States, in 1987 in the United Kingdom, and in 1999 in Japan. As of this writing, the Hong Kong commissions are scheduled to be deregulated on April 1, 2003.

Commissions vary substantially across brokers. Commission rates usually depend on how much service the client wants. *Deep discount brokers* offer the cheapest commissions but usually provide the least service. *Full service brokers* charge the highest commissions but offer substantial service and advice. Table 7-2 presents typical U.S. retail brokerage commissions for various instruments.

Discount and deep discount brokers typically specify standard commission schedules for their clients. They may further discount their commissions for their best clients. The commission schedules for full service brokers are generally just list prices. Although some clients pay these prices, most clients negotiate substantially lower commissions with their brokers.

Full service brokers increasingly charge a flat fee for accounts that they advise. The fee covers all trading commissions, investment research fees, portfolio management fees, and account maintenance fees that the client would otherwise pay. Clients prefer flat fee arrangements because they greatly reduce the incentives that brokers have to *churn* their accounts. Brokers churn accounts when they recommend trades primarily to produce commission revenue. The typical all-inclusive fees for managed accounts range between 1 and 3 percent of the total value of the account. Like straight commissions, they are negotiable. Fixed-fee accounts are sometimes called *wrap accounts* because the brokers wrap all commissions and expenses into a single fee.

In the United States, institutional stockbrokers typically charge a fixed price per share traded. The average U.S. institutional commission is about 5 to 6 cents per share, but can range between 1 cent and 12 cents per share. In most other countries, institutional stockbrokers base their commissions on the value of the transaction. In almost all countries, commission rates are negotiable. They may vary by the size of the trade, the difficulty of arranging it, and the soft dollars that the trade generates. (We describe soft dollars below.) Institutional clients also sometimes get volume discounts based on the total volume they trade during a month, quarter, or year.

Stockbrokers usually also broker options trades. U.S. deep discount brokers typically charge 1.50 dollars per contract with a 20-dollar minimum. Full-service brokers charge substantially more per trade.

TABLE 7-2.

Typical Retail Brokerage Commissions in the U.S. (2001)

BROKER	RELATIONSHIP AND SERVICE	INSTRUMENT	COMMISSION
Deep discount brokers	Clients must submit orders via the Internet	Stocks	$12 per trade for market orders $15 per trade for limit orders
	Some electronic investment information resources	Stock options	$1 per contract, minimum $15 per trade
	Little or no investment research	Corporate bonds	$3 per bond, minimum $35 per trade
	No investment or financial planning advice	Treasury bills, notes, and bonds	$40 per trade
		Futures contracts	$7 per contract round-turn
Discount brokers	Clients may submit orders over the phone or at a discount via the Internet	Stocks	$30 per trade
		Stock options	$29 plus 1.6% of principal
	Electronic investment information resources and stock reports	Corporate bonds	$5 per bond, minimum $35
	Some investment research	Treasury bills, notes, and bonds	$50 per trade
	Some fee-based investment and financial planning advice	Futures contracts	$10 per side per contract, or $20 round-turn
Full-service brokers	Clients and their personal brokers develop relationships in which the brokers know their clients well, and the clients trust their brokers	Stocks	8¢ per share, minimum $100–250 per trade, highly negotiable
		Stock optoins	$50–100 per trade
	Brokers supply investment research and give investment and financial planning advice	Treasury bills, notes, and bonds	Most full-service brokers trade fixed-income securities as principals rather than as agents. They therefore charge markups rather than commissions. The markups vary substantially.
	Directed account trading	Corporate bonds	
	Most retail full-service accounts are on an annual "fee basis." Clients pay between 1 and 2 percent of their assets in exchange for transaction services and research	Futures contracts	$80 to $125 per contract round-turn

Note: Commission rates vary substantially across brokers, and they change frequently.

Brokerages in the futures markets are called *futures commission merchants* (FCMs). Discount FCMs typically charge about 30 dollars per contract for a round-turn (two trades). They charge by the turn because they expect that their clients will close their positions before delivery. Many FCMs, however, charge for each side so that they can advertise lower commissions.

Soft Commissions

In the United States, before the final deregulation of stock brokerage commissions on May 1, 1975, brokerage commissions were much higher than they would have been had commissions not been fixed by exchange regulations. By then, automation of trading processes and growth in institutional trading had significantly lowered broker costs. Brokers who could obtain order flow could profit handsomely from the fixed commission rates. Brokers, of course, competed intensely for the orders.

Brokers in unregulated commission markets obtain order flow by lowering their commissions and by offering better service. In price-regulated markets, they can only offer better service or give their clients other things that they value.

To obtain order flow, stockbrokers gave their institutional clients free services. These services primarily included investment research, but brokers also gave away accounting systems, communications systems, computing systems, and staff training. In addition, brokers provided their clients with marketing incentives such as tickets to major ball games and all-expenses-paid trips to investment conferences that they organized at expensive resorts. The clients paid high fixed commissions and received various services besides trade execution.

To promote fairness, brokers and clients started to keep track of the commissions they paid and the services they received. They ultimately created a system of soft dollar accounting in which clients earned one *soft dollar* for a certain number of *hard dollars* they spent on commissions. They then used their soft dollars to buy various services from their brokers. They even asked their brokers to buy services for them from third parties.

The soft dollar accounting system allowed brokers to compete for order flow despite the fixed commissions. Clients benefited from more competitive markets and lower net trading costs.

The soft dollar system hastened deregulation by undermining the system of fixed commissions set by exchange rules. Commission deregulation in the United States started in April 1971 with deregulation for trades larger than 500,000 dollars. It continued in steps until all commissions were deregulated by May 1, 1975. (Traders refer to the deregulation as *May Day.*) Commissions dropped significantly following deregulation.

Interestingly, soft dollar usage has increased since deregulation. The U.S. Securities and Exchange Commission estimates that the total value of research paid for with soft dollars exceeded 1 billion dollars in 1998. To obtain soft dollars, many institutional traders willingly pay much higher commissions than they would otherwise have to pay for execution services. In 1998, soft dollar brokers offered an average of 1 dollar of soft dollar services for every 1.7 dollars of hard dollar commissions that they received.

Soft dollars persist in large part because of the way that investment funds account for their expenses. When an investment fund pays hard dollars for anything but a trading commission, the cost appears as an expense in its financial accounts. Since many investors prefer investment funds that have low expense ratios, funds try to minimize their hard dollar expenses. Although investment funds pay commissions with hard dollars, they do not treat them as direct expenses in their financial accounts. Instead, funds record their purchases and sales on a net price basis. Commissions raise their purchase prices and lower their sales prices. High commissions therefore lower their reported investment returns. Many investment funds prefer to buy things with soft dollars so that they can avoid reporting direct expenses to investors who are highly cost sensitive. The high volatility of portfolio returns ensures that such investors cannot easily identify expenses which reduce their investment returns.

The U.S. Securities and Exchange Commission recognizes this problem. In 1995, it adopted regulations that require investment companies (primarily mutual funds) to report the value of the goods and services that brokers pay on their behalf as expenses in their accounting statements. Many investment companies avoid the intention of this requirement by hiring investment advisers to manage their funds. The brokers allocate soft dollars to the advisers, who use them primarily to purchase research products. These soft dollars allow investment advisers to charge lower management fees to their investment company clients.

The SEC cannot close this loophole because Congress created a *safe harbor* in the 1975 amendments to the Securities and Exchange Act of 1934 that specifically protects it. Section 28(e) of the amended Act allows investment advisers to cause their clients to pay more than the lowest available brokerage commissions if the advisers determine in good faith that the amount of the commission is reasonable in relation to the value of the brokerage and research services provided. What otherwise might appear to be an improper kickback—the use of client commissions to obtain investment research that benefits their investment advisers—is therefore legal in the United States.

The U.S. Securities and Exchange Commission periodically considers regulations that would require funds to provide more extensive reports of their soft dollar expenses. Its efforts invariably encounter opposition from funds, their soft dollar brokers, and the investment fund industry trade association, the Investment Company Institute.

Soft commissions are common in other national markets where the same players debate the same issues. For example, in Britain, the Financial Services Authority (the British equivalent of the U.S. Securities and Exchange Commission) frequently is at odds with the Fund Managers' Association over the regulation of soft commissions.

Directed Brokerage and Commission Recapture

Many institutional investment sponsors direct their investment advisers to use specific brokers when trading for their accounts. Sponsors create *direct brokerage* relationships to support specific brokers. For example, political considerations force many state and municipal pension funds to use in-state brokers. Some sponsors ask their managers to direct orders to specific brokers so that the sponsors can obtain services which those brokers offer in exchange for the order flow.

Sometimes pension plan sponsors negotiate *commission recapture agreements* with the brokers to whom they direct their orders. These agreements provide that the brokers will return to the investment sponsor some of the commissions paid to them by the sponsor. The recaptured commissions may reflect volume discounts or they may simply be rebates. State and municipal plan sponsors generally use the money to pay for investment consulting services for which they otherwise would have no budget.

The *Employee Retirement Income Security Act* requires that the trustees of U.S. private pension plans treat commissions as fund assets. They therefore would have to return to their funds any recaptured commissions that brokers pay them. Consequently, private pension plans do not generally negotiate commission recapture agreements.

7.3.1.2 Payments for Order Flow

Payments for order flow are payments that dealers make to brokers to obtain orders from their clients. For many retail-based securities brokers, payments for order are a very significant source of transaction-based revenue. For example, in 1997, they represented 24 percent of total transaction revenue (commissions plus payments for order flow) at E*TRADE. Their importance has since dropped, however; dealers now pay less for order flow because decimalizaton has narrowed their spreads. In the second quarter of 2001, E*TRADE's payments for order flow had dropped to 15 percent of transaction revenue

7.3.1.3 Interest

Brokers earn interest on the margin loans that they make to their clients. Most brokers base the rate they charge their clients on the *broker call money rate*. It is generally about two and a half points higher than short-term Treasury bill rates. Margin loan rates typically vary from two points above the broker call money rate for small loans of less than 5,000 dollars to one point below the rate for large loans of more than 1 million dollars. The rates are negotiable for large loans.

Brokers also earn interest on the cash that their clients deposit with them. The interest that they earn on these balances, however, is offset to a significant extent by the interest that they pay to their clients on these balances. On net, the brokers profit from these balances because the rates at which they pay interest are less than the rates at which they invest the balances. Moreover, many brokers do not pay interest on all funds they hold on deposit. For example, many brokers pay interest only on balances that exceed some minimum figure, such as 1,000 dollars.

The interest that brokers can earn on cash balances can be quite significant. If the firm can invest money in margin loans at 7.0 percent, it earns 70 dollars per year for every 1,000 dollars on which it pays no interest.

7.3.1.4 Short Interest Rebate

When a trader wants to sell a security short, his broker must have the security to deliver to the buyer. Before brokers accept sell orders, they therefore must make an *affirmative determination* that the securities will be available to settle the trade. Brokers often can deliver securities that they hold in street name for their other clients. If they do not have the security, they must borrow it from someone who does.

When the broker delivers a security that he holds in street name, the broker keeps the cash proceeds of the sale as collateral to ensure that the short seller will be able to repurchase the security. The broker can invest these short proceeds and earn interest on them.

When the broker must borrow the security, the broker must deposit the cash proceeds of the sale (plus about 2 percent more) with the lender to col-

▶ Variation Margin and Cash Management in Futures Accounts

Futures traders must maintain margin in their accounts to ensure that they can cover any losses in their positions. *Margin* is cash or securities that clients post as bonds to cover their potential losses. Futures brokers require that their clients post an *initial margin* when they open their positions. The exchange or its clearinghouse usually sets minimum initial margins. Brokers may require higher initial margins from their clients.

When futures positions lose money, brokers deduct the losses from their clients' accounts. When positions make money, brokers credit the gains to the accounts. These monies pass through the clearinghouse every day from losers to winners. The margin in futures accounts is called *variation margin* because it allows brokers to collect or credit any variation in the value of their clients' positions.

Brokers require that their clients maintain a minimum margin deposit in their accounts. The minimum, called the *maintenance margin*, is usually lower than the initial margin. Like the initial margin, the exchange or its clearinghouse sets the minimum maintenance margin, and brokers may require higher maintenance margins from their clients.

When brokers require additional margin, they place a *margin call* on the account. If the trader does not supply the margin within the prescribed time, the broker will close his or her position.

Brokers allow their clients to post their margins with Treasury bills. When brokers need to deduct losses from an account, they first use any available cash in the account. If no cash is available, they then sell, as necessary, any Treasury bills posted as margin. This practice is called *breaking a T-bill*. Some brokers may allow their clients to borrow against their Treasury bills if they have sufficient equity in their accounts. The interest rate, however, tends to be high.

Brokers usually charge a fee when they sell Treasury bills. For small accounts, the fee is large relative to the interest that traders could earn on their free balances. Traders therefore tend to hold cash in their accounts to accommodate their variation margin payments without selling their Treasury bills.

Futures brokers generally do not pay interest on the cash balances that their retail clients place on deposit with them. The interest that brokers earn on these balances can be a very significant source of revenue for retail futures brokers. For example, at 5.0 percent interest, a typical retail client with 20,000 dollars in free cash in her account will generate 1,000 dollars a year in income for her broker. This revenue is equivalent to 50 round-turn commissions at 20 dollars per round-turn.

Large institutional traders usually manage the cash in their futures accounts carefully. They buy and sell Treasury bills on a daily basis as necessary to keep their free cash fully invested. They also may wire money in and out of their accounts to keep their cash fully invested in interest-bearing securities. ◀

lateralize the loan. The lender then can invest the cash and earn interest on it. Since the lending market is competitive, lenders must pay brokers interest on the cash collateral in order to obtain their business. This interest is called *short interest rebate*. In the United States, the short interest rebate rate is usually the federal funds rate or the LIBOR (London InterBank Offering Rate), less a small fee for borrowing the security. The borrowing fee depends on the availability of the security. If it is not difficult to borrow, the fee is only about 10 basis points per year. If the security is difficult to

▶ Synthetic Short Positions

Highly sophisticated retail short sellers can obtain some economic benefit from the short proceeds that they generate by constructing synthetic short positions instead of real ones. A *synthetic short position* is a position constructed from option contracts or from futures contracts that produces the same economic returns as an actual short position.

The *put–call parity theorem* proves that a long position in a put contract coupled with a short position in a call contract with the same strike and maturity, plus a long position in a bond with the same maturity, is economically equivalent to a short position in the underlying security. When options dealers receive short interest rebate on their short positions, and when competition forces them to price their contracts to reflect those rebates, traders who construct synthetic short positions in effect obtain short interest rebate. In practice, the transaction costs associated with constructing synthetic short positions can significantly reduce the economic benefits of this strategy. In any event, it can be used to short only securities for which option contracts trade.

Traders also can construct synthetic short positions by selling futures contracts and buying bonds with the same maturity. By a similar argument, this strategy also effectively produces short interest rebate. ◀

borrow, traders say that it is *on special*. The borrowing fees for such securities depend on their scarcity.

The interest that brokers directly or indirectly earn on the proceeds of short sales can be a very significant source of their revenue. For example, when interest rates are 5.0 percent, brokers receive 5,000 dollars per year on a 100,000-dollar short position. These revenues dwarf the commissions that they charge their clients to put on and take off these short positions.

Large clients and professional traders demand that their brokers rebate some of the interest on the proceeds of their short sales. Such interest is also called short interest rebate.

Almost all retail brokers refuse to pay short interest rebate to their clients as a matter of firm policy. Their nearly universal reluctance is surprising, given the interest that brokers can earn from the short proceeds. Brokers who pay short interest rebate, and who appropriately advertise this fact, should be able to garner significant short proceeds. If such brokers pay out only half the interest that they receive on these balances as short interest rebate, they should have extremely lucrative businesses.

7.3.1.5 Underwriting Fees

Investment banks receive *underwriting fees* when they help issuers sell securities. The fees vary by whether the broker *underwrites* the issue or merely sells it on a *best efforts* basis. In an *underwritten offering*, the investment bank guarantees that the issuer will receive the offering price for all shares or bonds issued. If it cannot sell the entire issue, it will buy the remainder for its own account. In a *best efforts offering*, the investment bank makes its best effort to sell the security. Most offerings are underwritten offerings because investment banks have a greater incentive to sell securities when they risk losing if they fail.

In the United States, the fees in an underwritten initial public stock offering tend to be around 7 percent of the transaction. Brokers often receive

▶ Brokerage Compensation

Most brokerage firms are highly entrepreneurial operations in which different units of the firm operate as substantially independent businesses. Such firms often base the pay of their senior employees on the performance of their unit. These compensation schemes ensure that key personnel have strong incentives to work hard for the firm. They also reduce the probability that key personnel will leave to start their own firms.

Most firms pay their brokers on a commission basis when they are responsible for obtaining their order flow. The more trades the brokers arrange, the better paid they will be. Highly productive brokers can easily make millions of dollars per year.

Compensation for the professional staff at brokerage firms generally consists of a low base salary plus a significant year-end bonus if the employee has been productive and if the firm has been profitable. This compensation scheme tends to keep employees attached to their firms (at least until year-end), it provides them with strong incentives to work hard, and it ensures that the firm will stay solvent when business is slow.

At firms where brokers are essentially well-trained telephone clerks, they are paid accordingly. Most firms, however, give year-end bonuses to all workers when the firm has done well. ◀

additional compensation in the form of options to buy additional shares at the offering price. These options are quite valuable if the share price rises following the offering.

The fees in underwritten offerings compensate brokers for their efforts and for the insurance that they provide issuers. Since brokers do not provide such insurance for best efforts offers, fees are usually lower for those transactions.

7.3.1.6 Merger and Acquisition Fees

Investment banks also broker mergers and acquisitions. The brokers who suggest and help arrange these transactions generally receive fees for their services. The companies involved may hire them as consultants or as underwriters of new securities created in the merger.

7.3.1.7 Security Lending Fees

Brokers who hold their clients' securities in street name often lend those securities to short sellers in exchange for security lending fees. The fees depend on the demand for short positions and on the availability of the shares. Security lending fees are highest for closely held securities that greatly interest short sellers. *Closely held securities* are securities for which a small number of investors hold a large majority of the shares or bonds. Such investors often will not lend their securities because they do not want short sellers to drive down their price. Widely held securities that do not interest short sellers generally command minimal lending fees.

7.3.2 Costs

Labor costs generally are the most significant costs of running a brokerage. Other important costs include interest payments on client cash balances and on money borrowed to finance client margin loans, marketing costs, accounting costs, clearance and settlement costs, data fees, and communications costs. Most of these costs are obvious and need no further comment.

▶ Economies of Scale in Trading Technologies

The back offices of brokerage firms must be highly automated to reduce labor costs. Brokerages therefore spend a lot on information technologies.

Most information technologies are characterized by *economies of scale*. The average cost of building and operating systems, per unit of output, declines with system usage.

Large brokerage firms therefore have significant cost advantages over small firms. They can spread fixed costs of creating and operating their information systems over many accounts, and they can provide many services at a lower cost because of their size. These scale economies explain much of the consolidation that has occurred in the brokerage industry since the introduction of automated information-processing systems. To compete in the presence of such scale economies, most small brokerage firms are *introducing brokers* that purchase trade execution and back office services from larger firms. ◀

7.4 THE PRINCIPAL–AGENT PROBLEM

Whenever someone works for someone else, a potential conflict of interest arises. This problem is the well-known *principal–agent problem*. It is the principal problem of management. Agents are supposed to do what their principals want them to do, but the agents often do what the agents want to do.

Brokers are agents who help their clients trade. The clients expect that their brokers will work hard and honestly. Brokers, however, may have other agendas. They may be lazy, they may cut corners, or they may even try to defraud their clients. Most brokers, of course, are honest and work hard on behalf of their clients.

Brokerage clients use several standard management techniques to solve the principal–agent problem. The techniques usually involve carrots and sticks. Clients reward their brokers for doing good work and penalize them for performing poorly.

Rewards may be explicit or implicit. Explicit rewards typically involve contractual payments that clients make to their brokers when they perform well. The formulas for these payments usually depend on explicit measures of productivity. Implicit rewards generally entail sending more orders to brokers who do better jobs.

Penalties likewise may be explicit or implicit. The most important explicit penalties that clients invoke are legal actions. Clients sue (or bring to arbitration) brokers who are negligent or dishonest. The most common penalty for poor performance is implicit: Clients take business away from brokers who serve them poorly.

7.4.1 Performance Measurement

Clients must measure the performance of their brokers in order to manage them effectively. Otherwise, they cannot reward brokers who serve them well or penalize those who serve them poorly. In general, managers cannot solve principal–agent problems when they cannot measure the performance of their agents. Accurate performance measurement therefore is a prerequisite for successful management. You cannot manage what you cannot measure.

Measuring broker productivity is quite difficult. To measure their productivity, you must compare their product to their commissions. Measuring commissions is easy, but measuring the quality of the transaction services that brokers produce is much more difficult. Brokers provide good service when they buy at low prices, sell at high prices, do not fail to buy when prices subsequently rise, and do not fail to sell when prices subsequently fall. Measuring these attributes is difficult because clients generally cannot easily determine whether their brokers obtained the best available prices. Clients also cannot easily determine whether their brokers failed to trade because no one was willing to trade or because their brokers were not aggressive enough. Consequently, measures of broker productivity are invariably imprecise. We consider how clients evaluate brokerage services in chapter 21. Without good measures of quality of service, brokerage clients cannot accurately judge whether they obtain service commensurate with the commissions that they pay.

Although traders cannot easily measure the quality of service they obtain from their brokers, others may do it for them. Rating agencies evaluate brokerages and sell the results to interested parties. Consultants likewise evaluate the transaction costs of their clients and compare them against those of their other clients. Increasingly, government regulators and exchange officials require that dealers and brokers publish order-handling data and execution price data that analysts can use to make meaningful comparisons among them. Traders often use the reports produced by these analysts to determine to which brokers they should direct their orders.

Clients who face principal–agency problems also benefit from the regulation of brokers by governments, exchanges, and trader associations. These agencies often supervise brokers to ensure that they do not engage in abusive or dishonest business practices.

7.4.2 Best Execution

When brokers take client orders, they assume an agency responsibility to obtain *best execution*. Unfortunately, best execution is not well defined. We devote much of chapter 25 to understanding best execution.

"Best execution" means different things to different people. To unsophisticated clients, "best execution" may mean "get the best price possible" for a market order and "trade as quickly as possible" for a limit order. This definition suggests absolute standards for best execution. In the U.S. equity markets, the term "best execution" generally refers to these standards.

More sophisticated traders understand that execution quality depends on the resources (effort, skill, and systems) brokers employ to obtain it. They know that in competitive markets, you do not get something for nothing. When they pay their brokers well for execution services, they expect better executions, on average, than when they do not pay much. For such traders, "best execution" means "Get me the execution I am paying you to provide." These traders define "best execution" in the context of their brokerage relationships.

The most sophisticated clients understand they cannot buy something that they cannot measure well. If brokers believe that their clients cannot measure execution quality, they are unlikely to provide it, whether they are paid for it or not: Any broker who spends resources to provide unrecognized execution quality will be undercut by those who do not. In competitive brokerage markets, such brokers cannot compete. They must either go out of business or quit providing high-quality service. The most sophisticated clients therefore pay only for the level of execution quality that they can audit. For them, "best execution" means "Get me the execution that I expect you to provide, given what I pay you and the limitations of my ability to audit your performance." These traders define best execution relative to the costs of auditing it.

7.4.3 The Dual Trading Problem

Dual traders trade both as dealers and as brokers. When they trade as dealers, they buy and sell for their own account. When they trade as brokers, they buy and sell for other people's accounts. Dual traders are also known as *broker-dealers*.

Dual traders face an unavoidable conflict of interest. The conflict is most obvious when they *internalize* orders. Dealer-brokers internalize orders when they fill client orders themselves. When internalizing client buy orders, broker-dealers want high sales prices and their clients want low purchase prices. When internalizing client sell orders, broker-dealers want low purchase prices and their clients want high sales prices. These price objectives are irreconcilable. What is best for the client is never what is best for the broker-dealer in the short run.

Dual traders also face a conflict of interest when both they and their clients want to trade on the same side of the market. Both want to trade first because the first traders usually get the best prices. They also want to trade first to benefit from the market impact of the others' trades. Traders who trade ahead of other traders to profit from the price impacts of their orders are known as *front runners*. We discuss the front-running strategy in section 7.5.1 below and in chapter 11.

In the long run, dealers who do not provide good service to their clients will not keep those clients. Clients, however, must be able to evaluate the quality of the service they receive. To the extent that they cannot do so, they must rely upon their brokers to represent them. When their brokers are also their dealers, the conflict of interest may become troublesome.

Many markets closely regulate dual traders because of the conflict of interest problem. In the U.S. futures markets, regulations prohibit dual traders from filling their agency orders for their own accounts. Instead, they must offer them to other traders. At a given price, they also must fill their agency orders before they can fill their own orders. This public precedence rule helps ensure that they do not front-run their clients.

Some markets prohibit all dual trading. In such markets, traders must trade either exclusively for their accounts or exclusively for their clients. The markets that prohibit dual trading typically are large markets in which everyone can specialize. Prohibitions against dual trading in small markets may significantly decrease liquidity by preventing traders who otherwise would be willing to offer liquidity from doing so.

7.4.4 Order Preferencing

Order preferencing is the routing of order flow by a broker to a preferred dealer. Most brokers preference orders based on the relations they have with various dealers. The routing does not normally depend on the prices that dealers quote or on current market conditions. The most commonly preferenced orders are small retail orders to trade stocks and options.

Brokers route orders to dealers who provide them with good service, who provide good prices to their clients, and who pay them for the order flow.

Brokers who own dealer subsidiaries often route orders to their subsidiary dealers when they internalize orders for execution. *Payments for order flow* are pecuniary and nonpecuniary inducements that dealers offer brokers in exchange for their order flows.

Sometimes in lieu of payments for order flow, two broker-dealers will exchange order flows. A broker whose dealer subsidiary does not deal in a particular instrument will route orders in that instrument to a broker-dealer who does. The other broker-dealer will reciprocate by sending orders that the first broker-dealer trades. The broker-dealers keep track of these reciprocal order flow exchanges to ensure that they are balanced.

In the U.S. stock markets, dealers often pay brokers about 1 cent per share for each market order that brokers send to them. Before the introduction of new order exposure rules in 1997 and decimalization in 2000, these payments often were substantially higher. The payments declined because the new rules and the decimalization caused bid/ask spreads to narrow, especially in Nasdaq stocks.

7.4.4.1 The Order-Preferencing Problem

Preferencing of order flow by brokers to dealers raises questions about whether brokers obtain best execution for their clients. To many people, payments for order flow seem like kickbacks. Likewise, the preferencing of order flow to a broker's own dealer subsidiary suggests an obvious conflict of interest, as does the exchange of order flows among brokerages and their dealer subsidiaries.

Since preferencing relationships generally benefit brokers directly, some clients and regulators suspect that preferencing brokers do not meet their agency obligations to their clients. In particular, since brokers rarely negotiate individual trade prices for preferenced order flows, and since the routing of preferenced orders rarely depends on the orders or on current market conditions, these clients and regulators question whether brokers actively search for best execution for their clients.

7.4.4.2 Best Execution Standards

Dealers and brokers involved in order-preferencing arrangements are aware of the conflict of interest. Brokers therefore demand, and dealers generally promise, certain levels of service that depend on order type and size. Since brokers negotiate these promises with their dealers, these agreements implicitly represent the brokers' definition of best execution. In general, brokers provide best execution when they ensure that their clients' orders fill at the best prices their clients can reasonably expect. In U.S. equity markets, this generally means that dealers will execute market orders at the national best bid or offer, or better.

Although clients always want their brokers to actively negotiate for the best price when filling their orders, such negotiations are prohibitively expensive for small orders: The small commissions that traders pay for small orders simply do not justify the individual attention that every client desires. Instead, many brokers direct their orders to dealers who use complex algorithms to provide best execution under various market conditions. Such brokers obtain best execution for their clients when they ensure that their clients receive good prices and high-quality service on average.

Large institutional traders who actively participate in the negotiation of their trades are less concerned about best execution standards than are small traders who must trust their brokers to obtain best execution. Large traders personally negotiate with their dealers, or they insist that their brokers negotiate actively on their behalf. Regulators therefore generally presume that such large traders can fend for themselves.

7.5 DISHONEST BROKERS

Although most brokers are honest, dishonest brokers occasionally exploit their clients. Markets therefore have developed mechanisms to detect and deter dishonest behavior among brokers. These mechanisms make dishonest broker problems uncommon in most places.

Brokers are most likely to be dishonest when their clients and their regulators cannot easily detect their frauds. The best way to deter fraud among brokers therefore is to have good mechanisms for monitoring their behavior. Markets detect dishonest brokers and deter dishonest behavior by having officials supervise their trading, by investigating suspicious trading practices reported by honest traders, and by maintaining reliable audit trails.

An *audit trail* records the submission and disposition of every order. A good audit trail includes detailed and unalterable information about everything that happens to each order. Complete audit trails also record market conditions at the times of submission and execution of every order. Regulators use audit trails to determine whether traders have violated trading rules. An accurate audit trail discourages dishonest behavior by brokers.

Brokers are most likely to engage in dishonest practices when the benefits of their fraudulent behavior are large compared to the expected costs of acting fraudulently. These costs include losing business from their defrauded clients, losing a reputation for honest dealings, acquiring a reputation for dishonest dealings, and suffering any criminal and civil sanctions that may ultimately arise out of their behavior.

These considerations suggest that traders will encounter dishonest brokers more often in unregulated markets than in well-regulated markets. They also suggest that brokers will be more honest in markets in which they have acquired valuable reputations for honest dealing than in markets in which they cannot develop—or have not yet developed—such reputations. Finally, brokers will be more honest in transparent markets with strong audit trails

▶ **Honesty Is the Best Policy**

The vast majority of brokers are honest. Nonetheless, brokers who work for large, well-established, and well-respected firms are more likely to behave honestly than are brokers who work for small, new firms. Firms with good reputations attract business because people trust them. The ability to attract and retain business makes these firms valuable. Their managers must be very vigilant to ensure that no rogue brokers exploit their reputations and thereby depreciate the values of their firms.

Since most newly established brokerages do not start with valuable reputations, their managers have less incentive to deploy resources to detect and prevent fraud by their employees than do the managers of firms with valuable reputations. Not surprisingly, most penny stock fraud takes place at small, relatively new brokerages rather than at large, well-established ones.

The value of a reputation for honesty makes it difficult to establish new brokerage firms. Clients naturally are wary of brokers who they do not know well and of firms they suspect could easily disappear tomorrow. ◀

▶ How to Check on a U.S. Broker

The regulatory arm of the National Association of Securities Dealers, *NASD Regulation*, or NASD-R for short, maintains a registration and licensing database called the *Central Registration Depository* (CRD). Regulators that collect data about securities firms and individual brokers deposit these data in the CRD. The data include information about employers; registrations; criminal events; actions taken by federal and state regulators and by self-regulating organizations such as exchanges; complaints; arbitrations; civil actions; bankruptcies; and unsatisfied judgments.

Anyone can access the public records in this database via the NASD-R Public Disclosure Program. Forms for conducting online research and for requesting disclosure reports appear at www.nasdr.com/2000.htm.

The National Futures Association (NFA) maintains a similar database through its *Background Affiliation Status Information Center* (BASIC). Forms for accessing BASIC appear at www.nfa.futures.org/basic/welcome.asp. ◀

▶ Front-Running Example

Doug is a dishonest broker, Fran is Doug's friend, and Earl is a large client of Doug's. Both Earl and Fran have given Doug market buy orders to execute. Earl's order is quite large and will likely cause prices to rise. Fran's order arrived after Earl's order but before Doug had executed Earl's order. The time precedence rules of the market require that Doug execute Earl's order before Fran's order because Earl submitted his order earlier.

Doug illegally trades Fran's order first so that her order front-runs Earl's order. She then profits from the price impact of Earl's order. The average fill price of Earl's order is worse because Fran takes some of the liquidity that otherwise would have gone to Earl. As a rule, front running harms the trader before whose order the front runner trades. ◀

▶ Front Running in Silver Futures

At a picnic hosted by a charitable organization, I met a wealthy man who told me the following story upon learning that I was writing this book.

In the mid-1960s, Jack (not his real name) traded silver futures for his own account on the floor of one of the two U.S. exchanges that trade silver futures contracts. He befriended a telephone clerk who worked for a large wirehouse that occasionally handled large orders for its industrial clients. He and the clerk conspired to front-run these large orders and share the profits.

By arrangement, the clerk would signal Jack that he had a large buy or sell order by how he carried the order when bringing it to his firm's floor broker. When Jack saw that the clerk was carrying a large order, he immediately bought or sold silver contracts according to the type of order the clerk was signaling. Jack said that they front-ran more than 50 orders this way before they quit. They profited on all of their trades.

I pointed out to Jack that the activity he was describing to me was illegal. He countered that everyone was doing it. Whether it was true or not, I imagine that Jack would not have told me the story if the statute of limitations had not run out.

The FBI conducted sting operations in the 1990s to detect front-running abuses in the futures markets. Agents posing as floor traders caught, convicted, and expelled several traders from the markets.

Front running in the futures markets is now much more difficult because audit trails have been substantially improved and because exchanges and buy-side traders now use electronic systems to monitor the quality of their executions. When execution quality is especially poor, or when it drops precipitously, they initiate investigations to determine why. ◀

▶ Inappropriate Order Exposure Example

Dishonest broker Doug shows Earl's large buy order to his friend Rick, who is a small trader. Since Doug knows Rick cannot fill Earl's order, it is inappropriate for him to expose it to Rick. Rick then buys in front of Earl's order before Doug fills it. The inappropriate order exposure allows Rick to make a profitable trade that hurts Earl.

Doug also exposes the full size of Earl's order to his friend Todd, who is a small dealer. Todd then raises his offer price to avoid filling Earl's order at a low price. Since Doug knows that Earl's order is too large for Todd to fill by himself, Doug should have exposed only a portion of the order. The inappropriate exposure ultimately causes Earl to pay a higher average price to fill his order. ◀

than in opaque markets in which traders cannot easily see what their brokers are doing.

The best way to avoid losing to dishonest brokers is to avoid doing business with them. Traders therefore should know their brokers well. In practice, many traders do not know much about their brokers. Most traders simply trust that brokers working for large, well-known firms will be honest.

If your broker proves to be dishonest, you may be able to avoid losses by recognizing the fraud before it gets out of hand. You therefore must be aware of how dishonest brokers can defraud their clients. The remainder of this section considers the most common ways that dishonest brokers defraud their clients.

7.5.1 Front Running

Front running occurs when a broker improperly allows one order to trade ahead of another. The order that goes first usually profits from the price impact of the following order. Front runners hurt the traders whose orders they front-run because they take liquidity that the front-running traders otherwise would have taken. These orders then fill at worse prices than those at which they would have filled.

Front running is most common when a broker holds a large order that will likely move the market. The broker then trades for his own account first, or he tips off a confederate who does the front running.

Front running also hurts the brokers who represent the orders that are front-run. Brokerage clients who pay close attention to how well their brokers perform will discover that their brokers who knowingly or unknowingly allow others to trade in front of their orders do not trade effectively on their behalf. When their poor performance becomes apparent, the clients often direct their orders to other brokers. Firms that employ brokers therefore must be vigilant to ensure that their brokers do not cheat their clients and thereby lose future business for the firm.

7.5.2 Inappropriate Order Exposure

Inappropriate order exposure occurs when a broker shows an order to another trader for the other trader's benefit rather than for his client's benefit. The other trader will typically act on the information, either by front running the order or by refusing to trade with it. Brokers must expose orders only for their client's benefit.

▶ Fraudulent Trade Assignment Example

After dishonest broker Doug fills Earl's buy order, the market rises. Doug then receives another buy order of the same size from his friend Alex. Doug fills Alex's order at a higher average price than Earl's order. To favor his friend, Doug assigns Earl's purchase to Alex and Alex's purchase to Earl. ◀

▶ Prearranged Trading Example

After dishonest broker Doug receives Earl's buy order, he arranges to trade it at a high price with his friend George. Although Doug could have obtained a lower price on the floor, Earl does not know this. ◀

7.5.3 Fraudulent Trade Assignment

Fraudulent trade assignment can occur when a broker executes orders on the same side of the market for more than one client. Each client should get the price at which his or her order filled. A dishonest broker, however, may assign the best prices to his favorite clients.

Fraudulent trade assignment may be especially problematic when brokers also act as dealers. Without appropriate safeguards, broker-dealers may be tempted to take the best trades for themselves and leave the worst trades for their clients.

7.5.4 Prearranged Trading and Kickback Schemes

Prearranged trading occurs when a broker arranges a trade without properly exposing her client's order to other traders who might be willing to offer better prices. Under such circumstances, the client often receives a worse price than he might have received if his broker had properly exposed the order.

Prearranged trading is illegal in floor-based futures markets. In such markets, traders must shout out their bids and offers so that all traders have an opportunity to trade. It is also illegal in most electronic futures exchanges.

Many equity markets and some futures markets allow block traders to prearrange trades that they want to print on the floor of the exchange. The matched trades must be brought to the floor to give floor traders an opportunity to offer better prices if they choose to. These special procedures allow brokers to profit when they have arranged both sides of a difficult transaction and at the same time protect both sides of the trade from potential abuse.

In a *kickback scheme*, a broker sends an order to a dealer with the understanding that the dealer will fill it at a poor price. The dealer gives the broker some consideration—the kickback—in exchange for the opportunity to cheat the client. The dealer may pay the kickback in cash or with nonmonetary considerations.

Brokers often arrange to send dealers order flow in exchange for monetary or nonmonetary payments. Although these *payments for order flow* arrangements appear a lot like kickback schemes, they generally are not. We discuss the economics of payments for order flow in chapter 25.

7.5.5 Unauthorized Trading and Churning

Brokers engage in *unauthorized trading* when they make trades for their clients that their clients have not authorized. Brokers generally make these trades to generate commissions or to manipulate prices. Not surprisingly, the problem is most serious among unsophisticated retail investors.

Clients must pay close attention to their accounts to ensure that their brokers are not making trades of which they do not approve. They must pay particular attention to the trade confirmations that they receive.

Unauthorized trading is especially difficult to detect if the broker has changed the mailing address on the defrauded account. In that case, the victim may not quickly detect the unauthorized trading. To prevent this problem, most brokerage firms do not allow their brokers access to the systems that maintain client mailing addresses. They also require signed instructions to change client mailing addresses, and they compare the signatures with those on file. Finally, they send letters to their clients to advise them when-

> ## Churn 'em and Burn 'em

The term *churn* means to actively agitate in place. Brokers churn accounts when they trade frequently without accomplishing anything. Since the clients suffer, traders call the strategy *churn 'em and burn 'em*.

Brokerages that use churn 'em and burn 'em sales practices must constantly seek new clients as they exhaust the resources or patience of their existing clients. They therefore devote much more of their resources to client acquisition than to client retention.

Not surprisingly, firms with such aggressive sales practices often advertise extensively and engage in endless *cold calling*. Salespeople make *cold calls* when they call upon prospects who have never indicated any interest in the firm's products and services.

The targets of these sales efforts generally are unsophisticated people with money. Aggressive firms especially target lonely people who are eager to form trusting relationships, gamblers who are looking for some action, and envious people who want to catch up with their successful peers.

P. T. Barnum's famous quote, "A sucker is born every minute," well characterizes the prevailing attitude at churn 'em and burn 'em brokerages. ◀

ever someone requests a change of address for their accounts. They address these letters to both the old and the new address to ensure that their clients have a chance to detect a fraudulent change of address. If a fraudulent change of address occurs, clients must respond immediately in order to protect their assets.

Brokers *churn* accounts when they advise their clients to trade more often than is prudent. Brokers suggest these trades to take advantage of opportunities that, they argue, will benefit their clients. The primary purpose of these trades, however, is to generate brokerage commissions. To help prevent these problems, many brokers monitor their client accounts and carefully investigate instances where trading seems excessive.

If the primary beneficiaries of the trading activity are the brokers rather than their clients, the brokers are acting unethically, regardless of whether their clients authorize the trades. In most legal jurisdictions, brokers acting as investment advisers must place the interests of their clients ahead of their own.

Churning is most common when unsophisticated, trusting clients give their brokers authorization to trade their accounts. To prevent churning, regulators require that brokerages know their clients and ensure that their trading is appropriate for them. To prevent abuses, the *compliance officers* at many brokerage firms monitor the turnover in client accounts to identify clients who may be trading too often.

7.5.6 Securities Theft

In extreme cases, dishonest brokers steal funds and securities that their clients entrust to them. Although the probability of theft is very small in most markets, the possibility of theft explains why many clearing and settlement procedures exist. These procedures ensure that securities theft is a small problem in well-developed markets.

Institutional traders prevent the theft of their assets primarily by contracting with *depositories* or *custodians* to hold them for them. When brokers arrange trades for clients who use depositories, the brokers report the

▶ Bearer Bonds

Bearer bonds are bonds for which the issuer does not register its bondholders. Like currency, whoever holds a bearer bond is its presumptive owner. Holders of bearer bonds obtain their interest payments and final principal repayments by presenting coupons clipped from their bonds to the bond issuer. Most banks help facilitate these redemptions.

In the past, almost all bonds were bearer bonds because keeping track of changes in bond ownership was quite costly. Now most new bonds are *registered bonds*. (U.S. government regulations now require that most bonds issued by public corporations in the United States be registered.) Investors like registered bonds because they can obtain new certificates if they lose the original ones and because the issuers can make their interest and principal payments by direct deposit or check. Tax authorities like registered bonds because they can compel issuers to report the interest payments that they make to investors.

Bearer bonds are popular with people who want to hide their assets or their income. Investors who hold these bonds must be especially careful not to lose them. ◀

trades both to their clients and to their clients' depositories. The clients then instruct their depositories to deliver or receive the securities, as necessary, to settle their trades.

The depository system protects traders from fraud by making it impossible for brokers to steal securities or funds, because brokers never hold them. Brokers simply arrange trades.

The depository system is attractive to institutional traders because it allows them to trade easily through any broker with whom they have an appropriate credit relationship. By relying upon a single agency to ultimately settle their trades, traders do not have to worry about whether they have adequately funded their brokerage accounts or whether the securities they want to sell are in their accounts with the brokerages that arranged their sales.

Almost all large institutional traders use depositories to hold their securities. In addition, most retail brokers place the securities that they hold on behalf of their clients in depositories. The brokers use depositories for the same reasons that institutions do. They want to protect themselves from rogues who might steal the securities or try to settle unauthorized trades. They also use the depositories to facilitate clearing and settlement.

Some investors guard their securities by holding them as paper certificates that represent their ownership. Most issuers employ *security registrars* to keep track of their shareholders and bondholders. The registrars issue and cancel certificates on behalf of their issuers. They also pay dividends and interest to security holders. When a paper certificate has been issued for a security, the certificate generally must be delivered to the registrar so that the registrar's record of who owns it can be changed. Investors therefore can protect their ownership by guarding their certificates. Traders who take certificates must be careful not to lose them because they can be expensive or impossible to replace.

Many issuers no longer issue certificates. Instead, their registrars keep electronic records of who owns their issues. This registration system is called *book entry registration*. Registrars have very strong procedures to secure their book entry records against loss and fraudulent changes.

▷ Can Investors Vote More Than 100 Percent of the Shares Outstanding?

When stocks are sold short, the number of shares that beneficial owners think they own is greater than the number of shares outstanding (not counting treasury stock). Consider an example.

BigBroker's client Cleo bought 100 shares of International Widgets, a perennial favorite of economists. Since Cleo leaves the stock in his brokerage account, BigBroker is the holder of record.

Shorty wants to sell short 100 shares of Widgets through his broker, SureBroker. Since SureBroker does not have the shares, it borrows them from BigBroker. Benny buys the shares from Shorty. Benny requests the certificate and holds them in his own name. Benny is now a shareholder of record for 100 shares. Cleo has no idea that BigBroker lent Widgets shares.

Benny and Cleo both believe that they own the stock and that they have a right to vote their shares in any matter that Widgets places before its shareholders. However, if they both could vote, more than 100 percent of the shares could be voted.

In fact, only shareholders of record have a right to vote their shares. Benny has an absolute right to vote his shares. As a beneficial owner, Cleo can only recommend to BigBroker how it should vote the shares.

Brokers usually follow the recommendations of their clients if they can do so. If they have not lent securities, they can vote exactly as their clients wish. Otherwise, they may have fewer shares to vote than their clients may direct them to vote. If this happens, brokers vote their shares in proportion to how their clients direct them to vote. In practice, since many clients do not issue voting instructions for their shares, brokers usually have enough shares to vote if they have not lent too many shares. ◁

7.5.6.1 Securities in Street Name

When traders have their brokers or depositories hold their securities, they hold their securities in *street name*. The issuers then register the brokers or depositories as the *holders of record*, and the brokers or depositories become responsible for keeping track of their *beneficial owners*, who no longer legally own the securities. Instead, the beneficial owners own claims that their brokers or their depositories give them for their securities.

These distinctions are important only with respect to custodial issues. For tax purposes, the government does not care how you hold your securities. These distinctions explain why issuers correspond directly with you when you hold securities in your own name and through your broker when you hold securities in street name.

When you execute a *margin agreement* with your broker, you can use your securities as collateral to borrow money from your broker. When you pledge your securities as collateral for a loan, you *hypothecate* them. Your broker requires that you hold hypothecated securities in street name so that he can sell them if you cannot or will not repay the loan.

Margin agreements also allow brokers to lend securities to short sellers. Clients generally do not know whether their brokers have lent their securities, and they generally do not receive any lending fees. (Some large institutions hold securities in their own name so that they can obtain security-lending fees.) After the short sellers use the borrowed securities to

▷ Cede & Co.

The Depository Trust Co. (DTC) holds about 20 trillion dollars in assets for its participants and their customers. Most of these securities are registered in the name of Cede & Co. as nominee of The Depository Trust Co.

According to folklore, Cede was a clerk at DTC. When DTC started to hold securities in street name, its filing system required a name for the shareholder of record. Not knowing what name to provide, Cede used his own name. In fact, Cede stands for Central Depository. ◁

▶ Sunpoint Securities

Sunpoint Securities was a full-service self-clearing broker-dealer based in Longview, Texas. It started its business in 1989. It ceased operations on November 18, 1999, when it became apparent that it did not have enough assets to cover liabilities owed to its clients.

In a civil lawsuit, the U.S. Securities and Exchange Commission charged the CEO and the CFO of Sunpoint with systematically stealing 25 million dollars from a money market account that the firm maintained for its clients. The SEC's complaint alleged that from December 1997 through November 18, 1999, Sunpoint illegally transferred money market funds, belonging to its clients, to the firm's clearing account. The firm then improperly transferred the funds to satisfy the firm's net capital requirements. The SEC further alleged that the firm's president and CEO also used the funds for their personal benefit. The diversion of client funds resulted in the firm having only 12 million dollars in its client money market account to cover 37 million dollars in money market obligations to its clients. Consequently, Sunpoint was grossly below its net capital and client reserve requirements. ◀

For more information, see SEC Litigation Release no. 16366, dated November 19, 1999 at www.sec.gov/enforce/litigrel/lr16366.htm.

settle their short sales, the lending brokers are no longer owners of record. The new purchasers become the holders of record on the issuer's registry.

7.5.6.2 Brokerage Bankruptcies

When a broker goes bankrupt, traders who deposited assets with the broker risk losing those assets. Bankruptcies often occur when the broker incurs significant trading losses on its own account, when one or more of its clients default on their obligations to the broker, or, most commonly, when someone steals assets from the broker. Traders therefore should carefully consider whether their brokers are creditworthy before they entrust their assets to them.

Brokers naturally want to assure their clients that they are trustworthy and creditworthy. To increase investor confidence, brokers publish their financial accounts for all to see. They may also take out *excess insurance* policies to protect their clients. The insurance companies help regulate brokers to ensure that they do not get into trouble.

Many other organizations subject brokers to regulatory oversight. Exchanges and clearinghouses regulate their members to ensure that they are financially viable, to minimize the costs that insolvent members can impose upon others, and to increase public confidence in their membership. Clearing members that clear for other broker-dealers regulate them to avoid losses that they may inherit if their broker-dealer clients go bankrupt. Broker-dealer associations and governments regulate brokers for similar reasons.

The various regulators ensure that brokers have adequate capital reserves to meet their obligations. They also ensure that brokers have well-functioning managerial controls in place to prevent unexpected losses due to negligence, stupidity, poor luck, or fraud. Finally, they require that brokers have accounting systems which can quickly detect such problems. Brokers accept these regulatory relationships in order to increase investor confidence in their financial integrity.

▶ The SIPC

The U.S. Congress created the Securities Investor Protection Corporation (SIPC) in 1970 to increase confidence in U.S. brokers. Almost all broker-dealers that register with the Securities and Exchange Commission are automatically members of the SIPC. (The only exempt brokers are those who exclusively distribute mutual fund shares, sell variable annuities or insurance, or conduct their business outside the United States.)

If a brokerage fails, the SIPC distributes all securities registered in clients' names and held by the firm to those clients. The remaining securities—those held in street name—and cash are then distributed on a pro rata basis to the clients. The SIPC will satisfy any remaining investor claims up to a maximum of 100,000 dollars for cash and a combined maximum of 500,000 dollars for securities and cash. The SIPC makes such distributions from a special fund it maintains for this purpose. The money comes from assessments that the SIPC levies on its members and from interest that the fund earns on its investments in U.S. Treasury securities. Should the SIPC need more money to satisfy claims, it can borrow up to a billion dollars from the U.S. Treasury.

The largest payout the SIPC has made was in the Sunpoint Securities liquidation. The SIPC paid 31 million dollars to restore stocks and cash that 9,738 investors apparently lost to theft at Sunpoint.

When a brokerage goes bankrupt, clients must quickly file their claims with the bankruptcy court. Most courts accept only claims filed within 30 or 60 days of the publication date of the bankruptcy. In any event, the law prohibits the SIPC from satisfying any claims that it receives more than six months after the bankruptcy is published.

Clients should be notified by mail when a brokerage with which they do business goes bankrupt. In practice, clients may not receive notice because their broker's records are poor or because clients failed to notify their broker of a change of address.

If you maintain an account with a brokerage whose bankruptcy might not immediately come to your attention, you should regularly open your mail to make sure that your brokerage has not gone bankrupt. You should also inquire quickly into your brokerage's financial health if you fail to receive your monthly statement. ◀

For more information, click on www.SIPC.org.

7.5.7 Summary

Most brokers are honest, trustworthy, and creditworthy. They behave well because most brokers are good and honorable people; because they know that a good name is good for their business; and because regulators, markets, competitors, clients, and broker associations have established systems to deter bad behavior.

Unfortunately, not all brokers behave well all the time. To weed out rogue brokers and to help traders recover losses, regulators maintain grievance programs.

Traders who suspect that they have been defrauded should complain to the appropriate regulator. Although many complaints are due to misunderstandings, some are due to dishonest or irresponsible behaviors that typically stop only when regulators take disciplinary actions. If you have been defrauded, your complaint may eventually lead to reparations. At a minimum, your complaint may prevent someone else from losing.

▶ What Works Best When You Never Use It?

All types of security systems—burglar alarms, guards, armies, criminal justice systems, and regulatory systems—work best when they deter bad behavior. Consequently, the better they work, the less necessary they seem. Unfortunately, many people do not fully appreciate the value of deterrence when confronted with its cost. The former is intangible, whereas the latter is concrete. ◀

▶ **How to Complain Effectively**

Regulators offer several programs that collect and attempt to resolve complaints that the public may have about the firms and brokers who carry their accounts. Full descriptions of these programs appear on the following web pages:

National Association of Securities Dealers Regulation	http://www.nasdr.com/2100.asp
Securities and Exchange Commission	http://www.sec.gov/complaint.shtml
National Futures Association	http://www.nfa.futures.org/dispute/index.html
Commodity Futures Trading Commission	http://www.cftc.gov/cftc/cftccomplaints.htm

In addition, most exchanges have grievance procedures.

7.6 SUMMARY

Brokers help their clients arrange trades. They match orders, they find traders willing to trade, and they clear and settle trades. Clients employ brokers for these tasks because brokers can do them more cheaply than they can themselves.

The principal–agent problem affects relations between brokers and their clients. Brokers may not always do what their clients pay them to do. Clients solve the problem by rewarding their brokers when they perform well and penalizing them when they do not.

Unfortunately, most brokerage clients cannot easily measure their brokers' performance. Regulators consequently concern themselves with best execution standards. These standards define minimum service guarantees that clients can expect from their brokers. The standards are meaningful only if clients or market regulators can audit broker behavior.

The structures of all mechanisms which facilitate trade reflect the unfortunate fact that not all traders are honest and reliable. Traders have created elaborate clearing, settlement, margin, custodial, and audit procedures to ensure that all negotiated trades settle, all parties honor their financial commitments, traders do not violate rules, and nobody steals assets that belong to others. In addition, government, exchange, and industry association regulators oversee trading to protect the integrity of the markets.

7.7 SOME POINTS TO REMEMBER

- Brokers help arrange and settle trades for their clients.
- Brokers and exchanges compete with each other to arrange trades.
- Cash management is a significant source of profits for many brokers.
- The principal–agency problem can be a significant problem in the brokerage industry because quality of service is hard to measure.
- Soft commissions allow institutional funds to use trading commissions to finance their expenses and thereby report lower expense ratios.

- Many aspects of brokerage operations and of clearing and settlement mechanisms reduce the potential for fraud among traders.

7.8 QUESTIONS FOR THOUGHT

1. Do brokers work for their clients or for themselves?
2. Are payments for order flow kickbacks?
3. What is best execution?
4. Why should a client value a broker's reputation?
5. Can you buy services that you cannot measure?
6. How can regulators distinguish between exchanges and brokers?
7. How do you solve the settlement credit problem when you want to buy a used computer advertised by an individual in an eBay Internet auction?
8. What is the difference, if any, between proprietary trading and dealing? Should we allow brokers or dealers to sell information about their order flows and their limit order books to proprietary traders? Should we allow dealers to use computers to process this information for their own benefit?
9. What obligations do brokers have to their clients when they send orders to dealers who have large proprietary trading operations?
10. Most people obtain advice about investments and about financial planning from brokers. The brokers usually do not charge them specific fees for these services. Instead, their clients pay them large brokerage commissions or annual fees based on their account balances. Why is this the case?
11. Brokers in most trading markets guarantee that their clients' trades will settle. Brokers in real estate markets almost never guarantee trade settlement. What differences between these markets account for the difference in how brokers participate in the trade settlement process?
12. Many exchanges limit the number of their members. Once the limit is reached, traders who want to become members must buy a seat from an existing member. Why would exchanges limit their memberships? Why might they expand the number of their members? What determines the value of an exchange seat?
13. Of what value is a large entertainment budget to a new broker?
14. How does a reputation for being a difficult negotiator affect trading profits?
15. Of what importance is a broker's reputation when many traders cannot measure the quality of service they receive? What if no traders can measure execution quality?
16. What is the practical difference, if any, between losing a reputation for honest dealings and acquiring a reputation for dishonest dealings?
17. Suppose that your futures broker allows you to borrow against T-bills you hold in your account. The T-bill yield is 5 percent; the broker will lend to you at 10 percent; the broker will not pay you interest on the cash in your account; and the broker charges you 40 dollars to buy or sell any number of 10,000 dollar T-bills. You have 200,000 dollars of equity in the account and you have futures positions that require only 100,000 dollars of margin. Your variation mar-

gin cash flows average about 10,000 dollars per day. How much of your equity should you invest in T-bills?

18. Most investment advisers have many clients. What fairness problems arise when an adviser uses soft dollars funded by client commissions to purchase investment research?

19. Can you explain why deep discount retail brokers typically charge a flat commission per stock trade, U.S. institutional equity brokers typically charge a fixed rate per share, and other institutional equity brokers base their commissions on the value of the transaction?

20. Some brokers have defrauded their clients and their employers by giving their clients false statements of their accounts. The brokers intercepted or misdirected official account statements and sent out fraudulent statements in their place. How can clients and brokerage firms detect such frauds?

The two chapters in this part discuss how trading benefits individual traders and the entire economy. Chapter 8 explains why traders trade. We introduce 32 types of traders and identify the benefits that each obtains from trading. Remarkably, traders often do not clearly understand why they trade. They therefore often trade when they should not or fail to trade when they should. Traders who understand why they trade will generally trade more effectively.

In chapter 9, we consider how well-functioning markets benefit the entire economy. The primary benefits come from informative prices and from market liquidity. We explain how well-functioning markets help market-based economies use their resources most efficiently. We also consider a framework for evaluating public policy.

Part II

▷

The Benefits of Trade

8

▷

Why
People
Trade

People trade to invest, to borrow, to exchange assets, to hedge risks, to distribute risks, to gamble, to speculate, or to deal. We consider each of these objectives in this chapter and explain how markets help traders achieve them.

You must understand why people trade in order to use markets effectively. Markets provide many valuable opportunities. To take advantage of them, you must first recognize them.

By considering why people trade, you will better understand why you trade and whether you should trade. Many traders do not fully recognize the reasons why they trade. Consequently, they pursue inappropriate trading strategies or they trade when trading is counterproductive to their true interests. The optimal trading strategy for a given trading problem depends on the problem. You cannot trade well if you do not know why you want to trade.

Knowing why people trade may also help you determine whether other traders understand why they are trading. This skill is very important because you can usually distinguish good money managers from poor ones by whether they understand well why they trade. It is also important because traders who do not fully understand why they trade often trade foolishly. If you can identify such traders, you may be able to profit from their foolishness.

If you engage in any trading strategy that depends on the volume of trade, you must understand why people trade in order to interpret volumes properly. Many factors cause people to trade. If your trading strategy depends on one of these factors, you will want to examine volumes carefully. However, you must be careful to recognize when other factors may cause people to trade. Otherwise, you may misinterpret volumes and trade when you should not.

Markets are successful only when people trade in them. If you want to design a new market, or if your business depends on trading in a successful market, you must understand why—and how—people trade.

Trading is a zero-sum game in an important accounting sense. In a *zero-sum game*, the total gains of the winners are exactly equal to the total losses of the losers. Trading is a zero-sum game because the combined gains and losses of buyers and sellers always sum to zero. If a buyer profits from a trade, the seller loses the opportunity to profit by the same amount. Likewise, if a buyer loses from a trade, the seller avoids an identical loss.

Successful traders must understand the implications of the zero-sum game. To trade profitably, traders must trade with people who will lose. Profit-motivated traders therefore must understand why losers trade in order to know when they should trade.

Finally, you must understand why people trade in order to form well-reasoned opinions about market structures. Different structures favor dif-

176

ferent trader types. If you intend to influence a decision about market structure, you should first consider how the decision affects various traders. The benefits that traders obtain from markets depend on why they trade. Regulators and other interested parties must therefore understand these reasons.

This chapter identifies the main reasons why people trade. We will refer to them throughout the rest of the book. Pay close attention to the distinctions between investing, speculating, and gambling. When traders confuse these important concepts, they often trade poorly. When regulators confuse them, they often adopt policies that hurt the markets. Also consider why liquid markets benefit most traders. When you understand why people trade, you will appreciate why all market participants care about liquidity.

For expository clarity, we will associate a stylized trader with each reason for trading, and we will assume that the stylized trader trades only for that reason. In practice, traders often trade for many reasons. The complexity of their motives explains why many traders get confused and fail to fully recognize why they trade. By considering stylized traders, we simplify our discussions and ultimately make it easier for you to identify the different reasons why people trade.

Our stylized traders are profit-motivated traders, utilitarian traders, or futile traders. *Profit-motivated traders* trade only because they rationally expect to profit from their trades. Speculators and dealers are profit-motivated traders. *Utilitarian traders* trade because they expect to obtain some benefit from trading besides trading profits. Investors, borrowers, asset exchangers, hedgers, and gamblers are utilitarian traders. *Futile traders* believe that they are profit-motivated traders. Although they expect to trade profitably, their expectations are not rational. They have no advantages that would allow them to be profitable traders. Utilitarian traders and futile traders lose on average to profit-motivated traders because trading is a zero-sum game.

Traders are either informed or uninformed. *Informed traders* can form reliable opinions about whether instruments are fundamentally undervalued or overvalued. The *fundamental value* of an instrument is the value that all traders would agree upon if they knew all available information about the instrument and if they could properly analyze this information. An instrument is *undervalued* when its market price is below its fundamental value. It is *overvalued* when its price is above fundamental value. Since nobody actually knows fundamental values, traders must estimate them. Informed traders typically form their opinions from insightful analyses of publicly available information or from simple analyses of information that is not widely known. Informed traders speculate on their information by buying undervalued instruments and selling overvalued instruments. Informed traders are therefore profit-motivated traders. *Uninformed traders* do not know whether instruments are fundamentally undervalued or overvalued. Either they cannot form reliable opinions about values or they choose not to. Uninformed traders include utilitarian traders, futile traders, and some types of profit-motivated traders.

Our discussion starts with, and primarily focuses on, utilitarian traders. At the end of the chapter, we will introduce the profit-motivated traders and the futile traders. Detailed discussions of how they behave appear in subsequent chapters devoted exclusively to their various styles.

▶ **Multiple Identities**

Many traders simultaneously invest, speculate, and gamble. They invest when they need to move money from the present to the future. They speculate when they try to use information about future security prospects to obtain a better return on their investments. They gamble when they focus more attention on favorable outcomes than on losing outcomes.

Their multiplicity of interests often compromises their judgment. Investors frequently speculate without thinking about whether they would be good speculators, and speculators often gamble without considering whether their emotional needs have influenced their judgment. ◀

8.1 UTILITARIAN TRADERS

Utilitarian traders trade to obtain some benefit besides trading profits. Investors and borrowers trade to move money forward or backward through time. Asset exchangers trade to exchange one asset for another asset of greater value to them. Hedgers trade to exchange risks. Gamblers trade for entertainment. Fledglings trade to learn how to trade. Cross-subsidizers trade to transfer wealth to other people. Tax avoiders trade to minimize their taxes by exploiting tax loopholes. We will consider each of these traders in turn.

8.1.1 Investors and Borrowers

People often need to move money from one point in time to another. Workers need to move their current earnings from the present to the future in order to finance their retirements. Students need to move their future earnings to the present to pay tuition. Young couples need to move their future earnings to the present to buy houses.

These problems are all examples of intertemporal cash flow timing problems. People face *intertemporal cash flow timing problems* when their incomes and expenses do not always coincide. When their incomes are more than their expenses, they *invest* money to move money into the future or they *repay* money that they borrowed in the past. When their incomes are less than their expenses, they *borrow* money from the future or they *liquidate* investments that they made in the past. People invest, borrow, liquidate, and repay to move money forward or backward through time.

Corporations and governments also face intertemporal cash flow problems. The most common problem that corporations face is inadequate current cash flow to pay for investments that will generate future revenues. To solve this problem, they borrow money from the future by selling bonds or stock shares. Governments most commonly borrow against their future tax revenues to finance current spending. They may use the money to fund projects that will produce benefits in the future, to fund current services, or to enrich poor people, disabled people, retirees, immigrants, and, in many cases, farmers and, manufacturers.

Although people, corporations, and governments invest and borrow to move money through time, in aggregate no money actually moves through time. Instead, for every dollar invested, someone must borrow a dollar. The assets that investors use to move money from the present to the future therefore are the same assets that borrowers use to move money from the future to the present. Traders buy assets when they want to move money to the future or when they repay money that they previously moved back in time from the current present to the past. They sell assets when they want to move money from the future to the present, or when they redeem money that they previously moved forward in time.

Investors use various financial and real assets to move money forward through time. *Financial assets* include stocks, bonds, mutual funds, insurance policies, certificates of deposit, demand deposits, and currencies. *Real assets* include real estate, machinery, commodities, precious metals, and going business concerns. Investors who cannot, or who would rather not, manage their own funds give their money to banks, mutual funds, retirement funds, insurance companies, and other financial intermediaries to invest for them.

▶ A Ballpark Estimate

How much trading volume in the U.S. equity markets is due to trading by pure investors? Much less than you might imagine! Here is a rough estimate.

Saving for retirement is by far the most important investment problem that people face. We can get a rough estimate of the annual dollar volume of private investment transactions by estimating how much retirees spend of their own money. In 2000, total personal consumption in the United States was 7 trillion dollars of which 1 trillion dollars was for health services. Assume that 20 percent of the non-health consumption was by retirees, and that retirees consumed 80 percent of the health services, so that retirees consumed a total of 2 trillion dollars. Retirees received about 0.7 trillion dollars in benefits from social security, Medicare, and Medicaid. They therefore had to finance 1.3 trillion dollars of consumption.

In 2000, the total dollar volume of U.S. equities trading was more than 43 trillion dollars (table 3-5). If retirees financed their consumption only by selling stocks, they would account for only 3 percent of all trading volume. Stocks, however, represent only about 20 percent of the capital assets of the country (table 3-4). If retirees sold all capital assets equally, their equity trading would account for only 0.6 percent of equity volume.

Workers who invest for their retirements also trade. If they expected no real return on their investments, if the population were not growing, if the retirement age were constant, and if the payments from Social Security and Medicare were expected to remain constant, workers would have to invest 1.3 trillion dollars per year to finance their retirements. Although these assumptions are obviously wrong (a positive expected real return lowers the estimate; a growing population raises it; a growing retirement age lowers it; and decreasing payments from government programs increases it), they give us a ballpark estimate for how much workers must be saving for retirement. If workers place 20 percent of their savings in the stock market, and if they buy and hold their securities, they will be responsible for another 0.6 percent of equity volume.

The total of 1.2 percent from retirees and workers overestimates the actual total investment-motivated trading volume because workers and retirees mostly invest and disinvest through private pension funds and mutual funds. These funds do not have to trade when the deposits made by (or on behalf of) workers offset the redemptions made by (or on behalf of) retirees. This happens much of the time so that the 1.2 percent investment-motivated trading volume estimate is much too high.

It is also too high because workers will occasionally trade directly with retirees. In which case, our estimate will double-count trading volume.

The assumptoins in this analysis are quite crude. Yet, even if we increased our estimate ten-fold, we would still only account for less than one-eighth of all equity trading volume! People clearly trade equities for many reasons besides investment. ◀

Borrowers create and sell various debt instruments to move money from the future to the present. These instruments include bonds, commercial paper, mortgage notes, home equity loans, bank loans, and credit card obligations.

Borrowers who create and sell debt instruments to public investors are *issuers*. Only creditworthy borrowers can successfully issue debt securities. The investors who buy their issues must be confident that the issuers ultimately will redeem them. Large corporations and governments are typically the only borrowers who can issue debt directly into the marketplace. Most

▶ Economic Proof That No One Will Ever Invent a Time Machine

To the list of logical contradictions associated with time travel, consider the following economic argument. If a time machine could freely move people and their money through time, the after-tax real rate of interest would always be zero. If it were ever positive, profit-motivated time travelers would carry money from the future to the present to invest. They would then go back to the future to liquidate their investment at a profit. The effect of their trading would be to depress real interest rates toward zero. If they carried enough money or if they repeated the cycle often enough, they would eventually force the real interest rate to zero. Since real rates of interest generally are positive, we can confidently conclude that either people will never invent time machines, or they will be too expensive for arbitrageurs to operate profitably. ◀

Source: Marc Reinganum, "Is Time Travel Impossible? A Financial Proof," Journal of Portfolio Management 13, 1 (1986): 10–12.

individuals and small businesses cannot issue public debt because most investors cannot easily determine whether they are creditworthy.

Borrowers who cannot issue debt instruments directly to the public borrow money from banks, finance companies, and other financial institutions that will loan them money. These financial intermediaries then often issue debt instruments to finance the loans that they make.

Banks and finance companies can lend money to individuals and small businesses because they are organized to cheaply determine whether their customers are creditworthy. Compared to public investors, they can more efficiently collect on small loans, especially if they are in default.

Corporations that need to finance projects may issue equity instead of debt securities. They may be unable to issue debt because they are not sufficiently creditworthy. They may choose not to issue debt because they do not want to assume the risks associated with highly leveraged balance sheets.

Firms that undertake very risky projects often cannot raise money through debt offerings because investors fear the company will be unable to pay off the debt. If that happens, the company will go bankrupt and the debt holders will own the remaining assets of the company. When this outcome is likely, investors prefer to start out as equity holders so that they can exercise some control over the management of the firm from the start. In addition, when substantial losses are likely, investors will not provide financing unless substantial returns are likely. Since only equity can provide such return distributions, very risky firms must raise money by issuing equity instead of debt.

Investors and borrowers carefully choose the assets that they trade to solve their intertemporal cash flow timing problems. Their decisions depend on the expected returns, risks, and transaction costs of the various assets. Investors naturally favor assets that have high expected returns, low risk, and low transaction costs. Borrowers favor assets that they expect will cost them the least to create, to service, and to repay. As a rule, the riskiest assets and those which are most expensive to trade have the highest expected returns. Traders must carefully consider these factors when deciding how to move money through time.

Textbooks about investments provide detailed discussions of how investors and borrowers weigh these various factors and of how their decisions affect asset prices and expected returns. For present purposes, merely note that investors and borrowers best solve their intertemporal cash flow timing problems when their transaction costs are low. Transaction costs are what people pay to move money from one point in time to another. Since transaction costs are low in liquid markets, investors and borrowers like liquid markets. When transaction costs are high, trading is an expensive method of moving money through time.

Investors expect to get a fair rate of return when using the markets to move money into the future. Indeed, many investors will defer their consumption only because of the investment returns that they expect to receive. Since investors are uninformed traders, the rate of return that they expect to receive does not depend on any private information that they may have. The fair rate of return is therefore an unconditional expected return.

The *unconditional expected return* to an investment has two components. The *real risk-free interest rate* is the return that investors expect to receive for deferring their consumption without risk of a real loss. (Investors suffer

▶ Wealth-Moving Technologies in Less-Developed Economies

In economies where property rights are poorly defined, and where people cannot effectively enforce contracts, financial markets do not function well. In such economies, strongmen often steal assets and many people refuse to settle their contracts when they have lost money.

To move wealth through time in such economies, people must resort to other methods. Most lending is within families because family bonds often ensure performance. Strongmen dominate public lending markets because they can use extralegal means to enforce their contracts. Investors typically invest in assets that they can hide or that only they can control. These assets include gold and silver, which they can easily hide, and human capital and housing, which thieves and corrupt officials cannot easily take. Finally, families tend to be large in economies with poorly developed financial markets because parents invest in children to provide for their retirement years. ◀

real losses if they cannot buy as much in the future as they could have bought had they not invested.) The real rate of interest depends on how much money investors and borrowers want to move through time. It is usually positive because people would want to move more money from the future to the present than vice versa if there were no cost of doing so. Since money cannot actually move through time, the real risk-free interest rate must be positive to discourage some borrowers and encourage some investors.

The *risk premium* is the additional expected return that investors demand to compensate them for the risk that their investment may not actually return the real risk-free interest rate. Risky assets have risk premiums because they are poor vehicles for moving money through time. Investors do not like them because they risk losing their wealth when using them. To get them to bear these risks, they must be compensated for holding these assets.

Although all traders hope to receive extraordinary returns from their investments, investors do not expect them. In this respect, they differ from speculators. *Speculators* trade because they expect to receive a higher return than the unconditional return that investors require to defer their consumption and to bear risks. They form these expectations based on private information they have about future returns. The expected returns of speculators are therefore *conditional expected returns*. Speculators expect higher returns from their positions than do investors.

8.1.2 Asset Exchangers

Asset exchangers use markets to exchange assets that they own for other assets that are of greater immediate use to them. Spot commodity markets and foreign exchange markets are the largest organized markets in which asset exchangers trade. In most asset exchanges, a buyer pays money or similar financial assets to a seller who delivers a commodity or a currency. In *bartered trades*, both traders exchange goods or services. In such trades, the distinction between buyer and seller is not always clear.

In a sense, all voluntary trades are asset exchanges. In a voluntary trade, traders acquire assets that are of greater value to them than the ones they give up. They would not trade otherwise. Investing and borrowing are special cases of asset exchanges. Investors exchange current money for assets that allow them to move money forward through time. Borrowers create

▶ Examples of Asset Exchanges

- U.S.-based Volkswagen importers use the currency markets to exchange U.S. dollars for the euros they need to buy Volkswagens in Germany.

- Photographic film manufacturers use the spot silver markets to purchase the silver they need to make their films.

- Feedlot operators use the spot soybean market to purchase the soybeans they need to feed their livestock. ◀

The Carryout Cash Market

One of the more interesting cash markets is the market for cash. ATM operators must regularly put currency into their machines so that their customers can withdraw cash on demand. These machines require properly formatted bills. If the bills are dirty, wrinkled, or sticky, they can jam the machines or cause them to dispense cash inaccurately.

A small industry has developed to package ATM-fit currency for use in ATM machines. The list price for a 20,000-dollar brick of 10 bundles of 100 20-dollar bills is 20,003.50 dollars. The 3.50 dollar premium over face value is the price that small ATM operators pay to have bank cash vaults recondition and package currency that they can confidently use in their ATM machines. (Large ATM operators negotiate better prices.) ATM-fit currency is thus a commodity in the same sense that silver is a commodity. ◄

debt instruments that they exchange for money they can use to buy things now. Although we could classify all trades as asset exchanges, we use the term only for trades that traders arrange because they have a current use for the item they acquire. Practitioners often call the markets in which such trades take place *cash markets* or *spot markets*.

Spot commodity and currency markets are some of the world's biggest markets. The foreign exchange markets are especially large. For example, according to the Bank for International Settlements, the average daily global volume in the spot currency markets was 1.2 trillion dollars in April 2001. This volume is about 10 times greater than global equities volume.

Asset exchangers like liquid cash markets. Such markets allow them to convert their assets from one form to another at low cost. Markets also must trade the assets that traders need. A liquid cash market for soybeans in Chicago is of little use to a Texas dairy that needs to buy soybeans for delivery in Texas. The dairy would benefit more from a liquid soybean market in Texas.

8.1.3 Hedgers and Hedging

Many economic activities expose people and businesses to serious financial risks. Consider four examples:

- Wheat farmers risk losing money if the price of wheat falls after they plant their fields but before they harvest them. The price they receive for their wheat might be too low to allow them to recover the costs of planting and cultivating it.
- Wholesale bakers risk losing money if the price of flour rises after they enter fixed-price contracts to supply bread but before they have purchased the flour necessary to make the bread. The cost of baking the bread might be greater than the fixed price they will receive.
- Traders who speculate in individual stocks risk losing money if the stocks they buy drop because the market as a whole drops. Speculators in individual stocks may be able to predict which stocks will beat the market, but they usually cannot predict what the whole market will do. If the market falls, they could lose money even if their stocks outperform the market.
- Banks that lend money at fixed long-term rates and borrow money at variable short-term rates risk losing money if interest rates rise. Their revenues would be fixed, but their borrowing costs would rise.

The risks in these examples are all very substantial. They can easily cause their holders to go bankrupt. Fortunately, markets and trading strategies have evolved that allow traders to avoid these risks.

Hedgers use the markets to reduce their exposure to substantial financial risks. They hedge their risks by selling or buying instruments whose values are correlated or inversely correlated with the risks that they face. Their positions in these instruments are their *hedges*, and the instruments are their *hedging vehicles*. When properly executed, the risks in their hedges offset their financial risks. Their *hedged positions*—the combinations of their positions in the original risk and in the hedging vehicle—are less risky than either position taken separately.

Traders use many instruments to hedge their financial risks. The remainder of this section examines how various hedging strategies can help solve the risk management problems in the above examples. These examples illustrate the use of forward contracts, futures contracts, option contracts, and swaps as hedging vehicles.

8.1.3.1 Some Commodity Hedging Examples: Wheat and Flour

The risk that prices will change for the worse is *price risk*. The price risk that traders face depends on whether they lose from an increase or a decrease in price.

Wheat farmers and bread bakers face complementary price risks. If the price of wheat falls, the farmers will lose money but the bakers, who have to buy flour made from wheat, will save money. Likewise, if the price of wheat rises, the bakers will lose money but the farmers will profit.

Wheat farmers and bread bakers are *natural hedgers* because they face complementary risks. They can eliminate their exposure to their respective risks by combining their operations or by entering contracts that allow them to assume each other's risks.

Hedging by Combining Businesses

Since the two risks are complementary, farmers and bakers can arrange to share their risks and thereby eliminate them. For example, by going into partnership, a farmer and a baker can eliminate their collective exposure to fluctuations in wheat prices. If the price of wheat rises, their farming profits will offset their baking losses. If the price falls, their farming losses will offset their baking profits. This partnership would be an example of a *vertically integrated firm*. Many firms integrate vertically to avoid exposures to price fluctuations in the markets for their intermediate goods.

Although a partnership would allow a farmer and a baker to manage their price risks, it may not be the best solution to their risk management problems. Most farmers do not know much about the wholesale baking business, and most wholesale bakers do not know much about farming. Their ignorance of each other's operations would complicate their management of the partnership.

Hedging with Forward Contracts

Farmers and bakers can also manage their price risks by exchanging forward contracts. A *forward contract* is an agreement to trade something in the future at a price that is set now. Hedgers frequently use forward contracts to hedge price risks.

In our example, a farmer would create and sell a forward wheat contract to a baker. The contract would specify a price at which the baker would buy the farmer's future harvest. The farmer then would be long wheat in the ground and short the forward contract. The baker would be short flour and long the forward contract. Since the value of the forward contract depends on the price of wheat, the two traders would have hedged positions. If wheat prices rise, the forward contract will rise in value. The farmer's greater farming profits will offset the losses on his short forward contract position, and the baker's profits on her long forward contract position will offset her

▶ Covering the Naked

Traders sometimes call unhedged positions *naked positions* because they expose them to risks. They call hedged positions *covered positions* because they cover the risks to which naked positions are exposed. ◀

baking losses. If wheat prices fall, the forward price will drop in value. The farmer's forward contract profits then will offset his farming losses, and the baker's greater baking profits will offset her short forward position losses. If the farmer and the baker can construct *perfectly hedged positions*, their total profits will no longer depend on future changes in the price of grain.

Although some farmers and bakers may manage their risks by exchanging forward contracts, three significant problems make this method infeasible for most farmers and bakers:

- To execute a forward contract, a farmer and a baker either must know each other or a broker must introduce them. Without a well-organized market, they may have trouble finding each other.

- Each of the two contractors must trust that the other will honor his or her commitment. If the price of wheat drops before the contract delivery date, the baker will prefer to ignore the contract and buy cheaper wheat. The farmer must trust that the baker will buy his wheat at the agreed-upon price. If the price of wheat rises, the farmer will prefer to ignore the contract and sell his wheat at a higher price. The baker must trust that the farmer will deliver his wheat anyway. The baker and the farmer must know each other well to confidently trust each other.

- The farmer and baker may find it difficult to arrange delivery terms that are convenient to both. The delivery terms of a contract specify where, when, how much, how, and exactly what the seller will deliver to the buyer. The farmer and baker may be geographically distant from each other, or the baker may be interested in a different grade of grain than the farmer can deliver. In addition, if the baker does not mill his own flour, he will prefer to receive flour rather than grain.

These problems ensure that forward contracts are attractive hedging vehicles only for traders who trade with each other in the normal course of business. Since such relationships are usually one-to-one relationships, forward markets generally are not liquid.

Hedging with Futures Contracts

To address these problems, markets have developed a special type of forward contract called a futures contract. A *futures contract* is a standardized forward contract for which a *clearinghouse* guarantees the performance of the buyer and seller by interposing itself between the buyer and seller of every trade. It acts as the seller for every buyer and as the buyer for every seller. The clearinghouse guarantee allows any buyer to trade with any seller without worrying about credit risk. Contract standardization ensures that all traders trade the same instrument. These features make futures markets very liquid.

All futures contracts traded in a given commodity market for the same delivery month are identical. In particular, they all have the same delivery terms. Few traders, however, make or take delivery because most traders prefer different delivery terms. To avoid delivery, buyers sell their contracts and sellers repurchase their contracts before delivery. Since the contracts have the same delivery terms, and since the clearinghouse is on the opposite side of all positions, traders can close their positions by trading with any other trader. To be released from their contractual obligations, they do not have to trade with the person with whom they originally traded.

Suppose that the wheat farmer in our example is in North Dakota. To hedge the price risk associated with his crop, he sells September Chicago Board of Trade wheat futures contracts short. These contracts call for the delivery of 5,000 bushels of wheat on the last business day of September. The contract specifies the types and grades of wheat that may be delivered. It also requires that the delivery occur in Chicago, Toledo, or St. Louis at specified grain elevators. The farmer does not intend to ship his wheat to any of these cities for delivery. Instead, he will sell it to a local grain elevator operator after he gathers his harvest. At the same time, he will repurchase his futures contract. Although the futures contract calls for delivery in cities distant from North Dakota, it is still a good hedging vehicle for the farmer because wheat prices in North Dakota are closely correlated with Chicago wheat futures contract prices.

Wheat prices in Chicago and North Dakota are closely related because shipping wheat between these two locations does not cost much. Under normal conditions, the difference in the two wheat prices can be no greater than the average cost of shipping a bushel of grain. If prices differ by more than the shipping cost, an *arbitrageur* would buy wheat where it is cheaper (typically in North Dakota), sell it where it is more expensive, and ship it to make the delivery.

The difference between the Chicago wheat futures price and a local cash wheat price is the *local basis*. Since cash prices vary slightly by location, the basis also varies by location. The local basis typically reflects the costs of shipping wheat from where it grows to where it is used. The basis obtained its name because grain traders throughout the Midwest typically express their local cash prices in terms of a premium to or discount from the Chicago futures price. The Chicago futures price is the *base price*, and the premium to or discount from the Chicago price is the basis.

The wholesale baker can hedge her price risk by buying wheat futures contracts when she enters a fixed-price contract to supply bread in the future. When she actually needs the flour, she will buy it from a local miller and simultaneously sell her futures contracts. The futures contract is a good hedging vehicle for her because Chicago wheat futures prices are closely correlated with the prices she pays for flour.

Traders hedge with futures when they want to reduce price risk. The futures hedge effectively locks in a future price so that hedgers will not lose from an adverse price change or profit from a favorable price change. A futures hedge therefore eliminates both downside risk and upside potential. Since the gains and losses on a futures contract are almost exactly proportional to changes in the underlying cash price, a futures hedge is a *linear hedge*.

8.1.3.2 Two Stock Hedging Examples

Given careful research, Jack expects that Apple's newest computer will be more successful than is widely thought. He therefore buys 550,000 dollars of Apple common stock (AAPL). The price of Apple depends on the success of the new computer and on other marketwide factors. Even if the new computer is successful, Jack may lose money if Apple falls in a marketwide drop.

> ### ▶ Pork Bellies on the Lawn
>
> Comedians occasionally tell stories about speculators who buy futures contracts and forget to close their positions before the delivery date. In these stories, a truck pulls up to the procrastinator's suburban house and dumps a 40,000-pound load of fresh pork bellies on his lawn. (A pork belly is an uncured side of pork.) The comedians then describe the resulting chaos.
>
> In practice, brokers attempt to contact their clients before delivery to determine their intentions. If a broker cannot reach a client and if the broker knows that the client does not intend to accept delivery, the broker usually will sell the contract to avoid delivery. In the event that the contract actually delivers, the delivery would be to a warehouse rather than to a front lawn. ◀

Hedging with Index Futures Contracts

To hedge against this risk, Jack sells December S&P 500 Index futures contracts at the Chicago Mercantile Exchange. The *S&P 500 Index* is an index of stock market values prepared by Standard and Poor's Corporation. The index is proportional to the total market value of 500 large stocks that Standard & Poor's believes broadly represent all large U.S. stocks. The final settlement value of the December S&P 500 Index futures contract is 250 times a special opening quotation of the S&P 500 Index computed from the opening values of the constituent stocks on the third Friday of December. The value of the contract therefore fluctuates with the value of the S&P 500 Index.

Jack believes that the average relation between percentage price changes in Apple and in the S&P 500 Index is approximately one to one. (The *beta* of the stock is 1.0.) Jack therefore wants to sell about 550,000 (550,000 × 1.0) nominal dollars of S&P 500 Index contracts to hedge his Apple position. Since the current value of the S&P Index is 1,084, Jack sells two contracts, which gives him about 542,000 (2 × 250 × 1,084) dollars of index risk exposure.

If Jack is right about Apple, the stock will outperform the market, whether the market moves up or down. If the market drops and pulls Apple down with it, Jack will lose on his Apple position, but he will profit on his short index futures position. If Apple indeed outperforms the market, Apple will drop less than the market, and Jack will make more money on his short position than he loses in Apple. If the market rises, Jack will lose on his short index futures position. If Apple indeed outperforms the market, Jack will make more money in Apple than he loses in the index futures contract. Regardless of what the market does, Jack will profit if Apple outperforms the market.

By hedging his bet with index futures contracts, Jack can limit his risk exposure only to whether Apple will beat the market or not. Since his research advantage is specific to Apple, the hedged position exposes him only to those risks where he has a competitive advantage. Since he cannot predict the market any better than anyone else can, he would like to avoid exposure to market risk. Speculators are generally most successful when they expose themselves only to the risks they understand best.

Hedging with Stock Option Contracts

Jack also could hedge his position in Apple by buying Apple put options. Put options would allow him to sell his position at a fixed *strike price* at any time before the option *expiration date*. If the price of Apple drops below the strike price, Jack would exercise his put options and thereby limit his losses. The purchase price of the options—the *options premium*—is the cost of this insurance. Jack would buy Apple put options rather than sell them because put option prices vary inversely with common stock prices.

An options hedge is a *nonlinear hedge* because the relation between option prices and their underlying stock prices is nonlinear. Put contract prices decrease as stock prices rise, but their rates of decrease decline as prices rise. (The relation would be linear if the rate of decrease were constant.) This nonlinear relation allows Jack to hedge his downside risk fully while preserving the potential for upside appreciation. When the stock price is well below the strike price, the put option is quite valuable. Changes in the put price are approximately the same size (but of opposite sign) as changes in the stock price, so that increases in the put option price almost completely offset further drops in the stock price. However, when the stock price is high relative to the strike price, the put option has little value. Changes in the put price, then, are much smaller than changes in the stock price, so that further losses from the put options hardly offset further increases in stock prices.

Jack may use put options to hedge his downside risk even if he never intends to exercise them. Since put option prices rise as the price of Apple falls, Jack can achieve his hedging goals simply by selling the options when he no longer wants to hedge.

According to the *options put–call parity theorem*, the combination of a long position in Apple and a long position in Apple puts is essentially the same as a long position in Apple call options. Both strategies would allow Jack to profit if the price of Apple rises and would limit his losses if Apple drops for any reason. If Jack wishes to hedge a preexisting position in Apple stock, he would probably buy puts. The strategy would be especially attractive if Jack has a large unrealized gain in Apple stock on which he does not want to pay taxes. If he wishes to establish a new position in Apple with upside potential and limited downside potential, he would probably buy call options.

The difference between hedging downside loss via futures and via options lies in the trade-offs made to eliminate the downside risk. In a futures hedge, the hedger gives up upside potential, but does not have to pay a premium for the hedge. In an options hedge, the hedger gives up a premium, but gets to keep the upside potential.

Jack might prefer the stock options hedge to the index futures hedge if he is uncertain about the quality of his information. The options hedge will limit his losses if he is wrong about Apple's value.

Jack might also prefer to use the stock options hedge if he believes that a decline in the market is more likely than an increase. The motivation for such a decision, however, is purely speculative. Jack also could act on this opinion by buying index futures contracts or index call option contracts.

8.1.3.3 An Interest Rate Hedging Example

Wilshire Savings and Loan borrows money from its depositors at variable short-term rates and lends money to homeowners at long fixed rates. If interest rates rise, Wilshire will have to pay more for its deposits, but it will receive no more from its portfolio of loans. A large increase in interest rates could cause the bank to go bankrupt.

Financial managers call this problem the *duration mismatch* problem. The duration of the bank's assets is greater than the duration of its liabilities. To manage this risk, Wilshire Savings and Loan needs to hedge its uncertain cash flows.

Hedging with Swaps

Wilshire can hedge its interest rate risk by entering an interest rate swap. An *interest rate swap* is an agreement between two parties to swap a fixed-rate cash flow for a variable-rate cash flow. The swap contract specifies both cash flows. A typical swap contract involves a five-year swap of semiannual payments. The variable-rate cash flow depends on some short-term interest rate index, like the London InterBank Offered Rate (LIBOR). The fixed-rate cash flow depends on the rate that the parties negotiate when they arrange their swap.

To reduce its interest rate exposure, Wilshire will swap a fixed-rate cash flow for a variable-rate cash flow. If short-term interest rates rise, the bank will have to pay more for its deposits, but an increase in the variable cash flow from the swap will offset this cost. The net effect on the income of the bank will be smaller than if it had not hedged. If the interest rate falls, Wilshire will have to pay less for its deposits, but it will receive less from the swap. The swap reduces the risk from an increase in interest rates, but it also reduces the benefits from a decrease in rates.

The natural other side of the trade might be a pension fund that holds a portfolio of long-term, fixed-rate bonds and wishes to hedge against possible future inflation. If inflation rises, interest rates will rise, and the value of the portfolio will drop. The pension fund can reduce this risk by swapping a fixed-rate cash flow for a variable-rate cash flow. This transaction effectively converts the fixed-rate interest payments to variable-rate payments. If inflation rises, the net cash flow from the portfolio will also rise.

Swaps provide imperfect hedges for the interest rate risks that banks face. The rates that banks pay for their deposits are rarely the same as the short-term interest rate index that determines the variable cash flows in the swap. Likewise, the cash flows that banks receive on their loan portfolios are not fixed. They depend on the numbers of borrowers who retire their loans early or who default on them. The hedged cash flows therefore still expose the bank to interest rate risks. The risks should be smaller, however, than would be expected if the cash flows were unhedged.

8.1.3.4 Hedging Markets

Hedgers like to trade in liquid markets where transaction costs are low. Low transaction costs allow them to set up and remove their hedges cheaply.

Hedgers also like markets that trade instruments which are closely correlated to the risks that they face. Such instruments *replicate* the underlying risks. A contract closely replicates a hedger's risk if the variation in his basis is small compared to the variation in the contract price.

The most successful hedging markets appeal to large numbers of natural hedgers. The hedging interest must be on both sides of the market, and the hedgers must all face large, highly correlated (or inversely correlated) risks. Consequently, successful hedging markets generally trade intermediate commodities that are largely undifferentiated and cheap to transport. *Intermediate commodities* are produced by one industry and used by another industry. They usually have two-sided hedging interest because producers and users face complementary risks. Some relatively new financial futures markets attract many hedgers. Hedgers use these contracts to hedge financial risks associated with transactions that they expect to do in the future. Table 8-1 presents examples of successful hedging markets.

Commodity futures markets constantly develop new contracts to offer to potential hedgers. A few new contracts are spectacularly successful. Most attract little interest and ultimately fail. The most successful recent contract introductions have involved energy and financial products. Some interesting failures have included contracts in sunflower seeds, wool, butter, eggs, high fructose corn syrup, boneless beef trimmings, frozen turkeys, crop yields,

TABLE 8-1.

Examples of Successful Hedging Markets

AGRICULTURAL PRODUCTS	INDUSTRIAL PRODUCTS	FINANCIAL PRODUCTS
Corn	Copper	U.S. Treasury bonds
Wheat	Gold	U.S. Treasury notes
Oats	Platinum	U.S. Treasury bills
Soybeans	Silver	Eurodollars
Soybean meal	Crude oil	Euroyen
Soybean oil	Heating oil	German government bonds
Live cattle	Gasoline	Various foreign currencies
Pork bellies	Natural gas	S&P 500 Stock Index
Lean hogs	Gas oil	Dow Jones Industrial Average
Coffee	Lumber	Nasdaq 100 Index
Cocoa		Various national stock indexes
Sugar		Various sector stock indexes
Cotton		Fixed/variable interest rate
Orange juice		differentials

Note: These markets all trade futures contracts or swaps contracts.

barge freight rates, anhydrous ammonia fertilizer, diammonium phosphate fertilizer, various Brady bonds, various yield curve spreads, the U.S. inflation rate, various catastrophe insurance indexes, aluminum, and U.S. silver coins. Table 8-2 lists some recent successful futures contract introductions.

8.1.4 Gamblers

Gamblers bet on future events. Their bets are contracts whose values depend on the uncertain outcomes of future events. Gamblers commonly bet on sporting events, horse races, lotteries, and card games. Although financial instruments are not gambling contracts, their values do depend on the uncertain outcomes of future events. Given the similarity, it would be surprising if some gamblers did not trade financial instruments.

Gamblers gamble because gambling excites them and makes their lives more interesting. Gambling entertains them.

TABLE 8-2.

Some Recent Successful Futures Contract Introductions

CONTRACT	YEAR	EXCHANGE
Swapnote	2001	Euronext LIFFE
Dow Jones Industrial Average	1997	Chicago Board of Trade
Natural gas	1990	New York Mercantile Exchange
U.S. Dollar Index	1985	New York Cotton Exchange
Crude oil	1983	New York Mercantile Exchange
S&P 500 Index	1982	Chicago Mercantile Exchange
30-year Treasury bond	1982	Chicago Board of Trade
Eurodollar	1981	Chicago Mercantile Exchange

▶ OTB and OTC

Some states and countries permit off-track betting (OTB) on horse races. OTB shops are similar to the storefront offices that many retail brokers maintain for their clients. In both types of offices, television sets broadcast the latest news. Computer screens present the latest information on prices and results. Clerks behind counters take orders. Customers mill about. They share tips with each other and discuss their strategies.

The similarity between the two types of offices, of course, does not imply that all retail brokerage customers are gamblers. Many are investors and some are good speculators. Their brokers provide them with facilities at which they can shoot the bull with new and old friends as a service to obtain their patronage.

Not all OTB patrons are gamblers, although I imagine that most are. Some may be well-informed speculators who appreciate the convenience of being able to bet on horse races at many tracks at the same time. ◀

Gamblers are different from speculators. *Speculators* are traders who use information to predict future price changes more accurately than most other traders can. Their superior information gives them an advantage when they trade. Speculators trade because they expect to make money. Depending on what they know, they may trade in betting markets or in financial markets. In contrast, gamblers are uninformed traders. Although they hope to make money, they have no rational reason to expect that they will do so. Gamblers who are honest with themselves trade for entertainment. Gamblers who trade because they believe that they will be successful speculators are foolish.

Few traders trade strictly for gambling entertainment. Instead, most traders who gamble also trade to invest, to hedge, or to speculate. Investors, hedgers, and speculators who gamble typically trade more intensely than they would otherwise. They may trade more often, they may trade more volatile instruments, and they may accept greater risks than they would given only their other objectives. Consequently, their gambling will compromise their performance as investors, hedgers, and speculators. People who allow others to trade on their behalf must carefully monitor their agents to ensure that they do not gamble.

Many—probably most—traders who gamble in the financial markets are unaware that they are gambling. Most believe that they are pursuing other objectives. Traders need great discipline to discriminate between prudent risk-taking behavior and gambling. Many traders who believe that they are speculating actually are gambling because they do not recognize that the information upon which they trade does not give them any advantage over other traders. Traders who gamble can sometimes be identified by their enthusiasm for trading and by their inability to clearly articulate their reasons for trading.

The notion that some traders are gamblers is controversial. Many regulators fear the damage that they can do to themselves and to the markets. They especially worry that gamblers may make the markets more volatile. We address these concerns in chapter 28 when we discuss the causes of excess volatility, and what regulators might do to reduce it.

Gambling is not necessarily bad for financial markets. Since gamblers are uninformed traders, they tend to lose to well-informed traders. When many gamblers are present, informed trading can be quite profitable. In chapter 10, we show that gambling may lead to less volatility.

Like all other utilitarian traders, gamblers like to trade in liquid markets. The low transaction costs in such markets allow them to acquire and divest their positions cheaply.

Gamblers also like to trade volatile instruments because they typically provide the greatest potential for exciting entertainment. The great popularity of public lotteries suggests that some gamblers like bets which win big with low probability and lose small with high probability. Since out-of-the-money options provide similar return distributions, gamblers may be especially attracted to these instruments.

8.1.5 Fledglings

Fledglings trade to learn whether they can trade profitably. They are willing to lose money when trading to answer this question. Fledglings may try a variety of trading styles, or they may concentrate on learning a single style.

Fledglings become profit-motivated traders if they learn to trade profitably. If they do not, they eventually quit or are fired. Fledglings who cannot trade well, and who continue to trade, are futile traders.

▶ A Common Fledgling Story

Brad traded a *paper portfolio* for several years as a hobby. Whenever he wanted to buy or sell a security, he pretended to do so at the closing market prices. His paper portfolio consistently outperformed the market, even after he accounted for the commission costs that he would have paid had he actually traded.

Brad's paper portfolio successes suggest to him that he might be able to make a lot of money trading securities. Figuring that every profitable trader has to start trading sometime, Brad begins to trade with real money. Since he believes that his trading will be most successful if he gives it all his attention, he takes a leave of absence from his work while he tries to make a go of it as a trader.

After several months, Brad has lost enough money to convince himself that further experimentation with his new career will not likely be productive. He quits trading and returns to work a much wiser, but less wealthy, man.

Trading on paper is not the same as actual trading. When real money is at risk, traders become more emotional about their trading. They become more risk averse. They allow their opinions about values to be influenced by their positions and by their past gains and losses in those positions. Many good paper portfolio traders cannot overcome these biases. Those who can, may become successful traders. ◀

Since measuring performance can be very difficult (see chapter 22), fledglings may falsely conclude that they are skilled when they are only lucky. A lucky, but unskilled, fledgling is still a fledgling. Many successful traders, including professional portfolio managers, may still be fledglings. Success does not necessarily imply skill.

Learning to trade profitably can be expensive. Most people do not succeed. Dealers, floor traders, and day traders in many different markets commonly say that fewer than 5 percent of fledgling traders survive to trade profitably. Some of those who do, however, may profit handsomely. Rational people therefore may be willing to lose money to learn whether they can trade profitably. In this respect, learning trading is similar to learning disciplines like medicine, engineering, the arts, sports, politics, and management.

8.1.6 Cross-subsidizers

Cross-subsidizers trade to produce commission revenues for their brokers in return for various services that they otherwise might purchase themselves. The commissions that they pay are higher than they would pay if they were not receiving services for them.

Cross-subsidizers are usually professional money managers. They and their brokers use *soft dollar* accounting systems to ensure that the services brokers provide are commensurate with the commissions they receive. Many money managers like soft commissions because they allow them to report lower expense ratios. Chapter 7 provides a detailed analysis of soft commissions.

Although few, if any, traders trade just to obtain soft dollars, soft dollar benefits undoubtedly encourage some traders to trade more than they otherwise would. Cross-subsidization therefore is a reason why people trade.

Other cross-subsidizers may trade to reward their brokers for friendship or companionship, or for their brokers' respect. These external benefits presumably offset the commissions and other transaction costs they incur when trading.

▶ Tax Deferral

Many countries tax capital gains only when traders realize them. Traders *realize capital gains* when they close profitable positions. Since capital losses generally offset capital gains, traders who have realized capital gains can cut their taxes by realizing capital losses. Clever traders can use this feature of the tax system to defer the taxation of their capital gains indefinitely. Consider the following example.

Susan is a U.S. investor who has already realized substantial short-term capital gains from her trading this year. It is now October. If she does not plan her finances carefully, she will pay substantial taxes at the end of the year. Susan needs short-term capital losses to offset her capital gains. Unfortunately—actually fortunately—she does not have any positions with losses that she can sell.

To solve her problem, Susan decides to buy the Mexico Fund (MXF) and short sell the Mexico Equity and Income Fund (MXE). These two funds are unrelated closed-end funds that own diversified portfolios of Mexican stocks. Although Mexican stocks are often quite volatile, the combined position is not very risky because the returns to these two funds are very closely correlated.

If the Mexican stock market rises before the end of the year, Susan will realize her loss on her short MXE position and carry her gain in MXF over into the next year. If she holds MXF long enough, she can obtain a second benefit of deferral: The government will tax her ultimate sale at a lower long-term capital gains rate.

If Mexican stocks fall, she will realize her loss on her long MXF position and carry her gain in the MXE short position into the next year, at which time she may close the position and realize the gain. Since the tax rate on profits from short sales does not depend on the holding period, deferral will be her only tax benefit.

Her strategy will fail only if the Mexican stock market does not move. Susan can protect against this possibility by holding a diversified portfolio of these matched positions.

The government is aware of this strategy, which traders call a *tax straddle*. Traders once routinely constructed tax straddles by trading futures with different maturity dates. To eliminate this loophole, U.S. tax law now requires that traders realize all gains and losses in futures contracts for tax purposes at year-end, whether or not they have closed their positions. Other rules prohibit traders from obtaining tax benefits from closely hedged positions constructed from essentially identical instruments. The IRS therefore may disallow the tax benefits from Susan's strategy. If challenged, Susan will claim that her position is actually a risky speculation on the relative values of different instruments. She will note that the two funds hold different portfolios and that they have different portfolio managers. Whether she would prevail is a question better addressed by a qualified tax attorney than by me. ◀

▶ Dividend Capture

When governments tax dividend income at a rate lower than the rate at which short-term capital losses reduce taxes, traders may try to *capture dividends* by using the following strategy. They buy a stock with instructions to settle on or before its *dividend record date*—the date on which the issuer notes which shareholders are entitled to receive the dividend. They simultaneously sell the stock with instructions to settle after the dividend record date. They thereby obtain the dividend but realize an offsetting short-term capital loss because the sale price is lower than the purchase price by the amount of the dividend. After taxes, the trade is profitable because the after-tax value of the dividend is greater than the after-tax value of the short-term loss.

In the 1980s, Japanese insurance companies traded extensively in the U.S. markets to take advantage of this strategy. Changes in Japanese tax laws have since made the practice less common. Since the United States taxes dividend income and short-term capital gains at the same rate for most people and corporations, Americans do not engage in much dividend capture. ◀

8.1.7 Tax Avoiders

Tax avoiders trade to take advantage of tax loopholes in order to minimize their taxes. Depending on the tax laws involved, their strategies can be very simple or very complex. The three adjacent boxes illustrate a few of these strategies.

8.1.8 Utilitarian Trader Summary

Utilitarian traders use the markets to solve problems that originate outside the markets. Investors and borrowers use the markets to move money for-

▶ Capturing the Capital Loss Exclusion

U.S. tax law allows individual investors to reduce their taxable labor income by up to 3,000 dollars of capital losses per year. Otherwise, investors can use capital losses only to offset capital gains.

Ron is an uninformed long-term investor. Since he is uninformed, he intends to buy and hold securities for the long run. To take advantage of the capital loss exclusion, he invests in a well-diversified portfolio of individual stocks instead of in a well-diversified mutual fund. Toward the end of each year, he *harvests his losses* by selling stocks that have dropped in value since he bought them. He replaces them with new stocks. Since his portfolio is well diversified, he usually has some stocks with losses. Ron never sells stocks with gains.

Using this strategy, Ron writes off 3,000 dollars of capital losses at his ordinary income rate. Since the government ultimately will tax his long-term capital gains at a lower rate, Ron effectively converts 3,000 dollars per year of his labor income into long-term capital gains. Given Ron's combined federal and state tax rate on his labor income of 40 percent, he saves 1,200 dollars a year in taxes. Over many years, the cumulative value of these savings will be quite significant. ◀

ward or back through time. Asset exchangers use the markets to obtain items that are of greater value to them now than those which they tender. Hedgers use the markets to offload risks. Gamblers use the markets to obtain entertainment. Fledglings use the markets to learn whether they can be successful profit-motivated traders. Cross-subsidizers use the markets to move money from one account to another. Tax avoiders use the markets to minimize their taxes. Table 8-3 summarizes these traders.

All utilitarian traders want to trade in liquid markets, which allow them to achieve their objectives at low cost. Economists sometimes call utilitarian traders *liquidity traders* because they need liquidity to accomplish their goals.

TABLE 8-3.
Utilitarian Trader Summary

TRADER	MOTIVE	TYPICAL INSTRUMENTS
Investors	Move money from the present to the future while obtaining a fair rate of return	Stocks, bonds, and notes
Borrowers	Move money from the future to the present at lowest cost	Bonds and notes
Asset exchangers	Obtain an asset of greater immediate value than the one they tender	Cash, commodities, and currencies
Hedgers	Reduce risk	Forwards, futures, and options
Gamblers	Entertain themselves	Volatile instruments
Fledglings	Learn whether they can be successful profit-motivated traders	Various
Cross-subsidizers	Compensate brokers for providing services	Various
Tax avoiders	Avoid taxes by exploiting tax loopholes	Various

Utilitarian traders want to trade instruments that best solve their problems. Investors trade only instruments that expose them to risks they can tolerate. Asset exchangers trade only for assets that they need. Hedgers trade instruments that are closely correlated to the risks they face. Gamblers trade instruments that excite them.

8.2 PROFIT-MOTIVATED TRADERS

Profit-motivated traders trade only because they expect to profit. Like all traders, they profit if they buy low and sell high. The key to trading profitably is to trade only when you have reason to believe that you will profit. Profit-motivated traders therefore must understand why they profit in order to predict when they will profit. This section introduces the various types of profit-motivated traders. We discuss them in detail in later chapters.

The two main classes of profit-motivated traders are speculators and dealers. *Speculators* attempt to profit by predicting how prices will change in the future. *Dealers* attempt to profit by selling liquidity to other traders.

8.2.1 Speculators

Speculators predict future price changes from information that they collect, analyze, and, in some cases, produce. To profit from their insights, they buy when they think prices will rise and sell when they think prices will fall. Although their predictions are often wrong, successful speculators are right more often than they are wrong. The more often they are right, the more they profit.

Two types of traders speculate. *Informed traders* trade on information about fundamental values. They make prices more informative. They also sometimes make markets more liquid. *Parasitic traders* profit from the trades that other traders do. They neither make prices more informative nor make markets more liquid.

8.2.1.1 Informed Traders

Informed traders acquire and act on information about fundamental instrument values. They trade when they believe that prices differ from fundamental values. They buy when they believe that prices are below fundamental values, and they sell when they believe that prices are above fundamental values. They then profit if prices adjust toward their fundamental values.

Informed traders differ by how they form and act upon their opinions about fundamental values. *Value traders* estimate fundamental values by collecting and analyzing all available information. *News traders* are the first to trade on new information. *Information-oriented technical traders* identify systematic patterns which indicate that prices differ from their fundamental values. *Arbitrageurs* compare fundamental values across instruments. Arbitrageurs include *pure arbitrageurs,* who trade instruments with values that depend on the same fundamental factors, and *statistical arbitrageurs,* who trade instruments with values that depend on both common and instrument-specific fundamental factors.

Informed traders are the only traders who cause prices to move toward fundamental values. All other traders add noise to prices. Economists therefore call them *noise traders.*

8.2.1.2 Parasitic Traders

Parasitic traders include *order anticipators* and *bluffers*.

Order anticipators acquire and act on information about the trades that other traders will make. They profit when they correctly anticipate how other traders will affect prices or when they can extract option values from the orders other traders offer to the market.

Order anticipators differ by the information they use. *Front runners* collect information about trades that other traders have decided to arrange. *Sentiment-oriented technical traders* use information to predict what uninformed traders will decide to do. *Squeezers* act on information about trades that other traders must do.

Although order anticipators use information to trade profitably, their information is not about fundamental values. They therefore are uninformed traders in the sense that we use this term.

Bluffers create information that other traders may misinterpret. They profit when they fool other traders into trading unwisely. Since the information they create is not about fundamental values, bluffers are also uninformed traders.

Bluffers differ by how they fool other traders. *Rumormongers* promote or discredit securities or commodities by disseminating misinformation. *Price manipulators* trade to create prices and volumes that they hope other traders will misinterpret.

8.2.1.3 Technical Traders

Our list of speculators includes two types of technical traders. *Technical traders* try to predict price changes from *technical data* that generally include past and current prices, volumes, short interests, money flows, block trading, and records of insider trading. Technical traders look for systematic patterns in technical data that allow them to predict future price changes.

Technical traders differ by the type of information that they try to discover. *Information-oriented technical traders* are informed traders. They try to identify when prices differ from their fundamental values. Their trades are profitable when prices move toward fundamental values. *Sentiment-oriented technical traders* are order anticipators. They try to identify what trades uninformed traders will want to make. They trade profitably when they can correctly anticipate the impacts that uninformed traders will have on prices.

8.2.2 Dealers

Dealers make themselves available so that other traders can trade when they want to trade. They supply liquidity. They buy at their bid prices and sell at their ask prices. The spread between these two prices is the price that they charge impatient traders for liquidity.

To trade profitably, dealers must buy and sell equal volumes. They therefore must discover the prices that equate supply and demand. Dealers know a lot about market values, but they generally do not know much about fundamental values. They are uninformed traders in our classification scheme.

Dealers vary by the size of the positions they take and by the time they are willing to hold their positions. *Market makers* provide liquidity on demand in small quantities. They often trade in and out of their positions many times a day. In many markets, market makers will provide liquidity to anyone. *Block facilitators* provide liquidity to large traders. They may take days or weeks to trade out of their positions. Block facilitators generally provide liquidity only to clients whom they choose.

8.2.3 Profit-motivated Trader Summary

Profit-motivated traders trade because they expect to profit from their trading. Successful profit-motivated traders must have some advantage that allows them to trade profitably. Their various advantages usually involve information they have that others do not have. Table 8-4 presents a summary of the various profit-motivated trading strategies.

TABLE 8-4.
Summary of Profit-motivated Trading Strategies and the Proprietary Information upon Which They Are Based

TRADER TYPE	TRADING STRATEGY	PROPRIETARY INFORMATION	CHAPTERS
Speculators	Predict price changes	Various	10–12
Informed traders	Buy undervalued or sell overvalued instruments	Fundamental information	10
Value traders	Estimate total value	All available fundamental information	10.5.1, 16
News traders	Estimate changes in value	News about fundamental values	10.5.2
Information-oriented technical traders	Identify patterns inconsistent with informative prices	Price patterns that indicate departures from fundamental values	10.5.3
Arbitrageurs	Simultaneously buy undervalued and sell overvalued instruments	Relative fundamental values	10.5.4, 17
Order anticipators	Trade ahead of other traders	Information about other traders	11
Front runners	Trade ahead of submitted orders	The trades that others want to do	11.1
Sentiment-oriented technical traders	Trade ahead of anticipated orders	Predictions about trades that others may decide to do	11.2
Squeezers	Trade ahead of trades that others must make	Positions that other traders have	11.3
Bluffers	Fool other traders into trading unwisely	Who can be fooled	12
Rumormongers	Spread rumors	The rumors they spread	12
Price manipulators	Have people misinterpret their trading	The true purpose behind their trades	12
Dealers	Supply liquidity	The relation between prices and the order flow	13–15
Market makers	Trade quickly in and out in small sizes	Short-term market conditions	13–14, 24
Block facilitators	Trade large blocks	Long-term market conditions; which securities interest their clients	15

Informed traders understand fundamental instrument values better than other traders do. They have better access to fundamental data than do other traders, and they can better analyze the implications of their data than other traders can. They profit when prices track fundamental values.

Order anticipators have information about what other traders intend to do. They profit when they can trade before other traders do.

Bluffers fool other traders into trading unwisely. They create information that other traders misinterpret. They profit when other traders do not recognize the false bases of their trading decisions.

Dealers supply liquidity. They allow other traders to trade when they want to trade. Successful dealers must be able to identify the prices at which buyers and sellers are equally willing to trade. Dealers profit when they understand market conditions well, and when they know which securities will interest their clients.

Profit-motivated traders do not always profit when they trade. Even the best traders often lose because of events that they could not anticipate. Successful traders win more often than they lose, however. Those who do not are futile traders.

8.3 FUTILE TRADERS

Futile traders expect to profit from trading, but they do not profit on average. They cannot recognize the difference between their expectations and their results. They may be irrational, they may have poor information about their results, they may rely on untrustworthy agents, or they may be of limited mental capacity.

Futile traders include inefficient traders and victimized traders. Inefficient traders are unable to produce the profits they desire. Victimized traders rely on brokers who do not trade in their interest.

Inefficient traders lack the skills, analytic resources, and access to information necessary to trade profitably. They may do everything that profit-motivated traders do, but they do not do it well enough to trade profitably. Although they may profit from trading with some types of traders, those profits are not sufficient to cover their losses to more skilled and better-informed traders. Inefficient traders generally make poor decisions about when to trade and when to refrain from trading.

The most common type of inefficient trader is the pseudo-informed trader. *Pseudo-informed traders* believe they are well-informed traders. The information on which they trade, however, is old news. Prices have already reacted to the news, but they do not realize it. Consequently, their trades are not profitable.

Victimized traders rely on brokers, advisers, or employees who fail to meet their fiduciary responsibilities. These agents may simply fail to provide services for which they are paid, or they may deliberately exploit their clients to their own advantage. Victimized traders believe that they will profit from trading, but they do not on average.

Traders who hire conscientious but incompetent managers to profit from trading are fledglings who have not yet learned how to manage their money. If they refuse to learn, they become inefficient traders.

Rogue traders victimize their employers or their clients. Rogue traders trade in ways that serve their own purposes but are not in the best interests

▶ A Trading Oxymoron

Investment managers help people manage their funds. They may help people invest, as their name implies, or they may help people speculate.

Passive investment managers pursue *buy and hold* strategies. Managers who buy and hold rarely trade. *Indexing* is the most common buy and hold strategy. Indexers try to replicate the returns to an index. Such strategies are often appropriate for investors.

Active investment managers are speculators who try to beat the market. Traders who "invest" with such managers actually speculate on whether the manager can beat the market. ◀

▶ Nick Leeson and the Fall of Barings Bank

In 1994, Nick Leeson was head trader and head of settlements for Baring Futures Singapore, a branch of Barings Bank. His supervisors thought that he engaged in arbitrage trades that would profit from differences in the prices of Nikkei 225 futures contracts listed on the Osaka Securities Exchange (OSE) in Japan and on the Singapore Monetary Exchange (SIMEX). Although such trades involve huge numbers of contracts, they are not very risky. A short position in one contract is an excellent hedge for a long position in the other contract.

In fact, Leeson was making substantial unhedged bets on the Nikkei 225. Following the Kobe earthquake of January 17, 1995, he even attempted to support the Nikkei 225 through huge purchases. His apparent motive was to protect a bonus that was to be set on February 24. The effort was not successful. A substantial fall in the Nikkei 225 created enormous losses for Barings. Leeson's trading losses of 1.38 billion dollars forced Barings into bankruptcy.

Barings fell in large part because Leeson was both head trader and head of settlements. As the head of settlements, he was able to hide his trading losses from his supervisors. The bank collapsed because senior management failed to properly supervise the trading of a rogue trader.

Singapore eventually convicted Leeson of forging documents and creating fictitious accounts to hide his unauthorized trading. He was sentenced to six and a half years in jail. In 1995, the Dutch bank ING bought Barings for the symbolic price of one pound. ◀

of their employers or their clients. They often are traders who know that they will lose their jobs when their employers discover they have incurred substantial trading losses. The rogues try to hide these losses while they take large positions in an attempt to trade out of their problems. If the positions prove to be profitable, and their subterfuges go undetected, they keep their jobs and may even receive substantial bonuses. If the positions create substantial losses, they lose the jobs that they would have lost anyway.

8.4 SUMMARY

Traders use markets for many reasons. Whether they are successful or not often depends on how well they understand the reasons why they trade.

Utilitarian traders trade because they expect to receive some benefit from trading besides profits. Investors and borrowers trade to move money through time. Asset exchangers trade one asset for another asset that has greater immediate use for them. Hedgers trade risks. Gamblers trade to obtain exciting entertainment. Fledglings trade to learn about trading. Cross-subsidizers trade to transfer wealth to others. Tax avoiders trade to take advantage of tax loopholes.

Profit-motivated traders trade only because they expect to profit from their trading. Profit-motivated traders include speculators and dealers. Speculators try to predict future price changes. Dealers sell liquidity to other traders. Speculators differ by the information they use to forecast future price changes. Informed traders use information about fundamental values, order anticipators use information about what other traders will do, and bluffers create information designed to convince other traders to trade foolishly.

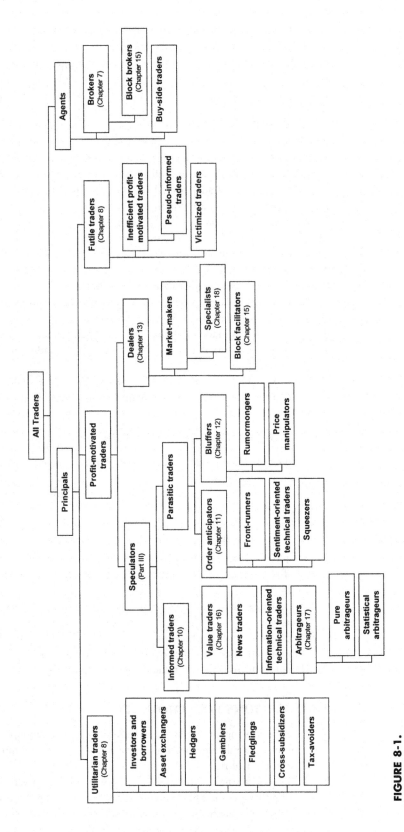

FIGURE 8-1.
Taxonomy of Trader Types

Futile traders are unskilled, irrational, or poorly advised. These traders consistently lose, even though they expect to profit.

Utilitarian traders and futile traders lose on average to profit-motivated traders. Without them, profit-motivated traders could not profit. Profit-motivated traders therefore need to understand why utilitarian and futile traders trade if they are to profit from their trading.

Many people confuse investing, speculating, and gambling. Investors are uninformed traders who trade to move money from the present to the future. They expect to receive a fair rate of return for the risks that they bear. Speculators are traders who use information to predict future returns more accurately than most traders can. They trade because they expect to profit from trading. Gamblers are uninformed traders who trade for excitement. Though they often think that they are speculators, they are not able to predict price changes well enough to trade profitably in the long run. Investors typically trade only in securities markets. Speculators trade in all financial markets and all gambling markets in which they can predict future returns. Gamblers trade in any market that interests them.

All traders except dealers like to trade in liquid markets. Liquid markets allow traders to achieve their objectives at low cost. Since dealers sell liquidity, they prefer to trade in illiquid markets. Their services are more valuable in illiquid markets than in liquid markets. Their trading makes markets more liquid.

Figure 8-1 presents a taxonomy of traders. We will examine many of these traders in greater detail throughout the remainder of this book.

8.5 SOME POINTS TO REMEMBER

- Utilitarian traders trade because they expect to obtain some benefit from trading besides profits.
- Investors and borrowers move money through time.
- Hedgers exchange risks.
- Asset exchangers trade to obtain assets of greater value to them than the assets that they tender.
- Gamblers trade for entertainment.
- Profit-motivated traders trade only because they expect to obtain profits.
- Speculators trade on information about future price changes.
- Dealers profit from offering liquidity to other traders.
- Futile traders believe that they are profit-motivated traders, but they cannot trade successfully enough to profit in the long run.
- Pseudo-informed traders trade on stale information.

8.6 QUESTIONS FOR THOUGHT

1. Besides saving for retirement and borrowing for education, what other intertemporal cash flow timing problems do people commonly face?
2. Can the real risk-free rate of interest ever be negative?
3. Suppose a wheat farmer sells a wholesale baker a forward contract. What happens if hail destroys the farmer's crop or if the baker loses a large contract to deliver bread in the future? Will their hedges protect them against these risks? How can they manage these risks?

4. In the stock hedging example involving Apple Computer, how would Jack's optimal hedge be different if the beta of Apple were 1.3? How would a beta different from 1 affect the analysis in the last two paragraphs of this example?

5. Is gambling in financial markets bad? Should gamblers be discouraged?

6. When traders capture dividends, they pay for the stock they buy, they receive payment for the stock they sell, and they receive the dividend on three different days. How do interest rates affect the difference between the purchase price and the sales price?

7. Sentiment-oriented technical traders anticipate the trades of uninformed traders. What type of trader can anticipate the trades of informed traders?

8. From whom do informed traders profit? From whom do order anticipators profit? From whom do bluffers profit?

9. From whom do dealers profit? To whom do they lose?

10. How can utilitarian traders reduce their losses to profit-motivated traders?

11. How does each type of trader affect volatility?

12. You have placed a 2 million dollar position limit on a trader who works for you. The trader has made the firm 0.5 million dollars in profit on a 4 million dollar position. What should you do?

9

▷

Good
Markets

Market structures have changed significantly in the last few years, and many more changes are under consideration. Throughout the world, people actively debate the following questions:

- Should regulators consolidate all orders into a central limit order book?
- Should markets use quote-driven or order-driven systems?
- Should regulators allow internalization and preferencing?
- Should regulators impose price limits or halts on trading?
- Should trading use floor-based or screen-based systems?
- Should dealers yield to their customers?
- Should regulators require that markets be linked electronically? How fast should those links be?
- What trading hours should markets adopt?
- Who should be able to see the limit order book?
- Who owns market data?
- What securities and contracts should regulators allow exchanges to trade?

The markets have wrestled with these and many other issues, and they undoubtedly will continue to do so.

Virtually any change in market structure will have significant economic effects on our markets. Trading rules, trading systems, and information protocols all affect liquidity, transaction costs, volatility, the quality of prices, and the distribution of trader profits. We therefore must carefully consider whether proposed changes in market structure are desirable. This chapter introduces a paradigm for how we should make these decisions.

Everyone has an economic interest in how markets should be organized because everyone—whether they trade or not—benefits from having well-functioning markets. Not surprisingly, opinions about market structure vary widely.

Many people try to influence market structure:

- Legislators pass laws that dictate structures.
- Regulators interpret those laws, propose new ones, and selectively enforce them.
- Government administrators propose laws, veto laws, and use their influence in myriad ways to promote their interests. In some countries, they also write the laws.
- Judges interpret laws and write new case law.
- Exchanges, brokers, clearing agencies, and information providers freely create any market structures that the legal system permits. They also

frequently propose—and sometimes even implement—structures that laws and regulations do not currently permit.

- Issuers influence market structure through the decisions they make about where to list their securities.
- Traders influence market structure through the decisions they make about where to trade.
- Investors and the general public influence market structure by voting for politicians who favor their interests and by lobbying those politicians.
- Finally, the leaders of trade organizations, public interest groups, and watchdog agencies often lobby on behalf of their constituents.

These people all discuss market structure with those who have power to promote or frustrate their interests.

Debate generally is most productive when conducted within a framework for making decisions. Welfare economics provides such a framework. *Welfare economics* is the branch of economics that considers how we should organize our economy. In this chapter, we consider principles by which we should organize our markets.

How markets should be organized is completely subjective. Everyone is entitled to his or her opinion. Many people think that markets should do well whatever it is that they do. Accordingly, we will closely consider the benefits that markets produce for our economy. At the end of this chapter, I provide a set of weak objectives that I believe regulators should use when evaluating alternative market structures. You may have your own opinion about what are good markets.

If you agree that markets should be organized to maximize the benefits they produce for the economy, then you must be familiar with these benefits so you can consider them when you evaluate alternative policies. If you believe that markets should be organized to promote other objectives, you should at least be aware of the costs to the economy of the policies that your objectives favor.

Even if you have no interest in influencing market structures, you should find these discussions interesting. Well-functioning markets are largely responsible for the tremendous wealth that free market-based economies have generated and continue to generate. This chapter helps explain why some countries are rich while other countries are poor.

We start our discussion with a brief introduction to welfare economics. The discussion then turns to the benefits that markets produce for individuals and for the wider economy. If your only interest in this book is to become a better trader, you can safely skip this chapter.

9.1 WELFARE ECONOMICS

Welfare economics involves positive and normative economic analyses. In *positive economic analyses*, analysts use theories and empirical evidence to predict the consequences of various economic policies. Positive economics is objective in the sense that analysts who use the same assumptions and the same data should obtain the same results. In *normative economic analyses*, analysts argue for specific economic policies. Normative economics is highly subjective. Everyone is entitled to his or her opinion about what should be.

▶ Do Economists Disagree Much?

The public widely believes that economists rarely agree with each other. Consider the popular joke, "Put two economists in a room, and you get three opinions."

Economists actually agree more than they disagree. They appear to disagree a lot because people remember controversies more than agreements. Since economic controversies interest us, economists often appear to disagree.

When economists disagree about positive analyses, they usually have based their analyses on different assumptions or different data. Since analysts must make many decisions about which assumptions and which data to incorporate into their studies, policymakers must be careful when interpreting economic analyses. They must ensure that the subjective biases of the analysts do not influence their results.

When economists disagree about assumptions and relevant data, we need a set of principles to evaluate the decisions that underlie their analyses. The norms of economic science provide us with these principles: We should evaluate assumptions by how well they represent the essential reality of the problem at hand rather than whether we like their policy implications. Likewise, we should evaluate data by how well they characterize relevant past experience rather than by whether we like their policy implications.

When economists disagree about normative analyses, they usually have employed different social welfare functions. Economists—like everyone else—have different opinions as to what is good and valuable. Policy makers must consider whether they agree with the analyst's values before accepting the conclusions of a normative analysis. ◀

Normative analysts arrive at their conclusions by finding the policy that maximizes a subjective measure of social welfare. The conclusions may flow from formal mathematical models based on rigorous statistical analyses or from simple heuristic arguments based on best guesses. Either way, a proper normative argument has four parts:

1. An identification of all reasonable alternative policies.
2. A specification of subjective criteria for evaluating the alternative policies. The criteria describe a *social welfare function* that measures the value of each policy. If the social welfare function is based on multiple criteria, it must specify the acceptable trade-offs among the various criteria.
3. A positive economic analysis that evaluates the social welfare of each alternative policy.
4. An identification of the policy that produces the greatest social welfare.

All normative analysts should follow this procedure. In practice, most follow it implicitly rather than explicitly. This procedure provides a valuable framework for debate because it clearly identifies the criteria upon which analysts base their conclusions. Without this discipline, proponents of a policy often argue for it as though it were the objective rather than the path to some commonly agreed-upon objective. When policy becomes the objective rather than the means to the objective, poor results often follow.

▷ Market Structure from Two Perspectives: Why Regulation Is Challenging

Dealers like markets in which they can trade profitably. Not surprisingly, most dealers favor quote-driven markets over order-driven markets because they make more money when they do not have to compete with public traders who offer liquidity.

Since trading is a zero-sum game in trading profits, dealer profits are buy-side transaction costs. Some buy-side traders do not value the liquidity services that dealers provide as much as these services cost them. They therefore favor order-driven markets over quote-driven markets.

The preferences of both types of traders are perfectly understandable. Given their different interests, no compromise on market structure can completely please them both. These conflicts make regulating markets very challenging. ◁

9.1.1 Market Welfare Economics

To decide public policy in the markets, we need a social welfare function by which we can measure the merits of alternative policies. Many people believe that we should design markets to do well whatever it is that they do. Whether you subscribe to this objective or not, you must understand what markets do in order to responsibly evaluate public policy.

We identify the economic benefits that markets produce in the next two sections. First, we describe the direct benefits that traders obtain from using the markets. These are *private benefits* because they accrue only to individual traders when they trade. We then consider how the wider economy benefits from having well-functioning markets. These benefits are *public benefits* because they accrue to everyone's benefit.

9.2 PRIVATE BENEFITS OF TRADING

Private benefits accrue directly to traders when they trade. We know that traders somehow benefit from trading because they trade voluntarily. They would not trade otherwise.

To appreciate the private benefits of trading, we have to understand why people trade. We considered this question in chapter 8. There we saw that people trade for two main reasons. *Utilitarian traders* trade because they hope to obtain some benefit from trading besides profits. *Profit-motivated traders* trade only because they expect to profit from trading.

Markets work best for utilitarian traders when they are liquid. In *liquid markets*, traders can accomplish their trading objectives at low cost.

Utilitarian traders use the markets less when transaction costs are high. Investors and borrowers use other methods to synchronize their cash inflows and outflows. Asset exchangers avoid activities that require assets they do not have. Hedgers rearrange their affairs to limit their exposure to risks that concern them. Gamblers find their entertainment elsewhere.

Markets also work best for utilitarian traders when the assets that they can trade are well suited to their needs. Investors and borrowers prefer to trade instruments that produce cash flows which occur just when they need them. Hedgers like to trade instruments that closely replicate the risks which worry them. Gamblers like instruments that excite them.

▶ Zero Coupon Bonds

Zero coupon bonds that mature at various dates are attractive to investors and borrowers because they use them as building blocks to construct any cash flow that they want. With enough different maturity dates from which to choose, traders can construct a portfolio of zero coupon bonds to represent any cash flow. ◀

Profit-motivated traders trade only because they expect to profit directly from trading. The primary profit-motivated traders are dealers and specu-lators. *Dealers* sell liquidity to impatient traders when they allow them to trade when they want to trade. *Speculators* trade to profit from future price changes that they can predict.

Since trading is a zero-sum game, speculators and dealers cannot profit on average if they trade only among themselves. They can profit only if util-itarian traders are willing to trade. Markets therefore exist only when util-itarian traders are willing to trade. This fact suggests to me that the welfare of utilitarian traders ultimately is more important than the welfare of profit-motivated traders. You may disagree.

9.3 PUBLIC BENEFITS OF TRADING

The *public benefits* of trading accrue to everyone regardless of whether they use the markets. Economists call these benefits positive externalities. *Posi-tive externalities* result when nobody compensates people for doing things that benefit others. Economists are especially interested in externalities be-cause they represent situations where regulations can often make people better off. In this section, we shall see that traders do many things which benefit people who do not even use the markets.

The public benefits of having well-functioning markets fall into two classes: those which come from having markets that produce informative prices and those which come from having liquid markets. We consider each in turn.

9.4 PUBLIC BENEFITS FROM INFORMATIVE PRICES

Well-functioning markets produce prices that accurately reflect the funda-mental values of the instruments they trade. *Fundamental value* is an imag-inary concept. It is the value that everyone would agree upon if everyone knew all relevant information about value, and if everyone knew exactly how to process that information to estimate value. In practice, nobody knows everything they need to know about value, and few people process infor-mation well. Fundamental values therefore are often poorly known. Fortu-nately, markets can aggregate information from many different sources to produce prices that are closer to fundamental values than anyone could con-sistently estimate by himself or herself. Markets produce *informative prices* when prices are close to fundamental values.

We discuss how prices become informative in chapter 10 when we exam-ine how informed traders trade. In this chapter, we consider how people—many of whom do not trade—benefit from living in economies in which mar-kets produce informative prices.

9.4.1 Production and Allocation Decisions

All economies must make *production and allocation decisions* about how to organize production and how to divide the goods and services produced. Economies that make and implement good economic decisions become wealthy. Those which cannot make or implement good decisions are poor.

To use their resources most efficiently, economies must allocate them to projects and managers that can derive the most value from them. A resource allocation is most *efficient* when the expected marginal benefit of a resource is the same for every project that uses it in the economy. The *marginal benefit* of a resource is the expected additional value that a project would produce if another unit of the resource were devoted to it. When marginal benefits differ across projects, moving resources from low marginal benefit projects to high marginal benefit projects can produce more efficient allocations.

Since millions of potential projects compete for resources in large national economies, allocating resources efficiently requires an extraordinary amount of information. Good decisions must reflect information about the goods and services people need, how best to produce them, and how best to distribute them. These decisions generally are highly interrelated. For example, truckers cannot deliver clothing if road builders do not receive cement because limestone miners cannot work without adequate clothing.

9.4.1.1 Command Economies

In *command economies*, central planners make production and allocation decisions. The planners may be individuals or they may be large planning bureaus. The planners collect requests for the use of capital, rank them, and then create production plans and resource allocation budgets for all projects. The planners then try to use their command authority to compel people to implement their plans.

Command economies suffer from several serious problems:

- Most obviously, planners must aggregate a fantastic amount of information to produce good plans. For a large economy, the information requirements of central planning generally overwhelm the capacity of any planning organization to collect and process information.
- A greater problem than the volume of information is its quality. Central planners often receive very low-quality information about capital requirements because the requests that managers submit are often unrealistic, fraudulent, or based on inconsistent assumptions. Improving the quality of the information is difficult, given the size of the problem, audit problems, and disincentives to comply.
- Political forces and personal biases often distort the planning process. Even if planners could solve their information problems, some would still distort allocations to meet their political objectives, to please their friends, or to get the job done quickly so they can go home early.
- Even when planners make good decisions, people may not implement their plans if the plans are unpopular. Central planners often find that people rebel against their authority when they must make sacrifices for which they feel inadequately compensated.
- Centrally planned economies often have serious accountability problems. When plans fail, the planners blame the implementers and the implementers blame the planners. Without good information about economic conditions, assigning and accepting responsibility for shortfalls is very difficult.

These problems cause all large command economies to perform poorly.

> **Some Important Production and Allocation Decisions in the Clothing Industry**
>
> - How much clothing should be produced, and in what styles and sizes?
> - How should the clothing be made?
> - Who should provide the raw materials and machines to make the clothing?
> - Who should operate the machines, and who should service them?
> - Who should receive the clothing?
> - Who should transport and distribute the clothing?

▶ Overlapping Benefits

Consider a very simple economy with three investors and four projects. Abby examines only projects 1 and 2, Barry examines only projects 2 and 3, and Charlotte examines only projects 3 and 4. Each project merits some capital investment. For each project, the marginal benefit of additional capital investment declines as the total capital invested increases.

Abby, Barry, and Charlotte all allocate their capital efficiently. Abby allocates her money to projects 1 and 2 so that the marginal benefit of a dollar invested in both projects is the same. Barry and Charlotte use the same rule to allocate to projects 2 and 3 and 3 and 4, respectively.

Since Abby and Barry both invest in project 2, the marginal benefit of an additional dollar invested in projects 1, 2, and 3 is the same. This result is interesting because no one evaluates both projects 1 and 3. Likewise, since Barry and Charlotte both invest in project 3, the marginal benefit of an additional dollar invested in projects 2, 3, and 4 is the same.

These equalities imply that the marginal benefit of capital in projects 1 and 4 is the same. This result is remarkable because the people who evaluate projects 1 and 4 evaluate completely disjoint sets of projects. ◀

9.4.1.2 Market-based Economies

In *market-based economies*, people and companies make production and allocation decisions as they look for the most profitable ways to use their time and money. Companies decide what products to produce and how to produce them by considering the prices that determine their revenues and costs. Managers who make good allocation decisions profit, and thereby retain the authority to make more decisions. Companies that cannot efficiently produce what others want lose money, and their investors thereby lose the ability to make more decisions. Because people risk losing when they make production and allocation decisions, they usually pay close attention to what they do, and they usually consider only projects about which they have some expertise.

Market-based economies work very well because decision making is distributed throughout the economy. Although no one examines more than a small fraction of all possible projects, the collective efforts of the millions of people who search for good investment opportunities place most projects under great scrutiny.

Market-based capital allocations are efficient because each person efficiently allocates his or her capital to those projects which appear best among the set of projects that he or she has examined. The resulting aggregate allocations are globally efficient because the sets of projects that investors examine overlap extensively.

In practice, most people do not compare projects directly against each other. Instead, they evaluate projects by comparison against a common standard called the *required rate of return*. Investors undertake an investment only if its expected rate of return is greater than its required rate of return. Since investors can always invest in risk-free government bonds, the required rate of return for an investment is equal to the risk-free interest rate plus an adjustment for the risk of the investment. Required rates of return thus depend on the supply of and demand for funds for savings and investment.

Market-based economies work well when prices convey information about values. Prices must indicate the values that people put on the goods that they consume, and they must indicate the values that producers put on the factors they need to produce their goods and services. Informative prices therefore play an extremely important role in market-based economies.

Prices in market-based economies generally reflect values because buyers or sellers try to trade when prices differ from values. When prices are too low, buyers try to buy more than sellers will offer. Buyers then bid up the prices of undervalued items as they compete to find scarce sellers. Likewise, when prices are too high, sellers try to sell more than buyers will buy. Sellers offer prices down as they compete to find scarce buyers. Market prices adjust to the point where *supply and demand* are equal. At that point, prices reflect a midpoint compromise between the high values that buyers place on the item and the low values that sellers place on it.

Not all economic decisions are best made in the marketplace. Markets work well only when the costs of negotiating are small relative to the costs of the goods or services that trade there. Markets work poorly when transaction costs are large or when activities need to be highly coordinated. All economies therefore use a mix of command and market-based allocation mechanisms.

Companies are the most important command organizations within a market economy. People form companies that managers control in order to avoid the excessive market negotiation costs. The managers create and implement plans for their companies. Within each company, the manager determines what the firm will do, who will do it, and how it will be done. (In large firms, managers generally delegate much of the responsibility and authority for planning and implementation to subordinates whose specific knowledge and proximity to information often make them better decision makers on smaller issues.) By consolidating authority with managers, firms avoid negotiating with their workers about who will do what and when. Most firms also own or lease the machines, properties, patents, and brands that they need to produce and market their goods and services. By putting these physical capital resources under management control, the firm avoids negotiating with owners of these factors of production.

Although firms are small command economies, they relate to the rest of the world through various markets. They sell their goods in product markets, they buy raw inputs in factor markets, they hire their employees in labor markets, they rent or buy their machines and property in asset markets, and they fund their business plans in the financial capital markets.

Markets that produce informative prices help make market economies wealthy by ensuring that resources are well allocated. Commodity and product markets produce information that helps people allocate goods and services to their best uses. The capital markets produce information that helps people make better capital allocation decisions.

Investors in market-based economies make two types of capital allocation decisions that involve firms. They must decide which firms will receive capital for new projects, and they must decide which managers will manage existing capital resources.

In the remainder of this section, we consider how investors use informative prices produced in primary and secondary capital markets to make capital allocation decisions. *Primary capital markets* are markets in which issuers sell stocks and bonds to raise capital for new projects. Investors allocate capital to new projects in primary markets. *Secondary capital markets* are

▶ **A Toll Booth on Every Corner**

We do not pay for using most streets and highways because collecting tolls at every intersection is too costly. Governments therefore build and maintain most roads, and taxpayers pay for them regardless of whether they use them. Since no one meters our usage and charges us for it, we overuse many streets in crowded cities and thereby cause traffic jams.

In the last few years, electronic devices for measuring highway usage have become much cheaper. These devices greatly cheapen the costs of collecting tolls. Many new tollways are now being constructed, and some old highways are being converted to tollways. In many places, the tolls vary by time of day to discourage usage when the traffic nears the road's capacity. ◀

▶ Primary Market Capital Allocation Example

A firm wants to sell stock to raise 1 million dollars of capital for a new project. The firm currently is financed entirely by 20,000 shares of equity. The existing assets of the firm are worth 2 million dollars. Since the firm has no debt, each share is worth 100 dollars. How many shares must the firm sell to finance the new investment, and at what price should it sell those shares?

The answers to these questions depend on what investors think about the new project. If they think that the project has great prospects, they will pay a high price for the shares, and the firm will not have to sell many shares. If they think that the project is a poor idea, the share price will be low, and the firm will have to sell a great many shares. If the project is a very poor idea, the firm may not be able to sell new shares at any price.

The solution involves two very simple equalities. First, the number of new shares times their price must equal the cost of the project:

$$\text{new shares} \times \text{price} = \text{project cost}$$

Second, the total market value of the firm's liabilities after the offering must equal the total expected value of the firm's assets. Since the firm has no debt, the total market value of the liabilities is just the new total number of shares outstanding times their price. The total expected value of the firm's assets is the sum of the value of the old assets plus the expected value of the project:

$$(\text{old shares} + \text{new shares}) \times \text{price} = \text{old assets} + \text{expected project value}$$

The prices that appear in these two equations are the same because the firm will not be able to sell the shares for more than traders expect they will be worth after the sale, and because the firm will not want to sell the shares for less than it can obtain. (For simplicity, we ignore the discounts that often are associated with seasoned offerings.)

Manipulation of these equations yields expressions for the number of new shares that the firm must sell and the maximum selling price:

$$\text{new shares} = \text{old shares} \times \text{project cost} \div \text{new value of old shares}$$

and

$$\text{price} = \text{new value of old shares} \div \text{old shares}$$

where

$$\text{new value of old shares} = \text{old assets} + \text{expected project value} - \text{project cost}$$

is the new aggregate value of the old shares.

If investors expect that the project will add 1.5 million dollars to the value of the firm, the firm will sell 8,000 shares at 125 dollars per share. The original investors will give up slightly less than 29 percent (8,000 ÷ 28,000) of the control of their firm to the new investors. The new investors receive stock worth 1 million dollars for their 1 million dollar purchase, and the original investors receive the entire benefit of identifying the profitable investment. The total value of the old shares increases by 0.5 million dollars, which is the difference between the expected value of the project and its cost.

If investors expect that the value of the project is only 0.5 million dollars, the firm should not undertake the project because it costs more than it is worth. If management insists on proceeding, the firm would have to sell 13,334 shares at 75 dollars per share to raise 1 million dollars. The existing shareholders would lose 0.5 million dollars, and they would give up 40 percent of the control of their firm to the new investors. The loss that they would experience is a tremendous disincentive to proceeding with the deal.

The price of the stock depends on the relation between the cost of the investment project and its expected value. If the difference is positive, the stock price will rise. Otherwise, it will fall. If the difference is negative and greater than the value of the existing equity, the equations suggest that the price will be negative. Investors would not finance such a poor project unless they were paid to do so. ◀

markets in which *seasoned securities* (previously issued securities) trade. Investors use information in secondary market prices primarily to help them choose and evaluate the managers of their firms.

9.4.2 Capital Allocation in the Primary Markets

The capital allocation problem in the primary markets is simply stated: Millions of ideas compete for capital, but not all ideas are good. New capital should go only to the best investment ideas.

The primary markets help to solve this allocation problem by pricing investment opportunities. When prices are informative, good ideas command high prices and poor ideas are worthless. Issuers with good ideas therefore can easily sell securities to raise capital to implement them. Promoters with poor ideas cannot sell their securities, or they must subsidize them with their own money in order to proceed. Since no one wants to subsidize other people's investments, poor ideas are rarely undertaken. New capital thus flows to the best ideas.

9.4.3 Secondary Markets:
The Manager Allocation Problem

The allocation problem in the secondary markets is also simply stated: Millions of managers compete to manage capital, but not all managers are good. Good management can produce a lot with a little. Poor management wastes resources. Only the best managers should manage capital.

The secondary market helps solve this allocation problem by providing investors with information about how well existing managers are using the resources available to the companies they run. If prices are informative and managers manage their companies well, their stock prices should be high relative to their asset values. If they are poor managers, their stock prices should be low. Investors use this information to obtain better management in three ways.

First, shareholders compensate managers based on share price performance. Through executive stock options, phantom stock, stock grants, and stock price-linked bonuses, shareholders encourage their managers to work hard. These mechanisms work well only if the link between managerial effort and managerial compensation is direct and noise free. Informative stock prices strengthen this link.

Second, shareholders remove managers who do not perform well and replace them with others who, they hope, will do better. Informative stock prices provide shareholders with useful information about how well their managers are performing.

Finally, when shareholders are unwilling to remove poor management, low stock prices may attract takeover attempts by speculators who believe that they can better manage the company. They may either run the company themselves or hire better managers to run it for them. This mechanism works best when stock prices are informative.

These three mechanisms all break down when stock prices are noisy. When prices do not reflect how well managers are performing, good managers may lose their jobs and shareholders may retain poor managers. Informative prices make that less likely.

Anyone who uses stock prices to evaluate managerial performance must be very careful when interpreting them. Stock prices depend on many factors besides the quality of management. For example, the stock prices of oil

▶ Indexed Options

Shareholders often give their managers *executive stock options* to encourage them to work hard. The options allow managers to buy stock in the firm at a specified *strike price*. If managers can raise the stock price above the strike price before their options expire, they can become quite wealthy.

The strike prices of these options generally are constant. When stock prices rise because the whole market rises—perhaps because interest rates fall— stock option values rise even if managers are performing poorly. Such compensation does little to encourage managers to work harder. Executive stock options would be more effective if their strike prices were indexed to the performance of comparable firms or, at a minimum, to the market as a whole.

Likewise, when stock prices fall because the market drops, executive stock options drop in value. If prices fall far below option strike prices, the options become worthless and thereby lose most of their incentive powers. To reestablish incentives, corporate directors often restrike options at lower prices.

Fixed strike prices and strike prices that adjust down but never up do not serve the interests of most shareholders. These characteristics of executive compensation schemes suggest that the independent corporate directors who sit on board compensation committees may not be as independent as many shareholders would prefer. Left unexplained is why shareholders routinely approve such compensation schemes.

Adverse tax treatment of indexed strike price options is one reason offered for why firms do not use them more often. The tax consequences, however, are small relative to the incentives associated with better compensation schemes. ◀

▶ The Great Semantic Irony of Communism

The words "communism" and "communication" have the same Latin root word, *communis*, an adjective which indicates that a group shares an object. Its direct translation to English is "common."

Ironically, communism failed in large part because Communists could not adequately communicate the information necessary to run their economies efficiently. Free market economies are very successful because markets facilitate the exchange and effective use of information necessary to organize production efficiently. Traders communicate more effectively than do Communists. ◀

producers rise and fall with the price of oil. A manager of an oil producer might be exceptionally skilled at yield enhancement and cost containment, yet still appear to perform poorly when the price of oil falls. Likewise, a poor manager may look great when the price of oil rises. These possibilities suggest that people who use stock prices to evaluate management must carefully account for other determinants of stock price performance. At a very minimum, performance should be measured relative to industrial peers rather than against an absolute standard.

9.4.4 Summary

Well-functioning markets produce informative prices that greatly benefit everyone in the economy, regardless of whether they trade. People use the information in prices to help solve production and allocation problems that are of first-order importance to the common welfare. Economies that cannot allocate new capital to the best projects, and the best managers to ongoing operations, waste their resources and are quite poor. Those which make these decisions well are much wealthier.

Perhaps nothing explains the failure of national Communist systems better than their inability to produce efficiently. Economywide planning problems are simply too complex to be solved well by any single agency, no matter how well intended and well prepared its managers are. Russia is poor compared to the United States largely because, for 70 years, it was unable to organize production as efficiently as the United States. Contrasts between North and South Korea, the former East and West Germany, China and Japan, and Albania and Greece provide clear evidence of the importance of free markets.

▶ Markets for the Air We Share

Clean air is a resource that we all share. We pollute that air when our cars burn gasoline. Since we do not pay for the free clean air that we use, we undoubtedly use more than we should. Many of our cities consequently are quite polluted. Governments can partially solve this problem by taxing gasoline so that its price to the consumer reflects both the value of the energy resource and the value of the clean air that cars consume when they burn gasoline. They can also partially solve the problem by taxing new car sales according to how much the cars pollute.

Increasingly, governments are creating tradable permits to emit fixed quantities of pollutants into the air and water. Industries that pollute must have permits to do so. Since holders can freely trade their permits, permit prices become a cost of doing business. Industries consider these costs when choosing how to produce their goods.

The resulting decisions tend to reduce pollution at the lowest total cost to the economy. Industries that can cheaply abate their pollution sell their permits and abate their pollution. Industries that cannot cheaply abate their pollution buy permits and pollute.

Since the cost of pollution becomes a cost of doing business, competition among firms forces them to pass their pollution costs along to the consumer. Goods that are produced with dirty technologies become expensive. Consumers avoid them when they have cheaper alternatives and use less of them when they do not.

Economic efficiency would rise whether the government initially sells the permits or whether it freely distributes them to polluters or to the public. If permits can be freely traded, industries will consider their value when they make production decisions, either because they can sell surplus permits or because they must buy permits to cover a deficit.

Pollution rights markets are becoming increasingly important commodity markets. The prices that these markets discover benefit everyone by allowing industries to mitigate pollution at low cost. They also force product prices to reflect environmental costs. ◀

Not surprisingly, one of the first things that countries do when they emerge from communism is establish capital markets. Although the markets often have few securities and contracts to trade, and no modern securities laws to regulate trading, they stand as symbols of changes to come.

Many people are attracted to communism because they like its values. Notions that everyone is economically equal, that each contributes according to his ability, and that each receives according to his needs are quite appealing. Unfortunately, running an economy on these principles is very costly. Proponents of communism must recognize the extremely high economic costs associated with the implementation of their values.

The benefits of free markets are sometimes lost in market-based economies when governments intervene with taxes, subsidies, quotas, and restrictive regulations to promote various agendas. These policies usually create prices that do not accurately reflect resource values. Although governments may enact them for good reason, they can be quite costly. Policy makers therefore need to consider whether the intended benefits of their interventions outweigh their often substantial costs to the economy.

When transaction costs are high or when the ownership of resources is not well defined, markets may not exist, and people may use resources inefficiently. In such circumstances, government interventions often improve economic efficiency. Since these problems are quite common, some government intervention into the economy is necessary to promote economic efficiency.

Many economists and political scientists study when and how governments should intervene in economies. They also consider the often unrelated issues of why governments intervene in markets. Their studies contribute to the fields of public finance, welfare economics, and public choice.

9.5 PUBLIC BENEFITS OF LIQUID MARKETS

Liquid markets benefit the public through the externalities that utilitarian traders produce when they use markets to conduct their businesses more efficiently. These externalities generally result from production efficiencies that traders can realize by using markets to exchange assets, hedge, or share risks.

9.5.1 Public Benefits of Exchange

Asset exchangers exchange things that are of less immediate value to them for things that are of greater immediate value to them. The people with whom they trade do the same. The resulting exchanges make both traders better off. Through such trades, market-based economies ensure that resources go to the people who most value them. Such economies are very productive because they allocate resources to the uses where they are most valuable. Without such exchanges, resources are wasted.

Transaction costs make such exchanges expensive. People will not trade if the difference in values between what they give up and what they receive is less than the transaction cost of the trade. High transaction costs therefore cause people to use resources poorly.

When transaction costs are prohibitively high, nobody trades. Economies in which nobody trades are *autarkies*. They are very poor because nobody can specialize to produce at low cost and because people waste resources.

Liquid markets benefit us all by allowing producers to specialize and by allowing resources to be committed to the processes for which they are most valuable. The resulting production efficiencies lower the costs of everything that we consume.

9.5.2 Public Benefits of Hedging

Many producers face a trade-off between the cost-saving benefits of specialization and the concentrated risk associated with specialization. They like to specialize, but they are afraid of the risk. Liquid hedging markets benefit such producers by allowing them to cheaply divest themselves of the risks that scare them. When hedgers can cheaply transfer risk, they specialize in the most efficient productive processes available to them. In competitive markets, we all benefit through lower prices.

9.5.3 Public Benefits of Risk Sharing

Many good projects are too large, and therefore too risky, for a single person to undertake. To undertake such projects, people form public corporations to spread the ownership and associated risks over a large number of people. Liquid markets benefit the public by allowing companies to raise new capital at low cost.

▶ Eggs in One Basket

Sam owns a farm in North Dakota, where the soil and weather are particularly well suited to growing wheat. Sam can also grow corn to feed chickens, but he does not have a competitive advantage in this industry. Chicken farming is more productive in warmer climates. After considering all alternatives available to him, Sam believes that his farm will be most profitable if he plants only wheat.

Sam is afraid of planting only one crop, however. If wheat prices fall or if his crop fails, he will suffer. To protect against these possibilities, Sam hedges his wheat by selling forward in the futures market. He also buys crop insurance from an agricultural insurance company. He uses these markets because they provide him with useful risk management tools at reasonable costs.

If Sam did not use these markets, he would not specialize in a single crop because of the risk. Instead, he would diversify his production, even though that would lower his expected profits. His profits would be lower because his land is best suited for wheat and because he can achieve significant economies of scale by specializing in one crop.

Judy owns a farm in Arkansas that is best suited to growing corn for chicken feed. She specializes in eggs and hedges her risks with corn futures contracts. If she could not cheaply lay off risk in the futures markets, she, too, would diversify her production and produce less value on average.

The whole economy is better off when Sam and Judy specialize in what they do best. Specialization allows farmers to produce more wheat and eggs in aggregate than they could produce if they all ran diversified operations. The abundant crops that they produce lower food costs for everyone.

Liquid hedging and insurance markets thus benefit people even if they do not trade in them. If trading in these markets were too expensive, hedgers would not use them and our economy would be less productive. ◀

Investors do not like to buy securities that trade in illiquid markets because the transaction costs lower their net investment returns. Security prices therefore are lower in illiquid markets than in liquid markets. Companies that have access to liquid markets thus have lower costs of capital. When product markets are competitive, companies pass along their lower capital costs to consumers so that people benefit even if they do not use the markets.

9.5.4 Other Public Benefits of Liquidity

Liquid markets also benefit investors who do not intend to trade but who take comfort in knowing that they could trade at low cost if they wanted to. Options to do things that you may not choose to do are valuable. People who have such options often arrange their affairs differently than they otherwise would. For example, investors will more likely invest in liquid markets than in illiquid markets when they are uncertain about when they will next need to use their funds for other purposes. Liquid markets benefit such investors even when they do not trade.

Liquid markets also provide indirect public benefits by facilitating profitable informed trading. Informed traders make more money when they can trade with little price impact than when their trades move prices. They then can afford to collect more information about fundamental values, and they can profitably trade on information of lesser significance than they other-

> ### Public Lotteries and Casinos Waste Liquidity
>
> Gamblers who bet on games of pure chance bet on events that have no consequence in our economy. Their trading produces no public benefits.
>
> Gamblers benefit from the entertainment they obtain. They also enrich the governments that run public lotteries, the corporations that run casinos, and the gangsters who run numbers on the street. These are all private benefits.
>
> Gambling on games of pure chance does not increase liquidity in trading markets. It does not help utilitarian traders solve their trading problems, and it does not allow informed traders to profit and thereby produce informative prices that improve production and allocation decisions in our economy. ◀

wise could. Prices therefore should be more informative in liquid markets than in illiquid markets.

Finally, and perhaps most controversially, liquid markets benefit the public by attracting gamblers. Gamblers like to trade in liquid markets because they lose less per trade in such markets. This benefit is a purely private benefit. The public benefit of having gamblers trade in financial markets comes from the wealth that they ultimately lose to profit-motivated traders. Recall that profit-motivated traders can profit on average only if they can trade with utilitarian traders. Without such traders, they will not trade. If informed traders cannot profit, they will not invest in their information, they will not trade, and prices will be less informative. If dealers cannot profit, they will not trade, and markets will be less liquid. Gamblers help make prices informative through their willingness to lose to informed traders and dealers. Liquid financial markets benefit the economy by attracting gamblers away from more traditional gambling markets in which informative prices provide little benefit to the economy.

9.6 SOME OBJECTIVES FOR EVALUATING MARKETS

The implications of welfare economics ultimately depend on the objectives that people use for evaluating issues. These objectives are opinions that people have about what is most important. In this short section, I present my opinion about how we should evaluate public policy issues that involve market structure. You may disagree with me.

We often evaluate opinions by whether they are reasonable. Philosophers have tried to derive criteria for evaluating opinions from basic principles, but these criteria, too, ultimately are subjective. You must decide for yourself whether my objectives are reasonable.

I believe that public policy should first promote the private interests of those traders whose needs cause markets to exist in the first place. These are utilitarian traders who use the markets to manage cash flow timing problems, hedge risks, share risks, and exchange assets. If these traders do not use the markets, the markets will not exist, and we will not obtain any other benefits from having markets.

I exclude gamblers from this list of utilitarian traders because they can entertain themselves elsewhere and because they have no natural reason to bet on economic events rather than on sporting events or random events. I do respect the liquidity that gamblers bring to the market. I therefore am willing to support policies that promote their interests, but only for the sake of obtaining their liquidity.

Second, public policy should strive to maximize the public benefits we all obtain from liquid markets that produce informative prices. These benefits are extraordinarily important to our common welfare. Perhaps this objective should appear first, given its importance. I list it second in order to emphasize that markets will not exist if utilitarian traders do not use them.

Third, public policy should support the interests of profit-motivated traders only when necessary to pursue the first two objectives. Since dealers help make markets liquid and since informed traders help make prices informative, these profit-motivated traders play important roles in our markets that we should support. However, we should support them only for the

▶ Recent Rule Changes in U.S. Equity Markets

The U.S. Securities and Exchange Commission appears to share my objectives. Under the leadership of Chairman Arthur Levitt, the Commission imposed the Order Handling Rules in 1997. These rules require dealers to expose all public orders that they hold when these orders are at the best bid or offer. These rules make it easier for public limit order traders to compete with dealers when offering liquidity. In effect, the Commission decided that when dealers and the public are both willing to supply liquidity, the public must have an opportunity to display their quotes.

The SEC adopted the Order Handling Rules shortly after the courts imposed the Manning Rule on dealers. The Manning Rule is a public order precedence rule. It prohibits dealers from trading before their customers at the same price. The Order Handling Rules and the Manning Rule taken together have substantially changed the character of the Nasdaq markets from essentially pure quote-driven to somewhat order-driven markets. These rule changes have benefited public traders at the expense of dealers.

In August 2000, the SEC adopted new rules concerning selective disclosure by issuers of material nonpublic information. Before their adoption, issuers would often disclose material information to the analysts who follow their stocks. The analysts or their clients then would trade on that information, often to the disadvantage of other public traders. Rule FD now prohibits such selective disclosure. Issuers must disclose all information to everyone at the same time. Although this rule undoubtedly hurts some informed traders, it should have little long-run effect on the information content of prices. ◀

---

sake of the benefits they provide other traders and the economy as a whole. We should not favor them when we can obtain liquidity and informative prices more cheaply elsewhere. For example, public policy should not support dealers to the exclusion of public traders who are equally willing to provide liquidity. Likewise, public policy should not allow informed traders special access to information that could as easily be granted to all traders.

Finally, public policy should be hostile to the efforts of profit-motivated traders who design trading strategies to exploit other traders. Price manipulators, bluffers, and front runners hurt other traders while doing nothing to make markets more liquid or prices more informative in the long run. This group also includes traders who employ very high-speed trading strategies to take liquidity from dealers who are slow to adjust their prices when values change. The value of the price discipline that they provide market makers over short intervals—typically, less than five seconds long—is small compared to the value of the liquidity that they take from the market.

9.7 SUMMARY

Most people would like to have the best markets possible. To obtain such markets, sometimes regulators have to intervene to impose necessary changes, and sometimes we have to defend our markets against harmful regulatory interventions. In either event, we can best justify our policies in public discourse by showing that they maximize social welfare.

Although the determinants of social welfare are subjective, most people would agree that we should organize markets to maximize the benefits that accrue to the traders who use them and to the economy at large. Accordingly, this chapter has considered the private benefits that traders obtain from the markets and the public benefits that we all enjoy when markets work well.

Traders benefit from highly liquid markets in which they can accomplish their purposes at low cost. Most people agree that public policy should strive to create liquid markets.

The economy benefits greatly from markets that produce informative prices. Informative prices help us to efficiently organize economic activity. People rely upon prices when deciding how to allocate capital to new projects and when deciding how to allocate managers to existing projects. Economies become wealthy when these decisions are made well, and they suffer when they are made poorly. Most people agree that public policy should strive to create markets that produce informative prices.

Public policy becomes quite interesting when these simple objectives conflict with each other. For example, in chapter 29 we show that rules which restrict insider trading usually increase liquidity while making prices less informative. In such circumstances, we need a more thorough understanding of our objectives to decide which policies promote our welfare.

Since the objectives of public policy are subjective, people will disagree about policies. Such disagreements typically arise when a policy affects someone's economic welfare. Although such conflicts are unavoidable, most people more willingly accept policies that hurt them if they are founded on deep principles which we all share. The ultimate challenge faced by honest public policy makers is to promote the public good against powerful and highly vocal private interests. The problem is most difficult when we poorly understand what constitutes the public good. I hope that this chapter has helped you to form well-reasoned opinions about what good markets are.

9.8 SOME POINTS TO REMEMBER

- Profit-motivated traders cannot profit on average if they trade only with each other.
- Markets ultimately exist only because utilitarian traders benefit from trading.
- Markets produce information used in production decisions and allocation decisions.
- Informative primary market prices help ensure that only the most promising projects receive new capital.
- Informative secondary market prices help allocate the best managers to existing capital.
- Many schemes that investors use to motivate their managers work best when secondary market prices are highly informative.
- The public benefits to the economy of well-functioning markets are largely responsible for the prosperity of market-based economies.
- Most people believe that markets work best when transaction costs are low and prices are informative.

9.9 QUESTIONS FOR THOUGHT

1. Is there a trade-off between informative prices and liquidity?
2. Should the government intervene to make the markets more liquid or less volatile? Can such interventions be effective?

3. Will stock prices reflect the value of the firm under poor management if everyone expects that the managers will soon be replaced in a takeover?

4. Why do some firms implement internal capital markets? What should be the relation between the costs of funds in internal and in external capital markets?

5. In the example that demonstrates how primary markets price investment ideas, how would the solution change if the new investors require a seasoned offering discount to fund their research into the value of the firm?

6. The text in the "Markets for the Air We Share" (p. 213) states that governments can partially solve the "free" air pollution problem by taxing gasoline or by taxing new cars according to how much they pollute. Why would these policies only partially solve the pollution problem? How might we arrange better solutions?

7. Do interest rates depend on how liquid money markets are? How would the answer to this question depend on the intertemporal cash flow misalignment problems that borrowers, as opposed to savers, face?

8. Gamblers make markets more liquid. Liquidity attracts informed traders. Since the profits that informed traders make come from other traders, informed trading must make markets less liquid. After considering the interactions between gamblers and informed traders, does gambling have a net positive or negative effect on liquidity?

We now turn our attention to the three main types of profit-motivated speculators.

We consider informed traders in chapter 10. Informed traders are well informed about fundamental values. Their trading makes prices more informative.

We study order anticipators in chapter 11. Order anticipators are well informed about what other traders intend do. They front-run other traders and thereby reduce their profits. Their trading often makes prices less informative.

In chapter 12, we examine bluffers. Bluffers try to fool other traders into believing that they have information about future price changes. Their trading usually makes prices less informative.

Part III
▷
Speculators

10

▷

Informed Traders and Market Efficiency

Informed traders are speculators who acquire and act on information about fundamental values. They buy when prices are below their estimates of fundamental value and sell when prices are above their estimates. Informed traders include *value traders, news traders, information-oriented technical traders,* and *arbitrageurs.*

In this chapter, we will consider how informed traders trade and how their trading makes prices informative. We will pay special attention to why some informed traders make money while others do not. We also will explain why prices cannot be completely informative. This chapter will help you understand how informed traders make money, when they make money, and the limits to how much money they can make.

Informed trading may interest you for at least three reasons. First, you may be an informed trader yourself. If your trading decisions depend in any way on opinions you form about fundamental values, you are an informed trader. Unfortunately, most traders who believe that they are informed traders do not trade profitably because they are not truly well informed. The principles we will discuss in this chapter should improve your trading by helping you predict when you will trade profitably.

Second, you must understand informed trading to understand the risks that traders face when they offer liquidity. In chapter 13, we show that dealers and other traders who supply liquidity lose to well-informed traders. The profitability of dealer operations therefore depends critically on how dealers cope with informed traders. If you intend to be a dealer, if you intend to trade with dealers, or if you intend to offer liquidity yourself, you must understand informed trading.

Finally, you must understand informed trading to see how prices become informative. A price is *informative* when it is near its corresponding fundamental value. Informative prices are extremely valuable to the economy because they help us allocate resources efficiently. To fully appreciate how market-oriented economies work, you must understand how informed traders make prices informative.

10.1 FUNDAMENTAL VALUES

To discuss informed trading, we must distinguish between market values and fundamental values. The *market value* of an instrument is the price at which traders can buy or sell the instrument. The *fundamental value* (or *intrinsic value*) is the "true value" of the instrument. In financial terms, fundamental value is the expected present value of all present and future benefits and costs associated with holding the instrument. Everyone would agree upon this value if they all knew everything known about the instrument, if they all used the proper analyses to predict and discount all uncertain future cash flows, and if they all perceived the benefits and costs of holding the instrument equally. Since these conditions never occur, traders often differ in their opinions about fundamental values. This chapter examines how informed traders estimate fundamental values and how they trade upon their estimates.

Fundamental values are not perfect foresight values. Fundamental values depend only on information that is currently available to traders. *Perfect foresight values* depend on all current and future information about values. Fundamental values are the best estimates of perfect foresight values.

Prices are completely *informative* when they equal fundamental values. *Efficient markets* produce prices that are very informative. The difference between fundamental value and market value (price) is *noise*. Informed traders try to identify the noise in prices by estimating fundamental values. Since we do not observe fundamental values, we cannot easily determine whether prices are informative or noisy.

Changes in fundamental values are completely unpredictable. Since fundamental values reflect all available information, they change only when traders learn unexpected new fundamental information. If fundamental value changes were predictable, current fundamental values would not fully reflect the information upon which the predictions are based. Fundamental value changes therefore must be unpredictable. Since prices are very close to fundamental values in efficient markets, price changes in efficient markets are quite unpredictable.

When traders cannot predict future price changes, statisticians say that prices follow a *random walk*. Plots of random walks through time look like paths that wander up or down at random because random walks are completely unpredictable.

10.2 INFORMED TRADERS

Informed traders estimate fundamental values. They may base their estimates on *private information* that only they have or on *public information* that any trader can obtain. Informed traders compare their value estimates with the corresponding market prices. They consider instruments to be *undervalued* if prices are less than their estimates of fundamental value, and *overvalued* if prices are greater.

Informed traders buy instruments that they believe are significantly undervalued and sell instruments that they believe are significantly overvalued. They hope to profit when the prices of their purchases rise and when the prices of their sales fall. Informed traders naturally hope that these price changes will occur quickly.

Informed traders lose money when they estimate fundamental values poorly. When their value estimates are wrong, they pay too much for instruments they have overvalued, and they sell too cheaply instruments they have undervalued. Informed traders who consistently estimate values poorly usually quit trading when they have lost more money than they can tolerate or when bankruptcy forces them out of the markets.

Informed traders also can lose money even if they accurately estimate fundamental values. This happens when prices move away from fundamental values rather than toward them. These losses, however, tend to be short-term. In the long run, prices usually revert toward their fundamental values, so well-informed traders ultimately profit.

▶ **Fischer Black on Noise**

Fischer Black was a mathematician who made many seminal contributions to the development of financial theory. Perhaps most notably, he helped develop option-pricing theory, for which Myron Scholes and Robert Merton received the 1997 Nobel Prize in economic science. Had Fischer not died two years before the prize was awarded, he undoubtedly also would have been a Nobel laureate.

In his 1985 presidential address to the American Finance Association, Black offered a now famous opinion about noise. He believed that we should consider stock prices to be informative if they are between one-half and twice their fundamental values! Most economists believe that the prices of actively traded securities are well within these extreme bounds, but no one can know for sure. ◀

Source: Fischer Black, "Noise," Journal of Finance 41, no. 3 (1986): 529–543.

Even if prices never adjust to their fundamental values, well-informed traders who have correctly estimated values still can profit from their trades if they are patient. When they buy an undervalued instrument, they acquire the rights of ownership for less than their aggregate value. By holding the instrument, they will eventually receive the benefits of these rights—typically interest, dividends, royalties, capital repayments, or liquidating distributions—at a lower price than they could otherwise obtain them. When they sell overvalued instruments, they can invest the proceeds in instruments with higher expected rates of return.

10.3 INFORMED TRADERS MAKE PRICES INFORMATIVE

Informed traders, like all other traders, often significantly impact prices when they trade. Their buying tends to push prices up, and their selling tends to push prices down. Since they buy when price is below their estimates of fundamental value and sell otherwise, the effect of their trading is to move prices toward their estimates of fundamental value. Their trading therefore causes prices to reflect their estimates of fundamental value. When informed traders accurately estimate values, their trading makes prices more informative.

Informed traders generally differ in their estimates of value. This often happens when they base their estimates on different data. Informed traders often trade with each other so that the price impacts of their trading tend to cancel. The net impact of their trading is a market price that reflects an average of their different value estimates. This price usually is more informative than are any of the individual value estimates. Markets aggregate data from many sources to produce prices that typically estimate fundamental values more accurately than any individual trader can.

Informed traders also may estimate different values when one or more traders make mistakes in their analyses. If many mistaken traders are in the market, or if one mistaken trader is quite large, their trading will make prices less informative. In the long run, however, the losses of error-prone traders cause them to exit the market so that prices become more informative.

Informed traders who most accurately estimate value eventually become wealthy while informed traders who estimate value less accurately lose wealth. Since wealthy informed traders take larger positions than do less wealthy informed traders, wealthy traders have more influence on price than do other traders. Prices therefore are closer to the value estimates of wealthy traders than to those of less wealthy traders. Since wealthy traders tend to be the best-informed traders, prices primarily reflect the value estimates of the best-informed traders more than those of less informed traders.

Although informed traders usually make prices more informative, they do not trade for this purpose. They trade to make profits. The price impacts of their trading are transaction costs to them. They make less money when their price impacts are large than when they are small. To trade profitably, informed traders need to trade in liquid markets in which prices differ significantly from fundamental values. They do not profit much in illiquid markets, where their trading quickly eliminates potential profit opportunities. Informed traders want prices to adjust toward their estimates of fundamental value only after they have established their positions.

▶ An Algebraic Illustration

This box presents an algebraic illustration of how markets aggregate information. If you are not comfortable with algebra and symbolic notation, skip it. The exercise only illustrates points made in the text.

Suppose that N traders each produce a different forecast of the true value of a security. Let f_i be the forecast of the ith trader and assume that it is an unbiased estimate of V, the true fundamental value. We can represent the forecast as $f_i = V + e_i$ where e_i is the error in the ith trader's forecast. The expected forecast error is 0 because the forecasts are unbiased. The individual forecast errors might be quite large in absolute value, however.

Let each trader's desired position in the security, D_i, be proportional to the difference between her forecast of value and the market price, i.e., $D_i = a(f_i - P)$ where a is some constant of proportionality and P is the market price. This assumption ensures that trader i will want a long position if her forecast is greater than the market price and a short position otherwise. It also ensures that the more different her forecast is from the market price, the more she will want to hold.

Finally, assume that the security is in *zero net supply*. Traders create such securities when they sell them short. Futures contracts and option contracts are examples of zero net supply securities. This assumption simplifies the arithmetic but does not affect our qualitative results.

We compute the market price by setting the sum of all desired positions equal to the net supply and solving the resulting equation for P:

$$\sum_{i=1}^{N} D_i = \sum_{i=1}^{N} a(f_i - P) = a \sum_{i=1}^{N} f_i - NaP = 0.$$

The market price $P = \dfrac{1}{N} \sum_{i=1}^{N} f_i$ is an average of the individual forecasts.

Substituting $f_i = V + e_i$ into this expression gives $P = V + e_M$, where

$$e_M = \frac{1}{N} \sum_{i=1}^{N} e_i$$ is the forecast error of the market price.

If the individual forecast errors are independent of each other, the law of large numbers implies that the market forecast error e_M will approach 0 as the number of traders N gets large. Even if the number of traders is not large, the average market forecast error will be less than the average individual forecast error if the individual forecast errors are not identical. The market price thus estimates the fundamental value of the security better than any individual trader can estimate it. Prices are most informative when many informed traders collect information independently. ◀

10.4 INFORMED TRADING STRATEGIES

Informed traders must minimize the price impacts of their trades to maximize their trading profits. They therefore must carefully consider how they trade. Their most important decision is whether to trade aggressively.

Informed traders should trade aggressively if they believe that their private information—and its implications for values—will soon become common knowledge. When values are well known, traders will not trade at any other prices. Since informed traders can profit only if they trade when prices differ significantly from values, they must complete their trades while they still know values better than other traders do.

Informed traders also should trade aggressively if they believe that many other informed traders will act on the same information. Each informed

▶ The Market Is a Statistical Calculator

Statisticians teach us that we can estimate most accurately when we have lots of data. For example, suppose you have two forecasts of value that you believe are equally accurate. The first forecast is 30 and the second is 50. Your best estimate of value given this information is the average of these two forecasts, or 40. This average would more accurately estimate value than either of the individual estimates.

If you knew that the first forecast was more accurate than the second forecast, your best estimate of value would be closer to 30 than to 50. It would be a weighted average of the two forecasts with a greater weight given to the more accurate forecast. (The actual weighted-average estimate would depend on the accuracies of the two estimates.) The combined estimate again would be more accurate than either of the other two estimates.

By combining information from different sources, markets generally produce more accurate estimates of value than any one source can. Moreover, since well-informed traders tend to take large positions, the market gives more weight to their more accurate estimates of value than to the less accurate estimates of less-informed traders who tend to take smaller positions. Prices thereby approximate an optimally weighted average of value estimates with varying degrees of accuracy. Markets are essentially statistical calculators that aggregate value estimates from various informed traders to obtain more accurate estimates of value. ◀

trader will push prices closer to fundamental value. The ones who trade first will profit the most. If the informed traders know that they are competing with each other, they all will race to complete their trades quickly. Unfortunately for them, the flood of their orders may alert other traders and suggest to them that prices do not equal values. The other traders then may become reluctant to supply liquidity, so that the informed trading has even greater price impacts.

Informed traders who are confident that they will not soon lose their informational advantages should trade slowly. By trading slowly, they make it difficult for other traders to infer that they are well informed. Economists call this strategy *stealth trading* because the informed traders want to complete their trades without anyone knowing that they are trading.

10.5 STYLES OF INFORMED TRADING

Informed trading styles differ according to the methods that traders use to estimate fundamental values. *Value traders* estimate the entire fundamental value of an instrument by using all available information. They determine whether instruments are correctly priced. *News traders* estimate only changes in fundamental values. They predict how fundamental values will change in response to new information. *Information-oriented technical traders* identify price patterns that are inconsistent with prices that fully reflect fundamental values. They identify systematic errors made by the other two trader types. Finally, *arbitrageurs* estimate relative differences in fundamental values. They examine the value relation between correlated instruments. This section describes how these four types of traders organize their operations.

10.5.1 Value Traders

Value traders estimate fundamental values. They gather as much information as they can about fundamental values. They then use economic models to organize this information and to estimate instrument values.

All information that can help value traders understand the value of an instrument interests them. They collect information about sales, costs, economic activity, interest rates, management quality, potential for competition, growth options, labor relations, input prices, and the prospects for new technologies. They then use this information to forecast and discount future cash flows, to value the options associated with the assets underlying the instrument, and to value any options associated with ownership of the instrument itself. When they do their job well, they know more about values than anyone else does.

Value traders may employ a variety of experts in their efforts to estimate values. These experts include financial analysts, statisticians, actuaries, macroeconomists, industry economists, marketing professionals, accountants, engineers, scientists, computer programmers, librarians, and research assistants. To support these experts, they often build significant libraries and run large information-processing operations.

Value traders must be very disciplined to minimize the biases that may enter their analyses. If they are overly optimistic, they may buy an overvalued instrument. When prices fall, they then will lose money. Likewise, if they are overly pessimistic, they may sell an undervalued instrument. When prices rise, they then will lose money (if they are short) or lose the opportunity to make money (if they sold a long position).

To avoid estimation errors, large value traders usually have *pyramid-shaped organizations* with many levels of management. Each level oversees the operations of the levels below it. The many layers of review in a pyramid-shaped organization help the organization make well-disciplined decisions. Unfortunately, they also ensure that the organization will make decisions slowly. At the bottom level are analysts who collect information and form opinions about security values. These analysts pass their opinions (and their supporting analyses) up to the portfolio managers, who consider their analyses. The portfolio managers (and other senior managers within the organization) must ensure that the analysts use comparable assumptions when forming their opinions about their securities. Otherwise, the firm will buy securities analyzed by optimistic analysts and sell securities analyzed by pessimistic analysts. They also must ensure that their analysts have not ignored important information. Otherwise, they will buy securities for which they failed to identify negative information and sell securities for which they failed to identify positive information. To avoid these biases, all successful value traders—whether large institutional money managers or individual investors—carefully review their research efforts to make sure that they use consistent assumptions based on all available information. Although these reviews make value traders slow traders, they protect them from making costly mistakes.

Since value traders know values very well, they often supply liquidity to large traders. In many respects, they are the liquidity suppliers of last resort. We consider this very important aspect of value trading in chapter 16.

▶ **The Effect of Inconsistent Assumptions on Value Trading**

Suppose that a value trader employs two analysts who separately specialize in the automobile and aviation manufacturing industries. If the automobile analyst believes that future interest rates will be 10 percent and the aviation analyst believes that future interest rates will be 5 percent, the automobile analyst will discount future Ford earnings more than the aviation analyst will discount Boeing's future earnings. The firm will therefore undervalue Ford relative to Boeing. If the organization does not recognize this inconsistency, it may sell Ford and buy Boeing. ◀

▶ **The Effect of Incomplete Information on Value Trading**

Suppose that an analyst estimates the value of an oil exploration firm without taking into account recent negative drilling results in one of its more important prospective oil fields. The analyst will overvalue the firm's stock. A value trader who buys the stock based on this analysis will likely pay too much for it. ◀

▶ Trading on Viagra

On March 27, 1998, the U.S. Food and Drug Administration approved Viagra for use as a prescription drug by men who suffer from penile erectile dysfunction. Pfizer launched the drug in April. By May 22, over 1 million U.S. men had already taken it. Each dose costs about 8 dollars. The speed and depth of Viagra's market penetration surprised many people.

The stock of Pfizer closed at 95¾ on March 27. By the end of the next week, its price had risen in roughly equal steps to 102⅞. One month later, on April 27, the stock closed at 113⁷⁄₁₆.

Although it is impossible to definitively attribute the increase in stock price to Viagra's introduction, the conclusion seems reasonable. The first traders to obtain, correctly analyze, and act upon the information made money. Later traders lost the opportunity to make money because prices had already increased to reflect the news. ◀

▶ Trading on Investigative Research into Aerospace Hiring

An aerospace firm is competing for an important classified contract. Analysts widely agree that the firm will be significantly more valuable if it obtains the contract. Although the firm may not reveal the status of its negotiations, a clever researcher may be able to infer how they are progressing by considering the numbers and types of people the firm is trying to hire. Such information will be valuable to a news trader if it is not already widely known. ◀

10.5.2 News Traders

News traders collect and act upon new information about instrument values. They try to predict how instrument values will change, given the new information. If they think that values will change significantly, they then buy or sell instruments, depending on whether the news is good or bad. *Material information* is information that significantly affects instrument values. News traders try very hard to discover material information before other traders do. Successful news traders employ experts in data collection who can quickly filter public data sources for valuable information, researchers with strong investigative skills who can produce useful new information, and traders who can quickly and accurately analyze implications of new information for instrument values.

Unlike value traders, news traders do not estimate the value of an instrument from first principles and all available data. Instead, they implicitly assume that current prices accurately reflect all information except their news. Their object is merely to estimate how values will change in response to their new information. They estimate total instrument values by adding to current prices their estimates of how their news changes values.

Successful news traders must collect information and act on it before other traders do. Those who collect and respond to publicly available information must be extremely quick, because much of the news that affects security and contract values is easy to obtain and interpret. These traders often compete with many other traders who simultaneously try to profit from trading on the same news. News traders who specialize in producing information through their own investigative research need not be so quick, but they still must be faster than their competitors. In either case, only traders who can trade before their news has its impact will profit.

Traders who trade on inside information are news traders. *Inside information* is material information that traders directly or indirectly obtain from the management of a company and that is not yet publicly available. In the United States, and in many other countries, trading on inside information is illegal. We consider how the prohibition on insider trading affects the security markets and the managerial labor markets in chapter 29.

Large money managers who pursue information-flow trading strategies usually have flat organizations with few management levels. In *flat organi-*

zations, managers are allowed (within limits) to make whatever decisions are necessary to pursue the firm's objectives. Flat organizations can make quick decisions with little deliberation. This structure is well suited to firms that trade on the flow of information because their traders generally must act quickly in order to trade profitably on their information.

Successful firms that trade on information flows use various systems to quickly collect and deliver information to portfolio managers, who analyze it and possibly trade upon it. These systems may include networks of reporters, brokers, or analysts whom the firms reward for providing them with valuable information. They may also include computerized systems that read and interpret electronic news feeds produced by news services like the Dow Jones Broad Tape. News traders may also employ clipping services to summarize newspaper articles from around the nation and the world. In addition, many news traders have television monitors on their desks tuned to financial news channels as well as computer monitors that scroll information distributed by electronic news services.

10.5.2.1 Information, Prices, and Pseudo-informed traders

To trade profitably, news traders must trade before prices adjust to reflect their information. A price *reflects* information if that information cannot be used to forecast future price changes. If that is the case, the information is *in the price*. Information gets into the price when all traders are aware of its significance or when informed traders push prices toward their estimates of fundamental value. Information that is already in the price is *stale information*. News traders cannot trade profitably on stale information.

The most common mistake that traders make is to trade on stale information. Economists call traders who trade on stale information *pseudo-informed traders*. Pseudo-informed traders think that they are well informed, but in fact they are not. They lose because they tend to buy when prices are already high and to sell when prices are already low. Pseudo-informed traders are actually uninformed traders.

Good news traders must know whether their information is already in the price before they trade. Unfortunately, they rarely know this. To answer the question directly, they must estimate instrument values from first principles. Although value traders routinely do these analyses, few news traders are well equipped to do so. However, traders often can make an educated guess about the quality of their information based on how they obtained it. If they are acting on unique information that others could not have anticipated, their information probably is not stale. If they have been slow to act, if their information is widely known, if others can obtain it cheaply, or if others could have reasonably anticipated it, their information probably is stale.

Since news traders generally do not estimate values as well as value traders do, they generally make more mistakes than value traders. Although news traders usually can accurately predict the direction in which values should change in response to their information, they often poorly estimate the sizes of the changes. In particular, they may under- or overestimate the implications of their information for instrument values. When they underestimate how much values should change, they lose the opportunity to make more money. When they overestimate how much values should change, they lose some, all, or even more than all, of what they gain as informed traders. In

▶ **Pseudo-informed Trading on Stale Information**

The price of Greasy Earth Oil (GEOL) is presently 90. GEOL should be worth 100 if it finds oil and 80 if it does not. From careful studies of the surrounding geology and of the discarded tailings from GEOL's main drilling rig, well-informed traders believe GEOL will find oil. They buy GEOL and push its price up to 100.

GEOL does indeed find oil. When news of the find becomes public, however, the information is already in the price.

If pseudo-informed traders buy on the stale information, they may push prices up to 110. Value traders will sell, and prices will fall back toward 100. The pseudo-informed traders will lose. ◀

▶ **Pseudo-informed Trading in Occidental Petroleum**

Armand Hammer was the Chairman and CEO of Occidental Petroleum (OXY) for 34 years, until his death at age 92 on December 10, 1990. Although many people criticized his management during the last years of his life, his control over the firm was nearly absolute. It was difficult to influence his decisions, and it appeared impossible to take over the firm from him. The day after he died, OXY's stock price rose by 10 percent as traders anticipated more favorable management. On the next day, the price dropped back to its former level.

Armand Hammer was a sick and very old man for a long time before his death. The fact that he died was not material news because many expected that he would die soon. The only uncertainty was on what date. The actual date was not material to the value of the firm. The traders who thought that they were trading on material information should have realized that their information was quite stale. Those who bought at high prices on the day after his death lost the next day. ◀

either case, value traders may recognize that prices do not accurately reflect values when they eventually learn the news and revise their value estimates accordingly. If prices have not changed enough, the value traders will profit directly from acting on the new information. If prices have changed too much, the value traders will profit by correcting the overreaction. Table 10-1 summarizes the mistakes that news traders make and how value-motivated traders respond to them.

10.5.3 Information-oriented Technical Traders

Technical traders attempt to predict the future course of prices by identifying recurring price patterns. Such patterns can arise when informed traders make systematic mistakes or when uninformed traders have predictable impacts on price.

When technical traders recognize and trade on mistakes made by informed traders, they effectively become informed traders themselves. By correcting these mistakes, technical traders cause prices to reflect more accurately the information that the informed traders have. This type of technical trading is *information-oriented technical trading*. We discuss it in this section.

TABLE 10-1.
Mistakes News Traders May Make and the Responses of Value Traders

REACTION TO NEW MATERIAL INFORMATION	INITIAL PRICE CHANGE	NEWS TRADER MISTAKE	VALUE TRADER RESPONSE	SUBSEQUENT PRICE CHANGE
Underreaction	Too small	Fail to exploit fully the profit opportunity	Trade on the new information and thereby become a news trader	Continuation
Overreaction	Too large	Lose some, all, or more than all of their trading profits	Trade against the overreaction	Reversal

▶ Technical Trading Following an Earnings Announcement

The value of Bethlehem Steel's common stock should rise when the firm reports better than expected earnings. Suppose that whenever this happens, news traders or pseudo-informed traders tend to overbuy the stock and push its price above its new higher value.

Technical traders who are aware of this systematic mistake will sell after prices rise following positive earnings announcements. They then will profit when prices fall to their proper (but still higher) levels. If they sell early enough, they will attenuate the overreaction. If they wait too long, they may lose the profit opportunity to other technical traders or to value traders who respond faster. ◀

▶ Tax Timing Strategies

Practitioners and academics have observed that U.S. stocks which have dropped significantly in one year tend to rise at the beginning of the next year. Such patterns may result when investors sell their stocks at year-end to realize capital losses for their taxes. Their sales tend to push prices below their fundamental values. Prices increase when value traders recognize that the stocks are mispriced.

Technical traders who try to profit from this information buy losers at year-end and sell them a few weeks later. Their buying, however, reduces the year-end price drop caused by the tax-loss sellers. As the tax-loss selling phenomenon becomes better known, it appears to be going away. ◀

When technical traders trade in response to predictable price patterns caused by uninformed traders, they effectively act as dealers or order antic- ipators. If they offer liquidity to the uninformed traders, they are essentially dealers. Their trading tends to make prices more informative. If they at- tempt to front-run the uninformed traders, they are order anticipators that we call *sentiment-oriented technical traders.* Their trading tends to make prices less informative. We discuss dealers and order anticipators in chapters 13 and 11, respectively.

Information-oriented technical traders identify violations of abstract statis- tical properties that characterize informative prices. When value traders and news traders efficiently acquire, process, and act on information, prices will not have predictable changes. Information-oriented technical traders profit by identifying predictable price patterns that result when other traders make mistakes. They are scavengers who pick up profit opportunities left by value traders and news traders.

Information-oriented technical trading is quite difficult because it is prof- itable only when informed traders make systematic mistakes. Since obser- vant traders correct their mistakes, opportunities for successful technical trading decrease as markets mature and traders become more experienced. Technical trading strategies that exploit informed traders' mistakes there- fore rarely are consistently profitable. Strategies that worked well in the past fail when informed traders learn from their mistakes.

Technical traders use many methods to identify predictable price pat- terns. They most commonly analyze price and volume charts. These tech- niques are not very effective because our eyes often see patterns where none truly exist. Some technical traders use computers to identify patterns in data.

▶ Pattern Recognition in the Food Chain

Simple principles of evolutionary biology can explain why we often see patterns that do not really exist. Our primitive ancestors needed to recognize signs of danger in order to survive. Those who could not recognize these signs undoubtedly had fewer children than those who could. For example, our ancestral aunts and uncles who could not recognize signs of a nearby saber-tooth tiger probably too often found themselves on the wrong end of the food chain. They did not survive to provide our ancestors with cousins. Since the costs of being wrong when a danger is present are much greater than the costs of being wrong when there is no real danger, survivors often identify more dangers than truly exist. As the descendants of those survivors, we are biologically programmed to identify patterns where none may exist.

Good traders must recognize this predisposition toward falsely identifying patterns. Otherwise, they often will trade foolishly. ◀

▶ The Psychology of Momentum Strategies

Financial economists have observed that stocks which have risen substantially over the last six months of the year tend to outperform the market in the next year. Stocks that have fallen substantially tend to underperform the market in the next year. These results are based on averages over many stocks and many years. The probability that any given stock beats or lags the market is close to 50 percent regardless of its previous performance. These results suggest that markets are not completely efficient.

Information-oriented technical traders try to profit from this information by buying extreme winners and selling extreme losers. Although each stock is quite risky, the risk is manageable when they buy and sell many stocks at the same time. This strategy is a *momentum* strategy because traders hope that prices continue moving in the same direction that they have moved. Momentum strategies are profitable when news traders and value traders underestimate the importance of significant new information.

The common tendency of people to resist changes in the status quo may explain why traders make these mistakes. When great news makes a stock much more valuable, or when terrible news makes it much less valuable, traders have trouble believing that the current value of the stock could be so different from its recent value. They find it difficult to buy stocks that have risen substantially because they are afraid that they may have become overvalued. They likewise find it difficult to sell stocks that have fallen substantially because they are afraid that they may have become undervalued.

The momentum strategy probably will become less profitable as the effect becomes better known. News traders and value traders will become more aggressive.

Technical traders who pursue momentum strategies must be extremely careful that they are the first to trade on the strategy and not the last. The price impacts of the first momentum traders will correct the mistakes made by other traders. Later momentum traders will simply cause prices to overreact. ◀

▶ Arbitrage in the Gold Market

An arbitrageur observes that the price of gold in London is lower than the price of gold in New York. If the price difference is greater than the cost of transporting gold from London to New York, plus the costs of trading it, the arbitrageur will buy gold in London and sell gold in New York. The arbitrageur will profit if the price difference grows smaller. ◀

They may tabulate frequency distributions, run regressions, or employ esoteric pattern recognition models like neural networks. Some technical traders even consider psychological models in their attempts to predict when traders make mistakes. Whatever the method, the defining characteristic of technical trading is its emphasis on pattern recognition rather than on economic analyses of material fundamental information.

Technical trading is not profitable in efficient markets. To trade profitably, technical traders must accurately predict price changes. In efficient markets, price changes are unpredictable because prices are close to values and because value changes are unpredictable.

10.5.4 Arbitrageurs

The final type of informed trader is the arbitrageur. *Arbitrageurs* simultaneously buy and sell similar instruments. They try to identify instruments that are inconsistently priced relative to each other. They then buy the cheaper instruments and sell the more expensive ones. Arbitrageurs profit if the cheaper instruments appreciate and the expensive ones depreciate, if the cheaper instruments appreciate faster than the expensive ones, or if the expensive instruments depreciate faster than the cheaper ones.

Instruments are similar when their values depend on common fundamental valuation factors. A *fundamental valuation factor* is a variable upon which instrument values depend. Common factors may include macroeconomic variables like interest rates, national income, unemployment, and expected inflation; industry variables like sales, wages, prices, product innovations, and competitive conditions; physical variables like the weather, agricultural pests, and solar activity; political variables like legislative, executive, judicial, and military interventions; and social variables like crime and social unrest. The actual factors upon which instrument values depend, vary substantially across instruments. Some examples appear in table 10-2.

Successful arbitrageurs must accurately estimate relative differences in value, but they need not form an opinion about which instrument, if any, is correctly priced. By simultaneously buying and selling similar instruments, they protect themselves against price changes due to common factors. If prices go up because all instruments are undervalued, they make money on their purchases and lose money on their sales. If prices go down because all instruments are overvalued, they lose money on their purchases and make money on their sales. In either event, they make money on net if the instruments they purchase are undervalued relative to the instruments they sell. They profit if their purchases are more undervalued then their sales, if their purchases are not as overvalued as their sales, or if their purchases are undervalued and their sales are overvalued.

Arbitrageurs use many methods to estimate relative differences in instrument values. Some arbitrageurs use statistical methods to characterize the normal relations among instrument prices. Others use economic

TABLE 10-2.
Some Common Valuation Factors of Similar Instruments

FIRST INSTRUMENT	SECOND INSTRUMENT	SOME COMMON VALUATION FACTORS
Gold in London	Gold in New York	The value of gold
Chrysler stock	Ford stock	Auto industry conditions General stock market conditions Labor relations
S&P 500 Index futures contract	An S&P 500 Index portfolio	All factors that affect the S&P 500 stocks
Soybean oil	Soybean meal	Weather Crop pests Livestock prices
Government bonds	Corporate bonds	Interest rates
Dollar/euro exchange rate	Dollar/yen exchange rate	U.S., European, and Japanese interest rates Trade relations Monetary and fiscal policies
Corporate bonds	Stocks	Expected inflation General economic conditions

Note: Two instruments have a common valuation factor if both instruments' values depend on that factor.

▶ The Law of One Price

The prices of live cattle and of pork bellies both depend on the price of corn because feedlot operators usually produce these commodities by feeding corn to animals. Although these prices also depend on many other common factors, the price of corn is especially important because corn often represents a significant fraction of the total value of all inputs used to create these products. In the long run, when the corn prices are high, cattle and pork prices are high.

The law of one price holds that the prices of live cattle and of pork bellies should both reflect the same information about corn prices. ◀

models to characterize how instrument prices depend on common underlying factors. Still others use psychological models to predict when and how traders will misprice one instrument relative to another. Regardless of their methods, all arbitrageurs trade when the relations between two or more prices differ significantly from the relations that their models predict.

Although arbitrageurs trade to make profits, the effect of their trading is to enforce the law of one price. The *law of one price* holds that identical instruments should have identical prices. For instruments that are similar but not identical, the law of one price holds that their prices should be consistent with respect to the values of their common factors. For example, if two instruments depend on the price of corn, the prices of both instruments should reflect the same price of corn. In general, the law of one price implies that all instrument prices reflect the same common factor values.

Arbitrageurs unwittingly enforce the law of one price when they arrange their arbitrage trades. Their buying tends to push up the prices of cheap instruments, and their selling tends to lower the prices of expensive instruments. When arbitrageurs correctly identify inconsistently priced instruments, their trading helps rationalize instrument prices and thereby makes prices more informative.

The price impacts of arbitrage trades are transaction costs. The less impact arbitrageurs have on prices, the more money they make. Once arbitrageurs have established their positions, they hope that prices will quickly adjust to their proper relations. These price changes make their trades profitable.

Arbitrageurs lose money when they mistakenly conclude that instruments are mispriced relative to each other. This often happens when the price of one instrument changes and the price of a similar instrument does not. If the price of the first instrument increases, an arbitrageur may sell it and buy the second one. If the first price drops, an arbitrageur may buy the first instrument and sell the second one. Whether these trades are profitable depends on the reason for the first price change. Three cases are possible:

- The two instruments were priced correctly relative to each other before the initial price change, and they are priced correctly relative to each other afterward.

  Although the instruments are similar, they are not identical. A change in some factor specific to the first instrument may have caused the price change. Arbitrage trades in this case are not profitable because the instruments are correctly priced relative to each other. These trades generate transaction costs, as do the trades necessary to unwind these positions. Arbitrageurs who trade in this case therefore tend to lose money.

- The two instruments were priced correctly relative to each other before the price change, and no instrument-specific factor changed.

  The two instruments therefore are no longer properly priced relative to each other. Either the first price should not have changed, or the second price should have changed in the same direction. If some common factor caused the first price to change, then the second price should have changed, too. If no common factors changed, the first instrument price should not have changed. Arbitrage trades in this case tend to be profitable because the instruments are not correctly priced relative to each other.

TABLE 10-3.
Informed Trader Types

TRADER TYPE	MOST SKILLED AT ESTIMATING . . .	INFORMATION SPECIALTY	TYPICAL TRADING SPEED
Value traders	Total value	All available information	Slow
News traders	Changes in value	News	Fast on public information; slow on private information
Information-oriented technical traders	Systematic valuation mistakes	Statistical anomalies	Fast
Arbitrageurs	Relative values	Relative factor prices	Fast

- The two instruments were not priced correctly relative to each other before the price change, but they are afterward.

  The price change corrected the price of the first instrument. Arbitrage trades in this case are not profitable because the instruments are correctly priced relative to each other. They merely generate transaction costs.

Successful arbitrageurs must discriminate among these three cases. Those who can accurately identify bona fide arbitrage opportunities trade profitably. Those who falsely identify too many arbitrage opportunities lose money through excessive transaction costs.

10.5.5 Informed Trader Summary

Each of the four types of informed traders acts on a different type of information. Value traders use the stock of all available information. News traders profit from learning new information before other traders do. Information-oriented technical traders profit by identifying predictable price patterns that result when value traders and news traders make mistakes. Finally, arbitrageurs trade on information about relative instrument values rather than absolute instrument values. Table 10-3 provides a summary of these informed traders.

10.6 COMPETITION, TRADING PROFITS, AND INFORMATIVE PRICES

The first half of this chapter describes how the various types of informed traders trade to profit from their information. We now examine when informed trading is profitable, where informed trading profits come from, and what determines how informative prices are.

10.6.1 Informative Prices

Prices become informative in two ways. First, when fundamental values are well known, prices reflect those values because no trader will trade at any other prices. No buyer will pay more than the known value of an instrument,

▶ Liquidity and Predictability

It may be better to be a slightly informed trader in a very liquid market than to be a very well-informed trader in an illiquid market. The following example illustrates this point. (You need not follow the algebra to understand the example.)

Futures contracts in the instructional Iowa Electronic Markets pay 1 dollar if some event occurs and nothing otherwise. Suppose all traders believe that an event upon which a contract depends has a 30 percent probability of occurring. If no one has any private information, and if traders care only about the expected value of the contract, the contract price will be 30 cents.

From very careful research, you believe the probability that the event will occur is greater than 30 percent. Let π represent your estimate of the probability. If π is 100 percent, you are extremely well informed. If π is only a little above 30 percent, your insight is not very good.

No one else knows that you are well informed. Other traders, however, suspect that some traders may be well informed. Consequently, the more contracts you buy, the higher their price will be. To keep this example simple, assume that you know you are the only trader with any private information.

For illustrative purposes, suppose that the following formula characterizes the average price of your purchases:

$$P = 0.3 + \frac{Q}{4\ell},$$

where P is your average purchase price in dollars, Q is the total quantity that you purchase, and ℓ is a parameter that characterizes the liquidity of the market. When ℓ is large, you can buy a lot without having much price impact.

How many contracts should you buy to maximize your expected profits? The answer depends on the quality of your information π and on the liquidity of the market ℓ. To derive the answer, your must compute your expected profits. The expected value of owning the contract, given your information, is simply π because it pays a dollar with probability π. The expected value of your position is therefore πQ. The total cost of acquiring your position is PQ, so your expected profits are

$$\pi Q - PQ = \pi Q - \left(0.3Q + \frac{Q}{4\ell}\right)Q$$

$$= (\pi - 0.3)Q - \frac{Q^2}{4\ell}.$$

The quantity that maximizes this expression is

$$Q = 2\ell(\pi - 0.3).$$

You can derive this result by using calculus or by observing that the profit formula is a quadratic formula which describes an inverted parabola with zero profits at $Q = 0$ and $Q = 4\ell(\pi - 0.3)$. Since parabolas are symmetric, the maximum is midway between these two values.

Substituting this quantity into the profit expression gives the maximum expected profits:

$$\ell(\pi - 0.3)^2.$$

This expression shows that you expect to make more money if the market is liquid and if your information is very good.

If you have poor information in a very liquid market, you may expect to make more than if you have excellent information in an illiquid market. For example, the expected profits for $\ell = 10,000$ and $\pi = 40$ percent are 100 dollars. They are only 49 dollars for $\ell = 100$ and $\pi = 100$ percent. ◀

You can learn more about the Iowa Electronic Markets at www.biz.uiowa.edu/iem.

and no seller will accept less than that value. Second, when values are not well known, informed traders make prices informative. The price impacts of their trading cause prices to reflect the information they collect. Prices therefore will be informative when fundamental values are well known or when informed traders collect and act fully on all available information. Since values are not common knowledge in most markets, informed trading is the more important process by which prices become informative.

10.6.2 Informed Trading Profits

The profits of informed traders depend on their ability to predict future prices and on the impact their trading has on prices. They are most profitable when they can accurately predict prices and when the price impacts of their trading are small. Their trading profits must cover their costs of acquiring and processing their information, their commission costs, the value of their time, and all other normal costs of doing business. Otherwise, their operations will not be economically viable, and they will quit trading.

10.6.2.1 Orthogonality

Since profitability of informed trading depends on liquidity, the most profitable informed traders are often those who want to trade when no other informed traders want to trade. Such traders do not have to compete with other traders to complete their trades. Liquidity therefore is relatively cheap for them.

Informed traders who want to trade when no other informed traders want to trade either have unique insights that other traders do not have, or they have estimated values incorrectly. If they have estimated values incorrectly, the cheap liquidity that they obtain often lowers the costs of their mistake. If they have estimated values correctly, the cheap liquidity increases their trading profits.

Traders who estimate values from the same information, using the same methods, tend to estimate the same values. Their estimates are *highly correlated*. They must compete with each other to profit from their insights. Traders whose estimates are not closely correlated with the estimates of other traders have *orthogonal* estimates. (*Orthogonal* comes from a Greek word that means "at right angles.") Traders obtain orthogonal estimates of value when they base their estimates on information that other traders do not use or when they analyze data using different methods than other traders use.

The most profitable traders have very accurate estimates of value that are uncorrelated with the value estimates made by other traders. Their value estimates are precise and orthogonal. They are right when nobody else is right.

Since precision and orthogonality both increase profits, a trade-off exists between them. Traders may be equally profitable with precise, highly correlated estimates of value and with imprecise, orthogonal value estimates. You can make a lot of money being right when nobody else is, even if it does not happen too often. You will not make much money, however, if you lose a lot when you are wrong and everyone else is right.

10.6.3 The Role of Uninformed Traders

Prices will not reflect information obtained by informed traders if they do not trade. We therefore must know when informed traders profit to understand the origins of informative prices.

First note that informed traders cannot trade profitably if they trade only with each other. Since trading is a zero-sum game, their aggregate profits would be zero. The better-informed among them would profit at the expense of the less well-informed. The losers eventually would stop trading. The remaining better-informed traders then would profit from the remaining less well-informed traders. Those losers eventually would stop trading. In the end, only the best-informed trader would want to trade, but no one would trade with him. There would be no informed trading, and prices would not reflect information gathered by informed traders.

Informed trading can be profitable only when informed traders trade with uninformed traders. Although uninformed traders lose on average to informed traders, they tolerate these losses because they obtain other valuable services from the market. (Chapter 8 discusses the reasons why uninformed traders—primarily investors, borrowers, hedgers, asset exchangers, and gamblers—trade.)

Uninformed traders naturally do not like to trade with informed traders because they do not want to lose to them. Uninformed traders therefore want to know who is well informed so that they can avoid trading with them. Informed traders, of course, do not want other traders to identify them. They try to trade anonymously, or they pretend to be uninformed traders. Informed trading is expensive in markets where traders can easily identify informed traders. Such markets may have less informative prices than other markets do.

Informed trading is most profitable in markets with many uninformed traders. In such markets, many informed traders compete to acquire information and act on it. These markets therefore have very informative prices. Of course, if prices are quite informative, informed traders may have few large profit opportunities. Uninformed traders therefore lose little individually, although they lose much in aggregate. When prices reflect fundamental values, uninformed traders most often trade with other uninformed traders.

10.6.4 A Market Paradox

This analysis suggests an interesting paradox. If prices are quite informative, informed trading will not be profitable. But if informed trading is not profitable, informed traders will not trade, and prices will not be informative! Since the conclusion of this argument is inconsistent with the assumption upon which it is based, some part must be wrong.

It may be that fundamental values are well known. In that case, prices would be informative even without informed traders. This simple solution to the paradox is not attractive, however, because values are rarely well known.

Alternatively, prices may not always be very informative. When prices differ significantly differ from fundamental values, informed traders trade and make money. Their trading makes prices more informative and eliminates further profit opportunities, at which point they do not trade further. If prices or values change, prices then may significantly differ from values so that informed traders can again profit by trading. Since prices and fundamental values change constantly, this resolution of the paradox seems most reasonable. Informed traders make prices informative, but prices are not always informative.

Prices move away from fundamental values when values change and prices do not change accordingly, or when prices change without a change in values. The former often happens when news arrives. The latter happens when trading by uninformed traders moves prices. Both situations create profit opportunities for informed traders.

Fundamental values change constantly as the world changes, and as people learn new information that they can use to predict what will happen in the future. News traders who learn news first profit most from these changes in value. If they under- or overreact to the news, value traders may recognize their mistakes and trade on the resulting profit opportunities. If the news traders or the value traders make systematic, predictable mistakes when estimating values, information-oriented technical traders may recognize them and trade profitably. If the changes in values are due to changes in common valuation factors, arbitrageurs may profit if they find that similar instruments are no longer priced correctly relative to each other.

Uninformed traders also cause prices to differ from fundamental values. When they make large trades or when many small traders all trade on the same side of the market, they often push prices away from fundamental values. Since uninformed traders are hard to distinguish from informed traders, most traders cannot determine whether prices are changing because uninformed traders are trading or because informed traders are trading in response to changes in values. The traders most able to make these distinctions are value traders. They profit when they recognize that prices differ significantly from fundamental values. They must be very sure, however, that no new information caused the price changes. If they miss an important development, their value estimates will be wrong, they will trade with news traders, and they will lose to them. Technical traders who can determine when uninformed traders have traded also may profit. Finally, arbitrageurs may profit if the price changes cause them to conclude that similar instruments are no longer priced correctly relative to each other. Like the value traders, however, they must be very sure that no new information about instrument-specific factors caused the price changes. Otherwise, they will lose to news traders.

10.6.5 Competition Among Informed Traders

Informed trading is a business in which traders compete for profits. Some succeed and others fail. The most successful informed traders collect material information more efficiently, and trade on that information with less price impact, than do less successful traders. Those traders who cannot collect material information at low cost or who trade poorly eventually fail. The least successful informed traders who stay in business have trading profits that just cover their total expenses.

If informed trading becomes particularly profitable, many traders enter the market to compete for those profits. Profits drop as more informed traders compete for the liquidity that they need to establish their positions. Their trading drives prices closer to fundamental values and thereby decreases informed trading profits. The increased competition eventually makes it impossible for additional traders to enter and profit.

The entry and exit of informed traders is a slow process because traders cannot easily predict how profitable their operations will be. Since informed

▶ The Dollar Price of a Five-dollar Bill

To buy a five-dollar bill, you must trade something for it. If you trade one-dollar bills, the price is usually five such bills for a five-dollar bill. The market in which five-dollar bills trade for single-dollar bills is strong-form efficient because the value of a five-dollar bill is common knowledge.

On very rare occasions, however, the price of five-dollar bills may vary. For example, suppose you need to rent a baggage cart from a machine at the airport that accepts only one-dollar bills. You have a five but no ones. You may be willing to sell your five-dollar bill for less than five single-dollar bills if no one is able or willing to give you its common price. ◀

traders do not share their information, they usually do not know how well informed they are relative to other informed traders. They therefore must use indirect methods to predict their profitability.

Many traders predict their profitability from their past performance. This method is not reliable, however, because poorly informed traders often profit by good luck, and well-informed traders sometimes lose through bad luck. Consequently, some poorly informed traders may trade for a long time before they realize they should not be trading, and some well-informed traders may refrain from trading because they do not recognize their advantages.

Predicting profitability is the most important problem that informed traders face. All traders who trade only for profits must address this problem if they have any doubts as to whether they will be successful. We consider the performance prediction problem in chapter 22.

10.6.6 Market Efficiency

Prices never fully reflect all information that informed traders could collect and act on. Informed traders will not collect information that is expensive to acquire if they cannot profit from that information. Some information may simply be too expensive, or of such little consequence, that it does not pay to trade on it. The information in prices therefore depends on the costs of obtaining that information as well as the opportunities to act upon it.

Financial economists have undertaken numerous empirical studies to determine how efficient various markets are. To classify their results, they have created three traditional definitions of market efficiency.

Markets are *weak-form efficient* if prices reflect all information in past prices so that no one can predict future price changes from knowing only past prices. In weak-form efficient markets, price charts and statistical analyses of past prices are useless. Prices simply appear to follow a random walk. Most published empirical studies have determined that markets are weak-form efficient. (Of course, if researchers found otherwise, they might trade on their results rather than publish them!)

Markets are *semistrong-form efficient* if prices reflect all publicly available information so that no one can predict future price changes using only public information. Publicly available information includes all public news, past prices, and volumes in all securities and contracts. If markets are semistrong-form efficient, informed traders can make money only if they have access to information that is not publicly available. The empirical evidence suggests that markets generally are semistrong-form efficient with respect to easily obtained and easily interpreted public information.

Markets are *strong-form efficient* if prices reflect all available public and private information as soon as it is known. Since informed traders can never profit in strong-form efficient markets, the only strong-form efficient markets are those which trade instruments for which values are commonly known. Such markets are rarely interesting.

These three traditional definitions of market efficiency do not recognize that acquiring and acting on information is costly. The following definition is more sensitive to these market microstructure issues. In an *efficient market*, prices reflect all information that traders can acquire and profitably trade upon. This definition implicitly incorporates the costs of acquiring information, the costs of acting on it, and the impact that informed trading has on prices.

10.6.7 The Trade-off Between Liquidity and Informative Prices

Although informative prices greatly benefit our economy by making production and allocation decisions more efficient, informative prices are not cheap. The money that uninformed traders lose to informed traders pays for much of the information that goes into prices. These costs lower the net benefits that uninformed traders obtain from using the markets for their utilitarian purposes—mainly to move money through time, to exchange risks and assets, and to gamble. Since these activities (with the possible exception of gambling) also benefit our economy, a trade-off sometimes exists between the benefits of informative prices and of liquid markets. In particular, policies that frustrate informed traders may make prices less informative while increasing market liquidity. Restrictions on insider trading (see chapter 29) are an example of such policies.

Deciding between price efficiency and market liquidity is very difficult when evaluating alternative market structures. Most regulators would balance the benefits of these two market characteristics. Unfortunately, these benefits are extremely hard to measure.

The total benefits to the economy of informative prices probably greatly outweigh the money that uninformed traders lose to informed traders. Informative prices are essential to efficient production and allocation decisions in market-based economies. When people make these decisions poorly, everyone suffers. In contrast, although the utilitarian services that uninformed traders obtain from our markets are also important to our economy, traders can obtain some of these services through other means. Moreover, if losses to informed traders merely tax the utilitarian uses of the markets rather than curtail them, no utilitarian benefits will be lost.

These observations about total benefits are instructive, but they are not very useful when we compare alternative market structures. To make such comparisons properly, we must know how these benefits change when switching from one structure to the other. A comparison of total benefits therefore is not relevant. Only a comparison of the changes in benefits is relevant. Such comparisons, unfortunately, usually are very hard to make.

10.6.8 The Benefits of Public Information

Some policies can increase both market liquidity and price efficiency. Policies that promote the publication of material fundamental information advance both objectives. They make informed trading less profitable while still producing prices that are more informative.

Publishing information allows traders to know values better. If traders can easily interpret the information, prices will immediately reflect the new information, and informed traders will not profit. If only informed traders can interpret the information, publication allows all such traders to act on the information. Since only the first traders to trade will profit, they all will try to trade quickly. Their race to profit causes prices to change quickly and makes it easy for uninformed traders to infer their estimates of value. The informed traders therefore do not profit as much as they would if they could trade at a slower rate. In both events, publishing information causes prices to become more informative while decreasing the profits that informed traders make from uniformed traders.

The publication of fundamental information also lowers the costs of

▶ Trading Halts for Impending Information

Many stock markets require that their listed firms contact them before the release of material information to the public. These markets then halt trading until after the information release. This rule allows all traders an opportunity to evaluate the new information before trading resumes. News traders consequently make less money from uninformed traders—particularly those who offer liquidity. This is especially true when all traders can easily interpret the new information.

Although trading halts for impending information protect uninformed traders, they also make prices less informative. Which effect is more important?

The protection of uninformed traders is probably more important than the lost price efficiency. Informative prices are extremely important to our economy, but it is hard to imagine that a few minutes' delay in price formation would significantly depreciate the quality of resource allocation decisions. Informed trading, however, clearly hurts traders who offer liquidity. The net benefits of this trading halt rule are probably positive. ◀

▶ *Trading Places* **and the USDA Orange Harvest Report**

One of the most famous trading scenes in a motion picture appears in the climax of the 1983 comedy *Trading Places*. (Do not read the next paragraph if you have not seen the movie!)

Don Ameche and Ralph Bellamy are evil commodity traders who have arranged to receive the U.S. Department of Agriculture's January *Monthly Estimate of Orange Production* before its publication. Their abused former employees, Dan Aykroyd and Eddie Murphy, learn of the illegal scheme. They intercept the report, alter it to make the harvest look worse than it is, and then pass it on to Ameche and Bellamy. In the climactic scene, the employers and their former employees trade frozen orange juice concentrate futures against each other on the trading floor of the New York Cotton Exchange Citrus Associates. Ameche and Bellamy buy heavily and push prices up. Aykroyd and Murphy sell heavily at the top. When the USDA releases the true report, prices drop precipitously on tremendous volume as Ameche and Bellamy try to sell out of their losing position. At the bottom, Aykroyd and Murphy buy to cover their short positions. The villains go bankrupt, and our heroes become multimillionaires.

Although the director, John Landis, exaggerated the scene for comic effect, it accurately represents the importance of the USDA orange production estimates. Since this report provides the most accurate estimate of the coming harvest, prices often change dramatically when the estimate is significantly different from what traders were expecting. The winter reports are especially significant when frosts have decreased crop yields.

The USDA National Agricultural Statistics Service takes extreme care to prevent the early release of its crop reports. Highly trusted statisticians prepare the report overnight in shuttered rooms that have no access to telephone or computer networks. The data they use arrives at the USDA encrypted. The statisticians decrypt the data only after they lock down to produce the report.

The USDA used to release the orange production report during the futures trading session, as shown in the movie. It now releases the report at 8:30 A.M., before the market opens. ◀

being an informed trader. Informed traders therefore can trade profitably on smaller differences between prices and values then they otherwise would, so that prices become more informative.

Many stock markets require that their listed firms publish substantial fundamental information in a timely manner. These reports make prices more informative and reduce the losses of uninformed traders to informed traders.

In markets that do not have such reporting standards, many firms voluntarily provide this information to make their stocks more attractive to investors. The managers of these firms know that investors will pay more for their stocks if the risk of losing to informed traders is small. Many firms are now placing their information on the Web.

Most governments have agencies that produce statistical information about the economy and about supply and demand conditions in various markets. Traders use this information to estimate commodity values and asset prices. When these agencies produce high-quality information, prices become more informative and farmers, manufacturers, retailers, and service providers make better production decisions. Generally, these public agencies freely distribute their reports.

Numerous private companies gather information about fundamental values to sell to others. Generally, only the traders who subscribe to their services can access their information. In the United States, these companies include BARRA, Bloomberg, Bridge Information Services, DataStream International, Dow Jones News Retrieval Service, Dun & Bradstreet, Edgar Online.Com, Ibbotson Associates, I/B/E/S, Moody's Investors Service, Reuters, Securities Data Corporation, Standard and Poor's Compustat, Standard & Poor's Equity Investor Services, Value Line, and Zacks Investment Research.

10.7 SUMMARY

Informed traders make prices informative. They acquire information that they hope will allow them to estimate values accurately. They buy when prices are lower than their value estimates and sell otherwise. Their buying and selling push prices up and down. They move prices closer to their estimates of value and thereby make prices more informative.

Four types of informed traders try to profit from information about fundamental values. Value traders estimate fundamental values by using all available information. News traders estimate changes in fundamental values from new information. Information-oriented technical traders identify patterns that are inconsistent with prices which reflect fundamental values. Arbitrageurs estimate differences in fundamental values across instruments.

Informed traders make markets efficient. In an efficient market, prices reflect all information that traders can acquire and profitably trade upon. How informative prices are depends on the costs of acquiring information, and on how much liquidity is available to informed traders. If information is expensive, or the market is not liquid, prices will not be very informative. Since trading is a zero-sum game, informed traders can profit only if uninformed traders lose to them. Prices therefore will not be informative in markets with few uninformed traders.

Informed traders compete with each other to profit from acquiring and acting upon information. Only those traders who can collect and analyze information at low cost, and who can trade effectively, are profitable.

No market is always completely efficient. Informed traders could not profit in such markets. Prices become more informative when informed traders push prices toward values. Prices become less informative when values change or when uninformed traders move prices. News traders tend to make money when values change. Value traders tend to make money when uninformed traders move prices.

Traders who intend to speculate should carefully consider why they expect to be successful. The most common mistake informed traders make is to trade when they have no comparative advantage. We consider how to predict performance in chapter 22.

10.8 SOME POINTS TO REMEMBER

- Informed traders make prices informative.
- Value traders estimate fundamental values.
- News traders estimate changes in fundamental values.

- Information-oriented technical traders estimate patterns that are inconsistent with fundamental values.
- Arbitrageurs estimate differences in fundamental values.
- Prices are most informative when the costs of obtaining information and the costs of trading are both low.
- When prices fully reflect all available information, nobody can forecast future price changes.
- Prices cannot always be completely informative.
- Trading is a zero-sum game when performance is measured relative to the market return.
- Informed traders profit only when other traders are willing to lose to them. Markets therefore require utilitarian traders in order to produce informative prices.

10.9 QUESTIONS FOR THOUGHT

1. What are the differences between data and information? How are the two produced?
2. In the short run, what effect do you expect an increase in the price of corn would have on the prices of cattle and hogs?
3. In the "Liquidity and Predictability" example, how would the analysis differ if you competed with other informed traders? How would it differ if you were risk averse?
4. Should regulators exclude gamblers from financial markets? How could they exclude them? What effect would their exclusion have on price efficiency in the long run?
5. Should stock markets impose financial reporting standards upon their listed firms?
6. Many government agencies and many private companies collect and publish fundamental information about supply and demand conditions in various markets. What is the purpose of these activities? What effect do they have on the markets? Should the government sector or the private sector conduct this research?
7. In their race to profit, informed traders often duplicate their research efforts. Since research is often very expensive, these duplicative efforts suggest that the competition among informed traders creates economic inefficiencies. Should informed traders collude to lower their costs? Would their collusion make prices more efficient? Should regulators address this issue? If so, how?
8. What is the optimal level of informed trading?
9. Do you have any reason to believe that you would be a profitable informed trader?
10. Futures, stock, and options exchanges constantly create markets for new instruments. What factors determine whether a market will be successful?
11. Can value traders make money if fundamental values follow a random walk?

*O**rder anticipators* are speculators who try to profit by trading before other traders trade. They make money when they correctly anticipate how other traders will affect prices or when they can extract option values from the orders that other traders offer to the market.

Order anticipators include front runners, sentiment-oriented technical traders, and squeezers. *Front runners* collect information about trades that other traders have decided to arrange. *Sentiment-oriented technical traders* try to predict trades that uninformed traders will decide to make. *Squeezers* try to exploit traders who must trade by cornering the market.

Order anticipators are *parasitic traders*. They profit only when they can prey on other traders. They do not make prices more informative, and they do not make markets more liquid. To trade profitably, you must avoid these traders. You therefore must understand how they trade.

Large traders are especially vulnerable to order anticipators. You must be familiar with parasitic traders to understand how large traders expose their orders.

Some front runners obtain their information about trader intentions from brokers. If you trade with brokers, if you are a broker, if you are interested in becoming a broker, or if you regulate brokers, you must know how brokers occasionally expose orders unwittingly or intentionally.

Trading by order anticipators often makes prices more volatile and markets less efficient. If volatility and price efficiency interest you, you must consider how order anticipators affect the markets.

Uninformed traders sometimes affect prices significantly. Traders who can predict what uninformed traders will do therefore can sometimes profit from that knowledge. If you have these skills, how sentiment-oriented technical traders trade should interest you.

Even if you cannot predict what uninformed traders will do, you may be able to identify what uninformed traders have done after the fact. Although you cannot profit directly from this information, you can use it to better understand why your trading strategies worked or failed. Understanding how sentiment-oriented technical traders collect and process information will help you to better understand uninformed traders.

In markets that enforce time precedence, order anticipators must improve price by at least the minimum price increment to trade ahead of other traders. The size of the price increment therefore greatly affects the profitability of order anticipators' strategies in such markets. You must be familiar with order anticipation trading strategies in order to form reasonable opinions about the proper size of the minimum price increment.

11.1 FRONT RUNNERS

Front runners collect information about trades that other traders have decided to arrange. They then try to trade before those traders complete their

▷ An Illegal Front-running Scheme Involving a Violation of Confidentiality

Rob is a runner who works for a large brokerage house on the floor of a futures exchange. Rob's job is to carry orders from his firm's telephone booth on the perimeter of the exchange floor to his firm's brokers in various trading pits.

Nate trades commodity futures for his own account in one of those pits. He and Rob have arranged a set of signals by which Rob can surreptitiously tell Nate that he is carrying a large buy or sell order. They may convey their signal by a glance at a clock, by the hand in which Rob carries the order, by the placement of a pen in a pocket or behind an ear, or by some other means. Rob and Nate employ a variety of signals to make it difficult for anyone to detect what they are doing.

When Nate sees the signal for a large buy order, he immediately buys contracts for his own account. After Rob delivers the order to his firm's broker, the broker buys contracts to fill it. Nate profits as the broker pushes the price up to fill the order. Nate sometimes sells his newly acquired contracts to the broker. Afterward, Nate and Rob split the profits.

Their profits come at the expense of the broker's customers. The customers pay higher prices when buying and obtain lower prices when selling because Nate takes liquidity that they otherwise would have taken.

This scheme is very difficult to detect in actively traded markets. To prevent it, brokerage firms, their customers, and exchanges must carefully watch how prices change before and after orders arrive. They must try to remember who traded before large orders arrived so that they can identify systematic patterns that might suggest a front-running problem.

Brokers also must secure their communications to prevent these schemes. At several exchanges, new wireless electronic order delivery systems eliminate the need for floor runners and thereby remove potential for fraud in that link of the order transmission chain. ◀

---

trades. Front runners may obtain their information from public sources, from the traders they front-run, or from brokers. Practitioners call them front runners because they hurry (run) to trade before (in front of) other traders.

Front-running strategies differ according to the type of trader that they front-run. Front runners may trade in front of aggressive traders or passive traders. *Aggressive traders* demand liquidity, and *passive traders* offer liquidity.

11.1.1 Front Running Aggressive Traders

Aggressive traders usually issue market orders. Their demands often push prices up when they buy and down when they sell. Front runners who trade ahead of aggressive traders profit from the price impact of the aggressive traders' trades.

In most markets, front running is illegal when the front runner improperly obtains information about the incoming order. Front runners obtain information improperly when they violate a confidential brokerage relationship or when they eavesdrop on confidential communications. These violations may take place at any point between the receipt of the order by the broker and its final execution.

Not all front running is illegal. Observant traders on the floor of an exchange can often infer an order from how a broker handles it. Brokers must be especially careful to avoid revealing their orders inadvertently.

▶ Legal Front Running by an Observant Trader

Rifka and Jon have traded on the same options floor for years. Although they are not friends, their proximity to each other has allowed them to become very well acquainted. Rifka trades for her own account. Jon is a floor broker for a large firm.

Rifka has noticed that Jon behaves slightly differently when he receives a large order than a small order. The differences are very subtle; Rifka cannot even articulate what she sees. She just knows from experience when Jon has a large order.

Jon's behavior does not reveal whether the order is a buy or sell order. Rifka often guesses correctly because she has noticed that Jon tends to buy after he has bought and sell after he has sold: At least one of Jon's clients probably splits his or her large orders.

When Rifka suspects that Jon has received a large order, she will try to front-run it. If she feels confident about the side of the order, she may try to beat Jon to the market. Otherwise, she will wait to see which side Jon needs to trade. She may then better his price and hope to make a profit when Jon's client returns to the market.

Rifka's trading is legal. Her profits come from recognizing Jon's shortcomings as a broker and from noting that Jon's clients tend to split their orders. She is a profitable trader because she is observant and because she acts quickly on her information. ◀

Front runners sometimes obtain information about orders when brokers call them to arrange trades. Brokers who want to arrange a large trade must call traders they think might be willing to take the other side. They often reveal their orders in these calls. Although front runners may legally exploit this information, those who do so risk harming their relationships with these brokers. Brokers must be very careful to expose orders only to traders who will most likely take the other side. They most avoid exposing their orders to traders who would front-run their clients.

Front runners capture the benefits of price discrimination that large traders would otherwise obtain. In continuous auctions, large traders typically split their orders so that they can discriminate among the traders who offer them liquidity. They want to trade first with those traders offering the best prices and then, if necessary, with traders offering inferior prices. Splitting their orders thus produces a better average price than they would obtain if they had to fill their entire order at a single price. Front runners appropriate the benefits of price discrimination by taking liquidity from the traders offering the best prices. They then offer this liquidity back to the large traders at inferior prices. The effect of a successful front-running strategy is to force large traders to pay more uniform prices to fill their orders.

Under some very limited circumstances, front runners can be valuable to large traders. If front runners can find liquidity more cheaply than large traders can, the front runners may lower the costs of trading large sizes. To be of value to large traders, front runners must consolidate the other side and then deliver it to the large traders at a lower cost than the large traders could obtain on their own. Large traders who believe this is true should widely publicize their orders in some credible manner. Those who do are *sunshine traders*.

Although front runners sometimes may be better traders than large traders are, large traders will not benefit from front runners if many front

▶ Shop the Block

Brokers *shop the block* when they expose large orders. Not surprisingly, prices tend to rise when they widely shop a large block buy order, and fall when they widely shop a large block sell order. ◀

▶ Front Running by Skilled Traders

Stuart wants to buy 150,000 shares of a somewhat illiquid security. If he buys it himself without interference from front runners, he may be able to buy 30,000 shares for 100 and 30,000 more at every 10 cents from 100.10 to 100.40. His average price will be 100.20, which is better than the 100.40 price he would have to pay if he had to fill the entire order at one price.

Suppose that front runners are better traders than Stuart is. If they buy before he does, they may be able to find 50,000 shares at each price from 100 to 100.20 so that their average price is 100.10. If the front runners then sell to Stuart for 100.20, he will be indifferent to the front running. He may actually prefer to be front-run if they save him the costs of searching. Moreover, if Stuart negotiates well with the front runners, he may be able to drive them down from 100.20 toward 100.10. (Although he may be able to drive the front runners below 100.10 on any given transaction, they will not continue to front-run for him if he consistently forces losses on them.) Of course, if the front runners have some market power, they may *squeeze* Stuart so that he has to pay more than 100.40 to fill his order. ◀

runners compete to front-run them. The impact on price of many traders competing to acquire the same positions tends to be much greater than that of a single trader who trades strategically. Front runners generally trade less efficiently than large traders do because they trade too quickly. Front running therefore generally hurts the traders they front-run.

When large traders recognize that they cannot trade as well as a professional trader can, they commonly hire a professional to help them trade. They may hire a *block broker* to act as their agent, or they may ask a *block dealer* to facilitate their trades. Block dealers who *facilitate* their customers' trades trade their blocks at uniform prices. The dealers then try to profit by trading the block in the market at a better average price. In a sense, block traders are front runners whom large traders hire to help them solve their trading problems. We discuss block trading in detail in chapter 15.

11.1.2 Front Running Passive Traders

Passive traders offer liquidity to the market. They give other traders options to trade when they want to trade. They usually offer limit orders or quotes to the market. Front runners who trade in front of passive traders try to extract the option values of the passive traders' orders. Economists call such front runners *quote matchers*.

Quote matching is a front-running strategy in which quote matchers try to trade in front of (and on the same side as) large patient traders. Once the quote matchers trade, the orders they front-run protect them from serious losses on their positions. If prices move against them, quote matchers limit their losses by trading with the passive traders. If prices move in their favor, the quote matchers profit to the full extent of the price changes. Since the decimalization of the U.S. stock markets, quote matching has also been called *penny jumping*.

The returns that quote matchers can obtain are option-like returns. They are unbounded on one side and limited on the other side. Quote-matching return distributions are similar to return distributions for option contracts because quote matchers extract the option values of the standing orders that

▶ A Case of Self-front-running?

One of several market makers who trade the Spider (SPDR) at the American Stock Exchange told me the following story:

Over a period of several months in 1998–1999, a broker well known to the SPDR market makers would come to the post to trade extremely large orders. The largest such orders were for approximately 850,000 shares, or about 85 million dollars at the then current price of 100 dollars per share. The first few times this happened, the market makers would fill the orders, only to discover that they would lose money as the market regularly moved against their positions.

They soon paid very close attention to this broker. The market makers discovered that whenever he traded large size, the market would almost invariably move in the same direction within five minutes. They also noted that the broker would usually unwind these trades the same day at a substantial profit.

The market makers therefore started to hedge their positions by trading S&P 500 futures immediately upon filling these SPDR orders. After completing their hedge, they immediately continued to trade the futures on the same side to profit from the correlation between this broker's orders and the subsequent price change.

My correspondent reported that this happened about 70 to 90 times over about nine months. It then stopped as abruptly as it started. The broker's client usually correctly anticipated subsequent moves in the S&P 500 Index. The market makers made a small fortune on these trades once they figured out what was happening. They did not know, however, how the broker's client knew what direction the S&P 500 Index would move.

The market makers presumed that the client was front running very large program trades in the stock market. The client may have been front running another trader. In that case, the client, the broker, or both would have been violating the law.

Alternatively, the client may have been front running his own orders in an attempt to lower the net cost of his program trades. If the client was a large equity fund with an investment policy that prohibited trading in the futures markets, the SPDR would have been the only feasible alternative to execute this strategy. Self-front-running may lower the cost of a program trade when highly correlated markets do not move in perfect lockstep. By submitting orders to both markets at the same time, a trader obtains the liquidity in both markets without either market realizing the full size of his trade. ◀

▶ Quote Matching

Jose places a large limit buy order at 20 pesos. Maria sees the order and immediately submits her own limit buy order at 20.01. An incoming market sell order arrives, and Maria's order is matched with it. If prices rise, Maria will profit to the full extent of the price rise. If prices fall, she will try to sell to Jose at 20, and her loss will be only 1 centavo.

Maria's potential return distribution is asymmetric. She has the possibility of significant gains, but her losses may be quite limited. If the probability of a price increase is about the same as a decrease, and if the probability that Jose cancels his order is not large, Maria's expected profits from this strategy would be positive. ◀

they front-run. When a quote matcher buys stock in front of a large buy limit order, the quote matcher has a long position in the stock and hopes to use the long put option offered by the buy limit order should she need it. The combination of a long stock position and a long put position has the same return distribution as a call option. Likewise, when a quote matcher sells stock in front of a large sell order, the quote matcher has a short stock position and hopes to use the call option implicit in the sell order should she need it. This combination has the same return distribution as a put option.

Quote matchers profit at the expense of passive traders. They take liquidity that otherwise would have gone to the passive traders. If the passive traders subsequently fail to trade because prices move away from their orders, they lose the profits that the quote matchers make.

▶ Trapping Quote Matchers

Jose knows that quote matchers often try to front-run his orders. To frustrate them, he occasionally cancels a standing order if he suspects that a trader has front-run him. He also sometimes traps quote matchers with the following strategy.

When Jose wants to be a seller, he baits his trap by submitting a large standing buy limit order. If a quote matcher posts a buy order in front of his order, he springs his trap by immediately selling to that order and simultaneously canceling his buy order. Otherwise, he cancels his buy order.

If the trap works, the quote matcher now has Jose's trading problem. The quote matcher needs to sell, but the apparent buyer upon whose order she was relying (Jose) has disappeared. ◀

Quote matchers will trade profitably only if the standing orders that they front-run are still standing should they need to close their positions quickly. If these trading options are no longer available, quote matchers will have trouble getting out of their positions when prices move against them. Quote matching will not be profitable if passive traders cancel their orders, if they adjust them frequently to reflect changes in values, or if other traders fill the passive traders' orders.

Since quote matchers must respond to changes in market conditions faster than the passive traders who they front-run, they must have excellent access to the markets. Successful quote matchers will tend to be floor traders in floor-based markets and computerized traders in screen-based markets.

Quote matching also will not be profitable if quote matchers must substantially improve prices in order to establish their positions. The price impacts of their trades are transaction costs. These costs decrease their profits if the strategy works, and they increase their losses if the strategy fails.

In markets that enforce time precedence, a large minimum price increment makes quote matching less profitable. In such markets, traders must improve prices by at least the minimum price increment to trade ahead of other traders. The minimum price increment therefore is the price that quote matchers must pay to front-run passive traders. They do not pay this price to the passive traders they front-run, however. Instead, they pay it to the traders with whom they trade to establish their positions. These traders would have traded with the passive traders if the quote matchers had not front-run them. In markets that enforce time precedence, front runners must pay traders on the other side a premium to prevent them from exercising the trading options that the quote matchers want to exploit.

To prevent losses to quote matchers, traders who supply liquidity must control how they expose their orders. They defend themselves from front runners by using floor brokers to hide their orders, by breaking up their orders, and by switching to market order strategies from limit order strategies. Unfortunately, these responses increase their transaction costs, lower displayed sizes, and reduce market transparency.

11.1.3 Front Runners and Market Efficiency

Whether front runners make prices more or less informative depends on whether they front-run informed traders or uninformed traders. In both cases, front running accelerates the price impacts of the traders they front-run.

When front runners front-run uninformed traders, their trades usually make prices less informative. When prices equal fundamental values before uninformed traders trade, their trading always make prices less informative. When prices differ from fundamental values, at best uninformed traders move prices toward fundamental values only by chance.

Front runners make prices more informative when they front-run informed traders. These trades move prices closer to fundamental values sooner than they would have otherwise.

The long-run effect of front running informed traders, however, may be to make prices less informative. Front running decreases the profits that informed traders make. Consequently, fewer informed traders will trade profitably. Those who can trade profitably will invest less in their information than they would if front runners did not front-run their trades. Front running of informed traders therefore will drive informed traders from the market, and prices will be less informative in the long run.

11.1.4 Front Runners and Liquidity

Front runners generally make markets less liquid. Since trading is a zero-sum game, their profits are transaction costs for other traders. If the front runners do not provide liquidity in exchange for these transaction costs, all other traders taken as a group would be better off if front runners did not trade.

Front runners generally provide no service to the traders they front-run. As noted above, front runners may benefit these traders only if they are better traders, if they do not compete with each other to quickly establish their front-running positions, and if they do not then squeeze the traders that they front-run. These conditions rarely are simultaneously true. If large traders thought they could benefit from front running, they would contract directly with block dealers or brokers to obtain these services. Rather than help traders, front runners generally hurt them by taking liquidity away from them.

Front runners benefit the traders with whom they trade when they improve prices to step in front of other traders. Front runners can offer better prices, however, only because they can extract more value from the traders they are front running. The increased costs that they impose on the traders they front-run therefore more than offset the benefits that other traders obtain from price improvement.

Front runners also affect liquidity through their effects on other traders. Traders alter their trading strategies to avoid losing to front runners. Some traders trade more aggressively. They may price their orders more aggressively, or they may demand liquidity rather than supply it. Both responses benefit traders on the other side of the market, but these benefits are exactly offset by the higher transaction costs of the more aggressive traders. Some traders trade less aggressively when confronted with the prospect of front running and the higher transaction costs it imposes on them. Their withdrawal from the market decreases liquidity.

Front runners are parasitic traders. They profit by extracting value from other traders, but they do not give back anything in exchange. The simplest proof of this conclusion lies in the observation that front runners do not offer to trade when they have no one to front-run. Front runners do not bring anything new to the table. Worse, they tend to drive away the orders from which they profit.

11.2 SENTIMENT-ORIENTED TECHNICAL TRADERS

Sentiment-oriented technical traders try to predict the trades that uninformed traders will decide to make. They then try to trade before the uninformed traders trade. Sentiment-oriented technical traders profit when they correctly anticipate the impacts that uninformed traders will have on prices.

Sentiment-oriented technical traders differ from front runners. Sentiment-oriented technical traders try to predict trading decisions that other traders have not yet made. In contrast, front runners trade on information about orders that other traders have submitted or intend to submit.

▶ **Predicting Investment Trades: The January Effect**

Historically, prices in the U.S. stock markets have risen more in January than in any other month of the year. Statistical analyses show that the difference between the average January return and the average of the other monthly returns appears too large to attribute just to chance. On average, over the 75-year period from 1926 to 2000, January returns have exceeded the other monthly returns by 0.85 percentage points.

One possible explanation involves year-end bonuses and pension fund contributions. Traders who invest these cash flows in January may be responsible for pushing the market up in that month. Tax selling in December also may be responsible for the January effect.

Sentiment-oriented technical traders who can predict these investment cash flows will buy in December or earlier to profit from the impact that these uninformed investors will have on price. If many such technical traders trade, they will push prices up well before January. ◀

Data source: CRSP combined NYSE and AMEX value-weighted, dividend-adjusted monthly return index.

Traders who can successfully predict the trades that informed traders will make are themselves well-informed traders. Since informed traders trade on information, only traders with their information can predict what trades they will decide to make.

Uninformed traders trade for many reasons (see chapter 8). Sentiment-oriented technical traders try to identify these reasons in order to predict when uninformed traders will trade. These reasons may be rational, or they may be the result of mistaken beliefs. Rational reasons to trade include investing, borrowing, hedging, asset exchanging, and gambling. Trading decisions based on mistaken beliefs typically involve mistakes that poor speculators make.

The information resources that sentiment-oriented technical traders use to make their predictions depend on the different types of trades that they try to predict.

- Traders who try to predict trades that investors and borrowers make examine data about intertemporal cash flows. These data include information about the timing and magnitude of paychecks, year-end bonuses, dividend payments, pension fund contributions, special subscriptions, and tax payments.

- Those who try to predict hedging trades consider the risks that concern people. They may collect data about production, inventories, and business commitments.

- Those who try to predict asset exchanges may study how production, sales, and international fund flows require traders to exchange assets.

- Those who try to predict what gamblers will do consider the factors that excite gamblers. They may collect information about what instruments are volatile and what securities are in the news.

- Those who try to predict the mistakes that speculators make consider how speculators form their opinions. These traders may examine data about past prices and volumes. They may also collect information from psychometric surveys designed to measure trader confidence and outlook.

▶ Predicting Hedging Trades: Dynamic Option Replication

Dealers who trade options often hedge their positions by buying or selling the underlying instruments. The effect of their trading is to replicate the returns to the options that they are hedging. The rates at which they make these trades depend on how underlying prices change and on several other factors that appear in mathematical formulas like the Black-Scholes option pricing equation. These hedging strategies are *dynamic hedges* because they require trades whenever the underlying prices change.

Some traders hedge assets by using dynamic hedges to simulate an options return. *Portfolio insurance* is an example of one such strategy.

Observant traders can predict the trades these hedgers make from recent price changes in the underlying instruments. These traders try to collect information about the size of the positions that the hedgers want to protect. They may obtain this information by examining option open interests, by surveying traders or their advisers, or by characterizing the relation between price changes and trading volumes. ◀

▶ Predicting Foreign Exchange Trades: IPOs in Asia

The mechanism for subscribing to an initial public stock offering in many Asian countries differs from that in the United States. In the United States, an investment bank allocates shares in an IPO before the offering. Only people who purchase the shares tender the cash to purchase them.

In Asia, traders who want to participate in an offering deposit the full purchase price with the investment bank before the offering. If the offering is oversubscribed, the bank allocates the shares on a pro rata basis. If the offering is very popular, it may be oversubscribed hundreds of times. Huge cash flows therefore may result.

If an Asian offering is very popular among international investors, the local currency may appreciate as investors buy it to tender to the offering. Traders who are aware of this phenomenon will try to predict when an offering will be very popular so that they can buy the currency before it appreciates. ◀

Sentiment-oriented technical trading can be quite risky because it involves front running uninformed traders. The impacts that uninformed traders have on prices often move prices away from their fundamental values. Such movements attract value traders to the other side of the market. If the value traders trade aggressively, they may drive prices back toward fundamental values, and sentiment-oriented technical traders then will lose. Sentiment-oriented technical traders therefore must know when to close their positions. If they hold their positions too long, they will lose when prices revert to fundamental values.

Since sentiment-oriented technical traders tend to lose to value traders, sentiment-oriented technical trading will be most profitable in instruments that are not easily valued. Value traders trade less aggressively in hard-to-value instruments than in instruments with values that they know well.

Perhaps the best examples of hard-to-value instruments are stocks in developing industries like the Internet. Their values are hard to estimate because they depend on uncertain technologies and on the development of unknown markets. Since these stocks tend to attract many uninformed traders, sentiment-oriented technical traders may occasionally identify profitable trading opportunities in them. The stocks and bonds of companies in emerging markets also may provide such opportunities for similar reasons.

▶ **Great Companies Are Not Always Good Investments**

Iomega makes high-capacity, removable media disk drives for personal computers. When it introduced the 100-megabyte Zip drive, it represented a very substantial improvement over existing 1.44-MB floppy disk drives. As investors became familiar with the product, the company's stock appreciated more than 1000 percent between June 1995 and May 1996. At its peak in May 1996, the total market value of the company was more than 10 percent of the value of IBM. It then fell by two-thirds over the next several months.

Many investors apparently mistook a good firm for a good investment. Investors make this mistake when they fail to consider whether the price of the firm already reflects the information that they believe they have. This often happens when investors are impressed with new technologies. Speculators who recognized the potential for this mistake early on could have made a lot of money buying the stock even when it was overvalued. To profit, however, they would have had to sell before the fall. The strategy therefore would have been quite risky. ◀

▶ **Asset Bubbles**

Investors often hold assets because they expect that they will appreciate. If many traders are overly optimistic about the prospects for capital gains, they will buy the asset, and the impact of their trades will make their expectations self-fulfilling.

An *asset bubble* exists when traders buy an asset because they hope it will continue to appreciate as it has in the past. In an asset bubble, the price of an asset may rise well above its fundamental value as long as traders continue to expect that it will keep on appreciating.

Traders who believe that uninformed traders will continue to buy an asset without regard for its fundamental value may buy the asset first. They must be extremely careful, however. When sentiment changes, the bubble will burst and prices will fall extremely quickly. ◀

Successful sentiment-oriented technical traders may trade successfully in instruments whose values depend on difficult-to-measure fundamental factors. The three most important such factors are expected inflation, future political uncertainty, and the equity risk premium. Stock, bond, and precious metal values depend crucially on these factors. Since these factors are very hard to measure, value traders do not know well the fundamental values of instruments whose values depend on them. Uninformed traders therefore may significantly affect prices in these instruments. Traders who can predict what uninformed traders will do may therefore be able to trade these instruments profitably.

11.2.1 Sentiment-oriented Technical Traders, Market Efficiency, and Liquidity

Sentiment-oriented technical traders are like front runners because they try to trade before other traders. They therefore accelerate the impact that other traders will have on price.

Since sentiment-oriented technical traders try to trade before uninformed traders, their trading tends to make prices less informative. This is especially true when they trade into a rising asset bubble.

Sentiment-oriented technical traders decrease market liquidity. They make markets less liquid for the traders they front-run. Although they sometimes improve prices, the additional transaction costs they impose on their victims more than offset the price improvements that they offer to the traders with whom they trade.

11.3 SQUEEZERS

Squeezers try to monopolize one side of a market so that anyone who must liquidate a position on the other side must negotiate with them. If they successfully *corner the market*, they can demand any price they want. Squeezers generally acquire their power by surreptitiously buying all available supply before other buyers realize they can buy only from them.

Squeezers are order anticipators because they trade before other traders have a chance to trade. They differ from front runners and sentiment-

▶ Benjamin P. Hutchinson and the Great Wheat Corner of 1888

In the spring and summer of 1888, Benjamin P. Hutchinson bought thousands of September wheat futures contracts on the floor of the Chicago Board of Trade. At the same time, he bought much of the available deliverable supply. At the end of September, he controlled most of the wheat in Chicago's grain elevators, and he was long several million bushels of September wheat.

As the contract delivery date approached, it became apparent that Hutchinson would demand delivery on his long futures positions. Traders who had sold the contract short needed to repurchase the contract or prepare to deliver the wheat. Hutchinson, however, refused to sell them his contracts or his wheat. The price of wheat therefore rose spectacularly as traders tried to cover their short positions. Between September 22 and September 30, the price rose from approximately 1 dollar to 2 dollars. Traders who were caught short suffered tremendous losses. Hutchinson ultimately specified the prices at which he released them. He made millions of dollars from this corner. ◀

▶ A Short Squeeze in a Penny Stock Fraud

XYZ is a thinly traded, low-priced stock with a small float. The *float of a stock* consists of those shares which the public can trade. A stock has a *small float* when management controls most of the shares outstanding or when legal restrictions prevent trading of most outstanding shares.

Ian is a value trader. Given his research, Ian believes with great confidence that XYZ is overpriced. He therefore borrows the stock and sells it short.

The stock is in fact overpriced. It has been promoted excessively by dishonest dealers who hope to sell it at high prices to unsuspecting traders. Ian's sales make their plan less profitable. His sales, in effect, allow him to participate in the profits of the fraud without paying the costs of setting it up and without bearing any legal risk if it is detected. The promoters do not appreciate his interference, and they do not want to share their profits with him. Unfortunately for Ian, he unknowingly borrowed some of the stock from the promoters.

The promoters decide to squeeze Ian. They buy stock in XYZ to raise its price. They then demand that Ian return the shares he borrowed. Other traders who lent Ian shares also demand that he return the shares so they can sell them to the promoters. Ian tries to borrow the shares from someone else, but none are available. He therefore must purchase the stock on the open market. Ian ends up buying the stock at a high price from the squeezers. Although Ian was right about XYZ being overpriced, he still lost much money in this short squeeze. ◀

oriented technical traders because they deliberately design situations that force other people to trade with them.

The largest and most notorious squeezes have occurred in commodity futures markets. Smaller squeezes occasionally take place in thinly traded stocks.

Squeezes are now illegal in United States. In the futures markets, the Commodity Futures Trading Commission carefully monitors trading and open interests as contracts expire. If the Commission believes that traders are not using the markets appropriately, they may intervene to prevent squeezes. They generally base their opinions on whether demands to deliver are reasonable, given market conditions.

Players lose the card game Hearts when they pick up the queen of spades or too many of the various hearts. However, if one player can pick up the queen of spades and all 13 of the hearts, that player wins big, and everyone else loses. Players *shoot the moon* when they try to execute this strategy.

To shoot the moon, players must conceal their intentions lest another player foil them. If they collect many—but not all—of the cards they need to shoot the moon, they will lose badly.

Traders who try to squeeze a market essentially shoot the moon. If they are successful, everyone else will lose. But if they do not control enough of the available supply, prices will drop before they can sell their positions. Since they typically push prices up to acquire their positions, they lose badly. ◀

In the U.S. stock markets, the Securities and Exchange Commission and the various exchanges monitor trading to detect and prevent squeezes. They cannot identify all stock squeezes, however. Squeezers often defend their actions by arguing that they are simply speculating on information. Since the SEC cannot easily discriminate between intentional squeezes and squeezes that result from price changes caused by honest speculators, short sellers always must beware of squeezes.

Squeezers are parasitic traders because they design trading strategies that profit only when they can exploit other traders. Their manipulations make prices less informative, and their trades greatly increase transaction costs for other traders.

11.4 MANIPULATION OF STOP ORDERS

Traders who use stop orders must be very careful about exposing their orders. Shrewd traders who know where stop loss orders are set can employ a manipulative trading strategy called *gunning the market* to profit from this information.

Market manipulators gun the market when they push prices up or down to activate stop orders. The stop orders then accelerate those price changes. The manipulators close their positions at a profit by trading with the stop orders.

Traders who use stop strategies can protect themselves from gunning strategies by hiding their orders and by trading only in very liquid markets that are expensive to manipulate. Otherwise, traders must monitor the markets to determine whether the price changes that hurt their positions are due to fundamental changes in value or to traders attempting to exploit stop strategies.

In some countries, including the United States, price manipulation of this type is illegal. The law, however, is virtually impossible to enforce because it is difficult to prove that a trader was gunning the market. When confronted, manipulators defend themselves by saying, "I bought because I felt that price was too low, and I sold when the market realized my expectations." If asked why they did not buy again when the market subsequently fell, they say, "Since I did not expect the market to fall, the fall demonstrated to me that I really did not understand what was happening. I was therefore unwilling to trade again." Without reliable evidence that documents the true purpose of their trading strategies, authorities cannot convict gunners of price manipulation.

11.5 SUMMARY

Order anticipators are speculators who attempt to profit from information about the trades that other traders will make rather than from information about fundamental values. They trade in front of other traders. They profit when other traders move prices to complete their trades.

Order anticipators are parasitic traders because they profit only by exploiting other traders. They generally do not make prices more informative, and they do not make the markets more liquid.

Order anticipators differ by what they know about the trades that other traders will make. *Front runners* know exactly what other traders have decided to do. *Sentiment-oriented technical traders* try to predict what other traders will decide to do. *Squeezers* force other traders into making trades at very disadvantageous prices.

Traders protect themselves from order anticipators in several ways. They protect themselves from front runners primarily by closely guarding information about the trades that they intend to do. They protect themselves from sentiment-oriented technical traders by trading quickly. They protect themselves from squeezers by always making sure that they have multiple ways to close their positions.

Markets can help protect traders from some types of order anticipators. Markets protect liquidity suppliers from quote matchers with order precedence systems that give time precedence to traders who expose their orders first. Such systems are meaningful only if they also have a significant minimum price increment that forces front runners to significantly improve prices if they want to trade first.

11.6 SOME POINTS TO REMEMBER

- Order anticipators profit when they can exploit information about other traders' orders.
- Since they do not offer liquidity or make prices more informative, order anticipators are parasitic traders.
- Front runners front-run orders that other traders have submitted.
- Quote matchers front-run traders who offer liquidity.
- Sentiment-oriented technical traders anticipate the orders that other traders will submit.
- Squeezers anticipate trades that other traders must make.
- Traders who are aware of stop orders may manipulate them.

11.7 QUESTIONS FOR THOUGHT

1. What are the advantages and disadvantages of splitting large orders?
2. What are the advantages and disadvantages of displaying large orders?
3. Consider the following front-running scheme: A dishonest block broker deliberately exposes large orders to an accomplice who front-runs the orders. The accomplice is a large trader who plausibly might be willing to fill these orders. Is this scheme illegal? How could anyone catch the conspirators? How can brokerage clients protect themselves from this fraud? How can brokerage firms protect themselves against employing such rogue brokers?
4. Time precedence with a large minimum price increment helps protect liquidity suppliers from quote matchers. How large should the minimum price increment be? What happens if it is too large?
5. Suppose that a market decreases its minimum price increment from 10 cents to 5 cents. How might a firm circumvent this change by splitting its stock?
6. How can quote matchers avoid being trapped?
7. When quote matchers front-run an order in markets that enforce time precedence, they improve prices for traders on the other side of the market and narrow bid/ask spreads. Should markets therefore encourage quote matching?

▶ **Gunning the Market**

Suppose that the price of silver futures contracts is presently 4.96 dollars a troy ounce. P. J. knows that many short sellers have placed stop loss buy orders at 5.00.

P. J. aggressively buys silver futures contracts to push the price from 4.96 to 5.00 in order to trigger the stop loss orders. She then sells her position to the traders who set those stop orders at 5.00 dollars per ounce. If the average cost of her purchases is 4.98 dollars, she would make a nominal return of 0.4 percent on the strategy.

The actual return on her capital will be much higher because she does not have to pay for the futures contracts when she buys them. She has to post only a small fraction of their notional value as margin. After this episode ends, the price of silver will probably drop again to 4.96. ◀

8. What effect does quote matching have on market liquidity?
9. Should exchanges try to discourage quote matching?
10. What is the relation between value traders and sentiment-oriented technical traders?
11. What is the relation between information-oriented technical traders and sentiment-oriented technical traders?
12. Short squeezes occur when traders with short positions are squeezed. Can traders with long positions also be squeezed?
13. What type of order anticipator is a trader who guns the market to exploit stop orders?

B *luffers* are profit-motivated traders who try to fool other traders into trading unwisely. The bluffers then profit from those foolish traders. To trade profitably, you must avoid trading with bluffers.

Bluffers use two techniques to fool their victims. *Rumormongers* spread information that they hope will encourage people to trade as the bluffers want them to trade. The information may be false information, or it may be true information presented in a manner or under circumstances that would cause traders to misinterpret it. *Price manipulators* arrange trades at prices, volumes, and times that they hope will change people's opinions about instrument values. The trades may be real market trades properly arranged at arm's length, or they may be *wash trades* arranged with confederates to create artificial market activity. Both bluffing techniques present the bluffers' victims with information that the bluffers hope will cause them to make false inferences about values. In both cases, bluffers try to convince other traders that they are well-informed traders.

Market manipulation occurs when bluffers or their victims cause prices to change from what they would be if the bluffers did not pursue their bluffing strategies. Market manipulation is illegal in the United States and many other countries. It is very difficult to catch, however. If the bluffers do not openly fabricate information or arrange wash trades with conspirators, they often can easily defend themselves by claiming that they were engaged in legitimate trading strategies.

Traders who offer liquidity to other traders must be especially careful not to offer liquidity to bluffers. To avoid losing to bluffers, liquidity suppliers must be very careful when they make inferences about values from prices and volumes. If they make these inferences poorly, bluffers may manipulate their trading and thereby profit. To fully understand how traders supply liquidity, you must understand how bluffers discipline liquidity suppliers.

This chapter starts with an illustration of a bluff. We then formally characterize bluffing. We discuss how bluffs work, why they sometime fail, and why regulators cannot easily enforce laws against market manipulation. The chapter concludes with a discussion of the implications of bluffing for traders who offer liquidity.

12.1 A LONG-SIDE BLUFF

Bluffing is best introduced with an example. In the following invented example, Bill undertakes a long-side bluff. In a *long-side bluff*, a bluffer tries to profit by buying at low prices and selling later at higher prices. Our example has two endings. In the first ending, Bill successfully completes his bluff and makes great profits. In the second ending, value traders call Bill's bluff, and he loses heavily.

After some careful research, Bill decides that the stock of a small firm named Bubbles Never Burst (BNB) is a good candidate for his bluff. BNB

▶ **Painting the Markets**

Traders say that price manipulators *paint the tape* when they trade to influence other traders. Traders coined this term when automated telegraph printers reported trades to off-floor traders. These printers—called *tickers* because of the sounds that they made—produced long paper ribbons called *ticker tapes*. Traders who paint the tape cause the price record to appear differently than it otherwise would appear.

Traders also say that price manipulators *paint a picture* when they produce information that does not reflect true market conditions. Manipulators hope that other traders will mistake their pictures for reality. ◀

is a young firm that has developed a new emulsifier with potentially valuable applications ranging from bathtub soaps to industrial foams. The stock is followed by many investors who are excited by its growth prospects. Most of them know little or nothing about the underlying chemistry. BNB currently has no earnings and is trading for 5 dollars a share. The firm has 8 million common shares outstanding, of which management holds 70 percent.

Bill starts his bluff by buying BNB shares as quietly as he can. Using limit orders, he patiently waits for the market to come to him. Because other traders also occasionally want to buy the stock, the price starts to rise. Over the next 40 trading days, Bill buys 200,000 shares at prices ranging from 5 dollars to 7 dollars. His average trade price is 6 dollars.

On the thirty-first trading day, and continuing thereafter, Bill starts to praise the stock extensively in messages he posts to various Internet message boards. He describes BNB's technology in substantial detail, as though he fully understood it. He also provides very optimistic cash flow projections for applications of the technology. His messages draw heavily on information presented in BNB's most recent 10-Q and 10-K reports. He posts these messages under several different user names, so that it appears that the stock is widely followed. He even has his various user names spar with each other on the message boards to strengthen the impression that they represent different people. Of course, his pessimistic user names eventually grudgingly concede winning points to his optimistic user names.

On the morning of the forty-first trading day, BNB independently issues a press release that announces it will be producing its new emulsifiers in China. The news is not surprising to anyone who read BNB's last 10-Q report, in which BNB provided a positive status report of its efforts to produce in China. Several electronic news services receive electronic copies of the press release. Most news service editors run the story by publishing an exact or slightly edited copy of BNB's press release.

Bill sees the news immediately because he subscribes to a real-time information service that he has programmed to alert him whenever stories about BNB appear. Although the announcement has no particular fundamental value, Bill quickly decides that it represents the opportunity for which he has been waiting. He immediately submits market orders to buy 50,000 shares of BNB stock. He divides the orders into several parts and submits them to different brokers without telling them about the other parts. When the orders converge on the market, the price rapidly rises. In 20 minutes, it goes from 7 dollars to 10 dollars as Bill buys 50,000 shares at an average price of 8.5 dollars. At the end of the hour, several news services are reporting that BNB is up substantially for the day on unusually large volume. BNB also appears on various electronic intraday lists of the largest daily price gainers.

Bill also starts posting notes to the Internet bulletin boards about the importance of the China information. His notes now project price targets of 20 and 25 dollars per share, with the possibility of more than 50 dollars a share by the time the new plant comes on line.

12.1.1 The Successful Ending: Bill Profits

Some traders who follow BNB closely see the price change. They immediately query their electronic information retrieval services to determine why the stock is moving, and when it started to move. They find the story about producing in China and see that the price increase immediately followed its publication.

Although the news has no particular fundamental value, many traders infer more from the story than they should because of the large positive price change that followed the announcement. They mistakenly conclude that other traders believe the story is extremely good news. They foolishly ask themselves, "Why else would the market have gone up?" They convince themselves that someone obviously thinks the stock is a good value. In light of this information, they reevaluate their opinions about BNB. BNB's technology now seems more promising, and the firm's prospects look much brighter than when they last thought about the company. They say to themselves, "Because I certainly am among the first to see this news, I probably can still profit by buying BNB stock. If I wait too long, the price will continue to rise, and I will have lost my opportunity." These traders then buy the stock. Since they are afraid that others may soon come to the same conclusion that they have, they submit market orders to trade quickly.

Traders who buy when the market is rising and sell when it is falling are *momentum traders*. They are particularly susceptible to bluffs.

These momentum traders primarily buy their stock from Bill! Bill lets the stock continue to rise to close at 12 as he sells 100,000 shares at an average price of 11 dollars.

By late afternoon, the stock exchange has contacted the CFO of BNB about the price rise. She reports that management is completely mystified by the events. The firm considers issuing a second press release stating that they have no idea why their stock price is rising. BNB's attorney, however, advises against doing so, for fear of exposing the firm to lawsuits. When news service reporters call, management declines to comment, stating that they have a policy of not commenting on market fluctuations.

By the next day (day 42), many other traders have seen the price rise. Some believe it indicates that the stock may do very well in the future. Others have read Bill's notes on the various Internet bulletin boards and now agree that the stock probably is undervalued. These traders also may have seen news stories reporting that BNB declined to comment on the burst in market activity. They interpret the refusal as a further indication that something is happening. These foolish traders try to buy the stock.

Other traders believe that the stock may be overvalued, but most are not willing to act on their opinion because they are not sure whether other, more significant, fundamental information might account for the large price rise. Still others think the stock is overvalued, but are unwilling to sell it because they expect that it will rise further.

Bill sells heavily throughout the day, along with a few value traders. The stock peaks at 13 dollars and then drops to 8 dollars on very high volume. Bill sells his remaining 150,000 shares at prices ranging from 13 to 8 dollars. His average sales price for these trades is 10.5 dollars. His total profit for the bluff, computed in table 12-1, is 1,050,000 dollars.

Over the next few days, more value traders enter and sell. Within a few weeks, the price has dropped back to 5 dollars. Those momentum traders who bought stock at high prices and held it, lost heavily. The value traders who sold the stock made money.

Given the unusual pattern of trading, the exchange where BNB is listed

TABLE 12-1.

Bill's Trading Profits in the Successful Ending to His Bluff

TRADES	SIDE	SHARES	AVERAGE PRICE	CASH FLOW
Days 1–40	Buy	200,000	6.0	−1,200,000
Day 41	Buy	50,000	8.5	−425,000
Day 41	Sell	−100,000	11.0	1,100,000
Day 42	Sell	−150,000	10.5	1,575,000
		0	Total Profit:	$1,050,000

initiates an investigation to determine who traded and who profited. Their investigators quickly determine that Bill was a significant player in the episode and that his trading was quite profitable. It appears to the exchange that Bill may have been manipulating prices. The exchange then provides the SEC with a brief of the case.

When exchange and SEC investigators confront Bill with this accusation, he acts astounded that anyone would accuse him of such a thing. Bill claims that he was simply a well-informed trader. In his defense, Bill tells the following story:

> After reading BNB's 10-Q and 10-K reports, and after doing other research into the emulsifier market, I became convinced that BNB had excellent growth prospects. I therefore bought a significant position in the stock. When I saw the China announcement, I decided to start trading aggressively. I believe that BNB's innovative emulsifier will be accepted quickly in China, where they do not already have large plants producing traditional emulsifiers. Moreover, given the huge potential of the Chinese market, I feel that the prospects there are extraordinary. I traded aggressively because I feared that other people would soon see the same announcement and realize that the company was significantly undervalued. I had read several positive stories about the China initiative on various Internet bulletin boards, and I assumed that others had as well. I broke up my order because I do not trust my brokers with large orders: I would rather front-run myself than let them front-run me. The subsequent price increase confirmed to me that I had been right about the stock. Although I undoubtedly was responsible for some of the price rise, others were buying, too. When I saw that so many others were buying the stock, I decided they were going to overreact and push the price above its fundamental value. When I met my price target, I decided to sell. It was much sooner than I expected, and I was thankful to have identified the stock while it was still undervalued.

Upon hearing his story, the investigators ask, "Why didn't you repurchase the stock when it fell to 5 dollars?"

Bill answered:

> I was surprised, and therefore a bit scared, when the price fell back to 5 dollars. I fully expected that the price would stay above 8 dollars. Obviously, the market does not believe that this stock is as valu-

able as I thought it was. Although I have been thinking of repurchasing it, I am reluctant to do so until I can figure out whether the market is wrong or I am wrong.

The investigators naturally suspect that Bill was the author of the Internet messages. Some messages contain information that Bill knew, or should have known, was incorrect or misleading. If the investigators can determine that Bill was the author, they can prosecute him for securities fraud. They therefore subpoena the message board hosts for information about who posted various messages about BNB. Bill is not concerned, however, since he opened his Internet accounts using false names and he always logged on using publicly available computers in libraries, schools, and Internet cafés. The investigators ultimately determine that the postings originated in Bill's hometown, but they cannot trace them directly to Bill.

The investigators conclude that they probably cannot convict Bill with the available evidence. After giving Bill an essentially toothless warning, they drop the case.

12.1.2 The Unsuccessful Ending:
Bill's Bluff Is Called, and He Loses

After the rapid run-up of the stock price immediately following the Chinese press release, many traders start to wonder just what is going on. Among them is a value trader named Valerie, who has long been skeptical about BNB's prospects. Valerie is intimately familiar with the firm, with its technology, and with the markets it hopes to enter. After consulting with an expert emulsifier chemist, she believes that the firm should be worth no more than 3 dollars per share, even though the new emulsifier has some valuable uses. At 5 dollars, she was unwilling to sell the stock due to the uncertainties inherent in her value estimate. At 10 dollars, however, the stock appears very overpriced. She is concerned about why the price is so high.

Valerie suspects that a bluffer may be responsible. She reads the Internet message boards and is aware that several authors are posting misleading messages which are overly optimistic. She wonders whether these messages might be the work of a single individual. Since she believes that the China story was not material, she finds the price reaction to the story surprising. Valerie suspects that a bluffer may have created it. To confirm her suspicions, she asks her broker to send a floor broker to the BNB post to determine what happened. The floor broker reports that several large buy orders arrived at the same time. The coincidence of large orders from several brokers arriving immediately after the announcement of seemingly insignificant news seems strange to Valerie. She believes that a bluffer may be responsible for the rapid increase in price.

Valerie is now quite confident that the stock is overvalued at 10 dollars. She believes that she understands both the fundamental value of the stock and why it is trading so high. She therefore starts selling the stock short. Since she thinks a bluffer may also start selling soon, she sells very aggressively. Her trading stops the price rise at 10 dollars.

Although Valerie may know more about BNB's value than anyone else does, other value traders also believe that BNB is overvalued at 10 dollars. They start selling, too.

Bill, who would like prices to advance further, tries to buy more shares.

Valerie and the other value traders sell as much as he buys, however, with no increase in price. Bill buys 100,000 additional shares at 10 dollars per share before the end of the day. The value traders sell 100,000 shares to Bill and another 75,000 shares to foolish momentum traders who fell for Bill's bluff.

At the start of the next trading day, Bill is very worried. If he cannot get the price to rise quickly, the stock will lose its momentum, and he will be the only buyer. If he stops buying, price probably will fall. If he starts selling, price probably will dive. His situation is desperate. He gambles and decides to place an opening order for 50,000 shares to move prices up.

Overnight, Valerie and other value traders have been calling around to obtain more shares to borrow to sell short. The institutions that hold these shares now consider what is going on. Some realize that the sudden interest in their shares from well-known value traders can only mean that they are overpriced. Rather than lend the shares, these institutions decide to sell themselves. They place large sell orders at the open for 75,000 shares.

The market opens at 9.5 dollars, and most of the momentum traders disappear. Bill now owns 50,000 more shares for a total of 400,000 shares. Price starts to fall as more shares come onto the market.

Things now look terrible for Bill. If he does nothing, prices will drop substantially, probably back to 5 dollars. If he starts to sell, prices will drop even faster. If he continues to buy, he might be able to regain the momentum he needs to draw other traders in, but he does not know how many shares it will take. If it takes more shares than he can finance, further purchases will only make his bad situation worse.

Bill concedes that that he has lost. Valerie has successfully called his bluff. He now must sell 400,000 shares at the best prices he can. Unfortunately, the only significant potential buyers are the value traders who want to close their short positions at a profit. At current prices, however, they are still sellers. They will not consider buying the stock until it drops significantly. Bill manages to sell 50,000 shares at an average price of 6.5 dollars as the stock plummets to close at 5 dollars. Over the next 18 days, he sells the remainder of his position at an average price of 4.5 dollars. His total loss for the failed bluff, computed in table 12-2, is 1.2 million dollars.

Given the unusual pattern of trading in BNB, the exchange initiates an investigation to determine who traded and who profited. Their investigators quickly determine that Bill was a significant player in the episode, but his trading was quite unprofitable. It appears to them that Bill manipulated

TABLE 12-2.

Bill's Trading Profits in the Unsuccessful Ending to His Bluff

TRADES	SIDE	SHARES	AVERAGE PRICE	CASH FLOW
Days 1–40	Buy	200,000	6.0	−1,200,000
Day 41	Buy	50,000	8.5	−425,000
Day 41	Buy	100,000	10.0	−1,000,000
Day 42 Open	Buy	50,000	9.5	−475,000
Day 42	Sell	−50,000	6.5	325,000
Days 43–60	Sell	−350,000	4.5	1,575,000
		0	Total losses:	−1,200,000

the market. The exchange provides the SEC with a brief of the case. Given its limited enforcement budget and the fact that the bluff failed, the SEC decides to take no formal action. Instead, it sends a stern letter to Bill warning him against conducting similar operations in the future.

12.1.3 Is the Example Realistic?

For expositional clarity, this invented example presents an extreme scenario in which Bill trades quite aggressively. Although the example nicely illustrates many issues involved in bluffing, we should consider how realistic it is.

The example is not as extreme as it may appear. The Securities and Exchange Commission was founded in large part in response to public concerns about similar market manipulations that plagued the markets throughout the nineteenth century and into the early 1930s. Although the SEC has greatly decreased the number of blatant market manipulations, it still devotes a substantial fraction of its enforcement budget to identifying and prosecuting market manipulators. The Commission now targets its efforts mostly at abuses in small, low-priced growth stocks that traders often call *penny stocks*. Many people widely believe that similar bluffing operations are still conducted frequently in less regulated markets throughout the world.

Had Bill's trading behavior not been so extreme, his bluff might have gone undetected. It is impossible to say how often traders actually conduct small, undetected bluffs in real markets.

Some traders probably commonly employ bluffing strategies. Bluffing can be profitable when many traders will respond to information that bluffers manufacture for their benefit, and when value traders are slow to react. Since many traders are foolish, and since value traders sometimes trade slowly, bluffing strategies often may be profitable. Cautious bluffers who are not so greedy that their trading draws attention to themselves therefore may trade profitably. Such traders may trade undetected in the markets.

12.2 THE FUNDAMENTALS OF BLUFFING

Bluffers profit by encouraging traders to sell when the bluffers want to buy and to buy when the bluffers want to sell. They do this by producing or distributing information that their victims use to form opinions about future prices.

For example, bluffers who want to sell stock may disseminate information about how valuable it is. Traders who see the good news may decide to buy the stock. The bluffers then sell the stock to them at higher prices than they otherwise would have been able to obtain. Alternatively, bluffers may quickly buy the stock at successively higher prices. Traders who see the price rise may conclude that informed traders are buying the stock, and then try to buy it themselves. The bluffers will sell the stock to them, again at higher prices than the bluffers otherwise could have obtained. Bluffers employ similar strategies when they want to buy stock.

12.2.1 Bluffers and Informed Speculators

Market manipulations are very hard to distinguish from legitimate speculative trading activities. Speculators who hold large long positions naturally want the market to value their securities and contracts highly. Like bluffers, they may use word-of-mouth, the press, newsletters, or Internet message

▶ Nathan Rothschild and the Battle of Waterloo

While the Battle of Waterloo was waged on June 18, 1815, British government bond traders in London awaited the outcome. If Napoleon's Grande Armée defeated the English–Prussian allies under the command of Lord Wellington, British consol bonds would fall. If Napoleon lost, the consols would rise. On June 18, however, the London traders did not even know that the battle had started. They learned the official outcome of the battle only after the Cabinet received Wellington's dispatch at 11 P.M. on June 21. Communications before the invention of the telegraph were much slower than now.

The Rothschild family of investment bankers ran a private system of couriers to move information, securities, currency, and bullion throughout Europe. Their system was very fast, given the available technology. The Rothschild brothers often were the first to learn news in their respective cities.

London-based Nathan Rothschild learned of Wellington's victory late on the night of June 19. He conveyed it to the government the next day. What happened next may be the most enduring myth in finance.

In the most common version of the story, Rothschild then went to the Stock Exchange to trade on his information. The bond traders believed that he would know the result of the battle before anyone else in London. They therefore looked to him for leadership. If Rothschild started to buy consols, they also intended to buy. If he sold, they would sell.

Nathan Rothschild knew that he could not profit from his information under these circumstances without bluffing. Accordingly, after arriving at the Exchange, he purportedly stood impassively as his agents started to sell consols. The traders quickly concluded that Rothschild was a seller. As they frantically tried to sell their consols, the price dropped dramatically. Rothschild then bought consols at low prices. When the news of Napoleon's defeat became public knowledge, consols rose substantially, and Rothschild profited handsomely.

Although academic historians believe the story is a myth, it nicely illustrates bluffing issues. Business rivals or anti–Semites probably created the story to discredit the Rothschilds. Rothschild did profit handsomely from buying consols following the war, but he apparently made his purchases well after the Waterloo news was common knowledge. ◀

Sources: Frederic Morton, The Rothschilds: Portrait of a Dynasty, New York: Kodansha International, 1998; and Niall Ferguson, The House of Rothschild, New York: Viking, 1998.

boards to explain to all who will listen why prices should be higher. Like bluffers, legitimate speculators also may buy instruments to show the market that confident buyers think their positions are undervalued.

The distinguishing difference between bluffers and informed speculators is that speculators trade on opinions about fundamental values that they base on fundamental information. Bluffers behave as though they are informed speculators, and they hope that others will believe they are well-informed speculators, but they do not have well-founded opinions about values. Instead, they try to fool other traders into thinking they do. Hence, the term "bluffer."

Because informed speculators trade on fundamental information, their trading activities make prices more informative. Since bluffers do not have such information, their trading more often than not makes prices less in-

▶ An Internet Stock Fraud in PairGain Technologies

On April 7, 1999, at 10:24 A.M., the following message (number 18,280) was posted to the Yahoo! message board for PairGain Technologies (PAIR):

> BUYOUT NEWS!!! ECILF is buying PAIR . . .
>
> by: stacylTN (32/F/Knoxville, TN)
>
> Just found it on Bloomberg . . .
>
> http://204.238.155.37/biz2/headlines/topfin.html
>
> GO PAIR!!!!
>
> SL

If you had clicked on the URL link, a seemingly properly formatted Bloomberg page would have appeared with a very credible news story about the acquisition agreement.

The story was false. The Web address does not point to a Bloomberg.com server, but rather to a free Web page service operated by Anglefire.com. Although the link is no longer active, you can read much of the story in Yahoo! PAIR message number 18,477.

Following the posting, the PAIR stock price rose to a high of 11⅛ from its previous close of 8½ on very heavy volume. For the day, the stock traded 14 million shares, which was about ten times its normal volume. Traders detected the fraud very quickly. (See messages 18,287 and 18,289.) When the company issued a statement denying the story, the stock fell to close at 9⅜.

PairGain provides Digital Subscriber Line (DSL) telecommunications products. At the beginning of 1999, the growth prospects of the firm seemed extraordinary to many people. The stock was very widely followed by small investors: The April 7 Yahoo! posting was the 5,079th message posted in 1999!

On April 15, the FBI arrested Gary Dale Hoke, 25, on charges of securities fraud for allegedly fabricating the news story. The SEC later also charged him in a civil suit.

Hoke worked for PairGain. His motive for the fraud is not obvious: He did not trade PairGain Technologies before or after this episode. Had he bought the stock beforehand, and sold it soon after releasing the story, he would have profited handsomely. Had he been more careful about how he posted the story, he might have avoided detection.

Many traders who relied upon his story lost money, as did many other traders who simply bought because the stock price was rising. Traders who quickly identified the fraud could have profited substantially. ◀

Sources: Yahoo! PAIR messages 18,280 and 18,477.

formative. Prices are more likely to reverse following a bluff than following a well-informed speculative trade.

Although bluffers generally are not well informed about fundamental values, they are informed traders in a special sense. They possess highly valuable information that other traders do not know. In particular, they know what they are doing as bluffers, whereas others generally do not. This knowledge allows them to better interpret market conditions—that they may have created themselves—than other traders can. Unlike fundamentally informed traders, who work hard to obtain the information upon which they can trade profitably, bluffers create their information!

▶ Bluffing and Poker

The game that bluffers play in the markets against value traders is similar in many respects to the game of poker.

In poker, players try to fool other players into believing that they have better cards than they do. The other players then consider whether this is likely. If they suspect not, they bet against the bluffer. The players take turns upping the ante until they drop out or until no one wants to bet further. Any remaining bets are resolved by comparing cards.

In trading, bluffers try to fool other traders into believing that they have material information about fundamental values that others do not have. Value traders then consider whether the bluffers are well-informed traders. If they bet against the bluffers, the bluffers and value traders take turns upping the ante until one group drops out or until no one wants to bet further. Values are resolved as time passes.

The similarities between these two games suggest that the best bluffers may also be good poker players.

The two games differ in several important respects. In most versions of poker, players must fold if other players challenge them to ante up and they refuse to do so. In trading, all players can stand on their positions as long as they can finance them. In poker, all players know with whom they are playing. In trading, most traders trade anonymously, and their trades are rarely identified. Traders can characterize their opponents only by the aggregate behavior of the market. In poker, the number of players is fixed. In trading, traders can enter the market whenever they want. Finally, players settle all poker bets when they reveal their cards. In trading, values are never resolved with certainty. ◀

12.2.2 Bluffers and Value Traders

Value traders foil bluffers. When bluffers cause prices to move far from their fundamental values, value traders may recognize the resulting profitable trading opportunities. If they then trade to profit from those opportunities, the bluffers may lose control of the market. Value traders make it difficult for bluffers to move prices far from their fundamental values. They also make it difficult for bluffers to profit from the price changes and order flows that they have created. When bluffers and value traders are on opposite sides of the market, the value traders stand in the bluffers' way. When bluffers and value traders trade on the same side of the market, value traders take liquidity that the bluffers need to trade profitably.

Bluffers can defeat value traders only if they have more capital than the value traders do. With enough capital, bluffers can retain control over the market and even force losses upon the value traders who trade opposite them. If the value traders are not sufficiently capitalized, they may be unable to bear these losses. If that is the case, large adverse price changes may force them to close their positions. Since such closing trades support the bluffer's bluff, bluffers always hope to force value traders out of the market. Even if bluffers profit from their manipulations, tenacious and well-capitalized value traders will eventually profit when the bluff collapses and prices eventually return to their fundamental values. The profits that value traders make diminish the profits that bluffers make.

Value traders risk losing to better-informed fundamental traders when they mistakenly attribute trading activity to a bluffer. Value traders must

▶ Jeffrey Vinik's Trading in Some Small Microcap Stocks

Jeffrey Vinik managed the Fidelity Magellan Fund for several years ending in June 1996. It was then the largest stock mutual fund in the world. Although it had underperformed the market during the last year of his tenure, Vinik was—and still is—widely regarded as a very well-informed trader.

After Vinik left Fidelity, he started his own investment fund in November 1996. In the next several months, Vinik bought stakes larger than 5 percent in 13 small and microcap stocks for his new 800 million-dollar hedge fund.

The SEC requires that investors disclose their positions when they have acquired more than 5 percent of outstanding shares of a company. These reports are publicly available.

When the public learned of Vinik's purchases, the prices of 11 of the 13 stocks increased substantially, presumably because investors felt that Vinik was well informed. However, shortly after these disclosures and their associated price increases, Vinik sold several of his new positions.

Vinik may have sold simply because his price objectives were realized. Alternatively, he may have been trading on his reputation as a well-informed trader to bluff the market into believing that these securities were more valuable than they were.

Interestingly, in 1994 and 1995, while still managing the Magellan Fund, Vinik was selling stocks that he apparently had been promoting at the same time in magazine interviews. The SEC considered whether his actions constituted market manipulation, but did not charge him. ◀

Sources: Susan Pulliam, Wall Street Journal, *January 24, 1997, p. C1; and Jeffrey Taylor,* Wall Street Journal, *May 9, 1996, p. C1.*

---

therefore be very certain that they fully understand fundamental values before they attempt to call a bluffer's bluff.

Bluffs are most likely to be successful when attempted in securities that value traders either do not follow closely or cannot trade easily. Value traders tend not to follow illiquid securities closely because they cannot trade enough to profit substantially from their costly fundamental research. Illiquid securities therefore may be good targets for bluffers. Value traders also tend not to follow securities that they cannot easily value. Bluffers therefore may target securities for which little fundamental information is available to the market. Finally, value traders generally cannot sell securities that they cannot borrow. Bluffs therefore are more likely in securities that are hard to borrow. These securities are often small stocks for which the bluffer controls a substantial fraction of the shares outstanding. Because value traders generally can buy securities more easily than they can short sell them, long-side bluffs probably are more common than sell-side bluffs.

12.2.3 Prosecuting Market Manipulation

Prosecuting market manipulators is very difficult because bluffers always claim to be well-informed speculators. The best bluffers probably are often well informed, though not necessarily about the objects of their bluffs. Since prosecutors, judges, and juries cannot easily determine whether an opinion is well founded or not, they cannot distinguish between informed speculation and bluffing. Moreover, a subsequent price reversal does not provide sufficient basis to conclude that the bluffer was uninformed, because even good speculators sometimes estimate values poorly. If bluffers are not caught disseminating false information or conducting wash trades, they can easily pass for the speculators that they hope others will take them to be.

To convict bluffers of market manipulation, prosecutors must show that bluffers are distributing information that they knew (or should have known) was false or that they engaged in wash trades. Well-informed testimony demonstrating manipulative intent also would help. Although such testimony might come from confederates in the scheme or from the bluffers' confidants, it must be quite rare.

12.3 BLUFFERS DISCIPLINE LIQUIDITY PROVIDERS

Traders who provide liquidity to the market must be extremely careful that bluffers do not fool them. As we shall see in chapter 13, many liquidity suppliers do not know fundamental values well. Instead, they simply follow the rule of supply and demand: They assume that prices should be higher or lower depending on whether liquidity-demanding traders are net buyers or net sellers. (Liquidity demanders are *net buyers* when they want to buy more than they want to sell, and *net sellers* otherwise.) Although this rule is generally sound, traders who use it to set the prices at which they are willing to trade must be very careful. By manipulating supply or demand, bluffers can cause liquidity suppliers to change their prices. Liquidity suppliers therefore must ensure that bluffers do not manipulate their trading to their disadvantage.

For example, suppose that bluffers know liquidity suppliers respond differently to large orders than to an equal volume of small orders. In particular, suppose that liquidity suppliers will raise (or lower) their prices by 10 cents per 100 contracts bought (or sold) for 1,000 contract orders, but by only 5 cents per 100 contracts bought (or sold) for 500 contract orders. A clever bluffer who is aware of this relation may buy 4,000 contracts with four 1,000-contract orders and then sell those 4,000 contracts with eight 500-contract orders. If the contract calls for the delivery of 1,000 units, the net result will be a profit of 1.5 million dollars.

To compute the profit, suppose that the last contract price before the bluffer started to trade was 10 dollars. (Any initial price will give the same answer.) The four 1,000 contract buys will take place at 11, 12, 13, and 14 dollars, so that the average purchase price for the 4,000 contracts will be 12.5 dollars. The eight 500 contract sales will start at a price of 13.75 dollars and take place at successively lower prices until the eighth and last sale takes place at 12 dollars. The average sales price will be 12.875. Since the average sales price is greater than the 12.50 average purchase price, this sequence of trades will be profitable. The total profit will be 4,000 times the 0.375-dollar difference in the average sale and purchase prices times the 1,000-unit contract size. The product of these three factors is 1.5 million dollars.

You can see that something is wrong here by noting that although the bluffer bought and sold an equal number of contracts, the last trade price of 12 dollars is far from the initial 10-dollar market price. The bluffer was neither a net buyer nor a net seller, but liquidity suppliers raised prices by

2 dollars in response to his orders. This difference indicates that the liquidity suppliers did not set their prices in a manner consistent with the principles of supply and demand.

Had the bluffer in this example initially sold short using four 1,000-contract sales and then covered his position by buying 500 contracts eight times, he also would have made 1.5 million dollars. In this case, however, the price would have moved from 10 dollars to 8 dollars.

Although this stylized example may not seem realistic, it shows clearly that liquidity suppliers can lose to bluffers if they do not adjust their prices carefully. To avoid these losses, liquidity suppliers must adjust prices up or down at the same rate per quantity traded, regardless of whether the quantities are large or small.

In our example, if the rate at which liquidity suppliers adjust their prices were the same for both large and small sell orders, no bluffing profits would be possible. Suppose that the liquidity suppliers raise or lower prices by 10 cents per 100 contracts traded, regardless of order size. A bluffer who buys 1,000 contracts four times and then sells 500 contracts eight times would cause prices to rise from 10 to 14 and then to return to 10. The average purchase price would be 12.5 and the average sell price would be 11.75, so that the total loss would be 3 million dollars. Had the bluffer first sold 1,000 contracts four times and then bought 500 contracts eight times, the resulting loss would be the same. The bluffer loses because all his orders individually have an impact on price but collectively have no net price impact. Since the buy orders push prices up and the sell orders push prices down, the average buy price must be greater than the average sell price if the trades are to have no net effect on price.

(If the bluffer had made many smaller trades, his losses would have been much smaller. For example, had he bought 100 contracts 40 times and sold 100 contracts 40 times, his losses would have been only 0.4 million dollars. The smaller trades are less costly because they do not move prices as much.)

In general, bluffers can trade profitably when the price impact of their purchases is different from the price impact of their sales. If selling has less price impact than buying, bluffers will buy first and then sell. If buying has less price impact than selling, they will sell first and then buy. In the successful ending to the BNB example, Bill profited because the price impact of his quick trades following the China announcement was greater than the price impact of his sales.

Figures 12-1 and 12-2 illustrate this principle. In figure 12-1, buys have greater price impact than sales. The bluffer first buys to raise prices and then sells to profit from the higher prices. The bluff is profitable because the average buy price is less than the average sale price: Although the price impacts of the bluffer's trades incur transaction costs, he profits because he can raise the price during the course of his bluff. In figure 12-2, sales have greater price impact than buys. The bluffer therefore sells first and then buys.

To avoid losing to bluffers, liquidity suppliers must be very disciplined when they adjust their prices in response to the flow of buyers and sellers that they serve. In particular, whenever liquidity suppliers cannot determine whether they are trading with bluffers, they must adjust their prices so that buy and sell orders have equal (but opposite) market impact per quantity traded. The market impact per quantity traded must be the same for trades of all sizes; it must be the same regardless of whether the orders arrive

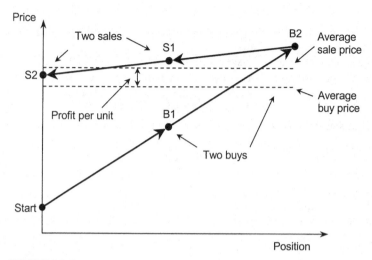

FIGURE 12-1.
Bluffing When Buys Have More Price Impact per Unit Traded
Than Sales
Each heavy arrow represents a trade. Arrows that lean to the right or left
represent buys or sells, respectively. Arrows that rise or fall represent
trades that increased or decreased prices, respectively. The slope of each
arrow thus represents the price impact per unit traded for the
corresponding trade. Buys B1 and B2 have greater price impact per unit
than sells S1 and S2. The bluff consists of buys B1 and B2 followed by
sales S1 and S2. The bluff is profitable because the average buy price is
less than the average sale price.

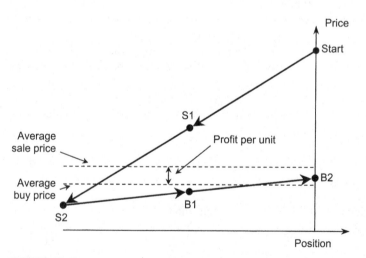

FIGURE 12-2.
Bluffing When Sales Have More Price Impact per Unit Traded
Than Buys
Sales S1 and S2 have greater price impact per unit than buys B1 and
B2. The bluff consists of sells S1 and S2 followed by buys B1 and B2.
The bluff is profitable because the average sale price is above than the
average buy price.

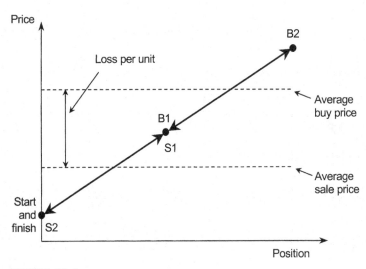

FIGURE 12-3.
Bluffing Is Not Profitable When Buys and Sales Have the Same Price
Impact per Unit Traded
Buys B1 and B2 and sells S1 and S2 all have the same price impact per unit.
A bluff consisting of buys B1 and B2 followed by sales S1 and S2 is not
profitable because the average buy price is greater than the average sale price.

quickly or slowly; and it must be the same regardless of when and how the
orders arrived. Otherwise, bluffers can arrange trades to manipulate prices
to their advantage.

In practice, bluffers may not be able to profit from small differences in
the market impacts of the buy and sell orders. Since bluffing is a very
transaction-intensive activity, the commissions and spreads that bluffers pay
when trading can significantly reduce the profits of their manipulations.
Like all traders, bluffers must control their transaction costs in order to
trade profitably.

Figure 12-3 shows that bluffing is not profitable when the price impact
per unit traded is the same for buys and sales. The bluffer loses because the
price impacts of his trades only generate transaction costs without producing a cumulative price change during the course of his trading. The loss
would be smaller if the bluffer broke his total volume into many smaller
trades, so that each trade would have less price impact.

12.4 SUMMARY

Bluffers try to fool traders into offering liquidity unwisely. They fool traders
by affecting the information that traders use to make their trading decisions. Rumormongers disseminate information about values. It may be false
information or it may be true information that they distribute in a manner
that they believe traders will misinterpret. Price manipulators trade at prices
and in volumes that they hope will fool traders into thinking market conditions are different from what they truly are. In particular, they try to fool
traders into believing that they are well-informed traders. Table 12-3 summarizes the techniques that bluffers use to fool other traders.

TABLE 12-3.
Bluffing Techniques

BLUFFER TYPE	BLUFFING TECHNIQUE	LEGALITY	PROSECUTION
Rumormonger	Spread false fundamental information	Illegal in most jurisdictions	Easy if caught
	Present true information in a manner or under circumstances intended to cause traders to misinterpret it	Questionable legality	Difficult to prove manipulative intent
Price manipulator	Arrange legitimate trades designed to change trader opinions about value	Questionable legality	Very difficult to prove manipulative intent
	Arrange wash trades with confederates	Illegal in most jurisdictions	Easy if caught

Bluffers generally can profit when the price impact of their purchases is different from the price impact of their sales. When purchases have greater impact than sales, they buy first and sell later. When sales have greater impact than purchases, they sell first and buy later. Such bluffing strategies are not profitable, however, when transaction costs are high.

The traders most vulnerable to bluffers are momentum traders and liquidity suppliers. These traders trade in response to trades that they see. Since bluffers can affect the trades that these traders see, bluffers may fool them into making poor trading decisions. To avoid these losses, traders must be very careful about how they interpret trade prices, sizes, and times.

Value traders can call a bluffer's bluff. If bluffers move prices away from fundamental values, value traders may identify profitable trading opportunities. Their trading makes it difficult for bluffers to control the market, and it diminishes the profits that bluffers make. Failed bluffs can be very expensive to bluffers.

12.5 SOME POINTS TO REMEMBER

- Bluffers profit by fooling traders into offering liquidity unwisely.
- Bluffers hope that other traders will mistakenly identify them as well-informed traders.
- Momentum traders must be especially careful to avoid trading with bluffers.
- When the price impacts of sales and purchases differ and transaction costs are not too large, bluffers can design profitable trading strategies.
- Bluffing destabilizes prices.
- Bluffers can lose when large value traders trade against their positions.

12.6 QUESTIONS FOR THOUGHT

1. What effect does bluffing have on price efficiency? On volatility?
2. What effect does bluffing have on price serial correlation?
3. How much volatility is due to bluffing?

4. Why are bluffers more likely to target growth stocks than value stocks?

5. How can traders avoid losing to bluffers?

6. Should bluffing and market manipulation be illegal? How should regulators enforce laws against bluffing?

7. Are bluffers informed traders? Do bluffers have valuable information?

8. Value traders who sell short are vulnerable to squeezes. How might a bluffer squeeze these traders?

9. In many jurisdictions, disseminating information about security values that you know is false is illegal. Although identifying and convicting violators may be expensive, the process is conceptually well defined. Should disseminating true information in circumstances that you believe would cause traders to misinterpret it also be illegal? How would you write and enforce such a law?

10. What effect would a shift to 24-hour trading have on bluffing?

11. Suppose that a rumormonger profits by short selling a security, circulating a false rumor that causes prices to fall, and buying to cover at lower prices. The rumormonger has clearly defrauded the market. Who should be entitled to damages in a civil suit? Does your answer depend on whether traders would have traded regardless of what the rumormonger did? Does your answer depend on whether traders traded with the rumormonger or with other traders?

This part of the book examines how and why traders supply liquidity to other traders. We start in chapter 13 by discussing dealers. Dealers make markets. They allow other traders to trade small size quickly. Dealers tend to be high-frequency traders who do not know much about with whom they trade or the fundamental values of the instruments that they trade.

Chapter 14 examines bid/ask spreads in dealer markets and in order-driven markets. The discussions in this chapter will help you to better understand the determinants of transaction costs.

Chapter 15 considers how block traders arrange large trades. Block traders find liquidity for traders who want to trade large sizes. They generally know their clients well.

We consider value traders in chapter 16. They are the ultimate suppliers of liquidity. These highly informed traders often supply great depth when they believe that prices do not reflect fundamental values.

We introduce arbitrageurs in chapter 17. Arbitrageurs are informed traders who move liquidity from one market to the other. You must understand their trading strategies well to appreciate the economic effects of competition among market centers for order flows.

Chapter 18 considers how buy-side traders create order submission strategies. These decisions determine whether they supply liquidity or take liquidity. When public traders are willing to supply liquidity, they can often displace dealers.

Part IV

▷

Liquidity Suppliers

13

▷

Dealers

Dealers are merchants who make money by buying low and selling high. What you already know about merchants will help you understand how dealers in the financial markets trade profitably.

Merchants may be dealers or distributors. *Dealers* buy from, and sell to, their clients. *Distributors* buy from their suppliers and sell to their clients. (In practice, many distributors are also commonly known as dealers. Consider, for example, new car dealers.) Traders act as dealers when they make a market in seasoned securities or in contracts. They act as distributors when they help firms sell new securities or when they help a client sell a large block of securities.

All dealers face the same problems regardless of what they trade. They must set prices, they must market their services to acquire clients, they must manage their inventories, and they must be careful that they do not trade with better-informed traders. The relative importance of these problems varies by what the dealers trade.

Dealers in the financial markets supply liquidity to their clients who want to buy and sell trading instruments. They allow people to trade when they want to trade. They buy when their clients want to sell, and they sell when their clients want to buy.

Dealers make money by buying at low prices and selling at high prices. They lose money when market conditions force them to sell at low prices or buy at high prices. These losses often occur after they trade with informed traders.

When dealers purchase something, they usually do not know to whom they will sell it or at what price they will sell it. If the price drops before they can sell the item, they lose money. Likewise, when they sell something, they usually do not know the price that they will pay to repurchase it. These unknowns make being a dealer challenging, exciting, and very risky. Dealers assume significant risks when they trade.

Dealers are passive traders. *Passive traders* trade when other traders want to trade. Since passive traders do not control the timing of their trades, they must be very careful about how they offer to trade and to whom they offer to trade. They must ensure that when they do trade, their trades benefit them and not just their clients. Dealers must be especially vigilant to avoid losing to informed traders and bluffers.

In this chapter, we will examine the principles by which dealers conduct their businesses. You will learn how dealers set their quotes, how they manage their inventories, how they respond to informed traders, and how they learn about the values of the instruments that they trade. The principles that we will discuss apply to all dealers, whether they trade securities, commodities, or retail goods. If you are—or intend to be—a dealer, understanding these principles will help you maximize your trading profits.

Even if you have no interest in being a dealer, you must understand how dealers behave in order to trade successfully in financial markets. Whether you trade with dealers or compete with them to offer liquidity, their trading decisions affect you. In particular, you must consider how dealers trade when you decide whether to take or offer liquidity.

In markets where dealers are the primary suppliers of liquidity, the cost of liquidity depends on the factors that determine dealer profits. If you are interested in market liquidity, you must understand how dealers trade and when they are profitable.

We start this chapter with introductory discussions about who dealers are, how traders negotiate with dealers, and how dealers attract order flow. We then consider how dealers control their inventories and how they set their prices. The chapter closes by examining how dealers relate to value traders and to bluffers.

13.1 WHO ARE DEALERS?

Dealers are profit-motivated traders who allow other traders to trade when they want to trade. The liquidity service they sell—immediacy—is valuable to impatient traders. Dealers profit when they buy from impatient sellers at low prices and sell to impatient buyers at high prices. The difference in prices compensates them for providing immediacy.

Many dealers are professional traders who work on the floors of exchanges or in the offices of trading firms. These professionals sometimes use computer systems to support their dealing or to implement their trading strategies.

Other dealers are individuals who access the markets through their brokers, often via Internet order entry systems. Such traders generally supply immediacy by issuing limit orders. These individuals often do not recognize that they are acting as dealers. They consequently do not always fully appreciate the risks that they face and the circumstances under which they will lose or profit.

Many markets officially register some traders as dealers. In exchange for special privileges, these markets may require that their registered dealers supply liquidity. We discuss these arrangements in chapter 24.

Dealers often are known by other names. At futures exchanges, dealers are often called *scalpers*, *day traders*, *locals*, or *market makers*. At many stock exchanges and options exchanges, they are known as *specialists* or *market makers*.

Many dealers are also brokers. We discuss brokers and the dual trading problem that broker-dealers present in chapter 7.

In addition to offering liquidity to other traders, many dealers speculate. Dealers sometimes can predict future price changes by inferring why traders demand to trade. They also can use quote-matching strategies to capture the option values of limit orders that they see. In many actively traded markets, competition among dealers may be so intense that they cannot profit only by providing liquidity to customers. In such markets, dealers must speculate successfully to stay in business. Such dealers are sometimes called *position traders* as opposed to spread traders. *Spread traders* profit exclusively from buying at the bid and selling at the ask.

In this chapter, we consider only how dealers supply liquidity. Although we discuss how dealers infer information from the order flow, and how they

▶ Example of a Small Realized Spread

Dell is a dealer who is bidding 35.0 and offering 35.3 for a security. A client arrives and sells at Dell's bid of 35.0. Dell now needs to sell the security to restore her former position.

Bad news about the fundamental value of the security subsequently arrives. To avoid buying from well-informed traders, Dell must lower her bid to 34.6. To encourage traders to buy from her so that she can sell the security, she must lower her ask to 34.9.

A buyer arrives and buys from Dell at 34.9. Although Dell's quoted bid/ask spread before both trades was 0.3, the realized spread for her round-trip buy and sell was −0.1 = 34.9 − 35.0. Dell lost money because she was holding the stock when its value dropped. ◀

react to it, we do not consider how they may speculate on it. Chapters 10 and 11 examine the speculative trading strategies that dealers most often employ.

Because dealing can be quite risky, successful dealers tend to be traders who tolerate risks well. They generally do not enjoy bearing them, however. The risks of dealing are serious and scary. Many dealers have gone bankrupt because they assumed risks that did not work out. Dealers constantly think about the risks that they bear and how to avoid them. Since bearing risk is unpleasant, dealers demand appropriate compensation when forced to bear large risks.

13.2 DEALER QUOTATIONS

The prices at which dealers are willing to buy and sell are their *bid* and *ask* prices. Dealers usually quote these prices to their clients before they trade. Dealers bid to buy at their bid prices and offer to sell at their ask prices. Sellers receive bid prices when they sell to dealers, and buyers pay ask prices when they buy from dealers. Ask prices are also known as *offering prices*.

Traders who want to buy from a trader who is offering to sell *take the offer*. Traders who want to sell to a trader who is offering to buy *hit the bid*.

Dealers always set their ask prices above their bid prices. The difference between the ask and the bid is the *bid/ask spread*. When the ask is close to the bid, the spread is *narrow* or *tight*. When the ask is much higher than the bid, the spread is *wide*.

Dealers make money by buying low at their bid prices and selling high at their ask prices. This strategy is profitable if dealers can fill orders on both sides of the market without changing their prices. In practice, this strategy is quite difficult to implement profitably because dealers rarely receive buy and sell orders in equal volumes, and because unforeseen price changes are very common.

The realized spreads that dealers earn are often smaller than their quoted spreads. The *realized spread* is the difference between the prices at which dealers actually buy and sell. Realized spreads are usually smaller than quoted spreads because dealers occasionally trade at better prices than they quote and because they often adjust their bid and ask prices between trades.

Dealers who quote both bid and ask prices quote a *two-sided market*. Their quotes *make a market*. Those who quote only one side quote a *one-sided market*. Although most dealers will quote a two-sided market, they usually aggressively price only the side on which they would prefer to trade. For example, dealers who want to buy usually quote high (aggressive) bid prices to encourage sellers to sell to them. They also quote high uncompetitive ask prices to discourage buyers from buying from them. Dealers who want to sell quote low bid and ask prices.

The *inside spread* is the difference between the highest bid and the lowest ask. The inside spread usually is much narrower than the average dealer spread. By definition, it can be no wider than the narrowest individual dealer spread.

The quotes that dealers offer are either *firm* or *soft*. Dealers who offer *firm quotes* must trade at their quoted prices, which are known as *firm prices*. Firm quotes are good only up to some maximum quantity that the dealer specifies. Dealers who offer *soft quotes* can revise their prices when asked to

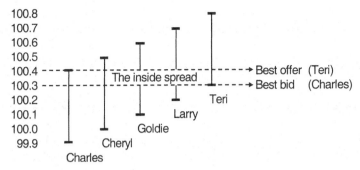

FIGURE 13-1.
The Inside Spread in RobertsonBooks.com

trade, or they can even refuse to trade. A soft quote is simply an indication of interest. Dealers who do not honor their indications risk alienating their customers.

Depending on the market, dealers may provide their quotes only on request, or they may quote continuous firm two-sided markets. Dealers in most corporate bond markets, and in some foreign exchange markets, quote only on request. Most organized quote-driven stock markets require that their registered dealers quote firm two-sided markets. For example, dealers in the Nasdaq Stock Market must continuously post firm prices at which they will trade.

When dealers quote only on request, their quotes are good only for some limited time. Customers must either trade while the quote is good or ask later for a new quote. They cannot assume that the dealer will continue to offer the same prices. The length of time that a quote is good depends on the rules or conventions of the market. In general, quotes expire quickly in actively traded markets with volatile prices or narrow spreads.

Dealers also quote sizes when they make firm quotes. Their *bid sizes* and *ask sizes* are the maximum quantities they must buy or sell when they make firm bids and offers. Upon request, dealers often agree to trade larger sizes at their quoted prices.

13.3 TRADING WITH DEALERS

Dealers frequently will trade at better prices than they quote to the public. Traders therefore often negotiate for the best possible price. Dealers may offer better prices to their smaller customers, to their more active customers, and to customers they believe are not well informed about fundamental values.

Many institutional traders negotiate directly with dealers without the intervention of a broker. Dealers usually do not charge these clients commissions to trade. Instead, they incorporate any fees for trading into their bid and ask prices. The resulting trades are on a *net price basis*.

Most retail traders and many institutional traders use brokers as intermediaries when trading in dealer markets. The brokers' job is to obtain the best possible price. For small orders, however, the benefits of actively negotiating prices are usually smaller than the costs of doing so. In such in-

▶ **The Inside Spread**

Charles, Cheryl, Goldie, Larry, and Teri are dealers in RobertsonBooks.com. Each quotes a two-sided market. Their quotes appear in table 13-1. Although each dealer's bid/ask spread is 50 cents, the inside bid/ask spread is only 10 cents. Teri is the best bidder at 100.3 and Charles has the best offer at 100.4. Figure 13-1 illustrates how the inside spread is composed from dealer quotations. ◀

TABLE 13-1.
Dealer Quotes in RobertsonBooks.com

DEALER	BID	ASK
Charles	99.9	100.4
Cheryl	100.0	100.5
Goldie	100.1	100.6
Larry	100.2	100.7
Teri	100.3	100.8

▶ **Warm Quotes in Oral Markets**

Futures traders say that the bids and offers they shout out in oral markets are good "only for as long as the breath is warm." Traders who want to hit a bid or take an offer must do so immediately after the bid or offer is made. ◀

stances, brokers will route their orders to dealers they believe most often offer the best combination of price and service. If their preferred dealers are not currently quoting the best price in the market, the brokers will insist that the dealers fill their clients' orders at the best quoted price. In some markets, brokers may occasionally expect to receive better prices. Orders that receive better than quoted prices receive *price improvement*.

When a broker sends an order to a specific dealer, the broker *preferences* the order to that dealer. In many markets, *preferencing* arrangements among brokers and dealers are quite common. Nasdaq is an example of such a market. By forming stable relationships, brokers and dealers often can lower the total costs of trading. *Wholesalers* are dealers who trade primarily with traders introduced by retail brokers. Wholesalers usually have preferencing relationships with many brokers. Preferencing raises important regulatory problems that we consider in chapter 25.

When experienced traders negotiate prices with dealers, they usually ask for a two-sided quote before they say whether they want to buy or sell. If the quoted spread is too wide, they may seek another dealer or refuse to trade. This strategy discourages dealers from quoting excessively high prices to buyers and excessively low prices to sellers. It is especially important in markets with few dealers because their limited competition may not provide adequate discipline against the exploitation of traders who are known to be buyers or sellers. In markets with many dealers, those who try to exploit known buyers and sellers lose their customers to dealers who quote better prices.

13.4 ATTRACTING ORDER FLOW

Dealers must attract order flow in order to trade profitably. A dealer's *order flow* is the stream of requests to trade that other traders make of the dealer. Dealers attract order flow by quoting aggressive prices and large sizes, providing high-quality service at low prices, advertising, creating marketing relationships, and purchasing it.

In many markets, dealers primarily attract order flow by quoting aggressive prices. Impatient buyers naturally look for the lowest ask prices, and impatient sellers look for the highest bid prices. Dealers who quote the best prices often get the orders.

Dealers also may obtain order flow by showing that they are willing to trade large sizes. Traders who want to trade large size generally prefer to trade with dealers who will commit to trading large size.

In markets where quotes are not publicly exposed, or where price improvement is common, dealers attract order flow by cultivating a reputation for providing good prices, good service, and large sizes. They acquire such reputations by consistently satisfying their clients. Dealers also may market their businesses by collecting and disseminating statistical evidence that documents the quality of their services.

In some markets, dealers actively advertise to acquire order flow. They design their marketing to promote their image, to provide information about their services, and to document the quality of their services. When clients choose the dealers with whom they trade, advertising is particularly important. When brokers choose the dealers with whom their clients trade, advertising may be less important.

Dealers also acquire order flow by cultivating relationships with clients who can send them orders. These clients are typically brokers and large institutional traders. Many dealers commonly provide their clients with market information in an attempt to attract their orders. They also may provide market research, training, electronic order-routing systems, accounting systems, and electronic information systems to develop their relationships. Many dealers also entertain their clients extensively. They take their clients to dinner, to the theater, and often to major sports events like the Super Bowl, the NBA finals, the NCAA basketball Final Four, and the World Series.

Finally, some dealers acquire order flow by buying orders from brokers who collect them. *Payment for order flow* arrangements are common in some stock markets. The dealers who pay for order flow typically only buy market orders. In the U.S. markets, the payments currently average less than 1 cent per share. In the past, they have been as high as 3 cents per share for certain stocks. Sometimes arrangements involve nonpecuniary payments of services, or reciprocal exchanges of order flows among broker-dealers. Payment for order flow raises difficult regulatory issues that we address in chapter 25, where we discuss internalization and preferencing.

13.5 DEALER QUOTATION DECISIONS

The most important decisions that dealers make concern their quotations. They must decide where to place their bid and offer prices, what the spread between them should be, and what sizes they will trade at their bid and offer. The remainder of this chapter considers how dealers decide where to place their quotes. Chapter 14 considers how dealers set their spreads.

Where dealers set their bid and ask prices is the most important and most difficult decision they make. When dealers set their prices poorly, they tend to buy and later wish that they had sold, or sell and later wish that they had bought. Dealers therefore pay very close attention to these decisions. We shall see that dealers set their quotes to control their inventories and to avoid losses to informed traders.

13.6 DEALER INVENTORIES

The positions that dealers have in the instruments they trade are their *inventories*. These positions may be long or short. Dealer inventories rise when they buy more than they sell, and they fall when they sell more than they buy. Since dealers allow their customers to determine the side on which they trade, dealer inventories fluctuate in response to the demands of their customers. Dealer inventories drop when traders buy from dealers, and they rise when traders sell to dealers.

Target inventories are the positions that dealers want to hold. Dealer inventories are *in balance* when they are near their target levels and *out of balance* otherwise. A dealer's *inventory imbalance* is the difference between his actual inventory position and his target inventory position.

If short and long positions are equally costly to create and hold, the target inventories of dealers who do not also speculate, hedge, or invest are zero. Dealers who hold no inventory avoid the costs of financing their positions, and they do not lose when prices move against their positions. In some markets, selling from a short position often costs more than selling

▶ **Imagine Being Fired for *Not* Spending Your Expense Account!**

Some firms partly measure the marketing efforts of their dealers and brokers by how much they spend in their expense accounts. These firms assume that employees who do not spend "enough" are not doing enough to cultivate their businesses.

Though it seems remarkable that people would need to be encouraged to spend their expense accounts, many traders tire of the constant entertaining they must do. When entertaining is essential to business development, young unmarried traders often have an advantage over married traders who want to be with their families in the evenings and on weekends. ◀

from a long position, and holding a short position often costs more than holding a long position. In such markets, dealers try to hold positive inventories in order to avoid these higher costs.

Dealers who speculate, hedge, or invest have target inventories that reflect these objectives. For example, the target inventories of dealers who also speculate are long when they think their instruments are undervalued or when they anticipate excess demand.

If dealers allow their inventories to get too far out of balance, they will not have enough capital to finance their purchases or secure their short sales. At that point, whoever clears their trades will force them to liquidate. If they have lost money, they may go bankrupt.

13.6.1 How Dealers Control Their Inventories

Dealers must *control their inventories* to keep them in balance. They must buy when their inventories are below their targets and sell when their inventories are above their targets.

Dealers control their inventories primarily by influencing the buying and selling decisions of their clients. When dealers want to decrease their inventories, they lower their bid and ask prices. Lower ask prices encourage traders to buy from them, which would decrease their inventories. Lower bid prices discourage traders from selling more to them, which would increase their inventories. Dealers also may decrease their bid sizes, and raise their ask sizes, to decrease their inventories. Smaller bid sizes discourage large traders from selling to them and larger ask sizes encourage large traders to buy from them. When dealers want to increase their inventories, they raise their bid and ask prices, increase their bid sizes, and decrease their ask sizes. Higher bid prices and larger bid sizes encourage traders to sell to them. Higher ask prices and smaller ask sizes discourage traders from buying from them.

Dealers who want to adjust their inventories quickly may not be willing to wait for another trader to come to them. Instead, they may initiate a trade with another trader who is offering to trade. This tactic quickly solves the inventory problem, but it is expensive. Dealers who demand liquidity from other traders typically buy at the ask price and sell at the bid price; thus their realized spreads will be negative.

Dealers must control their inventories in order to trade profitably. Large positions are expensive to finance. They also expose dealers to serious losses if prices move against them. Economists call this risk *inventory risk*. Traders must control their inventories to avoid inventory risk.

When dealer inventories are in balance, dealers want to buy and sell in equal quantities so that their inventories remain near their target levels. A *two-sided order flow* includes a mix of buyers and sellers who want to trade equal quantities. Dealers try to set their prices to obtain two-sided order flows.

The search for prices that produce a two-sided order flow is called the *price discovery process*. Dealers try to discover the prices which ensure that buying and selling quantities are just in balance. At these prices, supply equals demand. Prices that balance supply and demand determine *market values*. Dealers try to discover market values.

Dealing is most profitable when dealers can sell immediately after buying and buy immediately after selling. Dealers profit from these round-trip transactions if they can buy at lower prices than those at which they can

TABLE 13-2.
Tactics Dealers Use to Manage Their Inventories and Order Flows

CONDITION	TACTIC	PURPOSE
Inventories are too low or clients are net buyers	Raise bid price Increase bid size	Encourage clients to sell
	Raise ask price Decrease ask size	Discourage clients from buying
	Take another trader's offer (buy at another trader's ask price)	Immediately raise inventories
	Buy a correlated instrument	Hedge the inventory risk
Inventories are too high or clients are net sellers	Lower ask price Increase ask size	Encourage clients to buy
	Lower bid price Decrease bid size	Discourage clients from selling
	Hit another trader's bid (sell at another trader's bid price)	Immediately lower inventories
	Sell a correlated instrument	Hedge the inventory risk

sell. Dealers who can quickly rebalance their inventories minimize the probability that prices will move against their positions while their inventories are out of balance. Table 13-2 summarizes the strategies that dealers use to manage their inventories and order flows.

13.7 INVENTORY RISK

Dealers face two types of inventory risk. The risks differ according to whether future price changes are correlated with their inventory imbalances. If future price changes are independent of their inventory imbalances, the risk is a *diversifiable inventory risk*. If they are inversely correlated, the risk is an *adverse selection risk*.

13.7.1 Diversifiable Inventory Risk

Diversifiable inventory risks are due to events that cause price changes no one can predict. Such price changes are sometimes positive and sometimes negative. On average, they are zero. Otherwise, they would be predictable.

Diversifiable inventory risks are benign compared to adverse selection risk. Although dealers lose when prices unexpectedly move against their positions, they gain when prices unexpectedly move in their favor. Since the price changes are uncorrelated with their inventory imbalances, dealers gain and lose with equal probabilities. Diversifiable risks make dealing a scary business, but they do not cause dealers to lose in the long run.

Diversifiable risks are diversifiable because dealers can minimize their total inventory risk by dealing in many instruments. Unexpected gains in some instruments often offset unexpected losses in other instruments. The variation in total dealer profitability due to diversifiable inventory risk therefore is a lower fraction of their expected dealing profits than it would be if they traded only one security. Firms often deal in hundreds or thousands of instruments in order to diversify their exposure to diversifiable inventory risks.

13.7.2 Adverse Selection Risk

Dealers face *adverse selection risk* when they trade with informed traders. This risk is not benign. Dealers—like all traders—lose money when they trade with better-informed traders.

Informed traders buy when they think that prices will rise and sell otherwise. If they are correct, they profit, and whoever is on the other side of their trades loses. When dealers trade with informed traders, prices tend to fall after the dealers buy and rise after the dealers sell. These price changes make it difficult for dealers to complete profitable round-trip trades. When dealers trade with informed traders, their realized spreads are often small or negative. Dealers therefore must be very careful when trading with traders they suspect are well informed.

Since informed traders trade only on the side of the market that their information favors, they make order flows one-sided when they trade. Informed trading therefore causes dealer inventories to diverge from their target values. If prices change to reflect the informed traders' information before the dealers can restore their target inventories, the dealers will lose. Economists call these losses *adverse selection losses* because informed traders select the side of the market that is adverse to the dealers' profits.

Adverse selection from informed traders causes dealer inventory imbalances to be inversely correlated with future price changes. When informed traders buy, dealer inventories fall short of their targets, and prices subsequently rise. When informed traders sell, dealer inventories exceed their targets, and prices fall.

Dealers avoid adverse selection risk only by avoiding informed traders. The best way they can avoid informed traders is to set their quotes near fundamental values so that informed traders will not want to trade.

13.7.3 Market Values Versus Fundamental Values

Dealers avoid both types of inventory risk—diversifiable and adverse selection—when they keep their inventories under control. They usually do not care whether they trade with informed traders or uninformed traders as long as they can quickly restore their target inventories. Most dealers therefore devote much more attention to discovering the market values that produce two-sided order flows than to discovering fundamental values.

Many dealers are uncomfortable with academic arguments that explain their behavior in terms of asymmetrically informed traders. These dealers generally do not know much about fundamental values, they care even less about them, and they may not even believe that they exist. They are simply interested in discovering market values. These same dealers, however, will readily acknowledge that some traders are right more often than not, and that they trade more effectively when they are aware of such traders. However expressed, adverse selection is the most important determinant of dealer profitability.

The remainder of this chapter discusses how dealers respond to adverse selection from informed traders. We focus closely on adverse selection because informed trading is the most important—and most dangerous—cause of one-sided order flows. Dealers must have a thorough understanding of informed trading to best discover market values and avoid substantial losses. Dealers generally discover fundamental values as a by-product of their search for market values.

13.8 DEALER RESPONSES TO ADVERSE SELECTION

Successful dealers must confront the informed trader problem continuously. They must respond appropriately when they suspect that they have traded with an informed trader. They must quote properly when they expect that they may trade with an informed trader. Perhaps most obviously, they must try to avoid trading with informed traders. This section describes how dealers address these three objectives.

13.8.1 What Dealers Do When They Trade with Informed Traders

Dealers who suspect that they have traded with an informed trader must adjust their quotes to avoid further losses. If they do not adjust their quotes, informed traders will continue to trade with them, their order flow will remain unbalanced, and their inventory situation will worsen.

Dealers also must adjust their quotes to cover their positions quickly, before prices move against them. If they can rebalance their inventories before prices change, they will avoid losing when prices change. The traders to whom they unload their positions will lose instead.

When dealers suspect that they have bought from a well-informed seller, they must lower their bid and ask prices. They lower their bid prices to discourage informed traders from selling more to them. They lower their ask prices to encourage other traders to buy their inventory so that they can get back into balance before prices drop.

Likewise, when dealers suspect that they have sold to a well-informed buyer, they must raise their bid and ask prices. They raise their ask prices to discourage informed traders from buying more from them. They raise their bid prices to encourage other traders to sell to them so that they can replenish their inventories before prices rise.

Dealers who are especially concerned about holding positions that they do not like will quickly try to pass them to someone else. Instead of passively waiting until someone wants to take their positions, they actively put them to other traders by buying at the ask or selling at the bid. Although these trades are expensive, they allow dealers to quickly divest themselves of risks that they are unwilling to bear.

Table 13-3 presents the tactics that dealers can use when they suspect they have traded with a well-informed trader. The art of being a successful dealer lies in knowing when to use these tactics.

13.8.2 How to Quote to Avoid Informed Traders

Dealers avoid trading with informed traders by setting their prices close to fundamental values. Informed traders will not buy if they have to pay more than fundamental value, and they will not sell if they receive less than fundamental value. To avoid informed traders, dealers therefore try to set their

▶ **Two Brothers and a Piece of Cake**

How should two selfish brothers fairly divide a piece of cake between them? A clever solution has one brother divide the cake, and the other brother choose which half he wants. Since the chooser will take the larger piece, the divider must try to divide the cake exactly in half to maximize his share.

This solution is not entirely fair. The chooser has a slight advantage over the divider. If the divider cannot divide the cake exactly in half, a careful chooser will always take the bigger piece. The divider faces the adverse selection problem.

When dealers quote two-sided markets, they divide the number line of possible prices into two parts. If they set their prices too low or too high, informed traders will take the more attractive side. To avoid adverse selection, dealers must set their bids below fundamental values and their offers above them.

You can be confident that dealers offer fair prices when they quote tight bid/ask spreads before they know whether you want to buy or sell. Such quotes indicate that your transaction costs will be small and that your trade price will be close to the dealer's best estimate of the market value of the security. ◀

TABLE 13-3.

Tactics Dealers Use When They Suspect They Have Traded with a Well-informed Trader

SUSPECTED CONDITION	TACTIC	PURPOSE
Sold to a well-informed trader	Raise ask price Lower ask size	Discourage further sales to informed traders
	Raise bid price Raise bid size	Encourage clients to sell quickly and thereby restore inventory position before prices rise
	Buy from another traders at his/her ask price	Quickly restore target inventory; this strategy pays for liquidity, but the cost may be less than the loss that will result if prices rise while the dealer is short
	Buy a correlated instrument	Hedge inventory risk and speculate on information
Bought from a well-informed trader	Lower bid price Lower bid size	Discourage further purchases from informed traders
	Lower ask price Raise ask size	Encourage clients to buy quickly and thereby restore inventory position before prices fall
	Sell to another trader at his/her bid price	Quickly restore target inventory; this strategy pays for liquidity, but the cost may be less than the loss that will result if prices drop while the dealer is long
	Sell a correlated instrument	Hedge inventory risk and speculate on information

bid prices just below fundamental values and their ask prices just above fundamental values.

Although dealers rarely know fundamental values as well as the better-informed traders with whom they trade, clever dealers can infer values from the orders, prices, and quotes that they see. Dealers therefore always pay very close attention to market data when they set their prices.

Dealers make these inferences by using the simple principle that values probably are greater than current prices if informed traders are buying, and lower if informed traders are selling. Dealers therefore try hard to determine what informed traders are doing. If they suspect that informed traders are buying, dealers will raise their quotes. If they suspect that informed traders are selling, they will lower their quotes. These quotation price adjustments cause prices to reflect the informed traders' information about fundamental values.

To make these inferences accurately, dealers must form opinions about which traders are well informed, and how important their information is. Dealers need to adjust prices substantially when they are confident that informed traders are trading, and when they believe that their information is highly significant.

Unfortunately, dealers generally do not know which traders are well informed. Well-informed traders rarely reveal themselves because they do not want dealers to know that they have mispriced their instruments. They generally use brokers to represent their orders so that they can trade anonymously. Even when dealers know with whom they are trading, they still may be uncertain about whether their clients are well informed. Well-informed traders usually claim to be uninformed in order to fool dealers into offering liquidity cheaply. Dealers therefore cannot easily identify informed traders.

Dealers form opinions about how well informed their clients are by knowing them well, by paying close attention to their trading, by watching the order flow, and by observing market conditions. Dealers believe that traders who trade for large, actively managed portfolios are often well informed; that large traders are often better informed than small traders; that impatient traders are often better informed than patient traders; and that small retail traders tend to be uninformed. These rules are useful but not always reliable.

Since dealers usually cannot form reliable opinions about which traders are well informed, they must assume that all traders may be well informed. Dealers accordingly draw inferences about fundamental values from all orders. The significance that they attach to each order depends on how strongly they suspect that a well-informed trader submitted it. They adjust their prices more if they suspect that the order came from a well-informed trader than from an uninformed trader.

The amount by which dealers adjust their prices also depends on the significance of the information that they believe informed traders have. *Material information* is information that will significantly affect prices when it becomes well known. Dealers adjust prices more when they believe that informed traders have highly material information than when they believe that informed traders are unlikely to have any deep insights into fundamental values.

Dealers form opinions about materiality by paying close attention to fundamentals. They generally believe that well-informed traders are more likely to have highly material information about instruments for which publicly available fundamental information is scarce or highly ambiguous. Such instruments are hard to value and often are highly volatile.

13.8.3 The Adverse Selection Spread Component

Dealers do not simply adjust their quotes after they believe that they have traded with an informed trader. Before they set their quotation prices, they also take into account the possibility that the next trader will be an informed trader.

Successful dealers consider what they will learn about fundamental values when traders choose to trade with them. If the next trader is a well-informed buyer, prices should be higher. If the next trader is a well-informed seller, prices should be lower. Good dealers incorporate this information into their quotes beforehand rather than waiting until the next trader arrives. They base their ask prices on their best estimates of fundamental values, *conditional* on the next trader being a buyer. They base their bid prices on their best estimates of fundamental values, *conditional* on the next trader being a seller. Since these conditional estimates are different, ask prices are greater than bid prices. The portion of the bid/ask spread that is due to the different value inferences that dealers make—conditional on which side the next trader chooses to take—is the *adverse selection component* of the bid/ask

▶ How Madoff Controls Adverse Selection

Bernard L. Madoff Investment Securities is the largest dealer in NYSE-listed stocks in the United States. The firm is not a member of the New York Stock Exchange, however. The company trades approximately 15 percent of the transaction volume in NYSE-listed stocks. Its share of total volume is smaller because Madoff's average trade size is smaller than the average trade size at the NYSE.

Madoff obtains most of its order flow through order-preferencing arrangements that it negotiates with retail brokers. Since the firm is not a member of the New York Stock Exchange, it can choose with whom it is willing to trade. Bernie Madoff and his brother Peter have chosen to provide liquidity primarily to retail clients, and primarily in the common stocks of large firms. The Madoffs, along with most investment professionals, believe that retail traders generally are not well-informed traders when they trade large firm stocks.

Madoff's dealers are less exposed to adverse selection than are dealers who trade on the floor of the NYSE, who cannot choose their clients. The firm therefore often offers more liquidity to its clients than they can find on the NYSE floor.

Many institutional traders would like to trade with Madoff in order to access the liquidity that its dealers offer. The firm, however, will not accept them as clients unless it is convinced that they are generally uninformed traders.

Madoff offers its interested institutional clients a service it calls Time Slicing. Institutional clients who use Time Slicing send Madoff large orders that Madoff's computers break into small pieces to trade at periodic intervals. Time Slicing is attractive to institutions that do not want their orders to have immediate market impact. It is also attractive to institutions that want to have a time-weighted average price for their trades. Time Slicing is attractive to Madoff because it allows its dealers time to adjust their inventories while filling large orders.

Through its Time Slicing service, Madoff ensures that its large institutional clients do not include traders who demand immediate execution of their orders. The service thus is not attractive to well-informed traders who trade on material information that will soon become public.

Time Slicing allows Madoff to control the adverse selection problem that all dealers face. By refusing to offer immediate liquidity to well-informed traders, Madoff can offer more liquidity to uninformed traders. ◀

Source: www.madoff.com

---

spread. Dealers build these inferences into their quotes ahead of time in order to avoid regretting that they traded.

Since dealers generally do not know whether the next trader is well informed, they set their quotes based on their estimates of the probability that the next trader will be well informed. If they believe that the next trader is likely to be trading on material information, their ask prices will be substantially greater than their bid prices.

The dealers' response to adverse selection makes trading large orders very expensive. Dealers generally believe that traders with large orders tend to be well informed. They believe this because well-informed traders like to acquire large positions in order to maximize their profits and because large institutions can afford to be well informed because they can spread their research costs over a large portfolio. Dealers therefore quote wide spreads to fill large orders. They also adjust their prices substantially when they believe that traders have split large orders into small pieces to obtain better prices. The price adjustments that dealers make to avoid adverse selection cause large orders to have substantial market impact.

The substantial impacts that large anonymous orders have on price make it very difficult to trade large orders. We discuss how large traders solve this problem in chapter 15.

13.8.4 Dealers Sometimes Refuse to Trade with Informed Traders

Some dealers avoid adverse selection risks by refusing to trade with well-informed traders. Many dealers will not trade with informed traders if they can identify them and if regulations do not require that they trade with them.

Informed traders therefore prefer to trade anonymously, so that dealers cannot identify their trading. To hide their identities, informed traders use brokers to arrange their trades. Brokers often refer to this as *bearding the trade*.

Some dealers will trade only with clients they believe are relatively uninformed. For example, some dealers trade only with retail customers because retail customers are rarely well-informed traders. Other dealers refuse to trade with large institutions that actively manage their portfolios because such traders are often well informed. Still other dealers trade only with customers that they know. They do not offer liquidity to anonymous traders because informed traders tend to trade anonymously.

Most dealers prefer not to display large size. Instead, they hope that traders will come to them and ask for more size when they want it. By forcing traders to ask for size, dealers can better determine with whom they will be trading. If they believe that an informed trader wants the size, they will not offer it, or they will offer it at a substantial price concession. If they believe that an uninformed trader wants the size, they may be far more generous.

13.9 PRICING MISTAKES DEALERS MAKE, AND HOW THEY AVOID THEM

Dealers make two kinds of mistakes when adjusting their quotes. They may fail to adjust their quotes adequately when they have traded with informed traders. They then will lose when prices move against their inventories. Alternatively, they may adjust their quotes too much, thinking that they have traded with informed traders when they in fact have not. In that case, they may move prices away from fundamental values and thereby create profitable trading opportunities for well-informed value traders. Value traders quickly restore dealers to their target inventories following such mistakes, but the dealers will make smaller realized spreads on their round-trip trades than they otherwise would have.

Table 13-4 provides a summary of the responses dealers make, and the consequences they face, when trading with well-informed and uninformed buyers. Dealers make similar responses, and face similar consequences, when trading with sellers. Unfortunately, dealers rarely know whether they are trading with informed or uninformed traders.

Dealers use all information available to them to determine where to place their quotes. In addition to the information in their order flow, they extract information from orders that other dealers receive. Although they usually do not see these orders, they may see the trades that result from them and the changes in quotes that other dealers make as they fill them. This infor-

> ### Dealers as Card Players
>
> Good dealers are often excellent card players. The ability to remember which cards have been played in a game, and who played them, requires the same short-term memory skills as dealing in financial markets. Like card players, dealers must be able to estimate conditional probabilities quickly and accurately, they must be able to make quick decisions based upon all information available to them, and they must be able to conceal their intentions completely. If professional traders invite you to play poker with them, be prepared to learn more than you earn. ◄

TABLE 13-4.
Dealer Responses and Consequences When Trading with Well-informed and Uninformed Buyers

BUYER IS	DEALER RESPONSE		
	RAISE QUOTES	DO NOTHING	INITIATE BUY AT ASK
Well informed	**The correct tactic**	**A mistake**	**May be correct tactic**
	Prevents further informed trading	More informed buyers will follow	Correct tactic if prices will soon rise significantly
	Increases probability that dealer will cover before prices change	Dealer will lose when prices change	Dealer will limit subsequent losses
	Decreases realized spreads and dealer profits	Greatly decreases realized spreads	Decreases realized spreads, but not by as much as they might decrease otherwise
Uninformed	**A mistake**	**The correct tactic**	**Big mistake**
	Value traders will sell	Price presumably is still correct	Dealer unnecessarily pays for liquidity
	Decreases realized spreads and dealer profits	If the next client is a seller, the dealer will earn the full quoted spread	Greatly decreases realized spreads

▶ **Bagging a Front-running Dealer**

Dealers who try to speculate on information that they infer from their trades with informed traders must be very careful that informed traders do not try to manipulate their trading by bluffing.

For example, suppose that a clever informed trader knows a particular dealer will speculate on information that he infers from his trades. If the informed trader wants to sell substantial size, he might give a small buy order to the dealer. When the dealer then tries to buy substantial size to speculate on his "information," the informed trader can sell it to him anonymously through a broker. When prices fall, the dealer will lose. ◀

mation allows attentive dealers to infer information about the orders that other traders receive. Dealers also subscribe to electronic news services that publish information about their instruments. They pay close attention to these news stories to determine what effect they will likely have on fundamental values and to help them interpret the order flow.

13.9.1 Dealers Sometimes Choose to Trade with Informed Traders

Dealers occasionally choose to trade with well-informed traders. Although they take the wrong side of these transactions, the value of the information that they obtain by trading with a trader they know is well informed may more than offset the costs of being on the wrong side. When dealers trade with known informed traders, they learn whether their prices are too low or too high. Dealers can then adjust their prices to eliminate future adverse selection. They also may speculate on their secondhand information.

Dealers who trade with well-informed traders cannot offer them too much liquidity. To avoid losing, they must be able to trade out of their positions quickly. Otherwise, they may be holding the wrong position when prices move against them.

13.10 WELL-INFORMED AND POORLY INFORMED DEALERS

Dealers who are poorly informed about fundamental values are less able to judge whether their clients are well informed than are well-informed deal-

▶ Why Do Foreign Exchange Markets Trade Incredible Volumes?

The trading volumes in foreign exchange markets are remarkably large compared to the economic activities that motivate foreign exchange transactions. In April 2001, the total daily dollar volume in all major foreign exchange markets was approximately 1.21 trillion dollars! Placed on an annual basis, this figure is approximately 15 times the gross domestic product of the world economy and 40 times the dollar value of all international trade.

Most foreign exchange trades are among dealers. Why do dealers trade so much with each other in these markets?

Foreign exchange markets historically have been quite opaque. When dealers cannot see the trades and quotes made by other dealers, they must trade actively with each other to learn about market conditions. Any dealer who does not trade when called upon may not be called the next time. Dealers who are not called do not know what is happening, and will not stay in business long. In opaque markets, dealers often buy and sell positions that they do not want to have so that they can remain in the flow of information. After they take these positions, they very often immediately dispose of them by trading with another dealer.

Trades that could be easily arranged if a mechanism existed to match natural buyers to natural sellers often pass through the hands of many dealers. Each dealer takes the position and then passes it along until some dealer receives a position that restores his target inventory. This intense trading is possible because foreign exchange markets trade highly standardized instruments (currencies) for which trades can be settled very cheaply.

As foreign exchange markets become more transparent and as market mechanisms develop that allow natural buyers and natural sellers to be easily matched, volumes in these markets will probably decrease. Foreign exchange trading volumes decreased 19 percent between April 1998 and April 2001, most probably for these reasons. ◀

Data source: Bank for International Settlements, Triennial Central Bank Survey of Foreign Exchange and Derivatives Markets Activity at http://www.bis.org/press/p011009.pdf.

---

ers. Poorly informed dealers therefore more often mistakenly assume that an uninformed client is an informed trader than do well-informed dealers. Consequently, poorly informed dealers tend to trade quickly to keep their inventories near their target levels. Their efforts to stay in balance cause them to earn smaller realized spreads than well-informed dealers. Although their realized spreads are small, they may still be very profitable if they can turn their inventory quickly without holding large positions for long periods of time. These dealers trade most often in active markets. They are often known as *day traders* or *scalpers*.

Dealers who are well informed about fundamental values are better able to bear the risks of holding large positions than are poorly informed dealers. When dealer prices are close to fundamental values, most orders that dealers receive must come from uninformed traders. Since well-informed dealers can keep their prices near fundamental values, they are less exposed to adverse selection than are poorly informed dealers. They also depend less on the order flow when setting their quotes than do poorly informed dealers. With less concern about inventory risk, well-informed dealers do not have to balance their inventories as quickly as do poorly informed dealers.

▶ Dealing and Steamrollers

High-frequency dealing is a bit like picking up pennies in front of a steamroller. Sometimes you get in and out quickly, and profit a little. Sometimes you miss an opportunity or you pass because you have no safe opportunity. However, if you are not very careful, you get caught and lose everything! ◀

▶ Dealer Layoffs

A large uninformed trader buys stock in multiple transactions from many poorly informed dealers. (Equivalently, many small uninformed traders buy the stock.) Dealer inventories drop. The dealers raise their ask prices to avoid losing more inventory to traders they suspect are well informed. They raise their bid prices to try to restore their target inventories.

A value trader sees that prices have risen above their fundamental values. He sells to the dealers. These sales allow the dealers to restore their target inventories. The dealers effectively lay off their short positions on the value trader. The value trader then patiently waits until prices fall. ◀

They therefore are more willing to take larger positions and hold them longer than are poorly informed traders. Since well-informed dealers can patiently wait for traders to come to them, they earn larger realized spreads than do poorly informed dealers.

Traders who are willing to take large positions are often called *block traders*. We discuss them further in chapter 15.

13.11 DEALERS AND VALUE TRADERS

Dealers who are extremely well informed about fundamental values are essentially value traders. Value traders trade when prices diverge significantly from fundamental values. This often happens when poorly informed dealers mistakenly identify uninformed traders as informed traders. It also happens when risk-averse dealers demand and receive substantial price concessions to take large inventory positions. These events cause prices to diverge from fundamental values. Value traders then step in and typically trade with the dealers.

Value traders supply liquidity to the market when they trade in response to the demands for liquidity made by other traders. Unlike dealers, who primarily supply immediacy, value traders primarily supply depth. A market is *deep* when traders can buy or sell substantial size without significantly impacting prices. We discuss in detail how value traders supply liquidity in chapter 16.

13.12 DEALERS AND BLUFFERS

As noted in chapter 12, dealers must be especially careful when adjusting their prices to ensure that bluffers do not fool them into offering liquidity unwisely. Dealers adjust their prices in response to the order flow. Since bluffers can control the composition of the order flow, they can manipulate dealer prices. To avoid losing to bluffers, dealers must be sure that they adjust their prices in a manner that will not allow bluffers to trade profitably.

In particular, when dealers do not know well those with whom they trade, they must assume that a bluffer may be present. To avoid losing to bluffers, dealers must always adjust their prices at the same rate per quantity traded, whether they are buying or selling, with traders they cannot identify. The rate must be the same whether the orders arrived quickly or slowly, whether the orders are large or small, and without regard to whether the orders followed other orders of the same type.

13.13 SUMMARY

Dealers sell immediacy—the ability to buy or sell quickly when you want to—to their clients. Dealers acquire their clients by offering attractive prices and good service, by advertising, and by paying brokers to direct their client orders to them. The bid/ask spread is the price of liquidity that they sell.

Dealers try to buy and then quickly sell, or to sell and then quickly buy. They do not like to accumulate large inventory positions. When they hold large inventories, they risk large losses should prices change against them.

Dealers set their bid and offer prices to obtain and maintain two-sided order flows. Two-sided order flows allow them to keep their inventories at their target levels. When inventories deviate from their target levels, dealers must adjust their bid and offer prices to encourage their clients to initiate trades that will restore their inventories, and to discourage their clients from initiating trades that would cause them to deviate further. Dealers sometimes demand liquidity from other traders when they are especially impatient to adjust their inventories.

Dealers lose to well-informed traders who can predict future price changes. When informed traders are trading, the order flows that dealers receive are not balanced, dealer inventory imbalances become inversely correlated with future price changes, and dealers thereby lose money. Dealers avoid these adverse selection losses by setting their bid and offer prices so that they surround their best estimates of fundamental values. They estimate values by using all information available to them. Dealers pay particularly close attention to their order flows because they partially reveal what informed traders believe about values. Successful dealers also try to avoid trading with informed traders if they can.

When setting their bid and ask prices, dealers anticipate what they will learn about values when they discover whether the next trader is a buyer or a seller. If a buyer arrives, values may be higher than dealers otherwise estimated. Dealers accordingly set their ask prices slightly higher than they otherwise would. Likewise, they set their bid prices slightly lower than otherwise to reflect what they will learn about values should a seller next arrive. These price adjustments constitute the adverse selection spread component.

Dealing is a complex activity in which dealers try to discover who is informed, who is bluffing, and who wants to trade for other reasons. Dealers must constantly make these judgments as they try to discover the market prices that will generate the balanced order flows that they need to easily control their inventories.

13.14 SOME POINTS TO REMEMBER

- Dealers quote prices to control their inventories and to obtain two-sided order flows.
- Dealers attract order flow by quoting aggressively and by offering order flow inducements.
- Informed trading hurts dealers.
- Dealers learn about values from their order flow and adjust their quotes accordingly.
- Dealers often discover fundamental values in their search for market values.
- The inferences dealers make about future order flows create a spread between their bid and ask prices. This spread is called the adverse selection spread component.
- The adverse selection spread component increases with trade size.

13.15 QUESTIONS FOR THOUGHT

1. Which traders do you expect are more risk averse, dealers or brokers?
2. Which traders do you expect make better dealers, risk tolerant (mildly risk-averse) individuals or very risk-averse individuals?
3. Are preferencing arrangements good for brokerage customers?

4. How can dealers control the risk of trading with informed traders?

5. Could a proprietary trading firm program a computer to trade profitably as a dealer? What risks would such a trading operation encounter? In what markets would such systems be most successful? Would you be willing to trust a computer to trade on your behalf?

6. Would you expect that a dealer's inventory imbalance would be positively correlated with future price changes? Why or why not?

7. Why will dealers always quote the wrong prices if they do not know whether they will trade next with a well-informed trader or an uninformed trader?

8. When and why would uninformed traders cause one-sided order flows? How should dealers respond to one-sided order flows from uninformed traders?

9. Under what circumstances might market values differ from fundamental values for prolonged periods?

10. For what instruments would dealers have the most difficulty setting their quotes?

11. In what market structures would dealers have the most difficulty setting their quotes?

12. For what instruments would you expect informed traders to have highly material information?

13. Since all order flow is informative, dealers might want to change their quotes after every trade. In practice, most dealers do not change their quotes so often. Why might that be the case?

14. The minimum price increment employed in many markets limits the set of prices that dealers can use to quote their markets. If the increment is large, how might it affect dealer quotation behavior?

15. Traders who expose large sizes risk attracting quote matchers. Are dealers more or less vulnerable to quote matchers than are public limit order traders?

The bid/ask spread is the price impatient traders pay for immediacy. Impatient traders buy at the ask price and sell at the bid price. The spread is the compensation dealers and limit order traders receive for offering immediacy.

The spread is the most important factor that traders consider when they decide whether to submit limit orders or market orders. When the spread is wide, immediacy is expensive, market order executions are costly, and limit order submission strategies are attractive. When the spread is narrow, immediacy is cheap, and market order strategies are attractive. If you are interested in optimizing your order submission strategies, you must understand what determines bid/ask spreads so that you can judge whether they are wide or narrow, given current market conditions.

The spread is also the most important factor that dealers consider when they decide whether to offer liquidity in a market. If the spread is too narrow, dealing may not be profitable and dealers may quit trading. If it is wide, dealing will be profitable and other dealers may enter the market. If you are interested in dealer profitability, you must understand the factors that determine bid/ask spreads.

In this chapter, we will consider what determines bid/ask spreads in dealer markets and in order-driven markets. We will discuss when immediacy is expensive, when it is cheap, and why. The most important factors that determine spreads are adverse selection due to well-informed traders, volatility, and market activity. We will closely examine these factors and many others.

The most important lesson you may learn from this book appears in this chapter. You will learn why uninformed traders lose to well-informed traders whether they submit limit orders or market orders. Uninformed traders lose simply because they trade. If you are an uninformed trader and do not want to lose, you should minimize your trading.

14.1 DEALER BID/ASK SPREADS

Dealers set their spreads to maximize their profits. Their spreads must be wide enough to allow them to recover their costs of doing business. Otherwise, they will not be profitable, and they will quit dealing. Their spreads cannot be so wide, however, that no one will trade with them. Their revenues then would not cover their expenses.

Dealers profit when their revenues exceed their expenses. Dealer revenues depend on the effective spreads they earn on their round-trip trades, on how often they can turn their inventory, and on how much they lose to informed traders. Dealer business expenses reduce their profits. These expenses include financing costs for their inventories, wages for their staff, exchange membership dues, and expenditures for telecommunications, research, trading system development, clearing and settlement, accounting, office space, utilities, and other such items.

▶ **One Dealer Does Not Necessarily a Monopolist Make**

The specialists at the New York Stock Exchange are the unique dealers in their specialty stocks. Although their unique positions may give them some market power on the floor of the Exchange, they are hardly monopolists. They face competition from public limit order traders and from dealers at other exchanges that trade the same securities. ◀

14.1.1 Monopoly Dealers

When dealers face little competition, they may quote wide spreads in order to maximize their profits. The optimal monopoly spread depends on the demand for their services. If clients are willing to trade regardless of the spread, spreads will be wide. If clients are sensitive to their transaction costs, spreads will be low.

Monopoly dealers set their spreads so that the additional revenue from a slight decrease in spread is just equal to the additional cost of providing the additional liquidity that traders will demand at the slightly lower spread. A similar result appears in all introductory economics textbooks. We will not explain it here because dealers can rarely behave as monopolists in financial or commodity markets.

Monopolies are successful only when monopolists can prevent competitors from entering their markets. In most security and contract markets, the barriers to entry that dealers face are low. Dealers always look for markets in which they can make money. If dealing profits are excessively high in some market, they will enter that market and try to participate in the excess profits. Their entry tends to lower spreads, and thereby the profits of all dealers in the market. The threat of entry therefore may prevent a dealer from behaving as a monopolist even when no other dealers are in the market.

In many markets, dealers also face competition from public limit order traders. Limit orders are essentially the same as dealer quotes. Both are offers to trade that other traders may take when they want to trade. Dealers who compete with aggressive public limit order traders cannot earn large effective spreads because the limit order traders will undercut their quotes.

14.1.2 Spreads in Competitive Dealer Markets

In competitive dealer markets, dealer spreads ultimately depend on the costs that dealers incur in running their business. The free entry and exit of dealers ensures that spreads will adjust so that dealers just earn normal profits for providing their liquidity services. When spreads are too high, so that incumbent dealers earn excessive profits, new dealers will enter the market. Their competition for order flow will cause spreads to fall. As the spreads fall, so will the excess profits. If spreads are too low, so that dealers are losing money, some will eventually quit because nobody can lose money forever. With less competition, the remaining dealers will be able to raise their spreads and thereby decrease their losses. Only when spreads are set so that dealers earn normal profits will dealers neither enter nor leave the market.

Dealers earn normal profits when their revenues just cover their total economic costs of doing business. These costs include all costs described above, a fair rate of return on their invested capital, and fair compensation for their entrepreneurial efforts. Economists call the difference between revenues and the total economic costs of doing business *economic profit*. When dealers earn normal profits, economic profits are zero. Firms that make normal profits have accounting profits that just cover the value of the entrepreneurs' time and the rental of their capital.

14.2 SPREAD COMPONENTS

For analytic purposes, economists break the bid/ask spread into two components. The decomposition makes it easier to understand what factors determine bid/ask spreads.

The *transaction cost spread component* is the part of the bid/ask spread that compensates dealers for their normal costs of doing business. We enumerated these costs above. This component also funds any monopoly profits that the dealer may make and any risk premium that dealers may require for bearing inventory risk.

The *adverse selection spread component* is the part of the bid/ask spread that compensates dealers for the losses they suffer when trading with well-informed traders. This component allows dealers to earn from uninformed traders what they lose to informed traders. We also discuss this component in chapter 13 when we consider how dealers learn about values from the order flow. There we examine the component from an information perspective. Here we examine it from an accounting perspective. Remarkably, although the two perspectives are quite different, they both imply the same size adverse selection spread component.

The two components taken together constitute the total spread. Dealers never quote both components separately. They simply quote their bid and ask prices. To actually estimate the two spread components, analysts must use econometric methods.

14.2.1 The Transaction Cost Component

If all traders knew instrument values with complete certainty, the transaction cost component would constitute the entire spread. Prices would simply bounce back and forth between bid prices, which would be set slightly below instrument values, and ask prices, which would be set slightly above instrument values. Competition among dealers would cause the spread to equal the normal costs of doing business. If dealers had monopoly power, they would set wider spreads.

Economists also call the transaction cost spread component the *transitory spread component* because price changes associated with this component are transitory. *Transitory* price changes regularly reverse. Price changes caused by a jump from the bid to the ask most frequently follow price changes caused by a jump from the ask to the bid. Such price changes occur when the order flow includes a mix of buyers and sellers.

Traders call the bouncing back and forth between bid and ask prices *bid/ask bounce*. Bid/ask bounce is a minor form of price volatility caused by impatient traders who demand immediacy. The transitory spread component is responsible for bid/ask bounce.

14.2.2 The Adverse Selection Spread Component

Since dealers do not know fundamental values well, they expose themselves to adverse selection from better-informed traders when they offer liquidity. The better-informed traders choose the side of the market on which they trade, and the dealers end up losing money to them. When some traders are better informed than other traders, traders are *asymmetrically informed*.

If dealers set their spreads to reflect only their normal costs of doing business, their losses to well-informed traders would eventually force them out of business. Dealers must widen their spreads further to cover their losses to informed traders. This additional widening of the spread is the *adverse selection spread component*. It allows dealers to recoup from uninformed traders what they lose to informed traders. By widening the spread, it also decreases dealer losses to informed traders by ensuring that informed traders trade at less attractive prices.

Economists also call the adverse selection spread component the *permanent spread component*. Price changes due to the adverse selection spread component are permanent in the sense that they do not systematically reverse. Subsequent price increases and decreases are equally likely. Price changes due to the adverse selection spread component reflect changes in dealers' estimates of instrument values. When dealers efficiently use all information available to them to estimate values, the resulting sequence of estimate revisions should be unpredictable. (If their future revisions were predictable, the dealers would not be estimating values efficiently: They should have incorporated information upon which any predictable revision could be based in their earlier estimates.) A process with unpredictable changes is essentially a random walk. Every change in a random walk is permanent in the sense that it affects the levels of all subsequent values of the random walk.

14.2.3 Two Explanations for the Adverse Selection Component

The adverse selection spread component has two aspects. From an information perspective (see chapter 13), it is the difference in the value estimates that dealers make conditional on the next trader being a buyer or a seller. From an accounting perspective, it is the portion of the bid/ask spread that dealers must quote to recover from uninformed traders what they expect to lose to informed traders.

Remarkably, these two perspectives imply the same size for the adverse selection spread component. A simple proof of this result, known as the Glosten-Milgrom theorem, appears in the appendix to this chapter. You can easily understand the result by considering what determines the adverse selection component from both perspectives. To simplify our discussion, assume that dealers know exactly what values are if informed traders are trading. (Our result does not depend on this assumption.) The dealers, however, do not know when informed traders are trading.

From the information perspective, the adverse selection spread component is the amount that dealers should update their estimates of value when they learn whether the next trader is a buyer or a seller. If a dealer trades with a known uninformed trader, the dealer learns nothing and his estimate of value should remain the same. If the dealer trades with a known informed trader, the dealer should adjust his bid and offer to reflect the proper value of the instrument. This adjustment is the dealer's pricing error, the difference between the proper value of the instrument and the dealer's original estimate of its value. Since the dealer does not know which clients are well informed and which are uninformed, the dealer must adjust his estimate of value partially following every trade. In particular, he will discount the pricing error by the probability that his next client is well informed. From the information perspective, the adverse selection spread component thus is the product of the pricing error (assuming that the trader is informed) times the probability of trading with an informed trader.

From the accounting perspective, the adverse selection spread component is the amount that dealers should charge all their clients to recover their losses to informed traders. In our simple analysis, assume the dealer loses the difference between his original estimate of value, and the proper value, when he trades with an informed trader. Since the dealer incurs this loss only when he trades with a well-informed trader, the average loss per

▶ The Total Spread

Figures 14-1 and 14-2 illustrate the conceptual process by which dealers set and adjust their spreads. If charts intimidate you, skip them. The figures represent the same information presented in the text.

Figure 14-1 shows that the total spread is the sum of the two spread components. In principle, a dealer derives her bid and ask prices as follows:

- She first estimates the instrument value, using all information currently available to her. This estimate, V_0 in the figure, is the basis for her quoted bid and ask prices. It determines the level of her price quotes.

- Using this basis, she then estimates values, assuming that the next trader is a buyer (V_0^B) or a seller (V_0^S). The difference between these two estimates is the adverse selection spread component. If the probabilities of trading with informed buyers and sellers are equal, and if the expected pricing errors in both instances are equal, the two value estimates will be equally distant from her initial estimate, V_0. She then simply adds and subtracts half of the adverse selection spread component to V_0 to obtain them.

- She obtains her offer price by adding half of the transaction cost spread component to her value estimate for a buyer. She likewise obtains her bid price by subtracting half of the transaction cost spread component from her value estimate for a seller.

In practice, dealers set their bid and ask prices by using their experience to interpret current market conditions. Although they rarely form their estimates as described here, they regularly consider the issues discussed here.

When the next trader arrives, the dealer learns whether she wants to buy or sell. If the dealer learns nothing more about the trader or about values, the dealer's new unconditional value estimate will be the appropriate previous conditional value estimate.

Figure 14-2 illustrates the quotation adjustments following the arrival of a buyer ($P_0 = Ask_0$). The bid and ask both rise by half of the adverse selection spread component. ◀

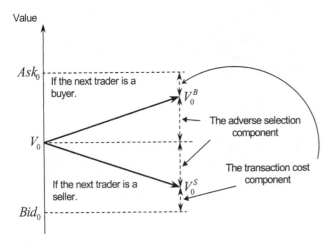

FIGURE 14-1.
The Components of the Total Spread

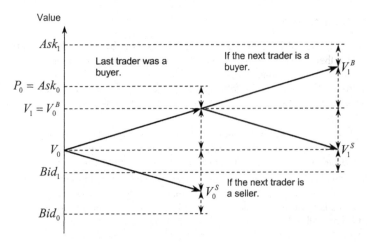

FIGURE 14-2.
Quotation Adjustments After a Buyer Arrives

trade to informed traders is the loss from trading with an informed trader times the probability of trading with an informed trader. This average loss is the adverse selection spread component.

These two expressions for the adverse selection spread component are the same if the loss from trading with an informed trader is the same as the pricing error when trading with an informed trader. This is true if dealers cannot restore their target inventories before prices change to reflect the informed traders' information.

If dealers can restore their target inventories, the result still holds with a caveat. If dealers do not recognize that they have traded with an informed trader, they will not fully adjust prices. Informed traders therefore will trade with them again. Dealers will continue losing until the price reflects the informed traders' information. Their cumulative losses will equal their original pricing error, so the Glosten-Milgrom theorem still holds.

If dealers do recognize that they have traded with an informed trader, but others in the market have not, they may be able to trade on the side that the information favors. They then will act as speculators rather than as dealers. They will be eager to trade on the informed side but unwilling to offer liquidity on the other side. We can restate the Glosten-Milgrom theorem to include this situation, but the restatement is beyond the scope of this book.

14.2.4 Discriminating Between the Two Spread Components

Econometricians have estimated the two components of the bid/ask spread so that we can determine their relative importance. The decomposition is possible because the two components give prices different statistical properties. The transaction cost spread component causes prices to bounce back and forth between bid and offer prices. The adverse selection spread component causes unpredictable price changes that have the properties of a random walk. In both cases, the price changes depend on whether a buyer or a seller initiated the transaction.

The most common decomposition method involves the estimation of an equation to explain current and future price changes using information about whether each trade was buyer- or seller-initiated. These analyses indicate that in most markets the adverse selection spread component accounts for more of the total spread than does the transaction cost spread component.

14.3 ADVERSE SELECTION AND UNINFORMED TRADERS: THE MOST IMPORTANT LESSON IN THIS BOOK FOR MOST READERS

Adverse selection explains why uninformed traders lose to informed traders, regardless of whether they trade with limit or market orders. In both cases, they suffer the effects of adverse selection.

When uninformed traders use limit orders, their orders fill quickly if they overprice their bids or underprice their offers. Informed traders then eagerly trade with them, and the uninformed traders ultimately will regret trading. In this case, uninformed traders directly suffer the effects of adverse selection, just as dealers do.

When limit order traders and informed traders compete to trade on the same side of the market, their limit orders often do not fill. Since informed traders tend to forecast future price changes correctly, prices often will move away from the limit orders, and the uninformed traders will regret not trading. In this case, adverse selection causes uninformed traders to lose profitable trading opportunities.

Uninformed traders thus often regret using limit orders. When they trade with informed traders, they regret trading. When they compete with informed traders to fill their orders, they often do not fill, and they regret not trading.

Uninformed traders who use market orders ensure that they trade, but they still suffer the effects of adverse selection. Since dealers widen their spreads to recover from uninformed traders what they lose to informed traders, uninformed market order traders trade at wider bid/ask spreads than they would if there were no informed trading. In effect, the adverse selection spread is a fee that dealers charge market order traders for bearing adverse selection risk.

Uninformed traders do not lose because they systematically want to trade on the wrong side. Even if they flip a coin to decide on which side to trade, uninformed traders tend to lose. A fair coin ensures that they will be right about future price changes half the time, but the costs of filling their orders will cause them to lose on average.

Uninformed traders thus ultimately lose to informed traders regardless of how they trade. They lose simply because they trade. They can avoid the problem only by not trading. Table 14-1 summarizes why uninformed traders lose when trading.

14.4 EQUILIBRIUM SPREADS IN CONTINUOUS ORDER-DRIVEN AUCTION MARKETS

Continuous order-driven auction markets arrange trades when they match an arriving market order (or marketable limit order) with a standing limit order. Traders who use these markets must decide whether to offer liquidity by submitting limit orders or to take liquidity with market orders.

TABLE 14-1.

Uninformed Traders Tend to Lose to Informed Traders Regardless of How They Trade

UNINFORMED TRADER'S ORDER	INFORMED TRADERS	ORDER DISPOSITION	SUBSEQUENT PRICES	CONSEQUENCES TO UNINFORMED TRADER
Limit order	Want to trade on the other side	Informed traders quickly fill the order	Price moves against the newly acquired position	Regrets trading
	Want to trade on the same side	The order competes with informed traders and does not fill	Price moves away from the limit order	Regrets not trading
Market order	Does not matter	Dealer quickly fills order at spreads made wide by informed trading	Bid/ask bounce causes price to move against the newly acquired position	Loses half of the spread

Chapter 4 discusses limit and market order properties in detail. Briefly, market order traders get immediate executions, but they pay the bid/ask spread to trade. Limit order traders get good prices if their orders execute, but they risk failing to trade if the market moves away from their orders. If they fail to trade and still wish to trade, they must replace their limit orders with more aggressively priced orders. In the end, they may trade at much worse prices than they would have received had they initially used market orders.

The bid/ask spread determines how attractive limit and market order trading strategies are. If the spread is wide, market orders will be expensive, and no one will use them. If the spread is narrow, market orders may be more attractive than limit orders.

This section describes how traders decide which type of order to use. We must understand their decisions in order to identify the determinants of bid/ask spreads in auction markets.

We will consider the problem by first analyzing a simple, but very unrealistic, situation in which we can easily predict how traders will behave. Once we understand that situation, we will be better able to analyze more interesting and realistic situations. The foundation for our analysis appears in a paper about equilibrium spreads by Kalman Cohen, Steven Maier, Robert Schwartz, and David Whitcomb.

14.4.1 A Simple Equilibrium Spread Analysis

Suppose that all traders in a continuous order-driven public auction are essentially the same. They all want to trade the same sizes, and no one is better informed than anyone else. No one is risk averse, no one values his or her time at all, and no one is in any hurry to trade. Everyone knows values instantaneously as they change, but no one can forecast changes in those values. In addition, everyone can submit and cancel orders instantaneously without any cost, and their trading commissions do not depend on order type. Our traders differ from each other only in that some want to buy and some want to sell. These traders are clearly like none that we will ever meet!

These extraordinarily unrealistic assumptions have two equally unrealistic implications. First, when deciding which type of order submission strategy to pursue, the traders care only about their expected trading costs. We explicitly assumed that they do not care about the value of their time, when they trade, or the risk of their strategies.

Second, when each trade takes place, the price will equal the current instrument value. Limit order traders will constantly adjust their limit prices to reflect any changes in value. They can make these adjustments because they instantaneously know values as they change. They will make these adjustments because they can cancel and resubmit their orders without any cost. They must make these adjustments to ensure that they trade if prices move away from them and to avoid trading at a loss if prices move through their orders. Although the market order traders would like to trade at prices different from values, limit order traders will not allow them to do so.

The expected cost of trading a market order is half the bid/ask spread less any profits that they expect to make by carefully timing their trades. Since market order traders cannot forecast price changes, and since limit order traders will not allow them to trade at any price different from value, they cannot expect to profit from timing their orders. The expected costs of trading a market order therefore will be exactly half the bid/ask spread.

We now introduce a very simple principle to obtain our results about bid/ask spreads. Since our imaginary traders can choose whether to submit limit orders or market orders and since they are all essentially identical, the spread must make both strategies equally attractive. Otherwise, every trader would want to use the more attractive strategy. If the spread is too narrow, everyone will want to use market orders, and no one will trade. If the spread is too wide, everyone will want to use limit orders, and no one will trade. The spread which ensures that traders are indifferent between using a limit order and a market order is the *equilibrium spread*. The traders discover the equilibrium spread through the following mechanism.

If most traders try to use market orders so that few traders use limit orders, the few limit order traders will set their limit prices far from the market. They do not need to be aggressive because the surplus of market orders ensures that they will trade. The resulting wide spreads, however, will discourage market order traders. Some will choose to submit limit orders instead. With more competition to supply liquidity, limit order traders will have to set their limit prices closer to the market, and spreads will narrow.

Conversely, if most traders use limit orders and few traders use market orders, bid/ask spreads will be small as limit order traders compete to trade with the few market order traders. The narrow spread will encourage some limit order traders to submit market orders instead. The reduced competition among the limit order traders will cause bid/ask spreads to widen.

In summary, spreads that are too wide cause traders to switch from market orders to limit orders and thereby narrow the spread. Spreads that are too narrow cause traders to switch from limit orders to market orders and thereby widen the spread. At some intermediate spread, traders are indifferent between submitting limit orders and market orders. This spread is the equilibrium spread.

With this principle, we can now determine that bid/ask spreads in this rather unusual market must be zero! Since the traders care only about their expected transaction costs, the equilibrium expected costs of using market and limit order strategies must be the same. Because trading is a zero-sum

▶ **Economists and Their Can Openers**

Economists often make highly unrealistic assumptions to simplify their analyses. Many people poke fun at economists for their propensity to create impossibly abstract models.

You may know the joke about the three hungry castaways on a deserted island who are trying to open a can of food. The chemist suggests heating the can until it bursts. The engineer proposes breaking it open with a sharp rock. The economist suggests, "Assume we have a can opener. . . ." The joke is unfair, but it reflects the discomfort people feel about many abstract economic models.

Economists make unrealistic assumptions when analyzing issues to ensure that they can create a simple situation (model) that they fully understand. They then consider what happens to their results when they replace the unrealistic assumptions with more realistic ones. This method allows economists to thoroughly understand complex situations that might otherwise elude them. It is especially useful for identifying the importance of the issues that affect the results. By starting with simple assumptions, economists can open many complex problems. ◀

▶ Market Manipulation of Quoted Spreads

Markets that wish to lower their quoted spreads can charge commissions only on market and marketable limit orders. If the commissions are proportional to the quantity traded, spreads will drop by exactly the difference between the limit and market order commissions. In equilibrium, this change would have no effect on order submission strategies or trader profitability.

In practice, markets can undertake this strategy only if they can control the commissions that all buyers and sellers pay. If a single broker within a multibroker market tried to raise the commissions on market orders and lower them on limit orders, traders would send only limit orders to that broker, and he would lose revenue. Only brokers who run their own markets and only exchanges that can regulate commissions can manipulate quoted spreads.

Cantor Fitzgerald organizes government bond markets for its customers through its eSpeed subsidiary. Since Cantor Fitzgerald charges commissions only on market orders, spreads in its markets are smaller than they would be if it evenly distributed the commissions between the limit order traders and the market order traders.

Some ECNs like Archipelago also charge different fees for market orders and limit orders. Although the fees are paid by the brokers who route orders to them, in perfectly competitive brokerage markets, the differential fees will be reflected in the commissions that traders pay for different types of executed orders. ◀

game, expected transaction costs to limit order traders are exactly equal to expected trading profits to market order traders and vice versa. To be equal, the expected costs of both order types therefore must be zero. Since the expected cost of the market order strategy is half the bid/ask spread, the bid/ask spread in this highly unrealistic model must be zero.

14.4.2 More Realistic Equilibrium Spread Results

We now obtain more realistic results by relaxing some of the remarkable assumptions made above.

14.4.2.1 Differential Commissions

If limit order traders pay greater trading commissions than market order traders, limit orders will be relatively less attractive. Without some compensating differential in the spreads, no trader will submit a limit order. Since traders must be indifferent between using both order strategies in equilibrium, spreads must widen so that limit and market order traders equally share the difference in commissions. In this simple model, the cost of trading a market order is half the bid/ask spread. It must equal half the difference in the commissions to make traders indifferent between the two trading strategies. The equilibrium spread therefore must equal the difference between the two commissions.

14.4.2.2 Costly Limit Order Management

In practice, canceling and resubmitting limit orders is costly. Brokers and exchanges may charge fees for canceling orders, and traders lose the opportunity to do other things while they manage their orders. Limit order traders therefore will not continuously adjust their orders. Instead, they will adjust their orders only when values diverge significantly from their limit prices. The divergence that triggers a limit price adjustment depends on the cost of canceling and resubmitting. If these costs are large, limit order traders will adjust their limit prices infrequently.

Costly limit order management makes limit orders less attractive than market orders for two reasons. First and most obviously, limit order traders incur costs to adjust their orders that market order traders do not incur. Second and more important, limit order traders give a valuable *timing option* to market order traders when they do not continuously update their limit order prices. Market order traders will wait to see what happens to values before they trade. If a market order trader wants to buy, he will wait to see if value rises. If value rises past the limit price of a standing limit sell order, he will then buy at the limit price and profit by the difference. If value falls, he will wait until limit order sellers drop their prices. He then can buy at a lower price. This timing option makes market orders more attractive than limit orders.

Market order traders who exercise the timing option subject limit order traders to a form of adverse selection. When the limit order traders trade, they wish they had been able to adjust their prices. When the limit order traders do not trade, they wish that they had. In a sense, the market order traders are better informed traders than the limit order traders. When they trade, the market order traders have more current information than the information that limit order traders had at the time they set their limit prices.

The timing option is most valuable when market order traders can respond to changing conditions faster than limit order traders can. If the limit order traders can adjust their limit prices before market order traders can take advantage of changes in value, the timing option will not be valuable.

The timing option is also most valuable when few market order traders compete to take advantage of it. When many market order traders try to exercise the same timing option, they must act quickly as soon as it becomes valuable. Market order traders who wait too long will lose the option to a quicker trader.

To ensure that traders are indifferent between using limit orders and market orders, the equilibrium spread must ensure that the limit order traders are compensated for the timing options that they give to market order traders. The equilibrium spread also must ensure that the two types of traders equally share the limit order management costs. Since the spread is the total cost of using two market orders to complete a round-trip trade, the equilibrium spread must equal the expected cost of managing the limit orders plus twice the value of the timing option.

In practice, limit order traders cannot instantaneously reprice their orders exactly when repricing would be optimal. The costs of paying attention ensure that values may change substantially before they notice the change. Order entry, order routing, and order handling delays also ensure that values may change before instructions to cancel limit orders become effective. These delays make the timing option more valuable. The equilibrium spread therefore also depends on the average time it takes limit order traders to successfully cancel their orders. If the order cancellation process is slow, equilibrium spreads will be wide.

When the order cancellation process is slow, equilibrium spreads also will depend on the volatility of the instrument. The timing option will be quite valuable for volatile instruments because prices may change substantially

▶ A Simple Timing Option Example

Suppose the value of a contract is 20 dollars. In the next five minutes, the value may stay the same, rise by 12 cents, or fall by 12 cents. These alternatives are equally probable.

Lisbet, a limit order trader, submits a sell order with a limit price of 20 dollars.

In the next five minutes, Mark, a price-insensitive market order buyer, may arrive and trade with Lisbet. The probability that Mark arrives is one-half. This probability does not depend on the value of the contract.

Tim is an opportunistic market order buyer who monitors the market to exploit timing options. He will buy from Lisbet if the opportunity looks attractive and if the opportunity is still then available. In particular, Tim will buy if values rise and if Mark does not arrive first. The probability that value rises is one-third. The probability that Mark arrives is one-half. Since the two events are independent, the probability that Tim buys is one-sixth. If Tim buys, he will earn 12 cents because he will buy at 20 dollars a contract worth 20.12 dollars. The expected value of his trading strategy therefore is one-sixth of 12 cents, or 2 cents.

Dieter is a dealer who is always willing to buy at 6 cents below the current value of the contract. Lisbet will trade with Dieter if her order does not fill after five minutes.

Consider Lisbet's expected trade price. We will first compute it assuming that Tim is not in the market and then assuming that he is present.

Assume that the probability that Lisbet trades with Mark at 20 dollars is one-half. If Mark does not arrive (and Tim is not in the market), Lisbet then would trade with Dieter. That trade price would be 19.82 if value falls, 19.94 if value does not change, and 20.06 if value rises. Since these events are equally likely, her expected trade price if Mark does not arrive (and Tim is not in the market) is 19.94. Accordingly, Lisbet's expected trade price when Tim is not in the market is the average of 20 (if she trades with Mark) and 19.94 (if she trades with Dieter), which is 19.97 dollars.

Now suppose that Tim is in the market. If Mark does not arrive, Lisbet will trade with Dieter at 19.82 if value falls, with Dieter at 19.94 if value does not change, and with Tim at 20.00 if value rises. Since these events are equally likely, her expected trade price if Mark does not arrive, and Tim is in the market, is 19.92. If Mark arrives, Lisbet will trade with him at 20 dollars. Since the probability that Mark will arrive is one-half, Lisbet's expected trade price is 19.96 if Tim is in the market.

When Tim is present, Lisbet's expected sales price is a penny lower than it would be if Tim were not in the market. If Tim is in the market, Lisbet loses a penny because she will never trade at 20.06. Otherwise, she will trade at 20 instead of 20.06 one-sixth of the time (when value rises, and Mark arrives).

Now consider how Tim affects Dieter's profitability. If Tim is not in the market, Dieter trades if Mark does not arrive. Since Dieter always buys at 6 cents below value, Dieter expects to make 3 cents profit. If Tim is in the market, Dieter trades only if Mark does not arrive, and prices fall or stay the same. The probabilities of these two events are both one-sixth, so that Dieter expects to make 2 cents profit if Tim is in the market. When Tim is present, Dieter expects to make 1 cent less than he would make if Tim were not in the market.

Tim's two-cent expected profit therefore comes partly from the timing option that he exercises against Lisbet (1 cent) and partly from quote matching in front of Dieter's order (1 cent). ◀

before traders can reprice their orders. Equilibrium spreads therefore must be wider for volatile instruments than for relatively stable instruments.

14.4.2.3 Valuable Time and Risk Aversion

When traders value their time, limit order strategies are more expensive than market order strategies because the former take longer to implement than the latter. Equilibrium spreads therefore must widen to make limit orders more attractive and market orders less attractive. When traders value their time highly, spreads must be wide.

Since the spread reflects the value of time, the spread is the price of immediacy. Traders say that market order traders *buy time* and limit order traders *sell time*.

Limit and market order strategies expose traders to different risks. Limit order traders risk having to chase the market if prices move away from their orders. Market order traders risk trading at unexpected prices. Quotes may change after they submit their orders but before they are filled. Their large orders also may have unpredictable price impacts. For small traders, limit order strategies are generally more risky than market order strategies. For large traders, market order strategies are probably more risky.

If risk-averse traders fear using one strategy more than the other, spreads will have to adjust to ensure that traders are indifferent between using the two strategies. In our simple model, all traders have equal-sized orders, and they all know the prices at which they can trade when using market orders. Using limit order strategies therefore is more risky to them than using market order strategies. If they are to offer liquidity, equilibrium spreads must widen to compensate limit order traders for the risk that they will not trade. The more risk averse traders are, the wider the equilibrium spreads will be.

In practice, since the sizes associated with inside spreads tend to be small, we can reasonably infer that small traders predominantly set inside spreads. Accordingly, limit order execution risk probably has a stronger effect on spreads than market order price risk.

In the real world, not all traders are equally risk averse, and not all traders value their time equally. In equilibrium, few traders will be indifferent between using a market order strategy and a limit order strategy. Traders who are the most risk averse or who value their time the most will use market orders. Traders who are most risk tolerant and for whom monitoring orders is least costly will use limit orders. Somewhere between these extremes will be traders for whom the equilibrium spread ensures that they are indifferent between using market order and limit order trading strategies.

14.4.2.4 Traders Do Not Know Values Instantaneously

To simplify our analysis, we assumed that all traders always know values as they change. This assumption is unnecessarily strict. With one caveat, we can obtain our equilibrium spread results merely if all traders are always equally well informed about values. In that case, they all always estimate the same values. Since nobody knows true values, knowing common value estimates is essentially the same as knowing true values.

The one caveat concerns results involving volatility. A theorem from statistics proves that the volatility of an estimate of a variable is less than the volatility of the variable being estimated. Value estimate volatility therefore

▶ Indexed (or Floating) Limit Orders

Some alternative trading systems like the Primex Auction System allow traders to submit *indexed limit orders*. These systems automatically change indexed order limit prices when the value of an index changes. The trader specifies the index and the linking formula. Traders also know these orders as *floating limit orders*.

By automatically adjusting limit orders, these systems reduce the cost of using limit order strategies. Equilibrium spreads in these trading systems therefore should be smaller than they otherwise would be. ◀

▶ Automated Limit Order Management Systems

Several data vendors, brokerage firms, and trading technology firms have products that allow traders to manage their limit orders automatically. Traders can program systems like ITG's Quantex to follow any set of instructions. For example, they can automate instructions to replace unfilled limit orders with market orders after a specified time.

These systems lower equilibrium spreads by decreasing the costs of implementing limit order strategies. Traders use these systems to submit aggressively priced limit orders that they otherwise probably would have submitted as market orders. ◀

is lower than value volatility. Consequently, spreads should be smaller when traders do not know values well.

This result is correct, but it does not seem right. Spreads generally are larger when traders are uncertain about values. The discrepancy has to do with the distribution of information. This unusual result comes from our assumption that all traders are equally ignorant. In practice, traders are asymmetrically informed.

14.4.2.5 Asymmetrically Informed Traders

In real markets, some traders are better informed than other traders. If the well-informed traders compete with each other to profit from their information, they all must trade quickly. Slow traders will find that faster traders have already caused prices to change. Well-informed traders therefore tend to submit market orders rather than limit orders. The well-informed traders subject the limit order traders to adverse selection. Their limit orders execute quickly if they are on the wrong side of the market, but they do not execute if they are on the informed side of the market. This adverse selection makes using limit order strategies relatively more expensive than market order strategies for uninformed traders. Equilibrium spreads therefore must widen to compensate. The additional widening of the bid/ask spread is the adverse selection spread we discussed earlier.

For most securities and contracts, the degree of information asymmetry varies inversely with how well traders estimate values. When most traders estimate values poorly, those traders who can estimate values well have a great advantage. Such traders typically have access to information that other traders do not have. Spreads therefore should be wider for instruments that most traders cannot easily value.

14.4.2.6 Summary

Equilibrium spreads in continuous order-driven auction markets depend on many factors. The most important factors are the degree of information asymmetry among the traders, how quickly traders can cancel their limit orders, and the volatility of the instrument. Table 14-2 provides a summary of the factors that determine equilibrium spreads in continuous order-driven markets.

When all traders are alike, the equilibrium spread will ensure that traders are indifferent between using market order and limit order trading strategies. This remarkable result is due to trader efforts to minimize their total costs of trading. These costs primarily include the spread (paid or received), commissions, order management costs, and the loss or exploitation of the trade timing option.

When traders differ, the equilibrium spread sets the supply of liquidity equal to the demand for liquidity. Traders who value their time highly, who trade on material information, or who are risk averse generally use market orders. Traders who can quickly adjust their limit orders with little cost, who are risk tolerant, or who do not value their time highly generally use limit orders.

14.5 SPREADS WHEN PUBLIC TRADERS COMPETE WITH DEALERS

In many markets, dealers and public limit order traders compete to offer liquidity. They compete unequally in two respects.

TABLE 14-2.
Equilibrium Spread Determinants in Continuous Order-driven Markets

FACTOR	EFFECT ON SPREADS	IMPORTANCE
Degree of information asymmetry among traders	Increases	Great
Time to cancel limit orders	Increases	High
Volatility	Increases	High
Limit order management costs	Increases	Moderate
Value of trader time	Increases	Moderate
Difference between limit and market order trade commissions	One for one	Depends on the difference
Degree of trader risk aversion	Increases	Low

Public limit order traders do not have the same business costs that dealers have. They therefore can quote more aggressive prices than can dealers who must fund their costs of doing business. In particular, public traders who are intent on filling their orders may use limit orders instead of market orders in an effort to lower their trading costs. Such traders price their orders aggressively in order to minimize their risk of not trading. The resulting spreads can be too small to allow dealers to recover their normal costs of doing business. Public limit order traders therefore may drive dealers out of the market.

Dealers, however, see more of the order flow than do most public traders. Most dealers also can change their quotes faster than public limit traders can change their limit prices. Dealers therefore may survive in markets with very narrow spreads by profiting from speculative trading opportunities that they can identify from analyzing their order flows. In particular, dealers may profitably employ quote matching, order anticipation, and trade timing strategies that public traders cannot identify or implement quickly enough. We discuss these strategies in chapters 11 and 24.

When dealers regularly exercise these strategies, limit order strategies become less attractive to public traders. Public traders will use market order strategies more often, and bid/ask spreads will be wider than they would be if dealers did not exploit their order flows.

14.6 CROSS-SECTIONAL SPREAD PREDICTIONS

The above analyses have many implications for bid/ask spreads. The implications all relate to three primary factors that determine whether spreads will be wide or narrow. These *primary spread determinants* are information asymmetries among traders, volatility, and utilitarian trading interest. (Chapter 8 shows that utilitarian traders trade because they obtain some value from trading besides profits.) If you know these factors, you can predict bid/ask spreads.

Unfortunately, two of the primary spread determinants are not easily measured, and none are easily predicted. We can easily measure volatility,

▶ Proxy Contests

When an observable variable varies with an unobservable variable, economists say that the observable variable is a *proxy* for the unobservable variable. Economists infer the values of unobservable variables from *proxy variables*.

Empirical economics is a contest in which economists try to convince us (and each other) that they have identified good proxies for variables that we wish we could measure well. ◀

but we cannot directly measure information asymmetries or utilitarian trading interest. To assess the importance of these factors, we must infer their values from observable instrument and market characteristics. We will call these characteristics *secondary spread determinants*.

Some secondary spread determinants are very highly correlated with spreads. For example, trading activity is an excellent proxy for utilitarian trading interest. In many markets, trading activity is the best observable predictor of spreads. Accordingly, many authors would classify it as a primary spread determinant. We do not because we want to preserve the distinction between theoretical and observable spread determinants. The distinction reminds us of the factors that ultimately determine spreads.

This section first summarizes the reasons why the three primary spread determinants affect spreads. We then consider predictions about how observable instrument and market characteristics (secondary spread determinants) affect bid/ask spreads.

Although the predictions specifically concern bid/ask spreads, most also apply to the provision of liquidity in general. The spread is only one of several aspects of liquidity. It measures the cost of immediacy for small orders. Other aspects of liquidity (discussed in chapter 19) include the cost of trading large orders (depth) and the ability of the market to recognize when uninformed traders have moved prices (resiliency). Since the factors that affect spreads typically also affect other aspects of liquidity, the predictions in this section are of more general interest than they might otherwise seem.

Since instrument prices vary considerably, spread comparisons are interesting only when we express the spreads as a fraction of price. For example, although a 10-cent spread on a 1-dollar stock is smaller than a 1-dollar spread on a 100-dollar stock, the spread on the 1-dollar stock is 10 percent of its price while the spread on the 100-dollar stock is only 1 percent of its price. The 1-dollar stock therefore is much more expensive to trade. The ratio of spread to price is the *relative spread*. When we compare spreads, we will implicitly refer to relative spreads.

14.6.1 The Three Primary Spread Determinants

The three primary spread determinants are asymmetric information, volatility, and utilitarian trading interest. Their effects on spreads are not independent of each other. For example, if information asymmetries are high, spreads will be wide. Wide spreads, however, discourage uninformed investors, decrease trading volumes (a secondary spread determinant), and thereby make spreads even wider.

Asymmetric Information The adverse selection spread model suggests that markets with asymmetrically informed traders will have wide spreads. Spreads will be widest when well-informed traders know material information about instrument values that would have an immediate and significant effect on values if it were common knowledge. When traders are asymmetrically informed, liquidity suppliers set their prices far from the market to recover from uninformed traders what they lose to well-informed traders.

Volatility The equilibrium spread model suggests that volatile instruments should have wide spreads. The spreads should be widest when limit order traders and dealers cannot easily adjust their orders. Since volatility increases limit order option values, traders widen their spreads when trading volatile instruments to minimize the value of the timing option.

Volatility also makes diversifiable inventory risks more frightening to risk-averse dealers. The transaction cost spread component therefore will be wider for volatile instruments than for stable instruments because dealers require a premium for bearing unpleasant risks. This effect probably is important only for highly volatile instruments.

Volatility and uncertainty about values undoubtedly are closely correlated. Instruments whose fundamental values change quickly are difficult to value because traders must be certain that they have all available information when they form their value estimates. Since it is harder for traders to be fully informed about volatile instruments than about stable instruments, asymmetric information problems are probably greater for volatile instruments than for stable instruments. Volatility therefore has a strong secondary effect on spreads because it is a good proxy for asymmetric information. The adverse selection spread component generally will be large for volatile instruments.

Utilitarian Trading Interest   Utilitarian traders—primarily investors, borrowers, hedgers, asset exchangers, and gamblers—trade because they expect to obtain some benefit from trading besides profits. Markets would not exist without utilitarian traders because purely profit-motivated traders cannot all profit when trading only among themselves. Actively traded instruments ultimately are those which interest utilitarian traders.

Utilitarian trading interest affects bid/ask spreads two ways. First, when utilitarian interest is strong, markets are very active. For reasons explained below, active markets tend to have narrow bid/ask spreads. Second, since utilitarian traders are uninformed, they dilute information in the order flow when they trade. The adverse selection spread component therefore will be small when utilitarian trading interest is strong. Since we discussed above how asymmetric information affects bid/ask spreads, we now focus on how market activity affects bid/ask spreads.

Dealers who trade frequently can spread their fixed costs of doing business over more volume than can dealers who trade infrequently. The transaction cost spread component therefore should be smaller for actively traded instruments than for infrequently traded instruments.

Dealers also face smaller inventory risks when trading in active markets than in inactive markets. In active markets, they can quickly lay off inventory imbalances. Since they can more easily control their inventories in active markets, they face less inventory risk—diversifiable inventory risk and adverse selection risk. They therefore can quote smaller spreads for actively traded instruments than they can for infrequently traded instruments.

Public traders who are committed to trading are also more willing to offer limit orders in active markets because the probability that their orders will execute quickly is larger in active markets than in inactive markets. They also are more willing to offer limit orders in active markets because the timing options that limit orders give up are less valuable when many market order traders compete for them. Public limit order traders therefore will make spreads narrower in active markets than in inactive markets.

Inactive markets cannot support many dealers. Dealers in such markets therefore may exercise some market power when setting their spreads. They will have more market power if the small size of the market makes other dealers reluctant to enter and if public limit order traders are unable or unwilling to offer liquidity. Spreads in such small markets therefore may be wider than we would otherwise expect.

▶ A Gap in Spreads Due to the Gap Between German and U.S. GAAP

The generally accepted accounting principles (GAAP) by which German corporations historically reported their financial results allowed them considerable latitude in how they presented their accounts. Using various hidden reserve accounts, they were able to smooth their earnings considerably, so that it was difficult or impossible for analysts to estimate firm values accurately. In contrast, U.S. GAAP do not allow U.S. corporations as much freedom in how they report their results. The difference in accounting standards suggests that firms which report using German GAAP will have wider spreads than will firms that report using U.S. GAAP (all other things being equal).

The New York Stock Exchange requires its listed firms to report their accounts using U.S. GAAP. They may also report using International GAAP, which are essentially similar. Although the NYSE would like to list many large German firms, it will not list them until they report their results using more transparent accounting standards.

German firms are increasingly reporting their results using International GAAP. The trend is due to the desire of German firms to trade in more liquid markets, and to efforts by the European Community to harmonize its financial markets. ◀

14.6.2 Spread Predictions Based on Secondary Factors

Various secondary factors allow us to draw inferences about the primary factors. This subsection examines these factors and considers how they are related to spreads.

Our presentation classifies the secondary factors by the primary spread determinant that they most closely represent. The classification, however, is somewhat arbitrary because many secondary factors are correlated with more than one primary factor. For example, firm size (a secondary factor) generally is both correlated with investor interest and inversely correlated with volatility.

The various secondary factors are often correlated with each other. The observed effect of a secondary factor in a statistical analysis therefore sometimes differs from its predicted effect. For example, we argue below that firms in emerging industries should have wider spreads than firms in established industries because of asymmetric information problems. However, firms in emerging industries tend to have substantial investment interest, which creates substantial volumes and therefore narrower spreads. Firms in emerging industries therefore may have narrower spreads than firms in established industries, although we predict otherwise. When factors are correlated, it is often necessary to use statistical methods to disentangle their conflicting effects.

14.6.2.1 Asymmetric Information Proxies

Information Disclosure Rules   Rules that require information disclosure decrease information asymmetries. Stock markets that require their listed firms to disclose reliable, comprehensive financial information on a regular and timely basis will have narrower spreads than those which do not require extensive disclosure. To decrease information asymmetries, many markets commonly require that their listed firms conform to audit, accounting, and reporting standards that are more demanding than the local legal standards.

Market Condition Reports   Commodity markets that compile and publish extensive reports of market supply and demand conditions will have smaller spreads than they would have otherwise. To reduce information asymmetries, many governments have agencies that collect and publish information on market conditions.

Analysts   Securities and commodities that many public analysts follow will have smaller spreads than will those which few analysts follow. Analysts evaluate the financial conditions and the economic prospects of various instruments. The information that they produce and publish reduces information asymmetries among traders.

Information Vendors   Stocks of corporations that the financial press covers closely will have smaller spreads than will those the press ignores. Like analysts, the press produces information that reduces information asymmetries.

Major Commodity Contracts   Spreads in contracts that represent economywide risks will be quite small. Traders rarely have significant material information about supply and demand conditions when information about those conditions is distributed throughout the economy. Oil, gold, silver, wheat, soybeans, currencies, and financial futures are examples of such commodities. Although traders occasionally have significant information about local supply and demand conditions, such information generally does not have a material effect on the whole market.

Diversified Portfolios Relative spreads will be smaller for contracts on well-diversified portfolios than for the individual assets in the portfolio. Although traders may have significant material information about individual assets, such information rarely is material to all assets in the portfolio. A large portfolio dilutes the importance of information about any single constituent asset. In addition, portfolios generally are easier to value than individual assets: Mistakes made valuing one asset may offset mistakes made in valuing other assets. For both reasons, stock index futures contracts have smaller spreads than individual stocks.

Diversified Stocks The stocks of well-diversified corporations will have smaller spreads than those of similar-sized corporations that focus on a single line of business. A well-diversified corporation is a portfolio of assets. Although traders may have significant material information about some of the asset values, such information often is not material to valuing all the assets. Conglomerates therefore have smaller spreads than undiversified firms.

Established Versus Emerging Industries (Value Versus Growth Stocks) Firms in established industries are easier to value than firms in emerging industries. Firm values in emerging industries depend primarily on uncertain future growth prospects. In contrast, firm values in established industries depend primarily on cash flows that are relatively easy to predict. Since valuing firms in emerging industries is more difficult than valuing firms in established industries, information asymmetries among traders are likely to be bigger in the former than in the latter. Firms in established industries therefore will have smaller spreads than firms in emerging industries (all other things held constant).

Age of the Firm Young firms are often harder to value than older firms doing business in the same markets. Young firms often use newer technologies. Although such technologies may be very promising, their values are often uncertain when they have not been fully tested. Even when the firms use the same technologies, younger firms are harder to value than older firms because new management systems are often less mature than old management systems. Bid/ask spreads will be wider for new firms than for old firms.

Insider-trading Rules Markets that effectively enforce insider-trading rules protect their liquidity suppliers from adverse selection. Insider-trading rules prevent traders from trading on certain types of material information. Bid/ask spreads will be smaller when such insiders cannot trade. We discuss this prediction further in chapter 29.

When Material Information Is Expected Spreads will be wider when liquidity suppliers expect that some traders may have material information. For example, stock spreads tend to widen before and after earnings announcements. They widen before because insiders sometime trade on the information before it becomes public. (Such trading is illegal in many jurisdictions.) They widen after because some traders are better able to evaluate the significance of the news than others.

14.6.2.2 Volatility Proxies

Since volatility is easily measured, we generally do not need to identify proxies for it when analyzing bid/ask spreads. However, if you want to predict

---

▶ **Why Speeches by Fed Chairmen Are Rarely Interesting**

Contracts on macroeconomic variables like stock index futures, Treasury bond futures, and T-bill futures typically trade with very narrow spreads. The values of these contracts depend primarily on expectations about interest rates and macroeconomic activity. Spreads are narrow because few people have reliable information about how these factors will change.

In the United States, the only people who may be able to predict future interest rates accurately are the Federal Reserve Board chairman and the other members of the Federal Reserve Open Market Committee. They, of course, may not trade on their information, and they may not offer it to other traders.

If you have ever listened to speeches by a Fed chairman or a Fed governor, you know that they rarely say anything interesting about interest rates. They do not want to reveal any information that would allow informed traders to predict the future course of interest rates. ◀

▶ Orange Juice Futures

Orange juice futures prices often become quite volatile during the winter when freezing weather in Florida threatens the orange crop. At those times, meteorologists and local farmers have an informational advantage over other futures traders. Accordingly, spreads on futures widen when cold air descends into Florida. ◀

future bid/ask spreads, you must predict future volatility. The problem is especially difficult when the instruments in which you are interested have not yet traded.

Practitioners use various methods to predict volatility. Since we describe these methods in chapter 20, we consider the issue here only briefly.

Many factors make instruments volatile. For stocks, the most important factors are financial leverage, operating leverage, and uncertain growth opportunities. Commodities are volatile when supply and demand conditions are uncertain. They are especially volatile when they are perishable, when the costs of storage are high, when inventories are low, or when the supply depends on weather conditions. Currencies are volatile when traders are uncertain about political stability, inflation, and interest rates. Finally, bonds are volatile when traders are uncertain about inflation, interest rates, and credit quality. These factors all cause spreads to be wide when they are significant.

14.6.2.3 Proxies for Utilitarian Trading Interest

Trading Activity   Measures of trading activity such as traded volumes and numbers of transactions are good proxies for utilitarian trading interest. Markets cannot sustain high volumes without traders who are willing to trade even when they do not expect to profit from trading. Markets that have high volumes therefore have many such traders. Actively traded markets usually have narrow spreads.

Firm Size   Large firms' stocks tend to have smaller relative spreads than do small firms' stocks. The substantial investor interest in large firms ensures that their stocks are actively traded. This interest also ensures that the press and many analysts follow them. Large firms also tend to be less volatile because they often are mature, well-diversified companies that use established technologies. Higher average trading activity and lower average volatility both suggest that large firms have smaller spreads than do small firms.

Debt Issue Size   Large debt issues often attract the interest of many investors. Investors are especially interested in government debt. Widely distributed debt issues tend to trade in active markets when they are first issued. Market activity quickly diminishes, however, as the issues age because many investors buy and hold debt until maturity. Spreads in large debt issues therefore start small and rise through time. Government debt issues are most liquid when they are *on-the-run*. On-the-run issues are debt issues that the government has most recently issued. They become *seasoned issues* when the government sells a new issue with the same initial maturity.

Risk Replication   Commodity contracts that closely replicate risks which bother many potential traders attract substantial hedging interest. Such contracts are most successful when the natural hedging interests on the long and short sides are approximately equal. Contracts that meet these criteria usually trade actively and therefore have small spreads. Accordingly, commodity markets try very hard to write standardized contracts that will appeal to many hedgers.

Volatility   In additional to its primary effect on spreads, described above, volatility may have a strong secondary effect on spreads through its effect on gambling interest. Gamblers like to trade volatile instruments. Volatility also may have a secondary effect on spreads through its effect on hedging interest. Hedgers often have to adjust their positions more in volatile markets than in stable markets. These effects both suggest that volatile instruments will be actively traded and therefore will have small spreads. This secondary effect of volatility on spreads works in the opposite direction to the primary effect.

14.6.3 Liquidity and Capital Structure

When the asymmetric information problem is particularly severe, or when utilitarian interest is very small, spreads may be so wide that no trading occurs. Dealers will not make markets in such securities because the losses they expect from trading with well-informed traders—and the costs of determining security values to avoid those losses—are greater than their potential trading revenues. When this happens, economists say that the market has failed. *Market failure* does not mean that something is wrong, but rather that the market fails to exist.

Market failure explains why small businesses rarely finance their operations by issuing publicly traded equity. Investors generally will not buy stock in firms that they cannot trade.

Small firms must therefore obtain their financing from banks and venture capitalists. Banks buy private debt securities (loans) and venture capitalists buy private equity issues. These agencies spend substantial time and money doing *due diligence* to determine whether their investments will be profitable. They also impose many restrictions on the management of the firm, foremost of which is the right to supervise the firm. These restrictions allow them to protect their interests. The due diligence, the managerial restrictions, and the special surveillance rights are possible only in the context of a confidential and trusting relationship between the investor and the firm. Such relationships are feasible in private financing markets, but not in public financing markets.

> ### ▶ Why Are Shares in Tommy's Burgers Not Publicly Traded?
>
> Tommy's Burgers is a small, single-outlet burger stand. Tommy is doing well and would like to expand his business. To finance his expansion, Tommy considers issuing equity shares and selling them to the public.
>
> One of Tommy's regular customers is an investment banker. Tommy asks him for advice. The banker explains that almost nobody will buy his stock because the secondary market will be highly illiquid. Dealers will not make a market in the security because they would be afraid of trading with much better informed traders.
>
> Tommy ultimately obtains his financing from the bank that provides him with transaction services. Since the bank can continuously monitor his checking account, it can easily supervise its investment. ◀

14.7 SUMMARY

Bid/ask spreads depend on numerous factors. The most important are asymmetric information, volatility, and utilitarian trader interest.

Information is asymmetrically distributed among traders when some traders are better informed than others. Asymmetric information makes the order flow informative and causes dealers to lose money to better-informed traders. Dealers widen their spreads to recover from uninformed traders what they lose to informed traders. Dealers also widen their spreads to anticipate what they learn from the order flow when they discover whether the next trader is a buyer or a seller. These two explanations imply the same adverse selection spread component. It will be large when the order flow includes many informed traders and when the informed traders have highly material information.

Volatility affects bid/ask spreads by increasing the option values of standing limit orders and dealer quotes. When liquidity suppliers cannot adjust their prices quickly, they give timing options to market order traders. The value of this timing option increases with volatility. Dealers widen their spreads, and limit order traders back away from the market, to decrease the value of the timing option. Volatility also indirectly determines bid/ask spreads because it is a good proxy for asymmetric information.

Utilitarian trader interest ultimately determines market trading activity. Actively traded instruments have narrow spreads because dealers can spread their costs of doing business over more trades, because dealers can more effectively manage their inventory risks, and because the competition to supply liquidity is intense. Measures of market activity, such as trading volumes and trading, frequency therefore vary inversely with spreads. Factors that determine market activity, such as firm size, hedging suitability, and volatility, therefore also are inversely correlated with bid/ask spreads.

The equilibrium model shows that spreads in order-driven markets adjust to ensure that some traders will be indifferent between taking liquidity with market orders (and marketable limit orders) and offering liquidity with limit orders. Those who value their time highly and those who are most risk averse will take liquidity. Those who can adjust their order prices quickly may offer liquidity. On average, limit order strategies will execute at slightly better prices than market orders strategies because market order traders must compensate limit order traders for the additional management time, price risk, and timing options associated with limit order strategies.

Adverse selection helps us understand why uninformed traders lose whether they submit limit or market orders. If they use limit orders, they suffer adverse selection. When they compete with informed traders, their limit orders do not fill, and they subsequently wish they had traded. When they offer liquidity to informed traders, their limit orders quickly fill, and they subsequently wish that they had not traded. If they use market orders, they avoid direct adverse selection, but they still suffer its indirect effects because they must pay dealers the adverse selection spread. The adverse selection spread is effectively a fee dealers charge uninformed traders for bearing their adverse selection risk. Uninformed traders thus lose however they trade. If they want to avoid losing, they must avoid trading.

Asymmetric information is extremely important in trading. In this chapter, we used it to explain bid/ask spreads, why uninformed traders lose no matter how they trade, and why small firms cannot obtain public financing. In subsequent chapters, we will use the model to help us understand block trading, why governments regulate insider trading, and why stock index contracts are so liquid.

14.8 SOME POINTS TO REMEMBER

- Competition among dealers and from limit order traders keeps spreads small.
- Dealer spreads depend on their costs.
- Informed trading makes spreads wide.
- Uninformed traders indirectly lose to informed traders when they pay spreads made wide by adverse selection.
- Spreads are small in active markets for well-known assets.
- Large anonymous traders are widely thought to be well informed.
- Limit order traders give away timing options to traders who can respond to changing market conditions more quickly.
- When all traders are identical, limit order strategies produce better

prices on average than market order strategies because traders value their time and do not like to risk failing to trade.

14.9 QUESTIONS FOR THOUGHT

1. Why do many securities markets, but not most futures markets, have insider-trading rules?
2. Does the risk of trading with informed traders vary by time of day? By time of year? By proximity to earnings reports?
3. Would the adverse selection spread be smaller if dealers sometimes could trade out of their positions before values are realized? What effect would this have on uninformed traders?
4. Would the adverse selection spread be smaller if dealers knew which of their customers were well informed?
5. Would a dealer ever knowingly want to trade with an informed trader?
6. What determines how many dealers will be in a market?
7. In some markets, a large minimum price increment puts a lower bound on the spreads that dealers can quote. When this constraint is binding, dealers cannot quote smaller spreads. Suppose that market making generates excess profits so that new dealers enter the market. If the spread is already equal to the minimum price increment, how can new entrants attract order flow?
8. Suppose dealers can obtain valuable information about future price changes through their dealing activities. In competitive markets, can dealers survive simply by offering liquidity, or must they speculate as well? What happens to bid/ask spreads when dealers speculate successfully on information obtained from their dealing operations? Which component of the bid/ask spread is affected?
9. Are there economies of scale in dealing? What advantages do dealers have when they see a large fraction of the order flow?
10. When limit order traders and market order traders trade at the same time and on the same side of the market, the limit order traders receive better prices. Why is this difference not sufficient to compensate limit order traders for offering liquidity?
11. When should limit order traders adjust their limit prices? How does your answer depend on the costs of adjustment, the number of market order traders who monitor the market, and the expected delay between the decision to adjust the order and its effective implementation?
12. Can you put an upper bound on the value of the timing option that limit orders traders give to faster market order traders? How does it depend on the cost of adjusting limit orders? Does it also depend on the number of market order traders who monitor the market?
13. If limit order traders could continuously monitor the market and if they could adjust their limit prices instantaneously, would the value of the timing option depend on volatility?
14. If spreads are set so that dealers expect zero economic profit, can public limit order traders expect to profit by randomly submitting limit orders at the best bid or best offer?
15. In the equilibrium spread model introduced in the text, what effect would diverse order sizes have on equilibrium spreads? Why is this question hard to answer?

16. Why might a corporation that is domiciled in a jurisdiction with lax financial reporting standards voluntarily report more information than is required?

17. Many corporations issue both debt and equity to finance their operations. Which issues would you expect to have smaller relative spreads? In practice, equity issues often have smaller relative spreads than the debt issues of the same companies. Why might this be so?

18. Suppose the values of two assets in two different markets are closely correlated. How would the liquidity in one market affect the liquidity in the other market?

19. Underwriters generally will refuse to underwrite equity issues in firms that are smaller than some minimum size that they each determine. In which industries do you expect that that minimum size would be smallest?

20. Legal systems vary considerably across countries. Some are quick, just, and thorough. Others are slow, corrupt, and incomplete. How does the legal environment affect cross-country bid/ask spread comparisons?

14.10 APPENDIX: A SIMPLE GLOSTEN-MILGROM MODEL OF THE ADVERSE SELECTION SPREAD COMPONENT

The information and accounting perspectives of the adverse selection spread component both imply the same size for the component. We can explore this result easily in a simple example based on the Glosten-Milgrom model.

Suppose that a dealer believes the following:

- The unconditional value of a security is V.
- The next trader is equally likely to be a buyer or a seller.
- The probability that the next trader is well informed is P, so that the probability that the next trader is uninformed is $1 - P$.
- The security is worth $V + E$ if an informed trader wants to buy it and $V - E$ if an informed trader wants to sell it.

The dealer knows neither whether the next trader will be well informed or not, nor whether the next trader will be a buyer or seller.

Consider first the derivation of the adverse selection spread component from the information perspective. What is the dealer's best estimate of value, given that the next trader is a buyer? If the next trader is an uninformed trader, the dealer will not learn anything, so his best estimate of the security value will remain V. If the next trader is an informed trader, he expects that the security value will be $V + E$. Since the dealer does not know whether the buyer will be well informed or not, his best estimate of the security value, given that the next trader is a buyer, is the probability-weighted average of these two values: $(1 - P) \cdot V + P \cdot (V + E) = V + P \cdot E$. Likewise, given that the next trader is a seller, his best estimate of the security value is $V - P \cdot E$. The difference between these two values, $2 \cdot P \cdot E$, is the adverse selection spread component.

The derivation of the adverse selection spread from the accounting perspective estimates the spread the dealer must quote to ensure that he expects to just break even, ignoring his normal costs of doing business. We derive this spread by computing the dealer's expected trading profits. Suppose first that the next trader is a seller. The dealer will buy the security at his bid price B. If the seller is uninformed, the dealer pays B for something worth V, so he expects his trading profits will be $V - B$. If the seller is well informed, the dealer likewise expects trading profits of $(V - E) - B$. Since the dealer does not know whether the seller is informed or uninformed, his best estimate of his trading profits, given that the next trader is a seller, is the probability-weighted average of these two values: $(1 - P) \cdot (V - B) + P \cdot ((V - E) - B) = V - B - P \cdot E$. If the next trader is a buyer, the dealer will sell at the ask price A. He expects trading profits of $A - V$ if he trades with an uninformed trader and $A - (V - E)$ if he traders with an informed trader. His best estimate of his trading profits, given that the next trader is a buyer, is therefore $A - V - P \cdot E$. Since the next trader is equally likely to be a buyer or a seller, the dealer expects that his profits on the next trade will be the equal-weighted average of the profits he expects given that the next trader is a buyer or a seller: $\frac{1}{2}(V - B - P \cdot E) + \frac{1}{2}(A - V - P \cdot E) = \frac{1}{2}(A - B) - P \cdot E$. The dealer expects to just break even when his expected profits are zero. Setting this expression equal to zero implies that the break-even bid/ask spread $A - B$ is $2 \cdot P \cdot E$. This expression is equal to the adverse selection component derived from the information perspective.

15

▷

Block
Traders

B *lock trades* result from orders that are too large to fill easily using standard trading procedures. Such orders generally demand more liquidity than is normally available at exchanges or in dealer networks. Traders who wish to trade large blocks therefore must look elsewhere for liquidity. They usually turn to block traders to arrange their trades.

Block traders include block dealers and block brokers. *Block dealers* arrange block trades when they fill their clients' large orders. *Block brokers* arrange block trades when they find other traders who are willing to fill their clients' orders. Both types of block traders usually arrange their trades by telephone in the *upstairs block market*. The traders who initiate large trades are *block initiators*. We will call the traders who fill their orders *block liquidity suppliers*. Block liquidity suppliers include dealers and large buy-side traders.

Although block trades represent a small fraction of all trades in most markets, they often account for much of the total trading volume due to their large sizes. Block traders arrange most block trades on behalf of large institutions and very wealthy individuals.

Large traders often have a significant impact on prices. They therefore must arrange their trades very carefully in order to control their transaction costs. Block traders must especially consider how they expose their orders so as to avoid losing to front runners and quote matchers.

Since block trades significantly affect volumes and prices, traders must understand block trading in order to interpret volumes and prices. If you intend to extract information from volumes and prices, you must understand block trading.

In this chapter, you will learn how large traders expose their orders and how block traders arrange their trades. You will learn that block dealers and block brokers want to serve only uninformed clients who honestly tell them the true sizes of their orders. Block initiators—whether they are uninformed or informed, honest or deceitful—therefore must convince block liquidity suppliers that they are uninformed and honest. We therefore will consider how traders convince others that they are uninformed and honest.

15.1 STATISTICAL DEFINITIONS OF BLOCK TRADES

For our purposes, a *block trade* is any trade that results from an order that is too large to fill easily using normal trading procedures. Such orders typically represent more than a day's normal trading volume. In thinly traded instruments, these orders may represent only a few thousand shares or tens of contracts. In actively traded instruments, such orders are many times larger. Most block traders think of a block as exceeding a quarter of a day's average trading volume in an actively traded stock.

For statistical purposes, exchanges often arbitrarily designate trades as block trades if they exceed some fixed size. These classification schemes vary by exchange. The New York Stock Exchange defines a block trade as 10,000 shares or more, regardless of trading activity or price level. Traders, however, routinely arrange such trades on the Exchange floor in actively traded stocks and in low-priced stocks. Although officially classified as block trades, these trades are normal trades in all other respects. In thinly traded stocks, or in very high priced stocks like Berkshire Hathaway (priced as of this writing above 70,000 dollars per share), trades smaller than 10,000 shares often cannot easily be arranged on the floor of the Exchange.

▶ **A Humble Suggestion**

Block trading statistics would be more useful if block trades were classified by whether they exceed some fraction of average daily volume rather than by whether they exceed some fixed size. ◀

15.2 BLOCK TRADING PROBLEMS

Block initiators face four problems when they attempt to arrange their traders. The *latent demand problem* makes it hard to find block liquidity suppliers who are not in the market. The *order exposure problem* makes block initiators reluctant to advertise for liquidity for fear of driving the market away from them. The *price discrimination problem* makes liquidity suppliers reluctant to trade with large traders because they fear that more size will follow. The *asymmetric information problem* makes liquidity suppliers reluctant to trade with block initiators because they fear that the block initiators are well informed.

15.2.1 The Latent Demand Problem

The most obvious problem that large traders face is finding traders to with whom to trade. Many block liquidity suppliers are unwilling to expose their interest. Many more might trade if asked, but they have not yet issued orders to trade. Block traders must find these traders in order to complete their trades.

Traders who would be willing to trade if asked, but who have not yet issued trading orders, have *latent trading demands*. They may not issue orders because writing orders is costly, or because they do not realize that they are willing to trade.

When the probability of trading is small, traders often do not issue orders because they are costly to manage. For example, a trader may be a willing buyer of hundreds of different stocks at prices 5 percent below their current market prices. If he creates and submits orders for each stock, he risks buying all the stocks if the market as a whole drops significantly. Since he cannot afford to buy all the stocks, he cannot allow so many orders to stand at once. Moreover, if all stocks drop together, he may not be a willing buyer in any stock. He therefore waits to see which stocks drop. He has latent trading demands for many stocks, but block traders must discover them before he will trade.

Other traders simply do not know that they are willing to trade. Forming opinions about thousands of securities is costly. Instead, they often wait until events force them to think about trading opportunities. When presented with an attractive opportunity, they may decide to trade.

Traders who are willing to trade but who do not initiate their trades are *responsive traders*. They respond to demands for liquidity. Most traders who supply liquidity are responsive traders.

Block traders must discover the latent demands of responsive traders

Hard Work Pays

Suppose that brokers can develop and maintain one buy-side trader client for each hour per week that they work. A broker who works only 20 hours per week has 190 ways to arrange trades among pairs of his 20 clients. If the broker works an additional 20 hours a week, he has 780 ways to arrange trades. If he works 60 hours a week, he can arrange trades 1,770 ways.

This illustration shows that well organized brokers become more productive the harder they work. Hardworking brokers benefit from the network externality. ◀

Block Traders Play Concentration Well

Block traders play a game similar to the card game Concentration, in which players take turns uncovering cards two at a time and attempt to match them. To match buyers to sellers, block traders must remember who was, who is, and—most important—who would be interested in trading hundreds of securities.

Unlike card players, block traders can take notes, and they obviously do not have to take turns when playing. Not surprisingly, good block traders spend most of their time on the telephone. Many enter copious notes into electronic contract management systems. ◀

when they cannot find adequate liquidity in the market. They find liquidity primarily by calling traders they think would be willing trade.

Block traders often move prices significantly to discover the latent demands of responsive traders. Buyers bid prices up, and sellers offer prices down to encourage responsive traders to pay attention and respond. Block initiators give *price concessions* to block liquidity suppliers so as to encourage them to trade.

Good block traders know where to look for traders willing to provide liquidity at the lowest cost. They keep track of who is interested in various securities, and who has traded those securities in the past. They also try to know what instruments will appeal to different traders so that they can predict who will be most willing to trade when presented with attractive trading opportunities.

Most large traders do not know as much about latent demands as do professional block traders who specialize in collecting this information. Large traders therefore often contract with block traders to arrange their trades.

Large traders do not initiate all block trades. Sometimes *sales traders* in large wirehouses broker block trades by identifying latent trading demands on both sides of the trade.

15.2.2 The Order Exposure Problem

When looking for liquidity, block traders must be very careful about to whom they expose their orders. Traders who know about impending blocks often use that information when trading, to the disadvantage of the block traders. Some traders create orders expressly to front-run pending blocks. Other traders who intend to trade on the same side as the block accelerate their trading to avoid the price impact of the block. Traders who intend to trade on the opposite side retard their trading to capitalize on the price impact of the block. These strategies accelerate the price impact of the block by demanding liquidity in front of the block or by withholding liquidity from the block. Block traders then ultimately obtain less favorable prices for their blocks. To avoid these problems, block traders try to display their orders first to traders who will most likely fill them.

Block traders *shop the block* when they expose their orders while searching for liquidity. Widely shopped blocks *hang over the market* as information about them *leaks out*. Block traders *spoil their market* when prices run away from their orders because they have foolishly exposed them. Table 15-1 describes strategies that clever traders use to exploit information about a block hanging over the market.

Successful block traders carefully consider whether the traders to whom they have exposed orders are front running them. They pay attention to prices, volumes, and any available information about who is trading. Block traders who suspect that traders are front running their orders must avoid exposing their orders to those traders in the future.

Traders who front-run block orders, or who allow information about block orders to leak, risk acquiring a reputation for being untrustworthy. Block traders do not make their first calls to such traders. Untrustworthy traders may thus lose the opportunity to participate in future blocks. They also lose early access to information that might allow them to better interpret market conditions. Since blocks initiators often give block liquidity sup-

TABLE 15-1.
Strategies Clever Traders Pursue When a Block Is Hanging over the Market

TRADERS	STRATEGY	PURPOSE	EFFECT
Front runners	Trade on the same side before the block trades	Profit from the price impact of the block	Accelerate the price impact of the block
Same-side traders	Accelerate their intended trades	Avoid the price impact of the block	Accelerate the price impact of the block
Opposite-side traders	Delay their intended trades	Take advantage of the price impact of the block	Reduce liquidity available to same-side traders so that their trades have greater price impact

pliers substantial price concessions, supplying liquidity to block initiators often is quite profitable. When block traders can identify front running, traders have substantial incentives to cultivate trustworthy reputations.

To avoid order exposure problems, block traders favor trading systems that do not expose their orders. Crossing markets like POSIT serve these traders by allowing them to arrange trades on a completely confidential basis. At exchanges that permit hidden limit orders (such as Euronext, GLOBEX, and Island), large traders frequently hide their orders to limit their impact upon the market. At exchanges that do not have such facilities, large traders give their orders to honest brokers who expose them selectively, or they break their orders into small pieces so that nobody can determine their full size.

15.2.3 The Price Discrimination Problem

Block initiators have trouble finding liquidity because block liquidity suppliers are afraid that they will price discriminate among them. Block liquidity suppliers do not want to be the first to offer liquidity to a large trader, only to see prices move against them when the large trader continues to trade. They therefore want to know how much the large trader truly wants to trade before they offer liquidity. Block initiators—especially those whose orders are not so large that they will greatly benefit from price discriminating—may obtain better prices from block liquidity suppliers if they can credibly convince them of the true sizes of their orders.

Traders cannot credibly reveal the true sizes of their orders in markets where they trade anonymously. Traders will lie in anonymous markets because lying has no negative consequences in such markets. The primary penalty for lying is losing an honest reputation. Since traders cannot cultivate reputations in anonymous markets, they will lie with impunity. Block initiators who want to solve the price discrimination problem must therefore trade in markets where they know with whom they are trading.

Since most large traders do not trade often enough to acquire strong reputations for being honest, they often use block traders who have such reputations to arrange their trades. Block traders acquire their reputations by consistently telling the truth. To protect their reputations, they must ensure that their clients do not lie to them. Dishonest clients improperly try to exploit the honest reputations of their agents.

▶ **A Quick Ticket to the Doghouse**

Blair tells Sawyer that he wants to buy 200,000 shares of IBM. Sawyer asks whether this is the full size of his order. Blair assures him that it is indeed. They arrange to trade IBM at 50 cents above its prevailing price.

Blair then contracts with another trader to buy 200,000 more shares of IBM at a price 50 cents higher than he paid Sawyer.

Sawyer immediately loses 100,000 dollars on his sale. Had he known Blair wanted to buy 400,000 shares, he would have demanded a higher price. Sawyer will now put Blair *in the doghouse*. He will not knowingly offer liquidity to Blair for a long time. ◀

▶ Untrustworthy Traders Do Not Get Shares in Hot IPOs

Buying a hot issue during its initial public offering can be extremely profitable. The prices of these issues often jump substantially on the first day of trading.

The investment banks that control the distribution of these shares can allocate the shares to whomever they please. They naturally will not allocate shares to customers who exploit them. Such customers include block initiators who are not honest about the full sizes of their trades and traders who front-run blocks displayed to them. ◀

Block traders keep their clients honest by knowing them well and by penalizing them when they are dishonest. They are most effective when they have well-established relationships with their clients. Block traders therefore often work for large investment banks that provide services besides transaction services to their clients. These other services may include investment advice, research, banking, and clearance and settlement. Through these relationships, block traders get to know their clients well, and they often can penalize clients who lie to them.

Since large traders can send portions of their orders to multiple block traders, block traders may not easily determine the full extent of their clients' orders. In the U.S. equities markets, many large institutions must report their portfolio holdings on a quarterly basis to the Securities and Exchange Commission. Data vendors such as CDA/Spectrum collect these *13F Holdings Reports* and disseminate the information in them to their clients. Block traders use this information to determine after the fact whether their clients were truthful in their dealings with them. Block traders also use information about portfolio positions to estimate the maximum amount that a large trader might trade. The information is particularly useful when the large trader is a seller whose investment policy prohibits short sales. Such traders can sell no more than they own. If they want to sell their entire positions, block traders know that no further size will follow.

15.2.4 The Asymmetric Information Problem

Block initiators have trouble finding liquidity because block liquidity suppliers suspect that they are well informed. They base their suspicions on two arguments. First, large traders can afford to invest more in information than can small traders because they can spread the fixed costs of research over larger portfolios. Second, well-informed traders want to trade large sizes in order to obtain the maximum profit from their information. Taken together, these arguments suggest that large traders are often well informed. Traders therefore do not like to trade with them. When they do, they demand very large price concessions.

Block liquidity suppliers demand these price concessions for the same reasons that dealer bid/ask spreads include an adverse selection component. These price concessions allow liquidity suppliers to recover from uninformed traders what they lose to informed traders. They also reflect the inferences about fundamental values that liquidity suppliers make when they suspect that they may be trading with well-informed traders.

Block liquidity suppliers especially suspect that large anonymous traders are well informed. Informed traders like to trade anonymously because they do not want to acquire reputations for being well informed. Such reputations would allow liquidity suppliers to avoid them. They also like to trade anonymously because they do not want front runners to profit from the fundamental information that their orders reveal. Since uninformed traders do not share these concerns, block liquidity suppliers suspect that anonymous traders tend to be well informed. Accordingly, block liquidity suppliers avoid anonymous traders.

Large block initiators solve the asymmetric information problem by convincing block liquidity suppliers that they are uninformed. To do this, they must reveal their identities. If they have a reputation for being uninformed, traders may then offer them liquidity that they otherwise would not have offered. If they do not have a reputation for being uninformed, they must submit to an audit of their trading intentions. If block traders conclude that the large traders are indeed uninformed, they may arrange trades for them.

15.2.5 Summary

Block initiators have trouble finding liquidity because most block liquidity suppliers do not express their trading interests, because block initiators cannot widely expose their orders without spoiling their markets, because block liquidity suppliers fear that block initiators will price discriminate, and because block liquidity suppliers fear that block initiators are well informed. Block initiators must address these issues in order to obtain liquidity.

To address each issue, block initiators must reveal credible information about themselves to block liquidity suppliers. They must tell them they want to trade to solve the latent demand problem. They must expose only to the most trustworthy traders to avoid order exposure problems. They must credibly reveal the full size of their orders to solve the price discrimination problem. Finally, block initiators must convince block liquidity suppliers that they are uninformed traders to address the asymmetric information problem.

Successful block trading therefore requires significant exchanges of information among traders besides the usual price and size information that all traders must exchange. Since most exchanges and dealer networks are equipped only to exchange price and order size information, block traders arrange most block trades by telephone in the upstairs market.

Block initiators choose between two strategies to convey information about themselves to the market. *Sunshine traders* try to communicate directly to the market. The sunshine trading strategy is rarely effective, however. We consider it because it allows us to better understand the alternative strategy in which large traders use the services of block traders in the upstairs market.

15.3 SUNSHINE TRADING

Traders who announce to the market who they are, what they intend to do, the full extent of their orders, and why they intend to trade are *sunshine traders*. Sunshine trading works well when sunshine traders are well known and are known to be uninformed and honest. In large markets, sunshine trading at best works only for the largest traders, since only those traders will be able to acquire credible reputations.

Sunshine trading does not work if traders suspect that the sunshine trader may be well informed or dishonest. If traders could always obtain more liquidity merely by revealing their identities, all traders would do so. Unknown informed traders would pretend to be uninformed traders, and well-known informed traders would create new identities to mask their trading. Well-informed traders who try to pass for uninformed traders are *wolves in sheep's clothing*. Sunshine trading generally does not work well because it is hard to determine whether sunshine traders are indeed uninformed traders and whether they have indeed revealed their entire trading interests. Good answers to such questions generally require thorough investigations of their motives for trading. Traders cannot conduct such investigations on exchange floors or in screen-based trading systems.

Although sunshine trading may solve the asymmetric information

▶ Ignorance Is Bliss

In almost everything we do, a reputation for being well informed serves us well. Trading is the notable exception. Although the most profitable traders are well informed, they must appear to be uninformed when they trade. Otherwise, they will not be able to trade at low cost. ◀

▷ LOR's Sunshine Trading in S&P 500 Futures

Leland O'Brien Rubinstein Associates (LOR) was an institutional money manager that popularized the portfolio insurance trading strategy in the early 1980s. The object of the strategy is to replicate the returns of a covered put position. Traders implement the strategy by buying securities when the market rises and selling them as it falls. A formula from the well-known Black-Scholes option pricing theory specifies the trade size.

LOR used S&P 500 futures contracts to provide portfolio insurance for clients whose portfolio returns were closely correlated with the S&P 500 Index. Since the strategy was extremely popular, LOR became a very large and very well known trader in the S&P 500 futures pit.

In an attempt to lower the cost of their trades, LOR would make public announcements of its orders and of when it would fill them. It thus hoped to notify other traders of the trading opportunities that it offered. Since traders knew LOR was an uninformed trader following a well-known and well-understood trading strategy, LOR hoped that its announcements would solve the price discrimination and asymmetric information problems that large traders normally face. ◁

▷ Wolves and Sheep

Traders sometimes call well-informed traders wolves and uninformed traders sheep. This biological analogy represents their relationship quite well. Just as wolves must eat sheep to survive, well-informed traders must trade with uninformed traders to profit.

Proprietary traders who use computers to implement trading strategies that offer liquidity write program codes they call *wolf detectors* to identify and avoid trading with well-informed traders. ◁

problem for some very well-known traders, it introduces another serious problem. By revealing their intended trades, sunshine traders give free trading options to the market. They therefore attract front runners, quote matchers, and, under some circumstances, squeezers. (Chapter 11 describes how these order anticipation strategies work.) Sunshine traders may therefore have higher transaction costs than they would have if they controlled their order exposure more carefully.

15.4 THE UPSTAIRS MARKET

The *upstairs market* serves large traders who cannot convey credible information about their trading motives and intentions to traders in the regular market. These block initiators use block dealers and block brokers to help them fill their orders. Both types of block traders investigate their clients to determine whether they are well informed and whether they have revealed the full sizes of their orders.

15.4.1 Block Dealers

Block dealers fill large client orders when they trade for their own accounts. Because they take their clients' positions, block dealers are also known as *block positioners*. They are also called *block facilitators* because they facilitate their clients' demands for liquidity.

After block dealers take their clients' positions, they then try to trade out of them. They may try to identify large traders who are interested in their new positions, or they may break their positions into small parts to distribute into the market over time.

Good block traders must carefully set the prices at which they facilitate trades with their clients to ensure that they will be able to trade out of their positions at a profit. To do this, they must be able to predict what their transaction costs will be when they liquidate their positions. Some block dealers therefore make substantial investments in transaction cost analyses so that they can predict future transaction costs.

Since block dealers take positions that they generally intend to liquidate, they must be very careful that they do not trade with well-informed traders or with traders who have more size to trade. If they trade with informed traders, they risk losing if prices change against their positions before they have liquidated them. If they trade with traders who have more size to trade, they must compete with their clients to liquidate their positions. Block dealers therefore have a very strong and direct interest in why their clients want to trade.

Many large traders choose to trade with block dealers because block dealers are better traders than they are. Although the block initiators might be able to handle the trade themselves by breaking it up, they presumably would incur greater transaction costs, especially if they want to trade quickly. To avoid these costs, block initiators pay block dealers to take their trading problems.

15.4.2 Block Brokers

Block brokers help block initiators identify traders who will fill their orders. Since they often must assemble many traders to fill a large order, block brokers are also known as *block assemblers*.

The traders whom block brokers organize to fill their clients' block orders care as intensely about whether they will lose when trading with block initiators as block dealers do. Block liquidity suppliers do not want to see prices rise after they sell or fall after they buy.

Block liquidity suppliers rely upon the block brokers who arrange their trades to determine whether the block initiators are well informed and whether they are honest about the full size of their intended trades. If subsequent events suggest that a broker failed to adequately screen his clients, block liquidity suppliers will be reluctant to do more business with that broker. To protect their reputations, block brokers therefore must know their clients well. To cultivate their reputations, block brokers often estimate transaction costs for their clients to demonstrate that they have served them well on average.

Block brokers charge block initiators commissions for their services. In many markets, they also collect commissions from the block liquidity suppliers.

15.4.3 Brokers Versus Dealers

Block brokers and block dealers tend to specialize in different segments based on their comparative advantages. Dealers have a comparative advantage when trading with impatient traders because dealers can take positions before they know where they will place them. They also have a comparative advantage filling small blocks because they often can trade out of their positions by patiently trading in the market. Brokers cannot compete well in these segments because they do not trade for their own accounts. Brokers have a comparative advantage assembling blocks for the largest traders because dealers are unwilling to hold very large positions.

In practice, most block traders act both as brokers and as dealers. Dual traders can better serve their clients than can pure brokers or pure dealers because they can do whatever is best for their clients at the moment. In addition, brokers who are willing to participate in a trade have an important advantage over brokers who will not. They can more credibly assure poten-

► **The Upstairs Market**

The upstairs market acquired its name because its traders arrange block trades at trading desks in the offices of the wirehouses for which they work. When traders used to have offices that were in the New York Stock Exchange building or across the street, these offices were generally above the street level on which the trading floor was (and still is) located. ◄

▶ A Finger in the Guillotine

Some magicians use trick guillotines to entertain their audiences. After demonstrating that the guillotine will easily cut a potato, the magician calls upon a volunteer to place her hand in the guillotine. The magician then drops the guillotine again. This time, of course, the guillotine does not cut off the hand, although it appears to the audience that it will.

Since a magician's guillotine will cut off a hand if not used properly, magicians must be very careful that they operate the guillotine correctly. To focus their attention, they commonly put one of their fingers in the guillotine along with the volunteer's hand.

When brokers propose trades to block liquidity suppliers, the suppliers must trust that the brokers are suggesting trades that benefit them and not just the brokers or the trade initiators. Brokers who put their finger in the guillotine by trading along side other block liquidity suppliers assure the block liquidity suppliers that they are acting in their interests. ◀

▶ Hot Potatoes

Dealing with informed traders is like passing a hot potato. A dealer who takes a position from a well-informed trader hopes to pass it along before its true value becomes well known. When traders can infer values from trade reports, trading with well-informed traders is more risky. ◀

tial traders that a trade will not hurt them when they also participate in it. Rather than staking just their reputations on their audits, as brokers do, broker-dealers also stake their wealth.

15.4.3.1 Trade Reporting Issues

Rules that require full and timely trade reporting favor block brokers over block dealers. Such rules have little effect on block brokers because their work is finished when they arrange trades for their clients. They affect block dealers because dealers must liquidate their positions after they facilitate their clients' orders.

When dealers must quickly report their block trades, clever traders may use this information to predict trades that dealers must arrange to liquidate their newly acquired positions. These traders may then front-run the dealers and thereby increase their costs of liquidating their positions.

Clever traders may also use trade reports to infer whether block initiators are well informed. Such inferences increase the probability that dealers will lose when they offer liquidity to well-informed block initiators. In particular, dealers may be unable to liquidate their positions before information about their trades causes prices to move against them. Timely trade reporting therefore increases the importance of the audit that dealers must make of their clients' reasons for trading.

Not surprisingly, the markets with the weakest trade reporting practices tend to be dealer markets. For example, most corporate bond markets are pure dealer markets. These markets have no trade reporting requirements. In the United States, the SEC has been pressing for the adoption of a bond trade reporting system, but the dealers are quite resistant.

15.4.4 The Trading Motive Audit

To avoid helping a well-informed trader, block traders research their clients' motives for trading to determine whether they are uninformed. Uninformed traders have utilitarian reasons for trading that are unrelated to fundamental values (see chapter 8). When these reasons are apparent, block traders may conclude that their clients are uninformed.

TABLE 15-2.
Examples of Trader Motives and Likely Interpretations

GIVEN REASON	INTERPRETATION	QUESTIONS
A firm needs to liquidate a diversified portfolio to fund a large project.	Probably uninformed	
A speculator needs to purchase stock to cover a short position that is losing money.	Probably uninformed	Can the speculator liquidate other assets?
An heir needs to diversify a recently inherited stock portfolio.	Probably uninformed	
An heiress needs to diversify a stock portfolio inherited two years ago.	Possibly informed	Why trade now?
A corporate insider needs to fund a college fund by selling founder's stock.	Possibly informed	Why trade now?
A legatee receives a large bequest and wants to buy a single stock.	Probably informed	Why buy only one stock when portfolio theory suggests a basket?
A baker needs to buy grain futures to hedge a newly won contract to feed the army.	Probably uninformed	
A large grain operator wants to sell grain futures to hedge millions of bushels in storage.	Possibly well informed	Does the firm speculate in its hedging accounts?
An electronics distributor needs to buy 50 million dollars of Bolivian bolivianos to fund a new joint venture.	Probably uninformed	Does the distributor need the money now?

Block traders are most confident that their clients are uninformed when their clients have easily verified utilitarian reasons to trade the instrument that they propose to trade when they want to trade it. When the block initiator has some discretion in choosing which instrument to trade, or when to trade it, the block trader may suspect that the trader chose the security or time to trade strategically. (See table 15-2 for trader motives.)

Some traders scoff at the notion that block brokers audit trader motives and total trading interest. Although they acknowledge that information about motives and total trade sizes is very important, they claim that block brokers are completely unreliable when it comes to providing this information. In particular, they assert that most block brokers are not trustworthy.

There may be some merit in their opinion. Since prices in many markets are quite volatile, block liquidity suppliers may be unable to determine whether adverse price changes are related to their trades or simply due to normal security price fluctuations. In such environments, block traders may not be able to cultivate reputations for effectively auditing trader motives and total order sizes. If that is so, block traders will shirk on their audits, and each block liquidity supplier will have to rely upon his or her own re-

▶ **Block Trade Reporting at the London Stock Exchange**

The London Stock Exchange historically has been a dealer market. It once allowed its dealers to report their largest blocks as long as seven days after the trade. The Exchange now requires that all traders report their trades within 90 minutes. By contrast, traders in the United States must report all equity trades within 90 seconds while the markets are open. ◀

▶ Block Traders and Brokerage Recommendations

Broker-dealers often recommend to their clients stocks the broker-dealers recently acquired by positioning blocks for their larger clients. If their clients listen to them, the brokers can then liquidate their positions by selling to their clients. Such dealers are called *distributors* because they distribute the blocks to their brokerage clients.

These recommendations often perform poorly. Stocks recommended by broker-dealers historically have underperformed the market.

Brokers who exploit their clients too often eventually lose them. Accordingly, the brokers most likely to exploit their clients are brokers who have the least to lose. These brokers usually employ hard sales tactics to acquire new accounts from unsophisticated retail investors.

Block distributions to retail brokerage clients are not necessarily nefarious. Honest broker-dealers do their clients a service by identifying and selling undervalued securities to their clients. ◀

▶ An Uninformative Divestiture

The Employee Retirement Income Security Act (ERISA) limits how much employer-sponsored pension plans may invest in their sponsors' stocks.

Suppose that a pension plan holds the maximum legal investment in its sponsor's stock. The sponsor then buys a firm in which the plan has also invested, and pays for the purchase by exchanging stock. Following the transaction, the pension plan will hold more of its sponsor's stock than the legal maximum. Since the law requires that it divest the excess stock, a block trader may reasonably conclude that the sale is not information-motivated. ◀

search to determine whether to offer liquidity. Traders who do not do their research risk offering liquidity foolishly.

15.5 A TELLING STATISTIC

We often can identify whether a seller or a buyer initiated a block trade by comparing the block trade price against the quotation prices that prevailed when the block traded. If the block trade price is closer to the bid than to the ask, it probably was seller-initiated. Otherwise, it was probably buyer-initiated. This classification scheme presumes that the block initiator paid a concession to fill the order. Since this presumption is reasonable, the classification scheme is quite accurate.

Using this classification scheme, analysts have determined that sellers initiate approximately 80 percent of all large block trades in the U.S. stock markets. The remarkable asymmetry between block buyer- and seller-initiated trades is consistent with three of the four block trading problems discussed in this chapter:

Consider first the latent demand problem. Block sellers can sell their blocks to any interested traders. In contrast, when short selling is difficult, block buyers generally can buy large blocks only from traders who own the securities in which they are interested. Buying large blocks therefore may often be harder than selling large blocks.

Now consider the price discrimination problem. Block sellers often can credibly reveal the full size of their orders if they cannot sell short. Few buyers, however, operate under such constraints. Although restrictions on the maximum quantities that institutional investors may hold in any one security may limit the purchases of some buyers, these restrictions rarely are binding. These observations suggest that block liquidity suppliers will more often trade with sellers than with buyers.

Finally, information asymmetries may also explain why block sellers initiate more trades than block buyers. Sellers generally can offer more convincing stories about why they are uninformed than can buyers. Sellers occasionally must sell specific securities to raise cash or to manage the risk of undiversified portfolios. Buyers, however, can buy any security. Since uninformed buyers should not construct undiversified portfolios, traders assume that most large buyers are well informed. Block liquidity suppliers therefore will more often offer liquidity to sellers than to buyers.

15.6 THE RELATION BETWEEN BLOCK MARKETS AND REGULAR MARKETS

Since block markets trade the same instruments that regular markets trade, regulators must consider how the two types of markets relate to each other. In particular, regulators must ensure that neither market has significant negative impact upon the other. Regulators are especially concerned about the potential for large traders to use block markets to subvert rules in the regular markets. Regulators generally want to protect the rights of traders in the regular markets and to protect block clients from potential trading abuses. The regulation of block trading markets is difficult because regulators must respect the needs of large traders who use the block markets to organize liquidity that they otherwise could not find in the regular markets. This short section considers some regulatory issues that arise when block markets trade alongside regular markets.

15.6.1 Equity Markets

In the U.S. listed equity markets, brokers and dealers who are members of an exchange must *print* their block trades in exchange-listed securities at an exchange if the trade takes place while the market is open. To print a trade, the block trader presents the matched buy and sell orders to the market. The purpose of these exchange rules is to expose all orders to the market so that the exchange order precedence rules protect the interests of all traders in the market.

Sometimes standing orders already in the market may have higher order precedence than some of the matched orders that block traders present. This happens when traders in the market have price priority because they are offering better prices or when traders have time precedence because they offered to trade at the block price before the matched block orders arrived. In such cases, the exchange must mediate between the interests of the block traders and the traders who submitted standing orders with higher precedence. The block traders want to cross their blocks without interference from other traders. Traders with higher precedence want to participate in the block trade.

The U.S. equity exchanges address this problem with a *size precedence rule*. For crosses that exceed 25,000 shares, the matched block orders are allowed to *outsize the book* at the trade price. In particular, large matched orders jump ahead of orders with greater time precedence. All orders standing on the book at better prices, however, are incorporated into the block trade at the block price. These orders displace some of the matched orders that the block trader presents. The block trader *cleans up the book* by filling these standing orders.

The size precedence rule represents a compromise between the interests of the block traders and those of the standing limit order traders. The block traders want to protect the efforts that they have made in arranging their blocks. When their block crosses are broken, they make less in commissions, they make less dealer profit, and they may have to tell some of their

▶ Block Trading at LIFFE

The London International Financial Futures and Options Exchange (LIFFE) introduced a block trading facility in April 1999. LIFFE's block trading procedures permit its members and their qualified clients—known as wholesale clients—to quickly trade large blocks at bilaterally negotiated prices. Traders may use the facility only for trades larger than a predetermined size. ◀

Source: www.liffe.com

clients that they did not trade when they expected to. Since the block traders provide services that are not generally available on exchange floors, exchanges are interested in protecting them. (They are also interested in collecting the print revenues that data vendors pay to exchanges in proportion to their trading volumes.) The standing limit order traders want to earn a return on the liquidity that they offer to the market. Since exchanges value the liquidity that they offer, exchanges are also interested in protecting these traders. By universally enforcing the price priority rule, the exchanges maintain strong incentives for traders to improve prices. The price priority rule also encourages block brokers to access liquidity on the exchange before they access other sources of liquidity. Block initiators like this incentive because identifying liquidity offered at the exchange is cheaper than identifying liquidity from traders with latent trading interest. The 25,000-share threshold for sizing the book ensures that only very large crosses may violate time precedence.

To avoid limit orders that might break up their blocks, block traders often print their crosses at regional exchanges. These exchanges usually do not have as many orders standing in their books as the primary stock exchanges do.

15.6.2 Futures Markets

Most futures markets require that traders arrange all trades in their contracts within their trading systems, whether they use floor-based or screen-based systems. These rules prevent abuses that can arise when brokers direct orders to confederates who offer prices inferior to those available at the exchange. Since block trading generally involves trades arranged away from the exchange, futures markets historically have had either no block trading procedures or cumbersome block trading procedures.

Various futures markets have experimented with block trading rules. These rules generally allow brokers to arrange block trades that exceed some specified quantity, but only among eligible participants. Exchange rules define *eligible participants* as sophisticated traders who presumably are aware of the problems associated with negotiating trades away from the market. Such traders typically include sell-side traders and buy-side professionals working for large institutional managers. Notwithstanding these qualifications, the exchanges still require the block prices to be fair and reasonable, given current market conditions and the circumstances of the trades.

Futures traders also use *exchange for physical* (EFP) trading procedures to arrange block trades. In an EFP, traders agree to exchange a long physical position for a long futures position plus cash. Exchange clearinghouses originally developed EFP trading procedures to allow commercial operators in the agricultural markets to transfer hedged cash positions.

The EFP trading procedure is attractive to block traders because it can be employed away from the exchange. The procedure therefore is also used to arrange after-hours trades. For example, traders in currency futures at the Chicago Mercantile Exchange (CME) often use the procedure immediately after trading closes to offset a position that they do not want to hold overnight. The CME floor traders generally execute these EFPs with currency traders at large banks. Exchanges call these EFPs *transitory EFPs* because the floor traders buy or sell the cash currency at the same time they execute the EFP.

▶ An EFP in Wheat

Frank is a North Dakota wheat farmer who has hedged his crop by selling wheat futures contracts at the Chicago Board of Trade. He intends to sell the crop to Oscar, his local grain operator.

Oscar owns wheat silos and facilities for loading wheat onto railroad cars. He knows much about wheat storage and shipping, but little about global wheat supply and demand. He therefore hedges his physical wheat positions to avoid exposure to price risks that he does not understand. Whenever he buys cash wheat, he sells futures contracts, and vice versa.

When Frank sells his crop to Oscar, Frank must close his short hedge and Oscar must create the same short hedge. Rather than separately trading futures in Chicago, they arrange an EFP. Frank gives his physical wheat to Oscar in exchange for cash and a long position in the futures contract. The long futures position that Frank receives offsets his short hedge. The long futures position that Oscar gives, leaves him short futures, so that his newly acquired cash wheat position is hedged. Through this mechanism, Frank transfers his hedged cash wheat position to Oscar. ◀

15.7 SUMMARY

Block trades are trades that are too large to arrange easily using normal trading methods. They usually involve more size than is typically available at an exchange or in a dealer network.

Four problems make block trades costly to arrange:

- Block liquidity suppliers may be hard to find because most traders do not express their trading interests.
- Block initiators are reluctant to advertise their interests for fear of spoiling their markets.
- Block liquidity suppliers fear that block initiators will try to price discriminate among them by breaking up their orders.
- Block liquidity suppliers fear that block initiators may be well informed.

Block traders solve these problems by keeping track of who might be interested in trading, by selectively exposing block orders, by determining the full size of their clients' orders, and by determining whether their clients are well informed. Since traders cannot easily undertake these activities on the floor of an exchange, traders arrange most large block trades off the exchange floors. Table 15-3 provides a summary of the skills that good block traders must have.

Block trading markets work well only when traders know each other well. Anonymous traders generally cannot credibly exchange the information that block traders require of each other. Since anonymous traders cannot establish reputations, they have no incentive to reveal information honestly. Trading systems that match anonymous buyers to anonymous sellers therefore cannot easily arrange block trades.

Block traders must be very careful when they agree to help a block initiator find liquidity. If they act as dealer and offer the liquidity themselves, they must be confident that prices will not move against them before they can divest the blocks that they facilitate. Otherwise, they will lose. If they act as broker and arrange to have other traders fill the order, they also must

▶ A Transitory EFP in German Marks

Geraldine trades German mark futures at the Chicago Mercantile Exchange. At the end of the trading day, she discovers that she is long more contracts than she is willing to hold overnight. To divest her position, Geraldine executes an EFP with a currency trader at a large money bank. She gives U.S. dollars and the futures contracts to the bank and in exchange receives German marks. She simultaneously sells German marks for U.S. dollars to the same currency trader. In effect, she has sold her futures contracts to the bank after hours. ◀

TABLE 15-3.
Block Trader Skills

REQUIRED SKILL	BLOCK DEALERS	BLOCK BROKERS
Ability to identify latent demands	Needed to trade out of their positions and to predict the costs of doing so	Needed to arrange block trades
Ability to conduct effective client audits	Needed to avoid trading losses	Needed to preserve their reputations
Ability to trade at low cost in the market	Needed when liquidating positions in the market over time	Not necessary
Ability to analyze transaction costs	Needed to predict transaction costs	Needed to cultivate reputation for delivering profitable trades
Ability to predict transaction costs	Needed to price block trades	Useful but not essential

be confident that prices will not move against their clients whom they have encouraged to offer liquidity. Otherwise, these clients will be reluctant to participate in future trades that the block brokers may propose.

15.8 SOME POINTS TO REMEMBER

- Block trading markets primarily serve large uninformed traders.
- Order exposure is very important to large traders.
- Informed traders may pretend that they are uninformed to obtain liquidity more cheaply.
- Large traders may split their orders to price discriminate among liquidity suppliers.
- To trade successfully, block dealers and brokers must determine whether their clients are well informed and whether their clients want to price discriminate.
- Block dealers lose their capital when they do not know their clients well.
- Block brokers lose their reputations when they do not know their clients well.
- Delayed trade reporting favors informed over uninformed traders, and block dealers over block brokers.

15.9 QUESTIONS FOR THOUGHT

1. Exchanges classify block trades as all trades larger than some threshold. The threshold can be a given trade size, a given trade value, a given fraction of daily trading volume, or a given fraction of shares/contracts outstanding. What are the advantages and disadvantages of these various alternatives?

2. Floor brokers on the floor of the NYSE often arrange institutional-sized trades. Do they offer their clients services that they could not obtain in an electronic trading system? Of what value is an honest reputation to a floor broker? How do they protect their reputations?

3. When a large trader splits his order among many block trades, should the trader submit the parts sequentially or simultaneously?

4. How might a block trader recognize when a large trader has split his order among many brokers?

5. When should exchanges allow size to take precedence over time at a given price?

6. Should regulators allow delayed reporting for large trades?

7. Which customers—informed or uninformed—favor delayed reporting?

8. How should an informed trader arrange his trades to obtain liquidity cheaply?

16
▷
Value
Traders

Value traders are speculators who form opinions about instrument values by using all information available to them. They buy instruments that they believe are undervalued and sell instruments that they believe are overvalued. We describe their speculative trading strategies in chapter 10.

Value traders are also liquidity providers, though they often do not see themselves this way. This chapter explains how and when value traders offer liquidity. We shall see that they are the ultimate suppliers of market liquidity. They trade when no one else will. We therefore must understand this aspect of value trading to fully understand who makes markets liquid.

Value traders who understand that they supply liquidity will trade more successfully than will those who do not realize this. By considering the implications of their roles as liquidity suppliers, value traders will make better decisions about when to trade and at what price to trade. If you are interested in being a value trader, the principles discussed in this chapter will be of particular concern to you.

Dealers often trade with value traders when they want to restore their target inventories. Dealers therefore have mixed feelings about value traders. On the one hand, they compete with them to provide liquidity. On the other hand, they depend upon them for liquidity when they are unwilling to carry large inventory positions. If you are a dealer or if you are interested in being a dealer, you need to thoroughly understand how dealers relate to value traders.

Value traders must confront an economic problem called the winner's curse to trade successfully. Traders suffer the *winner's curse* when they win an auction and subsequently regret that they traded because they paid too much or sold for too little. Everyone who competes with others to buy or sell items faces the winner's curse. You need to know about the winner's curse when you buy a house, when you trade on eBay, and when you bid on a job. Even if you do not intend to trade securities or contracts, you should find this chapter useful.

16.1 VALUE TRADERS SUPPLY LIQUIDITY

Although value traders trade to make speculative profits, the effect of their trading is to provide liquidity to the market. This characterization of their trading is apparent when you consider when they trade profitably.

Value trading is profitable only when price differs from fundamental value. Price can differ from fundamental value two ways:

- When new information causes fundamental value to change, and thereby deviate from price, or
- When uninformed traders push price away from fundamental value.

In the first case, news traders profit because—by definition—they are the first to receive new information. Their trading tends to push price to the new fundamental value. (Chapter 10 discusses information flow trading.) In the second case, value traders profit. Through their research, they are able to determine that price no longer reflects fundamental value. Their trading tends to push price back to its fundamental value. Value trading therefore is profitable only when value traders trade in response to demands for liquidity made by uninformed traders.

In the following discussion, we will need to refer frequently to "the uninformed traders whose demands for liquidity cause prices to change." To simplify our discussion, we will simply call them the *uninformed liquidity demanders*. They may be one or more large traders, or they may be numerous small traders who all want to trade on the same side of the market. They cause prices to change as they try to fill their orders.

16.1.1 Uninformed Traders Cause Prices to Deviate from Fundamental Values

Price deviates from fundamental value when uninformed traders demand liquidity, and when the traders who offer them liquidity do not realize that they are uninformed. This situation often happens when dealers do not know their clients well. To protect themselves from adverse selection losses to informed traders, dealers must make inferences from their order flow. If uninformed traders dominate the order flow on the same side of the market, dealers will mistake those traders for informed traders and adjust prices accordingly. These price adjustments cause price to deviate from fundamental value.

Dealers also may adjust prices even when they know that their clients are uninformed. When dealers supply liquidity only on one side of the market, their inventories diverge from their target levels. The resulting off-target inventories expose them to substantial inventory risks. If their uninformed clients demand more liquidity than dealers are willing to supply, dealers will demand substantial price concessions to bear the resulting inventory risk. These price adjustments will be especially large when dealers fear that they will not easily find traders on the other side of the market.

Uninformed traders may also cause prices to deviate from fundamental values in order-driven markets that do not have dealers. In such markets, prices change when traders demand liquidity on one side of the market and exhaust the liquidity supplied there.

16.1.2 How Value Traders Respond

Value traders may trade directly with the uninformed liquidity demanders, or they may trade indirectly with them through the intermediation of dealers and other traders who employ dealing strategies. Value traders trade directly with them when value traders offer limit orders that the uninformed liquidity demanders take, or when block brokers ask value traders to fill orders for their uninformed liquidity-demanding clients. In these situations, value traders supply immediacy to the uninformed liquidity demanders because they allow them to trade when they want to trade.

Value traders also indirectly supply liquidity to the uninformed liquidity demanders. We can best introduce this situation with an example.

Suppose that uninformed liquidity demanders want to sell stock in a hurry. They sell to dealers who offer them immediacy. The dealers accumulate large long positions as they buy the inventory. Since they do not know their clients very well, they suspect that the uninformed liquidity demanders may be informed traders. The dealers therefore adjust their prices accordingly. They also adjust their prices because they fear that they will not easily find traders on the other side of the market, in which case they will be exposed to more inventory risk than they would like to bear. These adjustments cause price to fall below fundamental value so that value trading becomes profitable. To restore their target inventories, the dealers lower their quotes. Value traders buy from the dealers at their ask prices when they see that they can buy substantial size at discounted prices.

The dealers solicit liquidity from the value traders by lowering their asking prices. When the value traders respond, they take liquidity from the dealers in the form of immediacy, but simultaneously supply liquidity to the dealers in the form of size or *depth*. In effect, the value traders indirectly supply liquidity to the uninformed liquidity suppliers through the intermediation of the dealers.

Even though the dealers lay off their inventory on the value traders, both sets of traders may profit. The dealers will profit if they sell their inventories at prices above what they paid to the uninformed liquidity demanders. The value traders will profit when prices return to fundamental values.

16.1.3 Market Resiliency

When uninformed traders cannot change prices substantially, the market is *resilient* to their trading. Value traders make markets resilient by standing ready to trade when prices move away from fundamental values.

Dealers will take larger positions when trading with their uninformed clients in resilient markets than in markets that lack resiliency. In resilient markets, dealers know that they can rely upon value traders to restore their target inventories if their order flows remain unbalanced.

16.2 THE OUTSIDE SPREAD AND ITS DETERMINANTS

The prices at which a value trader is willing to trade define his or her *outside spread*. Since value traders are well-informed traders, they rarely quote these prices. They do not want to reveal their value estimates, and they do not want to give free trading options to the market.

The spreads of value traders depend on the risks and costs of their business. When they are large, their spreads will be large. This section considers what determines the outside spread.

16.2.1 The Risks of Value Trading

Value traders face two serious risks when they trade: averse selection and the winner's curse. Like dealers, value traders face adverse selection when they supply liquidity to better-informed traders. They face the winner's curse when they have misestimated instrument values.

The two risks are closely related. Both arise when value traders are not fully informed. When they suffer adverse selection, they lack information that better-informed traders have. When they suffer the winner's curse, they have mistakenly valued their instruments.

16.2.1.1 The Adverse Selection Risk

Value traders are subject to adverse selection risk because they offer liquidity in response to other traders who demand it. They must be particularly careful that they do not trade with news traders who have new information that the value traders do not have.

When value traders trade with better-informed traders, they buy or sell instruments that they think are undervalued or overvalued but in fact are overvalued or undervalued. They eventually lose when prices move against their positions as traders learn the new information.

Value traders respond to adverse selection risk just as dealers do. They widen their spreads to recover from uninformed traders what they lose to better-informed traders. Equivalently, they widen their spreads to reflect the inferences they will make about values when they learn that other traders want to trade with them.

Value traders avoid adverse selection risk by trying to know everything that they can about instrument values. Because research takes time, value traders are often slow to respond to apparent profit opportunities.

16.2.1.2 The Winner's Curse and Value Trading

To understand how the winner's curse affects value traders, we must first describe the winner's curse. This subsection starts with a general discussion of the problem. Its implications for value trading follow.

The Winner's Curse

The winner's curse can affect buyers or sellers. To keep our discussion simple, we initially consider only how it affects buyers. Once we understand the problem from the buyer's perspective, the problem from the seller's perspective is obvious.

Buyers can suffer the winner's curse when they compete to buy something that has a common, but unknown, value. An item has a *common value* when its value is the same for everyone. Most trading instruments have common values because people value them only for the cash flows that they ultimately will produce. Artworks do not have common values because what is beautiful to one is often unattractive to another.

When the value of a common value item is uncertain, everyone interested in owning that item must estimate its value. Since people use different models and different information to estimate values, they typically obtain different value estimates. Some estimates will be closer to the true value than others. Unfortunately, since people do not know true values, they do not know the errors in their estimates.

Buyers suffer the *winner's curse* when they pay more for an item than it is worth. Although they win the auction, they are cursed by the price they pay.

The winner's curse arises because the highest bidders in an auction tend to be buyers who overestimate values. If they bid at prices near their value estimates, and if they pay those prices, they will regret trading if their estimates prove to be too high. On average, those estimates do prove to be too high because extreme estimates rarely are as accurate as estimates closer to the mean estimate. Bidders who pay prices near their estimates of value tend to pay too much if they win the auction.

Buyers avoid the winner's curse by considering the implications of being the highest bidder in an auction. The highest bidder learns that his value estimate may be the highest estimate among all buyers. If he knew this information beforehand, he could have improved his estimate by lowering it toward the common mean. Buyers avoid the winner's curse by lowering their

▶ The Winner's Curse in Oil and Gas Lease Auctions

The government often auctions oil and gas leases. The winners of these auctions have the right to explore for and develop oil within a particular tract.

Before an auction, each company interested in the tract has its geologists survey the site and produce an estimate of its prospects. The companies use this information to make their bids.

Until they learned better, oil companies systematically overpaid for these leases. The leases frequently proved to be less productive than the geologists expected. The winners confronted their geologists and asked why they were so optimistic. The geologists responded that they were correct, on average, about the various tracts that they had valued. Unfortunately, they overestimated values for the tracts that they won and slightly underestimated values for the tracts that they lost. The geologists also pointed out that they usually were glad that they had not purchased the tracts they had lost at the prices the winning companies paid for them.

With this evidence, the companies learned that they had failed to consider the winner's curse when setting their bids. ◀

bids to reflect the additional information that they will learn about their value estimates if they win the auction.

The adjustments that buyers must make depend on the expected sizes of their valuation errors, assuming that they win the auction. The expected winner's valuation error depends on the number of other buyers in the auction and upon their uncertainty about values.

The winning buyer learns more about his estimate when he wins an auction competing against many other buyers than against only a few buyers. When the winner outbids many people, he probably grossly overestimated value because all other bidders estimated lower values. To avoid the winner's curse, bidders therefore should lower their bids more when bidding against many buyers than against just a few.

This result is counterintuitive. Most people believe that they must bid more aggressively to win an auction when competing against many other traders. They forget that the object is not to win. The object is to win at a satisfactory price. It is better to lose than to win and pay too much.

Another reason why the result is counterintuitive involves market power. If you are the only bidder, or if you compete with very few bidders, you may underbid in the hope of winning the auction at a significant discount to value. If you compete with many other traders, however, this bidding strategy has little chance of success. Accordingly, you should bid more aggressively when competing against several traders than against just one or two. This result is important only if you compete with very few traders.

Buyers make larger estimation errors when they are uncertain about values than when they know them well. The most extreme estimation error therefore will likely be large when buyers do not know values well. To avoid the winner's curse, bidders should lower their bids more when values are hard to estimate than when they can easily estimate them accurately.

To summarize, buyers face the winner's curse when they bid in auctions for items with common value. They avoid the winner's curse by lowering their bids to reflect what they learn about their value estimates should they win the auction. They must lower their bids substantially when they compete with many other buyers and when they cannot estimate values accurately. Similar arguments suggest that sellers who will receive the prices they offer should raise their offers to avoid the winner's curse.

An important implication of the winner's curse is that you do not want to compete against foolish traders. When people bid foolishly, you have no choice but to accept that you should lose the auction. You cannot make money bidding against people whose bidding strategies ensure that they will lose money. Many Internet entrepreneurs in the late 1990s now wish that they had understood this principle better.

The Winner's Curse in Two-sided Auctions

The winner's curse does not pose a significant problem in a two-sided single price auction in which buyers and sellers both attempt to value the item sold. In such auctions, traders who estimate high values are buyers, and traders who estimate low values are sellers. The traders with the highest bids and the lowest offers trade with each other at the price that clears the market. Since the market-clearing price typically is near the median estimate among all traders, no one faces a serious winner's curse problem. The various traders are not trading at the prices they bid and offer. Buyers who

▶ If You Are Not a Buyer, Should You Be a Seller?

Some traders believe that they must act on everything about which they have an opinion. For example, if they own securities they think are overvalued, it is not sufficient for them to sell their long positions. They continue selling until they have established short positions.

The notion that you are either a buyer or a seller is inconsistent with the optimal response to the winner's curse. The uncertainties in your estimates of value imply that you should not speculate unless you believe instruments are very mispriced. Of course, the greater the mispricing you believe you have identified, the more likely it is that you have made a mistake. ◀

estimate the highest values are saved from serious losses by sellers who estimate the lowest values, and vice versa.

In continuous markets, traders do trade at the prices that they bid and offer, and their orders may have significant market impact. They therefore must be careful about the winner's curse. Although the market price aggregates the information held by all traders, the process of aggregation is sequential, not simultaneous. Traders who significantly under- or overestimate values may therefore lose when they push prices away from fundamental values. These losses are due to the winner's curse.

Value Traders and the Winner's Curse

Value traders are exposed to the winner's curse because they trade only when they believe that price differs significantly from their estimates of fundamental value. If their estimates are wrong, they may regret trading.

Value traders misestimate values when they use the wrong economic models to value their instruments, when they fail to consider significant information, and when they misinterpret the information that they have. When they make these mistakes, they trade when they should not. Although these mistakes do not necessarily cause them to buy overvalued instruments or sell undervalued instruments, the market impact of their trades may cause instruments to become undervalued or overvalued. When value traders value instruments poorly, they lose because their trades have market impact. They lose because they trade when they should not trade.

Value traders avoid these losses by widening the spread between the prices at which they are willing to buy and sell. When the winner's curse problem is very serious, value traders will have wide outside spreads.

The outside spreads of value traders overlap when their value estimates vary. The most aggressive value buyers and sellers are, respectively, the ones who estimate the highest and lowest values. In extreme cases, value traders will trade with each other when a very optimistic buyer is willing to buy at a price above the offer price of a very pessimistic seller.

16.2.2 The Costs of Value Trading

The outside spread must be wide enough to allow value traders to recover their direct costs of doing business. The most important of these costs are their expenditures for research.

Successful value traders must ensure that they are very well informed. They accordingly invest substantial sums to acquire and analyze data. Their outside spreads must be wide enough to recover these costs. Most instru-

▶ Why Were Internet Stocks So Volatile?

The winner's curse helps explain why Internet stocks were so volatile in the late 1990s. Since Internet stocks were hard to value and since so many traders tried to value them, the winner's curse problem was especially dangerous then to value traders. To protect themselves, they would trade only at very wide outside spreads. Some of the volatility was due to the bouncing of prices within the wide outside spreads of value traders. ◀

ments that value traders analyze are properly priced. Their outside spreads therefore must recover the costs that they incur analyzing the instruments that they ultimately trade and also the instruments that do not currently present profitable value trading opportunities.

16.3 OUTSIDE VERSUS DEALER SPREADS

The outside spreads of value traders are much wider than the spreads that dealers quote. The differences are due to differences in the speeds at which they trade, the sizes of their positions, their research costs, their exposures to adverse selection and the winner's curse, and their total volumes of trade.

Dealers can quote narrow spreads because they trade in and out quickly. When they can quickly and profitably restore their target inventories, they do not care whether the market price is close to or far from fundamental value. They only care about discovering current market values. When they make a mistake, they usually can correct it quickly, before prices change too much. Dealers learn about their mistakes when they see that the order flow is one-sided.

In contrast, value traders usually trade when the order flow is one-sided. Accordingly, they cannot easily use the order flow to determine when they are mistaken. When value traders trade, they set market values rather than simply try to discover them. They therefore have greater exposure to the winner's curse than dealers do. Value traders typically learn about their mistakes only after they have acquired significant positions. If prices subsequently change against them, they incur substantial losses.

Value traders generally take larger positions than dealers do. They therefore expose themselves to greater inventory risks than dealers do. Value traders control their exposure to adverse selection by trying to be the best-informed traders in the market and by trying to determine whether the traders to whom they ultimately offer liquidity are uninformed. Since these research activities are expensive, outside spreads must be larger than dealer spreads. In contrast, dealers control their adverse selection exposure by adjusting prices to find market values, by avoiding well-informed traders, and by refusing to take large inventory positions.

Since value traders speculate on fundamental values, they must hold their positions until market prices adjust to reflect the fundamental values. Such adjustments may take a long time when values are quite uncertain. During that time, they must finance their positions, which typically are larger than dealer inventories. Their financing costs therefore cause outside spreads to be wider than dealer spreads. In addition, while value traders wait for prices to revert to fundamental values, new information may arrive that changes values. Such changes make their positions risky. If the new information is inversely correlated with their positions, they have suffered adverse selection from news traders. If the new information is uncorrelated with their positions, it will be diversifiable. In either event, value traders must trade at wider spreads than dealers must because they face greater inventory risks.

Dealer spreads also are narrower than outside spreads because dealers typically trade much greater volumes than value traders do. They can therefore spread their fixed costs of doing business over greater volumes than value traders can.

Finally, dealer spreads are narrower than outside spreads because dealers often earn the entire spread when they complete a round-trip trade. The best that a value trader can hope for is to make half the outside spread when price returns to its fundamental value.

16.4 VALUE TRADERS AND NEWS TRADERS

Value traders and news traders are both well-informed traders. The bases for their trading profits differ, however. Value traders profit when prices deviate from fundamental values because uninformed liquidity demanders have pushed prices way. They offer liquidity to other traders. News traders profit when they know before others that values have changed. They generally take liquidity when they trade.

Value traders and news traders often profit at each other's expense. Value traders lose to news traders when they mistake news traders for uninformed traders. News traders lose to value traders when they do not realize that the information upon which they are trading is already in the price.

To trade successfully as a well-informed trader, you must know when you are trading as a value trader and when you are trading as an news trader. The two styles require different trading disciplines.

When you are a value trader, you must be sure that you offer liquidity only to uninformed liquidity demanders and not also to news traders. You can trade most confidently when you are certain that you have all available fundamental information, and when you clearly know that the traders to whom you are offering liquidity are uninformed. You will rarely have such information. At best, you should be sure that you have all publicly available fundamental information. You also should have some idea why uninformed traders are demanding liquidity. If you do not consider whether you are indeed best informed, your risk of losing to an news trader might be greater than you assume.

When you are a news trader, you must be sure that you are truly trading on fundamental information that is not yet in the price. You can trade most confidently when you know that nobody else has your information. You will rarely know this, however. At best, you should know how your information came to your attention, when it first became available, and who else might know it. You also should be familiar with the recent price history of the instrument in which you are interested. The price history will allow you to form a crude opinion as to whether your information is already in the price if you know when the information first became available. If you do not consider whether you are indeed best informed, your risk of losing to a value trader might be greater than you assume.

16.5 SUMMARY

Value traders supply liquidity to uninformed traders whose trading pushes prices away from fundamental values. Value traders are liquidity suppliers of last resort. When no one else will trade—when dealers have large positions or when liquidity suppliers fear informed traders—value traders may trade. Since they allow uninformed traders to trade large positions, they supply depth to the market. Since they often recognize when uninformed traders have caused prices to move from fundamental values, they also make markets resilient.

Value traders can afford to take large positions only by being the best-informed traders in the market. They risk being wrong, however. They suffer adverse selection when they lose to news traders who know news that they do not yet know, and they face the winner's curse when they under- or overestimate values. They widen their spreads to avoid these risks and to ensure that they recover from uninformed traders what they occasionally lose to news traders and to other value traders.

By making markets resilient, value traders allow dealers to offer more immediacy to uninformed traders than they otherwise would be willing to offer. Dealers know that they often will be able to lay off their inventories when value traders closely follow the market. Accordingly, they are more willing to take large positions because they know that they may not have to hold them long.

16.6 SOME POINTS TO REMEMBER

- Value traders are the ultimate suppliers of liquidity to uninformed traders.
- The winner's curse hurts traders who make the highest bids or the lowest offers if they do not anticipate what they will learn about the values that other traders estimate.
- The outside spread represents the prices at which value traders will buy and sell.
- The outside spread is wider than the inside spread.

16.7 QUESTIONS FOR THOUGHT

1. How does the winner's curse affect bidding strategies for single-family houses?
2. How does the liquidity provided by well-informed value traders affect the losses that other value traders incur when they are mistaken about instrument values?
3. Dealers suffer adverse selection when they trade with news traders. Do they also suffer adverse selection when they trade with value traders?
4. What arguments suggest that value traders should specialize in a single industry or commodity, and what arguments suggest that they should diversify across industries or commodities?
5. Can you compete in markets in which your competitors do not understand the winner's curse? Should you?

*A*rbitrageurs are speculators who trade on information about relative values. They buy instruments that seem relatively cheap and sell those which seem relatively expensive. Arbitrageurs profit when prices converge so that their purchases appreciate relative to their sales.

We introduced arbitrage trading strategies when we examined informed traders in chapter 10. There we described how arbitrageurs acquire information about relative values, how the price impacts of their trades cause prices to converge, and how they thereby unwittingly enforce the law of one price. This price characterization of arbitrage helps us understand how arbitrageurs trade as informed traders.

This chapter continues our study of arbitrageurs. Besides being informed traders, we shall see that arbitrageurs supply liquidity, move liquidity, and produce financial products. This quantity characterization of arbitrage helps explain why arbitrage opportunities arise.

Successful arbitrageurs must understand both the price and the quantity characterizations of arbitrage. Although many arbitrageurs can trade successfully merely by responding to arbitrage opportunities as they arise, arbitrage is more profitable when arbitrageurs also can predict when and where those opportunities will arise. Arbitrageurs who consider the quantity characteristics of their arbitrages will make better decisions about when and at what prices to trade.

This chapter characterizes different types of arbitrages and discusses the risks that arbitrageurs face. If you intend to be an arbitrageur or if you trade with arbitrageurs, this discussion should greatly interest you.

We shall see that arbitrageurs sometimes compete with dealers to offer liquidity. Dealers often lose to arbitrageurs because arbitrageurs usually are better-informed traders. If you intend to be a dealer, you must understand how arbitrageurs can hurt your business. If you merely wish to understand the origins of market liquidity, you also must understand what arbitrageurs do.

In chapter 26, we show that arbitrage is one of three processes that keep fragmented markets together. If you are interested in how markets compete with each other to trade similar or identical instruments, you must thoroughly understand why arbitrageurs trade. You must particularly understand arbitrage to estimate the costs of competition among marketplaces.

Commentators sometimes blame arbitrageurs when markets crash. For example, some people believe that index arbitrageurs were at least partly responsible for the 1987 stock market crash. To understand how traders transmit volatility among markets, you must consider what arbitrageurs do.

Complaints about arbitrage have led to restrictions upon arbitrage trading strategies in some markets. These restrictions can be costly because arbitrage trading benefits more than just arbitrageurs. It also benefits other traders and the economy as a whole. To estimate the sometimes significant

▶ Barter, Arbitrage, and Relative Values

Modern economies use money as a *medium of exchange*. Almost all trades involve money. The buyer pays it, and the seller receives it. When a trader wants to dispose of one item and acquire another, the trader usually sells the first and buys the second. The nice thing about money is that it allows us to buy and sell from different people.

Barter involves the exchange of two (or more) items without the use of money. Barter is not common because both traders must be interested in both items. Traders who want to exchange apples for oranges often cannot easily find traders willing to exchange oranges for apples.

Trades involving money can be considered special cases of barter in which one of the traded items is money. This characterization of trading reminds us that all trades are relative value trades. People buy things when they value the item more than the money they exchange for it. They sell things when they value the money more than the item. In a sense, all trades are arbitrages because all trades are relative value trades. ◀

costs of arbitrage restrictions, you must appreciate the quantity characteristics of arbitrage.

Our presentation starts with some definitions. We then characterize arbitrage so that we can understand it in light of trading strategies that we have already discussed. Next, we introduce and discuss various types of arbitrages. We follow this with discussions about the risks of arbitrage and about how arbitrageurs control these risks. We conclude the chapter with discussions about the quantity characteristics of arbitrage and about how dealers and arbitrageurs relate to each other.

17.1 DEFINITIONS

Arbitrageurs trade instruments whose prices are correlated. *Correlated prices* tend to rise or fall together. Instruments typically have correlated prices when their values depend on common fundamental factors. They also may have correlated prices when the demands of uninformed traders to buy or sell the instruments are correlated.

Arbitrageurs form opinions about the normal relations among correlated instruments. An *arbitrage opportunity* arises when the prices of correlated instruments diverge from their normal relations. Arbitrageurs then buy those instruments which have become relatively cheap and sell those which have become relatively expensive. The strategy is profitable if the prices of the instruments return to their normal relations. When that happens, the prices have *converged*. Arbitrageurs profit from *price convergence*.

When arbitrageurs take arbitrage positions, they *put on* the arbitrage. When they close their positions, they *unwind* their positions or *take off* the arbitrage. Arbitrageurs usually unwind their positions when the arbitrage converges. Since prices may again diverge after they converge, arbitrageurs need to watch their positions closely so that they can close them at favorable prices.

The portfolios that arbitrageurs construct are their *hedge portfolios*. The various positions in the hedge portfolio are the *legs* of the arbitrage.

Hedge portfolios usually consist of one or more long positions and one or more short positions in various correlated instruments. Arbitrageurs generally construct hedge portfolios to minimize the total risk of the portfolio, given some measure of its size.

(In some instances, hedge portfolios may consist only of short positions or only of long positions. Traders construct such hedge portfolios of instruments whose returns are inversely correlated. Such portfolios typically include put contracts. For example, a long position in a put contract is a hedge for a long position in the underlying instrument.)

Traders usually identify one leg of the hedge portfolio as the *arbitrage numerator* or *reference instrument*. They use the numerator to measure the size of the portfolio. The arbitrage numerator is usually the security, contract, or commodity that traders most closely identify with the common risk factor which causes the correlations among the various instruments in the hedge portfolio. The arbitrage numerator for hedge portfolios involving a derivative contract and its underlying cash instrument is usually the cash instrument.

The ratios of holdings in other legs to holdings in the numerator are the portfolio *hedge ratios*. Traders choose their hedge ratios to minimize the total risk of the portfolio.

Arbitrageurs may have long or short positions in the hedge portfolio. They are long the hedge portfolio when they have a long position in the instrument that serves as the arbitrage numerator. Since hedge portfolios usually have both long and short positions, a long hedge portfolio will have one or more short positions. A short hedge portfolio will likewise have one or more long positions.

Hedge portfolios have carrying costs. *Carrying costs* are the costs of holding a hedge portfolio. Depending on the arbitrage, these costs may include interest paid or forgone to finance positions in the hedge portfolio, dividends paid on short positions, fees paid to physically store commodities, and depreciation incurred as commodities age and spoil. Carrying costs are sometimes offset by dividends, interest income, and lending fees earned on long positions, or by interest earned on the proceeds from short sales. Carrying costs can make some arbitrages very expensive.

The difference in prices between instruments in the hedge portfolio is the *basis*. The *fair value* of the basis is the basis that would result if all instruments were correctly priced relative to each other. Fair values depend on carrying costs. Arbitrageurs must estimate fair values because they usually are not common knowledge.

The *arbitrage spread* is the difference between the basis and the fair value of the basis. Arbitrageurs trade when the arbitrage spread is sufficiently large.

The values of the basis at which arbitrageurs are just willing to trade are called *arbitrage bounds*. They are on either side of fair value. Arbitrageurs generally put on their arbitrages only when the basis is outside of the arbitrage bounds.

Hedge portfolios generally are less risky than the positions in the individual instruments from which arbitrageurs construct them. The reduction in risk is due to the offsetting effects of having long and short positions in instruments whose values depend on the same factors. When changes in these factors cause instrument values to fall, gains in the short positions offset losses in the long positions. Likewise, when changes in these factors cause instrument values to rise, gains in the long positions offset losses in the short positions.

The risk that an arbitrage hedge portfolio will lose value is called *basis risk*. Analysts also call this *residual risk* because it remains after the common factor risks in the various portfolio instruments cancel each other. Basis risk arises because prices depend on instrument-specific factors as well as common factors. The specific factors may be fundamental valuation factors, or they may be due to the price impacts that uninformed traders have on prices. Since specific factors are unique to each instrument, no combination of long and short positions can create a hedge portfolio that has no exposure to these risks. The contribution of instrument-specific factors to basis risk may be small, however, if the hedge portfolio is a well-diversified portfolio of many instruments. Most stock index arbitrage portfolios have very little residual risk.

17.2 A SIMPLE CHARACTERIZATION OF ARBITRAGE

Arbitrage is particularly easy to understand if you imagine that the arbitrage hedge portfolio is an instrument that traders buy or sell like any other instrument. When traders "buy" the hedge portfolio, they buy its long po-

▶ Some Confusing Nomenclature

Hedge funds are managed by speculators who sometimes hedge their positions to minimize exposure to risks that they cannot forecast. They may engage in arbitrage, but they often do not.

Long-short portfolios are actively managed portfolios that have no net exposure to marketwide risk. They typically consist of long and short positions of approximately equal aggregate sizes. Portfolio managers call the portion of an equity portfolio return that is correlated with the market index *deadweight*. Well-designed long-short portfolios have no deadweight. Since long-short portfolio managers construct hedged positions, they may be characterized as arbitrageurs. They rarely see themselves this way, however. Most simply see themselves as active managers who want to avoid exposure to market risk.

In the futures markets, a *long hedger* is a trader who holds the cash position and hedges it with a short futures position. His short futures position is his *short hedge*. Likewise, a *short hedger* is a trader who hedges a short cash position with a long futures position. Hedgers usually trade to reduce risks in their cash positions rather than to obtain arbitrage profits. ◀

▶ EFPs Are Hedge Portfolio Trades

Arbitrageurs buy one item and sell another when they believe that the first is cheap relative to the second. They sometimes do these transactions as a single barter trade. The most important example of an arbitrage barter trade is an *exchange for physical* (EFP) in the futures markets.

In an EFP, one trader offers a futures contract in exchange for the underlying physical commodity while the other trader offers the commodity in exchange for the contract. The trader offering the futures contract also must offer cash because the futures contract is only a commitment to buy the commodity in the future. The resulting trade is essentially a trade in the arbitrage hedge portfolio. Arbitragers who want to buy the commodity and sell futures contracts (or vice versa) often engage in EFPs. ◀

▶ Dice Are Mean-reverting

The completely random sequence of sums generated by rolling a pair of dice is mean reverting. The mean value of this sequence is seven. When a roll produces a sum above seven, the next sum will more likely be lower than higher. Likewise, when a roll produces a sum below seven, the next sum more probably will be higher than lower. ◀

sitions and sell its short positions. When they "sell" the hedge portfolio, they sell its long positions and buy its short positions. Viewed this way, arbitrageurs are simply traders who use various trading strategies to trade the arbitrage portfolio.

Arbitrageurs who employ high-frequency trading strategies are essentially dealers in the hedge portfolio. They buy and sell the hedge portfolio to profit from short-term reversals in its value. Such reversals typically occur when uninformed traders in one or more of the instruments cause prices in that instrument to change when they demand liquidity. Dealer-type arbitrageurs generally are less concerned about the fair value of basis than in its short-term behavior. They offer immediacy when they trade the hedge portfolio, but they usually are unwilling to trade large size when they do not know fair values well. Dealer-type arbitrageurs are usually professional traders who have very quick access to the markets.

Arbitrageurs who take large arbitrage positions must be very certain about the fair value of the basis. Such arbitrageurs are essentially value traders in the hedge portfolio. They supply substantial depth, but they may not be the fastest traders. When dealer-type arbitrageurs want to lay off positions in the hedge portfolio, they often trade with value-type arbitrageurs. (Chapter 16 describes the relation between value traders and dealers.)

17.3 TYPES OF ARBITRAGE

Arbitrages differ by the nature of the basis risk that arbitrageurs assume. *Pure arbitrages* involve instruments for which the value of the hedge portfolio is strictly *mean reverting*. *Speculative arbitrages*, also known as *risk arbitrages*, involve instruments for which the value of the hedge portfolio is *nonstationary*. This section defines these concepts and discusses their implications for arbitrageurs.

17.3.1 Pure Arbitrages

A variable is *mean reverting* if its values tend to return to some average value. Mean-reverting variables tend to drop when their values are above their long-run average values, and they tend to rise when their values are below their long-run averages. The best long-range estimate of the value of a mean-reverting variable is always the mean of the variable. Long-run value estimates never depend much on the current value of the variable.

Traders like pure arbitrages because a mean-reverting base eventually converges to its mean value. The mean typically is the fair value of the basis. Pure arbitrages therefore are not very risky in the long run. They may be quite risky in the short run, however, if the factors that have caused the wide arbitrage spread continue to widen the basis after arbitrageurs have established their positions.

Pure arbitrages typically involve instruments whose fundamental values depend on nearly identical factors and for which some mechanism ensures that the basis will eventually close. The mechanism generally places strong bounds on how wide the basis will be.

We can classify pure arbitrages by the type of mechanism that causes prices to converge. The basis in a *shipping arbitrage* depends on the cost of shipping an instrument from one market to another. In a *delivery arbitrage*,

▶ What Would You Do?

Cash corn is cheap relative to the near corn futures contract. You sell the futures contract and buy corn with the intention of delivering it. The price of corn then rises, and the basis continues to widen. The increase in price causes you to lose money on your futures position and to make money on your cash position. Unfortunately, since the basis widened, you lost more than you made.

You receive a margin call from your futures commission merchant (broker), who requires that you cover your loss in the futures contract. Should you close your position and limit your losses, hold your position and wait until the basis closes, or increase your position now that the basis is wider?

Suppose you increase your position. The next day, prices continue to rise, the basis continues to widen, and you continue to lose money. What should you do now?

The next day the same thing happens again. You are becoming financially distressed. If you are right about the basis, you now face an incredibly profitable arbitrage opportunity. If you are wrong, or if prices continue to move against you, you may be ruined. What should you do now?

Your answers should depend on how well you understand the arbitrage relation, on your ability to finance your positions, and on your degree of risk aversion. ◀

the basis depends on the costs of delivering on a contract. In a *conversion arbitrage*, it depends on the costs of converting a risk from one form to another. The next subsections discuss these types of pure arbitrages.

17.3.1.1 Shipping Arbitrages

Shipping arbitrages involve two essentially identical instruments that trade in different markets. Arbitrageurs buy the cheaper instrument and sell the more expensive one. If necessary, they then ship it between the two markets to settle their trades. The costs of shipping the instrument (and of financing it while in transit) generally determine arbitrage bounds for the arbitrage spread. When the spread is wider than these costs, arbitrage is essentially risk free.

In practice, arbitrageurs often do not have to ship the instrument. Instead, they hope to unwind their positions if the prices converge on their own accord. When this happens, they avoid the shipping costs. The competition among arbitrageurs for profits therefore often forces them to put on these shipping arbitrages at much narrower spreads than their shipping costs would indicate. Shipping arbitrage thus can be risky. If arbitrageurs can unwind without shipping, they profit. If they must ship, they may lose.

Shipping arbitrage opportunities arise when one market has an excess of buyers or another market has an excess of sellers. The effect of their trading causes the basis to widen. By trading on opposite sides of these markets, shipping arbitrageurs essentially connect excess demand in one market to excess supply in the other market. Since they supply liquidity in one or both of the markets, they compete with the dealers in those markets.

Two types of traders typically engage in shipping arbitrages. They differ by whether they will actually ship the instrument. *Virtual shippers* are arbitrageurs who do not ship. They try to hold their hedge portfolios until they

Persian—or Mexican—Gulf Oil

Crude oil futures trade in New York and in London. When the price of oil is significantly higher in New York than in London, traders sell oil in New York and buy it in London.

Although floor traders at the New York Mercantile Exchange and at London's International Petroleum Exchange are the first to engage in this arbitrage, the ultimate arbitrageurs are shippers who have oil in transit from the Persian Gulf or the Gulf of Mexico. These shippers typically hedge their cargoes by selling oil futures in the market near where they expect to deliver their oil. When oil becomes more expensive in New York than in London, these shippers reroute their ships from Europe to New York. They simultaneously buy crude oil futures in London and sell futures crude oil in New York to transfer their hedge from London to New York.

The normal basis between the two crude oil futures contracts reflects differences in delivery specifications between the two contracts. The contract that requires delivery of a higher grade will be more expensive. It also depends on local storage and delivery conditions. Oil will be more expensive in the port where it is more expensive to deliver.

After adjusting for quality, storage, and delivery differentials, the basis cannot be any larger than the costs of shipping oil across the Atlantic Ocean. In practice, it is smaller because oil companies never ship crude oil from one market to the other. Instead, they ship it from its source to one or both of the markets. The normal basis therefore depends on the difference in the costs of shipping oil to the two markets. When oil companies ship oil from the Persian Gulf to both Europe and New York, the New York crude oil price rarely exceeds the London price by more than the difference in the shipping costs. Likewise, when they ship oil from the Gulf of Mexico to both Europe and New York, the London price rarely exceeds the New York price by more than the difference in shipping costs from the Gulf of Mexico. ◀

A Wheat Delivery Arbitrage

If the wheat futures contract price is sufficiently greater than the cost of delivering cash wheat, arbitrageurs will buy cash wheat and sell wheat futures. If the basis closes before the delivery date, arbitrageurs then may offset these trades. Otherwise, arbitrageurs will deliver the wheat. This arbitrage is profitable only when the futures price is greater than the combined costs of buying the cash wheat, financing and storing it until delivery, and shipping it to the contract delivery point.

If the wheat futures contract price is substantially lower than the cash price, arbitrageurs will buy the futures contract and sell cash wheat short. To sell cash wheat short, they must borrow wheat from a grain operator. They return the wheat when they take delivery on the futures contract or when they reverse the arbitrage by selling the futures contract and buying cash wheat.

Since the options to demand or take delivery are often valuable to local grain operators, as contracts approach expiration, grain operators who can handle the cash wheat at the delivery points are the primary arbitrageurs. ◀

can unwind them at a profit. If they are unable or unwilling to bear the risks and costs associated with carrying their hedge portfolios, they *lay off* their positions (typically at a loss) to actual shippers. *Actual shippers* physically ship the instrument from one market to the other.

Stock Index Futures Arbitrage

Traders who want exposure to S&P 500 Index risk can hold a portfolio of index stocks, or they can hold index futures contracts. (Other alternatives also exist.) When traders want to hold more index risk in the form of futures contracts than contracts are available to them, futures prices rise relative to the underlying index. The wide basis encourages index arbitrageurs to sell futures contracts and buy a representative portfolio of the 500 index stocks, usually with a program trade. They reverse the transaction when the basis closes or when the futures contract expires. To avoid transaction costs in the individual stocks, arbitrageurs also may *roll* their futures positions from the current delivery month to a later expiration month. (Traders *roll a position* when they exchange a position in a near contract for a similar position in a more distant contract.)

The hedge portfolio that index arbitrageurs construct may not include all 500 stocks because trading 500 stocks is quite expensive. Instead, index arbitrageurs may trade a representative portfolio that they design to closely replicate the returns to the S&P 500 Index. The representative portfolio typically includes the largest firms in the index and a carefully selected set of smaller firms designed to provide broad industrial representation of the smaller firms in the Index. The included smaller firms are overweighted to compensate for the omitted ones. When two arbitrage trades follow one another on the same side of the market, the second program trade includes small stocks that the first program trade omitted so that the combined hedge portfolio will more closely replicate the Index.

Index futures contracts normally trade at slight premiums to the cash value of their underlying indexes. The premiums are necessary to compensate traders for the costs of financing long cash index portfolios. The dividends that traders expect to receive from holding the stocks in the cash portfolio slightly reduce these required premiums because traders who hold the futures contracts do not receive these dividends. Since traders cannot perfectly predict financing costs and future dividends, stock index arbitrage is not risk free. ◀

Virtual shippers are most successful when they can predict whether (and when) the arbitrage basis will close so that they can unwind their positions at a profit. Since they often compete with many other traders, they must be very quick to capitalize on arbitrage opportunities as they arise.

Actual shippers are most successful when they can ship the instrument cheaply between markets. Since shippers compete with each other, arbitrage spreads generally are no wider than the shipping costs of the most efficient (lowest-cost) shippers.

17.3.1.2 Delivery Arbitrages

Delivery arbitrages involve contracts for the future delivery of a commodity or, in some cases, its cash equivalent. The delivery mechanism causes the basis between the contract price and the underlying cash price to converge to zero—plus or minus the costs and benefits of delivery—on the maturity date. Before the delivery date, the basis depends on the carrying costs of the underlying commodity. When the cash commodity is cheap relative to the contract price, arbitrageurs buy the cash and sell the contract. When the cash commodity is expensive relative to the contract price, arbitrageurs sell the cash and buy the contract.

Financial Engineering

The term *financial engineering* has emerged to describe the highly technical body of knowledge that traders use to manage risk and to convert it from one form to another. The word *engineering* very accurately suggests that financial engineers engage in a productive process that consumes feedstock (various instruments) and produces products (other instruments). Unlike other productive processes, most financial engineering processes are completely reversible. ◀

▶ Manufacturing Stock Option Contracts

Public investors generally want to buy more option contracts than they are willing to sell. This is true for both calls and for puts. Since option contracts are in zero net supply, arbitrageurs generally fill the excess demands.

Arbitrageurs who sell option contracts manufacture them by constructing hedge portfolios. To do so, they must buy or sell enough of the underlying stocks so that the values of their hedge portfolios do not change when prices change. In effect, arbitrageurs convert equity risk from stock shares to option contracts.

The hedge is difficult to maintain because the value of an option contract is a nonlinear function of the value of the underlying stock.[1] As prices change, hedge ratios also change so that arbitragers must buy or sell stocks. Arbitrageurs therefore must constantly monitor their hedge portfolios to ensure that they remain well hedged when prices change.

Arbitrageurs do not actually adjust their hedge portfolios whenever prices change, because trading is costly. Instead, they adjust them only when their hedges become intolerably risky. Options arbitrage therefore is risky because prices often change when arbitrageurs are imperfectly hedged.

Options arbitrage is also risky because arbitrageurs cannot always trade when they want to rebalance their hedge portfolios. For example, an arbitrageur who is hedging a call option must sell stock when the underlying stock price falls. If the price drops too quickly, however, the arbitrageur may be unable to sell stock while the price is falling. The hedge portfolio therefore will have too much stock when stock prices are falling. The imbalance causes arbitrageurs to lose more money on their stock positions than they make on their short call positions. Arbitrageurs also face this problem when prices rise quickly. Their hedge portfolios then have too little stock to adequately hedge their short call positions. The imbalance causes them to lose more money on their short call positions than they make on their long—but too small—stock positions. Price changes in either direction therefore cause arbitrageurs to lose money.

Arbitrageurs are aware of the potential costs of their hedging programs. When they expect high volatility, they require substantial option premiums to cover their expected hedging costs. (This is another way of explaining why option values depend on volatility.) Once arbitrageurs have established their

continues next page

▶ Index Enhancement

Investors can very closely replicate the returns to an index by holding a properly weighted portfolio of the index stocks or by holding the corresponding stock index futures contract plus cash invested in secure short-term debt instruments like Treasury bills. Some index funds are indifferent between these two alternatives. When investing new cash, they will buy whichever is cheaper.

Some *index enhancement funds* try to produce an enhanced index return by switching between the cash index stock portfolio and the equivalent futures contracts when their prices diverge. They buy futures and sell stock when futures are relatively cheap, and they sell futures and buy stock when stock is relative cheap. The profits that they make from these arbitrage trades, conducted from a long position, allow them to ratchet up their returns. ◀

17.3.1.3 Conversion Arbitrages

A *conversion arbitrage* involves the purchase and sale of two or more instruments that embody essentially the same risks expressed in different forms. When buying one instrument and selling another, the arbitrageur in effect converts risk from one form to another. Viewed this way, the *conversion arbitrageur* is a manufacturer who produces financial instruments that interest traders.

Conversion arbitrage opportunities generally arise when traders are more interested in holding risk in one form than in another. The basis widens as traders attempt to buy the popular instrument or sell the less popular instrument. The wide basis is the signal that attracts arbitrageurs to their work.

The arbitrage bounds for a conversion arbitrage depend on the costs of doing the conversion and of carrying the hedge portfolio. When trading costs and carrying costs are high, traders must pay large arbitrage spreads to encourage arbitrageurs to convert risk from one form to another.

continued from previous page

positions, they hope that volatility will be small. Since volatility varies, options arbitrage can be quite risky. If prices prove to be more volatile than arbitrageurs expect, they lose money.

Options dealers do most stock options arbitrage. When making their markets, they limit their risk exposure by hedging with the underlying stock or with related option contracts. Although these dealers may engage in numerous arbitrages among many different instruments, they generally do not consider each one separately. Instead, when making trading decisions, they consider only how their decisions will affect the risk profiles of their combined positions. ◀

---

1. The relation between option values and underlying stock values depends critically on the difference between the option strike price and the stock price. It varies by whether the option is in, at, or out of the money.

An option is *in the money* when it would be valuable if it expired immediately. It is *out of the money* when it would be worthless if it expired immediately.

Standard call option contracts are in the money when the underlying stock price is above the strike price. Upon expiration, the option holder would exercise the option to buy stock at the strike price because the stock is worth more than the strike price. If the strike price were higher than the stock price, the option would be worthless: Option holders will not pay the strike price when they can buy the same stock at a lower price in the stock market. Put options are likewise in the money when the underlying stock price is below the strike price, and out of the money otherwise. Both types of options are *at the money* when the underlying stock price is equal to their strike prices.

When an option is far out of the money, a small change in the underlying price has little effect on the value of the option because the option will likely expire worthless. When an option is deep in the money, a small change in the underlying price will cause a nearly equal change in the option value. Option values therefore have a nonlinear relation to underlying instrument values.

The rate at which options values change in response to a change in the underlying instrument price is called the *delta* of the option. Deltas are positive for call options and negative for put options. They are near zero for far out of the money options and near 1 (in absolute value) for deep in the money options. The number of stock shares that an arbitrageur must hold in the hedge portfolio is equal to delta times the number of shares covered by the options contract. Arbitrageurs typically compute deltas by using complicated mathematical models. The Black-Scholes option-pricing model is one of the simplest of these models.

The traders who profit most from conversion arbitrages are those who can do the conversions at lowest cost and those whose costs of holding the arbitrage portfolio are lowest. They are often traders who have a natural reason to engage in the arbitrage transactions.

Many conversion arbitrages require that arbitrageurs continuously monitor and periodically adjust their hedge portfolios. Such hedges are *dynamic hedges*. They arise whenever the value of one instrument is not an exact linear function of the value of another instrument. (A variable is an exact *linear function* of another variable when all possible pairs of their theoretical values plot along a straight line.) The most common dynamic hedges involve option contracts. Dynamic hedges can be risky because price volatility makes them perform poorly.

Some conversion arbitrages are the financial equivalent of an underlying physical production process. The soybean crush may be the most interesting of these arbitrages. It is a three-legged arbitrage involving futures contracts for soybeans, soybean oil, and soybean meal.

▶ Crushing Soybeans on the Floor of the Chicago Board of Trade

Millers make soy meal and soy oil by crushing soybeans. They sell the meal primarily to feedlot operators for use as animal food. They sell the oil to food processors and chemical firms, which use it in a variety of products. (The process also releases a significant, but economically trivial, quantity of water.)

The Chicago Board of Trade trades futures contracts in all three commodities. The prices of beans, meal, and oil obviously are closely related. The notional value of the bean contract is approximately equal to the sum of the values of the meal and oil contracts less the cost of milling the beans and net difference in the costs of storing the three commodities.

The three soy contracts trade in adjacent trading pits. At the tops of these pits stand arbitrageurs who monitor prices in the three markets. When they determine that beans are cheap compared to oil and meal, they buy beans and sell oil and meal. Arbitrageurs thus crush soybeans on the floor of the Board of Trade!

Unlike the physical millers, arbitrageurs often reconstitute beans. They do this when they reverse the crush by buying oil and meal and selling beans.

Exchange locals do most of the arbitrage on the floor of the exchange because they are the fastest traders. When they are no longer willing to do arbitrage, either because they are unwilling to bear the risk or because they cannot finance additional positions, they often lay off their positions to millers for whom the soybean crush is a portfolio of three delivery arbitrages.

The costs of physically crushing beans place an economic bound on one side of the arbitrage spread. If beans are too cheap relative to meal and oil, millers will start to crush beans and thereby raise the price of beans and lower the prices of meal and oil. No such bound exists on the other side of the arbitrage, however, since millers cannot recombine oil and meal to sell as beans. Instead, when beans are expensive relative to meal and oil, millers stop crushing them until oil and meal consumption depletes supplies and thereby raises their relative prices. ◀

Perhaps the most intriguing conversion arbitrages are *cyclic arbitrages*, in which arbitrageurs exchange A for B, B for C, and C for A. When successful, these arbitrages seemingly create arbitrage profits from thin air. Currency cross-rate arbitrages are examples of cyclic arbitrages.

17.3.2 Speculative Arbitrages

Speculative arbitrages involve arbitrage hedge portfolios whose values are nonstationary. A variable is *nonstationary* if an increase or decrease in its current value causes us to expect that all future values of the variable will be higher or lower. Nonstationary variables tend to wander around without regularly returning to any particular value. The best estimate of a distant value of a nonstationary process always depends critically on the current value of the process. These estimates therefore change through time. Nonstationary variables do not have mean values. Long-run averages of their values do not converge. Instead, averages of their values also wander about.

Variables are either mean reverting or nonstationary; they cannot be both. The sum of a mean-reverting process and a nonstationary process is a nonstationary process because the properties of the nonstationary process eventually dominate the properties of the mean-reverting process. In the short-run, however, if the variation in a mean-reverting process is large compared

▶ A Three-legged Currency Money Machine

Various dealers make markets in the yen–euro, the euro–dollar, and the dollar–yen foreign exchange markets. The prices in these markets are codependent. Any two of the exchange rates imply the third exchange rate. For example, if the dollar–yen rate is 110 yen per dollar, and the dollar–euro rate is 1.10 dollars per euro, the implied yen–euro rate is 100 yen per euro.

On very rare occasions, an implied rate obtained from two of the markets is substantially different from the actual rate in the third market. When this happens, traders can do cyclic arbitrage. For example, suppose that the implied yen–euro rate obtained from the euro–dollar and dollar–yen markets is 100 yen per euro, as quoted above, but the actual yen–euro rate is 99.9 yen per euro. Arbitrageurs could buy 99.9 million yen for 1 million euro, buy 1 million euro for 1.10 million dollars, and buy 1.10 million dollars for 100 million yen. Following the three trades, the traders would have 0.1 million more yen—about 1,000 dollars—than when they started.

If these relations persisted forever, traders could become infinitely wealthy. In practice, price pressure from the arbitrage trades quickly causes the exchange rates to adjust so that further arbitrage will be unprofitable. In our example, the euro would appreciate relative to the yen, the dollar would appreciate relative to the euro, and the yen would appreciate relative to the dollar. The implied yen–euro rate thus would fall while the actual yen–euro rate would rise.

Dealers are the natural arbitrageurs in the currency markets because they are the fastest traders. These arbitrages typically arise when traders are unaware of price changes that take place in related currency markets. ◀

▶ Random Walks

A random walk is the best-known example of a nonstationary process. To generate a simple random walk, flip a coin repeatedly and keep track of the difference between the number of times it comes up heads and the number of times it comes up tails. This difference is a nonstationary process. After each flip, it is equal to its previous value plus 1 if the result is heads and minus 1 if the result is tails. Statisticians call this process a *random walk* because it describes the path a walker would take if after every step he flipped a coin to decide whether to next step forward or backward.

Fully informative prices seem to follow random walks because no one can predict future price changes from past information when prices fully reflect that information. When price changes are unpredictable, they appear random. ◀

to the variation in a nonstationary process, the process may appear to be a mean-reverting process.

Speculative arbitrages involve nonstationary hedge portfolios that arbitrageurs believe have a strong tendency toward short-term mean reversion. The nonstationariness is due to instrument-specific valuation factors that cause prices to follow a random walk in the long run. The mean reversion may come from inconsistent pricing of the common factors among the instruments in the hedge portfolio or from mispricing of one or more specific factors. Both types of errors cause mean-reverting price changes. Table 17-1 provides some examples of common and specific factors for several pairs of correlated assets.

Speculative arbitrages can be quite risky because the value of the hedge portfolio will not ultimately converge to some mean. Arbitrageurs should engage in speculative arbitrages only when they believe that mean reversion in the value of the hedge portfolio will dominate nonstationariness in the short run. Since speculative arbitrages are often quite risky, traders often call them *risk arbitrages*.

We can characterize the risk in an arbitrage by the volatility expected in the basis over a given period. Since the basis is nonstationary, its expected volatility over a given period increases with the length of the period. Speculative arbitrages that may not converge quickly therefore are more risky than are those for which traders expect quick convergence.

17.3.2.1 Spreads

Many common speculative arbitrages are spreads. *Spreads* involve the purchase and sale of instruments that are similar to each other in all respects

TABLE 17-1.

Common and Specific Valuation Factors of Some Correlated Instruments

SECURITY PAIR	COMMON VALUATION FACTORS	SPECIFIC FACTORS
Ford common stock GM common stock	Automotive industry fundamentals, interest rates, labor conditions	Consumer acceptance of their products, quality of management
IBM common stock S&P 500 futures contracts	Marketwide risk	IBM-specific risk
June gold futures contracts July gold futures contracts	Gold spot market conditions	Anticipated differences in gold market conditions between June and July, future interest rates

but one. In a *maturity spread*, the instruments differ by when they mature or expire. In a *credit spread*, the instruments differ by issuer credit quality.

Maturity spreads are some of the least risky speculative arbitrages. In a maturity spread, the arbitrageur buys and sells contracts that mature on different dates but are otherwise identical. The prices of such contracts are usually very highly correlated, especially if the contracts mature in the distant future and their maturity dates are near each other, so that most factors which determine their values are common to both contracts.

Fundamental contract values in a maturity spread differ only with respect to events forecast to occur between the different contract maturity dates. Since such valuation factors make the basis nonstationary, maturity spreads are speculative arbitrages. In practice, the mean-reverting component of the basis usually dominates.

The most common maturity spreads are calendar spreads and yield curve spreads. *Calendar spreads* involve futures contracts or option contracts that mature on different dates. *Yield curve spreads* involve bonds that mature on different dates.

17.3.2.2 Pairs Trading

Pairs traders try to identify pairs of instruments that they believe are mispriced relative to each other. They then buy the one that appears cheap and sell the one that appears expensive.

Pairs trading is profitable when the prices of the two instruments have diverged because their common fundamental valuation factors are not consistently priced or because traders have mispriced some instrument-specific factors. This often happens when informed buyers bid up the price of one instrument or uninformed sellers push down the price of the other instrument. It also happens when the price of one instrument has changed in response to a change in some common valuation factor, but the price of the other instrument has not yet changed. In these events, prices tend to converge. If the convergence occurs before specific factors cause the spread to widen, a pairs trade arbitrage will be profitable.

Pairs trading is not profitable when the change in relative prices is due to a change in instrument-specific valuation factors. When specific valuation factors change, the arbitrageurs cannot expect that the basis will converge.

▶ Calendar Spreads in Oat Futures Contracts

In North America, the oat harvest starts in late May in the northern Mexican states and moves north into Canada throughout the summer. Oat contracts trade at the Chicago Board of Trade for delivery in July, September, December, March, and May.

The December contract is normally cheaper than the March contract because sellers in March must carry their inventory for a longer period than sellers in December. This normal relation depends on interest rates, the costs of storage, and expected spoilage.

In September, after most of the crop has been harvested, Arnie sees that December contracts are trading at an unusually large discount to March contracts. He therefore sells March contracts, buys December contracts, and hopes that the normal relation will be restored. This calendar spread involves little risk because most factors that determine the value of oats for delivery in December also determine the value of oats for delivery in March.

The May contract normally trades at a very substantial premium to the July contract because traders generally deliver oats stored from the previous harvest for the May contract, whereas they deliver newly harvested oats on the July contract. The spread between the two prices can vary substantially, however, when traders are uncertain about the size of the new harvest or about whether supplies will be adequate for May delivery. If traders expect a small new harvest, July prices will be relatively high. If they expect unusually large May inventories, May prices will be relatively low.

In March, Arnie sees that the May contract is trading at a substantially higher premium to the July contract than he expects. He buys the July contract, sells the May contract, and hopes that their prices will converge. This calendar spread is highly risky because traders in March cannot accurately estimate the size of the new harvest and the oat inventory that will remain in May. ◀

▶ A Successful Pairs Trade in Washington Mutual and FirstFed

Bernie sees that Washington Mutual, a very actively traded large banking stock, rises following good macroeconomic news about interest rates. FirstFed Financial Corporation, a small and less frequently traded savings and loan, does not rise, however. Bernie knows that after taking into consideration their great difference in size, both firms have approximately the same exposure to interest rate risk.

Bernie concludes that Washington Mutual has moved in response to the news but that FirstFed has not. He therefore buys FirstFed and sells Washington Mutual short. The next day, traders interested in buying FirstFed arrive. Bernie sells them his position for a 3 percent profit and then immediately closes his Washington Mutual hedge position with a 0.2 percent loss. His net profit is 2.8 percent of the size of his long position. Since he borrowed half the money he needed to finance his position, his profit on the money he actually committed to the arbitrage was 5.2 percent. ◀

Pairs trading is risky regardless of whether the pairs trader has correctly identified a true arbitrage opportunity. While pairs traders wait for convergence, they are exposed to the possibility that some instrument-specific event will cause one or both of the prices to permanently move against their positions.

Fortunately, the opposite may also happen. Since good and bad events tend to offset each other, pairs traders do not expect to lose money, on av-

A Failed Pairs Trade in Ford and GM

Gerry sees that Ford has risen in value relative to GM, but he can see no fundamental reason to explain the change in relative prices. Gerry therefore buys GM and sells Ford short.

Unfortunately, the spread never closes. Ford soon reports that sales of its huge SUV, the Excursion, are soaring. The sales apparently are coming at the expense of GM's Suburban. Gerry eventually closes his arbitrage at a slight loss due to his transaction costs and to the costs of financing his positions. ◀

erage, when they fail to identify a profitable arbitrage opportunity. However, pairs traders may lose due to the costs of establishing and financing their positions.

Pairs traders are most successful when they can accurately predict whether changes in a spread will be mean reverting or permanent. They therefore pay close attention to the order flow to determine whether prices are changing in response to trades made by uninformed traders or informed traders. Since pairs traders generally do not know whether other traders are well informed, they often make mistakes when trading.

Pairs traders also pay close attention to how quickly and how efficiently markets respond, on average, to new information about common fundamental factors. Arbitrageurs generally should be reluctant to trade against markets that quickly and efficiently aggregate new information because the prices in such markets tend to accurately reflect fundamental values.

17.3.2.3 Statistical Arbitrage

Statistical arbitrageurs use factor models to generalize the pairs trading strategy to many instruments. *Factor models* are statistical models that represent instrument returns by a weighted sum of common factors plus an instrument-specific factor. The weights, called *factor loadings*, are unique for each instrument. The arbitrageur must estimate them.

Either statistical arbitrageurs specify the factors, or they use statistical methods to identify the factors from returns data for many instruments. Specified factors typically include macroeconomic variables such as interest rates, inflation rates, industrial production, credit spreads, stock index levels, and market volatility. The statistical methods that some arbitrageurs use to identify factors include factor analysis, principal components, and canonical correlations. These methods appear in books on multivariate statistics.

Statistical arbitrageurs estimate current factor values in order to determine which instrument prices appear to be inconsistent with their common factor representations. The arbitrageurs then sell those instruments which appear overpriced and buy those which appear underpriced.

Some statistical arbitrageurs also try to forecast future factor values. When they can successfully predict these values, they will speculate on this information by incorporating it into their trading models.

Statistical arbitrageurs carefully select the instruments and the quantities that they trade in order to control risk in their hedge portfolios while maximizing their expected returns. They also carefully consider how their transaction costs will affect their profitability. They employ sophisticated risk and transaction cost models, and they use numeric optimization methods to fine-tune their decisions.

17.3.2.4 Risk Arbitrage

Although *risk arbitrage* may refer to many different kinds of speculative arbitrages, traders most often use the term to refer to speculations and arbitrages that involve firms which may or will soon merge. In most mergers, a *bidder* (or *acquiring firm*) acquires a *target firm*.

Target firm share prices frequently rise because most bidders must pay a premium over current market value to obtain control. Since investors often suspect that bidders pay too much for their acquisitions, the stock prices of bidders sometimes fall on the announcement of an acquisition.

▶ Identifying Likely Arbitrage Opportunities in the GE–S&P 500 Futures Spread

General Electric common stock price changes are correlated with changes in the S&P 500 Index because the values of the two instruments depend on many common macroeconomic factors. These factors include interest rates, the general health of the economy, and trader sentiment about the future. When the spread between GE and the S&P 500 Stock Index futures contract widens (when GE rises relative to the Index), pairs traders may sell GE and buy S&P 500 futures contracts.

Clever traders discriminate between different causes for the change in the spread before they decide to trade. The spread may widen because (1) the price of GE has risen while the Index futures price has remained largely unchanged, or because (2) the price of GE has remained largely unchanged while the Index futures price has fallen. Successful traders consider which situation is more likely to offer a profitable arbitrage opportunity.

Situation 1 may occur when uninformed traders buy GE and push up its price. If that is the case, the arbitrage will probably be profitable. This scenario is probable because uninformed traders often trade GE and affect its price.

Situation 1 may also occur when the value of GE rises in response to a change in some factor specific only to GE. In this event, the arbitrage will not be profitable. This scenario is also probable because information specific to GE frequently changes the price of GE common stock.

Finally, situation 1 may occur when marketwide factors cause GE to rise while the futures market remains unchanged. If that is the case, the arbitrage will probably be profitable. This scenario, however, is unlikely, given the informational efficiency of the S&P 500 Index futures market.

Situation 2 may occur when a change in some common valuation factor causes the market to drop. GE may not drop, however, because the markets for individual stocks—even those as large as GE—generally respond to marketwide factors more slowly than does the S&P 500 Index futures market. The futures market responds faster to changes in marketwide factors because it focuses exclusively on those factors and because it is the more actively traded market. Arbitrage in this likely scenario probably would be profitable.

Situation 2 also may occur when changes in marketwide factors cause the S&P 500 Index to fall while offsetting changes in firm-specific factors cause GE to remain unchanged. Arbitrage in this scenario would be unprofitable. The coincidence, however, is unlikely.

Finally, situation 2 may occur when uninformed sellers in the futures market cause futures prices to drop. In this scenario, the arbitrage probably would be profitable. Although this scenario is possible, it is not likely because the S&P 500 Index futures market is highly liquid.

This discussion of the various alternatives suggests that arbitrage will more likely be profitable in situation 2 than in situation 1. In the first situation, the arbitrageur speculates that either GE rose improperly or the Index failed to rise. The former alternative is possible, but the latter is unlikely. In the second situation, the arbitrageur speculates that either GE failed to drop or that the Index dropped improperly. The former alternative is likely but the alternative again is unlikely. Table 17-2 presents a summary of the various contingencies discussed in this box. ◀

TABLE 17-2.

Event Contingencies When the Price of General Electric Common Stock Rises Relative to the Price of the S&P 500 Index Futures Contract

OBSERVED EVENT	POSSIBLE CAUSE	ARBITRAGE OPPORTUNITY	LIKELIHOOD
GE rises while the Index is unchanged.	Positive changes in GE-specific fundamental factors raise GE's price.	No	Possible
	Uninformed buyers push up the GE price.	Yes	Possible
	Positive changes in marketwide fundamental factors raise GE's price, but the Index market is slow to respond.	Yes	Highly unlikely
GE does not change while the Index falls.	Negative changes in marketwide fundamental factors lower the Index, but GE is slow to respond.	Yes	Likely
	Negative changes in marketwide fundamental factors lower the Index and GE, but positive changes in GE-specific fundamental factors coincidentally offset the negative market news.	No	Improbable
	Uninformed selling in the Index futures market drives down its price.	Yes	Possible but unlikely

Note: This table shows some possible events that could cause the spread between General Electric stock and the S&P 500 Index to widen. The likelihood assigned to each possibility suggests that arbitrages will be more profitable when the spread widens because the Index has fallen rather than because GE has risen. The table omits some very unlikely event contingencies.

Traders who can predict merger transactions therefore can profit from their insights by buying the target firms and selling the acquiring firms. Since the targets and the bidders usually are in the same (or closely related) industries, their equity values depend on many common fundamental valuation factors. Their prices therefore are closely correlated. The "hedge portfolio" thus has less risk than its component positions. Although called *risk arbitrage*, this strategy is more like a risky speculation than a mean-reverting arbitrage. It is highly speculative because the hoped-for merger may never take place.

When firms announce their intention to merge, they usually publish the terms of the merger negotiated by their respective managements. These terms fix the price of the target firm. In a *cash offer*, the price is either a fixed sum or a sum that depends on some observable variables. In a *stock offer*, the terms specify the number of shares the acquiring firm will exchange for each share of the target firm. In *a fixed rate stock offer*, the exchange rate is constant. In a *constant value stock offer*, the exchange rate varies in inverse proportion to the acquiring firm's stock price so that the value of the offer is constant. In *mixed offers*, the terms include both cash and stock.

The terms of the merger thus define the value of the target firm and, hence, a potential arbitrage relation. In a cash offer or in a constant value stock offer, the stock of the target firm essentially becomes a debt security that matures upon the successful completion of the merger. In such mergers, the arbitrage portfolio consists of a long (or short) position in the target stock offset by a short (or long) position in a short-term debt security. (The portfolio may also include other instruments if the cash payment depends on other variables.) In a fixed rate stock offer, the stock of the target firm essentially becomes the same as the stock of the acquiring firm. In such mergers, the arbitrage portfolio consists of a long (or short) position in the target stock offset by a short (or long) position in the acquiring firm. Risk arbitrageurs trade when the prices of the various instruments are inconsistent with the terms of the merger.

The risk in these arbitrages depends on whether the deal will fail, whether the terms will change, and whether the deal will close when scheduled. When the merger closes at the announced terms on schedule, the basis will revert to its theoretical fair value. The arbitrage then would be a pure arbitrage with no long-term basis risk. In the short run, the basis might differ from its fair value because traders may be unaware of prices in other markets, or because an excess of buyers in one market or of sellers in another market causes prices to diverge. The arbitrageurs connect the two markets and ensure that common risks expressed in essentially similar instruments are priced the same.

The merger may not close, however, if the shareholders do not support it, or if the merger requires government approval and the government does not approve. The basis under such circumstances will be nonstationary. If the deal fails, the price of the target firm will freely change in response to market conditions.

Target prices usually rise upon merger announcements, and they generally drop when deals fail to close. Accordingly, when traders doubt that mergers will close, target firms will often trade at discounts to their theoretical values implied by the terms of the merger. When the probability of failure is large, risk arbitrage is more like risky speculation than mean-reverting arbitrage. Well-informed traders who believe a deal will close, buy the arbitrage portfolio. Traders who believe that a deal will fail, sell the arbitrage portfolio.

Many merger agreements have collars. *Collars* are clauses in merger agreements that modify the terms of the agreement based on the price of the acquiring firm. Collars introduce optionlike characteristics into the arbitrage relation between the acquiring firm and the target firm share prices. Traders who attempt risk arbitrage in these situations usually implement dynamic hedges.

▶ A Rumored Merger

On June 8, 2000, CNBC reported that Broadwing was in talks to acquire Intermedia Communications. That day, Intermedia rose 16 percent, and Broadwing fell 13 percent, from their previous day's closing prices on very high volumes.

The next day, CNBC reported that the talks seemed to have failed over the treatment of a well-known accounting issue. Intermedia fell 14 percent, and Broadwing rose 7 percent.

Had Broadwing and Intermedia reached a deal, Intermedia might have risen even more than it did. As it happened, traders who bought Intermedia after the reported talks lost heavily the next day.

It is possible that traders who wanted to sell Intermedia stock fed the story to CNBC. As a matter of policy, neither firm would confirm that negotiations had taken place. ◀

17.4 ARBITRAGE RISKS

Several risks make arbitrage strategies difficult to implement profitably. *Implementation risk* is the risk that arbitrageurs will trade at worse than expected prices. *Basis risk* is the risk that the arbitrage basis will move against the arbitrageur's position. *Model risk* is the risk that arbitrageurs will fail to understand relative instrument values properly. *Carrying cost risk* is the risk that hedge portfolios prove to be more costly to carry than expected. Arbitrageurs must manage each of these risks in order to trade successfully.

▶ **How Definitive Is "Definitive"?**

In a February 7, 2000, press release, Lucent announced that it had reached a "definitive merger agreement" with Ortel. Under the agreement, Lucent would exchange 3.135 shares of Lucent for each share of Ortel. The press release stated that Lucent expected to complete the acquisition during the quarter ending June 30, 2000. The deal actually closed on April 28.

By the close of trading on February 8, the news was well known to all interested professional traders. Ortel closed at 161½ and Lucent closed at 54³⁄₁₆. Assuming that the deal would close, the implied value of a share of Ortel then was 169.88 = 3.135 × 54³⁄₁₆. Ortel therefore traded at a 5 percent discount to its theoretical value. This discount steadily narrowed to zero on April 28 when the deal closed.

If you bought Ortel and sold 3.135 shares of Lucent on February 8, you would have made 5 percent of the Ortel price. In addition, if you received interest on the proceeds of your Lucent short sale, you would have made another 1 percent in short interest. A 6 percent return over the 80-day period corresponds to a 32 percent annualized return.

Had the deal closed on June 30, you would have made 5 percent plus about 1.5 percent in short interest. You also would have had to pay the 2 cents per share dividend (0.04 percent) that Lucent paid on June 1 to its stockholders of record on April 30. Over this almost five-month period, your return would have been approximately 17 percent on an annualized basis. ◀

Since nobody likes exposure to risk, arbitrageurs must be compensated for taking risks. Arbitrageurs obtain their compensation when they trade at favorable prices. In particular, they will not enter a risky arbitrage if their expected profits seem small. Arbitrage price bounds therefore tend to be wide when arbitrage is risky.

17.4.1 Implementation Risk

Arbitrageurs face implementation risk when they establish and close their positions. *Implementation risk* is the risk that their transaction costs will be greater than they expect. Since transaction costs reduce trading profits, arbitrageurs must estimate their transaction costs before they trade. They must trade only when they expect that their transaction costs will be less than the profit they hope to obtain from reversion in the basis. If their actual transaction costs prove to be greater than they expect, arbitrageurs will make less arbitrage profit than they expect. If their transaction costs are larger than the expected basis reversion, arbitrageurs may lose money.

Arbitrageurs face implementation risk whether they use market orders or limit orders. When using market orders, their implementation risk is due to *execution price uncertainty*: Their market orders may trade at less favorable prices than they expect. Their orders may have greater than expected price impact, or prices may move against them during the interval between when they submit their orders and when their orders actually fill. Of course, arbitrageurs sometimes obtain better than expected execution prices. Unfortunately, the probabilities of trading at better than expected prices generally are less than the probabilities of trading at worse than expected prices. The asymmetry is due to competition that arbitrageurs face from other arbitrageurs and from other informed traders. Their trading tends to cause the basis to narrow.

▶ The Seagram-Vivendi Merger

On June 20, 2000, The Seagram Co. Ltd. and Vivendi S.A. entered into a merger agreement. Under the terms of the agreement, each share of Seagram would be exchanged for shares in Vivendi. The exchange rate would depend on an average of Vivendi's ordinary common stock daily closing prices at the Paris Bourse, expressed in dollars. The average would be computed over a 20-day period ending three days before the effective date of the merger. If the average price was less than 96.6875 dollars, the exchange rate would be 0.8 share of Vivendi for each share of Seagram. If the average was greater than 124.3369 dollars, the exchange rate would be 0.6221. If the average was between these two prices, the exchange rate would be equal to 77.35 dollars divided by the average Vivendi share price.

The value of the deal on the effective date of the merger depended on the exchange rate and the then current Vivendi share price. If the current share price was equal to the average share price and the average was between the two cutoff prices, the deal would be worth exactly 77.35 dollars per Seagram share. The deal would be worth more if the Vivendi average price was above 124.3369 dollars and less if the average was below 96.6875 dollars. Figure 17-1 plots the value of the deal as a function of the Vivendi average stock price.

If the Vivendi share price on the effective date of the merger was equal to its average closing price, a portfolio of the following three positions would produce an identical return to holding a share of Seagram:

- A long position in a pure discount bond worth 77.35 dollars on the effective merger date
- A long position of 0.6221 Vivendi calls struck at 124.3369 dollars expiring on the effective merger date
- A short position of 0.8 Vivendi puts struck at 96.6875 dollars expiring on the effective merger date

Given our price assumption, and assuming further that the merger will close, the value of a Seagram share therefore must equal the value of this portfolio.

The assumption that Vivendi's share price on the effective date will equal the average closing price is too unrealistic to produce useful valuation formulas and hedge portfolios for the risk arbitrage. This analysis, however, shows that the merger agreement introduces option characteristics into the valuation of Seagram shares. Financial engineers who undertake this arbitrage must derive appropriate formulas that do not depend on our simplifying assumption. They also must adjust for options to buy 19.9 percent of Seagram's stock at 77.35 dollars that Vivendi received in the merger agreement.

The July 26, 2000, NYSE closing price for Seagram was $57^3/_{16}$ dollars. Vivendi closed at 88.90 euros at the Paris Bourse. Given the then current exchange rate of 0.9429 euros per dollar, the dollar equivalent Vivendi closing price was 83.83 dollars. If the Vivendi average price were equal to this price, and if Vivendi was worth this amount on the effective date, each share of Seagram would be worth 67.06 dollars. Seagram traded at a discount to this value because subsequent increases in Vivendi's share price would have little effect on Seagram's value until Vivendi rose above 124 dollars. Any decrease in Vivendi's share price, however, would proportionally decrease Seagram's value. Seagram may also have been trading at a discount because traders doubted that the deal would close. ◀

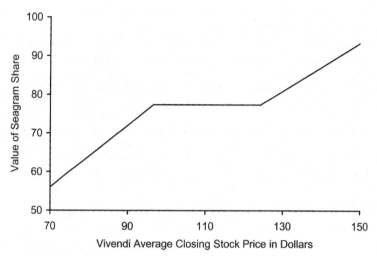

FIGURE 17-1.

Value of a Seagram Share at the Effective Date of the Merger

This analysis assumes that the Vivendi share price on the effective date of the merger is equal to its average closing price over the 20 trading days ending three days before the effective date.

▶ Arbitrage and Ice Floes

Arbitrageurs are like artic explorers who jump from one ice floe to another. When both legs are on the same side, they go with the floe! But if they straddle two floes, a foot on each, they face a substantial risk of being soaked.

Arbitrageurs likewise jump between relatively secure positions when they put on or take off their arbitrages. When they are fully hedged, they do not care where prices take them. They get into trouble when they are stuck in the middle with one leg on and one leg off. ◀

When using limit orders, arbitrageurs face implementation risk due to *execution uncertainty*. Their orders will not execute when prices move away from them. Arbitrageurs then must either cancel and resubmit their orders at less favorable prices or abandon their arbitrages. If they abandon their arbitrages before they have traded any instruments, they merely lose the opportunity to make arbitrage profits. If they abandon their arbitrage after trading one or more arbitrage legs, they must close those positions. These reversals usually generate additional transaction costs.

Failure to execute is an especially serious problem when arbitrageurs have already executed one or more arbitrage legs. Until they complete all the trades necessary to acquire (or liquidate) their hedge portfolios, their positions will be poorly hedged. Any price changes that occur during this time have a very significant effect on their trading profits. Arbitrageurs therefore try very hard to trade all legs of their hedge portfolio at the same time.

Some arbitrageurs try to keep their trades synchronized by using only market orders. This strategy is sensible when bid/ask spreads are small, and when the execution price uncertainty associated with market orders is small relative to the execution uncertainty associated with limit orders. These conditions generally hold in liquid markets.

When one instrument in an arbitrage trades in a liquid market and the other trades in an illiquid market, arbitrageurs often try to trade the illiquid instrument first. After that leg trades, they then trade the other leg. This strategy allows them to cancel their arbitrage cheaply if the basis closes before the illiquid leg trades.

When both instruments of an arbitrage trade in illiquid markets, arbitrageurs often split their orders into parts that they interleave to minimize their exposure to unhedged risks. In such markets, arbitragers often must use limit orders because the execution price risk of market orders can be quite large.

Implementation risk is greatest when the market is moving quickly and

▶ **Implementation Risk in a Takeover Spread**

When two firms agree to a merger in which one firm buys the other with an exchange of stock, the stock prices of the two firms become highly correlated. The price of the target firm times the agreed-upon stock conversion rate becomes approximately equal to the price of the acquiring firm. In practice, the target firm usually trades at a slight discount (or occasionally at a slight premium) to the acquiring firm. The difference may be due to relative mispricing of the two stocks or to speculation that the transaction will not close.

Risk arbitrageurs who wish to speculate on price discrepancies between the two stocks buy the relatively cheap stock and sell the comparatively expensive one. The spread that they earn for doing this transaction must compensate them for the loss they will experience if the transaction falls through, and it must cover the costs of financing the hedge portfolio.

When traders are quite certain that the transaction will close, the basis is usually small in comparison to the volatility in the stocks. Traders who try to buy one stock and sell the other risk failing to capture the arbitrage spread if prices change between the completions of their two trades. This can happen if they buy the long position first, and prices fall before they can sell the short position. They likewise may lose if they sell the short position first, and prices rise before they can buy the long position. Of course, if the opposite happens, they will profit by more than they expect. ◀

▶ **Building a Balanced Position Is like Loading a Small Boat**

Darlene wants to buy 75 contracts of ABC and sell 60 contracts of XYZ to implement an arbitrage in some illiquid markets. She enters the arbitrage by simultaneously submitting limit orders to buy 25 ABC and sell 20 XYZ.

Darlene's next trading decision depends on which order fills first. Suppose the execution report for ABC arrives first. If after a while the XYZ order still does not execute, she then may submit a second limit order to sell 20 XYZ, using a more aggressively priced order than the first XYZ order. This new order therefore should execute before the first XYZ order. When it executes, she will have a properly hedged portfolio. If both XYZ orders execute, she then will submit another order to buy 25 more ABC. If neither XYZ order executes, she will cancel and replace the first order with an even more aggressively priced XYZ order. Darlene will not submit another ABC order until she fills an XYZ order because she needs to hedge her 25-contract ABC position.

In this way, Darlene alternates fills between the two instruments to ensure that her positions are never too far from being properly hedged. If the basis closes while she is not fully hedged, she will cancel any unfilled orders and reverse one of her completed trades to establish a hedged position.

Building a balanced arbitrage position in illiquid markets is like loading a small boat. If you put everything in on one side first, you risk capsizing. ◀

when arbitrageurs cannot easily estimate the price impacts of their trades. It is a particularly significant risk when the arbitrage spread is small compared to short-term price volatility, and when the interval between when arbitrageurs submit their orders, and when they execute, is long.

17.4.2 Basis Risk and Arbitrage Scale

Basis risk is the risk that the arbitrage basis will move in the wrong direction. The hedge portfolio decreases in value when this happens. Adverse

▶ Index Arbitrage Program Trading

Index arbitrageurs use program trades to buy or sell a basket of index stocks while simultaneously selling or buying the corresponding index futures contracts. Because of differences in market structures, their futures orders usually fill faster than their stock orders.

Index arbitrageurs often split their futures orders to synchronize the execution of their program trades with the execution of their futures trades. They first submit their program trade. They then submit half of their futures order when the stock orders start to fill. They submit the remainder of their futures order when most of the stock orders have filled. ◀

price changes may occur when instrument-specific factors diverge or when common factors are not priced correctly. For many arbitrages, basis risk is the most important risk.

As noted above, basis risk differs by whether the basis is mean reverting or nonstationary. Mean-reverting arbitrages (pure arbitrages) generally are less risky in the long run than are nonstationary arbitrages (speculative arbitrages). In the short run, both types of arbitrage may be very risky.

Arbitrageurs can do little to control basis risk besides ensuring that they correctly understand the arbitrage relation. However, they can control their total exposure to basis risk by carefully choosing the scale of their arbitrage operations.

The total basis risk in an arbitrage is proportional to the size of the arbitrage portfolio. The larger the portfolio, the more risky it will be. When the basis is quite risky, arbitrageurs generally choose to hold smaller portfolios. When the basis risk is quite small, arbitrageurs often leverage their returns by creating large portfolios.

Arbitrageurs must be careful when they choose the size of their portfolios. Arbitrageurs lose money when the basis widens. If they cannot finance their losses, they may have to liquidate their positions earlier than they want to. Forced liquidations are especially costly when arbitrageurs engage in pure arbitrages because the liquidations take place when the arbitrage is most attractive. Arbitrageurs therefore should never leverage their positions to the maximum extent that their capital permits. Those who do, have no *staying power* if the basis moves against them.

17.4.3 Model Risk

Model risk, also known as *analytic risk*, is the risk that arbitrageurs will fail to properly understand the fundamental value relations among the instruments they trade. They then may mistakenly enter an arbitrage on the wrong side, they may construct a hedge portfolio that exposes them to risks that they do not recognize, or they may construct a hedge portfolio with the wrong hedge ratios.

The most common mistake that arbitrageurs make is to incorrectly identify a change in the basis as an arbitrage opportunity. Not all basis changes indicate that prices are inconsistent. Some changes move the basis toward its fair value. To determine whether changes in the basis move it closer to or further from its fair value, arbitrageurs must accurately estimate the fair value of the basis. Their estimation problem is especially difficult when the fair value of the basis changes frequently.

The fair value of the basis changes when any of the factors that determine it change. In all arbitrages, the fair value depends on the cost of carry factors such as interest rates, storage costs, and spoilage conditions. If the relation between the instruments is nonlinear, the fair value also depends on the common fundamental factors that cause the instrument values to be correlated. As these factors change, the theoretical values of the instruments either diverge or converge. Finally, if the arbitrage is a speculative arbitrage, the fair value of the basis also depends on any instrument-specific valuation factors. Changes in instrument-specific valuation factors by definition affect only the value of the specific instrument, and therefore must change the fair value of the basis.

▶ Wrong Way to Be Right

Long-Term Capital Management (LTCM) was a hedge fund that engaged in many pure arbitrages and highly mean-reverting speculative arbitrages. Most of their positions were in the bond and swaps markets, where it is possible to create very highly leveraged positions. LTCM employed substantial leverage to create very large positions in arbitrages whose bases it thought were not particularly risky.

On July 31, 1998, LTCM controlled approximately 125 billion dollars in assets from an equity capital base of only 4.1 billion dollars. The gross notional amounts of its contracts on futures exchanges exceeded 500 billion dollars, its swaps contracts exceeded 750 billion dollars, and its options and other OTC derivatives exceeded 150 billion dollars. Of course, the risks inherent in most of these positions substantially offset each other.

Most of LTCM's portfolio consisted of long positions in illiquid securities offset by short positions in highly correlated liquid securities. LTCM therefore was essentially selling liquidity to the market.

In August 1998, when Russia defaulted on its government bonds, credit and liquidity spreads widened considerably as investors sought more secure investments and shunned illiquid investments. Although LTCM lost substantially on its positions, most of them then appeared more attractive than ever before.

By September 21, LTCM's capital had deteriorated to the point that the firm would likely default within a few days. On September 23, a consortium of LTCM's primary creditors arranged to inject 3.6 billion dollars of new equity into the firm in exchange for 90 percent of LTCM's equity.

LTCM's partners lost nearly everything they had invested in the firm, yet their positions were still quite attractive. Although the subsequent performance of many LTCM's positions was not as good as the partners expected, many positions were still quite profitable by any measure. Had the firm been able to weather the crisis, its partners would now be much wealthier. ◀

Arbitrageurs can avoid model risk only by being very careful when they construct their valuation models. They must ensure that they estimate the fair value of the basis using as much information as they can practically acquire. Traders who do not have the appropriate tools and data to model financial relations should avoid trading arbitrages whose values are not easy to derive. In addition, traders who find that their positions are losing money should carefully examine their models to determine whether they are in error or whether market conditions have simply changed against them.

17.4.4 Carrying Cost Risk

Carrying cost risk is the risk that hedge portfolios will prove to be more costly to carry than arbitrageurs expect. The unexpected costs might be due to unexpected increases in the nominal size of the hedge portfolio, longer-than-expected holding periods, unexpected increases in interest rates, unexpected physical costs of carrying the hedge portfolio, or unexpected security borrowing costs.

17.4.4.1 Unexpected Costs of Carry

Arbitrage portfolios are costly to carry. Traders must finance their long positions. If the long positions consist of physical commodities, arbitrageurs

▶ Valuing Stock Stubs

Some publicly traded corporations own very substantial positions in other publicly traded corporations. In rare cases, the total market value of the parent's positions in its subsidiaries may be greater than the parent's total market value. The implied market value of the remainder of the firm's assets thus might appear to be less than zero.

Arbitrageurs who believe that those assets have positive values may attempt to profit in these circumstances by buying the parent firm and selling short their pro rata (undistributed) shares in the subsidiaries. This strategy, when properly executed, buys the parent's assets and liabilities exclusive of its marketable holdings. Traders call this strategy *buying the stub* of the parent.

When evaluating this strategy, it is extremely important to consider the parent's liabilities. If the parent is heavily encumbered by debt, the stub may have a negative implied price simply because of the debt. In that case, the apparent arbitrage opportunity may not be real.

The parent's liabilities may also include obligations to pay taxes in the future. If the parent sells its substantially appreciated assets, the parent will realize substantial capital gains. (It may be able to *spin off* its holdings in a tax-free pro rata distribution to its shareholders if it owns a sufficiently large fraction of the subsidiaries' shares.) The unrealized capital gains imply unrealized tax liabilities on the firm. In effect, the government shares ownership of the subsidiaries. Since these unrealized tax liabilities increase with the subsidiaries' values, arbitrageurs must account for them when computing their hedge ratios. Otherwise, their short positions will be too large. If the subsidiaries' values rise, the value of their hedge portfolios will fall, and vice versa.

Arbitrageurs who fail to properly evaluate stub values risk overpaying for their stubs. Those who fail to properly adjust their hedge ratios for the unrealized tax liabilities inadvertently take larger short positions in the subsidiaries than they should. ◀

must store them and insure them. If the commodities are perishable, they will spoil and depreciate. If the arbitrageurs must borrow securities to establish their short positions, they must pay borrowing fees to the lender. They also must pay lenders any dividends that they would have received if they had not lent their securities. These expenses may be offset by dividends paid on long positions, by lending fees that arbitrageurs receive by lending their long positions, and by interest that they may earn on the proceeds of their short sales. Table 17-3 presents examples of factors that determine carrying costs.

The fair value of the basis depends on the carrying costs of the arbitrage. When these costs increase, arbitrage profits will be less than arbitrageurs expect.

17.4.4.2 Unexpected Price Increases

For arbitrages with finite horizons, and for many other arbitrages as well, the most important carrying cost risk is a significant, unexpected increase in the prices of the instruments in the hedge portfolios. When prices rise, hedge portfolio positions increase in value. Arbitrageurs profit from the increases in their long positions, but they lose from the increases in their short positions. In many markets, arbitrageurs must immediately fund the losses

▶ How Fischer Black Destroyed the ValueLine Index Futures Contract

Fischer Black was an MIT finance professor when he decided to take a year's leave to work for Goldman Sachs in New York in 1984.

At that time, the Kansas City Board of Trade's ValueLine Index futures contract was still very actively traded. After its introduction in 1982 as the world's first stock index futures contract, it quickly became extremely popular.

The ValueLine Index is an unusual stock index. Most indexes are weighted arithmetic sums of stock prices. The ValueLine Index is based on a weighted sum of the logarithms of stock price relatives. A *stock price relative* is the ratio of the current stock price to a previous stock price.

Geometric indexes are easily approximated by arithmetic price indexes. Most ValueLine arbitrageurs used these approximations to value the futures contract and to compute their hedge ratios.

Fischer Black, however, knew that the mathematical properties of the geometric index implied that the exact theoretical fair value for the futures contract should depend on the volatilities of the individual stocks in addition to their prices. The formula he derived implied different theoretical values for the contract than those derived by traders who approximated the Index by an arithmetic average.

Goldman Sachs aggressively traded the arbitrage. Other arbitrageurs also aggressively traded the arbitrage, but on the other side. Many of them traded with Goldman. At one point, Goldman held 30 percent of the open interest in the contract.

Goldman Sachs prevailed in the end. The firm earned more than 125 million dollars on their trades!

The other traders reportedly said that they knew the theoretical value of the futures contract depended on the stock volatilities, but they assumed that the dependence was not economically significant. Had they attended Fischer's finance classes at MIT in 1982 and 1983, they would have known better. Fischer repeatedly told his MBA students about the pricing anomaly, and how he expected that it would soon go away. He probably had no idea then that he would make it happen.

Fischer Black remained at Goldman Sachs, where he ultimately was made partner.

After losing substantially in the ValueLine contract, other traders stopped trading it. The Kansas City Board of Trade quickly lost its market share in stock index futures trading to the Chicago Mercantile Exchange. The CME bases its most successful stock index futures contract on the S&P 500 Index, which is an arithmetic index. In an effort to regain market share, Kansas City changed the specifications of its contract to base it on an arithmetic form of the ValueLine Index. The reformulated contract never obtained any significant market share.

This is an unusual story about the analytic risks associated with proprietary trading. In this story, the market was wrong but Goldman Sachs was right. More commonly, a few traders are wrong and the market is right.

Goldman was able to profit from its minority position because the contract's cash settlement mechanism ensured that the basis would close by the contract expiration date. Had the arbitrage been a speculative arbitrage instead of a pure arbitrage, the valuation mistakes made by the majority of the traders probably would have influenced prices well into the distant future. In that case, Goldman would not have made its profits nearly so quickly. ◀

TABLE 17-3.
Carrying Cost Factors

FACTORS THAT INCREASE CARRYING COSTS	FACTORS THAT DECREASE CARRYING COSTS
Interest paid or forgone to finance long positions	Interest earned on proceeds from short positions
Fees paid to borrow securities sold short	Fees earned from lending securities
Dividends that must be paid on short positions	Dividends received on long positions
Storage costs of physical commodities	
Spoilage and depreciation of perishable commodities	
Costs of insuring physical positions	

in their short positions. These payments impose greater financing costs on the arbitrageur.

When arbitrageurs cannot fund the losses in their short positions when required, their brokers or their counterparts will liquidate the arbitrageurs' positions to satisfy their obligations. Unlike liquidations caused by adverse changes in the basis, these liquidations do not necessarily happen when the basis widens and arbitrageurs are least willing to give up their positions. However, the increase in prices is often correlated with increased volatility in the basis. Losing the option to continue the arbitrage therefore may be costly. The lesson is worth repeating: Successful arbitrageurs do not leverage their positions to the maximum extent that their capital permits. Instead, they leave themselves some margin to ensure that they have staying power if their hedge portfolios increase in value.

17.4.4.3 Slow Convergence

For arbitrages that have no finite horizons, the most important carrying cost risk is often an unexpected increase in the holding period. If the arbitrage basis takes longer to revert than expected, the costs of carrying the hedge portfolio will be greater than expected. Successful arbitrageurs not only must value the basis correctly, they also must be able to predict when it will close.

17.4.4.4 Unexpected Buy-ins

When arbitrageurs borrow securities to short sell them, they generally must return those securities when the lender demands them. Upon such demands, if the arbitrageurs or their brokers cannot arrange another loan, the arbitrageurs must repurchase their short positions in a *forced buy-in*. Such repurchases force them to terminate their arbitrages earlier than they would prefer.

Forced buy-ins often occur when the lender wants to sell because the security has appreciated significantly. Under such circumstances, the basis probably has moved against arbitrageurs. Such buy-ins therefore are especially costly.

On rare occasions, short squeezers may manipulate arbitrageurs. Short squeezes (described in chapter 11) are particularly costly to arbitrageurs.

▶ Not All Stubs Are Mean-reverting

Intermedia Communications owns about 62 percent of Digex. Between December 1999 and early June 2000, Intermedia's Digex position accounted for approximately 50 percent of its total market value.

During this period, Marcia observed that the relation between Intermedia and Digex appeared to be nearly linear, as theory would suggest. She also observed that the basis between the two—the Intermedia stub—appeared to be highly mean reverting.

Given these facts, Marcia decided to buy Intermedia and sell Digex when the stub fell from its average value of 16 to its historic low of 10 on June 30, 2000. Unfortunately, the stub did not revert to its former average value. Instead, Intermedia announced a few days later that earnings in its main line of business would fall substantially short of market expectations. The announcement specifically mentioned that its problems did not affect Digex. Intermedia shares fell very hard while Digex shares rose slightly. The Intermedia stub dropped below zero and reached a low of −3 on July 21.

Marcia lost heavily because she failed to recognize that firm-specific factors had caused the fair value of the stub to drop to 10. Given this mistake, she did not consider whether traders had already impounded the bad news in Intermedia's stock price. ◀

They typically occur when the basis has widened greatly. Arbitrageurs who are caught in a squeeze are forced to sell their positions after they have lost heavily, and when their positions look most attractive going forward.

17.5 THE CAUSES OF ARBITRAGE OPPORTUNITIES

Two sets of circumstances cause arbitrage opportunities. In the *slow price adjustment scenario*, arbitrage opportunities arise when common factor values change, but not all prices that depend on those factors change appropriately. Usually, one or more prices are slow to change. Occasionally, some prices may change too much in response to the news. Arbitrage trading in this scenario causes prices to adjust to their new fundamental values.

In the *uninformed liquidity demand scenario*, arbitrage opportunities arise when fundamental values are constant, but uninformed traders cause prices to change as they buy in some markets or sell in other markets. Arbitrage trading in this scenario connects demands for liquidity that traders make in different markets. The arbitrageurs sell to the buyers in markets where buyers have pushed prices up, and they buy from sellers in markets where sellers have pushed prices down. Their trading tends to restore prices to their fundamental values.

Although arbitrage generally will be profitable in both scenarios, arbitrageurs who recognize the causes of their arbitrage opportunities often will trade more profitably than will those who cannot recognize them. The former can formulate better trading strategies. In addition, since they know more about why they are trading, they are less likely to identify changes in the basis as arbitrage opportunities when those changes are due to changes in the fair value of the basis.

How arbitrageurs implement their trading strategies should depend on the cause of the arbitrage opportunity. When the opportunity arises because

▶ Carrying Cost Risk in Index Futures Arbitrage

When an index futures contract trades at a substantial discount to its fair value, index arbitrageurs sell the futures contract and buy the underlying index stocks. Carrying the hedge portfolio is expensive because the arbitrageur must finance the long stock purchases. The long positions, however, sometimes pay dividends, which reduce the carrying cost. Arbitrageurs therefore consider the expected costs of carrying their positions when they decide whether to trade. The fair value of the futures contract is the current value of the cash index, reduced by the expected interest costs of carrying the cash positions plus the dividends that the cash positions are expected to pay. Arbitrageurs buy the index contract when its price is below its fair value.

If interest rates unexpectedly rise while arbitrageurs hold their hedge portfolios, or if dividend payouts are smaller than expected, the arbitrageur's profits will be less than expected. ◀

▶ Financing a Losing Short Position in Plug Power

Mechanical Technology (MKTY) owns approximately 32 percent of the common stock shares of Plug Power (PLUG). On January 6, 2000, the market value of that position was substantially greater than the market value of all shares outstanding in MKTY. After accounting for MKTY's unrealized capital gains on its PLUG holdings, the MKTY stub—Mechanical Technology exclusive of its holdings in Plug Power—was worth approximately 30 cents per share.

Arbitrageurs who thought that the stub should be worth more would have bought shares in Mechanical Technology and sold shares in Plug Power. The proper hedge ratio depends on MKTY's corporate tax rate, its shares outstanding, its executive stock options outstanding, and its PLUG holdings. At that time, the hedge ratio was probably around 0.64 share of PLUG per share of MKTY.

The closing prices of MKTY and PLUG on January 6 were $23\frac{1}{2}$ and $36\frac{1}{4}$, respectively. If an arbitrageur bought 1,000 shares of MKTY and sold 640 shares of PLUG at their closing prices, he would have spent 23,500 dollars on MKTY and received 23,200 dollars from PLUG. The difference of 300 dollars for 1000 shares is the value of 1000 MKTY stubs at 30 cents per stub.

If this arbitrageur does not receive interest on the short proceeds of his sale, and if his cost of funds is 8 percent per year, the carrying cost of his position is 5.15 dollars per day, or 0.515 cents per stub per day. On average, the stub must appreciate every day by more than 0.5 cent for the arbitrage to be profitable.

By March 10, the prices of MKTY and PLUG had quadrupled! That day, MKTY closed at 90, and PLUG closed at $149\frac{3}{4}$. The arbitrageur now had a 90,000-dollar long position in MKTY and a 95,840-dollar short position in PLUG. The difference implies a stub value of -5.84 dollars. The arbitrageur lost 6,140 dollars on his positions. He also lost more than 325 dollars in financing costs for the 63 days between January 6 and March 10 that he held his position.

By March 10, the arbitrageur needed to give his broker a cumulative sum of 72,640 dollars to cover his losses in PLUG. If the arbitrageur could not have produced these funds, his broker would have closed his position. The increase in PLUG's price increased the arbitrageur's cost of carry to 21.01 dollars per day, or 2.1 cents per stub per day. The stub must now appreciate by more than a dollar every 50 days for the arbitrageur to avoid losing more money.

Fortunately, the arbitrageur's payday arrived a few days later. Over the next few days, MKTY and PLUG both fell substantially, with PLUG falling faster. At the close on March 14, the stub was worth 12.6 dollars per share. Had the arbitrageur sold then, he would have made a net profit after all costs of about 12,000 dollars. ◀

▶ Economists Must Be Patient Traders

Economists often correctly predict future events, but they frequently cannot accurately predict when they will occur. The laws of economic science are often suspended, but they are never rescinded. ◀

not all prices have appropriately adjusted to news about common fundamental factors, arbitrageurs should trade quickly. Otherwise, they may lose the opportunity to profit as news traders or value traders compete to trade first, and as dealers and limit order traders adjust their prices in response to the news. Arbitrageurs therefore should demand liquidity when trading in the slow price adjustment scenario.

When the arbitrage opportunity arises because uninformed traders cause prices to move from their fundamental values, arbitrageurs often have more time to trade. Indeed, they may sometimes wait to see whether uninformed traders push prices farther from their fundamental values. In this scenario, arbitrageurs compete primarily with value traders to supply liquidity to the uninformed traders. They also supply liquidity to dealers whose inventories are out of balance because they have already supplied liquidity to the uninformed traders. In the uninformed liquidity demand scenario, arbitrageurs offer liquidity when trading. They therefore should not trade too aggressively.

Arbitrageurs of course often compete with each other to offer liquidity. When their competition is intense, they must trade more aggressively and at smaller margins, regardless of the cause of the arbitrage opportunity.

17.6 QUANTITY CHARACTERIZATIONS OF ARBITRAGE

Arbitrage is best understood from two perspectives. The *price characterization of arbitrage* focuses on fundamental information. In this view, arbitrageurs are informed traders who trade on information about relative values. They trade when they conclude that instruments are inconsistently priced. The effect of their trading is to enforce the law of one price. This characterization holds regardless of the cause of the arbitrage opportunity.

The *quantity characterization of arbitrage* considers the economic roles arbitrageurs play when they trade instruments that are inconsistently priced. As noted above, inconsistent prices arise when prices are slow to adjust to new information about common factors, or when uninformed traders cause prices to move from their fundamental values.

When trading in the slow price adjustment scenario, arbitrageurs act as disciplinarians. Their trading tends to correct valuation mistakes that other traders make when common factor values change. This perspective explains why other traders often resent arbitrageurs. Nobody likes to take discipline from others.

When trading in the uninformed liquidity demand scenario, arbitrageurs act as shippers or repackagers of common factor risk. They act as shippers when they move the underlying risk from buyers in some markets to sellers in other markets. If the underlying risk is traded in different forms in the various markets, arbitrageurs also act as repackagers. When they buy an instrument in one market and sell a similar but different instrument in another market, they essentially repackage the underlying common factor risk.

In the derivative markets, risk repackaging is a productive process generally run by financial engineers. Arbitrageurs who buy cash instruments and then sell derivative contracts are essentially derivative contract manufacturers. They allow other traders to buy long contract positions. If the arbitrageur sells short to someone who is not covering a short position, the transaction increases the open interest in the contract. Likewise, arbitrageurs who buy derivative contracts and sell cash instruments essentially manufacture short derivative positions for other traders. If the arbitrageur is not short and if the seller is not covering a long position, the transaction increases the open interest. These processes also work in reverse. When arbitrageurs allow other traders to cover their positions, open interest usually drops.

The price and quantity characterizations of arbitrage are closely related. The price discrepancies that motivate arbitrage trading are signals to arbitrageurs to offer their productive services. The arbitrage spread—the dif-

▶ Crossed Markets

The simplest form of arbitrage involves crossed markets. In a *crossed market*, a buyer bids a higher price than a seller simultaneously offers for exactly the same instrument. An arbitrageur who can buy from the seller at the lower price and sell to the buyer at the higher price will make an immediate arbitrage profit. This arbitrage is especially attractive because it generally does not require a hedge portfolio.

Crossed markets typically arise when trading is active and prices move very quickly. Markets cross when sellers do not quickly withdraw their offers when prices are rising or when buyers do not quickly withdraw their bids when prices are falling. When these slow traders trade with an arbitrageur, they naturally regret it. ◀

▶ Time and Place

Traders say that liquidity is all about *time and place*. When buyers and sellers arrive at the same time and place, trades are easy to arrange. When they arrive at different times or at different places, they need the assistance of an intermediary to complete their trades.

Dealers and arbitrageurs are such intermediaries. Dealers use their inventories to match buyers and sellers who arrive at different times in the same place. Arbitrageurs use their hedge portfolios to match buyers and sellers who arrive at the same time in different places. ◀

ference between the basis and its fair value—is the compensation that arbitrageurs expect to receive for their services.

17.7 ARBITRAGEURS, DEALERS, AND BROKERS

Arbitrageurs often trade in response to demands for liquidity that uninformed traders make. When the price impacts of uninformed trades cause price discrepancies across markets, arbitrageurs enter to provide liquidity.

Since dealers also provide liquidity, arbitrageurs and dealers often compete with each other. The two types of traders, however, operate in different dimensions. Dealers offer liquidity to buyers and sellers who arrive at different times in the same market. In contrast, arbitrageurs offer liquidity to buyers and sellers who arrive at the same time but in different markets.

The two trader types also use different technologies to connect buyers to sellers. Dealers use their inventories to span time gaps between buyers and sellers. Arbitrageurs use their hedge portfolios to span spatial gaps between buyers and sellers.

Both traders need mean reversion in order to trade profitably. Dealers profit when prices have a strong mean-reverting component. Arbitrageurs profit when the basis has a strong mean-reverting component.

The competition among dealers and arbitrageurs explains why dealers often do not appreciate having arbitrageurs trade in their markets. Dealing would be more profitable if dealers did not have to compete with arbitrageurs to supply liquidity. Dealing also would be more profitable if arbitrageurs did not trade with dealers when dealers are slow to change their prices in response to new information.

Dealers do appreciate trading with arbitrageurs when the arbitrageurs help them solve inventory problems that trouble them. Such trades usually occur after a dealer fills a large order or a sequence of small orders on one side of the market. To reduce the resulting inventory imbalance, dealers often adjust their prices to encourage other traders to trade with them on the other side. When these price changes cause the basis to widen, arbitrageurs will trade and take the dealers' unwanted inventory positions.

Arbitrage also would be more profitable if arbitrageurs did not have to compete with dealers to supply liquidity. When dealers offer liquidity, they decrease the impact that uninformed traders have on prices. Arbitrageurs therefore see fewer profitable arbitrage opportunities than they otherwise would see. Stated differently, dealers make prices less mean reverting when they offer liquidity to uninformed traders. Less mean reversion in prices generally implies less mean reversion in the basis, and therefore less arbitrage profit.

Traders who can simultaneously act as dealers and arbitrageurs often have an advantage over traders who specialize in only one strategy. When confronted with an order flow imbalance, such traders can choose whether to supply liquidity by dealing from their inventories or by constructing hedge portfolios. This flexibility allows them always to choose the strategy with the greatest profit potential.

Arbitrageurs also compete with brokers. Arbitrageurs buy from traders in one market and sell to traders in another market. They therefore match

▶ Options Market Makers Like Options

Traders who make markets in stock option contracts typically quote every series within an options class. An *options class* includes all options that trade on the same underlying instrument. An *option series* is a specific option contract. Options series vary by their strike prices, by their expiration dates, and by their type—whether they are puts or calls.

When options dealers take a position in a given series, they may offset the risk in that position by a transaction in the same series or by a position in any other series in the class. They also may offset the risk by taking a position in the underlying instrument. The option to offset their risks in a multitude of different ways gives options market makers a great deal of flexibility. This flexibility allows them to take much greater positions in an individual series than they otherwise would take.

Options traders keep track of their total risk exposure by expressing the risk in each of their positions in terms of the underlying instrument. They do this by multiplying their options positions by their deltas.[1] The sum of their delta-adjusted positions is their net exposure to the risk in the underlying instrument. The delta of a perfectly hedged portfolio is zero. Options traders who do not want to speculate on price changes in the underlying instrument try to keep their net delta near zero.

Deltas change as the underlying instrument prices change. Options traders keep track of the net gamma of their positions so that they know how much of the underlying instrument they must trade to maintain their hedge when the underlying instrument price drops.

Option prices also depend on the volatility of the underlying instrument. Options traders keep track of the net vega of their positions so that they know how much they will gain or lose when volatility changes. Since most public traders buy puts or buy calls, options dealers typically have positions with negative net vega. They therefore make money when volatility falls or when prices do not change much before expiration. ◀

---

1. The *delta* of an option is the rate at which the option value changes when the price of the underlying security changes. (It is approximately equal to the change in option value that would result from a one-dollar increase in the underlying security price.) Calls have positive deltas, and puts have negative deltas. The *gamma* of an option is the rate at which its delta changes when the price of the underlying security changes. The *vega* of an option is the rate at which the option value changes when the volatility of the underlying security changes. Puts and calls have positive vegas.

buyers with sellers, which is essentially what brokers do. Brokers arrange matches on an agency basis: Their clients pay them commissions for arranging their trades. Arbitrageurs arrange these matches on a proprietary basis: The arbitrage spread rewards them for matching willing buyers with willing sellers. Since arbitrageurs are in some respects like brokers, the skills that make good brokers—being able to identify buyers and sellers who are willing to trade—also make good arbitrageurs.

17.8 COMPETITION AMONG ARBITRAGEURS AND EQUILIBRIUM ARBITRAGE SPREADS

Arbitrageurs compete with each other to make arbitrage profits. Although arbitrage is most profitable when the arbitrage spread is wide, arbitrageurs who wait for wide spreads often lose the opportunity to trade when more aggressive arbitrageurs trade first. Competition among arbitrageurs therefore tends to narrow arbitrage spreads so that only the most efficient arbitrageurs can survive.

When arbitrageurs can freely enter and exit, the resulting arbitrage spreads are just wide enough to ensure that most arbitrageurs make only normal economic profits on average. When arbitrage is more profitable, new traders enter and spreads narrow. When arbitrage is less profitable, some arbitrageurs give up, and arbitrage spreads widen.

Arbitrage spreads therefore reflect the costs of doing arbitrage. When arbitrage is expensive, arbitrage bounds will be wide.

Since only the most efficient arbitrageurs survive, arbitrageurs tend to be excellent traders and excellent estimators of relative values. In markets where the arbitrage relation is easy to understand, the most successful arbitrageurs are excellent traders who have very high-speed access to their markets. In markets where the arbitrage relation is difficult to understand, the most successful arbitrageurs are excellent analysts.

Arbitrageurs are often traders who have a natural interest in one or more legs of the hedge portfolio. Such traders are often the lowest cost arbitrageurs because they already are committed to doing one or more of the trades necessary to construct the hedge portfolio. For example, for agricultural delivery arbitrages, local operators near the contract delivery point are often the lowest cost arbitrageurs because they often need to buy or sell the commodity there anyway.

17.9 SUMMARY

Arbitrageurs play many roles in the markets. They enforce the law of one price, they discipline slow traders, they connect buyers to sellers, and they repackage risks into forms that other traders find most useful. These activities provide benefits to the economy and to individual traders.

Arbitrage trading strategies are special cases of more basic trading strategies. Arbitrageurs are simply traders who deal or speculate in their hedge portfolios. Trading two or more instruments simultaneously can be difficult, however, especially when price volatility is large relative to the basis. Good arbitrageurs therefore tend to be good traders.

Arbitrage is not easy. To trade successfully, arbitrageurs must properly understand the arbitrage relation, they must successfully implement their positions, and they must control their carrying costs. Arbitrageurs risk losing when the basis moves against them, when carrying costs are unexpectedly large, when they falsely identify arbitrage opportunities, and when they can no longer carry their positions because they have grown too large. Successful arbitrageurs must anticipate these problems and deal with them as they arise.

Arbitrageurs profit from mean reversion in the basis. In pure arbitrages, the basis must revert. Arbitrageurs can still lose, however, if the reversion takes too long. In speculative arbitrages, the nonstationary component of the basis may dominate the mean-reverting component, and the basis may never revert.

The most successful arbitrageurs understand why their arbitrage opportunities arise. They then know how best to trade, and they are less likely to trade when they should not trade.

Since arbitrageurs trade in more than one market, we need to consider their behavior when we consider how markets relate to each other. We discuss how arbitrageurs transmit volatility between markets in chapter 20, and in chapter 26 we show that arbitrageurs are instrumental in keeping fragmented markets together.

17.10 SOME POINTS TO REMEMBER

- Arbitrageurs trade similar risks in related markets.
- Arbitrageurs generally are dealers or value traders in their arbitrage hedge portfolios.
- Arbitrageurs convert assets and risks to different types, forms, or locations.
- Arbitrageurs are cross-sectional dealers.
- A large basis tells arbitrageurs to move liquidity from one market to another or to convert risk from one form to the other.
- The basis pays for the arbitrageurs' services.
- Arbitrage enforces the law of one price across fragmented markets.
- Successful arbitrageurs are low cost traders.

17.11 QUESTIONS FOR THOUGHT

1. What limits arbitrage profits?
2. Can you repeat the intermarket currency cross-rate arbitrage until you are rich beyond your wildest dreams? Why not?
3. What would happen to arbitrage spreads if the government taxed trading?
4. Would index futures contracts have more appeal to hedgers and arbitrageurs if they required short holders to pay long holders the amount of dividends that they would have received had they held the cash portfolio instead of the futures contract?
5. Can arbitrage trading cause prices in one or more markets to move away from their fundamental values? If this happens, which traders would restore prices to their proper values?
6. How are bid/ask spreads in option contracts related to bid/ask spreads in their underlying instruments?
7. When one market becomes volatile, arbitrageurs often cause prices in related markets to change. Does arbitrage therefore increase total volatility?
8. What effect does arbitrage have on total market liquidity?
9. What advantages do commodity operators have as arbitrageurs?
10. What can traders learn about future price changes from where prices lie within arbitrage bounds?
11. Is a spread between two option contracts with the same expiration date but different strike prices a speculative arbitrage or a pure arbitrage?
12. What are the missing event contingencies referred to in the footnote to table 17-2 about identifying likely arbitrage opportunities in the GE–S&P 500 futures spread?

18

▷

Buy-Side
Traders

Traders must pay close attention to their order submission strategies in order to trade effectively. Traders who optimize their trading strategies will
have lower transaction costs and higher portfolio returns than those who do
not carefully consider their trading problems.

Order submission strategy is the most important determinant of execution quality that traders control. Traders must decide when to submit market orders and when to submit limit orders. When they submit limit orders, they must know where to place their limit prices. If their limit orders
do not execute, they must know when, and how, to resubmit their orders.

Large traders also must pay close attention to how they display their orders. Traders who display large orders often attract front runners and scare
away liquidity suppliers. Large traders therefore must consider the following questions:

- Whether to actively look for the other side or to wait for it to come
  to them
- Whether to show their full interest or to hide it
- Whether to break up their orders and spread them over time or to
  bring their whole orders to market at once
- Whether to employ a single broker or to use multiple brokers to hide
  their total interest
- Whether to trade in one market or in many markets

Display decisions are the most important trading decisions that large buy-
side traders make.

The decision to use limit orders versus market orders is related to the
order display decision. Traders who want to display their trading interest often use limit orders to show that they are willing to trade. Those who do
not want to show their interest often use market orders. Traders do not have
to display their limit orders, however. They often can use the services of a
confidential broker, or they can submit their orders to electronic trading systems that permit undisclosed limit orders.

The strategies that traders should use, depend on their trading problems.
Informed traders who have material information that will soon become public will trade very differently from value traders who can identify mispriced
instruments. Both types of traders will trade differently from traders who
need to raise cash before a deadline or index traders who need to rebalance
their index portfolios in response to changes in the composition of their target indexes.

In this chapter, we examine the issues that buy-side traders weigh when
deciding how to trade. We start by considering the decision to use market
orders versus limit orders. We then analyze the benefits and costs of expo-

sure, and consider how traders can defend against parasitic trading strategies that order anticipators may exercise against them. Finally, we discuss how exchanges, brokers, and regulators can structure markets to promote the interests of buy-side traders.

Although these issues obviously interest buy-side traders, they also should interest anyone who wants to understand the origins of liquidity. Order submission strategies affect the supply and demand of liquidity. Traders demand liquidity when they submit market orders, and they supply liquidity when they submit limit orders. We therefore must consider how traders choose their order submission strategies in order to fully understand liquidity.

Chapters 4, 7, 11, 12, 14, and 15 introduce many of the issues discussed in this chapter. The value-added in this chapter comes from the discussion of these issues from the point of view of the buy-side trader. To avoid unnecessary duplication, the text in this chapter assumes some familiarity with some of these issues. Readers who are not familiar with the markets may want to read these other chapters first.

18.1 MARKET VERSUS LIMIT ORDERS

The equilibrium spread model presented in chapter 14 shows that order submission strategy does not matter when all traders have identical needs. Bid/ask spreads simply adjust to ensure that traders are indifferent between using market orders and limit orders. In practice, however, traders are not identical. Some traders need to trade faster than other traders. Impatient traders generally should use market orders and patient traders should use limit orders. Some traders are also more sensitive to order exposure issues than other traders. Those who do not want to display often use market orders to avoid exposing limit orders.

In all cases, the decision to use limit orders or market orders depends critically on the bid/ask spread. When the spread is wide, taking liquidity is expensive and offering liquidity is attractive. When the spread is narrow, market orders are attractive relative to limit orders. Traders judge whether spreads are wide or narrow from their experience in the market. They can much better organize that experience by being familiar with the bid/ask spread determinants discussed in chapter 14.

The prices at which traders place their limit orders depend on how they value the trade-off between execution price and execution probability. Aggressively priced orders will more likely execute than will less aggressively priced orders, but the execution prices will be inferior. Traders who are more concerned about price than about trading will more likely use limit orders. Traders who are more concerned about trading than price will more likely use market orders.

The decision to use market orders versus limit orders also depends on what will happen when limit orders do not execute. Traders who must fill their orders will trade at inferior prices when the market moves away from their limit orders. They can reduce their exposure to this risk by using market orders or by placing their limit orders close to the market to increase the probability that they will execute quickly. Traders who are not committed to trading, trade only if they can obtain a good price. These traders—primarily traders who employ dealing strategies—often use limit orders or firm quotes to profit from the bid/ask spread. When their limit orders do

▶ A Problem with Rules

The rule to take liquidity when the spread is small and offer it when the spread is large is valid only when you do not know anything about value. For example, suppose that the market is 48 bid, offered at 50. If the spread normally is 10, market orders would appear to be extremely attractive relative to limit orders.

Now suppose that you knew the true value of the instrument is 45. A market sell order would execute at an excellent price relative to value, but a market buy order would execute at a poor price.

This situation often arises when an impatient limit order trader places an aggressively priced order in the market. For example, suppose that the market was 40 bid, offered at 50, before an aggressive buyer placed a limit buy order at 48. The limit order buyer improves the market substantially for market order sellers, but provides no benefit to market order buyers. Sellers who can recognize this situation should take liquidity.

The new bid also affects the decisions that buyers make to offer or take liquidity. Since the new bid decreases the probability that limit orders placed below 48 will ultimately execute, limit order strategies which would otherwise place buy orders below 48 are less attractive. The new bid makes market orders more attractive to buyers, though not nearly as much as the abnormally narrow spread would suggest.

The rule is correct when traders know nothing about values. In our example, sellers benefit greatly if they use market orders rather than limit orders, and buyers may be slightly better off with market orders than with limit orders. The narrow spread makes market orders more attractive than limit orders—on average—to uninformed traders. ◀

not execute, they simply cancel them or replace them with orders placed at new prices.

To derive optimal trading strategies, traders must know how execution probabilities depend on limit order prices. The relation between these variables depends on market conditions. The most important factors include total limit order size at better prices, price volatility, and trader interest in the instrument.

Traders can acquire information about the relation between execution probabilities and limit order prices by using formal econometric models. Numerous vendors sell access to optimized order generators that suggest order strategies based on current market conditions.

Traders also acquire information about the relation between execution probabilities and limit order prices through experience. Experienced traders who pay close attention to the market get a feel for what may happen. Buy-side traders who give their brokers market-not-held orders give them timing discretion over their orders. They expect that their brokers will use their experience and knowledge of current market conditions to determine the best strategies for filling their orders and to continuously revaluate those strategies as conditions change.

18.2 THE ORDER EXPOSURE DECISION

Traders expose their intentions many different ways. On one extreme, traders can publicize their trading interests by submitting limit orders to systems that widely display their orders. They then hope that other traders will trade with them. On the other extreme, traders can hide their interests until an exchange or a broker presents an acceptable opportunity to trade. Traders may also trade only through brokers and exchanges that settle their trades on an anonymous basis so that neither side knows with whom it traded. A multitude of order exposure strategies lies between these two extremes.

Traders decide to expose by weighing the benefits of display against the costs of display. The benefits are obvious. Buyers and sellers can find each other most easily when they both show that they want to trade. This simple observation helps explain why trading tends to consolidate into a single central market. Traders who display their interests make it easy for other traders to find them.

The display decision would be simple if exposing trading interests did not often have significant negative consequences. For large traders, however, exposure can be quite costly. These costs are due to the actions that other traders may take in response to the exposed information.

We will call these other traders *parasitic traders* and *defensive liquidity suppliers*, depending on their response to the exposed information. *Parasitic traders* are order anticipators who profit only by exploiting other traders. We discuss their trading strategies in chapter 11. Parasitic traders use exposed information to create trading strategies that profit at the expense of the exposed traders.

Defensive liquidity suppliers use exposed information about trading intentions to step out of the way of large traders who would otherwise price-discriminate against them. Their response to exposed information is to refrain from trading so that the large traders ultimately pay more for liquidity.

Exposure issues generally do not concern small traders much. Their orders usually are too small to interest parasitic traders. Sometimes many small orders on the same side of the market may be the equivalent of a large order. The aggregate order size then may attract a costly response from other traders. Although small traders then would have a collective interest in managing their order exposure, no small trader has much incentive to do so because the benefits would accrue to all traders.

18.3 THE BENEFITS OF EXPOSURE

Trades are easier to arrange when traders publicize their interests. Traders who widely expose their orders make it easy for other traders to find them. They also attract traders with *latent trading interest* who are not able or willing to articulate their trading interests. These traders are *reactive traders* because they trade in response to trading opportunities that other traders present them. The opposite of a reactive trader is a *proactive trader*. Proactive traders articulate their interests.

Cost is probably the most important reason why traders choose to be reactive rather than proactive. Proactive traders express their orders and give them to their brokers before they know whether they will have an opportunity to trade. They may make many decisions and issue many instructions that produce no value if suitable trading opportunities do not arise. In contrast, reactive traders decide whether they want to trade only after they are presented with trading opportunities.

In trading situations where suitable trading opportunities are rare, many traders find it cheaper to be reactive than proactive. Reactive traders, however, risk that proactive traders may identify and act on valuable trading opportunities first.

▶ Dimensional Fund Advisors

Dimensional fund advisors often purchases large blocks of stock in small firms. Its traders find it cheaper to wait for opportunities to arise than to continuously search all small-firm markets for suitable trading opportunities. They obtain better prices by waiting until traders come to them. The firm has successfully provided substantially enhanced index returns to its investors by selling liquidity. ◀

Proactive traders expose their orders to attract liquidity from reactive traders. Without such exposure, the reactive traders cannot react. Two reactive traders will never trade with each other.

The reactive–proactive continuum is similar to the aggressive–passive continuum. The former represents the willingness of traders to bear the costs of searching, and the latter represents the eagerness of traders to arrange trades. Aggressive traders tend to be proactive and passive traders tend to be reactive. Traders who can search at low cost tend to be proactive, while traders for whom search is expensive tend to be reactive.

18.4 THE COSTS OF EXPOSURE

Large traders who display their interests may reveal three types of information useful to other traders: why they want to trade, the potential price impacts of their future trades, and valuable trading options. Traders may act on this information to the disadvantage of the exposing traders. This section examines these three situations.

18.4.1 Exposure May Reveal Trader Motives

Traders who expose their intentions risk that others will learn why they want to trade. Traders may use this information to compete with them, to withhold liquidity from them, or in some cases, to take other damaging actions against them.

Several types of traders do not want others to know why they want to trade:

- Well-informed traders do not want to reveal their unique information and proprietary analyses. They do not want other traders to compete with them or to refuse to trade with them.
- Traders engaged in corporate control battles avoid revealing their intentions because they want to minimize the time available for corporate managers to organize their defenses. They also do not want to reveal information that would allow others to infer the proprietary analyses of value upon which they base their choice of targets.
- Traders who must trade to satisfy various obligations do not reveal their obligations in order to avoid front runners and squeezers.
- Squeezers acquire power by surreptitiously cornering the market before traders realize that they have lost the option to negotiate with others. Squeezers therefore cannot reveal their intentions before they have established their corners.
- Finally, bluffers do not want to reveal their trading intentions because they do not want value traders to call their bluffs.

These traders must all be very careful about how they reveal their trading interests. If other traders can infer their motives from how they trade, their trading strategies will be much less effective.

Well-known traders who do not want to reveal that they are trading often use brokers as intermediaries. The brokers expose their orders without revealing their identities.

Even when traders trade anonymously, other traders may be able to infer their intentions in some instances. For example, order flows often con-

▶ The Better You Are, the Harder It Gets

Traders widely believe that Tom is well informed about security values. He has a strong reputation for the quality of his research and for his unique insights. His portfolios have consistently outperformed the market. Everyone understands that Tom buys when he thinks securities are undervalued and sells when he thinks they are overvalued.

Tom's competitors would like to know his estimates of security values. They would use this information to compete with him to establish profitable positions. Their competition would raise Tom's transaction costs and might prevent him from successfully completing his trading objectives.

The people with whom Tom would like to trade would also like to know Tom's intentions. Anyone who trades with Tom will likely be on the wrong side of the trade. Traders therefore try to avoid offering him liquidity. If exchange regulations, or their business plans, require that they trade with Tom, they will offer him inferior prices and little size. Even traders who are eager to trade with Tom will refrain from trading until Tom's trades impact the market. These responses to Tom's trading raise his transaction costs and may prevent him from achieving his objectives.

Well-informed traders like Tom have very difficult trading problems. If they expose their intentions, their transaction costs may increase. If they do not expose their intentions, they may find it hard to trade. Traders who have a reputation for success therefore must be very careful about how they expose their interest. The best-known traders often have the hardest time finding liquidity. ◀

tain information about values because well-informed traders buy when they believe prices are low and sell otherwise. Astute traders can make inferences about values just from observing the order flow.

Although well-informed traders generally do not want to expose their orders, they sometimes do want people to pay close attention to them. After they acquire their positions, informed traders want prices to move quickly in their favor. They then want prices to stabilize at their new level so that they can close their positions and realize their profits. Well-informed traders can achieve these objectives by sharing their information with other traders. They are most credible when they allow other traders to see that they are trading.

Bluffers also sometimes want to expose their trading. To profit from their bluffs, they must encourage momentum traders to follow their trades. Bluffers do this by trading aggressively, as though they were well-informed traders trading on material information that will soon be revealed to the public. At this point in their strategy, bluffers will expose their orders because they want other traders to notice their trading. When they later try to trade out of their positions, they will not want to be observed.

In summary, traders who expose their intentions make it easier for others to infer their motives. Exposed traders therefore risk having other traders compete with them, withhold liquidity from them, or otherwise act against their interests.

18.4.2 Exposure May Reveal Future Price Impacts

Large impatient traders often significantly affect prices when they trade. Other traders who know their intentions may therefore front-run them to profit from the market impacts of their large orders. Front runners increase large trader transaction costs by taking liquidity that might otherwise have gone to the large trader.

To trade profitably, front runners do not need to know why traders want to trade. They merely need to know that a large trader intends to complete a trade. Large impatient traders therefore carefully manage the exposure of their orders in order to control their transaction costs.

18.4.3 Exposure May Reveal Valuable Trading Options

Even if large traders patiently wait for the market to come to them, exposing their orders can still adversely affect their trading costs. Standing limit orders provide free trading options to other traders. Quote matchers can extract the values of these options.

Quote matching is a front-running strategy in which quote matchers try to trade before large patient traders. When the quote matchers trade first, the options offered by the large traders protect the quote matchers from serious losses on their new positions. If prices move in their favor, they can profit to the full extent of the movements. If prices move against them, they may limit their losses by trading with the large traders.

Quote matchers profit at the expense of the large patient traders by taking liquidity that otherwise would have gone to the large traders. If the large traders subsequently fail to trade because prices move away from their orders, they lose the profits that the quote matchers make. To prevent losses to quote matchers, large patient traders must control their order exposure so that quote matchers cannot exploit the trading options associated with their orders.

18.5 DEFENSIVE STRATEGIES

The preceding section shows that large traders must carefully control the exposure of their trading intentions in order to avoid losses that other traders can impose upon them. This section describes three strategies—evasive, deceptive, and offensive—that large traders use to deal with these problems. Large traders use evasive strategies to keep other traders from learning information about their trading intentions. They use deceptive strategies to fool other traders into making wrong inferences about their intentions. They use offensive strategies to attack parasitic traders.

18.5.1 Evasive Strategies

Traders may use several strategies to avoid exposing information to traders who might act on it to their disadvantage.

- Where traders negotiate face-to-face, large traders typically hire brokers to negotiate trades on their behalf in order to preserve their anonymity. Very large traders often will use multiple brokers to ensure that no broker knows the full extent of their interest, and to prevent other traders from inferring their interest by watching a single broker.
- To avoid front running that might be due to dishonest or incompetent brokers, large traders often prefer to use electronic trading systems that do not display their identities.
- When traders must show their interest in order to arrange a large trade, they, or their brokers, carefully select the traders to whom they first display their interest. They try to display first to those traders who will

most likely trade with them, and who are least likely to act on the information otherwise.

Being able to identify the best sequence of traders to whom to display interest is the most essential skill that institutional brokers and buy-side traders must master. This is the art of block trading. Traders develop this skill by cultivating reliable relationships, by observing market activity, by understanding what portfolio managers want, by keeping track of what traders hold, and by noting recent changes in their holdings. Among the most important brokerage services, selective order exposure is the service that computerized systems are least likely to provide efficiently.

- Large traders often limit their exposure by not showing the full extent of their interest in their orders. They, or their brokers, break their orders into small parts so that they display only a small part at a time.

- Large traders often use brokers and exchange systems that do not display their orders to other traders. eSpeed, POSIT, Global Instinet Crossing, GLOBEX, Euronext, and Island, among others, provide systems that accept and manage undisplayed orders. Traders can learn about these orders by committing to trade with them.

- Large traders often solicit interest without committing to trade by publicizing order indications on systems like Autex, Bridge, and Instinet. *Order indications* merely show that someone would like to talk about trading. Since they do not represent commitments to trade, any trader may indicate without intending to trade. (If contacted, traders who do not intend to trade say that they canceled or already filled their orders. They then apologize for failing to remove their indications. Alternatively, they quote prices so poor that no trades are likely.) Since the only cost of false indications is some loss in reputation if asked to trade, many traders do not take order indications seriously. Order indications therefore do not generally reveal much information.

- Finally, traders can avoid exposing their intentions by waiting until someone else exposes a trading opportunity that interests them. If another trader exposes a firm commitment, the trader can use a market order to trade with it. In this way, traders do not expose their interest until they actually trade.

If the other trader merely exposes an order indication, traders concerned about controlling the exposure of their interests should be wary. Inquiries about the indication may reveal their interests to the trader who posted the order indication.

18.5.2 Deceptive Strategies

Traders sometimes use deceptive strategies to confound traders who would try to infer their intentions. The following strategies are deceptive because traders actively disseminate false information or because they create situations in which other they may make false inferences:

- Traders may make a small trade on the side opposite the one in which they have substantial interest. If the small trade is widely publicized, the resulting confusion may make it harder for traders to identify the true interest. Traders may likewise post order indications on the opposite side to confuse other traders.

▶ **Fishing for Business**

Brokers sometimes post indications to solicit business. When a trader contacts such a broker, the broker either apologizes for failing to cancel the indication or says that he will check to see whether his client is still interested. The broker then tries to find someone who would be interested in taking the other side. Brokers who use this strategy can sometimes arrange trades without receiving formal orders from either side.

Traders who respond to indications only to discover that they cannot immediately trade become very annoyed. They object to the waste of their time and to being tricked into exposing their interest. When this happens, they often penalize the offending broker by refusing to do business with him for some period. ◀

▶ The Cost of Lying

Max sells 100,000 shares of a small stock through a block broker. To trade without substantially depressing prices, Max tells his broker that he has no further interest in selling the stock. The broker uses this information to encourage buyers to take the stock.

Max then uses another broker to sell an additional 100,000 shares at a substantially depressed price. The buyers of the first 100,000 shares lose money and are very upset at the first broker who arranged their trade. That broker's reputation will suffer accordingly.

Max successfully discriminated among the buyers, but he probably will not be able to use the first broker again in the near—and possibly distant—future. Brokers naturally do not want clients who damage their reputations. ◀

- Traders may say that they have finished trading when they have not, and they may say that they want a small position when they want a large one. These strategies may fool other traders into offering liquidity on better terms than they might otherwise.

- Traders may express interest away from the markets that truly interest them in order to divert attention from their true intentions.

- Traders may cancel orders that they want to fill so as to create uncertainty about their commitments to trading.

To increase the credibility of these strategies, some traders cultivate brokers they know cannot keep a secret, using them to unwittingly reveal false information.

Traders who actively deceive others risk damaging valuable relationships. Deceptions therefore must be weighed against the value of their relationships.

Because talk is very cheap, many traders discount information they receive if the source has little stake in its accuracy. For example, information obtained from brokers with whom you have no relationship is likely to be much less reliable than information obtained from brokers who depend upon you for their livelihoods.

18.5.3 Offensive Strategies

Traders may use offensive strategies to attack parasitic traders. Offensive strategies can increase the costs and risks of parasitic trading and thereby drive it away.

The most important offensive strategy involves a sting. If a trader realizes that someone is regularly front running his orders, he may want to sting the front runner to shake him off. To set up the sting, the trader displays an order on the opposite side of his true interest. If fooled, the front runner then tries to trade on that side ahead of the exposed order. The stinger then trades with the front runner—perhaps through a broker—and then cancels his false order.

If the sting is successful, the stinger will complete his desired trade with the front runner and leave the front runner on the wrong side of the market. To trade out of his position, the front runner must now solve the same trading problem that the stinger faced. In effect, the stinger transfers his trading problem to the front runner.

Not all stings are successful. Another trader may fill the false order, or the front runner may fill the order if he somehow recognizes the trap. In either event, the stinger will end up with a position just opposite to the one he wants to establish. To establish his desired position, the stinger will now have to trade twice as much as he originally intended, or three times as much if we count the trade made in the failed sting.

18.5.4 Summary

Traders use a variety of strategies to control the exposure of their trading intentions and to prevent losses to other traders who would act upon that information if they could infer it. Evasive strategies avoid revealing information to those who would use it against you. Deceptive strategies attempt to confuse these traders. Offensive strategies try to attack these traders. Unfortunately, all of these strategies are costly to implement.

Some of the deceptive and offensive strategies may not be legal in some jurisdictions. Traders who are concerned about such issues should consult a competent legal authority.

18.6 HOW MARKETS HELP TRADERS CONTROL EXPOSURE COSTS

Markets can reduce the costs of order exposure by adopting rules and trading systems that protect traders who expose their orders.

Markets can reduce front running by adopting a time precedence rule to make it impossible for traders to trade before a standing order at the same price. A large minimum price increment then would make front running expensive by forcing front runners to offer a significantly better price to trade first.

Markets can also protect large traders by allowing them to submit undisclosed orders. These facilities allow large traders to make firm offers to trade that other traders can discover only by committing to trade with them. Traders who look for these undisplayed orders can avoid exposing their own interest by attaching fill-or-kill instructions to their orders. If their orders discover undisclosed liquidity, they trade. If they do not, only the trading system knows that they inquired. Completely confidential trading systems work well when traders know what trades they want to do. They therefore primarily serve proactive rather than reactive traders.

Most markets maintain rules and procedures to protect traders against front running by dishonest brokers. A detailed and accurate audit trail is especially important for identifying and prosecuting front-running frauds. To further reduce the potential for encountering these problems, some markets prohibit dual trading (acting as both a broker and a dealer) by their members.

Finally, markets can protect some types of traders by allowing them to report their trades late. Delayed trade reporting helps traders who are in the middle of acquiring or divesting large positions by making it difficult for other traders to infer the full size of their interests.

Exchanges and regulators must weigh the benefits of delayed reporting against its costs. By obscuring the market, delayed reporting can greatly increase transaction costs for many types of traders. This result should not be surprising because traders can benefit from delayed reporting only if they hurt other traders. Since delayed trade reporting helps dealers more than brokers, it is more common in markets organized by dealers than in those organized by brokers and exchanges.

18.7 SUMMARY

Buy-side traders must pay close attention to their order submission strategies in order to trade effectively. The strategies that they choose depend on the problems that they solve. Traders who are impatient to trade generally use market orders, while those who are patient or who do not need to complete their trades use limit orders.

All traders pay close attention to the price of liquidity. When spreads are wider than normal, limit orders may be more attractive than market orders. When spreads are narrower than normal, market orders may be more attractive.

▶ **Order Exposure and Minimum Price Increments**

Large traders should expose more when time precedence and a large minimum price increment protect their interests. I examined this proposition by studying the propensity of large traders to display their orders at the Paris Bourse and the Toronto Stock Exchange in 1994 and 1995. Both exchanges then had electronic trading systems that allowed traders to submit undisclosed orders. (The Toronto Stock Exchange recently dropped this feature of its market.)

As expected, traders submitted more undisclosed orders when the minimum price increment was a small fraction of price than when it was a large fraction of price. ◀

▶ **The Liquidity in Liquidnet**

Liquidnet is an institutional equity broker that runs an innovative electronic alternative trading system. Clients plug the Liquidnet trading system into their electronic order management systems. Liquidnet then looks at the orders that their clients have placed in their order blotters. If Liquidnet sees that a client wants to buy a security that another client wants to sell, it suggests that they negotiate by placing an indication of this fact on their two workstations. Either of the two traders then can contact the other by sending an anonymous message through the Liquidnet system. If the receiving trader responds to the message, the two traders then try to negotiate a trade, using a Liquidnet messaging window designed for this purpose. If they agree to a price and quantity, they report the trade to Liquidnet. Liquidnet then crosses the trade so that neither trader ever knows with whom he or she traded. Liquidnet charges each trader 2 cents per share commission for its services.

To limit the number of potential negotiations, traders can specify a minimum fraction of their order size that other traders must have in their order books to negotiate with them. Liquidnet then suggests negotiations only among traders whose orders are adequately large.

To limit the number of unproductive negotiations, when Liquidnet suggests a negotiation, it presents traders with information about how often the other trader has responded and how often negotiations with that trader have produced a trade. Traders then can avoid negotiating with traders with whom they have not been able to trade in the past.

When traders can negotiate with more than one trader, Liquidnet ranks the traders by their order sizes. Traders use this information and the information described in the previous paragraph to choose with whom to initiate negotiations.

Otherwise, the Liquidnet trading system is completely confidential. The system does not present information about orders, prices, quantities, or trade negotiations to anyone.

Liquidnet became very successful very quickly because traders do not have to submit orders to it. Instead, Liquidnet observes the potential liquidity that traders have in their order blotters. ◀

Source: www.liquidnet.com.

Trades are easiest to arrange when traders broadly expose their orders. Unfortunately, exposure can reveal trader motives, the potential price impacts of future trades, and valuable trading options. Traders can exploit this information to their advantage and to the detriment of exposing traders.

Exposure decisions are the most important decisions that large traders make. Good traders know when and to whom to expose their interests. Poor traders expose to the wrong traders, they expose at the wrong times, or they fail to expose when they should.

Traders concerned about exposing their interests employ a variety of techniques to control their exposure. They use brokers to represent them anonymously, they split their orders, they use market orders instead of limit orders, and they selectively expose to those traders who are most likely to trade with them and least likely to front-run them.

Markets can help traders who are concerned about order exposure by adopting rules that protect them. Time precedence, in conjunction with an

▶ SOES Banditry

Some markets have rules designed to exclude parasitic traders. The response of the Nasdaq Stock Market to SOES banditry illustrates this approach.

SOES bandits were traders who used the Nasdaq Small Order Execution System (SOES) to submit orders designed to profit from very short-term price changes. The losers generally were Nasdaq dealers who adjusted their quotes a few seconds too slowly. These dealers naturally complained vociferously.

These high-speed trading strategies ultimately caused spreads to widen because dealers and other traders had to recover from other traders what they lost to the SOES bandits. Since Nasdaq wanted its markets to have narrow spreads, it tried to protect its dealers from SOES bandits. To this end, Nasdaq tried to classify SOES bandits as professional short-term traders and thereby restrict their access to the SOES system.

SOES banditry is no longer as controversial as it once was. Dealers are now more responsive to price changes. In addition, much more liquidity in Nasdaq now comes from public limit order traders than before. High-frequency proprietary traders undoubtedly exploit these traders when prices change quickly, but unlike Nasdaq dealers, public limit order traders are not organized to complain about it. ◀

economically significant minimum price increment, helps protect exposed orders by making front-running strategies less profitable.

Since regulators and exchanges can specify the size of the minimum price increment, they can control the degree to which traders expose their orders. Moreover, since traders clearly appear to be reluctant to display their large orders, exchanges that do not presently offer facilities to represent undisclosed orders may be able to obtain more order flow by offering these facilities. Without these facilities, traders tend to split their large orders into pieces.

18.8 SOME POINTS TO REMEMBER

- Buy-side traders must choose the best order submission strategies for the trading problems that they solve.
- The choice between limit order strategies and market order strategies depends on the price of liquidity, the size and price placement of standing limit orders in the trading system, and the consequences of failing to trade.
- In general, traders should offer liquidity when it is expensive and buy it when it is cheap. Experienced traders know when liquidity is expensive or cheap.
- Order exposure decisions are the most important decisions large traders make.
- Traders expose to encourage other traders to trade with them.
- Traders avoid exposing when they fear that other traders will front-run their orders or avoid trading with them.
- The art of trading large orders lies in knowing when and how to expose trading interest.

18.9 QUESTIONS FOR THOUGHT

1. Do defensive liquidity suppliers make prices more or less informative when they refrain from trading with well-informed traders?

2. Are parasitic traders truly parasitic? In the long run, do they make prices more informative, or do they make markets more liquid?

3. What is the difference between passive traders who wait for other traders to trade with them and reactive traders who trade in response to trading opportunities that other traders present them?

4. Why might exchanges want to protect the interests of large traders over smaller traders?

5. How would you construct a theoretical model to characterize the trade-off between limit prices and execution probabilities? How would you construct an econometric model to provide a statistical characterization of this trade-off? What would be the relative advantages and disadvantages of these two approaches to modeling limit order execution probabilities?

n the next two chapters, we provide broad characterizations of liquidity and of volatility. These concepts mean different things to different people. Consequently, people often are confused when they discuss them. The discussions in these chapters should give you a much more complete understanding of the origins of liquidity and volatility, and of their many dimensions.

Chapter 19 explains that liquidity is the successful outcome of a bilateral search in which buyers look for sellers and sellers look for buyers. This characterization of liquidity explains why liquidity has multiple attributes. The chapter concludes by showing how various types of traders cooperate and compete with each other to supply liquidity.

Chapter 20 breaks total volatility into fundamental and transitory components. Transitory volatility is closely related to the transaction costs that uninformed traders bear. Regulators therefore are quite interested in it. The chapter concludes with a discussion about how statisticians can discriminate between the two volatility components.

Part V
▷
Origins of Liquidity and Volatility

19

▷

Liquidity

▶ **Market Frictions**

Economists like liquid markets—securities markets, contract markets, product markets, and labor markets—because their models work better when they do not have to consider how transaction costs affect economic decisions. When confronted with transaction costs, people trade less often. If the costs are high enough, they do not trade at all.

Transaction costs in an economic system therefore are like frictions in a mechanical system. They both slow things down and can ultimately stop all activity. Economists therefore call transaction costs *market frictions*. ◀

▶ **The Most Important Bilateral Search**

For many people, finding a life partner is the most important bilateral search problem that they encounter. For others, it is finding a job. Although this book is not about how people form life relationships or obtain jobs, all bilateral search problems have similar structures. What you learn about how people trade securities and contracts may help you understand how people find partners and jobs. ◀

*L*iquidity is the ability to trade large size quickly, at low cost, when you want to trade. It is the most important characteristic of well-functioning markets.

Everyone likes liquidity. Traders like liquidity because it allows them to implement their trading strategies cheaply. Exchanges like liquidity because it attracts traders to their markets. Regulators like liquidity because liquid markets are often less volatile than illiquid ones.

Everyone in the markets has some affect on liquidity. Impatient traders take liquidity. Dealers, limit order traders, and some speculators offer liquidity. Brokers and exchanges organize liquidity.

Given its importance, you would expect that the term *liquidity* would be well defined and universally understood. In fact, liquidity means different things to different people. Traders and regulators talk about it all the time, but rarely are they clear about what they mean. Consequently, they often fail to communicate effectively about liquidity.

The confusion is due to the many dimensions of liquidity. When people think about liquidity, they may think about trading quickly, about trading large size, or about trading at low cost. Some dimensions of liquidity are more important to some people than to others. Unfortunately, people rarely distinguish among these dimensions when discussing liquidity.

In this chapter, you will see that liquidity—the ability to trade—is the object of a *bilateral search* in which buyers look for sellers and sellers look for buyers. The various liquidity dimensions are related to each other through the mechanics of this bilateral search. Traders must understand these relations in order to trade effectively.

Understanding liquidity is one of the primary objectives of this book. In this chapter, we will carefully define liquidity and its various dimensions. We then will identify the types of traders who supply liquidity and discuss how they compete with each other.

These discussions will be especially useful to you if you are a trader who needs to know where to look for liquidity. They also will be useful to you if you intend to offer liquidity. In that case, you must understand with whom you will compete so that you can predict when you can expect to be successful.

You also need to understand liquidity to measure it effectively. Many traders and regulators regularly measure liquidity. Traders measure liquidity to determine whether their trading strategies are sensible, given the available liquidity. They also measure liquidity to evaluate the service they obtain from their brokers. Brokers likewise measure liquidity to evaluate the service they obtain from their dealers. Regulators measure liquidity to determine which market structures are best. No one can answer these questions, however, without clearly understanding what they are measuring. As a rule, you cannot measure something that you cannot define. The concepts

▶ A Unilateral Search for a 35mm Camera

Fred wants to buy a specific camera model at a low price. His time is worth 30 dollars an hour.

Fred goes onto the Internet to search for the best price among mail-order photography stores that offer the camera. After five minutes of searching at A1ePhoto's site, he discovers that they will sell the camera for 112 dollars. After another five minutes, he discovers that BNDPicture will sell it for 109 dollars. He decides to search again. Six minutes later, he finds that CDBirD will sell it for 119 dollars. No bargain there.

Should Fred search more? He estimates that if he finds a lower price, it would be no lower than 99 dollars (i.e., no more than 10 dollars less than his current best price). He also estimates that the probability that he will find a price that low at less than 0.25. Fred's expected gain from searching again therefore is less than 2.50 dollars (10 × 0.25). Since it appears that each search takes at least five minutes, his expected cost of searching again is more than 2.50 dollars, given the 30-dollar value he places on an hour of his time. Since the expected cost is greater than the expected gain, Fred decides to stop searching. He buys the camera from BNDPicture for 109 dollars. ◀

presented in this chapter provide a basis for the measurement methods presented in chapter 21.

19.1 THE SEARCH FOR LIQUIDITY

Liquidity is the object of bilateral search. In a *bilateral search*, buyers search for sellers, and sellers search for buyers. When a buyer finds a seller who will trade at mutually acceptable terms, the buyer has found liquidity. Likewise, when a seller finds a buyer who will trade at mutually acceptable terms, the seller has found liquidity. To understand trading, you must understand the strategies that traders use to conduct these bilateral searches.

Bilateral searches are similar to—but more complicated than—unilateral searches. You will find bilateral search strategies easier to understand if you first understand unilateral search strategies.

19.1.1 Unilateral Searches

In a unilateral search, you actively search for a good match—a good price, for example. The main decision that you must make is when to stop the search. The general rule is to continue searching as long as the expected benefit from an additional inquiry is greater than the expected cost of the inquiry. The expected benefit depends on the probability that you will find a better match than you have already found. As the search proceeds, this probability declines as you find progressively better matches. The expected benefit also depends on how much better unfound matches might be than the best match you have already found. As the search proceeds, the possible improvement declines as you find progressively better matches. At some point, your expected benefit from an additional inquiry becomes less than the cost of the inquiry. You then stop the search and pick the best match that you have found.

If searching is expensive, you will often stop before you have found the best possible match. You may later discover that you could have arranged a

▶ The Economics of Divorce

Some people divorce because they learn that they have arranged a poor match. They either learn that their relationship did not develop as they expected, or that their opportunities to form other relationships were better than they expected.

Other people divorce because they are not mature enough to accept that even when they search optimally, they generally will not arrange a perfect match. When they later see other matches that they believe would have been better for them, they forget that they stopped searching because it was too costly. They also forget that the search for a spouse is a bilateral search. In particular, they forget that they cannot arrange every match that they might want to arrange.

In either event, people who initiate divorce presumably believe that the benefits from searching again, or from being single, are greater than the substantial emotional, social, and financial costs of not breaking their matches. Unfortunately, many subsequently learn that their expectations were poorly founded. ◀

▶ Exchanges Are Search Engines

A *search engine* is a system that collects information in which people may be interested. It allows people to search through that information at a low cost.

In the previous example, had Fred been able to use a search engine to locate the best price for his camera, he might have discovered that GR8 Film and Photo is offering the camera for 87 dollars. Search engines make markets more competitive by lowering the costs of searching.

Exchanges and electronic quotation services collect information about who wants to trade. They then organize it so that traders can easily find the best trading opportunities. They are search engines that allow buyers to cheaply find sellers who are offering the lowest prices and sellers to cheaply find buyers who are bidding the highest prices. ◀

▶ Librarians Are Information Brokers

Librarians help researchers solve unilateral search problems. Their training and experience help them make good decisions about where to look first for the information that their clients seek. ◀

better match had you known more about the alternatives. An optimal search produces the best possible result only if you are lucky enough to find it.

If you knew ahead of time where to find the best possible match, you would of course go there first. In that case, the costs of searching would be very low because you already know the outcome. In general, you will get a better outcome when your costs of searching are low.

Whether your search produces a good outcome or not depends to some extent on luck and to some extent on your skill as a searcher. Good searchers know the best places to look for what they want, and they look there first. A good trader knows where to look first for liquidity.

19.1.2 Bilateral Searches

Bilateral searches differ in two respects from unilateral searches. First, you may search either actively or passively. Active searchers try to find matches. Passive searchers wait for others to find them. Second, whatever your search strategy, you may not always be able to return to the best match that you identified during the course of your search. While you continue your search, so does the other side. When you decide that you want to return to your best match, you may discover that it is no longer available. These differences make bilateral search strategies significantly more complicated than unilateral search strategies.

The stopping rule for an active bilateral search is the same as for a unilateral search: You should stop when the expected benefit from an additional search is less than the expected cost of an additional search. Now, however, the cost of continuing to search must include the potential loss of your previous best match. This additional cost suggests that you will try to stop searching sooner when engaged in an active bilateral search than in an otherwise identical unilateral search. Your search may not end sooner, however: Your best match may no longer be available when you want to stop searching. In that case, you will have to continue your search.

The search strategies that traders employ to find liquidity vary by their trading objective. Impatient traders generally search actively. Patient traders usually are passive searchers. They wait for impatient traders to find them. Since impatient traders initiate trades, we say that they demand liquidity. Patient traders supply liquidity.

Passive traders often display their interest in trading to make it easier for active traders to find them. They offer limit orders, quote markets, post indi-

▶ **Sometimes You Can't Go Back**

Although John probably will not admit it, he has been looking for a wife for the last 10 years. As he sees his friends getting married, he realizes that he must get serious about his search. John fondly remembers that Ruth, a woman he dated seven years ago, would make an especially good match. Not surprisingly, she is no longer available. Although she liked John, she later met and married Boaz.

Even if Ruth were still available, she might not have welcomed John's renewed interest. How people value a match often depends upon how they conduct their searches. Ruth may never be able to trust John again because he once lost interest in her. ◀

cations on bulletin boards, or simply advise their brokers. Passive traders who most widely display their interests typically trade before those who do not.

In many markets, passive traders commit to trade at prices that they post. These commitments increase the probability that an active trader will call upon them. Active traders prefer to call upon such traders because they are confident that they can arrange trades with them and thereby reduce their overall search costs.

Problems that large traders encounter when they expose their orders often complicate their liquidity search strategies. Large traders generally do not like to show that they want to trade because they fear that front runners will trade ahead of them or that liquidity suppliers will retreat from before them. Large traders therefore either actively search for liquidity among traders who post firm quotes or become passive searchers who do not display their trading interests. Such passive traders have *latent* trading demands that active searchers must discover. Table 19-1 provides a summary of the different types of displayed and undisclosed liquidity.

Brokers often help traders solve their search problems. Brokers search more efficiently than their clients do because they know more about who

▶ **Order Exposure in the Marriage Market**

Many people are unwilling to expose that they are looking for a spouse for fear of appearing needy. Rightly or wrongly, people may make inferences about your position from how you search.

Matchmakers are marriage brokers who help solve this problem by confidentially proposing matches among people who indicate that they are interested in getting married. Matchmakers must know their clients well to propose successful matches. ◀

TABLE 19-1.
Types of Displayed and Undisclosed Liquidity

TYPE	EXAMPLES	SEARCH STRATEGY
Displayed quotes and orders	Dealer quotes Exposed orders in open limit order books	Take it
Not-displayed at market venue	Undisclosed order size in limit order books Undisclosed orders held by floor brokers	Offer to trade
Displayed indications	Order indications	Ask
Not-displayed at broker-dealers	Agency orders held by brokers in the upstairs market Liquidity dealers will offer but not display	Ask
Not displayed at buy side	Orders in buy-side desk order blotters that have not yet been sent to a broker, dealer, or exchange	Ask Use Liquidnet
Latent	Liquidity that buy-side traders will offer when asked	Ask

Source: This table expands upon a classification first created by George Sofianos of Goldman Sachs.

Dance Strategies

In many respects, the search for liquidity is similar to how teenagers find partners at a dance. Dancers employ three strategies to arrange their dances. Those most interested in dancing ask potential partners whether they would like to dance.

Other dancers stand on the side of the dance floor, tapping their feet and bouncing up and down to indicate that they are interested in dancing. These dancers display their interest, but they wait passively until others ask them to dance. They would have a greater chance of dancing if they were willing to commit to dancing if asked. Most, however, want to judge the partner before accepting the invitation.

Wallflowers use the last strategy. They lean against the wall, seemingly ignoring the dance floor. They may want to dance, but they will not ask to dance and/or display their interest. They may dance when asked, but only if they like the match. ◀

would want to trade. Large traders use brokers to arrange their trades to avoid displaying their orders to other traders.

The costs of finding liquidity vary substantially across instruments and often through time for a given instrument. Liquidity is easiest to find when many people on both sides of the market are looking for it at the same time. Widely held instruments therefore usually trade in very liquid markets. Instruments that are in the news and therefore are the subject of widespread interest also tend to trade in very liquid markets. Liquidity tends to dry up when people are paying attention to other things. For example, trading large size can be very difficult near holidays, when many traders are not working.

19.2 LIQUIDITY DIMENSIONS

Searches are productive processes in which searchers use inputs to produce outputs. In the search for liquidity, the primary input is the time spent searching. The main outputs are good prices and adequate sizes.

We can characterize the expected outcome of a search problem as a production function that explains how the inputs to the search are related to the expected products of the search. This characterization of the search problem allows us to easily recognize trade-offs among various dimensions of liquidity. In particular, when traders are willing to search longer, they can generally expect to find more size at a given price, or a better price for a given size. Likewise, when traders want to trade more size, they can expect to obtain a worse price or spend more time searching. Finally, when traders offer better prices to other traders, they can expect to find greater size or spend less time searching. Table 19-2 summarizes these trade-offs.

These inputs and outputs of the bilateral search process correspond to the following three dimensions of liquidity to which traders commonly refer:

- *Immediacy* refers to how quickly trades of a given size can be arranged at a given cost. Traders generally use market orders to demand immediate trades.
- *Width* refers to the cost of doing a trade of a given size. For small trades, traders usually identify width with the bid/ask spread. It also includes brokerage commissions. Width is the cost per unit of liquidity. Traders often refer to market width by the term *market breadth*.
- *Depth* refers to the size of a trade that can be arranged at a given cost. Depth is measured in units available at a given price of liquidity.

TABLE 19-2.
Liquidity Trade-offs

CHANGE	HOLD CONSTANT	IMPLICATION
Spend more time searching	Size of trade	Expect to find a better average price
	Price you are willing to pay or receive	Expect to find more size
Increase size of desired trade	Time spent searching	Expect to find a worse average price
	Price	Expect to spend more time searching
Offer a better price	Size of trade	Expect to spend less time searching
	Time spent searching	Expect to find more size

Breadth and depth are closely related. Mathematicians say that they are *duals* to each other. Traders who want to minimize the cost of trading a given size solve a problem that is essentially identical to that of traders who want to maximize the size they trade at a given cost. The strategies that best solve both problems are the same. In both cases, traders must search efficiently. Depth—the size that you can trade at a given price—and breadth—the price at which you can trade a given size—therefore summarize essentially the same information about liquidity conditions.

These three dimensions of liquidity help us understand why traders are often confused about the nature of liquidity. Impatient traders focus primarily on immediacy and its cost, which for small trades is represented by width. Large traders focus on depth. Different traders focus on different aspects of the search problem.

To summarize, liquidity is the ability to quickly trade large size at low cost. "Quickly" refers to immediacy; "size," to depth; and "cost," to width.

Since liquidity is the ability to trade, we can characterize liquidity as a function that tells us the probability of trading a given size at a given price, given the time we are willing to put into our search. This characterization allows us to consider many other factors besides size, price, and time that affect the probability of trading. Some of the more important factors involve the following issues:

- Why do you want to trade? Traders are far more willing to trade with uninformed traders than with well-informed traders. Liquidity thus is different for traders who are known to be uninformed than for those who are known as informed traders. Markets may be liquid for the former but not for the latter. In practice, traders often do not know who is well informed. Traders who can convince others that they are not well informed generally obtain better prices or more size.

- What is being traded? Instruments that interest large numbers of traders trade in much more liquid markets than do instruments that interest only a few traders.

- How well do traders know fundamental values? Instruments for which fundamental values are not well known tend to trade in illiquid markets because liquidity suppliers are afraid that they might trade with better-informed traders.

- When is the trade to be arranged? Trades are harder to arrange when markets are closed than when they are open. Markets are also less liquid when traders suspect that some traders have information that is not yet in the prices.

- What are other traders doing? It is easier to buy while prices are falling than when prices are rising.

- Is there an imbalance between displayed buying and selling orders? Imbalances often indicate that liquidity will be cheap for one side and expensive for the other side.

- Who is trading? All other things held constant, a good trader is more likely to complete a trade than is a poor trader. Good traders know how to display their interest, who wants to trade, and how to approach traders.

Traders, regulators, and academics often refer to a fourth dimension of liquidity called market *resiliency*. This dimension also is related to the bilateral search, but much less directly than are immediacy, width, and depth. *Resiliency* refers to how quickly prices revert to former levels after they change in response to large order flow imbalances initiated by uninformed traders. We will discuss it further below when we discuss the role that value traders play in offering liquidity.

19.3 THE WHO, HOW, AND WHY OF LIQUIDITY

We now will review who offers liquidity, why they offer liquidity, and the relation between their trading strategies and the various dimensions of liquidity. This review summarizes discussions about the various liquidity-supplying traders who appear in chapters 13–18. It provides an integrated view of all aspects of market liquidity.

19.3.1 Overview

Traders offer liquidity whenever they trade in response to orders that others initiate. Liquidity-offering traders may be market makers, block dealers, buy-side institutions, or individual investors. Market makers and block dealers offer liquidity when they fill marketable orders or do customer facilitations. Buy-side institutions and individual investors typically offer liquidity when they submit standing limit orders. They also offer liquidity when they use market orders to trade in response to requests for liquidity that others make. Order type therefore is not always the best indicator of whether a trader is offering liquidity or taking it. In general, traders offer liquidity when they want to exploit opportunities that liquidity-demanding traders create when they demand to trade.

Traders do not need to display their orders to offer liquidity. For example, a trader who submits an undisplayed order to an electronic trading system offers liquidity that traders can discover by submitting suitably priced orders. Likewise, a trader who will trade only if asked by a broker also offers liquidity. In both cases, these traders allow other people to trade, but they show their offers under very limited circumstances.

Traders offer liquidity because they hope to profit from selling at high prices and buying at low prices. Whether their trading is profitable or not depends on whether their orders execute, and on how prices change after their orders execute.

We can classify liquidity suppliers into two groups according to their primary motive for trading. Dealers and value traders trade primarily because they hope to profit. Dealers hope to profit from offering liquidity. Value traders hope to profit from speculating successfully on their information about fundamental values. These traders are *passive liquidity suppliers* because they generally will not trade unless impatient traders demand liquidity. Other traders offer liquidity only to lower the cost of trades that they already intend to make, but which they are in no hurry to complete. Such traders may want to trade to speculate, invest, hedge, exchange assets, or gamble. We will call these traders *precommitted liquidity suppliers* because they would demand liquidity if they did not offer it. Precommitted liquidity suppliers may eventually demand liquidity if their limit orders do not fill.

In the remainder of this section, we consider how market makers, block dealers, value traders, precommitted traders, and arbitrageurs contribute to market liquidity. Here, as before, we treat these traders as though they use only their single characteristic trading strategy. In practice, most traders use multiple trading strategies.

By focusing on characteristic strategies, we can analyze complex behaviors by breaking them down into simple components. If you are a trader, these analytic skills will help you to attribute your profits more accurately to the various strategies that you pursue. You therefore should be able to better identify when you have a comparative advantage.

19.3.2 Market Makers

Market makers are dealers who allow their impatient customers to trade at bid and ask prices that the market makers quote. Market makers often trade very frequently. They try to buy after they sell, and vice versa. They avoid large inventory positions because they generally do not know the fundamental values of the instruments that they trade very well. Large inventory positions expose them to losses if the market moves against them. Market makers simply try to discover the prices that produce balanced two-sided order flows.

Market makers primarily supply liquidity in the form of immediacy. They usually quote narrow markets, but only for small size. If asked to trade large size, they will quote wide markets to protect themselves from losses to well-informed traders.

Market makers are passive traders. They generally wait until their customers want to trade with them. They use their quotes to solicit trades that will help them reduce large inventory positions. If they are especially uncomfortable with their inventory positions, they may demand liquidity from other traders.

Market makers supply liquidity only when they are confident that they can recover from uninformed traders what they expect to lose to informed traders. They naturally try to avoid informed traders. Since they generally do not know their customers well, they occasionally trade with informed traders.

Market makers trade most effectively when they can identify whether they are trading with well-informed traders. They also have an advantage as order-anticipating speculators (see chapter 11) because they generally see more order flow than other traders.

Market makers need capital to finance their inventories. The capital available to them thus limits their ability to offer liquidity. Because market making is very risky, investors generally do not like to invest in market-making operations. Investors are less concerned about inventory risk—most of which is diversifiable—than about trader incentives. Financiers know that most people do not work as hard when working for others as when working for themselves. Since market making requires continuous attention in order to avoid significant losses, incentives are especially important. Market makers therefore often cannot easily raise capital by borrowing or by issuing equity.

Market-making firms that have significant external financing typically have excellent risk-management systems that prevent their dealers from generating large losses. These systems tightly limit the capital that each dealer can commit. Market-making firms also ensure that their traders' compensation contracts reward them for making profits and penalize them for generating losses. These contracts give traders equity-like positions and thereby align their interests with those of the firm's shareholders and bondholders.

Many exchanges and dealer networks require that their dealers meet minimum capital standards in an effort to make their markets more liquid. The strategy is not necessarily successful, however. Dealers who have more capital can offer more liquidity, but they may not choose to do so. Unless compelled to provide liquidity, dealers provide liquidity only to the extent that they feel comfortable. If they face too much adverse selection from informed traders, no amount of capital will make them willing to supply liquidity. Capital adequacy regulations therefore only ensure that dealers can offer liquidity if they desire to do so.

19.3.3 Block Dealers

Block dealers are traders who offer liquidity to clients who want to trade large positions. The positions may be large blocks of a single security or contract, or they may be portfolios of many instruments. Block dealers offer liquidity when they buy or sell the positions that their customers offer to them. Traders sometimes call these trades *facilitations* because the block dealers facilitate their customers' trading.

Since block dealers take large positions, they are especially concerned about trading with well-informed traders. To avoid this risk, they carefully consider with whom they trade. Block dealers usually know their clients well and facilitate trades only with clients they believe will not hurt them. Since block dealers need to study why their clients want to trade, they often do not trade quickly. They generally do not want to supply immediacy because impatient traders are often well informed.

Block dealers offer liquidity to their customers in the form of depth. By knowing their clients well, they can offer to trade much larger size than market makers will offer. They offer to trade only with clients they think are not well informed, however. Block dealers have no desire to facilitate trades for well-informed traders.

Block dealers need much capital to run their businesses. They must therefore have strong risk-management systems to ensure that traders do not take foolish positions. These systems tend to slow their trading. Since holding large blocks is quite risky, block dealers tend to work for large firms that can spread their inventory risks over many positions.

Block dealers have an advantage over market makers when offering liquidity to large traders because they know more about who wants to trade than do market makers. Market makers have an advantage over block dealers when offering liquidity to small traders because they can trade much quicker and because they know more about what prices will produce two-sided order flows over short intervals.

The best block dealers know how to trade out of their positions. Either they break them up and distribute them into the market, or they place them with other clients. Those who distribute their blocks must be excellent traders. Those who place their blocks must be excellent salesmen.

19.3.4 Value Traders

Value traders are informed traders who collect as much information about fundamental values as is economically sensible. They then use their information to form opinions about security and contract values. Value traders trade when prices differ substantially from their estimates of value.

Value traders typically trade only when they are supplying liquidity. To understand why they supply liquidity, consider the two scenarios under which prices may differ from fundamental values. In the first scenario, fundamental values differ from prices when fundamental values have changed but prices have not yet adjusted. Fundamental values change when events occur that change valuations. For example, the value of a factory will drop substantially if it burns down. Prices change to reflect changes in fundamental value when traders receive and digest news about events that change valuations. The traders who act on this information are news traders (see chapter 10) because, by definition, they trade on news that represents changes in the stock of information.

In the second scenario, fundamental values differ from prices when prices change but fundamental values have not. Prices often change when uninformed traders demand liquidity when trading. Such traders generally have an impact upon prices because dealers are unable to distinguish between informed and uninformed traders, because dealers require substantial rewards for taking large inventory positions, and because traders often require substantial price incentives to give up positions that they like or for which they have unrealized capital gains. Value traders exploit these opportunities when they buy underpriced instruments or sell overpriced instruments. When making these trades, value traders trade in response to the demands that other traders make for liquidity. Value traders therefore are liquidity suppliers.

Value traders are the ultimate suppliers of liquidity. When nobody else will trade, value traders will trade if the price is right. They supply liquidity in the form of depth. They are best able to supply depth because they are best able to solve the adverse selection problem. They solve it by knowing values better than anybody else does. They generally do not care with whom they trade as long as they are confident that they have all available fundamental information.

Value traders are usually slow traders. They must be very confident that they know everything relevant to estimating values. They therefore tend to trade after uninformed demands for liquidity have caused prices to change.

Value traders often compete with each other to supply liquidity. Frequently some event may cause many value traders to try to trade at the same time. In that case, the quickest value traders will be the most profitable because they will incur the lowest transaction costs.

Value traders make markets *resilient*. Markets are resilient when trading by uninformed traders has little effect on prices, and when the effects of their trading on prices are very short-lived. Markets are resilient when value traders are well capitalized, well informed, and willing to trade. Value traders cause prices to return to fundamental values after liquidity demanders cause them to diverge.

The prices at which value traders will buy and sell constitute the *outside spread*. Outside spreads tend to be much wider than market maker spreads because value traders generally trade much larger sizes and because they must fund their research costs. Although value traders trade with better-informed traders less often than do market makers, value traders expose themselves to greater adverse selection risk because they trade much larger sizes that they often must hold for much longer periods. Value traders lose only to news traders who are better informed than they are about the latest news concerning fundamental values. They also lose to other value traders who estimate values more accurately than they do.

Market makers who acquire inventory positions with which they are especially uncomfortable often lay off those positions onto value traders. Such layoffs occur after market makers have bought inventory from uninformed traders while lowering prices. The low prices may attract value traders who buy the market makers' inventories. Layoffs also occur after market makers have sold inventory to uninformed traders while raising prices. In that case, the high prices attract value traders who sell inventory to the market makers.

19.3.5 Precommitted Traders

Precommitted traders offer liquidity to obtain better prices for trades that they would like to complete. These traders typically offer limit orders in an attempt to buy at the bid or sell at the ask. They are successful only if their orders trade. If the market moves away from their orders, they may lose the opportunity to make a favorable trade, or they may ultimately make the trade at much worse prices. To avoid this risk, precommitted traders place their orders close to the market. (If they were especially afraid of not trading, these traders would demand liquidity with market orders.) Precommitted traders therefore are often the most aggressive suppliers of liquidity. Bid/ask spreads are small in public auction markets with many precommitted traders.

Precommitted traders can drive dealers out of a market because they can, and often do, price their orders more aggressively than dealers place their quotes. Dealers must quote spreads that allow them to recover their costs of doing business. Since precommitted traders do not face these costs, they can drive dealers out of business.

Dealers have an advantage over precommitted traders, however. Dealers generally can adjust their quotes faster than precommitted traders can adjust their limit orders. If they have limit order books, they also can decide whether they want to fill an incoming marketable order or allow it to fill with orders on their limit order books. Dealers naturally will make these decisions to their advantage. Limit order traders therefore often will find that they trade when they wish they had not, or that they did not trade when they wish they had.

Precommitted limit order traders supply liquidity in the form of immediacy. When they are especially aggressive, they may offer very narrow spreads. They typically do not offer significant depth, however, because large traders are reluctant to display their standing limit orders. Those who do display their large orders invite traders to employ quote-matching strategies against them.

19.3.6 Arbitrageurs

Arbitrageurs are traders who trade on price discrepancies between two or more markets. The effect of their trading is to connect demands for liquidity made in one market with offers of liquidity made in another market. Arbitrageurs therefore are not suppliers of liquidity but porters of liquidity. They demand liquidity in the market where it is most available and supply that liquidity in the market where traders demand it.

Since arbitrage is generally a low-risk strategy, arbitrageurs can move substantial liquidity from one market to another. Arbitrageurs increase the depth in a market by bringing in more liquidity from other markets when traders demand it.

Arbitrageurs are essentially market makers who connect buyers in one market with sellers in another market at same time. In contrast, dealers are market makers who connect buyers in one market to sellers in the same market who arrive at different times. Thus, arbitrageurs and dealers compete with each other.

19.3.7 Summary

To some extent, all liquidity suppliers compete with each other. Each type, however, specializes in a niche to which it is best suited to offer liquidity. Their advantages generally depend on their information about fundamental values or other traders.

- Market makers have little information about fundamental values or their clients. They specialize in offering immediacy to small traders.
- Block dealers know a lot about their clients. They offer depth to uninformed clients.
- Value traders know more than everyone else does about fundamental values. They generally do not care much about with whom they trade. Their confidence in fundamental values allows them to be the ultimate suppliers of depth.
- Precommitted traders trade for reasons other than to supply liquidity. Since they already intend to trade, they do not care much about with whom they trade. They typically supply immediacy.
- Arbitrageurs are well informed about relative instrument values. When their arbitrages involve very low risk, they ensure that traders can access the depth in any market that trades the instruments that interest them.

Table 19-3 presents a summary of the traders who offer liquidity.

19.4 AN ILLUSTRATIVE EXAMPLE

This section presents an example that illustrates many of the principles discussed in the previous section. Although the example is fictitious, the scenario described regularly occurs in many markets.

Suppose that an impatient uninformed trader wants to sell a large block of XYZ stock on the floor of the New York Stock Exchange. The trader is demanding more liquidity than traders can easily find there. He therefore will have a substantial effect on XYZ's stock price.

Although we assume that the trader is uninformed, the trader probably thinks that he is a well-informed trader who is trying to profit from material information that will soon become public. Otherwise, he would have been foolish to demand so much liquidity on the floor. If he knew that he was not well informed, and if he still wanted to do the trade, he should have traded using a less aggressive order submission strategy.

The trader sends his order to Florence, his floor broker on the floor of Exchange. When the order arrives, the XYZ NYSE specialist is quoting a tight market of 40 bid, offered at 40.05 for small size. The specialist's quote offers immediacy in a tight market for small size.

When Florence presents the order at the specialist's post, the specialist is the only trader standing there. Florence tells him that she has a large order to sell XYZ and asks for his assistance to fill it. The specialist asks about the order, and Florence tells him that she knows only that her client wants

TABLE 19-3.
Liquidity Suppliers

CHARACTERISTIC TRADER	CHARACTERISTIC STRATEGY	TYPICAL METHOD OF OFFERING LIQUIDITY	EFFECT ON LIQUIDITY	INFORMATION ADVANTAGES	PRIMARY COMPETITION	MOST OFTEN LOSES TO
Market makers	Complete quick round-trips without assuming much inventory risk	Publish quotes that anonymouse traders take	Offer immediacy for small size at narrow spreads	See order flow; can selectively commit to trading	Precommitted traders Arbitrageurs	Well-informed traders
Block dealers	Facilitate large trades for clients	Offer quotes on demand to known clients	Supply depth	Know with whom they trade	Market makers Value traders	Well-informed traders
Value traders	Buy and sell misvalued instruments	Trade with limit and market orders when prices differ from fundamental values	Ultimate depth suppliers; make markets resilient	Know values well	Other value traders	Better-informed traders
Precommitted traders	Offer liquidity to obtain better prices for trades they want to do	Offer standing limit orders	Offer immediacy for small size at narrow spreads	None	Market makers	Well-informed traders Quote matchers
Arbitrageurs	Trade on price discrepancies between two or more markets	Use limit or market orders	Increase market depth	Know relative values well	Market makers	Other arbitrageurs

it filled quickly. Under the circumstances, both the specialist and Florence assume that the client is well informed.

The specialist shows Florence that there is insufficient size in the book to fill the order. The specialist then tells her about some other floor brokers he suspects have clients who are interested in XYZ. They then page those traders. When they arrive at the post, Florence determines the extent of their interest. Some of the floor traders hold working orders issued by their clients. Others contact their clients to obtain instructions. Some of these clients express interest when presented with the trading opportunity. Given the information that the floor brokers collect and reveal, it becomes apparent that the price will have to drop to 37 dollars to fill the order. Florence agrees, and the specialist arranges the following trades.

The specialist first matches the large order with orders from traders on the book at prices between 37 and 40. These traders include some pre-committed traders and some value traders. They supply immediacy directly to the large trader, but they do not offer much size. The specialist matches them all at 37 dollars.

The floor brokers then arrange to fill some of the order for their clients at 37 dollars. Since the specialist brought these traders together, he acts as a broker for these trades. He will not collect a commission for his efforts, however. Brokering such trades is a responsibility of his position and a favor he does to please floor brokers. In any event, all he did was tell Florence about brokers who had previously inquired about the stock. The floor brokers' clients supply substantial depth to the large trader, but it comes at substantial cost.

Finally, the specialist buys the remainder of the order for his own account at 37 dollars. The specialist offers depth, but only at substantial cost.

The specialist now holds significantly more of XYZ stock than he wants to hold. To sell inventory and to avoid buying more, he lowers the market quote to 37 bid for moderate size, 37.30 offered for moderate size. The specialist bids for moderate rather than small size because he does not want other traders to suspect that the buy side of the book is empty. If traders suspect that they can drive the price down, they may try to do so, which could seriously hurt the specialist with his large long inventory position. The specialist hopes that the substantially lower prices will attract more buyers than sellers.

The specialist is using his quotes to solicit liquidity for his own account. There are no orders on the book on the buy side and none on the book on the sell side below 40 dollars.

Very soon afterward, an arbitrageur in the options markets sends a market order to buy moderate size through the SuperDot order-routing system. The specialist fills the arbitrageur's order from his own inventory at 37.30. At the same time in the options market, the arbitrageur sells XYZ calls and buys an equal number of XYZ puts struck at the same price and expiring on the same date. (This combination of long puts and short calls produces a short *synthetic stock* position that has essentially the same risk characteristics as a short stock position. The arbitrageur thus buys and sells positions that are essentially the same.)

Although the arbitrageur demands immediacy from the specialist, she also supplies depth to the specialist, and therefore indirectly to the large trader. The arbitrageur uses a market order because she wants to trade quickly so that she can synchronize her stock and options trades. She synchronizes her trades to reduce the risk in her arbitrage.

The buyers of the calls and the sellers of the puts also indirectly supply liquidity to the large uninformed trader through the intermediation of the arbitrageur and the specialist.

Hours, or perhaps days, later a value trader uses a market order to buy moderate size from the specialist at 38.25 when the stock is quoted for 38.10 bid, 38.25 asked. The value trader supplies liquidity (depth) directly to the specialist and indirectly to the large uninformed trader. The value trader uses a market order to demand immediacy, perhaps because other tasks compete for his time. The value traders help restore prices to their former levels. They make markets resilient.

Days, or perhaps weeks, later, the specialist is again quoting prices near 40 and his inventory is near its target level.

In this example, the large trader lost money because he traded too aggressively. His aggressive trading fooled the market into thinking that he was well informed. When traders concluded otherwise, prices rose. Depending on what he did with the money, he probably would have been better off had he not traded. He certainly would have been better off had he been able to convince other traders that he was uninformed.

19.5 SUMMARY

Liquidity is often discussed but rarely well understood. The confusion has its origins in the complexity of the bilateral search problem, in which buyers search for sellers and sellers search for buyers.

Liquidity is the object of this bilateral search. It is the ability to trade large size quickly at low transaction cost. This simple definition reflects the complexity of the concept. Liquidity has size, time, and cost dimensions. Traders generally refer to these respective dimensions as depth, immediacy, and width.

Impatient small traders easily solve the bilateral search problem because they typically trade at exchanges and in dealer networks that assemble information about who wants to trade and the prices at which they will trade. These trading systems act as search engines. To increase the probability that liquidity-demanding traders will trade with them, most liquidity suppliers in these systems provide firm quotes and orders. Small liquidity-demanding traders therefore need to search only for the best price. Order-driven trading systems that use price priority rules in their matching systems provide this service automatically.

Patient small traders offer limit orders, hoping that someone will find them. This trading strategy is more complex than simple market order strategies because their orders may not fill. When they do fill, however, they typically get better prices than do market order traders.

For large traders, the bilateral search problem is more complex. Many large traders are reluctant to expose their orders. Markets for large size therefore are not very transparent. Search costs can be high, and search strategies may greatly affect the ultimate execution prices.

Five types of traders offer liquidity. Market makers offer immediacy at narrow spreads to small anonymous traders. Block dealers offer depth to large uninformed traders. Value traders offer depth to all traders. Precommitted traders offer immediacy at very narrow spreads in an effort to lower the costs of trades that they already intend to do. Arbitrageurs move liquidity from one market to another market and thereby ensure that traders can find depth wherever they trade.

19.6 SOME POINTS TO REMEMBER

- Liquidity is the object of a bilateral search problem.
- Liquidity is the ability to trade when you want to trade, at low cost.
- Brokers and exchanges organize liquidity that traders offer.
- Liquidity has several related dimensions.
- Market makers primarily supply immediacy.
- Upstairs traders primarily supply depth.
- Value traders make markets resilient.

19.7 QUESTIONS FOR THOUGHT

1. How do the classified ads in a newspaper help traders search for each other?
2. How does eBay help traders find each other?
3. What are the advantages and disadvantages of open limit order books? Should exchanges have open limit order books?
4. Can traders spend too much time looking for liquidity?
5. Can a buyer and a seller find each other if neither is willing to display his interest?
6. If the cost of searching drops, will merchants charge lower prices on average? Does your answer depend on whether merchants can cultivate reputations for low prices?
7. Do market orders always demand liquidity?
8. In the example of section 19.4, why did the large trader not trade directly with the value trader?
9. Does the fact that securities are fungible make the bilateral search for liquidity qualitatively different from bilateral searches for life partners or for dance partners?
10. If you were a market regulator, how could you make markets more liquid?
11. Which dimension of liquidity do you believe is the most important? Which dimension is most important to large traders? Which dimension is most important to small traders? Which dimension should regulators most care about?

20
▷
Volatility

Volatility is the tendency for prices to change unexpectedly. Prices change in response to new information about values and in response to the demands of impatient traders for liquidity.

Volatility itself changes through time. Sometimes prices are very volatile. Other times, prices are very stable and hardly change at all. Large price changes sometimes occur in short time intervals. Regulators and traders refer to episodes of such price changes as *episodic volatility*. Episodic volatility concerns many people because it can be quite scary.

Volatility, risk, and profit are closely related. Every drop in prices creates losses for traders who have long positions and profits for traders with short positions. Likewise, every price rise causes losses for traders with short positions and profits for traders with long positions. Traders therefore are very interested in volatility because it can have a significant impact on their wealth. If risk scares you or profits interest you, you need to know about volatility.

Volatility especially concerns options traders. Option contract values depend critically on the volatility of the underlying instrument. Options traders must be able to measure and predict volatilities in order to trade profitably. Both skills require that they understand well the origins of volatility.

Technical traders who try to interpret trading volumes also pay close attention to volatility because volumes and volatility are often correlated. The relation between the two variables is not simple, however. It depends on the origins of the volatility.

Volatility greatly concerns regulators. Excessive volatility may indicate that markets are not functioning well. Since accurate prices are extremely important in the economy, regulators pay close attention to the markets when prices are highly volatile. They are especially attentive when markets crash.

In this chapter, we identify the origins of volatility and distinguish between its two types. *Fundamental volatility* is due to unanticipated changes in instrument values, and *transitory volatility* is due to trading activity by uninformed traders.

The distinction is important both for traders and for regulators. Traders must distinguish between the two volatility types in order to accurately predict future volatility, the profitability of dealing strategies, and transaction costs. Regulators must distinguish between them because they cannot have any lasting effect on fundamental volatility, but they often can substantially affect transitory volatility. Depending on the policies that regulators adopt, they may decrease or increase transitory volatility.

We start this short chapter with discussions about the origins of the two types of volatility. We then finish by considering how to distinguish between them. Chapter 28 considers what regulators can do about volatility when it appears excessive to them.

20.1 FUNDAMENTAL VOLATILITY

Since economies use prices to allocate resources, it is very important that prices reflect fundamental values. Values change when the fundamental factors that determine them change. Prices therefore should change when people learn that fundamental factors have unexpectedly changed. Such price changes contribute to fundamental volatility.

When new information about changes in fundamental values is common knowledge, prices may change without any trading. For example, suppose that an unexpected killer frost descends upon Florida overnight. The morning news will undoubtedly report the event. The next day, orange juice futures contracts will open at a much higher price than the last price of the previous trading day.

When only a few people know new information about changes in fundamental values, prices generally will change on high trading volumes. The well-informed traders will trade on their information. The pressures their trades put on prices will cause prices to change to reflect the new fundamental values.

Since informed traders generally hurt dealers, and since dealers generally do not know when they trade with informed traders, dealers try to infer information about fundamental values from their order flows. The inferences that they make contribute to the adverse selection spread component introduced in chapter 13. Price changes due to the adverse selection spread component thus contribute to fundamental volatility.

2.1.1 Fundamental Volatility Factors

Any factor that determines the value of a trading instrument can cause the price of that instrument to change. For a commodity, the most important factors are cash market supply and demand conditions. Other important factors are interest rates and storage costs. For a bond, the most important factors are interest rates and the credit quality of the issuer. For a stock, the most important factors are quality of management, the values of the company's resources and technologies, the supply and demand conditions in its product markets and in its input markets, and interest rates. For currencies, the important valuation factors include national inflation rates, macroeconomic policies, and trade and capital flows. Unexpected changes in any of these factors generate fundamental volatility in the instrument.

2.1.2 Predictability

Expected changes in fundamental factors generally do not change prices. Informative prices usually fully incorporate all available information about future values. Since people base their expectations on existing information, fully informative prices will already incorporate expected changes in fundamental factors. When the expected event occurs, it is not surprising, and it therefore should not cause prices to change. Only unexpected events cause fundamental price volatility. Consequently, the identifying characteristic of fundamental volatility in fully informative prices is unpredictable price changes. An unpredictable price process is called a *random walk*. Chapter 10 provides a more complete explanation of the properties of fully informative prices.

▶ Gasoline, Diesel Fuel, and Heating Oil Volatility

Gasoline, diesel fuel, and heating oil are expensive to store because they require very large tanks. The available producer storage in the United States amounts to only 9 days of consumption of gasoline and 18 days of distillate fuels (heating oil and diesel fuel). Since the demands for these fuels are highly inelastic, unexpected fluctuations in demand caused by weather, refinery accidents, or changes in the economy often cause substantial variation in the prices of these commodities. ◀

Source: Year 2000 consumption and refinery working storage capacity data obtained from the Energy Information Administration, U.S. Department of Energy, at www.eia.doe.gov.

The one exception to this rule involves price changes that are necessary to compensate instrument holders for their carrying costs and for bearing risk. For example, the prices of zero-coupon bonds creep upward over time as they approach maturity. Since they pay no interest, investors buy them at substantial discounts to their face values. The creep in prices compensates them for the interest payments that they would have received if they had invested in a straight bond. These creeping price changes are fully predictable, and therefore do not contribute to fundamental volatility. Note, however, that if interest rates unexpectedly fall, the prices of zero-coupon bonds will immediately rise to reflect the new interest rates. This unexpected price change would contribute to fundamental volatility.

2.1.3 Storage Costs

Commodities that are expensive to store are often quite volatile. The high storage costs ensure that producers and distributors generally will not hold large inventories. When demand exceeds supply, buyers can quickly deplete inventories. Prices then spike up until new production can relieve the shortage. Conversely, when inventories are large and new products will soon arrive, distributors may greatly discount the inventory to make room for the new arrivals.

Price volatility in high-storage-cost commodities depends on the time it takes to adjust the flow of product from producers to consumers. If the production pipeline is quite long, so that adjustments take a long time, prices may be quite volatile.

Price volatility in high-storage-cost commodities also depends on demand variation. When demand is highly variable, inventory imbalances may often occur. Production and distribution may be unable to adjust as quickly as demand changes. For low-storage-cost commodities, inventories generally buffer mismatches in the rates of production and consumption, so that prices are more stable.

Finally, price volatility in high-storage-cost commodities also depends on whether people can easily do without those commodities. If the demand is highly *inelastic*, people will demand approximately the same quantities at any price. Such goods often experience sharp price spikes when shortages develop.

Perishable goods are goods that become worthless if they are not used before they spoil or expire. The prices of perishable goods are often especially volatile because they cannot be stored indefinitely. Where a surplus of soon-to-perish goods exists, prices fall very quickly as their owners try to avoid a complete loss. If a shortage of perishable goods develops, prices may rise very quickly.

2.1.4 Fundamental Uncertainties

Uncertain knowledge about fundamental factors often causes substantial fundamental volatility. The stocks of companies involved in technological research tend to be highly volatile because their values depend critically upon the outcomes of their research and upon the markets for products that presently do not exist. Since even the best-informed traders have little information about these issues, the prices of technology stocks tend to vary substantially when new information arrives or when analysts develop new valuation models.

Generally, companies with high price to earnings (P/E) ratios tend to have volatile stocks. Most of these companies have high prices because people expect that their earnings will grow substantially through time. These growth expectations, however, generally depend on many future fundamental uncertainties. These uncertainties make high P/E stocks more volatile than low P/E stocks.

Instruments that are subject to substantial political risks likewise are quite volatile. *Political risks* are risks associated with government actions. For example, the prices of sovereign debt bonds in emerging markets depend on whether issuing governments will default on their debts and on whether they will inflate their money supplies to depreciate the real values of their bonds. The prices of firms in industries that may be subject to nationalization or to substantial government regulation likewise are quite volatile. The extreme example of political risk is war. Wars have completely destroyed the capital assets of many countries throughout the ages. Although governments generally can control the political risks upon which many security values depend, they often choose not to, in favor of other objectives.

Highly leveraged firms tend to have very volatile stocks because the ownership of their assets is divided between bondholders and equity holders. Since the equity holders must pay off the bondholders before they can benefit from the assets, equity holders bear most of the volatility in the asset values. Where there is little equity relative to debt, small changes in asset values will cause large changes in equity values.

20.2 TRANSITORY VOLATILITY

Transitory volatility results when the demands of impatient uninformed traders cause prices to diverge from fundamental values. These price changes are transitory because prices eventually revert to fundamental values.

The simplest form of transitory volatility is bid/ask bounce. *Bid/ask bounce* occurs when market order traders buy at the ask and sell at the bid. Their

▶ **Electrifying Moments in California**

Electricity is the ultimate perishable commodity because it is extremely expensive to store. Most electricity is either used as it is produced or lost forever. The spot market for electricity therefore is extremely volatile. California experienced an extreme example of this volatility in 2000–2001 when the price of electricity occasionally spiked dramatically upward for short periods when people demanded more electricity than generators could supply. ◀

▶ **Fundamental Volatility in Perishable Commodity Prices**

Price changes for perishable commodities often display extreme negative serial correlation because prices often spike up when shortages occur or collapse when surpluses occur. A casual observer may attribute this negative serial correlation to transitory volatility.

Such attributions, however, can be wildly mistaken. A sequence of spot prices is not a sequence of prices for the same item. It is a sequence of prices for a sequence of items that differ by their date of delivery. For example, the spot price of fish on Monday is the price of fish for Monday delivery. The Tuesday spot price of fish is for Tuesday delivery, and so on.

The sequence of spot prices can be highly negatively correlated when storage costs are high. The negative correlation reflects variations in fundamental factors over time as they affect delivery on different dates.

Many commodities have futures contracts written on them. These contracts price the delivery of the commodity on a specific day. When the underlying commodity is highly perishable, price changes in the futures contracts will not have nearly as much negative serial correlation as will price changes in the spot contract. Negative serial correlation in these contracts generally will be due primarily to transitory volatility. Negative serial correlation in the spot prices may be due either to changes in fundamentals across delivery dates or to transitory volatility. ◀

trades cause prices to bounce from bid to ask. These price changes reverse when traders arrive on the other side of the market. The transaction cost component of the bid/ask spread is responsible for bid/ask bounce. This spread component—which is also called the transitory spread component—therefore contributes to transitory volatility.

Large orders and cumulative order imbalances created by uninformed traders also cause prices to move from their fundamental values. The price changes reverse when value traders or arbitrageurs recognize that prices differ from fundamental values. Their trades then push prices back.

Transitory volatility includes both the price changes that impatient uninformed traders cause and the subsequent reversals of those price changes. Value traders, arbitrageurs, and dealers do not cause transitory volatility, but they do contribute to its ultimate resolution.

Transitory volatility and the transaction costs of uninformed traders are very closely correlated. The impacts that uninformed traders have on prices are transaction costs that they bear. These price changes contribute to transitory volatility. Transitory volatility therefore is small in liquid markets.

Regulators are very concerned about transitory volatility because high transitory volatility indicates that markets are illiquid. When volatility is high, people often pressure regulators to intervene to decrease it. Before doing so, regulators must be confident that the high volatility is due to the transitory component of volatility and not to its fundamental component.

20.3 MEASURING VOLATILITY AND ITS COMPONENTS

Total volatility is the sum of fundamental volatility and transitory volatility. People generally measure total volatility by using variances, standard deviations, or mean absolute deviations of price changes. The *variance* of a set of price changes is the average squared difference between the price change and the average price change. The *standard deviation* is the square root of the variance. The *mean absolute deviation* is the average absolute difference between the price change and the average price change.

Statistical models are necessary to identify and estimate the two components of total volatility. These models exploit the primary distinguishing characteristics of the two types of volatility: Fundamental volatility consists of seemingly random price changes that do not revert, whereas transitory volatility consists of price changes that ultimately revert. The transitory price changes are generally correlated with order flows of uninformed liquidity-demanding traders. Fundamental price changes may be correlated with order flows of informed traders, but need not be.

The reversion of transitory price changes causes price changes to be negatively correlated. In particular, increases tend to follow decreases and vice versa, so that price reversals are more common than price continuations. The presence of negative serial correlation in price series is therefore a strong indicator of transitory volatility.

Transaction-induced negative serial correlation in price changes may appear over various horizons. Bid/ask bounce causes negative serial correlation in transaction-to-transaction price changes. The price impacts of large orders and of order imbalances generated by uninformed traders may cause negative price change serial correlation measured over minutes, hours, days, or even months.

▶ Roll's Serial Covariance Spread Estimator Model

For readers who would feel unfulfilled learning economics without the use of some abstract notation, I offer the following analysis of Roll's serial covariance spread estimator model. (All other readers can safely skip this.)

Let

$$P_t = \text{Price of trade } t$$

$$S = \text{Spread}$$

$$V_t = \text{Fundamental value at trade } t$$

$$\varepsilon_t = \text{Change in fundamental value}$$

$$Q_t = \begin{cases} 1 & \text{if trader at } t \text{ is a buyer} \\ -1 & \text{if trader at } t \text{ is a seller} \end{cases}$$

Assume that

- Fundamental value follows a random walk so that the value innovation ε_t is independently distributed through time.
- The value innovation ε_t has zero mean and variance σ^2.
- The probability that the trader at t is a buyer is one-half.
- The probability that the trader at t is a buyer is independent of whether any previous trader was a buyer.
- The probability that trader t is a buyer is independent of ε_t and ε_{t+1}.

Let price at time t equal fundamental value plus or minus one-half of the spread depending on whether the tth trader is a buyer or a seller:

$$P_t = V_t + Q_t \tfrac{1}{2} S,$$

so that the price change is

$$\Delta P_t = \Delta V_t + \Delta Q_t \tfrac{1}{2} S = \varepsilon_t + \Delta Q_t \tfrac{1}{2} S.$$

These assumptions imply that the price change variance is

$$\begin{aligned} Var(\Delta P_t) &= E(\varepsilon_t + \Delta Q_t \tfrac{1}{2} S)^2 \\ &= E\varepsilon_t^2 + 2E\varepsilon_t \Delta Q_t \tfrac{1}{2} S + E(\Delta Q_t)^2 \tfrac{1}{4} S^2 \\ &= \sigma^2 + 0 + \tfrac{1}{4} S^2 E (Q_t - Q_{t-1})^2 \\ &= \sigma^2 + \tfrac{1}{4} S^2(EQ_t^2 - 2EQ_tQ_{t-1} + EQ_t^2) \\ &= \sigma^2 + \tfrac{1}{4} S^2(1 - 0 + 1) \\ &= \sigma^2 + \tfrac{1}{2} S^2. \end{aligned}$$

The two terms are the fundamental and transitory volatility components.

Roll showed that we can estimate the latter term from the expected serial covariance. It is

$$\begin{aligned} SCov(\Delta P_t, \Delta P_{t-1}) &= E(\varepsilon_t + \Delta Q_t \tfrac{1}{2} S)(\varepsilon_{t-1} + \Delta Q_{t-1} \tfrac{1}{2} S) \\ &= E\varepsilon_t\varepsilon_{t-1} + E\varepsilon_t \Delta Q_{t-1} \tfrac{1}{2} S + E\varepsilon_{t-1}\Delta Q_t \tfrac{1}{2} S + E\Delta Q_t \Delta Q_{t-1} \tfrac{1}{4} S^2 \\ &= 0 + 0 + 0 + \tfrac{1}{4} S^2 E(Q_t - Q_{t-1})(Q_{t-1} - Q_{t-2}) \\ &= \tfrac{1}{4} S^2(EQ_tQ_{t-1} - EQ_tQ_{t-2} - EQ_{t-1}Q_{t-1} + EQ_{t-1}Q_{t-2}) \\ &= \tfrac{1}{4} S^2(0 - 0 - 1 + 0) \\ &= -\tfrac{1}{4} S^2. \end{aligned}$$

Inverting this expression gives

$$S = 2\sqrt{-SCov(\Delta P_t, \Delta P_{t-1})}.$$

Roll's serial covariance spread estimator substitutes the sample serial covariance for the expected serial covariance in this last expression. ◀

The simplest statistical model that can estimate these variance components is Roll's serial covariance spread estimator model. Roll analyzed this simple model to create a simple serial covariance estimator of bid/ask spreads. The model assumes that fundamental values follow a random walk, and that observed prices are equal to fundamental value plus or minus half of the bid/ask spread. Total variance in this model is therefore the sum of variance due to changes in fundamental values and of variance due to bid/ask bounce. In the model, the latter variance is proportional to the square of the spread. The two components can be estimated from estimates of the total price change variance and of the serial covariance of price changes.

The main limitation of Roll's model is that it predicts that only adjacent price changes will be negatively correlated. If the reversion of prices takes longer than one transaction, price changes beyond the next one also will be negatively correlated with the current price change. Variance component estimates based on Roll's model therefore underestimate transitory volatility.

More complex variance component models identify transitory volatility by using various statistical methods that can decompose a series into a random walk component and a mean-reverting component that may have negative serial correlation over many intervals. These methods are quite complex, and well beyond the scope of this book.

20.4 SUMMARY

Traders pay close attention to volatility because price changes affect their profits and losses. Periods of high volatility are highly risky to traders. Such periods, however, also can present them with opportunities for great profits.

Regulators pay close attention to volatility because one form of volatility—transitory volatility—is correlated with transaction costs. Regulators generally try to create liquid markets that produce highly informative prices. High volatility suggests to them—and to many others—that markets need to be fixed. We discuss the regulatory responses to extreme volatility in chapter 28.

20.5 SOME POINTS TO REMEMBER

- Fundamental volatility is due to unexpected changes in fundamental valuation factors.
- Fundamental price changes are correlated with volume when only a few traders know new information about fundamental values. When such information is common knowledge, prices can change on little or no volume.
- Fundamental volatility may be scary, but it is necessary for the efficient allocation of resources.
- Prices must change as the world changes if they are to reflect all current information about instrument values.
- Transitory volatility consists of price changes caused when impatient uninformed traders seek liquidity.
- Transitory volatility and transaction costs are closely related. Both are high in illiquid markets.
- The price changes associated with transitory volatility tend to revert. Price reversion causes negative correlation in a price change series.
- Transitory volatility is identified by the negative serial correlation due to price reversals.

20.6 QUESTIONS FOR THOUGHT

1. What are the relations among liquidity, transaction costs, and transitory volatility?

2. To which volatility components do the adverse selection and transaction cost spread components contribute?

3. To which volatility component do the price impacts of news traders contribute? To which volatility component do the price impacts of value traders contribute?

4. What causes volatility to vary over time? How would you measure time-varying volatilities?

5. Why are absolute price changes correlated with volumes? Under what circumstances would you expect the correlation to be strongest?

6. Suppose that people trade—and prices change—whenever news arrives in the market. If the number of news events occurring each day were constant, would absolute price changes and volume be correlated? How would your answer be different if the number of news events varied each day?

7. One interpretation of episodic volatility is that it occurs when the flow of information quickly increases. If this were a complete explanation of episodic volatility, would we still care about episodic volatility?

8. How would Roll's serial covariance spread estimator be different if the spread were a random variable with a constant mean and variance, distributed independently through time and independently of all other variables?

n the next two chapters, we consider how traders measure and predict portfolio performance. Traders need to monitor their performance so that they can determine what they are doing well and what they are doing poorly. They then can better manage their trading. As a rule, you cannot manage what you cannot measure.

How well a portfolio performs depends on the instruments that are in the portfolio and upon the costs of constructing and maintaining the portfolio. The problem of choosing the best instruments to maximize portfolio performance is the *portfolio selection/composition problem.* The problem of implementing portfolio composition decisions is the *portfolio implementation problem.* Traders must obtain good solutions to both problems in order to perform well.

In practice, few profit-motivated traders consistently outperform the market. Most active traders lose because they trade too much and because they pay too much to trade. The costs of trading eventually overwhelm any informational advantages they may have. Traders therefore must understand their trading costs.

In chapter 21, we focus first on measuring and predicting implementation performance. For most traders, the portfolio implementation problem is easier to solve than the selection/composition problem. Because most traders cannot consistently outperform the market, the implementation problem is their more important problem. In chapter 22, we consider why superior selection/composition performance is difficult to achieve and even more difficult to predict.

Part VI

▷

Evaluation and Prediction

21
▷
Liquidity and Transaction Cost Measurement

Traders pay attention to their transaction costs because transaction costs make implementation of their trading strategies expensive. Transaction costs are most important to traders who trade frequently or who trade large sizes. For most active traders, transaction costs are the most significant determinants of their total returns. Speculators who perform poorly usually do so because their transaction costs exceed the values of their trading strategies.

Traders measure their transaction costs to evaluate how well they and their brokers have implemented their trading strategies. Traders must evaluate implementation in order to manage it effectively. They must know whether they have been trading too aggressively—or not aggressively enough—to optimize their order submission strategies. They also must know how well their brokers work on their behalf to decide which brokers should receive their orders in the future.

Traders also estimate future transaction costs to predict the costs of implementing various trading strategies. Clever strategies may not be profitable if the costs of implementing them are too great. Transaction cost prediction especially concerns large traders in illiquid markets. Their strategies may be profitable if implemented in small size, but the price impacts of implementing them in large size may cause them to lose on net.

Transaction cost measurement also interests exchanges, brokers, regulators, and investment sponsors for the following reasons:

- Exchanges conduct transaction cost measurement studies to document the quality of their markets. They use the results in their marketing efforts. They may also use them to evaluate their brokers, dealers, and specialists.

- Brokers conduct transaction cost measurement studies to document their performance. They use the results to identify their shortcomings, to market their firm's services, and to confirm that they obtain best execution for their clients. The last purpose is especially important when dealers pay brokers to route orders to them. Government regulations, exchange regulations, and common law require that brokers ensure that payments for order flow arrangements do not hurt their clients. Brokers therefore must regularly and rigorously examine execution quality to ensure the most beneficial terms for their customers' orders.

- Investment sponsors must ensure that they obtain value for the commissions that their investment managers spend on their behalf. The U.S. Department of Labor requires that pension funds covered by the Employee Retirement Income Security Act (ERISA) recognize that trading commissions are fund assets that they must conserve. Fund trustees therefore conduct transaction cost measurement studies to determine whether their funds obtain appropriate value for their commissions.

- Regulators often try to promote policies that lower transaction costs. Regulators therefore conduct transaction cost measurement studies to characterize the performance of various market structures. The U.S. Securities and Exchange Commission now requires that all market centers—exchanges, ECNs, and dealers—collect and publish highly disaggregated data that traders can use to evaluate average execution quality for various order types and sizes.

We consider how to measure liquidity in this chapter. We will examine both retrospective and prospective measures of transaction costs. We consider first retrospective measures of transaction costs. We then consider how traders use information about past transaction costs to predict future transaction costs.

21.1 TRANSACTION COST COMPONENTS

Defining and measuring exactly what we mean by the term "transaction costs" is difficult. This entire book is about understanding what transaction costs are, where they come from, and how to measure them. We explore these questions in detail throughout this book.

For our present purpose, *transaction costs* include all costs associated with trading. These costs include *explicit costs*, *implicit costs*, and *missed trade opportunity costs*.

Explicit transaction costs are all costs that a cost accountant would easily identify. These costs include commissions paid to brokers, fees paid to exchanges, and taxes paid to government. Explicit transaction costs also include any resources that traders devote to the trading process. For example, the costs of setting up, staffing, and running a buy-side trading desk are explicit costs of trading.

Implicit transaction costs are the costs of trading that arise because traders generally have an impact upon prices. For example, traders who buy at asking prices and sell at bid prices pay the bid/ask spread when trading. The spread is an obvious and important cost of trading. Likewise, when large buyers push prices up and large sellers push prices down, the price impacts of their trading are transaction costs.

Missed trade opportunity costs arise when traders fail to fill their orders or fail to fill their orders in a timely manner. Suppose that a speculator wants to buy 100 cotton futures contracts at the New York Board of Trade when the price is 65 cents per pound. In an effort to obtain a good price, the trader submits a buy limit order with a limit price of 64.95 cents. The price of cotton subsequently rises to 68 cents, and the order does not execute. Had the trader traded more aggressively and filled the order at an average price of 65.25 cents, he would have made 2.75 cents per pound, or 1,375 dollars for each 50,000-pound contract. Because the trader failed to trade aggressively, he lost the opportunity to make 137,500 dollars. Traders need to keep track of their opportunity costs so that they can determine whether they are trading aggressively enough.

Explicit transaction costs are the most easily measured of the three types of transaction costs. Measuring them is a simple cost accounting exercise in which the analyst identifies and sums all commissions, fees, and explicit expenses associated with trade process.

▶ The Flip Side

Transaction costs concern everyone in the trading industry. Sell-side institutions—brokers, dealers, and exchanges—try to sell low-cost transaction services. Buy-side institutions try to obtain transaction services at low cost. To a casual observer, it would appear that everyone wants low transaction costs.

Not so. Transaction costs to the buy side are revenues to the sell side. Sell-side institutions would like their revenues to be as high as possible. They market low-cost transaction services only because they compete with each other for buy-side business.

These comments suggest that sell-side institutions benefit from high transaction costs. While this might be true in the short run, it has not been true in the long run. Decreases in transaction costs have caused buy-side traders to greatly increase the volume of their trading. The increased volume, coupled with substantial decreases in the costs of providing transaction services, have increased sell-side profits even as buy-side transaction costs have fallen. ◀

Implicit transaction costs and missed trade opportunity costs are harder to measure because they require some benchmark against which to compare trade and no-trade prices. To measure the price impact of a completed trade, analysts must estimate what prices would have been if the trade had not taken place. To measure the opportunity cost of an uncompleted trade, analysts must estimate the average prices at which the trade would have taken place if it had been completed. These estimation problems make transaction cost measurement a difficult and imprecise science.

21.2 IMPLICIT TRANSACTION COST ESTIMATION METHODS

Traders estimate implicit transaction costs by using *specified price benchmark methods* and *econometric transaction cost estimation methods*. The price benchmark methods are the most commonly used. They are easier to implement than the econometric methods and generally more useful when traders need to evaluate transaction costs for specific trades. The econometric methods are most useful for estimating average transaction costs for a whole market.

Most traders measure transaction costs relative to specific price benchmarks. The price benchmark provides a basis for determining whether buyers paid, and sellers received, good or bad prices.

When traders use a specified price benchmark, they estimate the per unit transaction cost as the difference between the trade price and the benchmark price. For a purchase, the estimated cost is the excess of the trade price over the benchmark price. For a sale, it is the opposite. They then multiply this difference by the trade size to obtain the estimated transaction cost:

$$\text{Estimated Cost} = \text{Trade Size} \times \begin{cases} \text{Trade Price} - \text{Benchmark Price} & \text{for a purchase} \\ \text{Benchmark Price} - \text{Trade Price} & \text{for a sale} \end{cases}$$

Estimated transaction costs thus are high when buyers pay high prices and when sellers receive low prices.

Note that the estimated transaction costs for all buyers and sellers in a trade sum exactly to zero. Transaction cost to one side is trading profit to the other side. Traders who demand liquidity tend to pay transaction costs and those who offer liquidity have negative transaction costs.

For convenience, the difference between the trade price and the benchmark price is often called the *signed difference*, where the sign of the difference is understood to be 1 if the trade is a purchase and −1 if the trade is a sale:

$$\text{Estimated Cost} = \text{Trade Size} \times \text{Trade Sign} \\ \times (\text{Trade Price} - \text{Benchmark Price})$$

$$\text{where} \quad \text{Trade Sign} = \begin{cases} 1 & \text{for a purchase} \\ -1 & \text{for a sale} \end{cases}.$$

An ideal price benchmark would be the price that would have prevailed if the trader had not tried to trade. The difference between this price and the trade price would be entirely due to the trade, and therefore a good estimate of the implicit cost of trading. Unfortunately, no one can confidently specify such a price. Instead, traders commonly use a volume-weighted average price; the opening price; the closing price; an average of the open, high, low, and closing prices; or an average of bid and ask prices near the time of the trade. We discuss the virtues and drawbacks of each of these benchmarks in the next section.

Econometric transaction cost estimation methods use statistical methods to estimate transaction costs. The simplest econometric methods extract information about transaction costs from price reversals that traders cause when they have an impact on price. More complex econometric models extract information about transaction costs from the relation between executed orders and price changes. We can interpret both types of methods as benchmark methods in which the analyst estimates the benchmark instead of specifying it.

21.2.1 Trade Side Identification

Traders who conduct transaction cost measurement studies usually have a set of trades in which they participated for which they want to measure their transaction costs. They therefore know whether they were the buyer or the seller for each trade.

Analysts sometimes want to estimate transaction costs for trades in which they did not participate. Since all trades have at least one buyer and one seller, such analysts must identify the side of the trade in which they are interested. (Ignoring commissions, the sum of the costs on both sides is always zero.) They typically direct their interest exclusively to the side that appears to be taking liquidity.

Analysts typically identify that side by the relation between the trade price and the bid and asking prices. If the trade price is closer to the bid, they assume that the buyer was the aggressive trader. If it is closer to the asking price, they assume the seller was the aggressive trader. If the trade price was exactly in the middle between the bid and the ask, they look to the last price change. If the trade took place on an uptick or a zero uptick, they identify the trade as initiated by an aggressive buyer. Otherwise, they identify it as seller-initiated. This procedure is commonly known at the *Lee and Ready algorithm* after the two academic researchers who popularized it.

Analysts who use the Lee and Ready algorithm to measure transaction costs must recognize its two major shortcomings. First, it causes analysts to estimate higher transaction costs than most traders incur because most traders do not exclusively demand liquidity. Second, it cannot identify when an order has been filled with multiple trades. If the trades are at different prices because the order had market impact, the cost of filling the order will be underestimated. We discuss this problem further below.

21.3 MEASURING TRANSACTION COSTS WITH SPECIFIED PRICE BENCHMARKS

In this section, we introduce and discuss methods for measuring implicit transaction costs by using various specified benchmarks. Our presentation starts with a description of the various benchmarks. Then we consider the properties of the resulting estimators.

21.3.1 Benchmark Prices

Many traders estimate the cost of trading by the signed difference between the trade price and a *quotation midpoint*. The *quotation midpoint* is the average of the bid and ask prices in a quotation.

▶ **Money Flow**

Technical traders use a version of this trade identification procedure when computing *money flow* indicators. *Money flow* is volumes on upticks minus volumes on downticks. Technical traders believe that money flow indicates whether aggressive traders are net buyers or sellers. ◀

▶ **Passive-Aggressive Behavior in the Markets**

Analysts generally classify traders who offer standing limit orders as passive traders. They wait for the market to come to them. However, they also may be very aggressive traders. For example, a buyer can *peg the market* at his bid as long as he can afford to buy at that price. Although such traders may very aggressively accumulate or divest positions, the Lee and Ready algorithm will classify them as passive traders. ◀

Traders obtain different transaction cost estimates according to which quotation midpoint they use. The quotation midpoint that prevailed at the time of the trade produces a transaction cost estimate that analysts call the *effective spread* (or sometimes the *liquidity premium*).

Post-trade quotation midpoints produce *realized spreads*. Analysts most commonly compute realized spreads using quotation midpoints obtained 5, 10, 15, or 60 minutes after the trade.

Analysts also use pre-trade quotation midpoints. The most common transaction cost estimator based on a pre-trade quotation midpoint uses the quotation midpoint at the time the portfolio manager decided to trade. Analysts usually call this method *Perold's implementation shortfall* (after André Perold, who popularized it in an influential 1988 *Journal of Portfolio Management* article). Jack Treynor, writing seven years earlier, called it the *method of paper portfolios*.

Traders also estimate their transaction costs by using various dailyprices. The most common daily benchmark is the *volume-weighted average price* (VWAP). The VWAP is the average trade price of the day where each trade price is weighted by the size of the associated trade. Traders like the VWAP benchmark because they would like to trade at least as well as the average

▶ Consultant Benchmarks

Several investment consultants compute transaction cost estimates for their clients. The consultants generally use different price benchmarks.

Abel/Noser first popularized VWAP transaction cost estimates. Able/Noser is a U.S. discount institutional stockbroker. The firm started to measure transaction costs to show its clients that it could obtain good execution prices for discounted commissions.

SEI popularized transaction cost estimates based on closing price benchmarks. SEI provides investment consulting, investment software, and mutual fund management.

The Plexus Group computes implementation shortfall transaction cost analyses. Its clientele consists primarily of investment sponsors and investment managers who want to optimize their trade implementation or who need to demonstrate that they are not wasting their commissions. The Plexus Group primarily provides transaction cost analyses and trade process consulting.

The Transaction Auditing Group (TAG) computes effective spread (liquidity premium) analyses, among many other transaction audit functions. Their clientele consists primarily of broker-dealers who need to demonstrate to regulators and clients that they are obtaining best execution for their clients.

The Elkins/McSherry division of State Street computes transaction cost estimates primarily by using an average of the daily opening, high, low, and closing prices as the benchmark price. Their clients consist mostly of pension funds and investment managers who are interested in transaction cost comparisons across the 42 countries in the Elkins/McSherry universe. ◀

For more information, browse:
www.AbelNoser.com
www.SEIC.com
www.PlexusGroup.com
www.TAGaudit.com
www.Elkins-McSherry.com

trader on that day. The VWAP is computed most easily by dividing the total dollar value of all trades by the total trading volume:

$$
\text{VWAP} = \frac{\text{Dollar Volume}}{\text{Trade Volume}} = \frac{\sum_t \text{Trade Size}_t \text{Price}_t}{\sum_t \text{Trade Size}_t} = \sum_t w_t \text{Price}_t
$$

where weight $w_t = \dfrac{\text{Trade Size}_t}{\text{Trade Volume}}$. Traders also use the daily opening price, the daily closing price, or the average of the daily open, high, low, and closing prices as benchmark prices.

21.3.1.1 Effective Spreads

The signed difference between the trade price and the time-of-trade quotation midpoint is an intuitively simple transaction cost estimate. This method exactly measures the implicit cost of trading a round-trip when the quotation midpoint does not change. For example, if a trader buys at the ask and then sells the same quantity at the bid, the trader will have done nothing but trade. His per unit loss for the two-trade round-trip is the bid/ask spread. The cost of trading per trade therefore is half of the bid/ask spread. The quotation midpoint benchmark gives us this result: The cost of the purchase is the ask minus the quotation midpoint, or half of the spread. Likewise, the cost of the sale is the quotation midpoint minus the bid, which is also half of the spread.

The *liquidity premium* is the signed difference between trade price and the time-of-trade quotation midpoint. The *effective spread* is twice the liquidity premium. The effective spread equals the quoted bid/ask spread when all purchases take place at the bid and all sales take place at the offer. When trades take place within the spread because dealers or brokers arrange *price improvement*, the effective spread that traders pay is smaller than the quoted spread. Likewise, when large orders fill at prices outside the bid/ask spread, the effective spread is greater than the quoted spread.

The effective spread is the transaction cost estimation method that retail market order traders most commonly use. Retail traders primarily compare their trade prices against the bid and offer prices that prevailed when they submitted their orders. Most such traders are unaware that they engage in transaction cost analyses. They simply want to check whether they are receiving good prices.

21.3.1.2 Realized Spreads

The *realized spread* is twice the signed difference between the trade price and the quotation midpoint observed at some specified time following the trade. Realized and effective spreads are equal when the quotation midpoint does not change over the measurement interval. Prices often change, however, when traders raise prices in response to aggressive buyers or lower prices in response to aggressive sellers. Realized spreads therefore tend to be smaller than effective spreads.

Realized spreads interest dealers because their profits depend on the prices at which they establish their positions and the prices at which they subsequently liquidate their positions. The spreads that dealers actually realize are less than their quoted spreads because they often provide price improvement and because they sometimes trade with informed traders. The difference between quoted spreads and effective spreads measures the price improvement that dealers provide. The difference between effective spreads and realized spreads measures dealers' losses to well-informed traders.

21.3.1.3 Implementation Shortfalls

We can interpret implementation shortfalls as the difference in values between an actual portfolio and a corresponding paper portfolio. A *paper portfolio* is an imaginary portfolio that people construct on paper to see what would have happened if they had actually traded. People analyze paper portfolios for fun, to test new trading ideas, and to measure transaction costs.

To measure transaction costs, traders must specify a benchmark price at which they buy or sell instruments for their paper portfolios. The quotation midpoint at the time they decide to trade produces an easy-to-interpret measure of transaction cost. The midpoint quotation price represents a naive best estimate of instrument value at the time they decide to trade. The difference in value between their actual portfolio and the corresponding paper portfolio measures the costs of implementing their trading decisions relative to this benchmark. Since implementation generally is costly, paper portfolios typically are more valuable than the corresponding actual portfolios.

Analysts break the total implementation shortfall into components. The breakdown depends on whether the order was filled. If a trade occurred, the shortfall is the total trade size times the signed difference between the average trade price and the quotation midpoint at the decision time. If the trade did not take place, or if the order was not completely filled, the shortfall is the unfilled size multiplied by the difference between the current price and the benchmark price. The first component estimates the transaction cost of completed trades. The second component estimates the missed trade opportunity cost.

When they are constructing paper portfolios to evaluate new trading ideas, traders make assumptions about transaction costs that are often critical. If they assume costs that are too low, they may adopt unprofitable trading strategies. If they assume costs that are too high, they may reject otherwise profitable trading strategies. Traders typically assume that they pay the quotation midpoint plus some premium when buying. They likewise assume that they receive the quotation midpoint less some discount when selling. They obtain the premiums and discounts that they use for these analyses from transaction cost studies.

21.3.1.4 VWAP, Opening Prices, and Closing Prices

Many investment sponsors do not know when during the day that the trades made on their behalf by their investment managers took place. Unless they make special arrangements with their brokers and with their investment managers, they typically receive only daily reports of the share-weighted average prices of the trades they made that day. These investment sponsors therefore can conduct transaction cost analyses only with daily price benchmarks.

The daily market volume-weighted average price is an attractive transaction cost benchmark to such investment sponsors because it allows them to determine whether they received a higher or lower price than the average trader that day. Transaction costs measured relative to opening and closing prices likewise allow traders to compare their trade prices against the prices that prevailed before and after their trades. We shall see below that all three measures have serious problems which complicate their interpretations as transaction costs estimators.

21.4 PROPERTIES OF TRANSACTION COST PRICE BENCHMARK ESTIMATORS

In this section, we enumerate desirable properties for transaction cost estimators and consider which of the benchmark estimators have these properties.

21.4.1 Data Requirements

Transaction cost estimates should be easy to compute. Estimates that compare daily trade summaries against daily price benchmarks are easy to compute. Estimates that are based on quotation midpoints are more expensive because they require information about intraday trades and quotations.

21.4.2 Accuracy

Random events that are completely unrelated to the implementation of a trade should not affect the transaction cost estimate for that trade. For example, suppose that a buyer negotiates an excellent purchase price for a stock early in the morning. Later in the day, the market learns terrible news about the firm and the price drops significantly. If an analyst measures the transaction cost relative to the low closing price, the trader will appear to have negotiated a very poor price. Statisticians call such estimates noisy. In this example, if the transaction cost was measured relative to the opening price, it would have been much more accurate.

In general, the greater the time between the trade and the determination of the benchmark price, the noisier the transaction cost estimator will be. Transaction costs based on opening or closing prices therefore are noisier than transaction costs based on average prices. All daily benchmarks, however, are noisy because they use the same benchmark prices for all trades that take place within the day. The least noisy transaction cost estimator is the effective spread because it uses a contemporaneous price benchmark. The noise in realized spreads and in implementation shortfalls increases the further in time the benchmark price is from the trade price.

21.4.3 Trade Timing Issues

Many traders use transaction cost estimates to evaluate how well their brokers fill their orders. When managers give their brokers discretion over the timing of their trades, they expect that their brokers will try to trade when it is most advantageous. In particular, they hope that their brokers will use their experience, and the information available to them, to recognize and exploit predictable short-term price moves. For example, they hope their brokers will recognize that prices tend to be high after uninformed traders have bought. Under such conditions, brokers with timing discretion should immediately execute sell orders. Those with buy orders may wait until prices fall.

Traders who give their brokers timing discretion must pay close attention to their transaction costs to determine whether their brokers use their discretion appropriately. Since brokers generally are paid commissions only for completed trades, brokers may prefer to complete trades rather than wait for the best time to trade.

Good transaction cost estimators should produce information that allows traders to identify whether their brokers are skilled trade timers. The effective spread estimator is nearly useless for this purpose because it measures transaction cost only relative to the current quotation midpoint. If brokers can recognize any short-term predictability in the quotation midpoint, this estimator will not reveal it.

In general, a transaction cost estimator will best measure trade-timing effects when the benchmark price does not depend on the time of the trade. When it depends on the time of trade—as it does for the realized spread—the estimator will best measure trade-timing effects when the interval between the trade and the benchmark price is long.

Unfortunately, trade-timing considerations run exactly counter to estimator accuracy considerations. Accurate estimates require close benchmark prices, while estimates with the power to discover trade timing require distant price benchmarks. Analysts therefore must analyze many trades to accurately measure trade-timing effects.

21.4.4 Estimator Biases

Transaction cost estimates should be unbiased. They should measure only costs of implementing a trading strategy given current market conditions. Biased transaction cost estimators often produce cost estimates that depend on how or why the trade is made. Biases may arise when traders split their orders, when their decisions to trade depend on past price changes, when they are well informed about future price changes, and when brokers know that their clients will use transaction cost estimates to evaluate their trading.

21.4.4.1 Split Orders

Transaction cost estimates should measure the total transaction cost of an order that traders fill in multiple parts. Traders often split their large orders to avoid showing the market the full size of their interest. They also split large orders to price-discriminate as they push prices up or down. Accordingly, the last part of the order usually is the most expensive to execute. The transaction cost estimation method should estimate the total cost of executing the entire order and not just the sum of the apparent costs of executing each piece considered separately.

The liquidity premium (effective spread) is a poor transaction cost estimator for large trades that traders split into small parts. For example, suppose that a trader splits a 4,000-share buy order into two equal parts. The first 2,000 shares trade at 30.10 when the market quotation is 30 bid, 30.10 offered. The next 2,000 shares trade at 30.20 when the market quotation is 30.10 bid, 30.20 offered. The liquidity premium transaction cost per share for both trades is 0.05, or 200 dollars. The second trade, however, was more expensive than the first because the first had market impact. The impact of the first trade raised the bid and the offer associated with the second trade.

The VWAP transaction cost estimator also may poorly estimate the cost of executing a large order. In the previous example, suppose that the trader was the only buyer of the instrument that day. The VWAP transaction cost estimate then would be zero (ignoring commission costs) because the average price of the trader's purchases is exactly equal to the average price of all market trades that day. Although the buyer paid the bid/ask spread and had market impact, the VWAP estimator will not identify any costs.

In general, the split order problem arises when the price benchmark depends on the trades that fill the order. Since split orders tend to change subsequent quotation midpoints, the effective spread estimator underestimates total transaction costs. Likewise, since the price impacts of split orders affect the volume-weighted average price, the VWAP transaction cost estimator also underestimates total transaction costs.

The split order problem does not affect estimators—such as the implementation shortfall estimator—that use benchmark prices which are determined before the order has an impact on market prices. In our example, suppose that the decision to trade was made when the quotation midpoint was 30.05 (the first quotation midpoint). The implementation shortfall estimate of the total cost of filling the order would be 5 cents per share for the first trade and 15 cents per share for the second trade. The total cost of filling the order with the two equal sized trades therefore would be 10 cents per share, or 400 dollars.

The split order problem most seriously affects estimators based on benchmarks that are significantly affected by the market impact of the large order. In our example, suppose that the market closes at 30.20, the price of the second trade. Using the closing price as the benchmark price produces estimated transaction costs of −10 cents per share for the first trade and zero cents for the second trade, for a total of −200 dollars. Although the trader paid the bid/ask spread and had an impact on price, the closing price estimator makes it appear that he had negative trading costs.

When properly estimated, negative transaction costs are trading profits. The trader in our example made a 200 dollar unrealized profit. If the trader tried to realize the profit, however, he probably would have had a net loss. For example, suppose that the trader closed his position by selling 2,000 shares at 30.10 when the market quotation was 30.10 bid, 30.20 offered, and then sold another 2,000 shares at 30.00 when the market quotation had dropped to 30.00 bid, 30.10 offered. Since the trader sold all shares for 10 cents less than he bought them, his total loss for the round-trip would have been 10 cents per share or 400 dollars.

21.4.4.2 Momentum and Contrarian Traders

Transaction costs measured relative to some benchmarks may be systematically high or low, depending on whether the trader pursues *momentum* or *contrarian trading strategies*. Traders who use *momentum trading strategies* buy after prices rise and sell after prices fall. Traders who use *contrarian trading strategies* do the opposite.

Transaction cost estimates based on opening prices are particularly biased when traders use momentum or contrarian trading strategies. Momentum traders overestimate their transaction costs because they buy when prices have risen, so that the opening price benchmark is low. They likewise sell when the opening price benchmark is high. Conversely, contrarians underestimate their transaction costs because they buy when the opening price benchmark is high, and they sell otherwise.

Transaction cost estimates generally are biased when traders base their trading decisions on price changes that take place after the price benchmarks against which their trades will be measured have been determined. Transaction costs based on opening prices and—to a lesser extent—those based on the VWAP therefore produce biased results when used by momentum and contrarian traders.

21.4.4.3 Informed Traders

Prices tend to rise after well-informed traders buy and fall after they sell. Transaction costs that are based on price benchmarks which follow their trades therefore will underestimate their trading costs. For example, informed traders tend to measure smaller realized spreads than effective spreads. The difference is due to their successful speculations and not to the quality of their trade implementation.

The informed trader bias generally is greatest when the benchmark price is determined long after the trade takes place. The closing price and—to a lesser extent—the VWAP benchmarks therefore underestimate transaction costs for well-informed traders. The underestimation is most acute when the informed traders trade on short-term information that quickly becomes public.

21.4.4.4 Gaming

When traders use transaction cost estimates to evaluate their brokers, the brokers should not be able to manipulate the results by trading in ways that are not in the traders' best interests. Brokers who can affect their evaluations without delivering better prices to their clients are able to *game the measure*. Brokers who *game* their evaluations arrange trades to optimize their evaluations rather than to provide best execution services to their clients.

Brokers who have discretion over how aggressively they fill their orders can easily game the effective spread transaction cost estimator. To game this measure, brokers always offer liquidity and never take it. They then always buy at the bid or sell at the offer. If the market moves away from their orders, they adjust their order prices and try again to buy at the bid or sell at the offer. By only offering liquidity, these brokers ensure that their estimated transaction costs will always be negative. Unfortunately, they also fail to trade at prices that their clients would have preferred. Brokers who constantly chase after the market provide very poor service to their clients, especially if their clients are impatient to trade.

Brokers can game the effective spread estimator because the benchmark price depends on when the order executes. Every time the market moves away from the order, the broker fails to obtain a good price for the client. The broker, however, is not penalized for waiting because the benchmark price moves with the market.

Brokers who have discretion over the timing of their trades can game any measure of transaction costs for which the benchmark price depends on the timing of their trades. For example, suppose that a broker knows her client will evaluate her trades by using an opening price benchmark. Near the end of the day, the broker receives an order to buy. She will immediately fill the order at any reasonable price if prices have fallen during the day. If prices have risen, she will try to hold the order until the next day, so that she does not record a high-priced buy on a day when the market opened much lower.

This gaming problem is most serious when sponsors measure transaction costs relative to opening prices. To a lesser extent, it also arises for the

VWAP benchmark and other average price benchmarks that are partially determined by when the broker decides when to trade.

Measuring average price benchmarks over long intervals can mitigate gaming problems. For example, clients can compare their trade prices against the VWAP for the week surrounding their trades rather than only for the day of their trades. This procedure reduces the benefit to the broker of delaying a trade to obtain a new benchmark. Unfortunately, it also increases the noise in the transaction cost estimates.

Brokers with order timing discretion also can game transaction cost measures by timing their trades to coincide with the determination of their benchmarks. For example, brokers whose clients evaluate their trades by using a VWAP benchmark can ensure that their estimated transaction costs will be very near zero by spreading the execution of their orders over the course of the day so that their volume-weighted average trade price is approximately equal to the market VWAP. Likewise, brokers whose clients evaluate their trades by using a closing price benchmark can execute their orders only at the close so that they will have zero transaction cost estimates.

The gaming problem cannot arise when the benchmark price is firmly determined before the broker receives the order. The implementation shortfall therefore cannot be gamed.

When brokers blatantly game their evaluations, clients will easily recognize it. They then can appropriately discipline their brokers. Clever brokers can avoid this discipline by gaming judiciously. The gaming problem therefore may affect all measures that can be gamed. The size of the problem will depend on the difficulty of detection and on the propensity of the broker to exploit the game.

Few brokers game their measures even when they can do so without detection. Most brokers work honestly on behalf of their clients to provide the best service possible, regardless of how they are measured. They may advise their clients, however, when they make trades that are in their clients' interest but will generate unusually large estimated transaction costs.

21.4.5 Summary

Which price benchmark analysts use when evaluating implementation performance determines what they measure. Analysts who use the quotation midpoint at the time of the trade measure whether the quality of the trade execution was good relative to contemporaneous quoted prices. They learn nothing, however, about the cumulative market impact of split orders. They also learn little about whether traders can exercise valuable timing discretion. Analysts who use price benchmarks obtained long after the trade may learn about these issues, but they also measure whether portfolio managers made good portfolio composition decisions. Analysts who use price benchmarks obtained long before managers decided to trade are immune to the split order problem, but they also measure the degree to which their portfolio composition decisions depend on past prices.

No price benchmark is perfect for estimating implicit transaction costs. Analysts must make trade-offs between estimation cost and various estimator properties. When data acquisition costs are no consideration, the implementation shortfall is the best transaction cost estimator. It is not subject to any of the biases discussed above. When the costs of collecting data are significant, traders may prefer other estimators. Retail traders typically use the effective spread transaction cost estimator because it is generally unbiased for small orders. Institutional investment sponsors often use VWAP when they do not know when their managers ordered their trades. The VWAP transaction cost estimator has some bias, gaming, and estimation noise problems, but for most traders these problems are less significant than those found for the opening and closing price benchmarks. Table 21-1 provides a summary of the properties of price benchmark transaction cost estimators.

All transaction cost estimation methods produce noisy results when applied to single trades. Average transaction costs, measured over many transactions, therefore provide more reliable information about transaction costs than does the estimate from any one transaction. Averaging, however, does not solve any bias or gaming problems.

Traders who use transaction cost estimates to evaluate their brokers must carefully analyze their estimates. They cannot meaningfully evaluate their brokers without having some benchmarks against which they can judge their performance. To compare brokers, either traders must measure performance across many brokers, or consultants must provide them with meaningful comparison norms. In either event, comparisons across brokers are meaningful only when traders give brokers similar trading problems. Otherwise, brokers who receive difficult trading problems will appear to be less productive than are those who receive simple trading problems.

These problems make it imperative that clients evaluate their brokers by using quantitative methods. Traders use these methods because the information that they produce is very valuable when they can interpret it well.

21.5 MEASURING IMPLICIT TRANSACTION COSTS WITH ECONOMETRIC METHODS

Econometric transaction cost measurement models use statistical methods to measure the impacts that traders have upon prices. These models generally examine either price reversals or the relation between order flow and price changes.

Analysts usually use these models when they do not have quotation data or order flow data. For example, open outcry futures markets rarely record the bids and offers shouted in their pits. Their market reporters primarily record trade prices. Traders who want to measure transaction costs in these markets therefore must use methods that do not depend on bid and ask price quotations.

Econometric transaction cost measurement models generally estimate average transaction costs for the market as a whole. When traders are interested in the costs of specific trades, they typically measure them relative to a specified benchmark.

21.5.1 Price Reversal Models

The simplest econometric transaction cost models measure the price reversals that traders cause when they buy and sell. The most common price reversals are due to *bid/ask bounce*. Prices tend to bounce between bid and asking prices as impatient sellers and buyers demand liquidity. Traders also cause longer-term price reversals when an imbalance of uninformed buyers

TABLE 21-1.
Properties of Various Price Benchmark Transaction Cost Estimators

PRICE BENCHMARK	COMMON NAMES	DATA REQUIREMENTS	ESTIMATE NOISE	TRADE TIMING	POTENTIAL BIASES			GAMING STRATEGIES
					SPLIT ORDERS	CONTRARIAN/ MOMENTUM	INFORMED TRADER	
Quotation midpoint at time of trade	Effective spread; Liquidity premium	Trade price and time Contemporaneous quotation data	Generally quite precise	Does not estimate	Underestimates costs	None, if prices follow a random walk	No bias	Only offer liquidity Never use market orders when spreads are wide
Quotation midpoint following trade	Realized spread	Trade price and time Intraday quotation data	Noise increases with interval length	Estimates	Underestimates costs	None, if prices follow a random walk		None
Quotation midpoint at time of trade decision	Perold's implementation shortfall; Method of paper portfolios	Trade price and order time Intraday quotation data	None, if transaction costs are defined as the shortfall	Estimates	No bias	None, if prices follow a random walk	No bias	None
Volume-weighted average price	VWAP	Volume-weighted average trade confirmation price Daily market VWAP	Noisy	Estimates	Underestimates costs	Contrarians underestimate costs Momentum traders overestimate costs	Informed traders underestimate costs	Split large orders and fill throughout the day
Opening price	Opening benchmark	Volume-weighted average trade confirmation price Daily open	Very noisy for trades at the end of the day	Estimates	No bias if order is filled	Contrarians underestimate costs Momentum traders overestimate costs	No bias	Execute orders only when opening price is unfavorable Trade only at the open
Closing price	Closing benchmark	Volume-weighted average trade confirmation price Daily close	Very noisy for trades at the start of the day.	Estimates	Grossly underestimates costs	None, if prices follow a random walk		Trade only at the close

or sellers causes prices to rise or fall. Prices ultimately reverse when value traders recognize the resulting profit opportunities. These price reversals may occur over short intraday intervals or intervals as long as months.

The average absolute transaction price change is a very simple estimator of transaction costs. It exactly estimates the bid/ask spread when bid and ask prices are constant, and when all trades take place only at bid and ask prices. Bid and ask prices vary, of course, and not all trades take place at bid and ask prices. In practice, the average absolute transaction price change tends to underestimate bid/ask spreads when bid and offer prices change in increments that are smaller than the bid/ask spread, and it overestimates bid/ask spreads otherwise. Ignoring very small and very large price changes can improve the estimates.

Better transaction cost estimators are based on price change serial covariances. The *serial covariance* of a sequence of price changes is the average of the product of adjacent price changes. When prices tend to reverse, the serial covariance is negative because the product of adjacent positive and negative (or negative and positive) price changes is negative. Since the efficient markets hypothesis suggests that price changes should have no serial covariance if there are no transaction costs, negative price change serial covariance indicates transaction costs. Several econometric models exploit this insight. The best known of them is *Roll's serial covariance spread estimator*, which we describe in chapter 20. It is

$$\text{Effective Spread} = 2\sqrt{-SCov}.$$

Roll's estimator is unbiased when the sample size is large, when aggressive buyers and sellers arrive at random with equal probability, and when changes in the effective bid and offer prices are uncorrelated with the sequence of arriving traders. Violations of these assumptions typically cause the estimator to underestimate the bid/ask spread. Analysts therefore use Roll's method only when no quotation data are available.

21.5.2 Order Flow Models

More complex econometric models directly estimate the price effects that aggressive traders cause. These methods typically use regression models to characterize how prices change in response to order flow. These models exploit the principle that prices rise in response to aggressive buyers and fall in response to aggressive sellers. Analysts usually identify the more aggressive side in each trade by using the Lee and Ready algorithm described above. These regression models typically used signed trades to explain price changes.

21.6 MISSED TRADE OPPORTUNITY COSTS

Failing to trade is often more costly than trading. Informed traders lose profits when their orders go unfilled. Unfilled orders also may hurt uninformed traders, especially if they are hedging. Traders must pay attention to their missed trade opportunity costs in addition to their transaction costs in order to best manage their trading.

Analysts generally measure missed trade opportunity costs as the unfilled size times the signed difference between a subsequent price and a benchmark price. For example, suppose that a trader decided to sell 100,000 shares

▶ Glosten-Harris, Meet Glosten-Milgrom

Here is one more treat for the mathematically inclined.

The *Glosten-Harris spread components estimation model* is a simple example of an order flow transaction costs estimation model. This model is based on the Glosten-Milgrom spread component model introduced in chapter 14.

These models assume that aggressive traders have two effects on prices. The *permanent price effect* is due to inferences that dealers (and other liquidity suppliers) make about informed traders from the order flow. It corresponds to the adverse selection spread component introduced in chapter 13. Information theoretic considerations suggest that the permanent effect should be proportional to trade size. (See chapters 12 and 14.) The *transitory price effect* is due to costs of supplying liquidity to impatient traders. It corresponds to the transaction cost spread component introduced in chapter 14. The transitory effect probably has fixed and proportional effects on price.

The Glosten-Harris model represents these relations by specifying an equation that represents observed prices, P_t, as the sum of underlying fundamental value, V_t, plus the transaction cost spread component, θ_t:

$$P_t = V_t + \theta_t.$$

Another equation expresses the transaction cost spread component as a linear function of the sign of the trade, Q_t (1 for a purchase and -1 for a sale), and the signed size, $Q_t \text{Size}_t$:

$$\theta_t = aQ_t + bQ_t\text{Size}_t.$$

Finally, the permanent effect appears in an equation that describes how fundamental value changes in response to information inferred from the sign and size of the trade, and in response to other information that affect values, ε_t:

$$\Delta V_t = \lambda Q_t\text{Size}_t + \varepsilon_t.$$

Combining these equations produces the following equation for the observed change in price:

$$\Delta P_t = \Delta V_t + \Delta\theta_t = \lambda Q_t\,\text{Size}_t + \varepsilon_t + a\Delta Q_t + b\Delta(Q_t\text{Size}_t).$$

Econometricians estimate the coefficients λ, a, and b in this equation by interpreting the equation as a regression model in which the transaction price change, ΔP_t, is explained by three independent regressor variables and an error term. The regressors are $Q_t\text{Size}_t$, the signed size; ΔQ_t, the change in the trade sign; and $\Delta(Q_t\text{Size}_t)$, the change in the signed size. The error term is ε_t, the change in values that is unrelated to the order flow. The statistical properties of standard regression methods ensure that the regression error term is uncorrelated with the independent regressor variables. This is consistent with its interpretation as information that affects values independently of the trade process. Analysts can use the estimated coefficients to compute transaction cost estimates for any trade by evaluating the expressions for the permanent and transitory price components.

We can interpret the Glosten-Harris model as a benchmark price transaction cost estimation model. The price benchmark is the unobserved fundamental value, V_t. Although the model produces transaction cost estimates without estimating the benchmark, econometricians can easily estimate benchmark values if necessary. ◀

of DINE (Advantica Restaurant Group, owners of Denny's) when the quotation midpoint was 1.00 dollar. The trader submitted a limit sell order that filled 30,000 shares. The remaining 70,000 shares never filled. The price of DINE is now 82 cents. If we use the 1.00-dollar quotation midpoint at the time the trader decided to do the trade as the benchmark price, we obtain the implementation shortfall estimate of the missed trade opportunity cost. It is 12,600 dollars (70,000 shares × 18 cents).

Analysts who measure missed trade opportunity costs face two problems that they do not face when measuring transaction costs. They must decide when to measure their opportunity costs, and they must be sure that their orders are real and not just wishful.

Analysts will measure different opportunity costs depending on when they measure them. In the example above, suppose that one week after DINE dropped to 82 cents, it rose back 1.00 dollar. The estimated opportunity cost then would be zero. The measurement of opportunity costs depends on the date on which it is measured.

Even this result is not entirely clear. Had our trader originally sold the full 100,000 shares at 1.00, he might have bought 100,000 shares when the price dropped to 82 cents. If so, the trader lost the opportunity to make 18,000 dollars when the price went back up to 1.00.

In practice, traders measure opportunity costs at some interval after they first decide to trade, or after they finally give up trying to further fill the order. The interval may be one day, one week, or one month.

Opportunity cost analysts also must decide whether the orders that go unfilled are serious orders or merely wishful ones. Consider our example again. Suppose instead of wanting to sell 100,000 shares, our trader wanted to sell 4 million shares. Four million shares represents 10 percent of all shares outstanding and is 50 times the average daily volume of 80,000 shares. The implementation shortfall estimate of the opportunity cost of failing to sell the unfilled remainder of 3,970,000 shares is 714,600 dollars. This greatly overestimates the true opportunity cost because the trader probably could not have sold so many shares under any circumstances without depressing the price below 82 cents. The trader may have wished that he could sell those shares, but the wish is unrealistic. Even if he was certain that the price would drop to 82 cents, he did not lose the opportunity to make 714,600 dollars in profits because he never had that opportunity. Opportunity costs also must depend on the reasonableness of the order size.

The theoretically proper way to deal with this second problem is to use a benchmark price that reflects the average price at which the trade would have taken place if it had been completed under the most favorable conditions. Since the estimation of such a price is difficult, traders do not solve the problem this way. Instead, they simply monitor their orders to ensure that their sizes are reasonable.

Analysts can measure missed trade opportunity costs relative to any benchmark price. It is most sensible to measure them against the same benchmark price that they use to estimate their transaction costs. By using the same benchmark prices, they state their transaction costs and their missed trade opportunity costs on a comparable basis.

Traders should compare their transaction costs against their missed trade opportunity costs. If the additional transaction costs that they would incur if they traded more aggressively are less than the opportunity costs they

▶ The Plexus Iceberg of Transaction Costs

The Plexus Group provides its clients with a detailed breakdown of their implementation shortfalls into timing, market impact, commission, and missed trade opportunity costs. The firm measures two timing cost components for executed trades. The first is *manager timing*. Plexus also calls this component *system timing* or *model timing*. It is the signed difference between the decision price and the price at the time of submission of the order to the buy-side trading desk. The *decision price* is the market price at the time the manager determined that he or she wanted to trade. Most managers use the previous day's closing price as the decision price. Manager timing measures implementation shortfall while the order is still under the primary control of the portfolio manager. Portfolio managers who have high manager timing costs generally should submit their orders to their buy-side desks faster.

Trader timing is the second timing cost component. It is the signed difference between the price at the time of submission of the order to the buy-side trading desk and the release of the order to a broker. If the buy-side desk breaks up the order, the Plexus Group measures separate trader timing costs for each part. Trader timing measures implementation shortfall while the order is still under the primary control of the buy-side desk. Buy-side traders often have high trader timing costs when they shop a large block so that the market becomes aware that significant size will soon move prices. (See chapter 15.) They also may have high trader timing costs when they split orders into parts and stagger the release of the parts to brokers through time. The market impacts of the initial parts cause what the Plexus Group identifies as trading timing for the remaining parts.

The Plexus Group measures *market impact* as the signed difference between the price at the time of the release of an order to a broker and the execution price. If the order results in several trades, Plexus estimates separate market impacts for each trade. Market impact measures the implementation shortfall while the broker is managing the order. Since most traders will not let a broker sit on an open order overnight, market impact is an intraday effect. Interday timing effects contribute to the trader timing component.

Finally, the Plexus Group measures missed trade opportunity costs as the signed difference between the decision price and the price of the instrument 30 trading days after the decision to trade was made, for the part of the order that was not completed.

To illustrate the relative magnitudes of these various transaction cost components, the Plexus Group created and popularized their *Iceberg of Transaction Costs*. The visible costs of trading—commissions and market impact—correspond to the part of an iceberg that is above the water. The invisible costs—timing and missed trades—correspond to the bulk of the iceberg that is underwater. The Plexus Group estimates that their clients pay 12 basis points in commissions and 20 basis points in market impact. They lose 53 basis points in timing costs as prices move away from them, and they lose an additional 16 basis points due to orders that do not fill. The hidden costs of trade implementation (timing and opportunity costs) thus are much larger than the visible costs (commission and market impact).

The four Plexus components sum to the total implementation shortfall. Plexus believes that it is necessary to measure all these components because costs are readily shifted from one category to another. Traders need to avoid the mental trap where visible costs appear to have been reduced when in fact they have only been moved to the more subtle timing categories. ◀

Source: www.PlexusGroup.com

would save from trading more aggressively, they would earn more profit if they traded more aggressively. Likewise, if the transaction costs that they would save if they traded less aggressively are more than the additional opportunity costs they would incur from trading less aggressively, they would earn more profit if they traded less aggressively.

In practice, most traders do not estimate these marginal costs. Instead, they assume that their marginal costs equal their average costs. Accordingly, they try to trade more or less aggressively if, on a per unit basis, their missed trade opportunity costs are respectively greater or less than their transaction costs. Traders who are concerned about this issue should estimate their marginal transaction costs from the costs of executing the last trades that fill their orders.

21.7 TRANSACTION COST PREDICTION

Traders need to predict transaction costs in order to evaluate active trading strategies. To this end, traders develop, estimate, and use transaction cost prediction models. Most transaction cost prediction analyses use explicit and implicit information to predict transaction costs.

21.7.1 Explicit Information About Future Transaction Costs

Explicit information about future transaction costs consists of the contractual information about commissions and trading fees enumerated above. It also includes current market information about liquidity conditions that market quotations and exposed limit order books typically reveal. When traders seek to trade less size than markets display, they can confidently obtain an upper bound on the market impact of their orders. (These bounds, of course, assume that they can access the liquidity before other traders do.)

Quotation and limit order books rarely reveal the full liquidity available in a market, however. Traders often will not display the full size of their interest for the following reasons:

- They fear front runners.
- They do not want to give away option values.
- They do not want to reveal proprietary information about fundamental values or about their positions.
- They want to avoid offering liquidity to large price-discriminating traders or informed traders.

These issues ensure that traders often can trade at more favorable prices or for greater sizes than is apparent from displayed market information. Traders who want to accurately estimate their transaction costs therefore must estimate how much liquidity might be behind any displayed liquidity that they see.

21.7.2 Implicit Information About Future Transaction Costs

The implicit information that traders use to predict transaction costs consists of information about previous implicit transaction costs. Traders try to characterize this information by assuming that they can predict the market impacts of future orders from the market impacts of previous orders. The assumption is valid when liquidity conditions do not change. Substantial evidence, however, suggests that liquidity varies through time. To the extent that they can, some traders try to model this variation so that they can better predict their transaction costs.

The primary quantitative approach to implicit transaction cost prediction uses econometric regression models to explain past transaction costs by using observable variables. These variables characterize the orders, contemporaneous market conditions, and general market conditions.

The most important variables that characterize orders are order size and price placement. Large orders naturally generate higher transaction costs than do small orders. Likewise, aggressively priced orders typically generate higher transaction costs than do less aggressively priced orders.

The most important variables that characterize contemporaneous market conditions are bid/ask spread and current displayed size. These characterize width and depth. Other variables that traders use include recent volume, recent price changes (price momentum), and sums of volume on upticks versus volume on downticks (money flow). These variables measure transitory liquidity conditions.

The most important variables that characterize general market conditions are average volume and volatility. Transaction costs tend to be low in actively traded markets and in markets with stable prices. In equity markets, analysts often use market capitalization as a proxy for the size of the market. Large firm stocks tend to trade in more liquid markets than do small firm stocks.

21.8 CLOSING COMMENTS ON INTELLIGENT TRANSACTION COST MANAGEMENT

Institutional investment managers and investment sponsors commonly separately evaluate their trade implementation and portfolio selection/composition processes. The two processes are not dichotomous, however. Total performance often can be enhanced when the strategists who generate trading strategies regularly interact with the traders who implement those strategies.

As noted at the beginning of the chapter, portfolio strategists need to know what transaction costs will be before they adopt a trading strategy. Traders therefore need to advise strategists of what is feasible. Strategists must know how much they can trade, and at what cost, in order to form orders that will optimize portfolio values.

Strategists likewise need to tell their traders why they are trading, so that their traders can make good decisions about how aggressively they should trade. For example, when strategists base their orders on short-term information, they must tell their traders to trade aggressively. They also must provide their traders with price limits that reflect the value of their information. Well-informed traders should willingly incur substantial transaction costs, especially when they trade on very short-term information. Otherwise, they may fail to trade and thereby lose the opportunity to make substantial profits. Traders must know why they are trading in order to make the best decisions about how they should trade.

Portfolio strategists and the traders who implement their decisions must cooperate to maximize the value of their combined efforts. The schemes that investment sponsors use to evaluate their operations should not make their strategists and traders adversaries. Portfolio strategists should not be rewarded for blaming traders when they cannot profitably implement their trading strategies, and traders should not be rewarded for blaming strategists when they cannot fill unrealistically large orders. Instead, they should cooperate to obtain the most value from their joint operations.

Joint incentive contracts that reward everyone when the total performance is good provide strong incentives for cooperative behavior. Incentive contracts that attempt to separately identify and reward the contributions of the different participants in the trading process are counterproductive when managers cannot separately identify their contributions. Disentangling contributions is very difficult when personnel must cooperate to produce the best product.

21.9 SUMMARY

Traders estimate their transaction costs so that they can better manage their trading. Good information about their transaction costs allow them to do the following:

- Determine whether they obtain good value for the commissions they pay their brokers
- Balance their transaction costs and their missed trade opportunity costs to optimize their order submission strategies
- Ensure that their trading strategies are—and will be—profitable when implemented

Although transaction cost measurement is noisy, it can produce valuable information that traders can use to help solve these problems.

For many investment managers, reducing transaction costs through more effective trade implementation management improves performance more than would devoting the same resources to improving their portfolio selection decisions. Decreasing transaction costs is often easier and more reliable than improving portfolio section decisions.

21.10 SOME POINTS TO REMEMBER

- Total performance depends on portfolio selection and trade implementation.
- Transaction costs lower portfolio performance.
- Traders estimate transaction costs so that they can better manage them.
- Missed trade opportunity costs can be more significant than transaction costs. Good traders find a balance between the two types of costs when they decide how aggressively to trade.
- Transaction cost measurement depends on price benchmarks.
- Reliable inferences about transaction costs require reasonable benchmarks and many trades.
- Informed trading, contrarian trading, order splitting, and gaming may bias some transaction cost estimates.
- Brokers often can game a transaction cost measure by deferring trades or by mimicking their benchmarks.
- Transaction costs to the buy side are revenues to the sell side.

• Good managers consider transaction costs when making portfolio composition decisions.

21.11 QUESTIONS FOR THOUGHT

1. What services besides low transaction costs should brokers provide?
2. Analysts can conduct implementation shortfall transaction cost studies by using ask prices as price benchmarks when buying and bid prices as price benchmarks when selling. What advantages and disadvantages would this method have relative to the standard quotation midpoint benchmark method?
3. What is the relation between missed trade opportunity costs and transaction costs when traders optimize their trading?
4. Which types of profit-motivated traders would you expect should have high measured transaction costs? Which types should have low measured transaction costs?
5. In the extended example of section 21.4.4, the implementation shortfall transaction cost estimate for the four-trade round-trip was 400 dollars. If the market closed at 30.05 dollars, the closing price transaction cost estimate also would be 400 dollars. These two estimates are not normally equal. Why are they equal for the four-trade round-trip in this example?

22

▷

Performance
Evaluation
and
Prediction

Many people trade because they want to speculate successfully. They hope to profit by buying securities and contracts that will rise in value and by selling those that will fall.

Unfortunately for those of us who would like to get rich quickly, predicting future prices is quite difficult. Some people can do it, but most cannot. Successful speculators must predict future prices well enough to beat the market on average. Unsuccessful speculators eventually lose money when trading. At best, they make less money than they would have made if they had simply bought and held index funds. If they trade only because they want to earn speculative trading profits, they should stop trading.

In this chapter, we consider how to measure past performance and how to predict future performance. The two questions are closely related. Most people measure past performance primarily because they want to predict future performance. We shall see why predictions based only on past performance generally are quite unreliable. We can predict performance better by using other information.

You must be able to predict performance if you intend to speculate. Speculators trade only because they expect to profit. Successful speculators therefore must constantly consider whether their trades will be profitable. If you cannot predict whether you will trade profitably, you should not speculate. The most important decision speculators make is whether they should trade.

You also must be able to predict performance if you employ active investment managers to speculate on your behalf. *Active investment managers* speculate with their clients' money. They are *active*, as opposed to *passive*, because they actively try to identify and exploit speculative opportunities. Accordingly, they often trade frequently. You can hire their services by employing them as investment advisers or you can obtain their services indirectly by buying the mutual funds and commodity pools that they manage. In either event, when managers speculate on your behalf, you speculate on their success. To select good active investment managers, you must predict which ones will speculate successfully. If you cannot predict which managers will be successful, you should not employ active investment managers. The most important decision investment sponsors make is whether to employ active managers.

Investors who believe that they cannot speculate successfully often invest their money with passive investment managers. *Passive investment managers* use *buy and hold strategies*. They simply buy and hold securities. Passive managers therefore rarely trade. The most common buy and hold strategy is the index replication strategy. *Index replicators* buy and hold portfolios that they design to replicate the returns to a broad market index. We discuss how they do this in chapter 23.

Indexing is very popular because many investors have decided that they do not want to speculate. They do not believe that they would be successful traders, and they do not believe that they can pick successful managers. The limitations of performance evaluation and prediction help explain why index markets are so popular.

People often design investment management contracts so that the payments investment managers receive depend on their performance. Such contracts encourage investment managers to better serve their clients. You must appreciate the limitations of performance evaluation in order to understand how to best compensate investment managers and to understand the problems that arise in typical investment management contracts.

We begin with a discussion of the principal problem of discriminating between skill and luck. We then briefly consider the mechanics of performance evaluation. If you already know how analysts compute returns, and how and why they compare them against benchmark returns, you can skip this section. The discussion then turns to the problem of predicting performance. We first consider how statisticians approach the problem and explain why their approach is not very powerful. We then consider alternative approaches to performance prediction based on economic theory.

By the end of this chapter, you will understand why past performance does not necessarily predict future returns. You will also understand how sample selection biases affect the inferences you may make about investment decisions. Failures to understand these issues probably account for more trading losses than any other mistakes traders make.

22.1 THE PERFORMANCE EVALUATION PROBLEM

Portfolio performance depends partly on the quality of its management. Managers who perform well add value to their portfolios. Managers who perform poorly waste value.

Portfolio performance also depends on every factor that determines the values of the instruments in the portfolio. The factors may include macroeconomic, microeconomic, and firm-specific factors. *Macroeconomic factors* include changes in interest rates, general economic activity, productivity, and exchange rates. *Microeconomic factors* include industry supply and demand conditions, technological innovations, and government interventions. *Firm-specific factors* include a host of issues ranging from whether the firm is well managed to whether factories accidentally burn down to whether researchers make fortuitous discoveries.

Active managers try to foresee every factor that will affect values. They then buy instruments that they expect will appreciate and sell those they expect will depreciate. If they are very skilled, they will be able to add substantial value to their portfolios by selecting which instruments to buy and which to sell.

No one can anticipate most factors that affect portfolio returns. Unforeseeable factors therefore have a seemingly random effect on performance. Portfolios that perform well may be managed by skilled managers or by lucky managers. Likewise, poorly performing portfolios may be managed by unskilled managers or by unlucky managers.

The investment policies that govern many portfolios often have a substantial effect on portfolio performance. These policies may prohibit skilled managers from exploiting positive factors or from avoiding negative factors.

▶ Sizzler Sick with *E. Coli*

Sizzler International is an operator/franchiser of family restaurants that specialize in grilled meats. Sizzler operates 65 company restaurants in the United States, and it franchises another 200. In 1998, the company reorganized in a voluntary Chapter 11 bankruptcy. By the middle of 2000, its earnings were accelerating and many analysts, who had carefully studied the company and its prospects, believed that it had a winning strategy for revitalizing the chain. Based on their research, many investment managers bought Sizzler, expecting that it would outperform the market.

They did not immediately realize their expectations. In July 2000, the bacterium *E. coli* infected 42 patrons of a Milwaukee Sizzler franchise. Seventeen were hospitalized, and a three-year-old girl died from complications resulting from the infection.

Undercooked meats or food contaminated by raw meat spread the *E. coli* infection. The Milwaukee health commissioner believed that the infected patrons ate contaminated watermelon.

News about the outbreak was well publicized throughout the country. Following the announcement, Sizzler's stock fell 35 percent as investors feared the lawsuits and the lost reputation that would surely follow this tragic event.

The speculators who bought Sizzler may have been very well informed about its prospects. They undoubtedly knew that food poisoning episodes occasionally plague restaurant chains, and they probably discounted Sizzler's stock—and those of other restaurant chains—accordingly. Some may even have considered whether Sizzler designed and implemented adequate sanitation procedures to appropriately control the risks that they faced. Despite all these considerations, the Sizzler *E. coli* food poisoning episode probably was not predictable. These investors were simply unlucky. ◀

They also may force unskilled managers to unknowingly exploit positive factors or avoid negative factors. Portfolios that perform well therefore may be managed by skilled managers or simply by lucky managers subject to investment policies that the market currently favors. Likewise, poorly performing portfolios may be managed by unskilled managers or by skilled managers subject to investment policies that currently are out of favor.

For example, consider the performance of portfolios that must be fully invested in equity. These portfolios fluctuate in value with the market regardless of how management operates. When the market rises, even the most poorly managed portfolios may have high positive returns. A market rise can offset losses due to inept management. Likewise, when the market falls, the best-managed portfolios may have negative returns. A market fall can overwhelm gains due to superior management. Analysts often characterize this phenomenon by saying, "A rising tide lifts all boats."

Unforeseeable factors and unavoidable factors greatly complicate the performance evaluation problem. These factors make it difficult to estimate the manager's contribution to portfolio performance. Good performance evaluations must discriminate between skill and luck. Analysts must break total performance into separate components representing the contribution due to management and the contribution due to factors that no one could anticipate or control.

The task of estimating the contribution of factors that no one could anticipate or control is very difficult because so many factors affect portfolio

▶ The Combinations of Luck and Skill

Since luck is random, no relation exists between luck and skill. Skilled people are sometimes lucky and sometimes unlikely. Likewise, unskilled people are sometimes lucky and sometimes unlucky. For your amusement, consider the following characterizations of the four possible combinations of luck and skill:

	Skilled	Unskilled
Lucky	Blessed	Insufferable
Unlucky	Cursed	Doomed

returns. Even the best estimates of manager performance are quite noisy. Discriminating between skill and luck as explanations for portfolio performance is very difficult.

22.2 PERFORMANCE EVALUATION METHODS

These considerations suggest that relative performance evaluations are more valuable than absolute performance evaluations. *Absolute performance evaluations* simply compute total portfolio returns. *Relative performance evaluations* estimate how much portfolios have outperformed or underperformed the benchmarks or peers against which they are measured. By choosing benchmarks to represent how analysts expect portfolios would have performed without active management, they are better able to identify the contribution of management.

To measure the relative performance of a portfolio, analysts examine the difference between the total return to the portfolio and the concurrent total return to the benchmark. We therefore must consider how analysts measure absolute portfolio performance before we consider how to measure relative portfolio performance.

22.2.1 Absolute Performance Measurement

Analysts measure the *absolute performance* of a portfolio when they estimate how much the nominal value of the portfolio has changed over some measurement interval. The measurement interval may be a year, a quarter, a month, a week, or a day; or it may be a current period to date, such as *year-to-date* (YTD).

Measuring absolute performance is a relatively simple problem when investors have not transferred money or securities into or out of the portfolio. The *total return* to the portfolio is the percentage change in its value over the measurement interval. For example, if the value of a portfolio increases from 100 to 120 over a year, its total return for the year is 20 percent.

The *total return* includes the value of any cash and securities that the portfolio receives or pays in conjunction with its holdings. Cash inflows typically include dividends, interest, and security lending fees received. Outflows include brokerage commissions, management fees, interest paid to purchase securities on credit, security borrowing fees, and short dividends. Portfolio cash flows also include all *variational margin payments* that the portfolio receives, or must make, when holding long or short positions in futures, options, and swaps, and when holding short positions in securities.

▶ The Beardstown Ladies

Founded in 1983, the Beardstown Business and Professional Women's Club is a famous investment club composed of about 15 women. By 1993, most of its members were in or near retirement, but still actively managing their portfolio.

The club wrote several books and produced videos about their approach to investing. *The Beardstown Ladies' Common-Sense Investment Guide: How We Beat the Stock Market—And How You Can, Too* (1994) became an international best seller.

On the jacket of that book, the Beardstown ladies claimed that they earned an average annual return of 23.4 percent in the 10 years ending in 1993. When challenged, they recomputed their returns with the assistance of the Price Waterhouse accounting firm. Their actual annual average return was 9.1 percent, significantly less than the 14.9 percent average annual total return to the S&P 500 Index over the same period. Many people wondered how they could have thought that they were beating the market when they were actually underperforming it by an annual average of almost 6 percent.

The ladies reported that they failed to properly use investment accounting software with which they were unfamiliar. They consequently mistook a 2-year return for a 10-year return. Additional information in their explanation supports the conclusion that they did not have strong computer skills—which would not be surprising for professional women (or men) in or nearing retirement in 1993. Their apparent lack of computational sophistication suggests that their reported explanation may be accurate.

Many people, however, think that the women simply failed to account for the regular contributions that they made to their fund. Over 10 years, such a failure would lead to a gross overstatement of their total returns. Such a mistake would have been far more embarrassing to admit than the computational mistake that they reported. ◀

Sources: www.time.com/time/magazine/1998/dom/980330/business.jail_the_ beards12.html (Overview); www.better-investing.org/clubs/from-the-ladies.html (explanation by Betty Sinnock, Beardstown BPW Club senior partner).

Inflows and outflows of securities typically involve corporate reorganizations such as mergers, acquisitions, and spin-offs.

When investors transfer money (or securities) into or out of a portfolio, or when the portfolio distributes dividends to its investors, the total value of the portfolio changes. Without an adjustment, the change in portfolio value would misrepresent the actual performance of the portfolio. Capital additions would inflate the performance and capital distributions would deflate it.

Analysts use two approaches to address the problem of capital additions and distributions. The most common approach is to compute the internal rate of return for the portfolio. The *internal rate of return* (IRR) is the compounded rate of return that a savings account would have to earn to exactly replicate the capital flows into and out of the portfolio. The IRR calculation assumes that beginning and ending savings account balances are equal to the beginning and ending portfolio values. The IRR is approximately a time- and value-weighted geometric average of the total returns measured between each capital addition and distribution.

For many purposes, people would prefer to know the *holding period return* for a share of a portfolio rather than the average return earned by all investors in the portfolio. The holding period return estimates how much an investor would have made if he or she had invested a dollar in the portfolio at the beginning of the measurement period. Analysts typically compute holding period returns by assuming that all distributions are reinvested in the portfolio when they are paid.

The holding period return and the internal rate of return differ when capital additions and distributions do not occur on a pro rata basis within the measurement period. Capital additions and distributions are on a *pro rata* basis occur when all investors participate in the capital transactions in exact proportion to their ownership shares. Since pro rata additions and distributions do not affect the proportion of the portfolio that each owner owns, all investors have the same internal rate of return over the holding period.

Analysts often separate the total return into its *current yield* component and its *capital gains* component. The *current yield* of a portfolio (or of a security) is the total income—typically interest and dividends—that the portfolio receives from its assets divided by the value of the portfolio. For example, if the securities in a 100-million-dollar portfolio pay 10 million dollars in dividends to the portfolio in a year, the current yield for that year is 10 percent. The *capital gains return* of a portfolio is the difference between the total return and the yield. It is the percentage change in the value of the assets of the portfolio, exclusive of the income that the assets pay. The distribution of total return into the current yield and the capital gains return is of particular interest to investors for whom ordinary income and capital gains are taxed at different rates.

The current yield of the assets of a portfolio can be different from the current yield that owners of a portfolio receive. This happens when the portfolio pays its investors more or less income than it receives from its assets.

Analysts who measure performance must estimate values for all portfolio positions at the beginning and end of the measurement period. Estimating values for instruments that trade in active markets is quite simple. Analysts usually estimate such values by the last trade price or by the midpoint between the last bid and offer prices. The estimation problem is much more difficult for instruments that do not trade often. In that case, analysts must estimate values from the prices of related instruments. For example, estimating the value of a real estate portfolio can be extremely difficult. Managers must generally estimate values by means of appraisals that depend critically on the sales prices of comparable properties. Estimated valuations of infrequently traded bonds likewise depend on the sales prices of similar debt instruments.

22.2.2 Relative Performance Measurement

Raw returns are not useful for evaluating performance without some basis for comparison. For example, an equity portfolio that drops 10 percent when the market drops 20 percent has performed well relative to the market. In contrast, an equity portfolio that rises 15 percent when the market is up 30 percent has performed relatively poorly.

Analysts compute *relative returns* to facilitate performance comparisons. A *relative return* is the difference between a portfolio return and a corresponding *benchmark return*. Analysts choose benchmarks to represent how they expect the portfolio would have performed without active management.

▶ **When Is 100 – 50 = 0?**

Investors must be very careful when summing percentage returns. Suppose that a portfolio has a 100 percent increase in one year, followed by a 50 percent decrease in the next year. The summed arithmetic return over the two years is 50 percent. The actual holding period return over the two years, however, is exactly zero. (Prices double the first year and halve the second year.)

To properly compute a holding period return from a series of returns, you must compute their geometric sum rather than their arithmetic sum. You add 1 to each return, then multiply the resulting sums, and finally subtract 1 from the product. ◀

▶ **–94.7% + 95.6% = Very Bad News**

ProFunds UltraOTC Fund lost 94.7 percent between March 10, 2000, and April 4, 2001, and gained 95.6 percent from April 4 to May 2, 2001. Had you invested 10,000 dollars in the fund on March 10, 2000, your position would have been worth just 1,037 dollars on May 2, 2001. ◀

Source: Karen Damato, "Doing the Math: Tech Investors' Road to Recovery Is Long," Wall Street Journal May 18, 2001, p. C1 (Western edition).

▶ Smooth Sailing, Rapids Ahead

Investors generally like stable portfolios because they are risk averse. Their investment managers therefore hope to report stable values.

Managers of portfolios that include highly illiquid assets must estimate values for their assets when there are no sales prices. To create stable values, unethical managers may be slow to change their estimates when values change. They may be especially slow to adjust values when they fall. Investors in such funds therefore may believe that their funds are less risky than they actually are.

When true asset values differ significantly from the manager's estimated values, various processes may force the manager to revalue them quickly. For example, if investors try to withdraw funds from the portfolio, the manager may have to sell assets. The resulting sales may be at substantially lower prices than the manager last estimated. These sales will cause the reported value of the portfolio to drop significantly. Seemingly secure funds therefore may be quite risky.

Investors who are concerned about the valuation of illiquid assets should look at the sequence of reported portfolio returns. Returns display positive serial correlation when managers are smoothing values. ◀

▶ AIMR-PPS

Although performance measurement seems very straightforward, difficulties involving exotic contracts, infrequently traded instruments, foreign exchange rates, and complex portfolio ownership structures complicate many performance measurement problems. Reasonable people often can arrive at different results using the same data.

To ensure that performance measurements are presented on a comparable basis, the Association for Investment Management and Research (AIMR) developed performance presentation standards that they encourage analysts to use. The AIMR performance presentation standards (AIMR-PPS) allow investors to directly compare the performance of different investment managers. ◀

Source: The AIMR presentation standards appear at www.aimr. com/standards/pps/ppsstand. html.

The purpose of the benchmark comparison is to remove noise in the performance evaluation. A good benchmark adjusts raw returns to account for performance that should not be attributed to the manager. The remaining measure of performance therefore better represents the performance of the manager.

22.2.2.1 Market-adjusted Returns

The most common benchmarks that analysts use to evaluate performance for equity portfolios are market indexes. For example, analysts generally compare portfolios that primarily hold a diversified set of large capitalization U.S. stocks against the S&P 500 Index. They use specialized indexes to evaluate portfolios that invest in other asset classes. Table 22-1 provides a list of commonly used benchmark indexes.

Market-adjusted returns are portfolio returns minus corresponding market index returns. The market-adjusted returns in the above example are 10 percent and −15 percent. For most purposes, market-adjusted returns demonstrate how well the portfolio has performed better than raw returns do.

22.2.2.2 Risk-adjusted Returns

Analysts sometimes further adjust raw returns to account for the exposure of portfolios to known risks. For example, consider the exposure of a portfolio to *market risk*. Market risk is the risk that values will rise or fall with marketwide changes in value. It varies by security, and therefore also by portfolio. Analysts characterize market risk by the *market beta* of a security. Beta measures the extent to which the security fluctuates in value with the market. A stock with a beta of 0.5 tends to rise or fall only 0.5 percent for every 1 percent rise or fall in the market. It is only half as risky as the market. The beta of a portfolio is the value-weighted average of the betas of the various securities in the portfolio. Since the market has a beta of 1, and since the market is just a portfolio of all available securities, the value-weighted average beta of all securities is 1.

TABLE 22-1.
Some Common Benchmark Indexes

ASSET CLASS	BENCHMARK
Large capitalization U.S. equities	S&P 500 Index and S&P 100 Index Russell 1000 NYSE Composite Index
Small capitalization U.S. equities	Russell 2000 Wilshire Small Cap 1750 Index
Total U.S. stock market	Russell 3000 Wilshire 5000 Total Market Index
Utilities	Dow Jones Utility Index S&P Utility Index NYSE Utility Index
Oil industry equities	CBOE OIX Index AMEX XIO
U.S. large capitalization technology equities	Nasdaq 100 Merrill Lynch 100 Technology Index Goldman Sachs Technology Industry Composite Index
German equities	DAX
London equities	FTSE 100
Tokyo equities	TOPIX Nikkei 225 Stock Average
French Equities	CAC 40
European equities	Morgan Stanley Capital International (MSCI) Europe Index
World equities	MSCI World Index
Southeast Asian equities	MSCI Pacific Free Index
Commodity futures/Some hedge funds	LIBOR Goldman Sachs Commodity Index 3-month Treasury bill yields
Investment grade U.S. corporate bonds	Lehman Brothers Corporate Intermediate Bond Index Merrill Lynch Long-term Corporate Index
High yield U.S. corporate bonds (junk bonds)	Lehman Brothers High Yield Bond Index Credit Suisse First Boston High Yield Index Merrill Lynch High Yield Master Index
U.S. municipal bonds	Lehman Brothers Municipal Index
U.S. money market funds	6-month Treasury bill yields Merrill Lynch 6-month Treasury Bill Index

▶ Foolish John

John took money out of a savings account where it was earning 5 percent to invest in the stock market. He made 23 percent trading actively and was delighted with his performance. He thought that he could pick stocks really well!

That same year, the S&P 500 rose 33 percent. Had John invested in an S&P 500 Index fund, he would have made 33 percent.

John was pleased with his performance because he used the wrong frame of reference. He beat his measly savings account return by 18 percent. His performance was terrible, however, because he did not get the average return that other people got for bearing similar equity risks. He underperformed the market by 10 percent.

Satisfied with his expertise, John decided to continue to trade actively. The next year, he again underperformed the market by 10 percent. Unfortunately, that year the S&P 500 lost 10 percent. John lost 20 percent, which is 25 percent worse than he would have done had he kept his money in his savings account.

His total return for the two years was −1.6 percent. (The holding period is computed as $(1 + 0.23) \times (1 - 0.20) - 1$.) The corresponding two-year S&P 500 return was 19.7 percent. Had John kept his money in the savings account, he would have earned 10.3 percent. ◀

Managers who construct low beta portfolios tend to underperform the market when it is rising and outperform it when it falling. Likewise, those who construct high beta portfolios tend to outperform the market when it is rising and underperform it when it is falling.

To account for these effects, analysts compute *risk-adjusted excess returns* by subtracting the average portfolio beta times the market return from the raw portfolio return. The resulting measure is also called the portfolio's *realized alpha*. The realized alpha helps analysts determine whether a manager successfully selects winners and losers after accounting for market risk.

22.2.2.3 Market Timing

An equity manager *times the market* when she changes the portfolio beta to exploit her predictions about the future direction of the market. Managers change their portfolio betas by exchanging high beta assets for low beta assets or vice versa. For example, managers lower their portfolio betas by selling securities and leaving the proceeds in cash, by selling high beta securities and buying low beta securities, by selling index futures, by buying puts, by selling calls, or by selling securities short. They raise their portfolio betas by doing the opposite.

Risk-adjusted excess returns are best computed frequently because the portfolio beta changes whenever the manager exchanges assets that have different betas. To accurately estimate risk-adjusted returns, analysts must multiply market returns by concurrent portfolio betas.

Analysts who compute risk-adjusted returns often also compute *market-timing returns*. The market-timing return is the difference between the portfolio beta times the market return and the market return. It indicates whether the portfolio manager is a skilled market timer.

To summarize, raw portfolio returns can be broken into the sum of three parts: the market return, the market timing return, and the risk-adjusted excess return:

$$\text{Raw Return} = (\text{Raw Return} - \text{Beta} \times \text{Market Return})$$
$$+ (\text{Beta} \times \text{Market Return} - \text{Market Return})$$
$$+ \text{Market Return}$$

$$= \text{Excess Return} + \text{Market Timing Return} + \text{Market Return}.$$

Analysts use these decompositions to attribute performance to the market, to the manager's timing ability, and to all other factors—including, of course, the manager's risk-adjusted selection skills.

Analysts can easily generalize this decomposition to include other risk factors besides market risk. Finance courses and textbooks about investments describe these *multifactor risk models*. The most common additional risk factors that analysts use to analyze equity portfolios are factors that measure risks associated with firm size and with expected growth.

22.3 THE PERFORMANCE PREDICTION PROBLEM

People often evaluate past performance because they want to predict the future performance of a manager. Such analyses are valuable only if the factors that determined past performance will continue to determine future performance. Most people rarely think carefully about whether this will be true.

▶ Buy and Hold Benchmarks

The difference between the portfolio return and the return that the portfolio would have made had the manager not traded is a direct measure of an active manager's contribution to portfolio performance. This measure is intuitively attractive because it focuses only on the manager's decisions. The benchmark index for this approach to performance measurement is the beginning-of-period portfolio. Unfortunately, a serious problem complicates the use of this approach.

This approach identifies only superior performance that takes place during the measurement period. Any superior performance that accrues in subsequent periods contributes to the performance of subsequent benchmarks. For example, suppose a manager buys a stock at the beginning of the year. The manager believes the stock will appreciate significantly over the next two years. The appreciation in the first year will accrue to his benefit, but the appreciation in the second year will not. A similar problem applies to sales. This problem causes managers to focus on short-term ideas. It also causes them to delay the implementation of ideas generated near the end of the year.

Changing the definition of the benchmark index can reduce this problem. Instead of the beginning-of-period portfolio, a better benchmark would be the portfolio that would have been created if all trades made by the manager occurred one year later. With this benchmark, all trades get the benefit of at least one full year of evaluation. ◀

Whether the factors that determined a manager's past performance will continue to determine his or her future performance depends on three fundamental conditions. Each of the following conditions must be true to successfully predict future returns from past performance:

- *Past performance must reflect the manager's skills.* If past performance was due only to luck, it will have no bearing on future returns.

- *The manager's skills will continue to generate good future returns.* The skills necessary to perform well may vary by market conditions. For example, traders who succeed in bull markets may not succeed in bear markets. Past performance will have no bearing on future returns if the skills that generated it are no longer effective.

- *The manager still has the skills necessary for success.* Investment management firms often lose essential skills when they lose employees or access to valuable resources. Investment managers also often lose essential skills as they age or lose their drive. Past performance will have no bearing on future returns if the skills that generated it are no longer available.

If any of these conditions is not true, attempts to predict future performance from past performance will not be productive. People therefore should verify these conditions before attempting to predict future returns from past performance.

Analysts may use analytic or statistical methods to determine whether performance is due to luck or to skill (the first condition). In the analytic approach, analysts try to identify the skills that determined past performance. This task is quite difficult because analysts must understand the management process well enough to recognize what determined past performance. In the statistical approach, analysts use statistical methods to show that luck alone cannot reasonably explain past performance. Analysts often

▶ Regulation FD

Regulation FD requires that publicly traded corporations immediately disclose to the entire public any material information that they disclose to any unrelated person. Before the U.S. Securities and Exchange Commission adopted this regulation in 2000, investment managers who were skilled at arranging and conducting interviews with corporate insiders often could obtain valuable material information from them. These skills no longer are as valuable as they once were now that Regulation FD prohibits this practice. The past performance of managers who had these skills therefore is not a good predictor of their future performance. ◀

Our Faith in Past Performance

Why do so many people assume that past performance can predict future returns? This assumption is so pervasive and so wrong, it begs for an explanation. Perhaps behavioral biology can help us better understand ourselves.

During our evolutionary history as creatures that could learn from our environment, our ancestors survived by learning that things which happened in the past often would happen again. Our ancestral aunts and uncles who did not use the past to predict the future often did not survive to reproduce. Other creatures ate them, they fell off cliffs, they starved, or they froze to death. We are here today because our ancestral parents successfully used the past to predict the future. Natural selection has hardwired us to believe that performance is persistent. ◀

use the statistical approach to avoid the difficulties associated with the analytic approach. The statistical approach, however, has its own difficulties. We discuss them in the next section.

To determine whether the manager's skills will continue to generate good future returns (the second condition), analysts must first identify the skills that determined past performance. They then must decide whether those skills will continue to be useful. This second task is more difficult than the first task because explaining the past generally is easier than predicting the future. Predictions about the future necessarily depend on uncertain assumptions.

Analysts generally can determine whether the manager still has the necessary skills to perform well (the third condition) by direct inquiry. The determination, of course, is reliable only if the analysts know what skills to look for.

Since the verification of all three conditions is difficult, most people simply do not do it. Instead, they just assume that past performance can predict future returns. The prediction of future returns from past performance, however, is notoriously imprecise. We know this both from experience and from statistical theory.

22.3.1 Some Empirical Evidence

In the next section, we examine the problems that make statistical performance evaluation unreliable. Before we do so, let us consider some compelling empirical evidence.

Financial researchers have observed that essentially no correlation exists between the best-performing funds in one year and the best-performing funds in the next year. Good past performers are about equally likely to be good future performers as are poor past performers. Good past performance simply does not regularly predict good future performance.

(The very worst-performing funds, however, tend to remain at the bottom from year to year. These funds typically lose because they trade too much and because they have high management fees. As long as these conditions do not change, they stay at the bottom.)

These results are very robust. They are true for equity funds, bond funds, and commodity pools. The results are uniform across years and across countries. The results are similar when performance is measured by quarter or by month. The results do not depend on the criteria for identifying the best funds. These empirical results strongly suggest that statistical methods cannot reliably predict future performance from past returns.

22.4 STATISTICAL PERFORMANCE EVALUATION

Past performance poorly predicts future returns primarily because past performance generally is due more to luck than to skill. Unpredictable return factors very often obscure the value that skilled management can add to a portfolio.

This result is not surprising. Future price changes are largely unpredictable—even for well-informed traders—because informed traders make most instrument prices quite informative. Moreover, the competition among informed traders to profit from information ensures that few traders will have great insights into the future. We therefore do not expect that even highly skilled managers will have remarkably large returns on average.

We can see why past performance is so uninformative by considering how statisticians judge whether a manager can systematically beat the market. Their methods measure whether actual performance is greater than luck alone can reasonably explain. To determine what is reasonable, statisticians examine return distributions. The *distribution* of a variable tells us the probability of every possible value of the variable.

In a typical statistical analysis, statisticians use probability theory to characterize the distribution of possible returns that we would expect if managers were not skilled. This distribution therefore assumes that only luck determines performance. If the actual market-adjusted return is significantly greater than we would typically expect, based on luck alone, statisticians conclude that some factor other than luck probably contributed to the return. The likely factor is the skill of the investment manager.

This section presents the test that analysts most commonly use to determine whether managers are skilled. We describe the reliability of the test, and how analysts should use it when deciding whether to invest with an active manager. Although our presentation assumes that analysts will apply the test to equity managers, the methods apply equally well to all other types of managers.

I wrote this section so that any reader should be able to understand it. You do not need to know statistics to understand it. Without using mathematical notation, the text explains every statistical concept that you need to know to understand statistical performance evaluation.

If you do not want to have a deeper understanding of the statistical problems associated with performance evaluation, you may wish to skip this section. (You would be poorly advised to do so, however, if you work in, or intend to work in, investment management.) The most important principle that you need to know is that statistical performance evaluation is generally unreliable because unpredictable return factors make it very difficult to identify managerial skill. In practice, more than 20 years of returns data are typically required to obtain useful results for a given investment manager. Even more data are required to determine whether the most successful investment manager, selected from of a large group of managers, was skilled or just lucky.

22.4.1 The *t*-Test

To determine whether a manager can systematically beat the market, statisticians typically examine the ratio between the manager's average market-adjusted return and a measure of average size they call the *standard error of the mean*. The *standard error* is a number that statisticians compute based on results from probability theory. It is proportional to the average size of the market-adjusted return that we would expect to observe if only luck were responsible for the manager's returns. If this ratio—called *Student's t-statistic* or simply the *t-ratio*—is large, statisticians conclude that luck alone probably cannot explain the returns.

For example, if the manager has no skill, the probability that the *t*-statistic will be greater than 1.64 is only 5 percent. (The calculation of this probability assumes a one-sided *t*-test.) If statisticians conclude that the manager is skilled whenever the *t*-statistic for a manager's portfolio exceeds this *critical value*, they will be mistaken 5 percent of the time.

▶ **Student's Brew Samples**

W. S. Gosset first identified the *t*-test and the associated *t*-distribution. Gosset was a statistician who worked for Guinness Brewery in Great Britain. He invented the *t*-test in 1908 to analyze small brew samples for quality control.

The brewery did not want Gosset to publish under his own name. Gosset therefore published under the pseudonym Student. This restriction explains why the *t*-distribution is also known as Student's distribution. ◀

The *critical value* depends primarily on the *confidence level of the test*—in this example, 95 percent—and to a lesser extent on the sample size. The critical value for a less discriminating test is smaller. For example, the critical value corresponding to a 90 percent confidence level is only 1.31. The critical value corresponding to a 50 percent confidence level is zero. If luck alone determines market-adjusted returns, they will be positive 50 percent of the time.

(Statisticians generally express the confidence level of a test in terms of its *significance level*. The significance level of a test is 1 minus the confidence level. This exposition uses confidence levels instead of significance levels because they are less confusing.)

The test works because luck and skill have different long-term effects on average portfolio returns. Luck, by definition, is random and completely unpredictable. Good luck is as common as bad luck. Good luck increases returns and bad luck lowers them. Given enough time, however, the net effect of luck on average returns is small. In contrast, skill has a systematic positive effect on returns. Over time, a skillful manager should outperform the market.

22.4.2 A Power Calculation

This *t*-test is *powerful* when statisticians are likely to conclude that the manager is skilled, given that the manager is indeed skilled. The probability that the *t*-ratio will exceed the critical value, given that the manager is skilled, is the *power* of the test. Statisticians calculate power using probability theory.

The power of the test depends on several factors:

- Power increases when the confidence level of the test decreases. Low confidence level tests have low critical values for the *t*-ratio. If the manager is skilled, the probability that his *t*-ratio will exceed the critical value (the power of the test) is greater when the critical value is small.
- Power also increases with the skill of the manager. A highly skilled manager should have higher returns, and therefore a higher *t*-ratio.
- The power of the test decreases with the importance of luck as a factor that determines returns. When luck primarily determines returns, bad luck can cause a skilled manager to perform poorly, and therefore have a *t*-statistic that is smaller than the critical value.
- Finally, power increases with the years of data analyzed. Over a long period, good luck and bad luck tend to offset each other so that the manager's *t*-ratio depends more on skill than on luck. The probability that a skilled manager's *t*-ratio will exceed the critical value (the power of the test) therefore is greater when many years of returns data are included in the test.

To compute the power of the *t*-test, we must specify quantities for these four factors. We specify the confidence level when we create the test. The number of years of returns generally depends on what data are available. We specify the last two factors—the true skill of the manager and the importance of luck as a determinant of returns—by considering the economic context of the performance evaluation problem.

We quantify the true skill of a manager by how much we expect him to beat the market each year on average. A large number will imply a powerful test, but we cannot reasonably assume a large expected return. The competition among informed traders to profit from information, the costs of obtaining information, and the informational efficiency of most financial markets make large expected returns unrealistic. Given the competitive environment, most professional managers would be delighted beyond description if they were certain that they could beat the market by 2 percent per year, on average.

To put this number into perspective, consider the performance of two of the most successful equity managers ever. Over 36 years through 2000, Warren Buffet, chairman of Berkshire Hathaway, beat the market by an average of 11.8 percent per year. During much of this period, however, he may have been quite lucky as well as quite skilled. Between 1991 and 2000, his performance dropped to 6.8 percent per year over the market. I will comment more on his performance below.

Consider also the performance of Peter Lynch. During his 13 years as manager of the Fidelity Magellan Fund, the fund outperformed the market by an average of 12.7 percent per year. In his last five years, however, the Fund outperformed the market by an average of only 5.1 percent per year. Like Warren Buffet, Peter Lynch may have been quite lucky as well as quite skilled.

The performance of these superstars was quite remarkable. The fact that they have not been able to sustain their initial performance rates suggests that they may have been quite lucky in the beginning of their tenures. (The decline may also be due to the increased difficulties of managing ever-larger funds.) If we assume that their real skill is somewhere between 5 and 7 percent—this still seems high to me—it is reasonable to assume that the skill of a typical skilled manager is only 2 percent.

We quantify the importance of luck as a determinant of returns by the *standard deviation* that we would expect market-adjusted returns would have if only pure luck generated them. The *standard deviation* is a probability concept that measures the variation of a variable about its mean. The standard deviation of market-adjusted returns depends on the standard deviation of the portfolio returns, the standard deviation of the market returns, and the correlation between the two returns. An increase in either standard deviation increases the market-adjusted return standard deviation. A high correlation lowers the market-adjusted return standard deviation. Probability theory gives us a formula for the market-adjusted return standard deviation, σ_{Adj}. It is $\sigma_{Adj} = \sqrt{\sigma_{Port}^2 + \sigma_{Mk}^2 - 2\rho\sigma_{Port}\sigma_{Mk}}$ where ρ is the correlation. If the portfolio is well diversified, empirical experience suggests that reasonable annual values for these parameters are $\sigma_{Port} = 16\%$, $\sigma_M = 14.5\%$, and $\rho = 0.9$. These values imply a market-adjusted return standard deviation of 7.0 percent.

Table 22-2 presents power calculations for various combinations of these parameters. The results show that if we want to be 95 percent confident that we do not identify an unskilled manager as skilled, the probability that the *t*-test will identify a skilled (2 percent) manager using five years of monthly data is only 15 percent! An additional five years of data only raises this probability only to 23 percent. The test requires more data than are generally available to confidently separate skill from luck.

If we use a test with a lower confidence level of 75 percent, we will identify an unskilled manager as a skilled manager one time out of four. Even

TABLE 22-2.

The Power of a Standard One-sided *t*-Test of Manager Performance

TRUE MANAGER SKILL	TEST CONFIDENCE LEVEL	YEARS OF RETURNS	TEST POWER
0%	50%	Any number	50%
	75	Any number	75
	95	Any number	95
2	50	1	61
		5	74
		10	82
	75	1	34
		5	48
		10	59
	95	1	8
		5	15
		10	23
4	50	1	71
		5	90
		10	96
	75	1	45
		5	72
		10	87
	95	1	12
		5	35
		10	56

Notes: The t-*test attempts to determine whether a manager is skilled in the sense that he can beat the market on average. The confidence level of the test is the probability that the test does not identify an unskilled manager as a skilled manager. The power of the test is the probability that the test will identify a truly skilled manager as a skilled manager. We quantify the true skill of the manager by how much we expect him to beat the market each year on average. If the manager is unskilled, we assume that his expected market-adjusted return is zero.*

The calculations assume that monthly market-adjusted returns are normally distributed with an annual standard deviation of 7.0 percent. The power calculator used to construct this table appears at home.stat.ucla.edu/calculators/powercalc/normal/n-1/ n-1-power.html.

with this low standard, we will still only identify truly skilled managers less than one half of the time (48 percent) given five years of data and a bit more than half the time (59 percent) given 10 years of data.

If we use a 50 percent confidence level test, we will identify an unskilled manager as skilled half of the time. With this extremely low confidence level, the probability that we identify skilled managers as skilled is only 74 percent using five years of data and 82 percent with 10 years of data. For comparison, note that the probability of identifying a skilled manager as skilled is 50 percent if we merely flip a coin to decide the issue! Clearly, we require more data than are generally available to confidently separate skill from luck when using statistical methods.

22.4.3 How Much Data Are Required?

Power calculations can also tell us how many years of returns we need in order to conduct a test with a given confidence level and power. Table 22-3 presents the results of these calculations for several confidence levels and powers.

These results show that even tests with low confidence and power levels require more years of returns than are commonly available. For example, suppose that skilled managers can beat the market by 2 percent on average. A test that does not identify unskilled managers as skilled managers 75 percent of the time, and that identifies skilled managers as skilled managers 75 percent of the time, requires 22 years of monthly returns! If skilled managers were extraordinarily skilled, so that they could beat the market by 4 percent on average, we would still require six years of data to run a test with these low confidence and power levels.

22.4.4 The Statistical Argument for Indexing

Before we abandon the statistical approach to determining whether a manager is skilled, consider how we might sensibly choose the confidence and power levels of our test. These test characteristics depend on how the test results will be used.

For example, suppose that we will invest with an active manager if the test indicates he is skilled and invest in an index fund otherwise. If the manager is not skilled, but the test indicates that he is, we will expect to lose. If we expect large losses, the test confidence level should be high in order to avoid identifying unskilled managers as skilled managers. Likewise, if the

> ### ▶ One Year of Data Just Doesn't Cut It
>
> Many people make decisions about managers from just one year of data. If this were not so, the business sections of newspapers would not be full of ads that publicize last year's returns for various mutual funds. Of course, the only funds that advertise are those which performed well last year.
>
> The probability of correctly identifying a truly skilled manager with a year of data is less than 10 percent in any test that will not regularly identify an unskilled manager as skilled. Last year's return therefore is essentially worthless for judging managerial skill. ◀

TABLE 22-3.

Years of Data Required to Obtain Specified Confidence and Power Levels for the Standard One-sided *t*-Test of Manager Performance

TRUE MANAGERIAL SKILL	CONFIDENCE LEVEL	POWER		
		50%	75%	95%
Skilled manager adds 2% per year	50%	0	6	33
	75%	0	22	66
	95%	0	66	132
Skilled manager adds 4% per year	50%	0	2	8
	75%	0	6	17
	95%	0	17	33

Notes: The confidence level of the test is the probability that the test does not identify an unskilled manager as a skilled manager. The power of the test is the probability that the test will identify a truly skilled manager as a skilled manager. We quantify the true skill of the manager by how much we expect him to beat the market each year on average.

The calculations assume that monthly market-adjusted returns are normally distributed with an annual standard deviation of 7.0 percent. The power calculator used to construct this table appears at ebook.stat.ucla.edu/calculators/powercalc/normal/ n-1/n-1-samp.html.

manager is indeed skilled, and the test indicates that he is, we will expect to profit. If we expect high profits, the power of the test should be high to avoid failing to identify skilled managers. Finally, if the expected returns to investing in an index fund are large, the confidence level should be high.

The confidence and power levels that we choose therefore should depend on the costs and benefits associated with our decision. Depending on these consequences, good decisions may not require high confidence and power levels. In this subsection, we consider what should be the confidence and power levels for a given sample size. We will assume that we will use the test to choose between investing with an active investment manager and investing in an index fund.

Our analysis will choose the confidence and power levels to maximize our expected market-adjusted return. The results therefore will show how much we expect to profit from choosing between an active manager and an index function, assuming that we design the best possible test. If these expected profits are small, we should not consider choosing a manager based only on past performance.

To estimate the expected return, we must make some assumptions about the consequences of our decision and about how common skilled managers are. We start by assuming that a previously skilled manager can produce 2 percent market-adjusted returns per year, on average, before accounting for management fees and trading commissions. (We implicitly assume assumptions 2 and 3 of section 22.3, so that a skilled manager will continue to generate good future returns, on average.) Although 2 percent may seem low, it is a reasonable assumption given the competition among managers for trading profits. As noted above, most managers would be delighted beyond expression if they and their clients were certain that they could beat the market by 2 percent per year on average.

Since trading is a zero-sum game, unskilled managers must lose on average to skilled managers. Their losses will depend on the fraction of managers who are skilled. Assume that one-third of managers are skilled, so that the average unskilled manager underperforms the market by about 1 percent per year, before accounting for management fees and trading commissions: $\frac{1}{3} \times 2\% + \frac{2}{3} \times -1\% = 0\%$. This assumption seems generous to me.

All active managers—skilled and unskilled taken together—underperform the market by an average of more than 1 percent per year, after accounting for expenses. (The average U.S. equity mutual fund underperformed the S&P 500 Index by 1.4 percent between 1962 and 1997.) This average implies that commissions plus management fees for all active managers average at least 1 percent. Assume that they total just 1 percent. Accordingly, we expect that skilled managers will beat the market by 1 percent per year, on average, after expenses, and unskilled managers will underperform the market by 2 percent per year, on average, after expenses.

Finally, we assume that index funds underperform the market by -0.15 percent. This is typical for index funds that have very low management fees and tend to track the market extremely closely.

The consequences will vary according to whether the manager is truly skilled and according to whether the test indicates that the manager is skilled. We therefore must assign costs and benefits to four different states. Since we need to compute the overall expected return, we also need to specify the probabilities of these four states. Our assumptions allow us to specify these costs, benefits, and probabilities:

- If the manager is not skilled, and the test indicates that the manager is not skilled, we will invest in an index fund and our market-adjusted returns will be −0.15 percent. The probability of this situation is the confidence level times the probability that the manager is not skilled.
- If the manager is not skilled, and the test indicates that the manager is skilled, we expect to underperform the market by 2 percent per year, on average, by investing with the manager. The probability of this situation is 1 minus the confidence level times the probability that the manager is not skilled. Statisticians call this type of mistake the *Type I error* of the test.
- If the manager is skilled, and the test indicates that the manager is skilled, we expect the manager to beat the market by 1 percent per year, on average. The probability of this situation is the power of the test times the probability that the manager is indeed skilled.
- If the manager is skilled, and the test indicates that the manager is not skilled, we will invest in an index fund and our market-adjusted returns will be −0.15 percent. The probability of this situation is 1 minus the power of the test times the probability that the manager is indeed skilled. Statisticians call this type of mistake the *Type II error* of the test.

Table 22-4 summarizes this information.

The overall expected market-adjusted return associated with the decision is the average of the expected consequences weighted by their respective probabilities. For a given sample size, the resulting expected return is maximized by choosing a confidence level, which implies the test power. Table 22-5 presents results for several sample sizes.

The results show that the optimal tests require high confidence levels for all sample sizes. For small sample sizes, the optimal confidence level is very high because there is not enough information to reliably discriminate between skilled and unskilled managers. Since investing with an unskilled manager is costly relative to investing with an index fund, and since skilled managers are relatively rare, a trader who follows the optimal strategy will

TABLE 22-4.
Assumed Consequences and Probabilities of All Possible States

		TRUE MANAGER STATUS	
ASSUMED PROPERTY	TEST RESULT	SKILLED	NOT SKILLED
Annual expected	Skilled: Invest with active manager	1.00%	−2.00%
net excess return	Not skilled: Invest in index fund	−0.15%	−0.15%
Probability	Skilled: Invest with active manager	$\frac{1}{3} \times$ Power	$\frac{2}{3} \times (1 - \text{Confidence})$
	Not skilled: Invest in index fund	$\frac{1}{3} \times (1 - \text{Power})$	$\frac{2}{3} \times \text{Confidence}$

Note: This table presents the annual expected return consequences and occurrence probabilities of the four possible states associated with the decision to invest with an active manager if a t-test identifies the manager as being skilled.

TABLE 22-5.

Optimal *t*-Test Confidence and Power Levels and Maximized Expected Returns

YEARS OF MONTHLY RETURNS	OPTIMAL CONFIDENCE LEVEL	OPTIMAL POWER LEVEL	MAXIMIZED ANNUAL EXPECTED RETURN IN EXCESS OF INDEX FUND RETURN	PROBABILITY OF INVESTING WITH AN ACTIVE MANAGER
1	100%	0%	0.000%	0%
2	99	4	0.001	2
5	95	24	0.030	11
10	94	42	0.086	18
20	94	64	0.171	25
50	97	87	0.298	31

Notes: This table presents optimal test confidence and power levels for the t-test *of whether a manager is skilled. The optimal levels maximize the expected returns that result from investing with an active manager if the test identifies the manager as skilled, and from investing in an index fund otherwise.*

The costs and benefits of the four possible outcomes appear in table 22-4. The calculations assume that monthly market-adjusted returns are normally distributed with an annual standard deviation of 7.0 percent. The author derived these results using the power calculator at ebook.stat.ucla.edu/calculators/powercalc/normal/n-1/n-1-power.html.

almost always invest in index funds. Accordingly, the maximized expected return is essentially the same as the index fund return. For very large sample sizes, enough information is available to reliably discriminate between skilled and unskilled managers. The optimal confidence level remains high to avoid the mistake of investing with unskilled managers. The high power ensures that we invest with an active manager if he is skilled.

We assumed that a skilled manager will outperform an index fund by 1.15 percent on average. If the test could perfectly discriminate between skilled and unskilled traders, the expected value of conducting the test would be one-third of this value because—by assumption—only one-third of active managers are skilled. Note that even with 50 years of data, the expected return of using the test (0.298 percent) is still only 78 percent of its theoretical maximum ($0.383 = \frac{1}{3} \times 1.15$ percent).

The maximized expected return from using the *t*-test—expressed relative to the expected index fund return—is the value of the option to decide whether to invest with an active manager when the alternative is to invest in an index fund. It is always positive because you can always choose to invest in an index fund. For sample sizes of ten or fewer years, the value of this option is extremely low. With ten years of data, it is only 8.6 basis points. Not surprisingly, many investors choose to ignore these options. They invest in index funds because they do not believe that they can add significant value to their wealth by choosing managers.

22.4.5 Choosing Among Many Managers

In practice, investors rarely decide only between just one active manager and an index fund when choosing whether to invest with an active manager. Instead, they usually consider many managers, and generally, only those they know have done well in the past.

The best-performing managers of a large group of managers always will have performed very well. In a large group of people, extreme luck can produce very impressive results. Standard statistical tests of whether such managers are skilled or just lucky will invariably indicate that the managers are skilled.

Standard tests in this application, however, produce highly unreliable results. Standard tests consider whether a manager chosen at random is skilled. In this application, we already know that a manager has performed well, and we examine him or her only because we know that the manager has performed well. The proper test must consider whether the manager is skilled, given that we already know that the manager was among the best-performing managers of a large group of managers. Whether a given manager is skilled, and whether the best-performing manager among a group of managers is skilled, are different questions. To answer different questions, we require different tests.

Managers who have performed well may have been skilled, or they may have been exceptionally lucky. Unfortunately, the larger the group of managers from which we select the best performing managers, the more impressive are the performances of the luckiest unskilled managers. In a large sample of managers, some unskilled managers will be extremely lucky simply by chance.

Table 22-6 shows just how lucky the best-performing manager from a large group of unskilled managers can be. The calculations assume that all the managers have constructed well diversified portfolios which are closely correlated with the market. We therefore assume that the annual standard deviation of their market-adjusted returns is only 7 percent per year.

The results in the third column (labeled Median) of the first panel show that in half of all years, on average, the best-performing manager from a group of 10,000 unskilled managers will beat the market by almost 27 percent! The winner will beat the market by more than 28 percent in one year out of four (next column) and by almost 31 percent in one year out of 20 (column labeled 95th percentile). The results are even more impressive when the best manager comes from a larger group.

The second and third panels present results for five- and ten-year periods. On average, the luckiest of 10,000 unskilled managers will beat the market by an annual average of more than 8 percent in half of all ten-year periods, by almost 9 percent in one ten-year period out of four, and by almost 10 percent in one ten-year period out of twenty.

The last three columns show similar results for the 99th percentile manager in each group size. This manager's performance is also very impressive, although not nearly as extreme as the best-performing manager.

Exceptionally lucky managers perform very well in comparison to skilled managers of average luck. These returns are all greater than the 2 percent per year that we assumed a good skilled manager could produce on average. Even in ten-year periods, it is much better to be very lucky than skilled with average luck!

The results in this table indicate that if you want to be more than 95 percent confident that you do not identify an unskilled manager as a skilled manager when examining ten years of returns for the best-performing manager out of 10,000, you must classify as unskilled any manager whose average market-adjusted performance is less than 10 percent per year. Tests with such confidence have essentially no power to identify any but the luckiest—or most skilled—managers.

The results in this table greatly underestimate the actual performance of

TABLE 22-6.

Distributions of the Average Market-adjusted Performance of the Luckiest Managers of Various Group Sizes

PERIOD	MANAGERS IN GROUP	BEST MANAGER MARKET-ADJUSTED AVERAGE RETURN DISTRIBUTION			99TH PERCENTILE MANAGER MARKET-ADJUSTED AVERAGE RETURN DISTRIBUTION		
		MEDIAN	75TH PERCENTILE	95TH PERCENTILE	MEDIAN	75TH PERCENTILE	95TH PERCENTILE
1 year	10	10.5%	13.3	18.0	N/A	N/A	N/A
	100	17.2	19.3	23.0	16.1	17.8	20.4
	1,000	22.4	24.1	27.2	16.2	16.8	17.7
	10,000	26.7	28.2	30.9	16.3	16.5	16.7
	100,000	30.4	31.7	34.2	16.3	16.3	16.4
	1,000,000	33.8	35.0	37.3	16.3	16.3	16.3
5 years	10	4.7	6.0	8.0	N/A	N/A	N/A
	100	7.7	8.6	10.3	7.2	8.0	9.1
	1,000	10.0	10.8	12.2	7.3	7.5	7.9
	10,000	11.9	12.6	13.8	7.3	7.4	7.5
	100,000	13.6	14.2	15.3	7.3	7.3	7.3
	1,000,000	15.1	15.7	16.7	7.3	7.3	7.3
10 years	10	3.3	4.2	5.7	N/A	N/A	N/A
	100	5.4	6.1	7.3	5.1	5.6	6.5
	1,000	7.1	7.6	8.6	5.1	5.3	5.6
	10,000	8.4	8.9	9.8	5.1	5.2	5.3
	100,000	9.6	10.0	10.8	5.1	5.2	5.2
	1,000,000	10.7	11.1	11.8	5.1	5.2	5.2

Notes: This table presents three percentiles of distributions of average annual market-adjusted returns that we expect for the luckiest managers of a group of unskilled managers. Distributions are reported for the manager with the highest return and for the manager whose return was higher than 99 percent of the other managers' returns.

The calculations assume that annual market-adjusted returns are independently normally distributed with mean zero and standard deviation of 7 percent. The 99th percentile manager is not meaningful in a group of only 10 managers. The distribution of returns for the 90th percentile manager in a group of 10 unskilled managers is as follows:

PERIOD	MEDIAN	75TH PERCENTILE	95TH PERCENTILE
1 year	8.8%	11.1	14.5
5 years	3.9	5.0	6.5
10 years	2.8	3.5	4.6

Source: Author's tabulations of simulated returns.

the luckiest managers because the best (and worst)-performing managers typically construct undiversified portfolios. The annual standard deviation of their market-adjusted returns therefore is much greater than the 7 percent we assumed.

22.4.6 Summary and Discussion

The results in this section strongly demonstrate that past returns data are not very useful for determining whether a manager is skilled. For them to

▶ Is Warren Buffet Skilled or Lucky?

Berkshire Hathaway is a firm that Warren Buffet has managed since 1965. Although it has many operating divisions, in many respects it is essentially a closed-end investment fund. Because Berkshire Hathaway is primarily an insurance company, its reported book value is based on the market values of its holdings rather than on historic costs of its holdings. The book value therefore is essentially the net asset value of the firm.

Many people regard Warren Buffet as the most skilled investment manager of the late twentieth century. Since he took control of Berkshire Hathaway, its book value had appreciated 2,078-fold through December 2000. This corresponds to a compounded average growth rate of 23.6 percent per year. By comparison, the average annual total return (capital gains plus dividends) of the S&P 500 Index during this period was 11.8 percent. Berkshire Hathaway outperformed the market by an average of 11.8 percent per year. The firm exactly doubled the performance of the S&P 500 Index over this period.

Is Warren Buffet indeed a skilled investment manager, or has he simply been a very lucky manager?

A standard *t*-test indicates that he is exceptionally skilled. Over the 36 years, Berkshire Hathaway's annual market-adjusted return standard deviation was 14.3 percent per year, so that the standard *t*-statistic is 4.9. The probability that an unskilled manager would have a *t*-statistic larger than 4.9 is only 0.0011 percent.

This test, however, is not the proper test. Warren Buffet came to our attention only because he had exceptionally high returns. If his performance had not been exceptionally good, you probably would have never heard of him, and I certainly would not be writing about him. To properly address the question, we must consider whether Warren Buffet's investment performance is significantly better than we would expect from the best managers in a large group of unskilled managers.

Assume that Warren Buffet competed with at least 10,000 investment managers in 1965. Many of these managers underperformed the market and subsequently quit or were dismissed from their jobs. The total number of managers in 1965 would be much greater if we considered every amateur investor who would have become a professional investor if his or her investment performance had been better than it was.

If 10,000 unskilled managers constructed portfolios with normally distributed market-adjusted returns having mean zero and standard deviation 14.3 percent, the probability that the best-performing manager would beat the market by an annual rate of 11.8 percent or greater is only 0.5 percent. If there were 100,000 managers, the probability would have been 5 percent. These results suggest that Warren Buffet very likely is a skilled manager. ◀

Source: Author's calculations based on data at www.berkshirehathaway.com/2000ar/2000letter.html.

be of much value, we must base statistical analyses of past returns on more years of data than are normally available to us.

The problem is that skill is a far less significant determinant of portfolio returns than is luck. In particular, the additional return that we expect a manager can add to a portfolio is small relative to the variation in portfolio returns due to factors which managers cannot anticipate or act upon. Statisticians and engineers say that this problem has a low *signal to noise ratio*. The signal—whether the manager is skilled—is hard to find because it is lost in noise (variation due to other factors).

▶ A Last Word for the Statisticians

In practice, many managers pursue similar trading strategies so that they obtain similar results. The market-adjusted returns of these traders are correlated. I derived the results that appear in table 22-6 by assuming that the market-adjusted returns of all managers are uncorrelated. They therefore overstate the performance of the best-performing managers.

You can easily understand the problem by assuming that all managers pursue the same investment strategy so that they all obtain the same results. The distribution of the returns of the best-performing manager within a group of these identical managers does not depend on the size of the group because they all produce the same returns. Although many managers may be in the group, the effective size of the group is only one because they all pursue only one strategy. The correlation of trading strategies among managers therefore reduces effective group size.

Table 22-7 tabulates extreme average market-adjusted return distributions for varying degrees of correlation among the managers' market-adjusted returns. The results summarize 10-year average market-adjusted returns for the best manager and the 99th percentile manager within a group of 10,000 managers.

Comparing these results against the results in table 22-6 shows that when the correlation is 0.25, the return distribution for the best manager within a group of 10,000 managers is similar to the distribution for the best manager within a group of approximately 2000 managers with uncorrelated returns. (The approximation is based on a logarithmic interpolation.) For a given group size, if we account for the correlation among manager market-adjusted returns, the performance of managers like Warren Buffet appears more remarkable. ◀

The problem would be much easier to solve if we believed that skilled managers could add more, on average, than the 2 percent per year to a portfolio that we assumed in our analyses. Unfortunately, it is unreasonable to assume much greater skill than 2 percent because trading is a highly competitive zero-sum game. Even if we assume greater skills, we would have to assume that fewer managers have them. Although the test then would discriminate better, the greater scarcity of skilled managers would offset the improvement to some extent.

TABLE 22-7.

Distributions of the 10-year Average Market-adjusted Performance of the Luckiest Managers in a Group of 10,000 Managers for Varying Degrees of Correlation Among the Manager Market-adjusted Returns

CORRELATION AMONG MANAGER MARKET-ADJUSTED RETURNS	BEST MANAGER MARKET-ADJUSTED AVERAGE RETURN DISTRIBUTION			99TH PERCENTILE MANAGER MARKET-ADJUSTED AVERAGE RETURN DISTRIBUTION		
	MEDIAN	75TH PERCENTILE	95TH PERCENTILE	MEDIAN	75TH PERCENTILE	95TH PERCENTILE
0.00	8.4%	8.9	9.8	5.1	5.2	5.3
0.25	7.4	8.2	9.5	4.4	5.2	6.3
0.50	6.0	7.1	8.7	3.6	4.7	6.2
0.75	4.3	5.6	7.5	2.6	3.9	5.7
1.00	0.0	1.5	3.7	0.0	1.5	3.7

Source: Author's tabulations of simulated returns using the assumptions in table 22-6.

▶ Closet Indexers

Closet indexers are active equity investment managers who create portfolios that very closely replicate the benchmark indexes their clients use to measure their performance. Their clients presumably expect that their managers will choose portfolios to beat their benchmarks. It is very difficult, however, to significantly outperform an index with a portfolio that is very closely correlated to it.

Closet indexers choose closely correlated portfolios because such portfolios rarely significantly underperform their benchmark indexes. Closet indexers minimize the risk of significant failure.

Clients generally do not like closet indexers because they pay them high fees for their "active management" but they essentially receive only index portfolios in exchange. The management fees for index funds are much lower than those for actively managed portfolios.

Since the returns of closet indexers are very closely correlated to their benchmark indexes, analysts can determine whether closet managers are skilled managers with much less data than they require to determine whether true active managers are skilled. ◀

The problem would be much easier to solve if the variation due to other factors were smaller. In our analysis, we assumed that the variation of market-adjusted portfolio returns is 7 percent per year. We derived this number by assuming that the portfolio return standard deviation is 16 percent, the market return standard deviation is 14.5 percent, and the correlation between the two returns is 0.9. If the problem were characterized by lower standard deviations or by a higher correlation, stronger tests would be possible. For example, if the correlation were 0.95 instead of 0.9, the market-adjusted portfolio return standard deviation would be 5 percent per year. The power of a 95 percent confidence level test using five years of returns, assuming manager skill of 2 percent, would rise from 15 percent (assuming a 7 percent market-adjusted return standard deviation) to 22 percent. If the correlation were 0.99, the market-adjusted return standard deviation would drop to 2.6 percent, and the test power would rise to 52 percent. Unfortunately, the portfolio returns of most equity managers are not so highly correlated with the market.

To solve a low signal to noise ratio problem, we must either know more about the signal or somehow reduce the noise. In practice, analysts most frequently attempt to lower the noise by using factor models to explain unanticipated portfolio returns. The analysis of market-adjusted returns that we studied in this section is based on a simple one-factor market-adjusted model of portfolio returns. More complex models attempt to attribute returns to other factors, such as interest rates, firm size, and expected growth rates. Since the variation in the resulting factor-adjusted excess returns is lower than the variation in the market-adjusted returns, tests of manager performance will be more powerful for a given sample size. These tests, however, identify manager skill only after accounting for factor returns. They will not measure the value added by managers who can successfully predict factor returns, and who can adjust their portfolios to benefit from their skills.

With five years of monthly returns data, a test with 95 percent confidence and 75 percent power to identify 2 percent skilled managers requires an annual factor-adjusted excess return standard deviation of only 1.9 percent. Unfortunately, factor models generally cannot explain returns so pre-

▶ A Good Dissertation Topic

We know that skilled managers should perform better in liquid markets than in illiquid markets because the costs of establishing positions are lower in liquid markets. This observation is especially important for large fund managers and for skilled managers who pursue strategies that many other skilled managers pursue.

Since liquidity varies through time, so will the performance of such skilled managers. Tests of manager skill therefore should incorporate information about time-varying liquidity. To the best of my knowledge, no such tests have ever been done. ◀

cisely. Such models would have to explain 98.6 percent of the total variation in returns to achieve such precision.

The fraction of total variation that a statistical model explains is called the R^2 of the model. Factor models typically have R^2 of less than 90 percent in annual data. For comparison, the R^2 of the simple market-adjusted return model is 81 percent when the portfolio standard deviation is 16 percent, and the market-adjusted return standard deviation is 7.0 percent $\{0.81 = (0.9)^2 = (16^2 - 7^2).16^2\}$. (In the simple market-adjusted return model, the R^2 is equal to the square of the correlation coefficient of the portfolio returns with the market returns.)

In principle, analysts could construct stronger tests if they knew more about a manager's presumed skill. For example, suppose an analyst believes that a manager may be skilled only in rising markets but not in falling markets. This information would allow the analyst to construct a stronger test of whether the manager is skilled. In particular, the analyst would examine returns only in rising markets. In general, analysts can better identify skill if they can identify some variables that are correlated with it.

22.4.6.1 Length of Sample Versus Number of Observations

In most statistical analyses, the greater the number of observations, the more powerful the results will be. The results presented throughout this section illustrate this principle. The more years of data upon which statistical performance evaluations are based, the more powerful those evaluations will be.

For a given sample period, the number of observations can be increased by sampling more frequently. For example, in a 10-year period, analysts can examine 10 annual, 120 monthly, and approximately 522 weekly nonoverlapping returns.

In performance evaluations, however, statistical power depends primarily on the length of the sample period and not on the frequency of sampling within that period. This is because the total performance within a period is the same regardless of how often we observe it within the period. Analyses that attempt to discriminate between luck and skill need long sample periods to separate the systematic contribution of skilled managers from the noise of unanticipated factors. Sampling more often within a period does not address this need.

More frequent sampling, however, often produces slightly more powerful tests, especially when the total number of observations otherwise would be less than 20. The standard error of the mean—which appears in the denominator of the t-statistic—often can be estimated more accurately from more frequent observations for a given sample period. Whether it can or cannot depends on whether prices follow a random walk at various observation intervals. The issue is technical and need not concern us further. It explains, however, why I presented analyses for monthly returns instead of annual returns in this section.

22.5 MORE IMPORTANT PROBLEMS WITH STATISTICAL PERFORMANCE EVALUATION

Statistical performance evaluation often is even more difficult than the results in the previous section indicate. If the returns being analyzed are not well characterized by the assumptions upon which statisticians base their analyses, the conclusions that statisticians reach will not be reliable.

Two main problems may cause returns data to have substantially differ-ent properties than statisticians expect. These problems involve distribu-tional shape and the accuracy of the returns data. These issues are very im-portant because some investment strategies produce highly unusual return distributions and because—through malice, negligence, or simple over-sight—returns data sometimes do not represent true performance. Investors who fail to recognize these problems risk making decisions that often cause them to lose their entire investments.

22.5.1 Distributional Shape

The *shape* of the distribution of a variable refers to how the probabilities of different values of the variable are distributed. If the distribution is *flat*, all values have equal probabilities. If the distribution is *fat-tailed*, extreme val-ues are common.

Distributional shape is important because statisticians base their tests on assumptions about the return probabilities based on luck alone. If the shape they assume is different from the true shape of random returns, their infer-ences will be wrong.

The quantitative properties of the *t*-tests presented above were derived by assuming that portfolio returns are *normally distributed*. The *normal dis-tribution* is a specific bell-shaped distribution. (The probabilities of each outcome plotted against their corresponding outcomes trace the shape of a bell.) For reasons that need not concern us now, the normal distribution very often provides excellent characterizations of the distributions of a wide variety of random variables. Statisticians therefore most commonly base their analyses on this distribution.

22.5.1.1 Normality

The actual distribution of portfolio returns, however, is not normal. Many studies demonstrate that extreme values are more common for portfolio re-turns than we would expect if they were normally distributed. The actual distribution of returns therefore is fat-tailed in comparison to the normal distribution. Although the difference is not great, the unfortunate conse-quence of the more common extreme values is that *t*-tests are less power-ful than they would be if the returns were normally distributed. The results we discussed above, discouraging as they are, actually overstate the reliabil-ity of *t*-tests.

22.5.1.2 The Peso Problem

One particular property of the normal distribution is of critical interest to us. The normal distribution is a *symmetric distribution*. In a *symmetric dis-tribution*, outcome probabilities depend only on their distance from the me-dian value of the distribution. The probabilities of outcomes at equal dis-tances above and below the median therefore are the same. The returns of well-diversified portfolios are approximately symmetrically distributed. Al-though there are some systematic departures from symmetry (large nega-tive values are slightly more common than large positive values), these de-partures usually affect index returns as well. Accordingly, market-adjusted returns tend to be quite symmetric for well-diversified portfolios because the asymmetries in the portfolio and index returns offset each other.

Certain portfolio strategies, however, can produce highly asymmetric

How to Fool Most People Most of the Time: Sell Volatility

An equities manager can produce an enhanced index return in most years by holding an index portfolio (or a closet index portfolio) and writing out-of-the-money options. The index portfolio produces the index return. The out-of-the-money options produce a small additional return if the options are not exercised. If the options are exercised, the portfolio generally will suffer a significant loss. The options will be exercised when the market is highly volatile. Since it takes essentially no skill to set up this strategy, it is an example of an *informationless trading strategy*.

The market-adjusted returns of this portfolio will be small and positive most of the time. Only very rarely will the fund underperform the market. When it does, however, the underperformance will be very large.

If the manager has not been unlucky, *t*-tests will indicate that the manager is highly skilled, even in small samples. Clients therefore must be very vigilant to ensure that their managers have not given them a peso problem. ◄

return distributions. Unfortunately, *t*-tests applied to returns generated by these portfolios can produce highly unreliable results. The true confidence levels and power of *t*-tests based on highly asymmetric distributions are vastly different from those based on the normal distribution.

The *peso problem* is an extreme example of this problem. A *peso problem* arises when a trading strategy almost always produces a small positive return. Very rarely, however, the strategy produces a very large negative return that may more than offset the many small gains the portfolio normally produces. This distribution of returns is highly asymmetric.

The peso problem is of special concern to performance evaluation. Until a calamity occurs, a manager who holds a portfolio with a peso problem appears to be quite skilled. The manager, however, is lucky rather than skilled.

It is almost impossible to use statistical methods to evaluate managers who have peso problems. A reliable evaluation requires enough data to ensure that calamities are adequately represented in the sample. Since calamities are quite rare, the sample must be extraordinarily long. The only reliable way that clients can determine whether their managers are creating peso problems is to directly examine the strategies that their portfolio managers use.

The Peso Problem

The following story is part of the folklore of the Economics Department at the University of Chicago. I have no idea of its veracity.

In the 1960s and 1970s, inflation in Mexico was significantly higher than in the United States. Interest rates therefore were higher in Mexico than in the United States. Had there been a floating exchange rate regime then, the Mexican peso would have depreciated relative to the dollar at a rate that would have made investors roughly indifferent between investing in the United States and in Mexico. For example, a U.S. investor would have earned higher interest in Mexico than in the United States, but the premium would have been offset by a decrease in the dollar value of the peso over the period of the investment.

In fact, the Mexican government fixed the exchange rate so that it could not change. The continuing inflation, however, forced the government to devalue the peso on an irregular basis. Anyone who had assets denominated in Mexican pesos suffered a large loss every time the peso was devalued.

Investment in Mexican debt securities therefore created a *peso problem*. As long as there was no devaluation, the investment would systematically outperform similar dollar-denominated investments. Whenever a devaluation occurred, however, the gains would be lost overnight.

A certain Chicago professor is said to have invested in Mexican debt instruments to take advantage of the interest rate differential. When confronted by his colleagues about the peso problem, the professor was reported to have said that he was not worried: As an authority on international economics who had trained a significant number of Mexican economists, he was certain that his former students would call him for his advice before they devalued the peso. He therefore expected that he would be able to avoid the peso problem by selling immediately after he took their call.

He was right. His students did call, but they could not reach him because he was traveling! ◄

▶ The St. Petersburg Paradox: Why Not Double-down?

Bet a dollar on the outcome of a coin flip. If you win, quit with a 1-dollar profit. If you lose, bet 2 dollars on the outcome of another coin flip. If you win, quit. Your total profit from both coin flips will be 1 dollar. If you lose, double your bet again to 4 dollars. If you win this third flip, quit with a 1-dollar profit $(4 - 2 - 1)$, otherwise continue doubling your bet until you win.

This *doubling-down* betting strategy is called the *St. Petersburg paradox*. If you have infinite wealth, you will always win 1 dollar by playing it until you finally win. If your wealth is finite, however, you will eventually go bankrupt if you play the game often enough. It is a paradox because these results do not depend on whether the coin is fair.

An equities manager can produce an enhanced index return in most years by holding an index portfolio and making a short-term bet on some investment idea. The index portfolio produces the index return. If the bet does not work out, bet again with twice the money. Continue doubling down until you win. This simple trading strategy ensures that the fund manager outperforms the market as long as the fund does not go bankrupt.

The doubling-down strategy is very attractive to undisciplined investment managers because it usually allows them to avoid the psychological consequences of their poor decisions. They rationalize by thinking that they initially may have been wrong about an idea, but in the end they got it right.

The strategy is also attractive to unethical investment managers who fear that their clients will dismiss them if they perform poorly. They will play the strategy if they have performed poorly. Such managers are unethical because they do not care about the risks that they impose upon their clients, and because they manage their portfolios to benefit themselves rather than their clients. ◀

22.5.2 Fraudulent Returns

An implicit assumption of statistical performance evaluation is that the returns under analysis are true returns. Statistical tests applied to returns that are not accurate obviously will not produce accurate results. Computer scientists and statisticians are both fond of saying, "Garbage in, garbage out."

You need to be aware of two processes that can cause returns to be fraudulent. They involve return smoothing and pyramid schemes.

22.5.2.1 Return Smoothing

As noted in "Smooth Sailing, Rapids Ahead" (p. 448), managers who value portfolios of infrequently traded assets may adjust the values of those assets less quickly than they should. The portfolio returns that they compute from these values therefore will be inaccurate. In particular, they will change too slowly. Their variation from period to period will be less than it should be, and the ratio of return continuations to return reversals (return serial correlation) will be higher than it should be. Consequently, the returns will appear to be smoother than they should be.

Artificial smoothness affects statistical performance evaluation because smoothing decreases return volatility. The artificially low return volatility causes statisticians to conclude that large mean returns are more significant than they are. In particular, recall that the *t*-test is based on the ratio of the mean return to a measure of its expected dispersion called the standard error. Since statisticians usually estimate the standard error from the return volatility, artificially low return volatility causes artificially low standard error estimates, which cause artificially high *t*-ratios, and therefore overconfident conclusions.

When managers smoothe too much, their reported valuations may significantly differ from true valuations. At some point, their regulators, customers, brokers, auditors, or custodians may recognize the discrepancy and demand immediate adjustment. Since smoothing invariably delays the recognition of capital losses rather than of capital gains, the resulting revaluations produce very significant negative returns. Smoothing thus can produce an artificial peso problem. From the investors' point of view, however, there is nothing artificial about the problem.

22.5.2.2 Pyramid Schemes

A *pyramid scheme* is a fraud that dishonest investment managers commit against their clients. In these schemes, the manager explicitly or implicitly promises a high rate of return on an investment. Investors then place their money with the manager, who usually very actively promotes the scheme. The manager then uses their capital to pay high returns to initial investors. The apparently high returns realized by the initial investors attract new investors. As long as the manager can attract an ever-growing base of new investors, he can pay off earlier investors, and the scheme can survive. At some point, however, the fraud gets so large that the manager can no longer pay earlier investors. At that point, it collapses and anyone who has not yet been paid usually loses everything. The promoter profits either by stealing funds or by charging management fees. Pyramid schemes, of course, are illegal almost everywhere.

These schemes are called pyramid schemes because they are built upon an ever-enlarging base of investors. The investors at the top profit from the "support" provided by the investors at the base. They are similar to chain letters. Pyramid schemes are extreme examples of "robbing Peter to pay Paul." Pyramid schemes are also known as Ponzi schemes after Charles K. Ponzi, who ran an extremely large pyramid scheme in 1920.

Until pyramid schemes collapse, the returns that they generate are remarkably good. If you analyze these returns to determine whether a manager is skilled or just lucky, you will conclude that the manager is skilled.

The only way to protect against losing to a pyramid scheme is to determine whether the manager's accounting systems accurately report investment assets, account liabilities, investment income, and capital gains distributions. In a pyramid scheme, actual assets and actual investment income generally will be substantially less than reported.

If pyramid scheme promoters are not too greedy, if their excess returns are not too large, if they can convince their clients to not withdraw their funds, and if they can somehow control the audits of their portfolios, pyramid schemes can go undetected for a very long time. An investment manager's performance record therefore is no substitute for doing the *due diligence* that all prudent investors must undertake to ensure that they are not contributing to pyramid schemes.

22.6 THE SAMPLE SELECTION BIAS

The two preceding sections demonstrate that statistical tests for managers generally do not produce useful information about their skill. The proper-

▶ Ponzi's Ponzi Scheme

Charles K. Ponzi established the Securities Exchange Company in December 1919 in Boston. His company purportedly traded postal reply coupons.

Postal reply coupons are coupons redeemable for postage. People who wanted to enclose return postage used them when corresponding with people in other countries. The postal reply coupon system was set up in 1906 by a postal convention of over 60 countries. Participants in the system agreed to honor the coupons at fixed exchange rates. When the system was initially established, coupons everywhere sold for slightly more than they were worth in postage. Following World War I, however, changes in exchange rates made it possible to buy coupons in some countries and redeem them at a substantial percentage profit in other countries. Although the percentage profits could be quite large, the total amounts that anyone could earn this way were quite small because the coupons were not worth much.

To fund his operation, Ponzi sold bonds to investors that promised them a 50 percent return over 90 days. He claimed that he could produce this income through the 400 percent returns he was making by redeeming postal reply coupons. No evidence suggests that Ponzi ever redeemed more than a trivial quantity of coupons.

Ponzi repaid his bonds at face value in 45 days. The resulting excitement caused his business to grow exponentially. By July, the business was taking in 1 million dollars per week from offices in several cities in the Northeast.

The government forced Ponzi to halt sales of his notes on July 26. By that time, he had collected about 9.5 million dollars from more than 10,000 investors. On July 28, investors started to demand payment on their notes. Remarkably, instead of running away with the money, Ponzi paid the notes until he ran out of cash on August 7.

Ponzi was arrested on August 12 and charged with many counts of federal mail fraud. He negotiated a guilty to plea to one count, and the court sentenced him to five years in prison. Following his release, he engaged in other financial frauds for which he was caught and convicted. ◀

Source: Charles K. Ponzi Website: The Remarkable Criminal Financial Career of Charles K. Ponzi *by Mark C. Knutson at www.mark-knutson.com, May 31, 2001.*

ties of the tests described there were derived by assuming that analysts would use the tests under ideal circumstances. In practice, statistical performance evaluations rarely are applied under ideal circumstances. Consequently, the tests are still less useful than they seem.

The most important problem that plagues these tests is the sample selection problem. This problem can affect inferences whenever people learn from the past. Their learning may involve formal analyses like the t-test described above, or it may simply involve judgments that people make based on their experience. In either event, you must be very careful that the *sample selection bias* does not affect your conclusions.

The *sample selection bias* arises when some process selects the information that you see about some object. If the process does not randomly select the information that you see, you will see only selected aspects of the object and your impression of it will not be accurate. Decisions that you make based upon your information therefore very likely will be faulty.

▶ Blind Men Describe an Elephant

The story of the blind men who examine different parts of an elephant illustrates the sample selection bias: Each man feels only the trunk, leg, side, or tail, and each respectively concludes that the elephant is like a snake, a tree trunk, a wall, or a rope. Since each man examines only one aspect of the elephant, none of them appreciates the totality of the elephant. Each man would make a poor decision about elephants based only on the information produced by his examination of the elephant. ◀

22.6.1 Sample Selection in the Mutual Fund Industry

Suppose you examine the marketing literature of a company that manages and distributes a large family of mutual funds. Each fund accurately reports its performance relative to appropriate benchmarks. By reviewing the data, or by doing some formal statistical calculations, you conclude that their performance has been very impressive. On average, the funds in this family have substantially beaten their benchmarks. The performance obviously is both statistically significant and economically significant. The funds have performed much better than you would expect if their managers were not skilled. You therefore conclude that their managers are skilled and decide to invest your money with this company.

You may be very disappointed with your results. Many mutual fund distributors feature only their best-performing funds in their marketing literature. Although they may offer other reasons for why they select which funds to feature, they undoubtedly know that they will benefit from this presentation of their products. The average performance of all funds in the family actually may be negative. If you knew this, you might have concluded that it is unlikely the company's funds will beat the market on average, and that the managers of their best-performing funds probably were only lucky. If the managers indeed are not skilled, you probably will be disappointed with your decision. You would have made a better decision had you known about the other funds.

A sample selection bias affected your inference. You only saw the funds that the marketing literature presented and therefore only saw a selected view of the company.

Even if the company presents the results for all its funds, you still may not see the entire picture. Mutual fund distributors often kill their poorly performing funds, usually by merging them with better-performing funds. The reported performance of the survivor is based only on its performance and does not include the performance of the failed fund. Mutual fund companies may kill their losers because they become expensive to operate when they get small. They may also kill them because they do not want to report their performance. In either event, by killing poorly performing funds, they raise the computed average performance of the surviving funds. The average performance of all funds may be negative, but you could not know this without knowing about the other funds. This type of sample selection bias is called the *survivorship bias*.

Some large mutual fund companies start many new mutual funds every year. They keep the ones that perform well and kill the ones that fail. In this way, they are able to create the winners that they need to market their funds. If you are unaware of this process, you may give too much significance to past returns. You may not realize that the fund which generated superior past performance came to your attention only because it was among the best-performing funds of a large group of funds.

22.6.2 Avoiding the Sample Selection Bias

Sample selection biases may be responsible for more trading losses than any other cause. They usually arise because people do not see the whole picture or because they fail to ask the right questions when they interpret what they see.

Many people invest with active investment managers who have performed well. As noted in section 22.4.5, whether their performance is sta-

▶ My Favorite Fraud

The following scheme is illegal. Do not use it. I present it only so that you can better appreciate the sample selection bias, and so that you can avoid falling for this scheme should a con man ever try to target you.

Buy a mailing list of 20,480 wealthy and gullible people. Send them a letter in which you explain that you are a very successful trader who has more money than you can spend. Boast about how you correctly predicted what direction prices would move during nine of the last ten months. Tell some story about how you did it. Then tell them that you now crave their recognition for being a market genius, since money is no longer very meaningful to you. Give them your prediction for the next month.

Divide your names into two equal groups. To the first group, predict that the market will rise. To the second group, predict that it will fall.

One month later, write a letter to the 10,240 people for whom you correctly predicted the market. Continue boasting and remind them that you correctly picked the market for them. Tell them how much money they could have made if they had traded on your recommendation. Then give them another pick. Of course, you predict an increase to one half of the group and a decrease to the other half.

Repeat this for ten months until 20 people have seen you correctly predict the market 10 times in a row ($20 = 20480/2^{10}$). If they are not aware of your scheme, they will be convinced that you have correctly picked the market 10 times for them, and they will be prepared to believe that you did indeed do it correctly in nine of the ten months before you started to correspond with them. Such results are exceedingly unlikely to occur at random. They will swear that you are a genius.

You now have these people wrapped around your finger. If they are gullible, you may be able to abuse their trust.

If you also send letters to people for whom you incorrectly predicted the market, you can increase your yield. Simply tell them that you are only human and cannot get it right every time. You will have 200 people for whom you have correctly called the market exactly nine times and another 900 for whom you have correctly called the market exactly eight times. You probably will not want to continue corresponding with those for whom you failed to call the market three or more times.

The "lucky" ones for whom you correctly predicted the market cannot possibly make the proper inference about your skill without knowing your scheme. If they do know the scheme, the only rational inference is that you are not skilled. ◀

tistically significant must be judged relative to the entire sample of managers. What appears to be significant out of context may not be noteworthy in context. The important point to remember is that bad managers do not come to your attention. Nobody talks about them. Nobody writes about them. They do not write books. You learn about the best managers only because they had great performance. Everyone talks about them. Everyone writes about them. They write books that everyone reads. To make reasonable statistical inferences about whether great performing managers are skilled, you must know the total number of managers who might have been lucky but were not.

Similar comments apply to investment newsletters. Only the newsletters that have great records for recommending securities and contracts survive to come to your attention. The ones with poor records fail. The surviving newsletters may be written by insightful authors or by lucky authors. Unfortunately, you generally cannot assess the authors' skills from their performance record.

22.6.3 Regression to the Mean

Although sample selection can produce an upward bias in an average of past returns, it cannot affect subsequent returns. Perhaps the clearest evidence that sample selection has affected an average of past returns is the difference between that average and an average of subsequent returns. When selection has caused the past return average to be high, the subsequent return average is invariably lower. This phenomenon is called *regression to the mean*. Researchers have identified it in many different contexts.

22.6.4 Summary

Whenever some process filters the data that you see, you get only a selected aspect of reality. When you make decisions based on that view, you often will make poor decisions. The only way to avoid the sample selection bias is to understand how the data came to your attention. You must always ask whether an event is significant relative to the process that generated it, and not simply relative to what you know about it.

▶ The Regression of Public Commodity Pools

In the early and middle 1980s, approximately 2,000 commodity trading advisers were registered with the National Futures Association. The vast majority of these advisers managed private accounts.

Between July 1979 and June 1985, these advisers offered approximately 15 new commodity funds—commonly called *public commodity pools*—per year to public investors. The offerings were accompanied by prospectuses that reported the average returns for the adviser's accounts for at least the previous 36 months (if the adviser had been advising that long).

Their average monthly return in the 36 months before the offering was 4.1 percent. These funds had performed remarkably well!

In the first year after going public, their average monthly return was 0.23 percent. The results did not improve much in subsequent years. These returns were stunningly disappointing in comparison to the prior returns.

These results suggest that most of the advisers who offered public funds probably had simply been lucky in the previous 36 months. Once the funds went public, their average returns regressed to the mean.

To support this conclusion, consider how many of the 2,000 advisers we would expect would have average returns greater than 4.1 percent per month over the previous 36 months, purely by chance. During this period, all public commodity funds had a mean monthly return of approximately 0.7 percent per month with a standard deviation of 11.3 percent per month. If we assume that returns are normally distributed with this mean and standard deviation, by pure chance, a probability calculation (not reported) predicts that we would expect 70 of 2,000 advisers would have an average monthly return of greater than 4.1 percent over the last three years. Chance alone therefore provides more than enough advisers to explain the 4.1 percent monthly return average of the advisers who offered public commodity funds. (Note that the average includes managers with prior average returns both greater and less than 4.1 percent.) ◀

Source: Edwin J. Elton, Martin J. Gruber and Joel Rentzler, "New Public Offerings, Information, and Investor Rationality: The Case of Publicly Offered Commodity Funds," Journal of Business 62, no. 1 (1989): 1–15.

▶ Warren Buffet Reconsidered

In the 26 years between 1965 and 1990, the book value of Berkshire Hathaway increased by an average of 13.2 percent more than the total return on the S&P 500 Index. By 1990, Warren Buffet was widely acclaimed to be a highly skilled investment manager.

During the next 10 years, the book value of Berkshire Hathaway increased only by an average of only 6.84 percent more than the total return on the S&P 500 Index. Although this performance is still quite impressive, it is not as impressive as the earlier performance. The performance clearly regressed toward the mean. In his first 26 years, Warren Buffet probably was lucky as well as skilled. In the subsequent 10 years, he was either less lucky or it was much more difficult to produce the same extreme returns with a much larger firm.

Suppose that in 1990, you decided to collect returns data for the next ten years to determine whether Warren Buffet was truly a skilled trader. The standard *t*-test then would be appropriate because the subsequent returns would not be subject to the sample selection bias. Using only annual data from 1991 through 2000, the *t*-statistic is 1.95. The probability that an unskilled manager would have a *t*-statistic greater than this value is slightly greater than 4 percent. These results suggest that only one unskilled manager in 25 would have performed better than Warren Buffet over this period. Warren Buffet probably is a skilled manager. ◀

In trading, the sample selection bias is especially important because winners come to our attention much more often than losers do. Unless we are very disciplined, we may easily overvalue winners.

The sample selection problem is especially difficult to recognize because most of us want to believe that winners are skilled and not just lucky. Our natural inclination is to attribute performance to skill or the lack of it. Most of us believe that there is a reason for everything. We would rather that the reason be skill than luck. When making inferences, always beware of rose-colored glasses.

Our desire to attribute performance to skill or the lack of it applies primarily to others. When we consider our own performance, our natural inclination is to attribute good performance to skill and bad performance to luck. We do this because we want to feel good about ourselves. We therefore tend to remember good results and try to forget bad results. This may be the most dangerous selection bias that we face.

22.7 ECONOMIC APPROACHES TO PERFORMANCE PREDICTION

The difficulties associated with statistical performance prediction suggest that inferences based only on past performance will not be useful for predicting future performance. Past performance simply does not predict future returns with enough confidence to be of much use for most applications.

Fortunately, economic theory—simple game theory, actually—suggests another approach. In the long run, players win games when they have a *comparative advantage* over their opponents. Players have a *comparative advantage* when they have greater skills or greater resources than their opponents. The skills and resources, of course, must be those which will help the players excel. They therefore will vary by the strategies that the players pursue.

▶ More Caveman Psychology

Our evolutionary history has hardwired our brains to believe that everything has a cause. Our ancestral aunts and uncles who could not connect events to causes often failed to exploit opportunities that enhanced their survival, or to avoid risks that threatened their survival. They therefore did not survive to reproduce as often as did our ancestral parents. We know that our ancestral parents survived because we are here to speculate on how they did it. They must have been able to connect events to their causes better than our ancestral aunts and uncles. Our minds therefore are probably hardwired to seek an explanation for every event.

Many people think that the desire for an explanation for everything is the reason why many people are religious. Although I do not believe this, it seems reasonable to me that this hardwired desire to link causes to events explains why people want to believe that successful people are skilled and not just lucky. ◀

▶ It Seems Like Everyone Is a Winner

People talk about their successes far more often than their failures. They enjoy describing their winnings and they are embarrassed to admit their mistakes.

If you listen only to what people say about their trades, you will think that most traders are winners. If you draw inferences from what you hear, you might think that you, too, would be a winner, if only you traded. ◀

▶ **Winning the Olympic Marathon**

On average, *better* players win games. Good players and even great players do not generally win when they play against even better players.

A player has an *absolute advantage* when he or she can do something well. For example, a marathoner who can complete the marathon in less than 2:20 is incredibly fast. Unless you are involved in track and field, you probably have never met anyone so fast. A 2:20 marathoner will win the vast majority of marathons that are run every year.

Such a time, however, would have been good for only 36th place in the men's marathon at the 2000 Olympics. Most marathons do not attract world-class runners. Those which do, however, are highly competitive. You do not win such races by running extremely fast. You win them by running faster than every other runner.

To win a game, you must not just play it well. You must play it better than your opponents. ◀

Since trading is essentially a game, we should be able to predict long-run performance by identifying the factors that produce it. Those traders who have comparative advantages in those factors should be the long-run winners.

Tables 22-8 and 22-9 provide a partial list of the factors that may predict the performance of managers, traders and the organizations for which they work. These factors vary in importance depending on the investment styles and the trading strategies that the manager, trader, or firm pursue.

The most important comparative advantage that a manager or trader should have is a thorough appreciation of the need to have a comparative advantage. Traders who do not understand why comparative advantage is important will not consider whether they have a comparative advantage before they trade. If they do not consider this question, they can have no reason to expect that they will trade profitably.

Traders who appreciate the importance of comparative advantage consider both why their trading strategy should work, and why they expect other traders will lose to them. Since trading is a zero-sum game, the two issues are inseparable. Most traders, however, focus only on why they think they will profit and not also on why they think other traders will lose to them. Traders who understand both sides of their trades will undoubtedly be more successful than those who consider only the logic of their side.

Most people have trouble identifying comparative advantage. We often mistake absolute advantage for comparative advantage. We may err because absolute advantage is correlated with comparative advantage. The more skilled a manager is, the more skilled the manager will be in comparison with other managers. To identify comparative advantage, however, you must compare managers. The point bears repeating: To win a zero-sum game, you must not just be good, you must be better.

22.8 SUMMARY

People primarily examine past performance because they want to predict good future performance. Unfortunately, good past performance does not necessarily predict good future returns. In fact, it rarely does. Over human time frames, luck is generally a more important determinant of good per-

TABLE 22-8.
Factors Correlated with the Performance of Investment Managers and Traders

FACTOR	RATIONALE	INDICATORS
Intelligence	Intelligent managers and traders recognize theoretical opportunities and avoid theoretical mistakes	Intelligence test scores Insights expressed in written works
Experience	Experienced managers and traders recognize recurring opportunities and avoid past mistakes	Years of job experience
Education and training	Well-educated managers and traders and well-trained managers and traders understand the theoretical basis for the problems they solve	Formal education Participation in training programs Attendance at conferences
Creativity	Creative managers and traders solve problems well	Insights expressed in written works
Memory	Managers and traders who can recall what they have seen and known often can find seemingly hidden opportunities	Remembers facts, people, and history well Plays Concentration well
Discipline	Disciplined managers and traders make few mistakes; they focus on what they know they can do well and avoid what they cannot do well	Consistency The ability to articulate the importance of comparative advantage
Organizational skills	Organized managers and traders do not miss opportunities	Presentation skills Filing systems
Drive	Managers and traders with strong drive work hard and efficiently	Personality Attendance at conferences Working hours
Compensation and other performance incentives	Managers and traders generally work harder when their compensation depends on their performance	Compensation contracts
Interpersonal skills	People cooperate with, and try to please, managers and traders who have good interpersonal skills	Personality Club memberships
Presentation skills	Traders occasionally have to bluff or withhold information	Acting experience Skilled poker player

formance than is skill. In addition, the skills that may have been responsible for good past performance may not produce good future performance. Moreover, a formerly skilled manager may not still be skilled. These issues make the prediction of good future performance from good past performance an essentially worthless activity.

Even the most sophisticated statistical tests rarely can separate skill from luck. The typical contribution of skill to performance is simply too small.

TABLE 22-9.

Factors Correlated with the Performance of Investment Management Firms and Trading Firms

FACTOR	RATIONALE	INDICATORS
Qualified personnel	Investment management and trading depend critically on human-capital resources	The factors presented in table 22-8 Staff training programs
Information resources	Valuation and trading are information industries	Access to real-time and historic databases Data collection facilities Correspondent networks
Research	Research creates information from data	Good models Qualified analysts Research reports and conferences
Organizational structure	Resources are most valuable when their usage is well organized	Structure reflects functional needs Internal communications systems
Internal controls	Disciplined organizations do only what they intend to do	Good risk management systems Accounting and audit systems
Trading facilities	All ideas require implementation	Physical trading desk Communication systems
Leadership	Management is responsible for the morale of the firm and for all organizational issues	The factors presented in table 22-8

The contribution is small because many traders compete with each other to profit. Their trading makes prices quite informative, so that most price changes are not predictable. Statistical performance evaluation therefore is unreliable without more data than are generally available to us.

The importance of luck cannot be overemphasized. It is much better to be lucky than skilled. The luckiest managers in a large group of managers will certainly perform better than almost all skilled managers with average luck. Superior past performance—even that of the most acclaimed managers—by itself does not necessarily indicate skill.

These results do not imply that there are no skilled managers. The discussions in chapters 10–12 about speculative trading strategies suggest that skilled managers exist and are profitable. Some skilled managers may even be able to beat the market by more than the average 2 percent that we have assumed throughout this chapter. Unfortunately, we probably cannot identify these managers only from past returns.

To identify skilled managers, it is best to consider the characteristic factors that generate superior performance. These factors include intelligence, experience, education, training, creativity, memory, discipline, drive, and access to data. Managers who have these characteristics tend to perform better than those who do not.

Most professional managers have these characteristics and therefore appear to be good managers. They probably can manage better than most people. However, they mostly compete with other managers, not with the

▶ Why Do We Mistake Absolute Advantage for Comparative Advantage?

A very important difference between physical survival and trading explains why our successful evolutionary history has not prepared us to be successful traders.

Survival is primarily a game played against nature in which nature does not actively create adaptive strategies to defeat us. To survive, our ancestors merely had to be good at survival.

In contrast, trading is a zero-sum game in which our competitors constantly try to adapt to defeat us. Good competitors win only if they are the best competitors.

Our evolutionary history has trained us to appreciate absolute advantage but not to seek comparative advantage. ◀

▶ Handicapping a Horse Race

Handicapping a horse race involves essentially the same processes as choosing an investment manager. Handicappers and investment sponsors both try to predict the outcomes of zero-sum games. They both consider three classes of factors when they estimate the odds that a horse will win the race, or a manager will outperform other managers: past performance, absolute advantage, and comparative advantage. The similarity between the two problems explains why investment sponsors often call their searches for investment managers *horse races*. Table 22-10 illustrates these parallels. ◀

average person. Winning managers are those who have a comparative advantage. They are not just good managers, they are better managers. To identify a successful manager, you must therefore be familiar with many managers so that you can compare them. If you do not have the characteristics of a successful manager, you probably will not trade successfully in the long run.

TABLE 22-10.
Parallels Between Handicapping Horses and Choosing Investment Managers

FACTORS	HORSES	INVESTMENT MANAGERS
Past performance	How has the horse run in the past? How did it place against its competition?	What returns did the manager generate in the past? How did those returns compare with the market and with other similar managers?
Absolute advantage	Does the horse look like it will run fast? Does the horse possess characteristics that determine speed, such as stride, lung capacity, muscle fiber type, weight of horse, weight to be carried, time since last race, and race experience?	Does the manager look like he will generate high returns? Does the manager possess characteristics that determine performance, such as intelligence, education, experience, discipline, creativity, and access to data?
Comparative advantage	How do the horse's past performance and absolute advantage compare with those of the other horses in the race?	How do the manager's past performance and absolute advantages compare with those of the other managers in the market?

Perhaps the most important indicator of a skilled manager is whether the manager clearly understands that success comes from having a comparative advantage. Managers who are not constantly thinking about their comparative advantages cannot know when they should trade. I would be very reluctant to invest with managers who confuse absolute advantage with comparative advantage. Successful managers should be able to clearly articulate the comparative advantages that they believe will allow them to profit in the zero-sum game.

22.9 SOME POINTS TO REMEMBER

- Distinguishing skill from luck is very difficult.
- The skills that produced superior performance in the past may not produce such performance in the future.
- Past returns do not necessarily indicate future returns.
- Even when they have no skill, many traders will perform very well just by chance.
- Sample selection biases seriously affect common inferences.
- To avoid the sample selection problem, we must always consider how information came to our attention.
- An analysis of comparative advantage is probably the only reliable way to determine who can trade well.

22.10 QUESTIONS FOR THOUGHT

- Do equal-dollar investors always have greater returns than buy and hold investors? How does the answer depend on the serial correlation of prices? Which strategy is more attractive to contrarians? To momentum traders?
- Peter Lynch, former portfolio manager of the Fidelity Magellan Fund, was an extremely successful investment manager. During his 13-year tenure (May 1977 to May 1990), the fund outperformed the market by 1.03 percent per month. The standard deviation of the market-adjusted return was 2.21 percent per month. Was Peter Lynch skilled or just lucky? How did you first learn about him and about the Fidelity Magellan Fund?
- How is information in the newspaper subject to sample selection biases?
- How is selecting a manager like selecting stocks for a portfolio?
- Where do you get your investment ideas? Is your idea generation process subject to selection biases?
- Do you have any reason to believe that you would be a successful active manager?
- Do you have any reason to believe that you could choose a successful active manager?
- A highly skilled manager will probably demand higher compensation. How will the compensation affect his or her subsequent returns? If it were easier to determine whether managers are skilled, how would the labor market for investment managers be different? How would investment returns, net of managerial fees, be different?

- Corporate managers typically manage portfolios of real assets, whereas investment managers manage portfolios of financial assets. Are they otherwise similar? Do the principles discussed in this chapter about evaluating and predicting performance for investment managers also apply to corporate managers?

- Closed-end mutual funds are corporations that hold portfolios of financial assets. Unlike open-end funds, investors cannot buy or sell shares directly. Instead, they buy and sell shares in the secondary market. Accordingly, the market price and the net asset value of closed-end funds can differ significantly. What can the market discount or premium over net asset value tell us about the manager's skill?

- Why were so many investors willing to extend so much credit to Charles Ponzi?

- How might a statistician recognize when an investment manager is adjusting the valuations of illiquid portfolio assets too slowly?

The final chapters of this book examine the economics of market structures. The topics we consider encompass many active regulatory debates.

In chapter 23, we consider why index markets are organized as they are. Our discussion shows how uninformed traders benefit from trading indexes.

Chapter 24 examines the specialist trading system. Specialists are broker-dealers who supply liquidity and arrange trades at exchanges and at some proprietary trading firms. Exchanges, regulators, and their business models sometimes compel specialists to supply liquidity when they otherwise would not want to do so. To encourage them to offer such liquidity, they must receive some benefit from their unique positions.

The next three chapters examine how markets and dealers compete against each other for order flow. We examine internalization and order preferencing by dealers in chapter 25, why markets consolidate and fragment in chapter 26, and screen-versus floor-based trading in chapter 27. We pay special attention to the problems that result when traders can trade the same instruments in different places.

Chapter 28 discusses the origins of extreme volatility. There we consider how market structures contribute to—and mitigate—volatility. We also consider whether markets should have circuit breakers to control excess volatility.

Chapter 29 considers the benefits and consequences of prohibiting insider trading. Interestingly, the most important issues involve labor economics rather than market microstructure.

Part VII

▷

Market Structures

23
▷
Index
and
Portfolio
Markets

Index trading is one of the most important financial innovations of the twentieth century. The nominal dollar value of trading in equity index products now is greater than the total dollar value of trading in the underlying securities. The growth of index trading has had a profound effect on equity markets. It is also increasingly affecting debt markets.

Index markets trade index products. *Index products* include index futures contracts, index option contracts, and securities that represent ownership in index funds. *Index funds* are portfolios that their managers design to replicate the performance of various price indexes. Most index funds track market equity indexes. Some funds track debt indexes and sector equity indexes.

Index products and index markets are extremely popular. Many people have decided that they would rather invest in an index product than risk losing money investing with an active investment manager. Index products also are attractive to speculators who want to speculate only on index risks or only on firm-specific risks. The former buy or sell index products to establish their speculative positions. The latter sell or buy index products to hedge the index risk in their long or short positions in individual securities.

The widespread use of index strategies has changed the character of markets. Index markets are far more liquid than the underlying cash markets upon which their products are based. Price changes in index products generally lead changes in the cash index. Consequently, many people believe that index markets are the "tail that wags the dog." You must understand index strategies in order to understand the relation between index markets and their underlying cash markets.

In this chapter, we will briefly consider how indexes are computed and how index funds are managed. We will then turn to why index products and index markets are so popular. You may find this section particularly useful if you are unsure whether you should invest or speculate in equities. The chapter closes with a discussion of the various ways that traders exchange index risks.

23.1 PRICE INDEXES

People use *price indexes* to characterize the values of lists of instruments. The instruments upon which a price index is based are the *index components*. The index components determine the character of the index. Indexes exist for entire markets, for subsets of a market, and for sets of markets. The instruments may be equities, debt securities, commodities, or currencies. Indexes that include only a small subset of market securities are *narrow indexes*. Narrow indexes have been defined for small and large securities, value and growth securities, industry sector securities, and securities of firms that do business in narrow geographic regions.

Most price indexes are proprietary products that exchanges, brokers, or

▶ The Major Market Index and *The* Major Market Index

Dow Jones and Co. owns the Dow Jones Industrial Average (DJIA), which is a price-weighted index of 30 large U.S. stocks. The list originally included only industrial stocks. It now includes some stocks in the finance and services sectors of the economy. The Dow 30 is the best-known U.S. market index. It is *the* major market index.

For many years, Dow Jones refused to license the DJIA to options and futures exchanges that wanted to create contracts based upon it. The American Stock Exchange therefore created an index called the Major Market Index (MMI). The MMI is a price-weighted index of 20 blue chip stocks. Not coincidentally, most of the stock MMI stocks are also Dow 30 stocks. Changes in the MMI therefore are very closely correlated with changes in the DJIA. The American Stock Exchange trades options on the MMI using the ticker symbol XMI. It also licensed the index to the Chicago Mercantile Exchange, which traded futures on it.

In 1997, Dow Jones finally licensed the DJIA to the Chicago Board of Trade (CBOT) and to the Chicago Board Options Exchange (CBOE). The CBOT Dow Jones Industrials futures and the CBOE Dow Jones Industrials option contracts have been very successful. Both have killed their respective MMI competitors. The CME stopped trading its MMI contract in 1999. Although the AMEX MMI option contract continues to trade (as of December 2001), it no longer has significant open interest. ◀

data vendors compute. Although *index creators* sometimes sell their indexes, they often offer them to their clients to promote their businesses. Many index creators license their indexes to firms that base index products upon them.

All price indexes are essentially just averages of the prices of their index components. Indexes differ by the methods used to compute those averages, however. The two most common index types are price-weighted and value-weighted indexes.

A *price-weighted index* is proportional to the sum of the prices of the index components. The highest priced instruments therefore have the greatest influence over the values of price-weighted indexes. The Dow Jones Industrial Average (DJIA) and the Nikkei 225 Stock Average are the best-known price-weighted indexes.

A *value-weighted index* is proportional to the total capital value of all index components. Traders therefore also call value-weighted indexes *capitalization-weighted indexes*. Securities with the highest capital value have the greatest influence over the values of value-weighted indexes. Most price indexes are value-weighted. The S&P 500 Index is the best-known value-weighted index.

The value of an index is obtained by dividing the price or value sum by a constant *index divisor*. The divisor originally was a number that the index creator chose to ensure that the index started at an arbitrary initial value. Divisors now change only when necessary to ensure that the value of an index does not change when the creator adds or deletes index components or, in the case of a price-weighted index, when a stock splits. For example, the divisor of a price-weighted index must increase when a high priced stock replaces a low priced stock. Otherwise, the change would unnaturally increase the value of the index. Likewise, the divisor of a value-weighted index must increase when a high capitalization stock replaces a low capital-

They Each Manage About 3 Percent of All World Equity

Barclays Global Investors is the world's largest index fund manager. As of December 2000, the firm had 571 billion dollars under management in various U.S. and international equity index funds. (The firm had 802 billion dollars of assets under management, counting all asset classes.) By comparison, total world traded equity market capitalization was then approximately 31 trillion dollars. Counting only index funds, Barclays Global Investors manages a bit less than 2 percent of all traded equity in the world.

The world's largest equity manager is Deutsche Asset Management, which manages about 1 trillion dollars worldwide in many subsidiaries. ◀

Sources: http://www.barclays
global.com/about/who_we_are/
assets_rankings.jhtml;
http://www.fibv.com/
publications/Ta1300.pdf.

ization stock. The divisors of value-weighted indexes do not have to change when stocks split, because splits do not change total capital values.

You may occasionally encounter *equal-weighted* and *geometrically weighted* indexes. *Equal-weighted indexes* measure the returns from investing an equal dollar amount in each index component. The index values represent the cumulative returns to this hypothetical investment strategy. The best-known equal-weighted index is the CRSP (Center for Research in Security Prices) equal-weighted market index. It is used primarily in academic research. *Geometrically weighted indexes* average logarithmic returns rather than prices. The Value Line Geometric Index is a value-weighted index of logarithmic returns.

A price index is *dividend-adjusted* if it is adjusted upward when securities pay dividends. Traders also call dividend-adjusted indexes *total return indexes* because they measure the total return—capital gains plus income yield—that investors would receive if they could invest in the index without any transaction costs. People generally use total return indexes as benchmarks against which they measure the performance of their portfolios. The DJIA and the S&P 500 Index are not dividend-adjusted indexes. Corresponding total return indexes for these two indexes, however, are widely available.

23.2 INDEX FUNDS

An *index fund* is a portfolio that *index managers* design to replicate the performance of an index. *Tracking error* is the difference between the portfolio return and the corresponding dividend-adjusted index return. Index fund managers try to minimize their tracking errors. Most U.S. index funds try to replicate the S&P 500 Index, although other indexes are becoming increasingly popular.

Replicating a value-weighted equity index is quite simple. If the value of the index fund is 0.01 percent of the total capitalization of all the index components, the index fund manager simply buys 0.01 percent of the outstanding shares of each index component. The value of the fund therefore is exactly proportional to the total value of all index components, which is proportional to the value of the value-weighted index. Consequently, percentage changes in these three quantities will be identical. Index managers must rebalance a value-weighted portfolio only when the list of index components changes. Otherwise, the fund simply holds its securities.

Replicating a price-weighted equity index is equally simple. The index fund simply holds an equal number of shares in each index component. The value of the portfolio therefore is proportional to the sum of the prices of the index components, which is proportional to the price-weighted index. Percentage changes in these three quantities therefore will be identical. Index managers must rebalance price-weighted index portfolios whenever the index list is changed and whenever stocks split.

To replicate the returns to a dividend-adjusted index, index funds must reinvest their dividends as they are paid.

Index funds generally slightly underperform their target indexes because various *frictions* drag down their performance. These frictions include transaction costs resulting from dividend reinvestment, accommodating deposits

▶ The Price Impacts of the Annual Russell Reconstitution

Many U.S. stock index funds try to replicate the value-weighted Russell 1000, 2000, or 3000 Index. The Russell 1000 and 3000 Indexes respectively consist of the 1,000 and 3,000 largest publicly traded U.S. firms, ranked by their common stock market capitalization. The Russell 2000 Index consists of firms ranked between 1,001st and 3,000th in market capitalization.

The Frank Russell Company, an investment management consultant, annually reconstitutes its indexes at the close of trading on the last trading day in June, based on market capitalizations as of the close of trading on the last trading day in May. Stocks that have grown in size are added to the Russell 3000 or are moved up from the Russell 2000 to the Russell 1000. Stocks that have lost value are moved down from the Russell 1000 to the Russell 2000 or are dropped from the Russell 2000 and 3000. Stocks that stop trading due to bankruptcies or mergers are dropped when they stop trading.

Index funds that replicate the Russell Indexes rebalance their portfolios when the Indexes are reconstituted each June. Since these funds must buy the additions and sell the deletions near the same date, they often have substantial price impacts on these stocks during the months of June and July. In the six years from 1996 to 2001, the Russell 3000 additions outperformed the deletions by an average of 15 percent in June and underperformed the deletions by 5 percent in July.

The Russell 3000 reconstitution price impacts are quite large because these stocks are quite small. The reversal in prices in July indicates that some of the price impact is transitory. The remaining difference in June returns may be due to the increased value investors place on stocks in the Russell Indexes—perhaps because they trade in more liquid markets—or to a well-known momentum anomaly that affects the returns of small stocks. Some of the difference may also reverse in August and later months.

Portfolio rebalancing has similar effects when Standard & Poor's changes its stock index components. ◀

Source: Ananth Madhavan, "The Russell Reconstitution Effect," manuscript, 2002. To be published in Financial Analysts Journal.

---

and redemptions, and rebalancing transactions when the index list changes. Management fees also reduce fund performance.

Index funds can slightly improve their returns by careful management of their trading. In particular, they can supply rather than demand liquidity when trading, they can substitute nonindex components when index components are expensive to trade, they can rebalance only when accommodating deposits and redemptions and when reinvesting dividends, and they can hold only a subset of the index components to minimize the number of securities that they have to trade. Although these policies tend to increase returns, they also generally increase tracking error. Many funds therefore do not aggressively employ them.

23.3 THE ARGUMENT FOR INDEXATION

Active portfolio managers are speculators who try to beat the market by clever trading. Active managers may be informed traders, value traders, or technical traders. The *turnover* of a portfolio is the ratio between the total dollar

▶ A Perspective on Bad Active Management

Active managers do not lose because they consistently buy instruments that then fall and sell instruments that then rise. Funds that consistently make such mistakes could greatly increase their profits simply by selling whenever their research suggests that they should buy, and buying whenever their research suggests that they should sell. Bad research does not create systematically wrong signals—it merely creates random noise.

Active managers do not lose because they consistently buy losers and sell winners. They lose because they consistently buy and sell. ◀

value of all portfolio purchases (or sales, or average of purchases and sales) in a given period and the total value of the portfolio. Active managers often have turnover rates of more than 100 percent per year. They typically charge between 1 and 3 percent for their services.

In contrast, *passive managers* construct portfolios and then leave them alone. Since they rarely trade, passive managers usually have turnover rates between 0 and 10 percent per year. Passive managers typically charge less than 15 basis points (0.15 percent) for their services, whereas active managers charge 50 to 100 or more basis points.

Most active managers cannot beat the market because transaction costs—brokerage commissions and management fees—reduce performance in what is otherwise a zero-sum game. Without transaction costs, the value-weighted average return of all portfolios would be equal to the value-weighted market index return. Transaction costs ensure that the average portfolio return is always less than the market index return. Since active managers trade frequently, they tend to underperform the market.

These implications of the zero-sum game are logical conclusions based on simple accounting principals. They are always true.

Since these implications must be true, empirical results on the performance of active fund managers cannot be surprising: As a group, active fund managers underperform the market. In any given quarter, only one-fourth of all mutual funds beat the market. If there were no transaction costs, if mutual funds represented a random sample of all funds, and if small funds on average performed no better than large funds, we would expect that half of all mutual funds would beat the market. Indeed, if you add back transaction costs, about half of all mutual funds do beat the market. Funds underperform because of their transaction costs.

Interestingly, the set of winners varies from quarter to quarter. Funds generally do not persistently outperform the market. This result is not surprising: Our discussions in chapter 22 suggest that luck is a more important determinant of performance than skill.

The set of extreme losers does not vary as much as the set of winners. Extreme losers lose because they trade too much. It is much easier to consistently lose than to consistently win.

Some managers undoubtedly can beat the market on average, even after accounting for their transaction costs and management fees. Unfortunately, as we saw in chapter 22, identifying such managers is very difficult.

Many uninformed investors employ *buy and hold strategies* to avoid the difficulties of selecting skilled active managers and the costs of investing with unskilled active managers. Buy and hold investors avoid trading losses by not trading. They also avoid high management fees.

Since index funds implement buy and hold strategies, they are very attractive to investors who want exposure to index risk without the risk of substantially underperforming the market. The minor frictions associated with index fund management ensure that index funds will slightly underperform their indexes. Although index funds slightly underperform their indexes, they regularly beat three-quarters of all active managers.

Once again, note that this regularity is not simply an empirical fact. It is an implication of the zero-sum game.

Although investors can save transaction costs by pursuing any buy and hold strategy, they generally choose to invest in broad-based market index funds because they offer well-diversified portfolios that replicate the market. Since market index returns are widely published, index investors can easily audit whether their managers are doing what they expect them to do.

23.4 LIQUIDITY AND PRICE FORMATION IN INDEX MARKETS

Index markets and *index trading mechanisms* allow traders to trade index risk more cheaply than they could by trading each component instrument separately. Several factors ensure that index products have low transaction costs.

First, index dealers face little risk of trading with well-informed traders. Most index traders are uninformed investors. Few traders have valuable insights into the future direction of the entire market. Accordingly, index dealers do not have to quote wide spreads to recover from uninformed traders what they lose to informed traders.

Second, index markets tend to be very active because most people trade the same index products. Buyers therefore can easily find sellers. Moreover, since dealers can turn over their inventories quickly in active markets, they face little inventory risk, which allows them to quote tight markets.

Finally, traders of index products generally need to arrange, clear, and settle only a single transaction. Reducing trade to a single transaction saves time and effort. Index traders who trade the underlying component instruments have to arrange many trades, which is substantially more expensive.

Traders trade the index components when they need to assemble or disassemble index portfolios. These trades generally are arranged as *program trades*. A *program trade* involves the simultaneous submission of many orders at the same time. For statistical purposes, the New York Stock Exchange and the Securities and Exchange Commission classify program trades as any trades that involve 15 or more coordinated transactions having a total value of 1 million dollars or more. These trades represent about 27 percent of trading volume at the NYSE. Index arbitrageurs who need to construct or liquidate index portfolios do about 9 percent of the reported program trade volume at the NYSE and about 2.4 percent of total NYSE volume. The remaining 91 percent of program trading volume is due to other portfolio trading strategies, many of which are also index-based. Traders who do program trades generally use specialized *order list processing software* to manage their orders.

Price changes in index markets generally lead changes in the cash index. Index traders are concerned only about discovering the price of index risk. In contrast, traders in the component securities must concern themselves with pricing all of the risks inherent in their securities. Index risk is usually much less important to them than security-specific risks. Most index markets therefore discover the prices of index risk much faster than do the many individual markets in which their index components trade. Traders in individual security markets therefore look to index markets to get a sense of where the market is going.

23.4.1 Package Trading, Basket Trading, and Portfolio Trading

Package dealers make firm bids or offers for entire portfolios. When these portfolios are index portfolios, the costs of trading them are often quite low.

▶ The Program Trade Buzzer

The New York Stock Exchange used to print electronically routed (SuperDot) orders on the exchange floor. Each trading post had several dot matrix printers that printed the orders. Floor traders could easily recognize when program traders submitted their orders by the simultaneous buzz that these printers made when printing order tickets for the various stocks in the program trades.

The Exchange no longer prints Super Dot orders. Instead, it routes them directly to the specialists' electronic order books. ◀

▶ ESP at the NYSE

Following the stock market crash of 1987, the New York Stock Exchange decided that it would create an organized market for institutional-sized package trading in the S&P 500 portfolio. The Exchange created the *Exchange Stock Portfolio* (ESP), a portfolio of all S&P 500 stocks. Due to problems with fractional shares for smaller index stocks, the NYSE sized the ESP so that it was worth about 6 million dollars.

The NYSE enlisted five major investment banks to act as competitive market makers in the ESP. Each was required to make a firm bid and offer for the ESP.

The ESP started trading in October 1989. The product was not successful. Trades only occurred only when one dealer picked off another dealer who was slow to adjust his quotes in response to changing market conditions. During the 25 months that the ESP traded, fewer than 5 of the 269 total trades were agency trades arranged on behalf of a client.

The result was not surprising, considering that the price of S&P 500 Index risk then was (and still is) primarily discovered in the S&P 500 futures pit on the floor of the Chicago Mercantile Exchange (CME). The ESP dealers could never quote a market as tight as the futures market because they were away from the pit, and therefore away from the most recent and most reliable information about S&P 500 Index values. The ESP dealers were also at a disadvantage compared to the CME floor traders because the ESP dealers had to quote continuous firm markets for a 6 million dollar transaction. In contrast, CME floor traders were not—and still are not—obligated to quote firm markets for any size.

To facilitate trading of the ESP, the NYSE modified its trading systems to permit decimal pricing. Few people know that the NYSE was able to trade on decimals for 11 years before it switched its common stocks to decimal pricing. ◀

This market is variously known as the *firm bid/offer market*, the *package trading market*, the *basket market*, or the *portfolio trading market*.

The firm bid/offer market works as follows. A trader submits a characterization of the portfolio to one or more package dealers. The characterization indicates whether the portfolio is an index portfolio. If it is not an index portfolio, the characterization includes information about the securities in the portfolio. The information includes summary statistics about quantities, firm sizes, betas, price levels, average trading volumes, volatilities, primarily exchange listings, and index components. The package dealers use this information to quote firm prices for the portfolio. They typically express prices relative to the end-of-day value of the portfolio. For example, a package dealer may bid the closing value minus 15 cents per share to buy the portfolio, or ask the closing value plus 20 cents per share to sell the portfolio. The trader usually arranges the trade with the package dealer who offers the best price. To prevent market manipulations, the trader reveals the list of securities only after the market closes.

Traders often solicit firm bids and offers for portfolios because they can often obtain better prices and faster trades than if they traded each security separately. Package dealers generally offer better prices for portfolios than for individual securities because informed traders are less likely to trade portfolios than individual securities. Dealers therefore are less likely to be hurt by informed traders when trading portfolios than when trading individual securities.

Traders who do not have trading systems that allow them to easily do program trades especially benefit from the firm bid/offer market. They pay the package dealers to assume their trading problems. Package dealers can offer better prices than their clients can obtain because they generally are better traders than their clients are. Package dealers also may be able to place the portfolio, or significant parts of it, with their other clients. If so, they can facilitate the trade quite cheaply.

23.5 INDEX PRODUCTS

Index risks trade in many forms. Index products include several types of index securities and derivative contracts. Table 23-1 presents a summary of the major U.S. broad-based index products.

The most common index securities are open-end mutual funds that hold index portfolios. Traders buy these securities directly from the fund at

TABLE 23-1.
Major U.S. Broad-based Index Products

TYPE	PRODUCT	EXAMPLES	PRIMARY MARKET	OPEN INTEREST
Securities	Open-end mutual funds	Vanguard 500 Index Fund Investor Shares	By deposit to and redemption from the fund	$96 billion
		Fidelity Spartan 500 Index Fund	By deposit to and redemption from the fund	$10 billion
	Exchange-traded funds	S&P Depository Receipts, "Spiders"	AMEX	$27 billion
		Nasdaq 100 Trust, "Cubes"	AMEX	$28 billion
		Diamonds Trust Series 1 (DJIA)	AMEX	$2 billion
Derivative contracts	Cash-settled futures contracts	S&P 500 Futures Contract	CME	$290 billion
		Nasdaq 100 Futures Contract	CME	$11 billion
		Dow 30 Futures Contract	CBOT	$3 billion
	Cash-settled index options	S&P 500 Index Options (SPX)	CBOE	2.0 million contracts
		S&P 100 Index Options (OEX)	CBOE	0.3 million contracts
		Dow 30 Options (DJX)	CBOE	1.0 million contracts
	Options on futures contracts	S&P 500 Index Options	CME	0.17 million contracts

Source: Various Web pages.
The reported open interest is as of April 20, 2001.

closing net asset value prices. They likewise redeem their shares for cash by trading directly with the fund. The main disadvantages of these funds are that traders cannot trade them within the day, the funds must maintain cash balances to accommodate deposits and redemptions, and the funds must trade their underlying securities when deposits and redemptions do not net to zero.

Exchange-traded index funds (ETFs) are becoming increasingly popular. ETFs are trusts that typically hold index portfolios. Units of the trust trade like stocks. Most people buy and sell these trust units at exchanges and ECNs. Large traders, however, can create new units by depositing an index portfolio with the trust. They likewise can redeem units by giving them to the trust in exchange for their pro rata share of the index portfolio. Exchange-traded funds are growing in popularity because traders can trade them at any time and because they do not have to accommodate small investor deposits and redemptions. ETFs also generate fewer tax liabilities for investors than do open-end funds because they do not buy and sell securities when investors deposit and redeem shares. Finally, ETFs do not have to manage shareholder accounts as open-end mutual funds do.

The most important derivative index products are index futures contracts. Futures contracts are especially popular among hedgers and speculators because they can buy and sell them without posting large margins. Their main disadvantage as a vehicle for holding long-term index risk is that traders must *roll over* their positions into new contracts when their current contracts expire. These rollover transactions generate transaction costs.

Cash-settled index option contracts constitute the last major class of index products. Speculators, hedgers, and gamblers primarily use them.

23.6 SUMMARY

Interest in index markets has increased substantially since the early 1970s as investors have better understood the implications of the zero-sum game. On average, active managers cannot outperform the market. Transaction costs and high management fees ensure that they underperform the market on average. Investors who do not want to actively speculate—either by themselves or by choosing investment managers—find that index funds are quite attractive.

The removal of index order flow from underlying security markets to index product markets has greatly decreased the costs of pursuing index strategies. Index markets are quite liquid because they concentrate order flow and because few traders are well informed about broad-based index values. Index products are much cheaper to trade than the component instruments.

Low transaction costs in index markets have made these markets very attractive to speculators. They use them to speculate in index risk or to hedge out the index risk associated with their speculative positions in individual securities.

23.7 SOME POINTS TO REMEMBER

- Indexes characterize the average price performance of a set of index stocks.
- Index funds hold portfolios designed to replicate the returns of a price index.

- Index funds have very low turnover rates because managers rarely need to rebalance index portfolios.
- Investors hold index products to avoid transaction costs and to eliminate losses often associated with active management.
- Index markets provide low-cost ways to trade index risk.
- Index dealers are generally unconcerned about security-specific risks.

23.8 QUESTIONS FOR THOUGHT

1. What is the relation between a price index and a total return index?
2. What would happen to liquidity if buy and hold managers held 90 percent of all equity? Would prices become less informative? What active traders, if any, would benefit?
3. What effect do you think the switch of index trading from program trading to index products has had on liquidity in underlying markets?
4. Has the decrease in index transaction costs made new trading strategies possible? How do we all benefit from traders who pursue these strategies?
5. Index funds generally just slightly underperform the market. Is the quest for the average market index return an immoral search for mediocrity?
6. What strategies can index funds employ to improve their returns?
7. How can order anticipators and price manipulators profit from the Russell reconstitution?

24

▷

Specialists

Some exchanges assign special responsibilities to members they designate as specialists. The *specialists* must continuously quote two-sided markets so that markets always exist in their *specialties*. They must also ensure that their markets are orderly and that prices do not jump too quickly.

Exchanges that designate specialists have *designated primary market maker trading systems* or, more simply, *specialist trading systems*. The largest equity exchange that designates specialists is the New York Stock Exchange.

Exchanges with specialist trading systems believe that their specialists enhance market quality and thereby attract traders to their exchanges. They believe that continuous and orderly markets increase investor confidence so that investors are more willing to invest in the exchanges' listed companies. By attracting investor interest, these exchanges encourage issuers to list their securities with them. The exchanges thereby obtain greater revenues from *listing fees* and *transaction fees*, and their members make greater profits as brokers and dealers.

In this chapter, we describe the various obligations that exchanges impose upon their specialists. We show how these obligations often require that specialists trade when they do not want to trade and refrain from trading when they do want to trade. Such obligations therefore can be quite costly to specialists. To encourage traders to accept these obligations, exchanges give specialists various trading privileges. We describe these privileges and explain how specialists profit from them. To prevent abuses of these privileges, exchanges also impose restrictions on when specialists may trade.

Although all traders appreciate the liquidity that exchanges obligate their specialists to provide, many traders resent that they have special privileges. The special privileges can be quite valuable to specialists, and hence costly to other traders. The specialist trading system therefore is the subject of regulatory controversy. Regulators must consider whether the value that specialists obtain from their privileges is commensurate with the value of the services they provide. The traders who benefit when specialists fulfill their obligations usually are not the same traders who are hurt when specialists exercise their privileges. Regulators therefore also must consider whether the resulting transfers of wealth among traders are appropriate.

You must understand the specialist trading system if you trade at exchanges that employ such systems. At such exchanges, the execution of your orders will somehow involve specialists. They may act as your broker, they may act as dealers and fill your orders for their accounts, or they may conduct the auctions in which brokers match your orders to other traders' orders. You will make better trading decisions when you understand how specialists handle your orders.

You also must understand the specialist trading system in order to understand how markets compete with each other. The liquidity services that specialists offer are *public goods* in the sense that everyone benefits from them. Unfortunately, public goods are hard to obtain in competitive markets. Few people will pay for them when they can freely obtain them. Regulators who value the liquidity that specialists offer must therefore carefully consider how markets compete with each other. We introduce these issues at the end of this chapter and expand upon them when we consider how markets compete with each other in chapter 26.

Finally, you must understand the specialist trading system in order to responsibly consider whether floor-based exchanges that use specialist trading systems should convert to screen-based trading systems. Although exchanges can build a screen-based specialist trading system, many issues make such a structure unlikely. Analyses of conversions to screen-based trading therefore should consider the benefits lost and the costs saved if the specialist trading system were scrapped. This chapter will help you identify these benefits and costs.

Specialist trading systems differ across exchanges. The distinguishing characteristic of these systems is that they impose obligations on dealers to supply liquidity. The obligations vary, however. Most exchanges restrict the trades that specialists can do, but some do not. This chapter provides a general discussion of the principal economic and regulatory issues that arise in connection with all designated primary market maker trading systems. These issues are common to all variants of these systems. The examples that we will consider to illustrate these principles, however, are specific to the specialist trading systems that the New York and the American Stock Exchanges use.

24.1 OVERVIEW

Specialist trading systems are found primarily at U.S. stock and options exchanges. Some markets in other countries also use them. The specialist trading system is most important at the New York and American Stock Exchanges. The U.S. regional stock exchanges also have specialist trading systems, but most regional specialists are more like third market dealers than primary stock exchange specialists. The equity options markets organized by the Chicago Board Options Exchange (CBOE), the American Stock Exchange, the Pacific Exchange, and the Philadelphia Stock Exchange also use specialist trading systems.

Specialists are known by different names in various markets. The CBOE calls its specialists *designated primary market makers*. The Deutsche Börse calls its specialists *designated sponsors* in English and *Betreuers* in German. At the Paris Bourse, they are known as *animateurs*.

Third market dealers also often call their traders "specialists." The business models of these firms often obligate their traders to offer liquidity when they otherwise might not want to do so. These obligations are voluntary, however. The dealers propose and accept them as conditions for obtaining order flow from brokers. The NASD, the SEC, and some court decisions restrict the trades that these dual traders can do. These restrictions, however, usually are not as severe as those which exchanges impose upon their specialists.

Most specialists are dual traders who sometimes broker orders for their clients and at other times fill orders for their clients from their own inventories. Exchanges that permit dual trading generally employ many regulatory safeguards to solve the resulting conflict of interest problems introduced in chapter 7. Specialists therefore are subject to many regulations.

Exchanges with specialist trading systems usually assign only one specialist to each stock or options class. We will discuss below how they make these assignments.

Some exchanges use a *designated multiple market maker trading system* for trading their securities. These systems are similar to specialist systems except that the exchanges obligate multiple traders to offer liquidity that they otherwise might not want to offer. These obligations are best enforced in electronic markets because traders in open outcry markets will hide when they do not want to trade. When nobody wants to trade, a computer usually assigns the obligation to trade in rotation to each of the designated market makers.

The CBOE uses a designated multiple market maker trading system for its most actively traded index options series. Unlike most specialists, their designated market makers are not dual traders. They deal only for their account, and they do not broker agency orders. Like specialists, the market makers have some obligations to provide liquidity when markets are not trading normally. Similar structures appear at some European options exchanges and at some futures exchanges.

The number of stocks or option classes that each specialist trades depends on how actively traded the instruments are. Specialists who specialize in very actively traded securities usually trade only one security or option class. Those who specialize in less frequently traded securities trade larger lists. Most specialists trade only a few securities. For example, most of the 482 individual specialists at the New York Stock Exchange trade between three and six stocks each. They usually have one actively traded security and a few less actively traded ones.

Most specialists work for firms that employ many specialists. In December 2001, only eight firms employed all specialists at the NYSE. Five of these firms handled stocks representing 95 percent of all the NYSE dollar volume.

Specialists play three roles in most markets. They are dealers when they trade for their own account. They are brokers when they broker orders and trades for other brokers. Finally, they are exchange officials who are responsible for conducting orderly markets. We consider these three main roles in the next three sections.

24.2 SPECIALISTS AS DEALERS

Specialists act as dealers when they trade for their own accounts. Exchanges greatly regulate the trading that specialists can and must do for their own accounts.

Two sets of regulations govern specialist trading. *Affirmative obligations* obligate specialists to offer liquidity in various circumstances. *Negative obligations* prevent them from trading in other circumstances. Specialists accept these obligations because they enjoy the various privileges that come with them.

24.2.1 Affirmative Obligations

The specialists' primary affirmative obligation is to ensure that a reasonable market always exists in their specialties. When no one else is willing to trade, specialists must be willing to trade. They must quote two-sided markets when no one else will, and their quotes must be meaningful in the sense that the spread between the best bid and the best offer cannot be too wide. Since specialists often must trade when no one else is willing to trade, they are the *traders of last resort*.

Their obligation to make markets is limited, however. Specialists do not have to make firm quotes for large block sizes, and they are not required to support prices when values are falling or restrain prices when values are rising. They simply have to ensure that public traders can always trade some meaningful quantity.

Exchanges expect that their specialists will smooth prices by intervening to prevent large price reversals. A *price reversal* occurs when price rises and then falls or falls and then rises. Large reversals often result when uninformed traders demand liquidity that is not present in the market. If such traders insist upon trading, they often must move prices substantially to find someone with whom to trade. Prices then jump back to their former levels when someone else demands liquidity on the other side of the market.

A market has *price continuity* if prices move smoothly, without jumping too much. Specialists are responsible for creating price continuity. Exchanges like price continuity because it helps assure public traders that brokers fill their agency orders fairly.

Exchanges evaluate how well specialists meet their affirmative obligations by measuring the average width of the quoted bid/ask spread, the average depth of the quotes, the number of large price reversals, and the average size of price reversals. Specialists do their jobs well when the spreads in their

▶ Smoothing Jumps

An electronic order-driven market has the following limit book:

Aggregate buy size	Price	Aggregate sell size
40	22.1	
5	22.2	
	22.3	2
	22.4	
	22.5	
	22.6	
	22.7	8
	22.8	10

The market initially is 22.2 bid for 5; 2 offered at 22.3.

Suppose that a four-contract market buy order arrives, followed by a two-contract market sell order. The buy order will completely fill the sell order at 22.3. The remainder of the buy order will then fill two of the eight offered at 22.7. The market sell order will then fill two of the five bid at 22.2. The price will jump up from 22.3 to 22.7 and then down to 22.2.

The large reversal is due to the gap in sell orders between 22.3 and 22.7. If a specialist were in this market, she might have filled the remainder of the market buy order at 22.4. Had she done so, she could have filled the market sell order at 22.3 for a profit of 0.1 per contract. ◀

▶ Price Continuity and Telegraph Ticker Tapes

When telecommunication technologies were much less capable and much more expensive then they presently are, exchanges could not cheaply disseminate as much market information as they do now. For many years, most public traders did not know prevailing bid and offer prices at the time they submitted their orders. Instead, they knew only the last trade price transmitted by automated telegraph systems. Traders called these systems *ticker tapes* because they made ticking sounds as they printed on paper tapes.

With such limited information resources, traders could not easily determine whether they received fair trade prices. The best that they could do was check whether their trade prices were much different from the prices that immediately preceded and followed their trades. Exchanges therefore wanted to regulate price continuity to assure public traders that their orders were treated fairly.

Traders now can access much more information to determine whether their trade prices are fair. Traders are particularly interested in the quoted bid and ask prices. When dealers quote prices without knowing whether they will next trade with a buyer or a seller, they must quote fair prices. If they quote prices that are too high or too low, they risk trading with informed traders. Public traders therefore can be confident that their trade prices are fair when quotations are widely disseminated so that informed traders could take them if they wanted to trade. The width of the bid/ask spread therefore is a more important indicator of price fairness than price continuity is. ◀

markets are narrow, the quoted sizes are large, large price reversals are uncommon, and price reversals are small on average.

Creating price continuity is sometimes quite expensive. Specialists must trade when no one else is willing to trade. Whether these trades prove to be expensive depends on why no one else wants to trade. If no one wants to trade because informed traders believe that values are changing, specialists will trade on the losing side of the market. They will buy when prices are falling or sell when prices are rising. If no one wants to trade simply because no one is paying attention, specialist trades can be quite profitable.

Uncertainty about what prices will do in the future makes being a specialist very difficult. Consider what happens when specialists take prices down quickly because no one wants to buy in the face of strong selling pressures. If prices do not subsequently rebound, the specialists will have done a good job of finding market-clearing prices. If prices subsequently rebound, however, people may accuse them of failing to offer enough liquidity to ensure adequate continuity. This tension makes being a specialist difficult.

24.2.2 Negative Obligations

The specialists' *negative obligations* restrict their trading. At the New York and American Stock Exchanges, specialists are bound by exchange order precedence rules and by the principle that they should not take liquidity which would otherwise be available to public traders.

The exchange order precedence rules require that specialists yield to public orders at the same price or better. Specialists cannot trade at a given price unless no public traders are willing to trade at that price (the public order precedence rule), and no other traders are willing to trade at a better price (the price priority rule). These rules give precedence to public traders who offer liquidity over specialists.

Exchanges also discourage their specialists from trading with limit orders on their books. When specialists fill standing limit orders, they take liquidity that public traders could otherwise take. Since exchanges want to preserve this liquidity for public traders, we shall call this principle the *public liquidity preservation principle.*

The public liquidity preservation principle also protects traders who offer limit orders. For example, suppose that a limit order trader places a limit order to sell at 50 when the market is 49.80 bid, 50 offered. If good news arrives, if the market as a whole rises, or if the prices of similar stocks rise, the limit order trader may want to cancel the order and resubmit another at a higher price. In these circumstances, however, the specialist may want to fill the order. If the specialist can fill standing orders for his own account, the limit order trader probably will not have a chance to cancel his order. The specialist will generally fill the order before the limit order trader can cancel it because specialists can see and react to changing market conditions faster than most other traders can. Moreover, if the audit trail is not perfect, a dishonest specialist may fill the order immediately after receiving the cancel instruction. In that case, the specialist will claim that the order was filled first, and he will return the cancel instruction with a trade confirmation. The public liquidity preservation principle protects limit order traders by giving them more time to change their orders in response to changing market conditions.

The negative obligations ensure that specialists can only offer liquidity, and then only if no public traders are willing to offer liquidity at the same or better prices. Specialists subject to the public liquidity preservation principle therefore can trade only with incoming marketable orders—market orders and marketable limit orders. If they want to trade ahead of public limit orders, they must offer better prices. If they want to trade at the best quoted price, they can trade only after all public orders are filled at that price.

Since the negative obligations prohibit trades that specialists might otherwise want to do, these obligations must be costly to them. Specialists subject themselves to them because the value of their special privileges more than compensates for their inability to do certain desirable trades.

Third market dealers and regional specialists generally are not subject to the public liquidity preference principle. They can fill limit orders on their books for their own accounts whenever they want. The opportunity to trade with the limit order book is especially advantageous when the market is moving quickly and limit order traders cannot quickly cancel their orders. At such times, quick traders can buy at low prices when the market is rising and sell at high prices when the market is falling. Traders say that limit orders are *stale* when their prices no longer reflect current market conditions.

The *limit order price protection guarantees* that third market dealers and regional specialists give brokers to obtain their order flows require that these dealers fill limit orders on their books under certain circumstances. Chapter 25 describes these guarantees. When markets are stable, limit order price protection can be costly to dealers because they often must buy at the ask and sell at the bid to fill agency limit orders. These obligations therefore offset to some extent the benefits of trading with stale limit orders.

▶ Confirmation versus Cancellation

In floor-based markets with poor audit trails, traders sometimes say that a request to cancel a limit order is actually a request for a trade confirmation. Their experience has led them to believe that floor traders often fill their orders when presented with requests to cancel.

Limit order traders undoubtedly think that this abuse happens more often than it actually does. Long delays between the execution of an order and the receipt of the associated trade confirmation, and long delays between the submission of a request to cancel and its receipt by the specialist, ensure that specialists often may receive requests to cancel *after* the orders have filled. Traders then receive trade confirmations instead of their desired order cancellations. Markets can avoid these misunderstandings by ensuring that their order-routing systems, trade reporting systems, and trade confirmation systems all operate at very high speeds. ◀

▶ Tick Size, Negative Obligations, and Specialist Participation Rates

Specialist trading is especially difficult when only one tick separates the best-priced public buy and sell limit orders. The public precedence rule prohibits specialists from buying at the best bid until all public orders at that price are filled, and the public liquidity preservation principle prohibits them from buying at the ask by trading with sell orders in their limit order books. Specialists who want to buy ahead of their booked orders therefore must wait until an incoming marketable sell order arrives and then fill it at the asking price. Likewise, specialists who want to sell ahead of their booked orders must wait until they can fill an incoming marketable buy order at the bid price.

As a rule, traders do not profit by buying at ask prices and selling at bid prices. Specialists will make these trades only when they want to speculate on future price changes or when they are very uncomfortable with their inventory positions.

A decrease in tick size relaxes the public order precedence rule by decreasing the cost of stepping in front of booked orders. When the tick size is small, so that more than one tick separates the best public bid from the best public offer, specialists who want to trade can step ahead of their books while still trading within the best bid and offer. Since these trades are less costly, they will tend to be more profitable.

The *specialist participation rate* is the fraction of orders that specialists fill (or partially fill) while trading as dealers. When tick sizes decreased in the United States from one-eighth dollar to one-sixteenth dollar in 1997, and to 1 penny in 2000, specialist participation rates and specialist profitability both increased substantially. ◀

24.3 SPECIALISTS AS BROKERS

Exchange specialists often broker orders for other brokers. Specialists receive orders from brokers via exchange order-routing systems and through direct contacts.

Most exchanges maintain electronic order-routing systems that allow brokers to cheaply deliver customer orders to them. Electronic order-driven exchanges deliver these orders directly to their order-matching systems. Floor-based exchanges deliver these orders either to their specialists or to exchange officials called *order book officials*. In either event, the recipient then acts as the broker for these *system orders*. Brokers route orders through exchange order-routing systems when they do not have a presence on the exchange floor or when they do not want to tie up their floor brokers with small orders.

Exchanges regulate the commissions that specialists can charge for representing the system order flow. At the NYSE, specialists can charge commissions only on limit orders that they hold for more than five minutes. They receive no commissions for representing market orders and limit orders that fill within five minutes.

Floor brokers also often give their agency orders to specialists to manage so that they do not have to stand around waiting for traders to arrive with whom they might arrange their trades. The specialists then *work* these orders. This procedure allows floor brokers to handle more orders and to direct their attention to the orders that most require their skills and immediate action. Specialists generally charge brokers commissions for these services. The brokers' clients never see these commissions.

Specialists also broker trades by acting as oral bulletin boards for other brokers. Brokers sometimes tell specialists that their clients are large buyers or sellers. The specialists then tell the brokers whether somebody else has expressed substantial interest on the other side. If somebody has, the specialist will page the other side and put the parties together. Otherwise, the specialist will promise to page the brokers if someone with interest appears. Brokers usually do not pay specialists for the trades that specialists arrange this way, but all traders value the goodwill that the specialists create.

24.4 SPECIALISTS AS AUCTIONEERS AND EXCHANGE OFFICIALS

Markets that designate specialists usually make their specialists responsible for conducting orderly markets in their specialties. The specialists ensure that all traders follow the exchange rules so that all orders are fairly represented. At markets that open with a single price auction—such as those organized at the New York and American Stock Exchanges—the specialists are responsible for conducting those auctions. To assist them, the electronic systems that maintain their limit order books also summarize the excess demand or supply at each possible auction price.

The obligation to act as an auctioneer can be costly when specialists want to direct their attention to other issues. Specialists, however, receive no direct compensation for assuming these responsibilities. Instead, they accept them in exchange for the privileges that come with being a specialist.

24.5 SPECIALIST PRIVILEGES

Specialists have several privileges that allow them to profit from their unique positions. These include access to information about order flows, the right to make decisions after others make their decisions, the ability to create the market quote, the ability to create and exercise certain look-back timing options, and the right to collect brokerage commissions from executing system order flow.

Perhaps the greatest advantage specialists have comes from their access to information about orders. Specialists see the entire system order flow as it arrives. They also see much of the order flow that floor brokers handle, either because they observe the floor brokers or because the floor brokers give them their clients' orders to work. Finally, they also see their limit order books, in which they have placed the orders that they cannot immediately execute.

Although specialists must sometimes share this information with other traders, they always have an advantage because they see it first. In markets where specialists do not have to share the information, they obviously have a greater advantage. The next several subsections provide examples of how specialists may act upon information about orders.

24.5.1 Speculative Strategies

Information about order flows may allow clever specialists to forecast short-term price changes better than other traders can. Specialists may use this

TABLE 24-1.
How Specialists Affect Their Participation Rates

DESIRE	ACTION
Increase their probability of buying	Quote the most aggressive bid price
	Improve prices for incoming marketable sell orders
	Augment the quotation bid size
Increase their probability of selling	Quote the most aggressive offer price
	Improve prices for incoming marketable buy orders
	Augment the quotation offer size
Decrease their probability of buying	Quote only the best bid on the book and no more than the aggregate order size on the book at that price
Decrease their probability of selling	Quote only the best offer on the book and no more than the aggregate order size on the book at that price

information to speculate on the side that their information favors or to refrain from offering liquidity on the other side. If they can indeed predict short-term price changes, they will be able to make more profitable trades and avoid costly trades.

To exploit their information, specialists must alter the probabilities that they will next be a buyer or a seller. The specialists' affirmative and negative obligations complicate their efforts to trade and avoid trading:

- To increase the probability that they trade, specialists must get in front of the orders on their books. They may quote more aggressive prices than their books offer and hope that their quotes attract other traders, or they may step in front of the book when an incoming market order arrives with which they want to trade.

- To decrease the probability that they trade, specialists hide behind their books. When marketable orders arrive that they do not want to fill, they match these orders with booked limit orders. They can avoid trading as long as the limit order book holds orders that are not too far from the market.

Table 24-1 summarizes the strategies that specialists use to trade and avoid trading.

24.5.2 Quote-matching Strategies

Specialists do not need to predict future price changes to profit from information in their limit order books. Their information allows them to predict what trades they may—and may not—have to make to satisfy their affirmative obligations. For example, when their books are heavy on the buy side but not on the sell side, they know that that they are somewhat protected on the buy side. Unless their market drops quickly on high volume, they will not need to provide liquidity on the buy side in the near future.

Specialists who see such asymmetries may engage in the quote-matching strategies described in chapter 11. For example, they may try to buy in front of a limit order book that is heavy on the buy side. If values subsequently rise, they will profit with the price rise. If values fall, they will not need to buy until market order sellers exhaust the liquidity on the buy side of their books. During that time, the specialists may sell their positions to any market order buyers who arrive.

The quote-matching strategy does not need to be profitable on its own to increase specialist profitability. Whenever incoming marketable orders arrive, specialists must decide whether to improve prices or to let the orders go to their books. The information they have about orders in their books allows them to make better decisions than they otherwise would make. Better decisions lead to greater profits.

The quote-matching strategy is more profitable in markets where dealers can freely trade with limit orders that they hold. In such markets, the dealers can immediately trade with their books when they want to close losing positions.

24.5.3 Cream-skimming Strategies

Specialists also can profit from knowing who wants to trade. Specialists—like all other dealers—generally will supply more liquidity to uninformed traders than to well-informed traders. Traders who offer firm orders and quotes must fill marketable orders as they arrive without regard to whose they are. In contrast, when specialist quotes simply reflect the best bids and offers in their books, specialists can decide whether they want to trade with an incoming market order *after* they see where it comes from. If they want to trade, they step in front of their books by improving the price.

Since small retail traders tend not to be well informed, specialists improve prices for retail traders more often than for large institutional traders. Because specialists can see the order flow before they commit to trading, they can discriminate among the different types of liquidity-demanding traders. This trading option can be very valuable.

Specialists also see the size of the incoming marketable orders before they decide to trade. They therefore can avoid the price discrimination—described in chapters 6 and 15—that large order traders try to exercise against liquidity suppliers. Accordingly, specialists are more likely to let large orders go to the book than small orders.

Traders call selective filling of orders *cream skimming* because the specialists take the richest orders and leave the less desirable orders for their books. Cream skimming makes limit order strategies less attractive than they otherwise would be. Since cream skimming benefits small market order traders who obtain improved prices, the practice makes market order strategies relatively more attractive than limit orders strategies for small traders.

The cost of exercising the option to step in front of the book is the minimum price increment. Specialists must improve prices by the increment to free themselves from the constraints of the public order precedence rule. When the minimum price increment is very small, specialists fill market orders that they believe will be profitable to fill, and they let their limit order books fill the market orders that they do not want.

24.5.4 Another Order Anticipation Strategy

Dealers may manipulate their trading to profit from stop orders in their books. Suppose that a dealer has a large sell order with a stop price of 20 in his book. Suppose further that no buy orders are on the book at 20 or

▶ An Accidental Shooting When Gunning Against a Stop Order

The SPDR (pronounced "Spider") is an exchange-traded fund that holds an S&P 500 index portfolio. (SPDR is an acronym for Standard & Poor's Depository Receipt.) It trades primarily at the American Stock Exchange under the ticker symbol SPY. A specialist manages trading in the SPDR. The specialist competes with several market makers who stand before his post. The specialist does not display his order book to the market makers.

A trustworthy source told me the following story. (The numbers in the story are all approximate, but they represent the essence of the event.)

One day in 1998 or 1999, the SPDR specialist received a very large market order to sell 500,000 shares with a stop price of 100. The SPDR was then trading at about 100½. Soon after receiving the order, the specialist aggressively sold the S&P 500 futures contract in Chicago to gun the market. The futures price fell. This fall caused other traders to sell the SPDR. These sales cleared buy limit orders priced above 100 from the SPDR order book. Soon the best bid in the SPDR was 100.

The specialist then waited for an incoming market sell order that he could fill at 100. A trade at that price would activate the 500,000-share stop order. The specialist then would buy the 500,000 shares at 100 to hedge his short futures position. Since the specialist sold the futures at higher prices (even after accounting for the normal fair-value premium), this purchase would lock in a substantial profit.

A moment before a market sell order arrived, however, one of the market makers in the crowd bid 100¹⁄₁₆ for 100,000 shares. Her firm probably issued the order in an attempt to exploit the price discrepancy between the SPDR and the underlying index stocks.

Price subsequently rose, and the specialist was unable to execute the stop order. He therefore lost substantially on his short futures position.

The ethics of his behavior are questionable. It appears that the specialist gunned the futures market to exploit the stop order. Such behavior would appear to violate his agency obligations to the trader who gave him the stop order. If a regulator confronted him, however, his response would have been that he believed the market was dropping, and he sold the futures so that he could give a better price to the stop order if it were activated. ◀

above, and that some sell orders are in the book at 20.10. When an incoming market buy order arrives, the dealer may sell in front of the limit sell orders because he knows that he may be able to repurchase his inventory from the stop order at 20. The dealer can make this happen when a market sell order arrives by filling the order at 20, which will activate the stop sell order. If the dealer does not want to activate the stop order, he will fill the market sell order at a price above 20. The stop order allows the specialist to be a more aggressive seller than he otherwise might be because it gives him an option to easily offset his position.

24.5.5 Specialists Control the Market Quotes

At many exchanges, specialists establish the market quotes that the exchanges disseminate to the public. This privilege is most valuable at markets that publish only the best bid and offer—the *top of the book*—as opposed to markets that publish the entire book or a summary of the book—*market by price.*

At markets that publish only the best bid and offer, specialists can set these quotes however they want, within some constraints. Of course, they must honor the quotes that they set.

▶ A Defensive Quotation Strategy

Jack is the specialist for a small stock that has the following thin limit order book:

Aggregate buy size	Price	Aggregate sell size
4	11.00	
10	12.00	
	12.10	18

Jack quotes the book. His market is 12.00 bid for 10 100-share lots, 18 lots offered at 12.10.

A market order to sell 2,000 shares arrives. Jack fills the first 1,000 shares of this order by matching it with the buy limit orders on his book at 12. He then fills the remainder of the order for his own account at the same price.

Jack now holds 1,000 shares that he hopes to sell at a profit. He will not profit, however, if traders decide that the stock is worth less than 12 dollars.

Jack now considers what market he should quote. His affirmative obligations prohibit him from quoting the best prices on the limit order book (11.00 to 12.10) because the spread would be too wide. At a minimum, Jack will have to supply a firm bid for his own account. He considers bidding 11.95 for 100 shares because he does not want to buy more stock. He also considers offering 1,000 shares at 12.05 because he wants to sell his inventory. He is reluctant to offer these quotes, however, because he does not want to show the weakness in the stock. He is afraid that if he lowers the price, he may panic sellers and cause buyers to wait to see what happens. Instead, he decides to leave the quote unchanged to hide the weakness. Jack hopes that a market buy order will next arrive to which he can offer an improved price of 12.09. ◀

The main constraints on specialist quotations come from *order exposure rules*. These rules require that specialists expose the most aggressively priced offers to trade. They may come from orders on their books, traders on the floor, or the specialists themselves.

The order exposure rules in the U.S. equity markets require that specialists quote prices which are at least as good as the best bid and offer prices in their limit order books. The quotation sizes must be at least as large as the aggregate order sizes at the quoted prices. Floor traders also can request that specialists include their orders in the market quote.

Specialists can quote better prices or greater sizes to represent their own market-making commitments. Exchanges, however, discourage them from quoting a market for small size that hides large size offered by the public.

Within these constraints, specialists can set their quotes to influence the inferences some traders make about values. The specialists may thereby influence their order flows.

24.5.6 Stopping Stock and the Look-back Timing Option

Specialists at some exchanges can *stop* the execution of an incoming marketable order. When they stop an order, they guarantee that the order will eventually execute at a price that is at least as good as the best price at which

▶ Why Stopped Stock Look-back Timing Options Are Valuable

Johanna is an NYSE specialist who is quoting a market that reflects the orders on her limit order book. The market is 50 bid for 20, 27 offered at 50.10.

When an incoming limit market order to buy 10 arrives, Johanna decides to stop the order at 50.05. The NYSE requires that she then adjust her quote to reflect the stopped stock. She therefore quotes the market as 50.05 bid for 10, 27 offered at 50.10. Johanna now waits to see what happens. If no marketable sell orders arrive, she will have to fill the stopped buy order by selling from her inventory.

Suppose that while she is waiting, the prices of stocks that are similar to her stock start to rise. Johanna expects that her stock also will rise in value. She therefore does not want to sell her inventory. Instead, she waits and hopes that some other seller will arrive who will fill the stopped order and thereby relieve her of the obligation to do so. If this happens, she will not lose the opportunity to profit as prices rise.

Suppose instead that the prices of similar stocks start to fall. Johanna now fears that the value of her inventory will fall. She therefore executes the stopped order for her account. She must act quickly, before a public trader takes the option from her.

The stopped stock timing option is valuable to Johanna because she can look back to see whether prices are falling or rising when she decides whether to exercise the option. Although she ultimately may have to trade the stock when she would rather not, some other trader may arrive who will relieve her of this responsibility. The option to wait for such traders when she would rather not trade, and the option to exercise quickly when she does want to trade, make the stopped stock look-back timing option valuable. ◀

the order would execute if it filled immediately. Specialists provide this guarantee by committing to execute the order for their own accounts if no one else is willing to take the other side.

While an order is stopped, if an incoming market order on the other side arrives, the specialist must match it with the stopped order and execute the trade. If no such orders arrive, specialists must execute stopped orders for their own accounts before the end of the trading day. Otherwise, specialists may execute stopped orders for their own account at any time they wish.

A stopped order is a trading option that specialists may exploit to their advantage. For example, when specialists stop market sell orders, they create call options. They can exercise these options as long as no market order buyers arrive first. Unlike most options, however, specialists cannot abandon them when they expire. Instead, they must then exercise them.

The stopped stock trading options is a timing option. *Timing options* allow people to choose when they want to do something. Stopped stock timing options are valuable because specialists can continuously decide whether they want to exercise them now or risk—or hope—that someone else will do so. Since they can decide after they have seen what has happened in the market, these options are *look-back options*. The specialists can look back at what has happened before they decide whether to execute them.

Specialists often stop stock to improve prices without trading when spreads are wide. They then hope that another trader will arrive on the other side who will fill the order. Such traders will also receive an improved price.

We will call such traders *subsequent traders*. Although specialists could make more money by filling the stopped and subsequent orders themselves at their bid and ask prices, they cannot do so when public limit orders are on their books at these prices. Since exchanges and brokers rate specialists by how often they provide price improvement, the stopped stock strategy often allows them to improve prices without trading when they could not trade profitably otherwise.

24.5.6.1 Whom Does the Stop Harm?

Since trading is a zero-sum game, someone must lose if specialists profit from creating and exercising stopped stock options. Who loses is not immediately obvious, however. The only possibilities are the traders whose orders are stopped, the subsequent traders who fill stopped orders before the specialists must fill them, and the limit order traders whose orders would have filled the stopped orders if the specialist had not stopped the stock or immediately filled the orders at improved prices. We will now consider the interests of each of these traders.

The stops do not harm the traders whose orders the specialists stop. These traders receive the same or better prices than they otherwise would have received. Since specialists guarantee their executions, they usually do not even know that their orders have been stopped. As soon as specialists stop their orders, they receive reports of their guaranteed trade prices. Retail customers then receive normal execution reports.

The subsequent traders who fill stopped orders before the specialists fill them will regret trading on average. As a rule, specialists will quickly fill their stopped orders when they believe that filling them will be profitable, and wait otherwise. Therefore, if specialists have any skill at forecasting future price changes, filling stopped orders that specialists do not want to fill should not be profitable on average.

Specialists also may be reluctant to fill stopped orders when filling them would cause already out-of-balance inventories to move further from their target values. Under such circumstances, filling their stopped orders will be harmful if their inventories are inversely correlated with future price changes, as we would expect if the specialists have been trading with informed traders.

Whether the public traders who fill stopped orders are harmed depends on whether they would have traded anyway or whether their decisions to trade were influenced by the improved prices that the specialists quote to reflect the stopped orders. If they would have traded anyway, they are no worse off than they would have been. They may even obtain better prices than they otherwise would have obtained. However, if the improved prices influenced their decisions to trade, they will regret that they traded. These traders take the specialists out of positions that the specialists do not want.

The expected costs of filling stopped orders that specialists do not want to fill are greater when the order has stood unfilled for a long time than when the order has stood unfilled for a short time. The more time that passes without the specialists filling their orders, the more likely is it that the specialists have learned information that makes them reluctant to fill such orders.

Order stopping also harms the limit order traders who would have filled the stopped orders if the specialists did not choose to stop them. Consider the position of a limit order buyer on the book at the best bid who fails to trade when a specialist stops an incoming market sell order. If the market then moves up, this limit order trader will regret not trading. Stopping stock thus harms limit order traders by decreasing their opportunities to trade profitably. In the long run, when specialists frequently stop stock, limit order trading strategies become less attractive, so that public traders submit more market orders.

24.5.7 The Market Open

Specialists conduct the opening single price auction at the NYSE. When the order flow at the open is imbalanced, as it often is, specialists step in to supply liquidity on the weak side of the market. Since this side is weak, the market-clearing price generally favors it. For example, if traders want to buy more than they want to sell at the previous closing price, the market-clearing price will be lower than the previous close, and the specialist will typically be a buyer. Prices often reverse in these circumstances, so that specialists often profit from their opening trades.

Specialists have a unique advantage at the open relative to other traders because they can see all the orders. They also have an advantage because they can decide how much they want to trade after everyone else has submitted their orders. Since their participation in the auction can determine the trade price, they have a significant advantage over other traders.

24.5.8 Brokerage Commissions

Receiving commissions for brokering orders is a valuable specialist privilege. Specialists receive and represent orders that brokers route though exchange order-routing systems. As noted above, specialists can charge brokerage commissions on some of these orders. Specialists also charge floor brokers commissions on the orders that they leave with them to work. The combined brokerage revenues can be significant.

24.5.9 Dealer Profits

The final privilege that specialists have is not uniquely theirs, but one at which they have a distinct advantage due to their unique positions. Specialists can supply liquidity to marketable orders when no one else is present. In thinly traded markets and occasionally in actively traded markets, market orders may arrive when no aggressively priced limit orders are present to supply liquidity. Specialists supply liquidity to these marketable orders by buying at the bid and selling at the offer. If their spreads are sufficiently wide, if they receive enough marketable order flow, and if the order flow is not too well informed, they will profit from filling marketable orders.

Specialists compete with other traders to supply liquidity to marketable orders. In thinly traded markets, they have an advantage over other traders because they are always at their posts. Traders who might compete with them can fill marketable orders only when they are present, either by being in the crowd or by being in the limit order book. Most floor traders, however, will not wait at a post for orders in thinly traded securities to arrive because they cannot make enough money that way. Many limit order traders likewise are reluctant to offer liquidity in thinly traded stocks because their costs of managing these orders are too high. Compared with specialists, off-floor traders do not have as much information, they cannot adjust their prices as quickly, and they cannot cream skim.

▶ The Opening Option

The previous close was 35.2. To manage his inventory, the specialist would like to sell 16 lots at the open. Just before the specialist opens the market, the following supply and demand schedules summarize the order book:

Price	Demand schedule	Supply schedule	Excess demand
35.1	31	14	17
35.2	30	15	15
35.3	18	34	−16

If the specialist does not participate in the auction, the auction clearing price will be 35.3; 18 lots will trade; and there will be excess supply of 16 lots at that price.

If the specialist opens the market at 35.3, he may feel obligated to buy the 16 lots to fill the excess supply. Since the specialist does not want to buy, this option is not attractive.

If the specialist sells 16 lots, the opening price will be 35.1 and the specialist will probably sell 17 lots to ensure that all orders at 35.1 fill. If the specialist sells just 15 lots, the opening price will be 35.2. Although the specialist wants to sell 16 lots, he sells only 15 because he does not want to depress the price on his sales. The option to choose the clearing price after all other traders have submitted their orders is quite valuable. ◀

Electronic proprietary traders use computers to create, submit, cancel, and adjust limit orders in response to changing market conditions. These traders are becoming increasingly important in markets that have fast electronic interfaces to their trading systems. As these systems grow and as more electronic information about market conditions becomes immediately available, the advantages that floor-based specialists have as dealers will diminish.

24.6 WHO ASSIGNS SPECIALISTS?

The specialist system originated when some traders found that they could trade more successfully if they focused their attention on a small number of stocks. Those early specialists better understood who was trading, why they were trading, and the value of what they were trading than did other traders. Their specific knowledge helped them trade more successfully as dealers. It also made them attractive to traders who needed knowledgeable brokers.

As the specialists became well known, they were able to obtain something of a natural monopoly in their specialties. The more that specialists knew about their specialties, the more effectively they could compete with others who might want to replace them. The most effective specialists were the ones who obtained the most order flow. Those who obtained the most order flow learned the most about their specialties, and thereby became more effective specialists. This circularity is an example of the *order flow externality* that influences market structures.

When exchanges started installing electronic order-routing systems, their specialist systems were well entrenched. Specialists naturally become the recipients of the system order flows.

In principle, specialties at most exchanges are still contestable by any exchange member who wants to specialize in a stock. In practice, it is now

▶ Boyd's Broken Leg

Folklore at the New York Stock Exchange holds that the first specialty started there when a man named Boyd broke his leg in 1875. Not being able to walk around the floor, he sat down on a chair on the exchange floor and announced that he would trade only Western Union, a popular stock of the time. Brokers who felt sorry for him, and brokers who valued the fact that he would not miss any trading opportunities in Western Union, left their orders with him. He thus became the first specialist by providing good service to his fellow brokers. ◀

Source: Robert Sharp, The Lore and Legends of Wall Street (Dow Jones-Irwin, 1989), p. 139.

▶ Consolidation among NYSE Specialist Trading Firms

The number of firms employing NYSE specialists has decreased very substantially through mergers and acquisitions. In 1933, 230 specialist trading firms traded at the NYSE. This number shrank to 59 by 1983, and to 8 at the end of 2001.

Many factors probably explain the consolidation of specialist firms. Large, well-capitalized firms are better able to carry large inventory positions, to diversify their inventory risks, and to finance expensive information systems than are smaller firms.

Allowing newly listed issuers to pick their specialists undoubtedly has caused many small specialist firms to merge. Since issuers generally do not know much about specialists, large firms with large capital bases are more attractive to them than are small firms. ◀

virtually impossible to obtain a specialty through direct head-to-head competition. The main impediment to competition is the assignment of the electronic order flow. Without that order flow, new specialists cannot successfully challenge incumbents.

When an exchange lists a new stock or options series, the exchange asks its members to apply to be the specialist. A committee evaluates the applicants based on their prior performance and on their ability to make liquid markets in the security. The committee then chooses either the winning applicant or a set of finalists from whom the issuer chooses the winning applicant.

Exchanges periodically evaluate the performance of their specialists. They base their evaluations on objective criteria and upon subjective ratings provided by floor brokers. The objective criteria measure the width and size of quoted spreads, the frequency and size of price reversals, and price improvement rates for market orders. The floor brokers rate the specialists on various dimensions which characterize the quality of the service that the specialists provide to them and to their clients. In very rare cases, exchanges take specialties away from specialists who provide very poor service or who break exchange rules.

24.7 REGULATORY ISSUES AND PERSPECTIVES

Regulators must consider whether the value specialists obtain from their privileges is commensurate with the value of the additional liquidity they provide. If the privileges are more valuable than the additional liquidity, many traders will resent the money and profitable trading opportunities that they lose to specialists.

Given the difficulties of measuring and valuing liquidity services, regulators cannot easily find the proper balance between privileges and obligations. In practice, exchanges squeeze their specialists when specialists are making lots of money and public traders are complaining about their trading costs. Exchanges then demand more service, they further restrict specialist trades, and they limit the commissions that specialists can collect for executing system orders. Of course, the specialists scream loudly and threaten to quit if things get too bad. Since they rarely quit and since many traders want to be specialists, exchanges probably do not squeeze them too hard.

Regulators also must consider whether the distribution of the benefits and costs of the specialist system are equitable. The public traders who benefit most from the liquidity that specialists offer generally are not the traders whose trading costs increase when the specialists exercise their privileges. The beneficiaries of the specialist trading system are primarily small, uninformed market order traders who receive price improvement from specialists. Momentum traders who can quickly submit orders into rapidly rising or falling markets also benefit from the liquidity that specialists offer in order to maintain price continuity when the markets are volatile. The benefactors of the specialist system are the limit order traders in front of whose orders the specialists often step. These traders often generally do not understand the system well enough to appreciate how it increases their transaction costs. Since the beneficiaries and the benefactors generally are not the same traders, the specialist system transfers wealth from one group to another. How regulators regard these transfers often depends on which group is more able to lobby for its interests.

The beneficiaries and benefactors of the specialist system also differ by where they trade. The liquidity that specialists provide benefits all traders, regardless of whether they normally trade at the specialists' exchange or elsewhere. The benefactors of the specialist system, however, are only those traders who trade where the specialists trade.

This mismatch is problematic for specialists and for their exchanges. The profits that specialists normally make must fund the losses that they typically incur when no one else will supply liquidity. However, when trading is normal, competition from dealers in other markets reduces specialist profits. When increases in uncertainty and volatility cause liquidity suppliers to withdraw from the markets, the specialists are the only traders who remain to supply liquidity. At such times, the dealers with whom the specialists normally compete to offer liquidity may demand liquidity from them.

Exchanges can afford such generosity when their market shares are substantially greater than 50 percent. In that case, the beneficiaries and benefactors of the specialist system mostly trade at the same exchange. When their market shares are smaller, however, specialists may be unable to earn enough from their customers during normal times to fund the liquidity they provide to the entire market when no one else will. Exchanges with small market shares therefore cannot expect that their traders will provide much price continuity.

If regulators believe that markets should provide price continuity, they must somehow require that all dealers who supply liquidity in normal conditions also supply liquidity when markets are volatile. Since regulators cannot effectively prevent traders from free riding, markets with many competing dealers will not have much price continuity.

Exchanges impose *capital adequacy standards* on their specialists to ensure that their specialists have enough capital to conduct their businesses. The exchanges monitor these standards closely in order to identify and quickly correct problems before they affect their customers.

The capital adequacy standards also ensure that specialists will have adequate capital to provide liquidity if no one else will. Without such standards, specialists may distribute the profits that their firms make in normal markets so that they are unavailable for providing liquidity in extraordinary markets.

▶ Nasdaq's Partial Solution to the Free Rider Problem

To discourage its dealers from hiding when volatility rises, the Nasdaq Stock Market requires that they wait 20 trading days before they resume trading a stock in which they stopped making a market. Although the rule does not compel dealers to offer aggressively priced quotes, it does keep them attentive when markets are volatile. ◀

24.8 SUMMARY

Exchanges and third market dealers designate specialists who must supply liquidity when no liquidity would otherwise be available. Traders like continuous, liquid markets. Exchanges and dealers hope to attract customers by offering such markets.

Specialists do not willingly take these obligations upon themselves without compensation. The compensation that specialists obtain is access to order flows which allow them to earn dealing profits and brokerage commissions. Information in the order flows also allows them to speculate successfully on short-term price changes.

The profits that specialists make are transaction costs for other traders. Specialist trading is most costly to limit order traders with whom they compete to offer liquidity. Specialists harm them by selectively stepping in front of their limit orders when specialists believe the resulting trades will be profitable.

Specialists consider many factors when deciding whether to trade. They prefer to trade with small uninformed traders. They like to trade in front of the heavy side of the limit order book in order to extract order option values. If exchanges allow specialists to stop market orders, they do so to create valuable look-back timing options.

In markets that enforce public order and time precedence rules, the profitability of specialist trading strategies depends on the minimum price increment. When the increment is small, the cost to specialists of stepping in front of other traders is small.

Although traders value the liquidity that specialists offer, they do not like to pay for it if they can avoid it. Since the specialist system transfers wealth from limit order traders to market order traders, not all traders appreciate it. Regulators must therefore decide whether the liquidity supplied by specialists to some traders is worth the costs of the system to other traders.

Many traders and commentators believe that the regulatory problems associated with the specialist trading system are intractable. They believe that the special privileges which specialists enjoy allow them to take too much value from the markets, and that regulators can never adequately compel specialists to return commensurate value to the markets. These people lobby to replace the specialist trading system with a multiple designated market maker system or with a pure price-time priority screen-based trading system.

24.9 SOME POINTS TO REMEMBER

- Specialists are dual traders.
- The specialists' affirmative obligations require that they provide liquidity when no one else will.
- The specialists' negative obligations require that they refrain from providing liquidity in competition with the public.
- Specialists accept their obligations in exchange for some special privileges.
- Regulators and exchanges must balance the value of the special privileges with the value of the services that specialists provide.
- Price continuity can be expensive to provide.
- Price continuity is a public good that competitive markets generally will not provide.

24.10 QUESTIONS FOR THOUGHT

1. Are specialists monopolists in their specialties? Do their unique positions give them economic power? What limits their power?
2. How can exchanges enforce affirmative obligations by using a multiple designated market maker system?
3. Can specialists compete with third market dealers who do not face similar obligations?
4. How valuable is price continuity? How could you estimate its value?
5. Who should pay for the liquidity services that specialists provide?
6. Can specialists survive and thrive in electronic exchanges?

7. Of what importance are quick trade confirmations when the only prices you can see are last trade prices?

8. When evaluating specialists, should exchanges give more weight to price continuity or to narrow spreads?

9. What effect does order stopping have on the order placement decisions that public traders make?

10. What effect would an increase in the minimum price increment have on specialist profitability? How large should the minimum price increment be?

11. Perhaps specialists should be required to improve prices by at least 5 cents to trade in front of their books when trading in stocks that trade on pennies. What long-run effect would such a *step-ahead increment rule* have on the spread between the best bid and offer in the limit order book? Should exchanges apply such a rule to all limit order traders? Should the step-ahead increment ever be different from the minimum price increment?

12. How do the specialists' negative obligations help solve conflict of interest problems that arise because specialists are dual traders?

13. Exchange-based U.S. equity traders use the Intermarket Trading System (ITS) to route orders from one market to another. Should exchange specialists be allowed to use the ITS to route orders for their own accounts to other exchanges? Would a prohibition on such usage prohibit specialists from trading with each other?

14. Dealers who provide limit order price protection must often buy at the ask and sell at the bid. Such trades are unprofitable when the market is stable, but they can be quite profitable when the market is moving. Under what conditions do you expect that the opportunity to fill agency limit orders, coupled with the responsibility to provide limit order price protection, is profitable on net?

15. Are the regulatory problems associated with specialist trading systems intractable? Should exchanges with specialist trading systems convert to other market structures?

Dealers *internalize* orders when they fill their clients' orders. Brokers *preference* orders when they route their clients' marketable orders to dealers in exchange for various monetary or nonpecuniary *payments for order flow*. Brokers also preference when they route their clients' limit orders to electronic communications networks (ECNs) that pay them *liquidity fees* when standing limit orders execute. Brokers *cross* orders internally when they arrange trades among their clients.

Internalization, order preferencing, and internal order crossing all arrange trades away from organized markets. Traders say that these practices *fragment* the markets.

Internalization, preferencing, and crossing practices raise important regulatory questions. Most notably, clients and regulators wonder whether brokers who engage in these practices meet their obligations to obtain best execution when filling their clients' orders. Less obviously, traders and regulators wonder whether these practices hurt markets by making it more difficult for traders to find each other. All three practices decrease order transparency. Many people wonder whether the markets would be better off with a single, consolidated limit order book to which brokers would send all orders.

In this short chapter, we discuss the issues that underlie these processes. We shall see that internalization and preferencing may benefit small market order traders. The practices generally harm limit order traders, however. Internal order crossing tends to benefit crossing brokers and their clients at the expense of traders with whom the clients might otherwise have traded.

Internalization, preferencing, and crossing affect all markets in which traders can trade away from a central exchange. These practices have attracted the substantial attention in U.S. equity markets. The attention undoubtedly comes from the high volumes traded in these markets, the high degree of transparency in markets, and the ease with which traders and regulators can compare dealer and public auction markets that simultaneously trade similar securities. Most of the discussion that appears in this chapter therefore draws on examples from U.S. markets. The forces that cause internalization, order preferencing, and internal order crossing, however, are present in all markets. If you understand how these forces work in U.S. equity markets, you will be able to identify them in all other markets.

We start by discussing best execution and the effects of internalization and preferencing on commissions. We then turn to the anticompetitive aspects of internalization and preferencing. The chapter ends with a short discussion of issues associated with internal order crossing.

25.1 BEST EXECUTION PRACTICES

Brokers who internalize and accept payments for order flow have a significant conflict of interest that concerns clients and regulators. Brokers address these concerns by trying to provide *best execution* to their clients. They provide best execution when they ensure that their clients' orders fill quickly at the best available prices.

Definitions of best execution are controversial because determining whether dealers fill orders at the best available prices is difficult. It is especially difficult when willing traders do not display their orders and quotes.

Definitions of best execution are also controversial because price is only one dimension of execution quality. Traders value speed of execution as well as price. The relative importance of speed and price depends on order type. Market order traders are primarily concerned with speed, whereas limit order traders are most concerned about price. All traders, however, value both dimensions and accept reasonable trade-offs between speed and price.

Brokers and the dealers to whom they preference orders have created a standard set of order handling practices that they claim assures best execution if followed. You may disagree. The procedures vary by order type.

In U.S. equity markets, dealers claim that they provide best execution when they fill marketable orders at the national best bid or offer (NBBO)—the best bid or offer quoted by any other dealer or limit order trader. This standard applies only to marketable orders that are smaller than the total displayed quotation size at the best price. Best execution for larger marketable orders is harder to define because undisclosed size might also be available at the best price. To attract order flow, some dealers guarantee to brokers that they will always fill orders at the NBBO up to a specified maximum size, regardless of the size displayed in the market.

In some markets, small market orders often trade at better prices than the best quoted price. In such markets, brokers must obtain average rates of *price improvement* for small market orders in order to ensure best execution. Dealers who fill their orders generally use complex algorithms to provide price improvement given various market conditions. These algorithms often expose an order to the market at an improved price. If anyone trades anywhere at that price, dealers then fill the order at that price.

Best execution standards for standing limit orders also are difficult to define. Since standing limit orders typically execute at their limit prices, brokerage clients are most concerned about whether and when their orders execute. Best execution for orders that are not marketable upon submission therefore depends on whether and when they execute.

In markets that match public orders to public orders, best execution standards for standing limit orders are especially difficult to define. Clients generally expect that their brokers will represent their orders wherever they have the highest probability of executing. Brokers who internalize their agency orders or who preference them to dealers must ensure that they execute at least as soon as they would otherwise execute in the primary markets. Many dealers who accept limit orders have *limit order price protection* procedures to provide this standard of best execution.

The fact that dealers pay for marketable orders suggests—but does not necessarily imply—that they could provide better execution services than they do. In particular, dealers may not be providing as much price improvement for marketable orders as they might. They also may be extracting too much option value from standing limit orders that brokers often force them to accept as a condition of receiving marketable orders. If brokers demanded more price improvement and better limit order executions, dealers would pay less for their preferred order flows.

▶ **The Primex Auction System**

The Primex Auction System allows participants to expose their marketable orders to an electronic crowd of traders who may offer improved prices. The Nasdaq Stock Market operates the system as a facility under an agreement between Nasdaq and Primex Trading.

Several large financial services firms, which have very large dealing operations, own Primex Trading. They include Bernard L. Madoff Investment Securities, Goldman Sachs, Merrill Lynch, Morgan Stanley Dean Witter and Co., and Salomon Smith Barney. ◀

Source: www.primextrading.com.

▶ **Best Execution of Limit Orders by Third Market Dealers in NYSE-listed Stocks**

Many third market dealers who accept agency limit orders for NYSE-listed stocks use some version of the following algorithm to provide best execution for limit buy orders. They use similar procedures for limit sell orders.

If the limit order bids a better price than the dealer is bidding, the dealer will adjust his bid to reflect the limit order price and size. If the two prices are the same, but the limit order bids for more size than does the dealer, the dealer will increase his bid size to the order size.

While the limit price matches the best bid in the market, the dealer will match any marketable sell orders that he receives with the limit buy order. If a trade occurs anywhere at a price below the limit order price, the dealer will fill the limit order for his own account at the limit price. The dealer may fill all of the order, or just the size of the trade that occurred below the limit order price.

When the limit order price is first equal to the best bid in the market, and the NYSE quote is also at the best bid, the dealer will record the size of the NYSE bid. If the NYSE bid is behind the best bid, the dealer will record zero NYSE size. He then will count volume traded everywhere at the limit price. When that total volume exceeds the recorded NYSE size, the dealer will execute the limit buy order for his own account.

The dealer also may place a limit order into the NYSE specialist's limit order book at the same price. If the NYSE order fills, he will fill his agency limit order. If he fills the agency order first, he will immediately cancel the NYSE order. By placing the NYSE order, he ensures that he will obtain no worse execution for the agency order than it would have received if it had gone to the NYSE. He also can query the SuperDot order-routing system for the size ahead of the order. ◀

To fully understand how payments for order flow affect retail traders, we must consider more than just that the payments exist. We also must consider how those payments are determined, and what effect they have on retail brokerage commissions. The next subsection describes the economic factors that determine payments for order flow, and how they affect brokerage commissions.

25.2 THE ECONOMICS OF BEST EXECUTION

We start our discussion with a well-known property of all competitive markets. In *perfectly competitive markets*, nobody earns profits in excess of a fair rate of return on their dedicated resources. Perfectly competitive markets arise when suppliers with identical cost functions can freely enter or exit the market at low cost. When suppliers in such markets make excess profits, they tend to lower price or provide better service to attract more business. New suppliers also enter to share in the excess profits. These responses drive excess profits to zero. When suppliers earn less than their required profits, they raise prices, cut service, or leave the market. These forces tend to raise profits. As a result, excess profits are zero in equilibrium.

Consider now the application of this principle to wholesale and retail order flow markets in which dealers and brokers, respectively, compete. Both markets are highly competitive. Dealers compete with many other dealers to fill orders; brokers likewise compete with many other brokers to arrange trades. In both markets, entry and exit are not too costly.

Dealers compete to obtain wholesale order flow from brokers. Orders are valuable to dealers when brokers are unable or unwilling to enforce high execution standards. Dealing is especially profitable when dealers can execute market orders at wide bid/ask spreads. To earn these profits, however, dealers first must obtain wholesale order flows from brokers. In perfect competition, dealers will compete away any excess profits by offering various inducements to brokers to obtain their client order flows. If executing the order flow is profitable, the payments to brokers for obtaining that order flow will be high.

Brokers compete to obtain order flow from their retail clients. Retail order flows are valuable to brokers because they can preference these orders to dealers in exchange for payments. They also can internalize them and thereby directly profit from them. To earn these profits, however, brokers must first obtain retail orders. In perfect competition, brokers will compete away any excess profits by offering their clients various inducements to obtain their orders. These inducements include low commissions and a wide variety of ancillary services, such as free or discounted investment information and investment advice. If brokering retail order flow is profitable, the inducements that brokers offer their clients to obtain their orders will be valuable.

In perfectly competitive markets, if brokers or regulators demand that dealers provide higher execution quality, wholesale payments for order flow and retail inducements for order flow will fall. A trade-off thus exists between execution quality and the price and level of brokerage services offered. Holding everything else constant, if traders demand greater price improvement for market orders, commissions will rise by a corresponding amount. In perfectly competitive markets, net transaction costs for small market orders (bid/ask spread plus commissions) will not depend on how brokers and dealers define best execution.

Consider now the forces that determine the allocation of net transaction costs between bid/ask spreads and commissions for market orders. We start by explaining why retail traders pay more attention to low commissions than to good prices. We then explain why bid/ask spreads tend to be wide.

25.2.1 Low Commissions

Retail traders pay more attention to low commissions than to good prices because you cannot buy anything that you cannot measure. Suppliers who offer expensive quality that buyers cannot recognize can be undercut by those who claim to do so but do not. If buyers cannot tell the difference between high quality and low quality suppliers, suppliers can give them low quality products regardless of what they promise. As a result, buyers in such markets tend to purchase from low cost suppliers. Price reflects the costs of low quality suppliers, and high quality suppliers will not be able stay in business.

Consider the implications of this principle for retail market order traders: Good execution for marketable orders means good prices and quick service. Retail market order traders can easily audit response times, but not the quality of the prices that they receive. Reliable transaction cost measurement is very difficult for most traders, and especially difficult for retail traders who trade in very active markets (see chapter 21). To effectively measure execution price quality, traders must carefully assess their execution prices in

▶ SEC Rules 11Ac1-5 and 11Ac1-6

To help retail investors deal with these measurement problems, the SEC adopted two rules to improve public disclosure of order execution and routing practices. Rule 11Ac1-5 requires market centers (dealers, exchanges, and ECNs) to make monthly electronic reports that include uniform statistical measures of execution quality. Rule 11Ac1-6 requires broker-dealers who route customer orders in equity and option securities to make publicly available quarterly reports that, among other things, identify the venues to which they route their customer orders for execution.

These rules allow rating agencies to compile reports that rate dealers and brokers. The resulting reports give dealers and brokers substantial incentive to provide high quality service, at least as it is defined by the uniform execution quality measures that they must report. ◀

Source: SEC Release no. 34-43590 (17 CFR Part 240) at www.sec.gov/rules/final/34-43590.htm.

▶ The SEC Mandate

"The Commission believes that broker-dealers deciding where to route or execute small customer orders in listed or OTC securities must carefully evaluate the extent to which this order flow would be afforded better terms if executed in a market or with a market maker offering price improvement opportunities. In conducting the requisite evaluation of its internal order handling procedures, a broker-dealer must regularly and rigorously examine execution quality likely to be obtained from the different markets or market makers trading a security. If different markets may be more suitable for different types of orders or particular securities, the broker-dealer will also need to consider such factors." ◀

Source: SEC Release no. 34-37619A (17 CFR Part 240) at www.sec.gov/rules/final/37619a.txt.

relation to nearby trade and quotation prices. Most retail traders cannot easily access the relevant data or are unwilling to spend the time necessary to analyze the data. Unless their trade prices are unusually good or bad, most retail traders have no idea how well their market orders execute.

The execution audit problem for limit order traders is even more difficult because it can be hard to determine whether a limit order that matches or improves the NBBO should have executed. The uncertainty associated with limit order executions greatly complicates the execution audit problem.

Even if traders accurately estimate execution price quality, without norms against which to compare their estimates, they cannot judge whether their trades are well executed. To benchmark their trades, they must trade with several brokerages, or they must compare their results with other traders. In either event, they must be careful to compare apples with apples and oranges with oranges because some securities are harder to trade than are others. Retail traders rarely make such comparisons because they are too costly.

Since retail clients generally do not know whether they receive good executions on average, brokerage firms have little direct incentive to demand that dealers provide better execution than whatever is generally accepted as best execution. If they did, they would obtain fewer order flow inducements from dealers. Instead, brokers accept the prevailing best execution standards and use the resulting order flow inducements to lower their brokerage commissions, which their clients can readily audit.

The brokerage industry is not particularly concerned about this result. When deciding to trade, most clients give more weight to visible commission costs than to largely hidden bid/ask spreads that they pay. The brokerage industry therefore prefers low commissions to good executions because low commissions encourage clients to trade.

Although retail brokers have little incentive to demand higher best execution standards, they have a very strong incentive to ensure that dealers provide them with best execution. Brokers who do not ensure that their customers obtain best execution expose themselves to regulatory discipline and civil lawsuits. Brokers therefore pay close attention to the quality of execution that they obtain for their clients. A small consulting industry has grown

▶ The Industry Response

Several consultants provide transaction audit services to retail brokers. Brokers use these services to ensure that the dealers to whom they route their orders provide them with best execution. The leading consultants in this area are the Transaction Auditing Group (TAG) and Market Systems Inc. (MSI).

Both companies nightly collect all transactions from their subscribing brokers. They then compare them with trade price and quote data to determine whether dealers properly handled the orders sent to them. These analyses produce F+1 *exception reports* that list trades which do not conform to execution standards that the brokers specify. The brokers use these reports to demand explanations or adjustments from their dealers. Both companies also produce monthly and quarterly reports that characterize various aspects of execution quality. ◀

Source: Full descriptions of the TAG and MSI products and samples of their reports appear at www.tagaudit.com and www.marketsystems.com.

to help brokers measure best execution and manage their order preferencing relationships.

25.2.2 Wide Bid/Ask Spreads

In chapter 14, we show that the competition among dealers and limit order traders to attract orders which traders route to the best displayed prices determines bid/ask spreads. Spreads therefore critically depend on the orders that brokers do not preference or internalize. Most brokers internalize and preference all orders that interest dealers. They send the remaining orders to whoever offers the best prices. These orders therefore are the ones that determine bid/ask spreads.

Dealers who offer firm quotes do not want to receive orders from well-informed traders, or from large traders, many of whom are well informed. Well-informed traders force them to acquire positions on the wrong side of the market. Large traders often price discriminate against dealers and force them to take large positions that they cannot easily divest.

Dealers expose themselves to well-informed traders and to large traders when they offer firm quotes that any trader can take. They therefore quote wider spreads than they would quote if they traded only with small uninformed traders. The wider spreads compensate dealers for their losses to informed traders and to price discriminating traders. These spreads also compensate dealers for the costs incurred when searching for traders to take large unwanted positions.

Small uninformed traders who trade at quoted bid and offer prices therefore are indirectly hurt by the presence of well-informed traders and large traders because of the wider spreads that they must pay. They pay higher prices when buying and receive lower prices when selling than they would otherwise pay and receive.

Payments for order flow benefit small uninformed traders when dealers can determine who they are, and when the wholesale and retail markets for order flow are highly competitive. When dealers can *skim the cream* of the order flow by offering liquidity only to small uniformed traders, payments

▶ Hot Order Flows

Dealers who pay for order flow pay close attention to the orders they receive. They regularly measure the profits that they make handling these orders by considering, among other things, what happened to prices after they received the orders. Order flows are hot when prices tend to rise following the submissions of market buy orders and fall following the submissions of market sell orders. When dealers find that they are receiving hot order flows, they will not pay for them unless brokers force them to take the hot orders in exchange for other, more profitable orders. Obviously, brokers who force hot order flows on dealers will not obtain as generous payments for order flow as they would have if they sold only benign order flow. ◀

▶ We Will Meet or Beat Any Advertised Price!

Retailers often offer to meet or beat any advertised price in town for the products they sell. In practice, they simply match the quoted price, less some small amount.

Although this practice suggests that these retailers will aggressively compete on price in order to obtain orders, it is actually quite anticompetitive because it weakens the incentives to advertise low prices. The incentives to offer low prices are strongest when the retailers who offer them attract orders. When other retailers are willing to match prices, retailers who offer the lowest prices do not get as much order flow. Consumers would be better off if retailers could attract orders only by offering the lowest prices, rather than by offering to match the best prices. ◀

for order flow ensure that these small traders ultimately obtain lower commissions in compensation for the high spreads that they pay.

25.3 ANTICOMPETITIVE ASPECTS OF INTERNALIZATION AND PREFERENCING

Dealers and limit order traders will more likely offer aggressive prices when their quotes and limit orders attract order flow than when they have no effect on the orders that come to them. The internalization and preferencing of order flows take orders away from traders who price aggressively. Internalization and preferencing therefore place aggressive dealers and limit order traders at a disadvantage, and thereby weaken incentives to quote aggressively. Internalization and preferencing thus increase bid/ask spreads relative to what they would be if brokers routed all orders to the traders who offer the best prices. This result would occur even if all traders were equally well informed and traded the same size.

In Nasdaq stocks, brokers increasingly preference their market orders to dealers and their limit orders to ECNs. The dealers pay brokers for market orders and the ECNs pay brokers *liquidity fees* for standing limit orders that execute. The liquidity fees are funded by the fees that traders pay to the ECN when they use marketable orders to take liquidity. Since ECNs represent their orders in Nasdaq, and since all Nasdaq participants can trade with those orders, brokers can claim that they are properly representing limit orders that they send to ECNs.

Limit orders in ECNs, however, are undoubtedly subject to serious adverse selection. When they are at the NBBO, preferencing and internalization ensure that they will not often be matched with marketable orders. If prices move away from them, they also will not execute. However, if prices move toward them, they will quickly execute, and the traders who submitted these limit orders will regret trading. Adverse selection hurts these traders by reducing their opportunities to profit from trades that are followed by price changes which benefit their positions.

Dealers and public limit order traders compete with each other to offer liquidity. By decreasing the probability that limit orders will execute, internalization and preferencing shift the balance of power in this competition toward dealers.

25.4 INTERNAL ORDER CROSSING

Brokers cross orders internally when they arrange trades among their clients. They may use formal order-driven trading systems or more traditional methods to match orders that their clients give them.

Brokers arrange internal order crosses when they run crossing networks, alternative trading systems, and electronic communications networks (ECNs). Block brokers also often arrange internal order crosses.

Brokers who arrange internal crosses for their customers generally provide them with services or service prices that they cannot otherwise obtain. If their clients were not pleased with the combination of service and price that they obtain, they generally would not use these brokers.

Regulatory concerns about internal order crossing involve order exposure and agency problems. The order exposure problem arises because brokers who cross internally may expose their client orders to their clients only, and not also to other traders who might be willing to fill the orders if given the chance. Because brokers want to receive commissions from both sides of the trade, they are reluctant to expose their orders to traders represented by other brokers. The order exposure problem concerns regulators because it makes the trade search problem more difficult for buyers and sellers.

Brokers defend the practice by noting that they work harder to fill orders when they get two commissions rather than one. Clients, however, note that they need not work harder if they can easily find the liquidity necessary to fill the order elsewhere.

The agency problem arises when brokers favor some clients over other clients. The brokers may then arrange trades to the advantage of their favored clients. If the harmed clients cannot easily estimate the costs of their transaction, they may not easily recognize that they received poor prices. Exposure of orders to markets helps protect traders from these abuses.

You can view order preferencing as internal crosses. When a broker preferences an order to a dealer, the broker essentially arranges a trade between the client and the dealer. Although we do not normally consider dealers to be clients of order preferencing brokers, this characterization of their relationship is completely consistent with our understanding of what brokers do. Payments for order flow are essentially commissions that dealers pay brokers to arrange trades for them. From this perspective, regulatory concerns about preferencing are easy to understand. Regulators fear that brokers will favor dealers—with whom they do much repeated business—over their clients, with whom they do much less business on an individual basis.

Regulators can prohibit internal crossing, or they can require that brokers represent their clients' orders to the market. Although these restrictions would consolidate order flows, they would not necessarily be desirable. Brokers who cross orders internally often provide services to their clients that they could not—or would not—provide if they were required to expose their orders.

25.5 SUMMARY

Brokers internalize and preference order flows in order to extract value from largely uninformed orders that execute at wide spreads. Payments for order flow ensure that dealers in perfectly competitive wholesale dealing markets do not obtain excess profits from trading these orders at wide spreads. The commissions and other order flow inducements which brokers must offer their clients to obtain their orders ensure that brokers in perfectly competitive retail brokering markets do not profit excessively from internalization or payments for order flow. When competition is perfect in retail and wholesale order flow markets, low commissions offset poor execution so that net prices do not ultimately depend on best execution standards.

In no market is competition perfect, however. Dealers and brokers with market power will exploit that power and ultimately obtain excess profits from public traders. How much excess profit they obtain depends on how competitive these markets are.

Wholesale dealers have some market power by virtue of the economies of scale associated with their operations. These economies have led to substantial consolidations through mergers and acquisitions in the dealing

▶ Exclusive Listings

Real estate agents usually try to arrange trades exclusively among their clients when they first obtain a listing. To minimize the probability that they may have to allow another broker to participate in the trade, brokers almost always show newly listed properties to their clients before they post them on multiple listing services, before they post a for-sale sign, and before they advertise the property.

Real estate trade organizations are well aware of the problem. They often set standards to which their members must adhere to prevent serious abuses. ◀

▶ The Open Outcry Principle

Floor-based futures markets require that traders arrange all their trades in the pit, in front of all other traders. By allowing anyone to offer a better price, this procedure ensures that a broker cannot arrange an unfair internal order cross.

Some futures markets now permit their traders to negotiate block trades off-floor for qualified clients. The qualification standards ensure that the clients are sophisticated traders who can look out for their own interests. ◀

▶ ACATS

Procedures that allow retail traders to transfer their accounts cheaply from one broker to another are essential to prevent brokers from accumulating market power over their retail clients. In the United States, brokers and their clients use the *Automated Customer Account Transfer Service* (ACATS), operated by the National Securities Clearing Corporation to facilitate the transfer of customer accounts from broker to broker. This automated system generally can move an account in less than six business days. Verification of the trader's authorization to request the change takes most of the time.

Brokers try to accumulate market power through various programs that make switching brokers expensive for their clients. For example, some brokers encourage their clients to store personal financial data with them. Clients who have done so are reluctant to switch brokers because they cannot transfer their data. ◀

Source: www.nasdr.com/2500_trans_proc.htm.

---

segment of the trading industry. Although the remaining firms undoubtedly increased their market power, the economies of scale have also made them more efficient. These economies of scale make it difficult for new entrants to compete aggressively in the wholesale order flow market.

Generally, the more convoluted a competitive system is, the less efficient it will be. The wholesale and retail order flow market system is a more complex competitive system than a centralized market. We therefore can presume that it will be less efficient.

By taking orders away from common market mechanisms, internalization, preferencing, and internal order crossing practices make it harder for natural buyers and sellers to find each other. Internalization and preferencing also weaken central markets by reducing incentives to quote aggressively. These practices therefore must ultimately increase the total transaction costs of all buy-side traders. Internalization and preferencing, however, probably provide small uninformed traders with better net prices—spread plus commission—than they would otherwise obtain. Internal order crossing likewise provides many traders with services that exchanges and brokers would not otherwise provide. Regulators who would restrict internalization, order preferencing, or internal order crossing must consider the trade-offs between the benefits and costs of these practices.

Many people believe that the benefits some traders obtain from internalization, preferencing, and order crossing practices do not justify the damage these practices do to central markets. They would instead prefer a *consolidated limit order book* market structure that would bring all traders together in the same place. In chapter 26, we further consider the economic forces that consolidate and fragment markets.

25.6 SOME POINTS TO REMEMBER

- Competition among dealers and brokers ensures that payments for order flow reduce commissions.
- Retail customers can easily audit commissions but cannot easily audit trade executions.
- Internalization and preferencing decrease incentives to quote aggressively.

- Internalization and preferencing probably provide better net prices (spread plus commission) to small uninformed traders.
- Internalization and preferencing shift power from public limit order traders to dealers.
- Brokers like internal order crosses because they often can collect commissions from both sides of the trade.

25.7 QUESTIONS FOR THOUGHT

1. Should the payments that dealers make for order flow depend on the characteristics of the stocks that they trade? How so?
2. The economic analysis of payments for order flow presented in the text assumes that the wholesale and retail order flow markets are perfectly competitive. How would the analysis differ if competition in these markets is less than perfect?
3. Why do you suppose that dealers who receive preferenced order flow and broker-dealers who internalize order flow founded Primex?
4. Why do dealers generally not pay to obtain limit orders?
5. What effect does internalization have on price discovery in the primary markets? How would prices be determined if all orders were internalized?
6. Why do corporate bond markets and equity markets have such different market structures? How do the differences in their structures affect their qualities?

26

▷

Competition Within and Among Markets

In the last few years, many exchanges, brokers, electronic communications networks (ECNs), and dealers have created innovative trading systems to provide traders with better services at lower costs. The competition among these *market centers* is significantly changing how all markets operate, and the pace of change is accelerating.

The competition among market centers has some worrisome consequences, however. The proliferation of market centers is fragmenting the markets. Buyers and sellers often are in different places, so that they may have trouble finding each other. Their transaction costs therefore may be higher than they would be if all traders traded in the same place. The benefits of competition among market centers may be offset by the increased costs it creates for traders who are searching for the best price.

A market in which people can trade essentially the same thing in different market centers is a *fragmented market*. A market in which all traders trade in the same market center is a *consolidated market*.

Regulators and practitioners wonder whether markets should be consolidated or fragmented. Regulations can produce either alternative. Most futures markets are fully consolidated, as are some national stock markets.

The issue is quite complicated. The competition among traders to obtain the best price works best in consolidated markets. The competition among market centers to provide low-cost services to traders, however, implies fragmented markets. The two competitions therefore are inconsistent with each other. Any reasonable attempts to address competitive issues must consider why market fragmentation occurs, and the benefits and costs of market diversity.

In this chapter, we consider the economic forces that cause markets to consolidate and to fragment. Our discussion starts with a short description of how technology has changed trading markets. This section presents the technological context of the main issues. The economic analysis starts with a discussion of why markets consolidate. We then consider why markets fragment, and how fragmented markets coalesce into segmented markets. Finally, we address the public policy problems related to externalities among market segments.

26.1 TRADING SYSTEMS AND TECHNOLOGY

New trading systems have proliferated largely due to advances in communications and computing technologies. New communications technologies have given traders instantaneous presence in markets that they formerly could not attend. Traders no longer need to be on an exchange floor to know what is happening there or to trade effectively. Instantaneous market data reporting systems and order-routing systems now allow traders anywhere in the world to see and act upon opportunities wherever they occur.

▶ Where Is the Market for AOL?

AOL Time Warner common stock trades in each of the following market centers:

- The New York Stock Exchange, its primary listing market
- All U.S. regional exchanges: Boston, Chicago, Cincinnati, Pacific, and Philadelphia
- Most ECNs and alternative trading systems. The most important of these are Island, Instinet, REDIBook, Archipelago, Bloomberg Tradebook, BRUT, and POSIT.
- The third market and Nasdaq—Bernard Madoff Investment Securities and Knight Capital Markets are the largest dealers in these markets
- The upstairs block trading market
- Some large foreign stock exchanges

The risk in AOL common stock also trades in the following derivative contract markets:

- U.S. options exchanges all trade AOL stock option contracts cleared by the Options Clearing Corporation. These include the Chicago Board Options Exchange, the American Stock Exchange, the Pacific Exchange, the Philadelphia Stock Exchange, and the International Securities Exchange.
- Futures contracts on AOL common stock shares will trade at several exchanges starting in late 2002.
- Many large investment banks will write individually tailored synthetic derivative contracts in AOL for their clients. ◀

New computing technologies have allowed market centers to organize sophisticated algorithm-based order-matching systems that would be impossible to implement by hand. These systems provide traders with complex order management tools that permit traders to more effectively solve their trading problems. Examples of such features include systems that

- Display orders only to traders who commit to filling them
- Ensure that a trader buys and sells equal dollar values
- Ensure an order that is part of a larger strategy will fill only if all orders in the strategy fill
- Allow traders to submit orders with limit prices indexed to market conditions
- Substitute orders in one instrument for orders in another instrument based on market conditions.

Trading systems that incorporate these features use complex rules to treat all traders fairly, subject to various constraints. They could not be implemented without the assistance of a computer. New computing technologies therefore have allowed markets to develop new applications that formerly would have been economically infeasible.

Even when clerks can effectively operate a trading system by hand, they are not as cost effective as computers. New computing technologies therefore have allowed market centers to lower the costs of existing services in addition to providing new services.

▶ Slogans Don't Help

All languages promote wisdom with slogans. Slogans, however, will not resolve debates on market structure. For example, "United We Stand, Divided We Fall" suggests that consolidated markets are good, but "Strength Through Diversity" suggests that fragmented markets are good. When applied to market structure, these two slogans promote the two different competitions that take place in the trading industry. The first slogan promotes the competition of traders to find the best price, and the second promotes the competition among market centers to provide the best services. ◀

▶ From Dispatch Messenger to ECN

In the beginning, markets reported some trade prices—and almost no quotations—by dispatch messengers. They usually traveled by horseback and ship. Later they reported prices by carrier pigeon, semaphore, telegraph, telex, and telephone. Now most organized markets continuously report all trade prices and all quotations as they occur via dedicated communications systems run by computers. Information that once moved at equine speed now moves at the speed of light.

Likewise, traders once made all trading decisions themselves and brokers once arranged all trades manually. Now computers commonly make and implement trading decisions while dedicated exchange, ECN, broker, and dealer trading systems arrange trades automatically. ◀

26.1.1 A Very Short History of Fragmentation and Consolidation

In the beginning, most trading occurred on the trading floors of regional exchanges. Professional traders wanted to belong to these exchanges because only by being on these floors could they learn about market conditions and access trading opportunities. Nonmembers traded through member-brokers because that was the only way they could trade in these markets. Although no single market structure can simultaneously best serve the needs of all traders, most traders traded at exchanges because everyone traded there.

Trading in many instruments fragmented across regional exchanges because impatient traders would not send their orders to distant exchanges. These traders incurred high transaction costs to compensate dealers who moved liquidity through time and arbitrageurs who moved liquidity from market to market. Wide arbitrage spreads reflected the high costs of obtaining information and acting upon it across large distances.

When new communications technologies reduced the costs of transmitting market information and orders, regional exchanges consolidated to form large international markets. Where permitted, many alternative trading systems operate on the periphery of these markets. These systems provide special services to traders whose needs vary substantially. Arbitrageurs ensure that prices in all systems reflect market conditions throughout the world.

Traders now trade in whatever trading system best serves their particular needs, confident that prices in that market segment will reflect liquidity conditions in all other segments. New trading systems have proliferated as entrepreneurial exchanges, brokers, dealers, data vendors, and software providers compete to help satisfy the liquidity demands of diverse traders.

26.2 MARKET CONSOLIDATION

Markets are *consolidated* when all traders trade in the same place. Markets naturally consolidate. Since trades are easiest to arrange on good terms in liquid markets, traders gravitate to the most liquid market. Each trader who joins a market adds liquidity to that market. The additional liquidity then attracts more traders, who add more liquidity. Economists call this phenomenon the *order flow externality*. It causes markets to consolidate without any regulatory intervention.

We can best understand the implications of the order flow externality by momentarily adopting a simple but highly unrealistic assumption. Assume that all traders are essentially identical. In particular, assume that all traders trade for similar reasons; they trade the same sizes, they are equally patient—or impatient—to trade; they are equally creditworthy; and they pursue roughly the same investment strategies.

If this extreme assumption were true, the same exchange services would interest all traders. Whatever market pleased one trader would please all other traders. No trader would want to trade anywhere but where all other traders trade. Traders would find the best terms for their trades there because all interested traders would be there. With all interested traders in the same market, the search for best price would be least costly.

The market in which identical traders would trade need not convene in any one physical location. It could reside anywhere that traders can expose their orders to everyone and trade with any order. Electronic trading systems are becoming increasingly common because electronic networks often provide cheaper and more efficient communications than face-to-face networks do.

This consolidated market would treat each trader equally. No one would receive any special preferences based on size, creditworthiness, or experience because we assumed that no such differences exist.

26.2.1 Innovative Markets

Occasionally, someone may want to create a new market with different trading rules or with a new technology. If the innovation lowers transaction costs or provides more service, all traders would join the new market, and the market would remain consolidated. All traders would want to join the new market because all traders are identical. If one trader decides that it is optimal to join, all other traders will reach the same conclusion.

It may be difficult to convince all traders to switch to the new market at the same time, even if everyone would be better off trading there. The order flow externality gives the incumbent market a tremendous advantage over new rivals. No trader wants to be the first trader in a new market, no matter how good it might be. If the new market structure is not substantially better than the incumbent one, or if it is too costly for traders to redirect their orders, it may not be possible to convince enough traders to switch to make the new market viable. An innovative market may fail simply because it cannot take the order flow externality away from the incumbent market. The order flow externality may allow an incumbent market to survive even if another market structure could provide better service.

▶ **The Optimark Experience: 406 Million Dollars Lost!**

Optimark was a highly innovative trading system that permitted traders to create "profiles" for their orders. Using a graphical interface, traders could express degrees of preference (trader satisfaction) for various combinations of price and quantity. A Cray supercomputer processed these profiles to match buyers to sellers according to a complex set of preference rules.

Many people—especially institutional traders—were very excited by the system when it was under development in the mid-1990s. The novel means by which the system could allow them to express their preferences, and the novel ways in which these expressions could facilitate negotiation of cheap, mutually satisfactory trades, particularly enchanted them.

Unfortunately, their excitement did not generate much order flow. After a couple of years of very poor performance, Optimark closed the U.S. equities segment of its business in September 2000. Accumulated deficits for the entire firm through September 2001 totaled 406 million dollars. Much of the loss was due to technology development and marketing.

How you interpret this story depends on what you think about the technology that Optimark introduced. If you believe that the technology represents a significant improvement over existing exchange technologies, then you learned that the order flow externality is extremely hard to overcome, especially for systems that traders cannot easily understand. If you believe—as I do—that the technology was inferior to existing exchange technologies, then you learned that traders enthusiastically support interesting development efforts as long as they do not have to pay for them. ◀

Source: www.sec.gov/Archives/edgar/data/1062023/000095012301500801/ y47391a2e10-ka.txt.

▶ **Why ECNs Compete Well with Nasdaq but Not with the NYSE**

Several ECNs provide electronic order-driven markets for U.S. equity traders. ECNs get around the order flow externality problem through clever manipulation of their linkages with the Nasdaq trading system. ECNs can route orders to Nasdaq, and they can post and quickly revise quotes on Nasdaq. They use these facilities to expose their clients to the liquidity available in Nasdaq.

When an ECN receives a market order, it determines whether the order would be best executed by crossing it with standing orders in the ECN order book or by sending it to Nasdaq. If the order would obtain a better execution through Nasdaq, the ECN sends the order there. Otherwise, it crosses the order internally. This procedure ensures that market order traders who send their orders to ECNs obtain execution that are at least as good as they would obtain on Nasdaq.

When an ECN receives a limit order, it first determines whether it is marketable in Nasdaq or in its own system. If it is marketable, the ECN treats it like a market order and sends it to the best market. If the order is not marketable, the ECN places it in its order book. If the order matches or improves the best price on the ECN book, the ECN revises its Nasdaq quote to reflect the improved price or size of the new order. If a market order then arrives at the ECN with which the ECN can match the standing limit order, the ECN crosses the order and adjusts its Nasdaq quote. If Nasdaq routes a marketable order to the ECN, the ECN fills the order if it has not already been filled. This procedure ensures that limit orders sent to ECNs are exposed to the entire market.

The exposure of a limit order in two markets at once puts the order in *double jeopardy* of executing twice. The problem is especially serious if either market has slow execution, quotation, order-routing, or trade reporting systems. In that case, both markets may try to execute the order before either market can cancel an order or adjust a quote.

Since most traders will not bear the risk of double execution, one market must take precedence over another. Existing order-routing systems ensure that ECNs have precedence over Nasdaq but not over the NYSE. This difference explains why ECNs have taken significant market share from Nasdaq but not from the NYSE. An ECN cannot cross a market order with a limit order that it has routed to the NYSE until it cancels the NYSE limit order and receives a report confirming that the order is canceled. This process generally takes much longer than most market order traders are willing to wait. ◀

To initially compete with an incumbent market, a new market must find a way around the order flow externality problem. The new market must be closely integrated with the incumbent market so that traders can easily obtain liquidity in either market, or the new market must have an extremely effective advertising campaign that can convince many traders to switch at the same time. The ECNs that started to complete with Nasdaq in the late 1990s took the first approach.

26.2.2 The Order Flow Externality, Order Exposure, and Preferencing

When a market fully displays its orders and quotes, dealers can compete against the order-flow externality held by that market by filling market orders on the same terms available in that market. Since their clients get the same execution that they otherwise would have received, they do not care where their market orders fill.

If permitted to do so, dealers frequently establish preferencing arrangements to compete against such markets. If they arrange to fill orders that primarily come from uninformed traders, dealers may be able to offer better terms than are available in the primary market. Dealers then will take much of that order flow away from the primary market.

When dealers take market orders away from the primary market, the primary market becomes less attractive to limit order traders. Traders then either send their limit orders elsewhere or use market orders instead.

The order flow externality is strongest when traders are uncertain about what orders and quotes are available in a market. If so, traders need to be in that market to take advantage of whatever opportunities are present there. These issues are of greatest concern to traders who want to fill large orders because other traders generally are unwilling to display large sizes. To fill their orders, they therefore must participate in the market where other large traders trade.

Facilities that allow traders to control the exposure of their orders strengthen the order flow externality where it is strongest. Strong markets do not want to display their quotes and orders because doing so only allows dealers to compete along side of it. Electronic markets that permit traders to place undisplayed orders, and floor-based markets in which brokers hold undisplayed orders, force traders to come to them to trade. Strong markets do not benefit from exposing their orders.

The order flow externality is very strong at the New York Stock Exchange because much of the liquidity there is in the hands of floor brokers who do not fully disclose their orders. Dealers successfully compete against the NYSE market only when filling small market orders that come primarily from uninformed traders, and very large orders that require more liquidity than is available on the floor of the exchange.

In contrast, the order flow externality is weak at the Nasdaq Stock Market because traders who route their orders cannot learn any more about market conditions than do traders who preference their orders to specific dealers of ECNs. Dealers and ECNs therefore have competed very successfully against the Nasdaq Stock Market.

26.2.3 Public Policy Implications

The role for public policy would be quite limited if all traders were identical. Good public policy would simply allow traders to choose for themselves the trading system that they prefer. Although the best market system would be a consolidated system, regulators would not need to impose one on identical traders: They would choose it for themselves.

Regulatory efforts to impose a consolidated system risk choosing the wrong market structure or stifling innovation. When regulators consolidate by fiat, they have to determine what structure to use and when to change it as new technologies and demands for service emerge. Should the consolidated system enforce strict price-time precedence, as the Tokyo Stock Exchange does? Open-outcry futures markets generally do not. Should the consolidated system display all orders, as the CATS system in Toronto does? Most trading systems do not. Should displayed orders have precedence over undisclosed orders that were submitted first, as is the case in the GLOBEX

> ### Order Exposure on the NYSE Floor
>
> Floor brokers generally handle large market-not-held orders on the floor of the NYSE. The floor brokers often reveal their orders only after identifying traders likely to be interested in trading, and then only to the extent that they believe the interested traders are willing to trade.
>
> Try as they might, exchange floor brokers do not always manage order exposure perfectly. They may misjudge who might be interested in trading or the size that a trader will trade. They may inadvertently expose their orders by the way they walk, talk, or otherwise present themselves. They also may deliberately reveal their orders to reward friends or to exchange favors with traders with whom they must deal, shoulder-to-shoulder, every day of the year.
>
> Large traders protect themselves against these risks by breaking their orders into parts. They then sequentially submit the parts to their broker as each part fills. They may also submit the parts to different brokers. ◀

and Paris CAC trading systems? Most systems do not even allow undisclosed orders. These differences in market structure are very significant. The public welfare depends on the market structures that regulators chose.

When traders choose where they trade, the competition for their orders helps reveal the market structures that best serve them. This competition occasionally fragments the market as innovative systems take order flow from incumbent systems. If traders are identical, however, the fragmentation will be transitory. The best market structure will eventually garner all the order flow, if new markets can overcome the advantages of the order flow externality.

Regulators can help ensure that competition reveals the best market structure by helping disseminate reliable and unbiased information about competing market structures. Such information makes it easier for traders to switch to better trading systems as they become available.

It also might appear desirable for regulators to require that incumbent trading systems permit fast linkages between their trading systems and those of their rivals. Although such policies make it easier for rivals to overcome the advantage of the order flow externality, they can seriously disrupt incumbent trading systems that use slow trading technologies. If the slow technology is slow because the market has failed to innovate, requiring fast linkages will promote efficiency-enhancing competition. But if the technology is slow because traders need time to arrange trades that they could not otherwise arrange, requiring fast linkages will disrupt the incumbent market and possibly destroy its valuable trading system. The decision to require fast linkages therefore is not merely a decision to promote competition; it can unintentionally impose an inferior market structure upon certain markets.

26.3 MARKET FRAGMENTATION

Markets fragment because traders are not all identical and because their trading problems differ considerably. Some market structures therefore better serve the needs of some traders than other market structures do. Consequently, identical instruments—and very similar instruments—may simultaneously trade in multiple market centers.

Although different traders prefer different market structures, they all greatly appreciate the order flow externality. Every trader wishes that all other traders would trade exclusively in his or her preferred market structure. Traders naturally want their preferred market to be as liquid as possible.

In the remainder of this section, we identify how traders differ, and how these differences cause them to prefer different market structures.

26.3.1 Unequal Sizes

Traders differ in the quantities that they want to trade. Some traders are so large that their orders can significantly move the market. Others are so small that their individual orders rarely have any price impact.

Large traders are reluctant to reveal their trading plans. They fear that if their orders were widely revealed before they arranged their trades, other traders would front-run them and thereby increase their trading costs. Large traders manage this risk by controlling the exposure of their orders. They prefer to expose their orders only to traders who will commit to trading with them.

▶ Order Exposure in Cantor Fitzgerald's Government Bond Trading System

eSpeed, the government bond trading system used by Cantor Fitzgerald, is an electronic trading system designed to serve the needs of large traders. Traders confidentially indicate to eSpeed that they are willing to trade at a given price. The system continuously publishes the best bid and ask prices. When a trader indicates that he will take a standing bid or offer, the taking trader and the standing trader take turns revealing how much they want to trade. They reveal increasing sizes until one of the two traders no longer wants to increase the size of the trade. At that point, the eSpeed system executes the trade at the last agreed-upon size.

All traders are able to see the agreed-upon size of the trade as it is growing, but no one except the two parties to the trade and the broker can see the negotiations. The system thus allows the two traders to see each other's orders only to the extent that they are willing to trade while ensuring that neither trader knows with whom he or she is trading.

Some large traders are so sensitive about revealing size that they split their orders so that no one can confidently infer the full size of their orders. Occasionally, two such traders will unknowingly trade with each other two or more times in a row simply because neither trader is willing to let any other trader know the full size of the order. ◀

Executing large orders can be difficult and expensive in markets that widely display orders. If traders do not expose their orders, finding the other side is difficult. If they expose their orders, they may scare away traders who might otherwise supply liquidity to them, and other traders may front-run them. Large traders therefore prefer market structures that allow them to find traders willing to trade while minimizing the information they must expose to find these traders.

Large traders also prefer markets that enforce strict time precedence rules in conjunction with an economically significant minimum price increment. These rules protect them from quote-matching front runners when they expose their orders. Chapter 11 discusses front-running strategies.

In contrast, small traders like to expose their orders. They do not fear front runners because front running a small order is not generally profitable. Wide exposure allows small traders to fill their orders quickly, at the best prices available. They prefer market structures in which they can expose their orders.

Small market order traders like markets that have small minimum price increments because they pay the bid/ask spread when they trade. Since spreads cannot be smaller than the minimum price increment, a large price increment can force them to pay artificially high spreads.

26.3.2 Asymmetric Information

Well-informed and uninformed traders generally prefer different market structures. Most traders want to avoid trading with well-informed traders. Well-informed traders therefore prefer to trade in fully consolidated markets, in which all traders trade anonymously, so that they cannot easily be identified as informed traders.

In contrast, uninformed traders prefer to trade in markets that expose trader identities so that they can avoid informed traders. They also prefer to trade in markets where they can try to convince other traders that they are uninformed. Retail traders benefit from the preferencing of their orders

▶ Order Exposure in Crossing Networks

Electronic crossing networks, such as POSIT, allow large traders to avoid exposing their orders. These computerized trading systems take electronically transmitted orders and match them at prices determined elsewhere. The systems are completely confidential. They reveal only the aggregate sizes of the matches they have arranged. ◀

▶ Hybrid Trading Systems

The New York Stock Exchange and the Nasdaq Stock Market both have hybrid trading systems. The NYSE is essentially an order-driven public auction in which specialists ensure that impatient traders can always trade. Nasdaq is essentially a quote-driven dealer market in which public traders can offer liquidity by exposing their orders. Both systems are hybrids designed to meet the needs of all types of traders. ◀

to dealers who discriminate between their orders and more informed orders. Chapters 15, 23, and 25 discuss how fragmented market structures have evolved to benefit uninformed traders.

26.3.3 Unequal Patience

Some traders are more patient than are others. Impatient traders want to trade quickly. They generally will pay bid/ask spreads and high commissions to increase the probability that they trade. Impatient traders like market structures in which dealers are always available to provide them with liquidity when they want to trade. In contrast, patient traders are cost-sensitive and willing to wait for the market to come to them. They tend to supply liquidity through their limit orders and through the floor brokers who represent them.

Some market structures serve the needs of impatient traders better than those of patient traders. For example, Nasdaq's Small Order Execution System (SOES) is a quote-based system that allows small impatient traders to trade immediately whenever they want to. Users of this system, however, generally must buy at the ask and sell at the bid. Since Nasdaq allows traders to preference their orders to specific dealers, and thus does not enforce time precedence, Nasdaq does not best serve the needs of patient traders. Patient traders instead prefer consolidated order-driven trading systems that enforce universal time precedence. Such systems increase their probability of trading when they expose their orders.

All traders must decide whether they value execution certainty more than they value transaction cost savings. Those who value the former opt for quote-driven market systems that provide execution certainty at the expense of transaction costs. Those who value transaction cost savings opt for order-driven market systems that provide lower transaction costs for executed trades, but lower certainty that orders will trade. Diverse market structures exist because no single trading system best serves the needs of both patient and impatient traders.

26.3.4 Unequal Access

By design or historic accident, markets often deny some traders access to information or facilities that other traders have. For example, exchange members may have direct access to floor information or trading opportunities that are unavailable to off-floor traders. The latter group of traders generally can trade only by purchasing brokerage services from exchange members.

Many large institutions and sophisticated individual investors believe that they could execute their trades at a lower cost if they had the same access to information and trading facilities that exchange members have. Disadvantaged traders naturally favor market structures in which they have stronger and more equal roles. Diversity in market structures is partly due to competitive responses to their disenfranchisement. Trading systems like Instinet and POSIT attract order flow, in part, because users can arrange their trades without the intermediation of traditional brokers.

26.3.5 Unequal Creditworthiness and Trustworthiness

Traders differ in their creditworthiness and trustworthiness. Trades settle only if traders acknowledge and fulfill the terms of their agreements. Traders who do not settle, impose costs upon other traders.

Trustworthy and creditworthy traders therefore prefer to trade with each other and exclude less worthy traders. When they cannot do so, they bear the costs that less worthy traders impose upon them. Depending on the market, they may directly bear these costs when a deadbeat fails to settle properly with them, or they may indirectly bear these costs by settling their trades through a clearinghouse that guarantees their performance.

Markets exclude individuals who would impose costs upon others if allowed to trade. The excluded individuals may still trade, but usually they must trade through intermediaries who guarantee their trades. Exchanges, dealer networks, and clearinghouses impose financial and ethical standards upon their members in order to exclude traders who might impose unnecessary settlement costs upon others. Any consolidated trading system that imposes the same standards on all traders requires the more creditworthy and more trustworthy traders to subsidize the less worthy ones.

26.4 MARKET SEGMENTATION: HOW FRAGMENTED MARKETS CONSOLIDATE

The two preceding sections suggest that a trade-off may exist between the cost-reducing benefits of market consolidation and the service-enhancing benefits of market diversity. Within any given market structure, liquidity is greatest and transaction costs are lowest when all traders trade in that structure. All traders therefore want all other traders to trade in the market structure that they prefer. Differences among traders, however, cause them to prefer diverse market structures. Unfortunately, no single market best meets the service needs of all traders; thus, in many markets, a diversity of market structures has evolved to serve the various needs of different traders. The resulting fragmentation suggests that some of the cost-reducing benefits of market consolidation may be lost. In particular, regulators and practitioners fear that fragmented markets substantially increase transaction costs.

These concerns would be well founded if traders in various market fragments did not know about—and respond to—market conditions in other fragments. Each fragment then would constitute an isolated market in which price formation would take place independently of all other fragments. The resulting prices would depend only on market conditions within each fragment. Prices would not efficiently incorporate all available information about fundamental asset values because information in one fragment would not affect trading in other fragments. Transaction costs would be high because liquidity demands in one fragment could not meet liquidity supplies in other fragments. Traders thus would have to satisfy all liquidity demands separately within each fragment.

Market diversity, however, does not necessarily imply inferior price formation and high transaction costs. Traders can obtain the benefits of consolidation in fragmented markets when information flows freely between market fragments, and when some traders can choose which fragment in which to trade. These two conditions are sufficient to coalesce a fragmented market into a unified complex of diverse segments. The first condition ensures that traders know what is happening in each market segment. The second condition ensures that some traders can act on that information when prices or liquidity conditions diverge.

The Route to Best Execution

Many trade facilitators sell sophisticated order-routing systems to their clients. These systems take client orders and route them to the best available market. They are particularly useful to large traders who want to *sweep the market* by taking liquidity from all sources at once. Most of these vendors bundle their order-routing systems with buy-side order management systems that they offer to their clients. Table 26-1 provides a partial list of these vendors. ◀

Three mechanisms consolidate a fragmented market. First, within each market segment, traders adjust their orders to reflect information that traders reveal in other segments. These adjustments cause prices to reflect information from all segments.

Second, some traders route their orders to market segments where they expect to obtain the best prices. Traders who demand liquidity route their orders to segments that are currently most liquid. Traders who supply liquidity route their orders to segments with the greatest current demands for liquidity. These order-routing decisions help balance the supply and demand for liquidity in all market segments.

Finally, arbitrageurs specialize in moving liquidity among market segments. They trade whenever prices in one segment are inconsistent with prices in another segment. Their trading enforces the law of one price across market segments as they connect buyers in one segment to sellers in another segment. Chapter 17 discusses how and why arbitrageurs move liquidity among market segments.

The forces that consolidate market segments are quite robust. Even if some traders can trade only in one market segment, the market will remain consolidated if other traders can freely route their orders to other market segments. In the worst case, if an order cannot move to its best market, arbitrageurs will move the best market to the order.

These three mechanisms will consolidate a fragmented market only if information about trades and orders in each market segment is publicly available at low cost. Without this information, traders cannot easily search for the best price across market segments.

Traders will consolidate fragmented markets only if they always seek the best prices for their orders. Problems may arise, however, when traders use brokers to arrange their trades. Although traders expect that their brokers will seek the best prices for their orders, brokers may not always do so. If they do not, market fragmentation may reduce liquidity and make the price formation process less efficient. Chapter 7 discusses this agency problem in detail.

TABLE 26-1.
Buy-Side Equity Order-Routing Systems

PRODUCT	VENDOR	LINK
Blackwood PRO	Blackwood	www.blackwoodtrading.com
Bloomberg Tradebook	Bloomberg	www.bloomberg.com
IOE	Bridge Trading, a unit of Reuters	www.bridge.com
RouteNet	Investment Technology Group	www.itginc.com
Lava ColorBook	Lava Trading	www.lavatrading.com
REDIPlus	Spear, Leeds & Kellogg, a unit of Goldman Sachs	www.redi.com
Smart BRASS; PowerNet	SunGard Data Systems	www.trading.sungard.com
RealTick	Townsend Analytics	www.realtick.com

Agency problems at their worst involve frauds that brokers perpetrate upon their clients. For example, brokers may arrange to have confederates fill orders at inferior prices. Such frauds are much easier to commit in fragmented markets than in consolidated markets because fewer people monitor trading in small market segments than in fully consolidated markets. Any consideration of the trade-offs between market consolidation and market diversity therefore must consider the potential for fraud in fragmented markets.

Public policy makers who consider whether to consolidate fragmented markets by regulation should compare the benefits and costs of diversity. Unfortunately, both are hard to measure.

We can identify a lower bound for the costs of diversity. The total costs of trading in a segmented market must exceed the trading costs in a fully consolidated market by at least the cost of the information systems necessary to consolidate the market plus the resources that arbitrageurs use to move liquidity among market segments. If this lower bound is high, market diversity is very expensive.

In very active markets, information usually is quite cheap relative to the volume of trade, and the competition among arbitrageurs to profit from trading opportunities ensures that they provide cheap and efficient service. The benefits of complete consolidation in such markets therefore are small relative to the benefits of market diversity. Active markets therefore can support more diverse market structures than less active markets can.

> **Anyone Care to Swim?**
>
> Traders say that they access *liquidity pools* in fragmented markets. The order flow externality causes a pool of liquidity to form in each market fragment. ◀

26.5 EXTERNALITIES IN THE COMPETITION AMONG MARKET CENTERS

The discussion in the preceding section suggests that competition among market centers to satisfy different service needs of diverse clienteles is generally beneficial. The resulting segmentation helps traders solve their various trading problems at minimum cost. If information flows freely between market segments and if no serious agency problems are present, segmentation is unlikely to have any overwhelmingly negative effects on price formation and transaction costs.

The conclusion that competition among market centers is beneficial, however, depends on the assumption that no significant externalities affect the competition. An *externality* arises whenever someone does something that has an impact upon others for which he or she is neither adequately compensated nor properly penalized. When no one compensates people for the benefits they provide others, they tend to do less than would be socially desirable. Likewise, when no one penalizes people for the costs they impose upon others, they tend to do more than would be socially desirable. Unfortunately, competition among market centers involves several such externalities.

26.5.1 The Order Flow Externality

We have already discussed the most important externality that affects competition among markets. The order flow externality makes it very difficult for new markets to compete effectively against incumbent markets.

The order flow externality is an example of a *network externality*. Network externalities arise whenever the value of a system to a user increases as more people use the system. For example, a phone network is more valu-

▶ How Many Disks Have You Received from AOL?

When a new market with a network externality opens, competitors must rush to quickly build their networks. AOL is the best-known example of a recent winner in a new market with a network externality. People once joked about how many computer disks AOL mailed to potential subscribers. Those disks, however, helped to create AOL's unassailable market position. ◀

able to each subscriber when the network connects many subscribers as opposed to few subscribers.

Trading systems are networks that link many potential buyers to many potential sellers. The more buyers and sellers who participate in the system, the more valuable it is to everyone who uses it.

Network externalities can create tremendous barriers to entry. Usually, one trading system grows large, and no other system can become large enough, quickly enough, to be a viable economic competitor. Markets with network externalities are *winner-take-all markets*. Without government regulation, new entrants often cannot get a toehold.

The U.S. government requires that all phone companies allow all other phone companies to access their networks. Without such linkages, new phone companies could not compete with existing companies. The cellular telephone, telephone-over-cable, and telephone-over-Internet industries would not exist today were it not for these open access regulations. The government, of course, specifies the *interconnect access fees* that companies can charge each other for access to their networks.

Governments can acquire, and have required, linkages among trading networks. In 1975, the U.S. government required that U.S. equity exchanges establish the Intermarket Trading System (ITS) to link their trading floors. The exchanges created a rather inefficient system, so ITS has had little effect on the markets. A redesign of the system is presently very high on the political agendas of many market centers. For example, the ECNs would like to have access to a revised ITS system through which they can route firm commitments at high speed. Most incumbent exchanges, of course, are not interested in improving the system.

Order routing systems created by various data vendors also link traders with various trading systems. These links connect to the *application programming interface* (API) of each trading system. (APIs are portals through which computer systems talk with each other.) This approach to market center linkage may ultimately accomplish all that coordinated regulatory linkages attempt to accomplish.

26.5.2 Secondary Precedence Rules

The second most important externality in exchange competition is also due to the option values implicit in orders. Traders who offer standing limit orders benefit other traders, but no one compensates them for the benefits that they provide. They therefore provide less liquidity than would be socially optimal.

The liquidity offered by limit order traders benefits markets because it attracts traders. Exchanges and ECNs therefore try to encourage traders to offer limit orders. Traders will offer liquidity when they are rewarded for—and not hurt by—offering liquidity.

Some ECNs reward limit order traders by charging lower fees for limit orders than for market orders. In effect, market order traders pay limit order traders a fee for their liquidity in these systems. In chapter 14, we show that in competitive order-driven markets, such differential fees simply narrow equilibrium bid/ask spreads so that the long-run incentives to supply or demand liquidity are unchanged.

In general, any preference given to limit order traders will have no net effect on the supply of liquidity in a competitive equilibrium in which all

▶ Lost Time Precedence

Time precedence rules govern trading in U.S. exchange-listed stocks at exchanges, but not among exchanges and over-the-counter dealers. Regional exchange specialists and third market dealers like Bernard Madoff regularly fill market orders at the same bid or ask prices that traders at the New York and American Stock Exchanges first quoted. Likewise, exchange traders occasionally fill market orders at prices that regional specialists and third market dealers quoted first. In either event, the trader who quoted first does not receive a trade that he or she would have received if time precedence were universally enforced across markets.

Order crossing by brokers also often violates time precedence. Many brokers like to match orders internally for execution because internal matching ensures that they obtain two commissions for the trade instead of one. These brokers then print the trade at a market with a thin limit order book to ensure that no standing limit order interferes with the trade. Traders who place their orders in exchange order books would be better off if the brokers had to print their crosses in a consolidated market.

In both examples, limit order traders would be better off if time precedence were universally enforced. ◀

traders are precommitted to trading. In such models, spreads adjust so that traders are indifferent between offering and taking liquidity.

In most markets, however, not all potential traders are committed to trading. In particular, quote-matching order anticipators trade only if they can extract option values from limit orders. (Chapter 11 discusses the quote-matching strategy.) Their trading therefore taxes liquidity. In equilibrium, quote matchers' profits imply higher transaction costs for precommitted traders whether they use limit orders or market orders.

Since quote matchers directly hurt limit order traders, and thereby indirectly hurt market order traders, markets have an incentive to exclude quote matchers. The only effective way that they can do so is by maintaining secondary precedence rules—time precedence and public order precedence—that give precedence to limit order traders who display their orders. An economically significant minimum price increment, of course, must be set to make these precedence rules meaningful.

An externality problem arises when market segments compete with each other because a market segment cannot meaningfully enforce secondary precedence rules when other segments trading the same—or essentially the same—instruments do not. Quote matchers simply place their orders and quotes in other markets when they do not have precedence in a given market. If they can get their orders filled in these other markets, they get around the secondary precedence rules.

Markets that attract few limit orders have little incentive to maintain an economically significant minimum price increment to protect limit order traders. On the contrary, with a small increment, they can attract orders of quote matchers who will improve the consolidated quote in order to obtain market orders. Since brokers generally must execute orders at the best available prices, they often route to markets that display the best prices. A small market with little volume may therefore obtain order flow by offering a small minimum price increment. Although larger markets may want to protect limit order traders, they cannot do so: To remain competitive, they must

▶ The Race to the Bottom

Reduction of the minimum
price increment in U.S.
equities markets started in the
1990s and culminated in the
full decimalization of the
markets in 2001. As the
above analysis suggests, the
first markets to offer smaller
minimum price increments
were weaker markets like the
American Stock Exchange
and the ECNs. They moved
first because they had little
incentive to protect limit order
traders. (They then had few
such traders.) The larger
markets had to decrease their
price increments to remain
competitive in the face of best
execution standards that
require brokers to obtain the
best available prices for their
clients' orders. ◀

lower their minimum price increments to equal the smallest minimum increment offered by any market.

Unregulated competition among markets therefore does not permit markets to enforce trading rules that would solve the order exposure externality problem. Consequently, public limit order traders offer less liquidity than they would have if they traded in a fully consolidated trading system that used an economically meaningful minimum price increment to enforce secondary order precedence rules.

26.5.3 Regulatory Services

Markets compete for order flow by offering services that they believe will be attractive to their clienteles. We can divide the services that markets offer into two groups, according to whether the benefits they provide are private or public services.

Private services benefit only the traders who use the market. Order-routing systems and accounting systems are examples of such services. Since usage of these services is easy to measure, markets can charge their traders to cover the costs of providing these services. Markets therefore will provide whatever private services their users demand.

Public services benefit everyone, regardless of where—or sometimes whether—they trade. The promotion of price continuity, and the regulation of insider trading, manipulative trading practices, and capital structures, are examples of services that produce public benefits. These services improve market quality for everyone. Exchanges fund them through fees that they charge traders who use their markets. Traders can avoid these fees by patronizing markets that do not provide these regulatory services. Since markets can charge only their traders for these services that benefit everyone, unregulated competition among market centers produces fewer public services than would be socially desirable.

26.6 CONSOLIDATION OF MARKETPLACES

The preceding sections discuss consolidation and fragmentation of trading in a single instrument. In this section, we identify additional forces that cause market centers—exchanges, ECNs, brokers, and dealers—to consolidate through mergers, acquisitions, joint ventures, and joint operating agreements.

Two major waves of such consolidations have occurred. The first followed the invention and widespread adoption of the telegraph and telephone. These communications technologies greatly decreased the costs of knowing what was going on in distant markets and of routing orders to those markets. Once, every major city had exchanges that traded many of the same securities, and many of these cities also had futures markets that traded similar contracts. With improvements in telecommunications, traders seeking better prices eventually caused markets to consolidate. The markets that lost order flow failed or merged with other exchanges.

The second wave of consolidations started in the early 1990s and is continuing to this day. This wave is occurring largely in response to three factors. The first factor is the order flow externality mentioned above. It is responsible for much of the consolidation among dealers and among some ECNs.

The second factor is related to changes in the costs of operating trading systems. Advances in computing technologies have caused the ratio of vari-

▶ An Academic Proposal for Exchange Competition

Consider the following proposal for competition among equity markets:

1. Regulations would completely consolidate all trading in an equity issue into a single market. Different equities might trade in different markets, but all trading in a given equity would be in the same market.
2. Shareholders would decide each year at which market their equity issues will trade.

This proposal would produce many benefits of regulatory consolidation while preserving the benefits of competition among markets. Instead of competing for order flow, markets would compete for listings. Although the proposal provides a simple and attractive solution to a complex problem, only academics have shown any interest in it. ◀

able costs to fixed costs to decline. Consequently, the economies of scale in operating trading systems have increased. Operating small trading systems has become more costly relative to operating large trading systems. To reduce costs, many exchanges and brokerages have consolidated.

Finally, much consolidation is taking place because regulatory restrictions on cross-border cooperation and competition have loosened. These changes are most obvious in the European Community. Markets there are quickly consolidating to take advantage of the order flow externality and economies of scale in operating large trading systems. Likewise, the relaxation of regulatory restrictions has led to several international joint operating agreements among futures exchanges.

26.7 SUMMARY

Markets consolidate because traders attract traders. Trading is easiest and cheapest where most traders of an instrument or similar instruments trade. Liquidity attracts liquidity.

Markets fragment because the trading problems that traders solve, differ. Different market structures serve some traders better than others. Markets fragment when, for enough traders, benefits from differentiation exceed benefits from consolidation.

Some traders are small and unconcerned about the price impacts of their trades, while other traders are large and very concerned about front running. Small traders prefer market structures that widely expose their orders so that everyone can see and react to them. Large traders prefer market structures that allow them to control how and to whom their orders are exposed.

Some traders are well informed about fundamental values and therefore very concerned about revealing their information, while others are relatively uninformed and very concerned about minimizing transaction costs. Uninformed traders prefer markets where they can be identified and given better prices. Informed traders prefer consolidated markets with anonymous trading so that they can hide in the order flow.

Some traders are impatient to trade and therefore willing to pay for liquidity, while others are patient and willing to wait for their price. The former prefer quote-driven markets, while the latter prefer order-driven markets.

▶ Should Apples and Oranges Trade Together?

The order flow externality most obviously applies to a single instrument. Traders interested in trading a given instrument are attracted to the market with the most order flow in that instrument.

This principle also applies to instruments that are similar to each other. Instruments are similar when their values largely depend on the same common valuation factors. Many traders therefore regard them as good substitutes for each other. Such traders are attracted to markets that actively trade any of these instruments. Markets that actively trade many similar instruments are especially attractive to traders who are interested in exposure to the common valuation factors. The order flow externality thus applies to common factors as well as to individual instruments.

Markets that trade similar instruments often merge to take advantage of the order flow externality. By concentrating order flow in similar instruments, they increase the liquidity of underlying common factors. This effect explains why mergers of markets within a country generally have been quite successful. It also helps explain why stocks generally do not trade well outside of their national markets. ◀

▶ RISC versus CISC

Issues involving market structure are similar to issues involving computer microprocessor architecture.

The reduced instruction set computing (RISC) approach to microprocessor design uses a simple processor to process a limited set of instructions very quickly. Software parses complex instructions into simpler instructions for execution. This architecture can be very efficient because RISC processors are very fast.

The complex instruction set computing (CISC) approach uses a complex processor to process complex instructions. This architecture can be very efficient when complex instructions are quite common.

The RISC approach corresponds to fully consolidated markets. A simple market structure that receives all order flow can work very quickly and efficiently, but it can solve only simple trading problems. Traders with complex trading problems typically break up their orders into smaller pieces when trading in these markets.

The CISC approach corresponds to fragmented markets. Fragmented markets can provide more service to diverse clienteles than can fully consolidated markets. ◀

▶ The Libertarian View

Although enlightened regulation of the markets might benefit everyone, many people are reluctant to give regulators much power to regulate. They fear that regulators—through ignorance or malice—may abuse their power. The history of regulation is replete with examples of regulations that have been more costly than beneficial. ◀

Not withstanding these differences, all traders appreciate the benefits of consolidation. Traders often trade in markets that they do not like simply because those markets are most liquid. Conversely, no market will attract and keep liquidity if it does not provide good service to many traders. Competition among market structures generally reveals the market structures that best serve various types of traders.

Fragmented markets consolidate when traders can access information about market conditions within each segment. Traders use this information to adjust their orders, reroute their orders, or issue new orders. Prices and liquidity in each segment thereby reflect information from all other segments.

Traders naturally enforce price priority in segmented markets when they seek the best prices for their orders. Traders do not enforce secondary order precedence rules, such as time precedence, across market segments. Only coordinated regulation can implement such rules.

Fragmented markets generally will provide less regulatory oversight than is socially optimal. Good regulatory activities benefit everyone, but exchanges can charge only those traders who trade in their segments. Only coordinated regulation can ensure that markets provide adequate regulatory oversight.

Two types of competition characterize segmented markets. Traders compete for the best price, and market centers compete to serve diverse traders. Unfortunately, policies that promote the benefits from one competition can decrease the benefits from the other. Regulators therefore must balance the benefits obtained from these two types of competition.

26.8 SOME POINTS TO REMEMBER

- Markets consolidate because traders attract traders. Liquidity attracts liquidity.
- Consolidation maximizes competition among traders and thereby most efficiently reveals the best price.

- A better market structure may never emerge if it cannot attract enough traders to move away from an incumbent market to make it liquid.
- The order flow externality is strongest when search costs are highest.
- When a market displays enough information about orders and quotes to accurately predict the average execution price of a market order, preferencing to dealers of such market orders can weaken the order flow externality held by that market.
- Markets fragment as exchanges, brokers, ECNs, and dealers compete to meet the diverse service requirements of different traders.
- Fragmented markets consolidate when traders can observe and act upon information in all market segments.
- Arbitrageurs help consolidate fragmented markets.
- Externality problems affect the competition among market centers to provide exchange services. Unregulated competition therefore may not create the best market structures.

26.9 QUESTIONS FOR THOUGHT

1. Should regulators consolidate all trading to maximize price competition among traders and to lower liquidity search costs? If so, to what market structure should they consolidate?
2. How important are the externalities that affect the competition for order flow? Is time precedence valuable? Is order exposure valuable? Is market surveillance valuable? Is price continuity desirable?
3. Are regulatory services valuable? Should laws compel exchanges to provide regulatory services, or should governmental agencies directly supply these services?
4. Who should pay for market regulation?
5. How should regulators trade off the interests of diverse traders? Should we favor small individual traders over large institutional traders? Should we favor impatient traders over patient traders? Should we favor informed traders over uninformed traders? Should we favor public traders over exchange members?
6. Can domestic regulators regulate market structure when market centers compete globally to provide exchange services?
7. How does market fragmentation affect the information in prices?
8. Why is the order flow externality called an externality?
9. Before decimalization, the Nasdaq Stock Market had a smaller minimum price increment than the New York Stock Exchange. Can you explain this fact in light of their different market structures?
10. How does the order flow externality make the provision of price continuity possible?
11. What problems do you see with "An Academic Proposal for Exchange Competition?" How might clienteles specialize in various stocks? Would market structure affect portfolio allocation decisions or corporate control decisions?
12. Can markets consolidate even if no coordinated mechanism, like the Intermarket Trading System (ITS), routes orders from one market segment to another? Do proprietary electronic routing systems that allow traders and brokers to quickly select and route to the best markets for their orders make coordinated intermarket routing systems unnecessary?

13. Innovative markets fail if the cost of convincing traders that they are beneficial is too high relative to the additional benefits they provide. What is the exact condition for failure? How does it depend on who bears the cost of educating traders? How does it depend on the ability of the new market to charge traders for the additional benefits that they receive?

14. The proponents of CISC and RISC microprocessors compete with each other in the marketplace. How does their competition differ from the competition among markets for order flow?

A dvances in communications and computing technologies now allow exchanges to completely automate their trading systems. Many exchanges have done so, and many brokers, ECNs, and dealers have created automated trading systems.

Despite these developments, many of the most liquid exchanges in the world still employ floor-based trading systems. The New York Stock Exchange, the Chicago Board of Trade, the Chicago Mercantile Exchange, the New York Mercantile Exchange, and almost all U.S. options exchanges primarily use floor-based trading systems. Although traders on their floors now rely extensively on electronic systems to route orders and report confirmations, they still arrange trades essentially as they did when these markets first started.

If the floor-based market structures at these exchanges encourage traders to offer liquidity, eliminating their floors would be foolish. However, if other reasons account for the liquidity in these markets, switching to electronic trading may be desirable.

When floor-based trading systems and electronic trading systems have competed head-to-head, the results have been mixed. During the 1980s, the London Stock Exchange was the most important market for large French stocks. In 1989, the Paris Bourse introduced an automated electronic trading system. Since then, much of the trading in French stocks has migrated from London to Paris. More recently, the electronic German DTB futures exchange wrested trading in German T-bond futures from the floor-based London International Financial Futures Exchange (LIFFE). Neither example, however, provides definitive evidence for or against floor-based trading because other events have influenced the outcomes. The market share of the Paris Bourse grew following the 1994 repeal of a French transaction stamp tax that traders formerly avoided by trading in London. Likewise, the German T-bond futures contract moved from LIFFE to DTB in response to an effort by German banks to repatriate their market.

In contrast, brokers, dealers, exchanges, and ECNs have created many automated systems for trading NYSE stocks and U.S. equity options. Some of these systems have been notably successful. Optimark—discussed in chapter 26—failed spectacularly. The Arizona Stock Exchange proved to be a disappointment to people who believe that markets would benefit from electronic call markets. Instinet, Archipelago, and Island ECN have not taken substantial market share from the New York Stock Exchange despite their tremendous success competing against the electronic Nasdaq Stock Market. The electronic International Securities Exchange obtained a 16 percent share of U.S. equity option trading in the issues it trades, within 18 months of its 2000 launch. However, it has not yet displaced the traditional floor-based options markets. The most successful electronic competitors of the NYSE have been third market dealers, like Bernard L. Madoff Investment

The Bangladeshi Stock Exchange and the New York Stock Exchange

In 1999, the Bangladeshi Stock Exchange replaced its trading floor with an automated trading system. At the same time, the New York Stock Exchange considered where to build a new trading floor.

The continued commitment of the New York Stock Exchange to its trading floor may be its most important decision at the turn of the millennium. The members and officers of the Exchange are fully aware of its significance. They believe that the tremendous success of the NYSE is due in large part to its floor-based market structure. They also know that they may lose much, if not all, of their franchise if they are wrong. ◀

Securities and Knight Capital Markets. Their automated trading systems provide very quick service primarily to retail traders represented by discount brokers.

Floor-based oral auctions and automated rule-based auctions are very similar. Both are order-driven markets that match buy orders to sell orders using very similar rules. Their primary difference lies in the technologies they use to arrange these matches. Traders in oral auctions arrange trades by personally exchanging information among themselves, whereas in automated markets, computers arrange the trades.

Since the two market structures are so similar, exchange officials, regulators, and traders naturally consider which is best. There is no simple answer. Both structures have strengths and weaknesses.

In this chapter, we consider the arguments for and against these two trading structures. Our discussion examines how they differ in fairness, convenience, capacity, speed, efficiency, and cost.

27.1 FAIRNESS

Two concepts of market fairness concern traders. Traders want their markets to operate fairly, and they want fair access to those markets. In *operationally fair markets*, trading rules are uniformly applied, and no cheating occurs. In *fair access markets*, all traders have an equal chance to take advantage of any opportunities that arise.

27.1.1 Operational Fairness

Many traders believe that automated trading systems are the fairest of all market structures. Automated systems do only what they are programmed to do. They implement their trading rules exactly and without exception. They expose orders only as instructed, and only to those traders to whom the system permits orders to be exposed.

In contrast, fairness in oral auctions depends on the skill and honesty of the traders who arrange the trades. Traders must be highly skilled to follow the trading rules faultlessly when the market is active, and when prices are moving quickly. They must follow those rules honestly even when doing so may cause them to lose an advantage.

Although most oral auctions are quite fair, all oral auction markets have suffered from well-documented trading scandals. These scandals usually involve front running, inappropriate order exposure, fraudulent trade assignment, or prearranged trading by dishonest brokers.

Although these problems can also arise in automated markets, they cannot take place within their automated trading systems. Instead, dishonest brokers must conduct their frauds on the side.

Markets prevent these frauds by having officials supervise trading, by investigating suspicious trading practices reported by honest traders, and by maintaining—and reviewing—reliable audit trails. An *audit trail* records the submission and disposition of every order. Good audit trails include detailed information about everything that happens to each order. Regulators use audit trails to determine whether traders have violated trading rules. An accurate audit trail helps keep brokers honest.

Floor-based markets have extensive rules that govern how traders process orders and record trades. Markets design these rules to make the audit trail complete, reliable, and accurate. These rules require traders to time-

▶ What Would You Think?

Eli needed to roll a 10-contract short futures position in the Dow Jones Industrial Average Index futures from June to September contracts. Via the Internet, he submitted a spread order to buy 10 June contracts and sell 10 September contracts with a limit of 75, premium to the sell side. The DJIA index futures contracts trade in a pit on the floor of the Chicago Board of Trade.

About a half hour later, Eli queried his broker's Internet site and discovered that he bought the June contracts for 11,060 and sold the September contracts at 11,130. The 70-point difference was less than the 75 points that Eli specified.

Since the nominal size of the DJIA contract is 10 times the Dow index, each point is worth 10 dollars per contract. For ten contracts, the five-point difference between the reported spread and the limit represents 500 dollars.

Eli naturally called his broker and inquired about the discrepancy. Since the broker did not follow his instructions, Eli could have refused to accept the trade, or he could have demanded that his broker make up the difference. The sales broker who answered the phone asked him to hold the line while she called the floor to inquire about the problem. One minute later, she reported that the floor incorrectly reported the trade price of the sale. She said that the September contract actually sold for 11,137 so that the spread trade occurred at 77 rather than 70. Eli was pleased with the result.

What really happened? Consider the following four alternatives:

A. Somebody incorrectly reported the trade, most probably due to a typo or a transcription error. Had Eli not reported the discrepancy, someone would have noted it later, and the broker would have properly adjusted Eli's account.

B. Somebody incorrectly reported the trade. Had Eli not reported the discrepancy, the broker might have pocketed the difference.

C. The floor trader executed the trade incorrectly by mistake. The trader or Eli's broker made up the difference and added two points to keep Eli happy.

D. The floor trader intentionally executed the trade incorrectly and hoped that Eli would not notice the mistake. The trader or broker made up the difference and added two points to keep Eli happy.

Most probably, A characterized what happened. However, if you believe that brokers may conspire to steal from their clients through fraudulent trade assignment or prearranged trading, and that the audit trail cannot detect all such frauds, the other alternatives are possible. Stories like this one tarnish the image of floor-based trading systems regardless of whether their origins are innocent or nefarious. If an automated trading system had arranged the trades, this story simply could not have occurred. ◀

stamp their orders when they receive them and when they fill them, to record trades sequentially, and to report trades immediately.

Automated trading systems easily produce complete and flawless audit trails of all activity that takes place within them. Many traders and regulators especially like these systems for this reason.

27.1.2 Fair Access

Markets provide fair access when all traders have equal access to the market. In such markets, no traders have special advantages over other traders. Few trading systems provide pure fair access.

In floor-based trading systems, floor traders have an advantage over off-floor traders. Floor traders can see and react to market developments well before off-floor traders can. Off-floor traders must obtain their information through market data systems, and they must respond through an order-routing system. The best market data systems report information in less than two seconds. The best order-routing systems pass orders from the client to a broker in less than five seconds. If the routing system requires a *runner* to physically deliver the order to a floor broker, the delay can be substantially longer. These delays allow floor traders to take advantage of opportunities before off-floor traders can.

Floor traders also can observe all market information revealed on an exchange floor, and not just what market data systems report. They are particularly interested in who is trading. This information can be valuable if you can guess why they want to trade or whom they represent. Floor traders also often ask whether an order represents the full size that a client wants to trade. Brokers who have a reputation for reliably reporting this information often can obtain better prices than other traders can. Traders who have access to floor information that market data systems do not report have a significant advantage over other traders.

In large, actively trading futures pits, being able to see and be seen, and being able to hear and be heard are very important. Thus, in some floor-based markets, human anatomy also affects the fairness of the trading. Physically large traders have some advantage over smaller traders because they can control the "real estate" within the pit that offers the best sight lines. They simply move to where they want to be and plant themselves. Although futures markets have rules against physical contact, bumping is common in futures pits. Big traders tend to get the best spots. Tall traders have some advantage over short traders because they can see and be seen more easily. Traders with loud voices have some advantage over less audible traders because they can more easily attract attention when yelling. Traders with shrill voices—typically women—have an advantage over traders with bass voices because high-frequency sounds are highly directional. Their voices penetrate through the noise and easily attract attention. These anatomical characteristics give some traders an advantage in oral markets. They are meaningless in automated markets.

Automated markets favor traders with good keyboard skills and abstract visualization skills. These issues worry some traders when markets convert from floor-based systems to electronic systems.

Automated markets also favor traders who use computer systems to generate their orders. Such systems can monitor electronic data feeds and respond instantly to new information. Although this advantage is a natural consequence of faster trading technologies, many manual traders resent competing with such automated traders.

27.2 THE CONVENIENCE OF DISTRIBUTED ACCESS

A primary advantage of automated trading systems is that they allow traders to trade from their office desks rather than on an exchange floor. Aside from the obvious physical convenience, distributed access allows traders to sit next to their telephones, talk with their colleagues, and consult any data systems they want in support of their trading.

Such facilities are often difficult or impossible to arrange on an exchange floor. Floor traders who want instant access to telephone and data services must carry cell phones and portable terminals onto the trading floor. These instruments are often cumbersome, and a few markets still do not permit them.

27.3 SYSTEM CAPACITY

Electronic order matching technologies are much more scalable than oral order matching technologies. A technology is *scalable* when it can operate with equal or greater efficiency as it grows.

More traders can directly participate in an automated auction than in an oral auction. The number of traders who can effectively communicate with each other simultaneously limits the size of an oral auction. When too many traders try to participate in the same oral auction, they exceed its capacity to process information in an orderly fashion. When the number of traders bidding and offering is large, traders in an oral auction cannot easily keep track of who is quoting the best prices. They then may arrange trades that violate time precedence or even price priority.

Futures and options markets designate such disorderly markets as *fast trading markets.* The designation tells brokerage customers that they cannot expect their brokers to fill their orders at the best available prices when the market is trading fast. In the confusion of a fast market, the brokers may be unaware of the best trading opportunities.

Great numbers of traders can simultaneously interact in automated trading systems because these systems process order messages much faster than people can. Traders who use automated systems do not have to keep track of the best bid and offer. The system does it for them. They also do not have to arrange their trades. The system does it for them according to the market's trading rules. By supporting these functions, automated trading systems allow traders to focus their attention exclusively on creating and submitting their orders.

27.4 NEGOTIATION SPEED

Some floor dealers believe that they can trade more quickly on a floor than in an electronic market. They claim that they can shout a bid or offer, or accept a bid or offer, faster than they can enter this information into a computer. Although this probably is true, modern trading systems with graphical interfaces allow traders to enter information almost as fast as they could shout it out.

In any event, automated trading systems can complete trades much more quickly than individual traders can. In an oral auction, traders must manually record the price, size, counterpart, and instrument traded for each trade. In many markets, they also must record the time of the trade for the audit trail. Since trading requires both order entry and trade record keeping, traders can complete trades more quickly in electronic markets than in oral markets.

Oral trading, however, is undoubtedly faster than screen-based trading when traders want to negotiate their trade sizes. In such negotiations, traders often will not reveal the full size of their order unless they are sure that the other trader will trade the same size. After agreeing on a price, they often

▶ **Why Doesn't Microsoft Trade at the New York Stock Exchange?**

Before 1990, most large U.S. corporations listed their stocks at the New York Stock Exchange when they grew large enough to meet its listing standards. Since then, Microsoft and some other large technology companies that list on the Nasdaq Stock Market have not switched to the NYSE.

Although there are many reasons why Microsoft has remained a Nasdaq stock, one is of particular note to this discussion. Microsoft creates and sells distributed access computing systems. Although Nasdaq does not organize automated auctions, it is a distributed access communications facility. Microsoft may have chosen to stay at Nasdaq for ideological reasons, among others.

The New York Stock Exchange hopes that Microsoft soon will choose to list its stock there. Many people believe that the NYSE is reserving the single character symbol "M" for Microsoft's ticker symbol. ◀

take turns proposing successively higher sizes. Negotiations stop when one trader proposes a greater size than the other trader will accept. The trade size is then the last agreed-upon size. This back-and-forth negotiation is very fast in oral auctions. When conducted through a computer that accepts only firm orders, the negotiation is much slower because the traders must split their orders into pieces to avoid displaying their full sizes.

Some electronic trading systems solve this order display problem by providing messaging systems that allow buyers and sellers to negotiate their trade sizes by exchanging messages on their screens. Liquidnet and Instinet are two such systems.

A second way some automated exchanges solve this order display problem is by allowing large traders to place limit orders with undisclosed size. The automated trading system is aware of the full order size, but it does not display the size to other traders. When the system arranges a match between an undisclosed hidden order and another order, the trade size is set to the minimum of the buy and sell order sizes. This procedure automatically accomplishes what oral traders must accomplish through their back-and-forth negotiations. Euronext, GLOBEX, and Island are markets in which traders often use undisclosed orders.

27.5 EXCHANGE OF INFORMATION ON TRADING FLOORS

Floor-based trading systems dominate electronic trading systems when brokers need to exchange information about buyers and sellers to arrange their trades. This is especially important when traders want to know information about their counterparts before agreeing to trade. Most electronic trading systems cannot provide this information. These issues are most important for traders who want to avoid trading with well-informed traders and with large price-discriminating traders.

All traders want to avoid trading with traders who are well informed about instrument values. When a well-informed trader wants to sell or buy, prices respectively are either too high or too low. Whoever trades with a well-informed trader therefore will probably regret trading. Since it usually is better not to trade than to trade at a poor price, traders prefer to trade only with uninformed traders.

Large traders often direct their brokers to trade only with institutions that they deem to be uninformed. They prefer to trade with institutions that have no research staffs, and that trade only to invest and disinvest rather than to speculate. They often refuse to trade with the proprietary trading groups of investment banks for fear of losing to them. Large traders can issue these instructions to their brokers because they can afford the significant commissions necessary to obtain these services, which require a lot of personal attention. When arranging large trades, traders carefully audit the motives of their trade counterparts.

Traders also do not want to trade with a large trader if that trader intends to continue trading on the same side. The market impact of the large trader's subsequent trades will generate immediate losses for the first traders who trade with the large trader. Traders therefore instruct their brokers to ask how much more size the other side wants to trade. If traders expect that more size will follow, they will offer less favorable terms to the large trader. Chapter 15 discusses these price discrimination issues.

On an exchange floor, a broker who has no additional size to fill will freely offer this information to obtain a better price. Brokers who have substantial additional size usually indicate that they either do not know, or cannot tell, how much additional size remains. If they say that they have no additional size, but soon return to do more size, they depreciate their reputations, and traders will no longer trust them. Brokers therefore do not like clients who lie to them about the full size of their orders. In most electronic trading systems, no similar mechanism allows traders to credibly indicate to each other how much additional size remains in their orders.

Finally, brokers often know of traders who might be interested in trading but have not yet submitted orders. Such traders may be unwilling to display their orders, or may not realize that they want to trade, until a broker approaches them with a suitable trading opportunity. Brokers in possession of this information often can arrange trades that otherwise might not be possible in an electronic environment.

27.6 MARKET DATA REPORTING

Automated systems report market data to the public much faster and much more accurately than floor-based trading systems. In floor-based systems, traders or market reporters must manually enter quotes and trades into the market information system to report them to the public. In automated systems, these data are already in electronic form. Automated systems therefore report faster and more accurately.

27.7 COST

Screen- and floor-based trading systems have different cost structures. Both systems have high initial creation costs. Screen-based systems generally have low operating costs, while floor-based systems are quite costly to operate.

27.7.1 Electronic Trading Systems

Fully automated trading systems require the construction of extensive data networks and data processing systems. These systems must validate users, accept orders, process orders, report trades, and report order status. These functions must be reliable, secure, and fast.

Reliability

Automated trading systems must be reliable because trading stops when the computer or network is down. If only part of the network is down, the affected traders will be extremely upset. Traders generally prefer that all trading halts if they cannot trade. Traders will not use unreliable systems.

To build reliable trading systems, markets must make substantial investments in redundant hardware and software systems. They must eliminate all single points of failure. Since failures are inevitable, given current technologies, markets also must invest in systems that allow them to recover from service interruptions. Markets—as well as brokers and dealers—employ many of the following processes to create reliable trading systems:

- They use fault-tolerant computer hardware.
- They build redundant computer systems.
- They build redundant network connections.

▶ Some Examples of the Risks of Trading Through Unreliable Data Networks

- A trader submits a limit order to an electronic market. After the order is accepted, but before it trades, the trader's network connection fails. The trader does not know whether she has traded. If she knew that she had not traded, she would do the trade in another market. If she goes elsewhere without knowing whether her trade has executed, she risks trading twice.

- An arbitrageur uses an electronic order-routing system to buy Nasdaq 100 futures contracts and sell S&P 500 futures contracts. The arbitrageur initially buys the Nasdaq 100 contracts. His network connection then fails before he can sell the S&P 500 contracts to establish his hedge. If the Nasdaq 100 falls, he may suffer a great loss. If he had hedged his position, a correlated decrease in the S&P 500 probably would offset his loss.

- A short-term speculator uses an electronic market to buy a stock whose price he believes is momentarily depressed by a large uninformed seller. If he is right, he will profit when the price rebounds. If the large seller is well informed, however, the price probably will continue to fall. The speculator therefore intends to sell his position if it does not show a profit in the next 15 minutes. His network connection fails immediately after he buys the stock. If the market drops significantly before he can sell his position, he will lose substantially. (To protect against this possibility, the speculator could issue a stop loss order immediately after he purchases the stock. The stop order would represent his interests even if he cannot communicate with the market.) ◀

- They route network connections through different vendors and through different physical paths.
- They provide backup power supplies.
- They replicate all systems at a remote "hot disaster recovery site," to which all activity can switch instantly if a disaster affects the primary processing site.
- They build significant excess capacity to protect against unexpected surges in demand.
- They maintain high-quality controls in software development.
- They maintain redundant data backup procedures.
- They test software thoroughly, using independent quality assurance groups.

Security

Automated trading systems must be secure because traders enter contracts involving large sums of money. Traders must be confident that computer hackers cannot tamper with their systems and that impersonators cannot fraudulently trade in their name. Markets build secure systems by using various data encryption systems and user authentication systems.

Speed

Automated trading systems must be fast because traders want instant access to markets. They want to see everything as it happens, and they want everything they do to happen instantly. These are reasonable requests. In active markets, prices may change every second. Traders who do not have the latest information will make poor decisions.

Costs

Several vendors sell fully automated exchange trading systems off the shelf. These have been particularly popular in emerging markets. Such systems typically are pure price-time precedence systems. They cost about 5 million dollars to purchase and set up.

Most electronic trading systems trade over private data networks. These networks are generally quite secure, and they provide high-quality service. They are quite expensive to operate, however, because they usually require dedicated leased lines that traders rarely use to their full capacity. In the future, many electronic trading systems probably will send encrypted data over the Internet. Which traders use Internet connections will depend on the speed they require, and the quality of service they can obtain from the Internet.

Once set up, electronic trading systems have small operating costs because everything is automated. The main operational costs are telecommunications costs and costs of adequately backing up data.

27.7.2 Floor-based Trading Systems

Exchanges that use floor-based trading systems must acquire or build suitable trading floors. Trading floors can be quite expensive, especially where real estate is expensive. A floor-based market also must have adequate telecommunications systems to route orders and to report market data and trade confirmations. These systems are comparable to those that electronic trading systems use. Floor-based markets also must invest in information display systems to assist their floor-based traders. Data vendors often provide these systems.

Actively traded floor markets must employ automated systems to support their trading. These systems may include electronic limit order books, broker paging systems, wireless order-routing systems for floor brokers, electronic reporting systems, and automatic execution systems for small orders. Costs of designing and implementing these systems can be quite high. When faced with these costs, many exchanges have chosen to switch to completely automated trading systems.

Floor-based trading systems are often quite expensive to operate. They require substantial labor to run. Brokers must arrange trades, reporters or traders must report the trades, officials must watch for trading abuses, and runners often must carry messages to and from brokers. Although new electronic trading systems are increasing broker productivity in some markets, floor-based trading systems will always be labor-intensive.

To operate well, floor-based trading systems require well-trained floor brokers. The brokers must know and follow the trading rules and procedures. They also must know how to best expose their orders and negotiate their trades. Although floor brokers provide special services that distinguish floor-based from automated trading systems, their substantial training makes employing them quite expensive.

Since floor brokers are often quite busy on the floor, they often cannot communicate directly with their clients. In that case, their clients give their orders to sales brokers who forward them to the floor brokers. The depen-

▶ Communications Delays in GLOBEX

GLOBEX is an electronic trading system in which the futures contracts of the Chicago Mercantile Exchange and the MATIF (Marché à Terme International de France) trade after hours. It is located in Chicago. During development, traders in Australia were concerned that they would have slower access than traders who were close to Chicago. The system designers therefore designed the system to ensure that all traders would receive a minimum quality of service regardless of where they are in the world.

The issue is particularly important in computerized trading systems that allow their users to submit computer-generated orders. Computerized traders who can act most quickly on new information take advantage of market opportunities first. When two computerized trading systems employ the same trading strategies, the first to submit its orders will be the more profitable system. Since the difference in their submission times may be less than a millisecond, speedy connections are essential to trading successfully.

Although the GLOBEX communications network is extremely fast, traders for whom reaction time is of the essence undoubtedly place their computers in Chicago. ◀

dence on sales brokers increases the costs of floor-based trading systems. It also slows them down.

In contrast, electronic trading systems do not require well-trained brokers to operate. In many such systems, brokerage clients can access the market themselves, without the intermediation of their brokers. In such *direct access* systems, brokers merely guarantee and settle their clients' trades. Skilled brokers can provide valuable services to their clients in electronic environments by forming and implementing good order submission strategies. These brokers, however, are not necessary to run the system. Electronic trading systems are cheaper to operate because they do not require floor brokers and sales brokers.

27.8 SUMMARY

Floor-based trading systems and automated trading systems have different strengths and weaknesses. Consequently, they appeal to different clienteles. It is unlikely that one market structure will dominate all trading. Table 27-1 summarizes strengths and weaknesses of floor-based and automated trading systems.

Fully automated systems are very fast and generally cheap to use and

TABLE 27-1.
Floor Versus Automated Trading Systems

ISSUE	FLOOR-BASED SYSTEMS	AUTOMATED SYSTEMS
Speed	Relatively slow	Very fast
Information exchange	Floor-based traders can exchange any information they want	Traders can communicate only through a limited set of order instructions
Potential for order exposure strategies	Limited by floor brokers' skills	Limited by the set of order instructions
Trader convenience	Traders must be on floor	Distributed access
Buy-side access	Through floor brokers and possibly sales brokers	Direct access is possible
System scalability	Limited by difficulties of physically exchanging messages	Highly scalable
Initial costs	High costs to acquire and construct floor High costs to train floor brokers and exchange officials	Relatively lower costs for the exchange software
Communications costs	Low if based on telephones Moderate if based on electronic data systems	Moderate costs for electronic data systems
Labor costs	High labor costs	Low labor costs
Fairness	Requires substantial surveillance of floor trading	Very fair
Audit trails	Require substantial efforts	Perfect

operate. These characteristics ensure that active markets and markets that serve small traders will use automated trading systems extensively. In the U.S. equities markets, Bernard L. Madoff Investment Securities, Knight Capital Markets, and other dealers who offer automated execution systems provide excellent service to high volumes of small traders. Options markets tend to have high order volumes and small transaction sizes. We can expect that these markets will increasingly automate their trading.

Fully automated systems also allow traders to exercise direct control over their orders. They therefore appeal to traders who do not trust their brokers or who do not want to pay for brokerage services. Large institutions that are concerned about how brokers expose their orders often favor automated systems if they are willing to employ their own buy-side traders.

Floor systems work best when traders need to exchange information about each other before they trade. They also work best when brokers need to actively search for traders to fill their orders. Since these advantages are most important to large traders, floor-based markets will serve primarily large institutional traders. The NYSE increasingly is an institutional market. Although people have been predicting the demise of the NYSE floor since the mid-1960s, it will not disappear as long as the NYSE floor traders continue to provide valuable services to traders that other systems cannot provide.

The communications and computational technologies that have enabled automated electronic markets allow these markets to exploit huge economies of scale. Consequently, many exchanges have merged to take advantage of scale economies. Many more will probably merge in the future.

In chapter 26, we noted that the order flow externality can make an incumbent market highly liquid even if it employs an inefficient trading technology. The continued existence of large floor-based markets therefore does not necessarily imply that their trading systems are better than fully automated trading systems.

27.9 SOME POINTS TO REMEMBER

- Electronic trading systems provide much better audit trails than floor-based trading systems.
- Electronic trading systems provide faster access to markets than floor-based trading systems.
- Floor-based trading systems are not as scalable as electronic trading systems.
- Floor-based trading systems allow brokers to exchange information that they cannot easily exchange in electronic trading systems. This information often is essential for arranging good trades for large traders.
- The order flow externality makes it impossible to conclude that large floor-based trading systems survive because their floor-based trading technologies are superior to electronic trading technologies.

27.10 QUESTIONS FOR THOUGHT

1. How would you start an automated exchange that will compete with an established floor-based exchange? In particular, how can a new exchange overcome the order flow externality enjoyed by an incumbent exchange?

2. What are the labor savings when a floor-based exchange converts to an automated exchange? What jobs no longer need to be done? What is the impact of the change upon dealers, floor brokers, sales brokers, exchange clerks, and surveillance officers? Where do the people who still have jobs work? Who pays for their office space and their communications infrastructure?

3. Does the decision to use screen-based versus floor-based trading systems depend on the assets to be traded? Which type of trading system would be best suited to trading instruments in the following asset classes: futures, stocks, bonds, currencies, spot commodities, pollution credits, and options?

Bubbles and crashes occur when prices differ greatly from fundamental values. The wealth that these events create, destroy, and redistribute is often enormous. Bubbles and crashes thus are quite scary when prices change quickly.

Extreme volatility concerns many people:

- Traders pay close attention to it because large, unexpected price changes expose them to tremendous risks and opportunities.

- Clearinghouses worry about extreme volatility because traders who experience large losses may be unable to settle their trades or contracts. Clearinghouses and their members must bear the costs of resulting settlement failures.

- Exchanges and brokers plan for extreme volatility because extreme price changes usually generate—or are generated by—huge volumes that can overwhelm their trading systems and cause them to fail. Large sustained price drops especially concern them because trading volumes usually shrink substantially and remain low for a long time afterward.

- Microeconomists fret over extreme volatility because very large price changes often appear to be inconsistent with rational pricing and informative prices. They wonder whether excess price volatility causes people to make poor decisions about the use of economic resources.

- Macroeconomists fear that the wealth effects associated with large, broad-based changes in market values may adversely affect the investment and consumption spending decisions that companies and individuals make. Poor spending decisions can cause unsustainable booms and protracted contractions in economic activity.

These concerns explain why market regulators regularly examine trading practices and trading rules that might induce or attenuate extreme volatility. Some policies that they consider can create markets which are more resilient. Other policies have little value, and many policies can harm the markets. Regulators therefore must carefully analyze how market structure affects volatility before adopting new policies.

In this chapter, we consider what causes extreme volatility, and how regulations might make it less likely or less dangerous. Not surprisingly, analysts generally understand the causes of extreme volatility better after the fact than beforehand. Volatility episodes rarely have common causes. They do, however, tend to follow a common pattern. Traders who can recognize conditions that may lead to extreme volatility can take positions that are highly profitable. Regulators who can recognize these conditions can occasionally adopt policies to reduce the harmful aspects of extreme volatility.

We start our discussion by distinguishing among the types and causes of extreme volatility, and then illustrate these points by considering several

▶ The Price Accelerator

Increases in prices transfer wealth from pessimistic traders who have short positions to optimistic traders who have long positions. These transfers can cause accelerated price changes.

When prices rise, optimistic traders get wealthier. The most optimistic traders may buy more. If they do, they may cause prices to rise further.

When prices rise, pessimistic traders lose. The losses of the most pessimistic traders may force them to buy back short positions to cover margin calls. Their buying may cause prices to rise further.

In both cases, the sellers will be traders who do not have such strong opinions. Mild pessimists will sell because the increase in market price makes their short positions more attractive. Mild optimists will sell because the increase in market price makes their long positions less attractive. ◀

Source: "The Canonical Bubble," manuscript by Jack Treynor.

examples of bubbles and crashes. We next examine how changes in market structure can affect extreme volatility. Finally, we briefly consider how politics affects regulatory policies taken in response to extreme volatility.

28.1 BUBBLES AND CRASHES

Bubbles occur when prices rise to levels that are substantially above fundamental values. (Fundamental values, of course, are not common knowledge. If they were, crashes and bubbles would not occur.) Some bubbles occur very quickly. Others occur over long periods. Many bubbles end with a crash. Traders say that such bubbles pop.

Crashes occur when prices fall very quickly. Crashes often follow bubbles, but they also occur in other circumstances. Crashes sometimes are called *market breaks* because the price path breaks when prices fall very quickly. They also are called *market meltdowns* when they overload the order handling capacity of a market.

Bubbles and crashes may affect an individual trading instrument or many instruments at once. Those which simultaneously affect many instruments are *broad-based events* or *marketwide events*. Very large price changes most commonly affect only an individual instrument. Broad-based bubbles and crashes are quite rare.

28.1.1 Typical Bubble and Crash Dynamics

Bubbles start when buyers become overly optimistic about fundamental values. The potential of new technologies and the potential growth of new markets can greatly excite some traders. Unfortunately, many of these traders cannot recognize when prices already reflect information about these potentials. They also may not adequately appreciate the risks associated with holding the securities that interest them. If enough of these enthusiastic traders try to buy at the same time, they may push prices up substantially.

The resulting price increases may encourage momentum traders to buy, in the hope that past gains will continue. Some momentum traders may buy because they hope to obtain the profits that their neighbors and friends have already earned. If enough traders follow them, they will realize their hopes. The last buyers, however, will lose badly.

Order anticipators may buy in anticipation of new uninformed buyers. They will profit if they can get out before prices fall.

The combined trading of these traders can cause a bubble in which prices exceed fundamental values. Momentum traders and order anticipators, in particular, tend to accelerate price changes. Prices also accelerate when early buyers grow more confident as their wealth increases, and when early sellers repurchase their positions to stop their losses.

Value traders and arbitrageurs may recognize that prices exceed values, but they may be unable or unwilling to sell in sufficient volume to prevent the bubble from forming. These traders may be unable to sell as much as they want to sell if they do not have large positions to sell, if they do not have enough capital to carry large short positions, or if they cannot easily sell short. They may be unwilling to sell if they suspect that uninformed traders will continue to push prices up, or if they lack confidence in their abilities to estimate values well.

Eventually prices rise to a level that causes sellers to start trading ag-

▶ You Believe You Are Right, but . . . (Confidence Is Everything)

Even when value traders believe that prices greatly differ from fundamental values, they may lack the confidence to trade on their opinions. Trading against the majority opinion requires great courage. Since markets generally aggregate information from diverse sources extremely well, value traders must always wonder why they believe they understand values better than everyone else does. Value traders will not trade unless they are confident they are right, even after considering that the majority of traders think otherwise.

Value trading is especially difficult when unresolved uncertainties make it impossible for anyone to estimate values well. In that case, value traders will not trade until price is far from their estimates of value. This observation explains why bubbles often form in the stock prices of companies that hope to profit from highly promising, but unproven, technologies. ◀

gressively. The sellers may be long-term holders, early buyers who want to realize their gains, contrarians, value traders, or arbitrageurs. Once their selling causes prices to fall, momentum buyers lose their interest. Overly optimistic buyers lose their confidence, and sellers become more confident. Late buyers especially worry about their positions, and often start selling to stop their losses. Traders who financed their positions on margin may have to sell their positions to satisfy margin calls from their brokers. Other long holders who have placed stop loss orders also will start to sell. Order anticipators may anticipate these margin calls and stop orders, and sell before them. A crash occurs when the combined effect of all their selling causes prices to fall quickly.

The uncertainty associated with crashes, and the great demands for liquidity that panicked sellers make during crashes, can cause prices to drop below fundamental values. A bounce back in price therefore follows many crashes when traders recognize that the market overreacted. Traders call this bounce a *dead cat bounce*, for reasons that you can speculate on privately.

28.1.2 Fundamental and Transitory Volatility

Bubbles and crashes—like all price changes—may be due to fundamental or transitory factors. Unexpected information about fundamental values causes fundamental volatility. The demands for liquidity by uninformed traders cause transitory volatility. Most bubbles and crashes involve both types.

The two volatility types have different effects on prices. Fundamental price changes have a permanent effect in the sense that subsequent price changes are unrelated to previous price changes. Transitory price changes tend to reverse when value traders and arbitrageurs act on the differences between prices and fundamental values.

Bubbles generally start when prices rise on good news about fundamental values. These initial price changes contribute to fundamental volatility. Pseudo-informed traders then overreact to the news and to the resulting price increases. They eventually cause prices to exceed values. This portion of the bubble contributes to transitory volatility.

Bubbles often burst when traders react to bad fundamental news that causes prices to fall. The combination of bad news and falling prices shakes trader confidence and becomes a focal point for rational thought. As traders start thinking more carefully about values, many conclude that prices are

▶ You Know You Are Right, but . . . (Timing Is Everything)

Consider the trade timing decisions that value traders must make when they believe that prices are too high.

If they initially have long positions, and they sell them too soon, they will lose the opportunity to sell at higher prices as uninformed traders cause prices to continue to rise.

If they initially have no positions, and they sell short too soon, they initially will lose on their short positions. If they cannot finance their losses, their brokers will force them to buy to cover their losses, and they will lose the opportunity to profit when prices fall.

If value traders wait too long to sell, they will lose the opportunity to profit. Other value traders will enter and push prices down, early buyers will try to realize their gains, or the flow of uninformed traders necessary to maintain the bubble may end. ◀

▶ The News Just Wasn't Good Enough

In 1999 and 2000, the prices of many Internet companies fell after they reported record earnings. These earnings announcements caused traders to think carefully about values. Prices crashed because these companies could not produce the extremely high earnings growth necessary to sustain overly optimistic price expectations. ◀

too high, and sell. The resulting volumes and decreases in price are vastly disproportionate to the volumes and price changes that we would normally have expected in response to the news. The extreme response is due to the initial overpricing rather than to overreaction to the news. The bad fundamental news merely triggers the crash. The true causes of the crash lie in the bubble that preceded it. Although these events move prices toward their fundamental values, this reversion in prices contributes to transitory volatility. It occurs only because uninformed traders caused prices to rise during the bubble.

Panicked sellers sometimes cause prices to drop below fundamental value at the end of a crash. These price overreactions, and the price reversals that follow them, create additional transitory volatility.

28.2 SOME BUBBLE AND CRASH EXAMPLES

This section describes several bubbles and crashes to illustrate how bubbles and crashes occur. I selected these events because they involve important market microstructure issues.

Traders and regulators are very familiar with the most important of these examples. If you intend to work in the markets, you should be as well. The seven events that we discuss here do not include all important examples of bubbles and crashes. You may wish to consult other sources to learn about the Dutch tulip bulb mania and crash of 1637, the British South Sea Company bubble and crash of 1720, and many similar events of great interest to economic historians.

As you read through these stories, consider the role that investor sentiment played in these bubbles and crashes. In most cases, you will find that sentiment was a more important cause of these events than any issue involving market structure. The public, however, often demands changes in market structure following crashes. We discuss regulatory proposals to deal with crashes in the following section.

28.2.1 The 1929 Stock Market Crash

On October 28–29, 1929, the U.S. stock markets crashed in what may be the most famous stock market crash of all times. The Dow Jones Industrial Average (DJIA) dropped 13 percent on October 28 and another 12 percent on October 29. Although it rose 12 percent on October 30 and 3 percent more on October 31, the market continued to drop substantially over the next several weeks, months, and years. Figure 28-1 shows that by July 8, 1932, the DJIA had dropped to only 11 percent of its previous maximum closing value, reached on September 7, 1929.

This crash followed tremendous growth in prices in the late 1920s. The DJIA steadily rose by almost 300 percent from the beginning of 1924 to the September 1929 peak. Following the crash, the DJIA did not make a new high until more than 25 years later, in November 1954.

Many commentators attribute the bubble that preceded the 1929 crash to uninformed speculators who borrowed excessively to buy stocks. Traders were very excited by the prospects of new technology and media companies that were developing radio. In hindsight, traders clearly overvalued these stocks. For example, RCA—which proved to be one of the strongest radio stocks—did not rise to a new high until 34 years after the crash.

FIGURE 28-1.
Dow Jones Industrial Average, 1900–1950
Source: Dow Jones and Co., at www.djindexes.com.

The crash partly occurred because traders needed to sell stock to satisfy margin calls following the decline in stock prices over the previous month. Much selling undoubtedly also was due to value traders who sold the market short, and to speculators who anticipated the sell orders that the margin calls would create.

Panicked sellers also caused prices to drop. Although panicked traders generally do not make good decisions, in hindsight, those who sold in the crash were quite lucky. Had they held their positions, they would have lost even more money in the next months and years. We shall shortly see that the same was not true in the 1987 stock market crash.

In response to concerns about excessive speculation on margin, the U.S. Congress gave the Federal Reserve Board authority to regulate the margins upon which speculators could buy stock. (The authority appears in the Securities Exchange Act of 1934.) The Fed immediately set stock loan margins at 45 percent, so that speculators had to have at least 45 cents of equity for every dollar of stock they purchased.

The 1929 stock market crash preceded the Great Depression of the 1930s. Many people associate the two events and believe that the crash caused the Great Depression. Few economists believe this, however. The Great Depression was more likely caused by excessively tight monetary policy that led to widespread banking failures from late 1930 through early 1931, and again in 1933. Most economists also believe that spending cuts the government made in 1937 further extended the Great Depression.

28.2.2 The October 1987 Stock Market Crash

The U.S. stock markets crashed most dramatically in October 1987. (See figure 28-2.) The DJIA lost 23 percent on Monday, October 19. This loss was—and remains—its largest daily percentage loss. The loss followed a 5 percent loss on the previous Friday, a cumulative loss of 9 percent in the previous week, and a cumulative 17 percent loss from its previous all-time high, achieved on August 25.

▶ **Market Failures or Market Corrections?**

Analysts generally cannot attribute the large price changes that occur in broad-based market crashes to unexpected bad fundamental news of commensurate importance. Many people therefore believe that crashes demonstrate that markets do not produce informative prices. When they see prices change substantially on seemingly trivial information, they conclude that crashes represent market failures.

Most crashes, however, more likely represent corrections to previous pricing errors rather than market failures. They generally bring prices closer to fundamental values rather than move prices further from them.

Evidence for this conclusion lies in the behavior of prices following crashes. If crashes represented market failures, prices would generally rebound completely when traders discovered that prices were below values. In fact, prices generally rebound little following most crashes. Most crashes therefore more likely correct previous problems than create new ones. ◀

Portfolio Insurance or Portfolio Manager Insurance?

In principle, portfolio managers use portfolio insurance to protect their investment sponsors from losses that would result if the values of their portfolios drop below the values of the liabilities that the sponsors must fund. These liabilities typically are future pension benefits. In this application, the target guaranteed minimum portfolio value—the strike price of the put—should be the value of the liabilities that the sponsor must fund. Since these liabilities do not change much over time, neither should the target guaranteed minimum portfolio value.

In practice, portfolio insurers often increased the put strike price as the market value of their portfolios increased. This practice caused many people to refer to portfolio insurance as "portfolio manager insurance" because managers—and their sponsors—appeared to be locking in past successes rather than insuring against future shortfalls. The unfortunate consequence of these strike price increases was that portfolio managers would have to sell more when the market dropped than they would have needed to sell had they not ratcheted up the strike prices.

FIGURE 28-2.
Dow Jones Industrial Average, 1980–1992
Source: Dow Jones and Co., at www.djindexes.com.

These losses followed a substantial price increase. From the beginning of 1987 through August 25, the Dow rose 44 percent.

The market recovered quite quickly. The Dow rose 2 percent and 10 percent, respectively, on October 20 and 21. Although the market experienced many violent swings up and down over the next couple of months, it quickly resumed its previous growth. The Dow achieved a new all-time closing high less than two years later, on August 24, 1989. Remarkably, the Dow rose 2 percent in 1987 despite the crash.

The 1987 stock market crash was a very complex event with many causes. The most notable cause of the crash was the use of portfolio insurance by institutional investors. *Portfolio insurance* is a dynamic trading strategy that portfolio managers use to replicate the combined returns of a portfolio plus a put option. When correctly and successfully implemented, the strategy ensures that the total value of the portfolio will not fall below a value that the manager specifies. The specified value corresponds to the strike price of the dynamically replicated put option.

The strategy depends upon a formula that tells managers how much they should buy or sell given changes in the value of the portfolio. The formula, which comes from the Black-Scholes option-pricing model, depends on the volatility of the portfolio, the period over which the managers wish to protect the portfolio, and the minimum value that they wish to guarantee. Since managers must trade whenever prices change, the strategy is a *dynamic trading strategy*.

Portfolio insurance is highly destabilizing to market prices. When prices rise, portfolio insurers must buy stock. When prices fall, they must sell stock. Portfolio insurance therefore has the same effect on the market as stop orders. Indeed, many portfolio managers implemented their strategies using stop orders.

Portfolio insurance can work well when the total money covered by the strategy is small. Portfolio insurers then can execute their orders without much price impact. Great problems arise, however, when managers try to insure a significant fraction of the market. When sellers want to sell large quantities at the same time, prices can fall very substantially. Moreover, when everyone knows that large sellers will come onto the market when prices fall, order anticipators will quickly sell at the first sign of a price drop. Likewise, buyers will withdraw from the market until prices have dropped substantially. Expectations about portfolio insurance selling therefore can drive the market down, even if no portfolio insurance selling occurs.

Many commentators believe that unrealistic expectations about how well the portfolio insurance strategy would perform caused the crash. By October 1987, portfolio insurance had become very popular. A rough calculation—presented in the box below—suggests that portfolio insurers would need to sell 10 million shares for every 1 percent drop in the market. This potential sell order volume is very large compared to the then current daily average volume of only 160 million shares. It is especially large because it represents money that managers would completely take out of the market rather than simply reallocate among other stocks. Many people wondered who would buy that equity risk.

Many traders were aware of the portfolio insurance problem. Several academics had written widely circulated papers about the problem, and it was a major topic of discussion at several practitioner conferences. Unfortunately, everyone was uncertain about how much money managers devoted to the strategy. This uncertainty undoubtedly contributed to the crash because nobody would want to buy before he or she believed that all sellers were either satisfied or discouraged.

The uncertainty would not have been so severe had portfolio insurers bought exchange-listed put option contracts instead of trying to replicate put options with dynamic trading strategies. Had they used contracts, everyone would have known the total open interest in the contracts. Traders therefore could have better estimated how much risk would be transferred when prices fell.

The 9 percent decline in prices in the week leading up to the crash, and especially the 5 percent decline on Friday before the crash, undoubtedly suggested to many traders that the markets faced great downside risk. Not surprisingly, the market fell hard when it opened on Monday, October 19. (See figure 28-3.)

The price declines before the crash may have been due to bad news about economic fundamentals. Traders were concerned about the trade deficit, trade tensions with Germany, international interest rates, the value of the dollar, and anti-takeover legislation pending in Congress. Moreover, just before the market opened on October 19, the United States announced that it had attacked Iranian oil platforms in the Persian Gulf. Although each of these stories should have decreased fundamental values, even when taken together, they were not so significant or so surprising that they could have reasonably accounted for the 36 percent drop in the Dow from its August 25 high to its October 19 close.

Several factors besides portfolio insurance selling probably contributed to the crash. First, prices may have been above fundamental values before the crash. Managers who believed that portfolio insurance protected them from significant loss may have switched their asset allocations from bonds to stocks in the months before the crash. The pressure of their purchases

The Overhang of Portfolio Insurance on the Market

The total U.S. stock market capitalization before the 1987 stock market crash was about 2 trillion dollars. Institutional management controlled about 50 percent of this total. About 10 percent of these institutional funds were subject to portfolio insurance strategies. These figures imply that about 100 billion dollars was subject to portfolio insurance.

The delta of an option indicates how much the value of the option will change when the value of the underlying instrument changes. The typical option delta for portfolio insurance was probably about 0.4, so that a 1 percent drop in the market would require that managers sell 0.4 percent of their portfolios. At an approximate average price of 40 dollars per share, 0.4 percent of 100 billion dollars represents 10 million shares. ◄

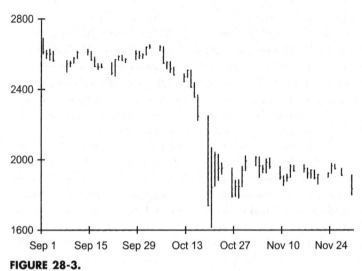

FIGURE 28-3.
Dow Jones Industrial Average, September–November 1987
Source: Bridge Information Systems.

may have created a small bubble as prices quickly rose in the first three quarters of 1987.

Second, the huge volumes that traders wanted to trade during the crash exceeded the trade processing capacity of the New York Stock Exchange and its floor traders. The most significant capacity problem involved dot matrix printers on the floor that printed orders which traders sent to the Exchange through the SuperDot order-routing system. During the crash, these printers could not print orders as fast as they arrived, which created an order backlog in the Exchange computer print queues. Breakdowns of several printers further compounded the problem. Consequently, many SuperDot orders had to wait more than an hour until they could be printed and executed. The traders who submitted them had no idea whether their orders were filled. Many undoubtedly telephoned sell orders to their floor brokers when they could not confirm that they had sold via SuperDot. The uncertainty associated with the capacity problem surely contributed to feelings of panic that many traders experienced.

Third, traders may have panicked as they watched the index futures market lead the stock market down. In normal trading, the index futures market generally leads the stock market because the futures market employs a faster trading system than the stock market. It also leads because index futures traders are interested only in finding the price of index risk. In contrast, the cash stock market consists of thousands of markets for individual stocks in which most traders are more concerned about firm-specific risk than index risk. When prices started to drop, they dropped first in the index futures market. Traders who saw those decreases in price knew that prices in the stock market would soon drop.

When capacity problems slowed the stock market, the spread between the cash index and the futures contract widened to unprecedented levels as the futures dropped faster than the stocks. The two markets, which generally follow each other very closely, became *disconnected*. Before the October

▶ Where's the Price?

The markets almost never give away anything for free. When traders want to buy an option contract, they must pay a premium to the seller. When traders want to replicate an otherwise identical option with a dynamic trading strategy, they likewise must incur some cost. Otherwise, no well-schooled trader would ever buy option contracts.

Unfortunately, traders can neither observe nor easily estimate the price of a dynamically created option. Dynamic option replication is expensive because traders always buy or sell after the price changes that require them to trade. They therefore trade later than they wish they could. Understanding exactly why dynamic options replication is expensive requires high-level mathematics that most portfolio managers and investment sponsors do not know.

Option replication is also expensive due to the impact that traders have on price when they trade to replicate options. Traders frequently underestimate these costs. When transaction costs are high, options replication is very expensive.

Many traders who adopted portfolio insurance undoubtedly ignored or underestimated these costs of option replication. For such traders, portfolio insurance must have appeared to be a tremendous bargain that gave them unlimited upside potential with limited downside potential for little cost.

Few traders now use the portfolio insurance strategy. Now that they know the full cost of portfolio insurance, most traders choose not to buy it. ◀

19 close, the S&P 500 Index futures contract was trading at a discount of more than 10 percent to concurrent value of the cash index!

Index arbitrage normally would ensure that such a huge discount would never exist. Arbitrageurs, however, largely stopped trading because they could not obtain quick executions of their sell orders in the stock market. They would not trade because they had no idea whether their stock sales would trade at the high prices the market was currently indicating or at lower prices that they feared would prevail when their orders actually executed.

The huge discount of the futures to the cash market undoubtedly caused some traders to submit more sell orders to the stock market. The unprecedented discounts also confused many traders and thereby contributed to their panic.

Finally, many buy-side traders could not contact their Nasdaq dealers during the crash. Before the 1987 crash, most Nasdaq dealers took their orders over the phone. During the crash, many traders could not reach their dealers because the dealers were overwhelmed with client orders. Moreover, some dealers simply took their phones off the hook because they did not want to trade. The inability to contact the Nasdaq dealers while the market was falling also must have contributed to trader panic.

In summary, the 1987 stock market crash had many causes. Chief among them was the confusion that traders felt when confronted with uncertainty about risk. Traders were uncertain about portfolio insurance selling, their ability to execute their orders, and the meaning of the extremely large spread between the cash index and the index futures contract price. These uncertainties undoubtedly caused many panicked traders to order sales that they later wished they had not.

▶ Global Confusion

The 1987 stock market crash was a global event. Prices fell in almost every world market. In many cases, the percentage falls were greater than in the U.S. market.

This fact suggests that we cannot base any complete explanation for the 1987 crash only on U.S. factors. Either the crash had causes that affected all international markets, or some mechanism must have transmitted the volatility from the U.S. markets to other markets. Analysts have carefully examined this issue, but no clear picture has emerged. We do not all agree upon the causes of the 1987 global stock market crash.

Some analysts believe that common factors must have caused the crash throughout the world. Since the Asian and European markets crashed on Monday, October 19, before the U.S. markets opened, these analysts believe that the U.S. markets did not *transmit* their volatility to the foreign markets.

Analysts who believe that the causes of the crash lie in the U.S. markets suggest that the Asian and European markets may have crashed in anticipation of the U.S. market crash. As we noted above, over the weekend, many traders expected the Monday crash. Indeed, their expectations may have helped cause the crash.

All analysts agree on some relevant facts. First, the U.S. stock and product markets are extremely important because they are so large and because the United States engages in so much world trade. Fears that recession in the United States would cause recession in other countries were reasonable, and could account for the crashes in the other markets. Second, cross-border ownership closely links international stock markets. International investors often use the same trading strategies in many markets. They also may have satisfied margin calls that they received in one market by selling in another market. Third, prices in all stock markets are correlated because the capital market is an international market. Changes in the real rate of interest in one country ultimately will affect the real rate of interest in all other countries that have open economies. Although these facts cannot resolve the debate, they do suggest that U.S. factors could have been responsible for the global crash. ◀

28.2.3 The October 1989 Mini-Crash

On the afternoon of October 13, 1989, the U.S. stock markets dropped 7 percent. The abrupt drop occurred immediately after a consortium of banks announced at 2:54 P.M. that they would not finance a levered buy-out of UAL Corporation, the parent of United Airlines. UAL quickly fell, as did several other stocks that traders had identified as potential takeover targets. The index futures market also fell abruptly. As usual, the index futures market led the cash market down. This event became known as the *October 1989 Mini-Crash.*

A very quick recovery followed the Mini-Crash. Figure 28-4 shows that the market returned to normal within just a few weeks of the event.

The cause of this crash is hard to understand because it clearly seems linked to the bad news about UAL. The bad UAL news easily explains why that stock dropped. If traders assumed that the news indicated that takeover financing would become more difficult for other firms to obtain as well, the news may also explain why the stocks of other potential takeover targets fell. (Although with hindsight, we now know that the UAL failure did represent the end of the merger and levered buy-out wave that occurred in the

FIGURE 28-4.
Dow Jones Industrial Average, September–November 1989
Source: Bridge Information Systems.

1980s, it is not obvious that traders then knew this.) It is hard to understand, however, why the UAL news caused the broad market to fall.

Although no adequate explanation exists for this event, some intriguing information may help us understand what happened. Until the UAL information arrived, trading had been quite uneventful. By 2:30, many traders in the New York stock and index futures markets, and in the Chicago index futures markets, had left early to go home for the weekend. The warm Indian summer weather that both cities enjoyed that day undoubtedly influenced their decisions to leave early: Many traders probably were either consciously or subconsciously aware that they might not enjoy such good weather again until after the coming winter. The departure of many traders from the markets thus removed much liquidity. If no unusually large demands for liquidity had occurred, the day surely would have ended normally. The market dropped because the UAL news arrived when the market was not well prepared to handle the large demands for liquidity that sellers subsequently placed upon it.

The early departure of many traders, however, does not adequately explain why the whole market fell. One highly speculative explanation was rumored but never confirmed. Traders who recognized that the market would be vulnerable to a downside bluff may have deliberately caused the Mini-Crash. (Chapter 12 describes how bluffers can profit from manipulative trading strategies.) Under this scenario, these traders recognized that the market was weak, or they were waiting for some bad information that they thought other traders might misinterpret if it were associated with a large price fall. In either event, the conditions for a marketwide bluff were ideal: The market was unusually illiquid; the negative news about UAL grabbed everyone's attention; and traders undoubtedly were sensitive to volatility near the second anniversary of the October 1987 stock market crash. If a bluff did take place, the bluffers would most likely have executed the bluff by selling aggressively in the index futures pits.

▶ **No Quorum**

Following the 1987 stock market crash, the Chicago Mercantile Exchange adopted a rule to halt trading for an hour in its S&P 500 Index futures contract in the event of a large price change. The rule required that a quorum of the members of the S&P 500 Index Futures Price Limit Committee determine that the market was limit down. The members of the Committee are Exchange members who trade in the pit. Their primary responsibility is to report the time of the halt so that the Exchange can determine when trading should resume. The quorum was not necessary to stop trading because the rules prohibited trading at prices below the price limit.

When the market dropped on the afternoon of October 13, 1989, the CME could not quickly obtain a quorum of the Price Limit Committee. It was rumored that too many members had left the pit early to enjoy the late Indian summer afternoon. ◀

▶ An Appeal for the Truth

Since the statute of limitations on market manipulation expired a long time ago, someone may someday write a credible memoir in which he or she explains how he or she participated in a marketwide bluff on October 13, 1989. Of course, if no such bluff occurred, any such memoir would be fictional rather than autobiographical. ◀

The SEC and the CFTC did not cite any evidence of manipulation in the public reports of their investigations into the Mini-Crash. Any index futures sellers that they may have contacted undoubtedly explained that they sold because they recognized the implications of the UAL news. Unless these agencies could prove beyond a doubt that manipulation took place—an essentially impossible objective, given the UAL news and its potential implications—they could not have publicly acknowledged that they strongly suspected bluffing without severely shaking confidence in the markets. To date, no publicly available evidence has surfaced to suggest that there is any truth to this rumor.

28.2.4 The Palladium Cold Fusion Bubble

On March 23, 1989, electrochemists Martin Fleischmann and Stanley Pons announced that they had achieved cold fusion by supersaturating a palladium cathode with deuterium in an electrolytic cell. They claimed that the process produced excess energy at room temperatures. They also provided an intriguing conjecture as to why the process worked.

The announcement was extremely exciting. If the results were correct, the new process might very likely provide a clean, cheap, and inexhaustible source of energy.

Unfortunately, other researchers have not reliably replicated their results. Although some electrolytic cold fusion research continues to this day, most physicists do not believe that the research will ever lead to a reliable source of power. Intriguingly, some responsible physicists believe that electrolytic cold fusion experiments have revealed new physics.

The press widely reported the announcement by Fleischmann and Pons, as well as the skepticism of some high-energy physicists. A few days afterward, some enthusiastic traders started buying palladium futures contracts. They presumably concluded that the demand for palladium would increase

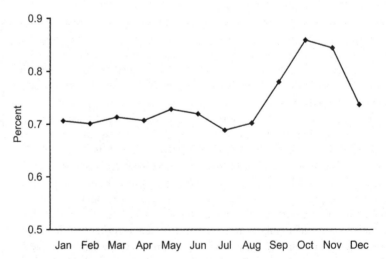

FIGURE 28-5.
Mean Absolute Daily Returns to the Dow Jones Industrial Average, by Calendar Month, 1901–2000

Source: Author's calculations, using index data from Dow Jones and Co. at www.djindexes.com.

▶ Why October?

October has been one of the most volatile months of the year in the U.S. stock markets. The 1929 and 1987 stock market crashes, as well as the 1989 Mini-Crash, took place in October. More recently, October 1997 was quite volatile as well. Four Octobers (1929, 1931, 1932, and 1987) appear in the list of the 10 most volatile months of the twentieth century. Why are Octobers so volatile?

If you are a probabilist, you might want to consider whether volatile Octobers are simply coincidental. If we assume that three extreme events occur at random among the 1,200 months in a century, the probability that they all would occur in the same calendar month (not necessarily October) is only 0.68 percent.[1] The probability that any month would be represented—at random—four or more times in the top 10 list of volatile months is less than 8 percent. It is not likely that these events happened only by chance.

If you are a social historian, you might explain that history repeats itself. Perhaps traders are more likely to reflect on valuations in months when history reminds them that they may be at risk. The first extreme event could have taken place in any calendar month. Subsequent extreme events may have occurred in the same calendar month because the anniversary of the first event served as a psychological focal point for traders. The high volatility that markets experienced in October 1997—the ten-year anniversary of the 1987 crash—is consistent with this theory.

If you are a political scientist, you might note that October is the month when the government gets down to business after its summer recess. The government often intervenes in the economy, and these interventions often have strong implications for stock values.

If you are a psychiatrist or an evolutionary biologist, you might note that people most notice the end of summer and the approach of winter in October, when changes in the weather and in the total hours of daylight are most obvious. The darkness and thoughts of the coming winter depress many people and make them more risk averse. These influences may cause prices to fall in October. (The change from daylight savings time to standard time may also be important.) Although this theory predicts that prices in southern hemisphere markets should be most volatile in April, the strong correlation between price changes in southern and northern hemisphere markets—due in part to share ownership of southern hemisphere companies by northern hemisphere investors—probably would make tests of this prediction inconclusive.

The last two theories suggest that other fall months should also be volatile. Figure 28-5 shows that they indeed have been. ◀

Source: Author's calculations using index data from Dow Jones and Co. at www.djin-dexes.com.

1. If you are indeed a probabilist, you may appreciate the derivation of this probability: The total number of different ways to choose three of 1,200 months is

$$\binom{1200}{3} = \frac{1200!}{1197!\ 3!} = \frac{1200 \times 1199 \times 1198}{6}.$$

Likewise, the total number of ways to choose three years from 100 years of a given calendar month is $\binom{100}{3}$. Finally, any one of the 12 calendar months could be the given calendar month. The probability that three events occur in the same calendar month at random in a century is therefore

$$12 \times \binom{100}{3} \bigg/ \binom{1200}{3} \approx 0.0068.$$

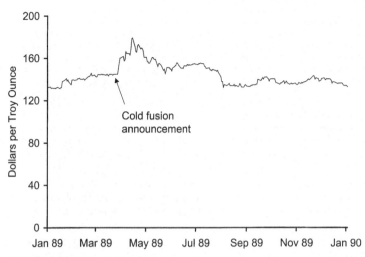

FIGURE 28-6.
London Daily Palladium Price Fixings, 1989
Source: DataStream.

substantially if other researchers confirmed the results. The price of palladium quickly spiked upward by 24 percent over the next three weeks. On several days, the futures contract closed up the daily price limit of 6 dollars. Figure 28-6 shows that the price fell back as laboratories throughout the world announced that they were unable to replicate the results.

Although the palladium bubble appears to be an example of transitory volatility, it is better classified as an unusual example of fundamental volatility. The traders who bought palladium probably formed rational expectations about the future value of the metal, given all available information. Although they were not physicists, they knew that many physicists were skeptical about the results. They also knew, however, that if the results proved true, palladium might become many times more valuable. With hindsight, we know that these speculators were wrong. However, given the information people had at the time, their trading decisions seemed quite sensible. The palladium bubble therefore was an example of unexpected extreme good fundamental news followed by a stream of bad fundamental news that ultimately resolved uncertainty about the discovery.

28.2.5 The Iomega Bubble and Crash

Iomega is a removable media computer disk drive manufacturer. Its best-known product—the Zip drive—uses disks just slightly larger than standard $3^1/_2$-inch floppy disks to store almost 70 times as much data. Soon after Iomega introduced the Zip drive, many people became wildly excited about prospects for its stock. They expected that the Zip drive would replace floppy disk drives in all new computers.

In early 1996, eager buyers pushed Iomega's stock price up to an intraday high of $55^1/_8$ dollars per share. (See figure 28-7.) At that price, the price to earnings ratio for the stock, based on Iomega's 1995 earnings, was almost 1,000. Buyers clearly expected phenomenal earnings growth. Such extreme growth, however, never materialized. In its best year, the company earned only 1.26 dollars per split-adjusted share. (The company's earnings and share

> ▶ **Great Companies and Great Investments**
>
> The traders who bought Iomega at prices substantially above values made one of the most common investing mistakes. They mistook a great company for a great investment. In 1996, Iomega produced excellent products that served extremely large markets. The firm, however, was a poor investment then because it was overpriced.
>
> A good company is a good investment only if the price is not too high. A poor company can be a great investment if the price is low enough—assuming, of course, that the prospects of the company are not so bad that the company has no value at all. ◀

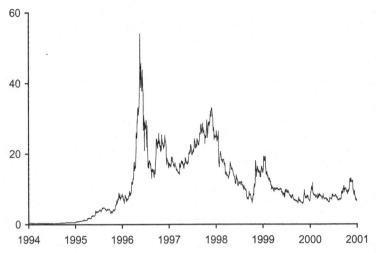

FIGURE 28-7.
Iomega Split-adjusted Closing Share Prices, 1994–2001
Iomega's all-time high closing price occurred on May 23, 1996, three days after the stock split 2 for 1. The stock also split 2 for 1 on December 23, 1997, 3 for 1 on February 1, 1996, and 5 for 4 on November 25, 1994. I adjusted earlier and later prices in this plot for these splits so that you can compare them to the May 23 high.
Source: Center for Research in Security Prices.

price crashed in 2001 when its removable media drives experienced withering competition from cheap CD and DVD optical drives that can record and rewrite on much less expensive media.) Perhaps the most convincing measure of the bubble appears in the following comparison: At its peak, the entire value of Iomega stock was worth more than 10 percent of the entire value of IBM stock! Not surprisingly, Iomega's stock price crashed.

28.2.6 The Nasdaq Bubble

The Nasdaq bubble (figure 28-8) was in many ways similar to the bubble that preceded the 1929 stock market crash. Traders who were excessively optimistic about prospects for new technology companies caused both bubbles. In the Nasdaq case, these were companies primarily in the Internet, telecommunications, computer, and biotechnology sectors. Momentum traders who wanted to participate in the gains made by their friends and acquaintances also fueled both bubbles.

The Nasdaq bubble was fueled in part by many momentum investors who placed money in largely undiversified mutual funds that had performed well in the recent past. These funds often invested the avalanche of new money that they received in the same stocks that they held. The new money pushed up the prices of their holdings, which ensured that the funds would continue to produce high returns. The high returns led to more inflows of new money. The small fraction of shares available to public investors in many of the technology companies exacerbated the phenomenon. In the end, of course, many investors learned the hard way that past performance is a poor predictor of future returns.

To some extent, a new faith taught to investors by investment advisers (and by some academics) also contributed to the Nasdaq bubble. These

FIGURE 28-8.
Nasdaq Composite Index, 1991–2002
Source: Bridge Information Systems.

▶ You Should Live So Long!

It is impossible to say now whether Nasdaq stock returns will eventually catch up with bond returns. Investors who bought the Nasdaq market near its 5132.52 peak on March 10, 2001, undoubtedly will have to wait a long time until their investments catch up with the bond investments they otherwise might have made then. Let us hope that they will all live long enough to see it happen. Of course, they will not be waiting alone. Among others, investors who bought Japanese equities around December 1989 when the Nikkei 225 Stock Average was near its peak of 38,916 (see figure 28-9) will keep them company.

Once again, many investors learned the hard way that past performance is a poor predictor of future returns. ◀

advisers told long-term investors not to worry about equity market risk because, over the long run, stocks have always beat investments in all other broad asset classes. Many investors were emboldened by the idea that they could not lose if they waited long enough.

Interestingly, the empirical results upon which the equity faith is based come primarily from the U.S. markets. Stocks in many other markets have not performed as well as comparable alternative investments.

A final factor worth noting involves new traders who traded over the Internet. Giving orders to brokers by phone intimidates many people. Many people are afraid that their brokers will judge them for the trading decisions they make, for their inability to properly articulate their desires, or for taking too long on the telephone. Even though their brokers may forever be strangers to them, the fear of trading with a judgmental broker undoubtedly inhibited many uninformed traders. The advent of Internet trading allowed many of these timid traders to access the market at their leisure, without worrying about what others would think of them. Widespread Internet-based trading therefore probably brought many new uninformed traders into the market. The money these traders put into the market probably contributed to the Nasdaq bubble.

28.2.7 The Japanese Asset Bubble

Japanese equity and Japanese real estate markets experienced a large bubble that peaked in the end of 1989. Figure 28-9 shows that the equity markets fell to a fraction of their peak levels and have not recovered. The real estate markets likewise have not recovered.

Like all bubbles, the Japanese asset bubble had many causes. Investors both in Japan and in the rest of the world were extremely confident in the Japanese economy. In the late 1980s, Japanese companies were widely cited as examples of efficiency and productivity. Many people undoubtedly invested in Japan to participate in what was then known as the Japanese economic miracle.

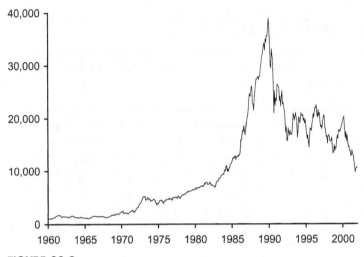

FIGURE 28-9.
Nikkei 225 Stock Average, 1960–2000
Source: Bridge Information Systems.

Japanese monetary policy probably contributed to the bubble. Interest rates in the mid- and late 1980s were extremely low, and the money supply grew very quickly. Many commentators said that there was simply too much money in Japan. Since Japanese investors—both individual and institutional—historically have not placed much of their money abroad, they invested the excess money locally. This money pushed up equity and real estate prices.

Although it is interesting to speculate on why Japanese monetary policy was so loose, doing so is beyond the scope of this book. The answer undoubtedly lies in the complex relationships among Japanese firms, banks, monetary authorities, and political parties.

28.2.8 Summary

Market crashes are like automobile and airplane crashes. In both cases, crashes usually do not occur for a single simple reason. Instead, a number of factors cause people to become confused about what is happening. Their confusion becomes most dangerous when they are uncertain about risk. They then pay attention to the wrong issues, they ignore important risks, and, if things happen too quickly, they panic and lose their ability to make good decisions. In all types of crashes, the survivors rarely make the same mistakes again. When crashes reoccur, it is often because new participants have failed to learn lessons learned by others.

The examples in this section show that most major market crashes are not short-term transitory trading problems. More often, the conditions that led to the crash started creating a bubble long before the crash occurred. Crashes more often represent a final restoration of rational pricing rather than a transitory problem in need of correction.

Regardless of these observations, political passion for change is often quite high following some crashes. Many people demand that regulators do something to prevent future occurrences. We next consider public policy responses to extreme volatility.

28.3 REGULATORY RESPONSES TO EXTREME VOLATILITY

Policy makers have responded to extreme volatility primarily by proposing circuit breakers to restrain traders. *Circuit breakers* are trading rules that limit trading activity:

- *Trading halts* stop trading when prices have moved, or will imminently move, by some specified amount. Trading may remain halted until the order imbalance is resolved or until some specified period passes.
- *Price limits* require all trade prices to be within a certain range on a given day. If traders are unwilling to negotiate prices within that range, trade stops until traders are willing to trade within the limits.
- *Transaction taxes* restrict trading by taxing it.
- *Margin requirements* and *position limits* restrict the size of positions that traders can accumulate.
- *Collars* restrict access to trading systems.

In this section, we consider how these rules may affect volatility, liquidity, and price efficiency. We shall see that some of these proposals are economically sensible while others are quite controversial.

28.3.1 Trading Halts and Price Limits

Arguments in Favor

Proponents of trading halts and of price limits believe that these circuit breakers reduce short-term volatility by slowing price changes. Whether this is desirable depends on the cause of the volatility.

If new fundamental information causes the volatility, the halt will merely postpone the inevitable. While the markets are closed, prices will be less informative, and no one will be certain of the new price levels. Worse, the uncertainty associated with the halt may cause uninformed traders to panic, which may generate unnecessary transitory volatility when the market reopens. On the other hand, if uninformed traders panic when price is moving quickly, the trading halt may cut them off before they can act.

If an order imbalance originating among uninformed traders causes the volatility, a trading halt that stops their trading may be beneficial. The benefits come from protecting the market from their volatility-inducing trades and from protecting uninformed traders from trading losses that they can incur in poorly functioning markets.

Trading halts also can give informed traders an opportunity to enter and provide liquidity. Traders who are willing to supply liquidity may not be able to do so if the market is moving quickly and they are not paying attention. Markets therefore may attenuate volatility by halting trading to publicize order imbalances.

A trading halt rule may make order-driven markets more liquid by switching the trade pricing rule from the discriminatory pricing rule used in continuous trading to the uniform pricing rule used in the single price auctions that resume trading. In a continuous auction, standing limit orders typically trade at their limit prices. When price is dropping quickly, buyers with standing limit orders suffer immediate losses when their orders execute and prices continue to fall. A trade halt can prevent these losses by

▶ Coordinated Trading Halt Rules

Following the 1987 stock market crash, U.S. stock and index futures exchanges adopted a set of coordinated trading halt rules. These rules halt trading for various periods, based on how much the market has dropped and when it has dropped. The New York Stock Exchange version of this rule is known as Rule 80B.

The current version of these rules calls for a Level 1 halt if the Dow Jones Industrial Average drops by more than approximately 10 percent from its closing value on the previous day. In that case, the markets will halt for one hour if the event occurs before 2:30 P.M., and for half an hour if the event occurs after 2:30 P.M. but before 3:30 P.M. If the event occurs after 3:30, and there is no Level 2 halt, the market will not halt.

A Level 2 halt will occur if the DJIA drops by more than 20 percent from its previous closing value. In that case, the markets will halt for two hours if the drop occurs before 1 P.M. and for one hour if it occurs between 1 P.M. and 2 P.M. If the 20 percent drop occurs after 2 P.M. and there is no Level 3 halt, the market will not halt.

A Level 3 halt will close trading for the rest of the day at any time the Dow drops by more than 30 percent from its previous closing value.

These coordinated trading halt rules have halted trading only once. On October 27, 1997, the DJIA had dropped 350 points, or 4.5 percent, by 2:35 P.M. The then current version of these rules halted trading for 30 minutes. When trading resumed, the DJIA dropped 200 more points by 3:30 P.M., which halted trading for the day. Many people felt that these halts occurred too quickly. The various exchanges therefore amended their coordinated halt rules in early 1998 to provide for halts at 10, 20, and 30 percent thresholds, as described above. ◀

Source: NYSE Rule 80B at www.nyse.com/pdfs/lm9815.pdf.

---

forcing the market to clear at a single price when it resumes trading. All limit order buyers who participate in the single price auction receive the same price, regardless of their limit order prices. When protected by an effective trading halt rule, limit order traders therefore may be more willing to offer liquidity under normal circumstances. A trading halt rule therefore can decrease transitory volatility by encouraging traders to offer more liquidity.

Finally, a trading halt rule may decrease transitory volatility by allowing traders greater time to respond to intraday margin calls and to remove stop loss orders. When traders are unable to satisfy their margin calls, brokers will trade to stop their losses. Since stop loss orders further imbalance an uninformed order flow, a halt that reduces their numbers may reduce transitory volatility.

Arguments Against

Opponents of trading halts and price limits offer two arguments that suggest these circuit breakers may actually increase transitory volatility. First, if traders fear that a halt will occur before they can submit their orders, they may submit their orders earlier to increase the probability that they execute. Greater volatility therefore will result as the price limit attracts orders from rationally fearful traders. Economists and traders call this effect the *gravitational effect*.

▶ **Am I Bankrupt?**

Suppose that Spencer has a 1 million-dollar long futures position for which he posted a 100,000-dollar margin. For convenience, assume that the contract is denominated so that each point in price is worth 10,000 dollars to Spencer. Spencer has 100,000 dollars in other assets in addition to his margin. He therefore knows that he will be bankrupt if the price drops by 20 points.

If the futures price were to drop immediately by 25 points, he should lose everything. In practice, he would immediately lose only his 100,000-dollar margin. His broker would then try to collect the additional 150,000 dollars. Although Spencer would be able to pay 100,000 dollars, he probably would be reluctant to pay his broker anything. The broker might be able to collect Spencer's debt only at great expense. If Spencer can hide his remaining wealth, the broker might not even collect Spencer's remaining 100,000 dollars. In that case, the broker would lose 150,000 dollars plus collection expenses.

Now suppose instead that the futures exchange limits the price drop to five points per day. On the first day, the contract would close limit down five points. Spencer's broker would collect 50,000 dollars from Spencer's 100,000-dollar margin. He also would ask Spencer to post an additional 50,000 dollars to cover his losses. If Spencer does not realize that the total drop will ultimately be 25 points, he might voluntarily post the margin.

The next day, the contract would again close limit down five points. Spencer's broker would again ask him to post additional margin to cover his losses. If Spencer still does not realize that the price will ultimately drop 15 more points, he might make the margin call with his last 50,000 dollars and hope that price rebounds when trading resumes.

On the third, fourth, and fifth days, the contract would again drop by the limit. Spencer's broker would ask for more margin, but Spencer would not be able to cover his losses. The broker would then deduct the third- and fourth-day losses from the 100,000-dollar margin. Since Spencer could not meet the margin calls, the broker would close the position when the market restarted, trading 25 points down. Spencer then would owe the broker 50,000 dollars that he does not have. ◀

If the gravitational effect is strong, a discretionary halt procedure may be better than a price triggered trading halt rule because the former is less predictable. For example, the New York Stock Exchange allows floor officials to halt trading if, in their opinion, trading would otherwise become disorderly. They usually do this when an order imbalance exists or when they know that a company will soon release material information. Since off-floor traders generally cannot predict when floor officials will halt trading, this discretionary trading halt rule has little gravitational effect.

Second, value traders may reduce their surveillance of the market if they know that the media will notify them when a trading halt occurs. If so, a trading halt rule would make the market less liquid between trading halts. Transitory volatility would increase and more trading halts would occur.

Other Issues

When several markets trade essentially the same risk, the imposition of a trading halt or a price limit on one market will have consequences for the other markets. In particular, when only one market halts trading, traders will divert order flow to other markets. If circuit breakers are desirable, exchanges should coordinate their regulations. Otherwise, uncoordinated circuit breakers may increase volatility by forcing traders to resolve all excess demands for liquidity in a single market.

Trading halts and price limit rules also benefit the markets by making it easier for brokers and clearinghouses to collect margins. Traders who know that they are bankrupt generally do not make margin payments. Traders who are uncertain about being bankrupt may make margin payments to avoid losing their positions. Trading halts make it difficult for traders who are near bankruptcy to determine whether they are bankrupt because the halts prevent traders from knowing at what prices trading will ultimately resume. Markets that have trading halt rules therefore can have lower margin requirements.

28.3.2 Increased Margin Requirements and Transaction Taxes

Throughout history, many people have believed that excessive trading increases volatility. Some commentators therefore have proposed that regulators increase margins or impose transaction taxes to reduce trading in stocks, futures, and options.

Margins and transaction taxes have related but slightly different effects on trading. Large margins decrease position sizes by increasing carrying costs and by preventing capital-constrained traders from acquiring large positions. Transaction taxes reduce trading by making it more expensive. Taxes penalize high frequency trading strategies more than buy and hold strategies.

To evaluate the merits of these proposals, we must review why people trade. Since people trade for many reasons, we must consider several types of traders.

Restrictions on informed traders would make prices less informative. News traders cause prices to reflect the latest fundamental news. Restrictions on their trading slow fundamental price changes. Value traders cause prices to move back toward fundamental values when uninformed traders push prices away. Since value traders ultimately offer liquidity to uninformed traders, and since they make markets resilient to the price impacts of uninformed traders, restrictions on their trading would increase transitory price volatility.

Dealers offer liquidity to other traders. Any measures that increase their transaction costs will decrease market liquidity and increase transitory volatility.

Order anticipators trade in front of other traders. When they front-run uninformed traders, they increase transitory volatility. When they front-run informed traders, they may make prices more informative in the short run. In the long run, however, the additional transaction costs that they impose upon informed traders are the same as a tax on informed trading. Measures that would decrease trading by order anticipators therefore would decrease transitory volatility and make prices more informative.

Bluffers manipulate prices to trick uninformed traders into offering liquidity foolishly. Since their price manipulations are not related to fundamental information, they contribute to transitory volatility. Regulations that increase their trading costs would decrease transitory volatility.

Utilitarian traders use markets to help them solve problems that they face. In particular, investors and borrowers use markets to move money through time, hedgers use them to exchange risks, and asset exchangers use them to obtain instruments that are of greater value to them than the instruments that they tender. Since utilitarian traders are uninformed traders, their trading generally increases transitory volatility. Restrictions on their trading therefore would decrease transitory volatility in the short run. Such restrictions would be highly undesirable, however, because they would obstruct utilitarian traders from solving important problems that they face. Since good solutions to their problems benefit the economy as a whole, restricting their trading would be foolish.

Gamblers trade for entertainment. Many gamblers, however, do not realize that they are gambling. Instead, they generally believe that they are well-informed traders. (If they traded successfully, they would indeed be well-informed traders.) In practice, gamblers usually trade on stale information that prices already reflect. Gamblers therefore increase transitory volatility. Measures that would discourage them from trading would decrease transitory volatility.

These discussions suggest that the markets would be best served if regulators could restrict trading by order anticipators, bluffers, and gamblers without unduly affecting trading by dealers, informed traders, and the utilitarian traders, for whom the markets ultimately exist. It is difficult, however, to imagine how regulators could design regulations that would effectively discriminate among these types of traders.

Taxes on trading fall more heavily on high frequency traders than on low frequency traders. Since most utilitarian trading problems do not require many trades to solve, a transaction tax would have less effect on utilitarian traders than on gamblers, bluffers, and order anticipators, who may trade frequently. A transaction tax, however, would fall disproportionately on dealers, who trade quite frequently. Although it might be possible to exempt dealers from a transaction tax, fair and meaningful regulatory distinctions between dealers and other high frequency traders can be difficult to establish.

Removing uninformed traders from markets may actually increase transitory volatility in the long run. Informed traders can profit only when uninformed traders trade and lose to them on average. Without these profits, informed traders would not invest in the research necessary to estimate values, and prices therefore would be less informative. In the long run, a decrease in the number of uninformed traders may actually increase transitory volatility by discouraging traders from doing the research necessary to identify fundamental values, and thereby discriminate between transitory volatility and fundamental volatility.

28.3.3 Trading Collars

Trading collars are rules that explicitly prevent traders from trading under certain conditions. The only significant trading collar of which I am aware is NYSE Rule 80A.

28.3.4 Circuit Breaker Summary

The theoretical effects of circuit breakers on volatility are mixed. We can confidently say that circuit breakers slow price changes associated with changes in fundamental information. Their effects on transitory volatility are less certain. They decrease transitory volatility when they restrain the trading of the traders who most contribute to it. These traders are typically uninformed traders, order anticipators, and bluffers. They increase transitory

▶ NYSE Rule 80A

NYSE Rule 80A prevents index arbitrageurs from using market orders to trade their index arbitrage program trades in S&P 500 Index stocks after the Dow Jones Industrial Average has moved up or down by approximately 2 percent. Instead, when the collar is in effect, arbitrageurs must use tick sensitive orders to trade S&P 500 stocks.

The primary effect of Rule 80A is to make index arbitrage more difficult and expensive when the collar is active. It probably increases transitory volatility because it forces the cash and futures markets to operate more independently. When arbitrage is unrestricted, arbitrageurs move liquidity from the market where it is in greatest demand to the market where it is in greatest supply. Their efforts reduce transitory volatility because order flow imbalances in the two markets sometimes cancel. When the collar restricts arbitrage, each market must separately satisfy demands for liquidity. The collar therefore discourages arbitrageurs who try to cross a buy order placed in one market with a sell order placed in another market.

In practice, index arbitrageurs can subvert the collar in several ways. They can submit their program trades through floor brokers, they can submit fewer than 15 orders through SuperDot to avoid classification as a program trade, and they can construct their hedge portfolios using stocks that are not in the S&P 500 Index. These methods all increase arbitrage costs and risks, but not appreciably so. The collar therefore probably does not have much effect on the markets.

Proponents of the collar argue that it decreases volatility at the NYSE by preventing the more volatile futures market from transmitting volatility to the cash market. Although this is undoubtedly true, the argument fails to distinguish between fundamental and transitory volatility. The futures market is more volatile than the cash market over short time intervals because it is better organized to discover fundamental index value quickly. Unlike cash market traders, futures traders are not concerned about price continuity or firm-specific risks in the markets for 500 securities. ◀

volatility when they restrain the trading of the traders whose trading normally limits transitory volatility. These traders include informed traders, dealers, and arbitrageurs. Since we do not know which effect is larger, the theoretical net effect of circuit breakers on transitory volatility is indeterminate.

Some circuit breakers may increase transitory volatility while others decrease it. For example, the NYSE Rule 80A collars probably slightly increase transitory volatility because they primarily restrict the trading of arbitrageurs while having almost no effect on uninformed traders. Conversely, trading halts may decrease transitory volatility because they primarily protect liquidity suppliers while frustrating uninformed traders.

Economists have conducted numerous empirical studies to determine what effect circuit breakers have on volatility. These studies generally have been inconclusive. Extreme volatility events have not occurred often enough for investigators to confidently evaluate how well circuit breakers perform.

28.3.5 Other Responses to Extreme Volatility

Regulators and market organizers have been quick to respond when excess volatility appears to have been related, at least in part, to deficiencies in trading systems. For example, following the 1987 stock market crash, the NYSE invested billions of dollars in its information infrastructure to ensure that it would not experience capacity problems again.

The Nasdaq market likewise improved the Small Order Execution System (SOES) to ensure that its dealers would always be available to handle orders. Before the 1987 crash, dealer participation in the SOES system was voluntary. The system therefore was not well used because dealers did not want to accept the trade liabilities it imposed upon them. Following the crash, Nasdaq made participation in SOES—now SuperSoes—mandatory. Nasdaq market makers who withdraw from SuperSoes in the middle of a trading day must wait 20 trading days until they can resume dealing in that stock.

Markets also have introduced new products in response to extreme volatility. The most notable of these have been various long-dated options that entrepreneurs created to meet the needs of portfolio insurers. These securities have not been very successful because portfolio managers apparently will not buy insurance when they can easily observe its high cost.

28.4 THE POLITICS OF REGULATORY INTERVENTION

The clamor for regulatory responses to crashes undoubtedly influences the policies that regulators ultimately adopt. When regulators and traders understand the political aspects of regulation well, better regulations probably result. This section therefore briefly discusses the political economy of regulation.

We consider two models of regulation. The first involves regulatory risk, and the second involves rent seeking. The first model helps us understand why regulators may regulate even when their regulations will produce little or no economic value. The second model helps us understand how regulated people and institutions can use the regulatory process for their private benefit. We illustrate these discussions with two regulations that came out of the 1987 stock market crash: New York Stock Exchange Rules 80A and 80B.

28.4.1 Regulatory Risk

Following the October 1987 stock market crash, the markets adopted a coordinated trading halt rule that was almost meaningless. At the time of its adoption, NYSE Rule 80B would halt trading only if the Dow dropped by more than 12 percent. Such a large drop had occurred only once in the life of the U.S. markets (during the October 1987 crash). Why did the markets adopt this mild trading halt rule?

In the days and weeks after the 1987 crash, many people demanded that regulators act to prevent future crashes. Fewer people considered whether regulators could prevent crashes or whether their efforts to do so would impose serious costs upon the market. In this environment, we can easily imagine that government and exchange regulators reasoned as follows:

- If we fail to adopt any circuit breakers and another crash occurs, the public will hold us responsible for failing to protect them, regardless of whether the circuit breakers would—or even could—have made a difference.

- If we fail to adopt any circuit breakers, and no crash occurs, we will have saved whatever costs the circuit breakers might impose upon the markets, but nobody will credit us with our wisdom.

TABLE 28-1.

Perceived Costs and Benefits to Regulators of Their Decision to Adopt Circuit Breakers

	REGULATORY ACTION	
SUBSEQUENT EVENTS	ADOPT CIRCUIT BREAKERS	DON'T ADOPT CIRCUIT BREAKERS
Another crash follows	No cost	High cost
No crash follows	Some benefit	No cost

- If we adopt circuit breakers and another crash occurs, people will learn that we cannot prevent crashes, but they will not blame us for not trying.
- If we adopt circuit breakers, and no crash occurs, people may credit us with preventing another crash, even if the circuit breakers are not effective. Although we will be responsible for imposing potentially costly and unnecessary restrictions on the market, people may not recognize these costs, and they probably will not attribute them to us.

Table 28-1 summarizes these costs and benefits. If regulators act to maximize their personal welfare, these costs and benefits imply that they would be better off adopting circuit breakers, whether or not another crash occurs.

Consider now the decision to adopt mild or severe circuit breakers. Mild circuit breakers are unlikely to change trading practices significantly, whereas severe circuit breakers will alter the character of trading. Regulators may have reasoned as follows:

- If we adopt mild circuit breakers and another crash follows, people may blame us for not acting more strongly. They may reserve their judgment, however, because many may conclude from the second crash that regulators cannot prevent crashes.
- If we adopt severe circuit breakers and another crash follows, most people will conclude that regulators cannot prevent crashes. Some, however, will claim that had the severe circuit breakers not been in place, the unconstrained market would have been able to handle the crisis. People may blame us for causing the crash.
- If we adopt mild circuit breakers, and no crash follows, we will have had little effect on the markets.
- If we adopt severe circuit breakers, and no crash follows, people will blame us for overreacting.

Table 28-2 summarizes these costs and benefits of the decision to adopt mild or severe circuit breakers. These assumptions imply that regulators would be better off if they adopt mild circuit breakers, whether or not another crash occurs.

The conclusions in these simple analyses obviously depend on the costs and benefits that I assumed. If you make other assumptions, you may obtain different conclusions, or you may be unable to obtain any conclusions without making additional assumptions about the probabilities of future crashes. These assumptions seem reasonable to me, but you may think otherwise.

▶ **Odd/Even Gas Rationing**

The imposition of odd/even gas rationing during the 1974 oil crisis is an extreme example of an ineffective regulatory action. Following the October 1973 war between Israel and most of its Arab neighbors, many Arab states embargoed exports of oil to the United States. The embargo would have raised gasoline prices in the United States if they had not been regulated. Instead, long lines formed at gas stations as consumers tried to purchase scarce gasoline.

Rather than raise the price of gas to ration it, the government imposed odd/even rationing. Motorists could buy gas only on odd-numbered days for cars with odd-numbered license plates and only on even-numbered days for cars with even-numbered license plates. This rationing scheme had little effect on gas lines because almost no drivers buy gas everyday. It did prevent panicked drivers from filling up every day, however. ◀

TABLE 28-2.

Perceived Costs and Benefits to Regulators of Their Decision to Adopt Mild or Severe Circuit Breakers

	REGULATORY ACTION	
SUBSEQUENT EVENTS	ADOPT MILD CIRCUIT BREAKERS	ADOPT SEVERE CIRCUIT BREAKERS
Another crash follows	Some cost	Possibly high cost
No crash follows	No cost	High cost

The conclusions are consistent with well-recognized regulatory behavior. Regulators often respond to crises with policies that have little or no actual impact. When the public demands action, regulators tend to act. However, when faced with uncertainty about the consequences of regulatory actions, regulators frequently do not act decisively. They do not want the public to blame them for exacerbating a problem or for creating new problems. When regulators do act decisively, they usually have a strong political mandate based on a clearly defined ideology or unambiguous empirical results. (Consider, for example, deregulation in the Reagan years or the ban on the birth defect-causing sedative Thalidomide.) No such mandate for extreme change followed the 1987 crash.

28.4.2 Regulatory Capture

The other circuit breaker adopted by the New York Stock Exchange following the 1987 stock market crash was the Rule 80A collar on index arbitrage program trading. Although a similar analysis of regulatory risks may explain why the Exchange adopted this rule, an analysis of rent-seeking behavior (self-interest) is more insightful.

Arbitrageurs compete with specialists to supply liquidity. Both traders move liquidity between buyers and sellers who are unable or unwilling to trade with each other. Arbitrageurs construct hedge portfolios to move liquidity from one market to another at one point in time. Specialists use their inventories to move liquidity from one point in time to another within their market. The two types of traders compete in the following sense: When either trader cannot act, the profit opportunities for the other are greater. Since Rule 80A restricts index arbitrage, it benefits specialists at the expense of arbitrageurs.

Specialists also benefit from Rule 80A because it helps them avoid trading with arbitrageurs. When a specialist provides liquidity to an arbitrageur, the specialist is often on the wrong side of the market. For example, if the futures market is falling, and the cash market is lagging behind, arbitrageurs will be selling to specialists. The specialists will be buying stock at prices that very likely are too high, and will thereby lose money. These arguments suggest that specialists had a strong interest in adopting Rule 80A.

The Exchange adopted the rule, at least in part, because specialists have more power at the NYSE than do arbitrageurs. If power were based only on relative numbers, specialists certainly would dominate over arbitrageurs. Far more members of the NYSE conduct specialist operations than arbitrage operations. In November 1997, 470 of the 1366 members of the Exchange were full-time specialists. In contrast, only 20 members then conducted 95 percent of the program trades. These numbers were similar in

1988. Although this comparison is overwhelming, it is not necessarily conclusive. Many arbitrageurs are very large wirehouses whose influence at the Exchange may be disproportionate to their numbers.

Two other arguments also support the conclusion. First, the loyalties of independent floor broker members lie primarily with specialists, with whom they regularly deal, rather than with wirehouses, with which they compete. Second, the interests of the senior management of the exchange are more likely aligned with specialists than with arbitrageurs because specialist trading exclusively benefits the NYSE, whereas arbitrage trading also benefits competing futures markets. These arguments suggest that specialists have more political power than do arbitrageurs at the NYSE. We therefore should not be surprised that the NYSE adopted Rule 80A.

This analysis helps explain two significant differences between the Rule 80A collars and the Rule 80B trading halts adopted by the NYSE. First, Rule 80A is triggered by much smaller price changes than those triggering trading halts. Until the Exchange amended the rule in 1999, the collars were imposed almost every trading day in the years prior to the amendment. Second, Rule 80A applies both to price decreases and to price increases, as opposed to just price decreases. These differences ensure that Rule 80A is triggered much more often than Rule 80B. The difference should not surprise us, given the specialists' interest in restricting arbitrage trading.

28.5 SUMMARY

Extreme volatility is quite scary. Large price changes can quickly create, destroy, or transfer enormous wealth. Although people do not like extreme price changes, they can better accept them when they are due to fundamental valuation factors than when they are due to human folly. Rarely, however, is news about fundamental values so important and so surprising that it can explain dramatic price changes. Large price changes therefore often are the result of mistakes that people make. People pay close attention to these events because they do not want to repeat their mistakes.

Perhaps the most common mistake that traders make is to overvalue assets. They make this mistake when they are overly optimistic about future prospects, or when they do not fully appreciate risks. If enough traders share their enthusiasm, they push asset prices beyond fundamental values. Although well-informed value traders may recognize the problem, they may be unwilling or unable to trade in sufficient quantities to prevent a bubble from forming. The bubble pops when traders lose confidence.

Most regulatory initiatives associated with extreme volatility come too late. They also tend to address problems that have more to do with crashes than with the formation of the bubbles that ultimately lead to crashes. Trading halts and price limits, for example, at best only ensure that extreme price changes occur in an orderly fashion. They mainly attenuate volatility only to the extent that they prevent traders from overreacting.

The best way to prevent the formation of bubbles is to empower value traders who can recognize and trade against bubbles. Value traders are most willing to trade when they are confident that they understand values well. Regulators therefore should direct their policies toward lowering the costs of obtaining high quality information that value traders need to form reliable opinions about fundamental values.

Regulators also should try to remove any impediments to short selling that value traders may face. In particular, U.S. regulators should consider eliminating the short-sale rule that requires short sellers to sell stock on an uptick. They also should consider policies that would make it easier for short sellers to obtain short interest on the proceeds of their sales.

28.6 SOME POINTS TO REMEMBER

- The most common mistake traders make is to identify a good company as a good investment.
- Momentum traders are especially susceptible to losing in bubbles and crashes.
- Traders should not speculate if they cannot value the instruments that they trade.
- The portfolio insurance trading strategy is destabilizing when many traders use it, and when traders are uncertain about the total funds under portfolio insurance management.
- Portfolio insurance does not reduce fundamental equity risk. It merely attempts to transfer risk among traders.
- Trade halts and price limits protect liquidity suppliers when prices change quickly. These rules change the trade pricing rule from discriminatory pricing to uniform pricing.
- Traders can panic when they are uncertain about risk, and when unusual situations confront them with new trading problems that require quick solutions.
- Trade halts and price limits can stop a panic by giving traders time to obtain and analyze more information.
- Price limits can protect the clearing system by increasing the margin payments that bankrupt traders pay before they default.
- The gravitational effect associated with trade halts and price limits can increase volatility if traders fear that they will not be able to complete their trades before trading stops.
- After a crisis, regulators often adopt regulations that have little economic value simply to respond to public demands for action.

28.7 QUESTIONS FOR THOUGHT

1. What role do pseudo-informed traders have in the formation of bubbles?
2. What effect do circuit breakers have on public welfare?
3. Was the 1987 stock market crash a problem or a correction to a problem?
4. How can a stock market crash cause a recession?
5. How might the normal correlation among security prices affect prices when the price of one security falls dramatically?
6. Do price correlations rise or fall during extreme volatility events?
7. The 1987 stock market crash showed that portfolio insurers grossly underestimated their trading costs. Why did they make this mistake?
8. Should the government try to prevent traders from trading foolishly? How can it do so?

9. How can the government help investors better understand their trading problems?

10. To what extent, if any, would the susceptibility of a market to crashes and bubbles depend on whether it uses a floor-based trading system versus a screen-based trading system? Would the use of a quote-driven trading system versus an order-driven trading system make any difference?

11. The SEC, the CFTC, and the various exchanges adopted some circuit breakers following the 1987 stock market crash. Despite many calls for higher margins, the Federal Reserve Board, which is responsible for setting margins for securities borrowing and lending, left margins unchanged. Why did the Fed not act when the other agencies did?

12. In the United States, the margins required to obtain equivalent-sized risk exposure in equities, equity options, and equity futures are quite unequal. Should margin rates be standardized across similar instruments? What accounts for the differences in margin rates in these markets?

13. During crashes, volume often rises to very extremely high levels. How much excess capacity should markets design into their systems to ensure that they are not overwhelmed in a crash? How would you balance the very high costs of building system capacity with the very high costs of failing to meet demands for that capacity which may never occur?

14. Can circuit breakers lower the optimal design capacity of a trading system?

15. Immediately following the terrorist atrocities on Tuesday morning, September 11, 2001, all trading in U.S. financial markets was halted. Trading in bonds and in all futures but equity index futures resumed on Thursday. Trading in equities and in equity options and futures resumed on Monday, September 17. Was it wise to halt trading everywhere in the United States? Should trading have resumed earlier? Why did the over-the-counter bond markets resume trading before the exchange stock markets?

Insider
Trading

Traders engage in *insider trading* when they base their trades on material information about the value of an instrument that is not publicly available. Most insider trading involves private information that corporate managers know about the prospects of their companies. Insider trading also may involve information that traders improperly obtain from other sources.

In most countries, insider trading is illegal and punishable by fines or imprisonment. Insider-trading laws are very difficult to enforce, however. Only a few countries—primarily the United States, Canada, and Great Britain—regularly and seriously attempt to enforce their insider-trading laws.

Insider trading has many economic effects. In the financial markets, it affects investor confidence, price efficiency, and liquidity. In the overall economy, insider trading affects the labor market for senior corporate managers, and the quality of management decisions that these executives make.

In this chapter, we define insider trading and explain how regulators enforce insider-trading laws. We then consider the debate over whether to restrict insider trading. As we debate the two sides of the issue, we will identify the effects that insider trading has on the markets and on the overall economy.

If you trade, you must recognize insider information in order to avoid making illegal trades. More generally, you must understand insider trading to fully understand market liquidity. Finally, and perhaps most unexpectedly, you must understand the effects of insider trading on managerial labor markets so as to fairly interpret comparisons of senior executive compensation across countries.

29.1 INSIDE INFORMATION
AND INSIDER TRADING

Insider trading and inside information are hard to define. Both are complex legal concepts that are subject to substantial interpretation. If you are confronted with an issue that may involve insider trading, you should consult a competent attorney.

The primary purpose of this chapter is to help you understand the economic issues that surround insider trading. For this purpose, we define *inside information* as material information about the value of a security that is not available to public traders. *Material information* is information that would cause prices to change if it were widely known. In the equity markets, corporate managers control most inside information.

In jurisdictions that prohibit insider trading, nobody can trade on inside information until after the information is publicly available. In particular, corporate managers cannot trade on the information nor can their friends nor can the friends of their friends. Inside information generally retains its

▶ An SEC Definition of Insider Trading

Statutory laws, the government regulations that implement them, and the case law created by successful and unsuccessful attempts to prosecute inside traders define insider trading. As a public service, the U.S. Securities and Exchange Commission provides a one-paragraph summary definition of insider trading on its Web page:

> "Insider trading" refers generally to buying or selling a security, in breach of a fiduciary duty or other relationship of trust and confidence, while in possession of material, nonpublic information about the security. Insider trading violations may also include "tipping" such information, securities trading by the person "tipped" and securities trading by those who misappropriate such information. Examples of insider trading cases that have been brought by the Commission are cases against: corporate officers, directors, and employees who traded the corporation's securities after learning of significant, confidential corporate developments; friends, business associates, family members, and other "tippees" of such officers, directors, and employees, who traded the securities after receiving such information; employees of law, banking, brokerage and printing firms who were given such information in order to provide services to the corporation whose securities they traded; government employees who learned of such information because of their employment by the government; and other persons who misappropriated, and took advantage of, confidential information from their employers.

This summary nicely illustrates the complexity of the law on insider trading. ◀

Source: www.sec.gov/divisions/enforce/insider.htm, January 4, 2002.

▶ Texas Gulf Sulfur

In late 1963, Texas Gulf Sulfur discovered very valuable deposits of copper, zinc, and silver in Ontario. Between November 12, 1962, and April 16, 1964, officers, directors, employees, and their friends bought Texas Gulf Sulfur stock and call options. During this period, the stock price rose from $17\frac{3}{8}$ to $29\frac{3}{8}$ dollars.

The company, however, did not disclose information about the find until April 12, 1964. On that date, it merely revealed that its drilling had "not been conclusive" and that "the rumors about the discovery were unreliable . . . premature and possibly misleading." Four days later, on April 16, the company announced a major ore discovery. Following the announcement, the stock price rose to 71 dollars.

The Securities and Exchange Commission sued various directors, managers, and employees of Texas Gulf Sulfur, alleging insider trading and deliberate efforts to mislead the public. The suit was successful. ◀

Source: Facts paraphrased from Jie Hu and Thomas H. Noe, "The Insider Trading Debate," Federal Reserve Bank of Atlanta Economic Review, Fourth Quarter 1997, p. 36.

status regardless of how many people have passed it. You may not trade on a stock tip that you receive from your barber, who received it from another client, who received it from a corporate insider, if the tip is based on inside information. Inside information loses its special status only when it becomes available to the public. After a firm releases information to the public through a broadly distributed press release or a public filing, the information is publicly available.

Sometimes, information that traders do not obtain directly from management is inside information. For example, suppose that a financial printer prints a prospectus for a takeover offer. While operating the presses, a pressman reads the copy and calls a friend to tell him to buy the target. The friend will be trading on insider information.

Managers must control the dissemination of material information. In particular, they must either keep it secret or distribute it widely. When they distribute confidential information to business associates, they must execute confidentiality agreements. If managers distribute inside information to their friends, who then trade upon it, the managers risk prosecution.

Many analysts produce valuable private information by carefully analyzing publicly available information. If they base their analyses only on information that is available to the public, the private information that they produce is not insider information.

In general, traders may not trade on information that they obtain unfairly. In particular, traders may not profit from misappropriating (stealing) information. For example, traders who know the contents of an economic

▶ Vincent Chiarella, the Printer

In 1975 and 1976, Vincent Chiarella worked as a "markup man" in the New York composing room of Pandick Press, a financial printer. Among the documents that he handled were five announcements of corporate takeover bids. When these documents were delivered to the printer, the identities of the acquiring and target corporations were concealed by blank spaces or false names. The true names were sent to the printer on the night of the final printing.

Chiarella, however, was able to deduce the names of the target companies before the final printing from other information contained in the documents. Without disclosing his knowledge, he purchased stock in the target companies and sold the shares immediately after the takeover attempts were made public. By this method, Chiarella realized a gain of slightly more than 30,000 dollars in the course of 14 months. Subsequently, the Securities and Exchange Commission began an investigation of his trading activities. In May 1977, Chiarella entered into a consent decree with the SEC in which he agreed to return his profits to the sellers of the shares. On the same day, Pandick Press discharged him.

Chiarella was later convicted of 17 counts of violating section 10(b) of the Securities Exchange Act of 1934 and SEC rule 10b-5, under the principle that Chiarella owed a responsibility to the sellers to disclose his information. In 1980, the U.S. Supreme Court reversed the conviction because he had no fiduciary duty to the acquiring or target firms.

The law has subsequently changed. If Chiarella were brought to trial now, he would be convicted of insider trading because he misappropriated information. ◀

———————

Source: The first two paragraphs are taken almost verbatim from section I of the Supreme Court decision in Chiarella v. United States, 445 U.S. 222 (1980). The decision appears at caselaw.lp.findlaw.com/scripts/getcase.pl?court=us&vol=445&invol=222.

▶ A Noble Cause and a Base Explanation

In the fall of 2000, the U.S. Securities and Exchange Commission adopted Regulation FD. This regulation requires that "whenever an issuer . . . discloses any material nonpublic information regarding that issuer or its securities to any person . . . , the issuer shall make public disclosure of that information . . . simultaneously, in the case of an intentional disclosure; and promptly, in the case of a non-intentional disclosure."

Before the adoption of Regulation FD, corporations would frequently tell their analysts material information before they reported it to the public. The analysts, their clients, or both would then trade on this information.

Not surprisingly, analysts adamantly opposed the new regulation. They claimed that it would make security prices less informative. In particular, they argued that their reports would be much less informative if they could not privately interview management and ask them probing questions. Without this privilege, they claimed, they would not be able to discover incompetent or dishonest management.

They undoubtedly also opposed the new regulation because it eliminated a valuable privilege that they formerly enjoyed. ◀

———————

Source: The complete text of Regulation FD appears at www.law.uc.edu/CCL/regFD/index.html.

▶ Heard on the Street

In 1982 to 1984, R. Foster Winans was one of two regular authors of the *Wall Street Journal* column "Heard on the Street." This popular column regularly reported news, analyses, perspectives, and rumors about companies. Although much of the material was public information, the prices of stocks featured in the column often moved following the publication of the column.

From October 1983 through March 1984, Winans conspired with Kidder, Peabody and Co. stockbrokers Peter N. Brant and Kenneth P. Felis to provide them with information about the content of his upcoming "Heard on the Street" columns. They made 600,000 dollars on the information. Winans was paid 31,000 dollars for his part in the scheme. An observant investigator at the SEC identified the pattern of their trades. Two others were involved in the conspiracy.

In 1985 Winans was convicted of 59 counts of securities fraud and conspiracy, even though he claimed that his columns did not contain inside information about the corporations discussed in his column. However, he did violate the *Wall Street Journal*'s confidentiality policy. The legal doctrine under which he was convicted is called the *misappropriation doctrine*. Brant and Felis also were convicted of fraud and conspiracy.

Winans was sentenced to 18 months in federal prison and fined 10,000 dollars. Felis was sentenced to six months and fined 10,000 dollars. Brant, who cooperated with the prosecution, was sentenced to eight months and fined 10,000 dollars. Both Felis and Winans were permitted to serve their time over consecutive weekends. All three disgorged their profits to the government. ◀

report that the government will soon release may not trade on such information until the government releases the report. Likewise, traders who improperly obtain a report written by a widely read analyst may not trade on the information in that report until the analyst publishes it.

29.1.1 Trading by Insiders

Corporate insiders are senior managers, corporate directors, large shareholders, and key employees. Insiders generally know material information about a firm that is not publicly available. Insiders also include anyone involved with corporate activities that will materially affect the value of the firm.

Insiders may trade stock in their companies, but insider-trading laws prevent them from trading on nonpublic material information. How managers could make trading decisions that are not influenced by confidential information in their possession is hard to imagine.

In the United States, insiders must report their insider trades to the Securities and Exchange Commission. They must report their initial purchases within ten days of making the trade. They must report any subsequent purchases or sales within the first ten days of the month following these trades. To prevent insiders from resigning their positions in order to trade on inside information, traders must report their trades for six months after they lose their insider status. Many countries have similar requirements.

Studies of insider trades generally indicate that insiders are well informed about the long-term prospects for their firms. Accordingly, many traders closely follow insider-trading reports.

Because managers often know nonpublic material information, all their trading could be construed to be insider trading. To permit insiders to trade, the U.S. Securities and Exchange Commission allows insiders to avoid prosecution by establishing prearranged trading programs. Although insiders cannot establish these programs because they want to profit from nonpublic material information, these programs allow them to trade when they know such information. Interestingly, insiders do not have to disclose these plans to the public.

Some insider-trading laws restrict insiders from profiting from short-term price swings in their stocks. In the United States, the law also requires insiders to return to issuers any profits they make on positions they open and close within six months. These profits are known as *short-swing* profits.

Most insider-trading laws also restrict insiders from taking short positions in the stocks of their employers. These restrictions ensure that insiders do not benefit when the firms they manage and oversee perform poorly.

Some corporations execute agreements with their employees that restrict their trading. These agreements often require that employees obtain corporate approval before they trade. If the proposed trade would occur before the corporation releases information, the corporation may not allow the trade.

Some firms allow their employees to trade only during specific intervals. The *trading window* is usually for one or more weeks following the week of their quarterly earnings announcement. Firms design these rules to reduce the probability or perception that their managers trade on material information that is not available to the public.

29.2 PRACTICAL JUDICIAL ISSUES

Enforcing insider-trading laws is quite difficult. Insiders rarely trade on their information themselves because it is illegal. Instead, they give their information to confederates who trade on their behalf. Identifying who is trading on insider information therefore is often impossible.

Exchange officials identify most insider-trading cases. In the United States, each stock exchange has a market surveillance department that monitors its markets for trading irregularities. The surveillance officers look for suspicious events—typically, large price changes on large volumes. When they identify unusual trading, they next try to determine whether a recent release of public information would explain it. If they cannot find an obvious explanation, they call the listed firm and ask whether it is aware of information that could have caused the price change. If the surveillance officers learn that the firm will soon release information, or if they later learn that the firm released information soon after the unusual trading activity, they may suspect insider trading. In general, large price changes associated with high volumes that occur before releases of significant unexpected news often indicate that insiders or their confederates were trading.

When surveillance officers suspect insider trading, they pass the case to investigators for further study. The investigators may work for the exchange or for the government. Exchange investigators generally can subpoena and question only exchange members. Government investigators can obtain greater subpoena powers from the courts. In the United States, the government agencies most responsible for enforcing the insider-trading laws

▶ Degrees of Separation

If you do not know the president, but you know someone who does, the president is one degree of separation from you. A popular play, *Six Degrees of Separation*, addresses the notion that no more than six people connect all people to each other.

Computer programs that access large databases of related names can determine the degree of separation between you and another person. Investigators searching for insider trading use these programs to identify potential relationships between people who knew inside information and people who may have benefited from such knowledge.

Many databases link individuals together. Here are a few examples of publicly available databases:

- Address databases identify current and former neighbors.
- E-mail address databases identify coworkers.
- College yearbooks identify classmates, fraternity brothers, sorority sisters, teammates, and members of the band.
- Databases of vital records permit the construction of family trees and the identification of in-law relationships.
- Databases collected by direct-order marketing firms and their consultants classify people by their hobbies and their religions.

In addition, governments can access confidential databases that include armed forces service records and employment records. ◀

---

are the Securities and Exchange Commission and the Department of Justice.

The investigators form a list of everyone who knew the insider information and a list of everyone whose trades—in stocks, options, or bonds—benefited from the ultimate revelation of that information. Anyone who appears on both lists may be guilty of insider trading. For obvious reasons, the same people rarely are on both lists. To identify insider trading, the investigators must try to determine how people on the first list might know people on the second list. Such relationships do not prove insider trading, but they may provide clues about how information passed from an insider to a trader.

Occasionally, investigators will find that someone engaged in highly unusual trading. For example, a gardener may have bought a substantial position in a security that subsequently was taken over at a large premium. Such a trade would be very unusual if the gardener had never traded before or if the gardener's position represented a very large fraction of his wealth. In that case, investigators may interview the gardener to ask him why he traded. Such interviews often allow investigators to work backward to the source of the information.

When the investigators are convinced that they have identified insider trading, they turn their cases over to the Securities and Exchange Commission enforcement officers for civil action and to the Department of Justice prosecutors for criminal prosecution. These prosecutors then must try to resolve these cases by negotiated settlement, plea bargain, or trial.

Prosecutors often will grant immunity to the last person in a chain of informed traders in exchange for his or her testimony. These traders may not even know that they were trading on insider information. Prosecutors

▶ Colt Industries

On July 20, 1986, Colt Industries announced that it would recapitalize by purchasing most of its outstanding stock shares. On the next day, the price rose by almost 30 dollars.

Israel Grossman apparently learned about the recapitalization from a colleague at his law firm with whom he shared a secretary. Colt's pension plan trustees retained the law firm on July 9 to represent their interests in the recapitalization. Grossman, however, did not work on the case.

Between July 11 and 18, Grossman called 40 friends and relatives, who together bought 1,400 "deep out of the money" options. Following the announcement of the plan, these options, which were purchased for 38,000 dollars, became worth 1.5 million dollars.

The Philadelphia Stock Exchange market surveillance unit discovered their trades. Newspaper articles credit the Exchange surveillance computers with discovering the fraud. Undoubtedly, traders who sold the options also brought the matter to Exchange investigators.

The Exchange investigators solved the case by placing pins in a map to mark the homes of each person who bought the options. All the buyers lived within a few blocks of each other in Brooklyn.

Grossman was convicted of 38 counts of mail fraud and securities fraud. He was sentenced to two years in prison and fined 25,000 dollars. ◀

Source: "Insider Trading: There's Just No Stopping It," *Los Angeles Times*, September 3, 1989 p. 4-1.

▶ Inside Information, Skilled Speculation, or Good Advice?

Spencer Speculator buys shares in ABC just before XYZ announces that it will buy ABC at a substantial premium. Spencer and Charles E. Officer, the CEO of ABC, are close confidants. What happened?

A. Charles told Spencer about the pending transaction, so Spencer traded on inside information.

B. Through careful and completely independent analysis of publicly available information, Spencer concluded that ABC would be a good takeover target for XYZ. He bought it, and events soon proved that he was correct.

C. Through careful and completely independent analysis of publicly available information, Spencer concluded that ABC would be a good takeover target for XYZ. He bought it. He then told Charles why the deal made sense. Charles agreed, and soon arranged the deal.

D. Alternative A is true, but when accused of insider trading, Spencer claims that alternative B is true. ◀

Suppose that Alternative D is true. How would the government prove its case?

▶ Bounty Hunting in the Financial Markets

To encourage people to report insider trading, U.S. law permits the Securities and Exchange Commission to offer up to 10 percent of the civil penalty eventually collected for insider trading as a bounty to anyone who provides information that leads to the imposition of such penalties. ◀

Source: www.sec.gov/divisions/ enforce/insider.htm.

therefore cannot easily convict them of insider trading. By obtaining their cooperation, prosecutors often can build stronger cases against traders who were closer to the inside information.

Proving that a trader traded on inside information is very difficult without clear evidence about how the trader obtained inside information. When the government accuses a sophisticated speculator of insider trading, the speculator will claim to have acquired his or her information strictly through insightful analysis of publicly available data. If the inside information involved a decision that management made as a result of some calculation, the speculator often can credibly claim to have independently made the same calculation. When confronted with the fact that the trades were very well timed, the insider trader will attribute the coincidence to chance.

Detecting and prosecuting insider trading is almost impossible if the information is not revealed in a discrete event. For example, suppose that management recognizes that its firm's prospects are exceptionally good, perhaps because some basic research has been much more successful than expected. The firm may not report this information for months or years, however. It does not want to give its competitors information that would allow them to catch up or that would discourage them from pursuing less successful lines of research. Insiders or their confederates who trade on this information are essentially impossible to detect only from prices and volumes. The only exception would be if many insiders all traded at the same time. If their trading causes prices to change substantially, a subsequent investigation might identify the inside information.

Since catching insider traders is quite difficult, the penalties for insider trading must be severe. Rational criminals engage in crime when the expected benefit is greater than the expected cost. The expected cost of insider trading equals the product of the probability of being caught times the penalty for being caught. If the probability of being caught is low, the penalty must be large. Otherwise, the expected cost of insider trading will be small.

The typical penalty for insider trading includes the disgorgement (repayment) of any profit that the trader made. In addition, the insider trader often must pay a fine. In rare cases, traders go to jail. The penalties usually are greater for traders who are closest to the source of the inside information. Traders who benefited from acting on a tip without knowing its source rarely are penalized severely. In the United States, the maximum criminal penalties for insider trading now are ten years in prison and a 1 million-dollar fine. The maximum civil penalty is three times the profit gained (or loss avoided) due to the insider trading.

29.3 THE DEBATE OVER INSIDER TRADING

Efforts to restrict insider trading have been very controversial. Regulators, attorneys, and economists have created a substantial legal and economic literature on the issue. In this section, we survey many of the arguments that they offer for and against restricting insider trading.

29.3.1 Why Restrict Insider Trading?

People opposed to insider trading offer three main arguments in defense of their position. They believe that effective restrictions on insider trading increase investor confidence, lower transaction costs, and solve corporate control problems which arise when insiders can trade on inside information.

29.3.1.1 Fairness

The most commonly offered reason for restricting insider trading is to satisfy the public's sense of fairness. That insiders can profit from access to information others do not have bothers many people. Many people favor insider-trading rules because they believe that these rules help create fair markets. For them, fair markets reward traders for insightful research that anyone could do rather than for personal connections that only some people have.

Traders avoid markets that they do not believe are fair. Restrictions against insider trading therefore benefit the markets by increasing investor confidence. Greater investor confidence increases the funds that investors will invest in stocks, raises prices, and thereby lowers corporate costs of capital.

Rebuttal

If restrictions on insider trading benefit listed firms, firms will place these restrictions in their employee labor contracts. Since many do, there may be no role for government regulation.

Rejoinder

Restrictions on insider trading primarily benefit firms that need to raise new capital. To a lesser extent, they also may benefit existing shareholders by increasing the value of their shares. Corporate directors, however, are unlikely to enact and enforce restrictions that limit their ability to engage in insider trading. In addition, since insider trading is difficult to detect, effective restrictions require the backing of the government to enforce.

29.3.1.2 Liquidity

Insider trading—like all informed trading—hurts traders who supply liquidity. Insider trading consequently increases dealer bid/ask spreads and thereby increases transaction costs for uninformed market order traders.

(Chapters 13 and 14 explain how dealers and limit order traders respond to the adverse selection due to informed traders.)

Insider trading also increases transaction costs for uninformed limit order traders. Like dealers, limit order traders lose when they trade with insiders. When they try to trade on the same side the insiders trade on, their orders often do not execute because they compete with insiders to fill their orders. They thus often fail to profit when they want to trade on the side of the market that will prove to be profitable. When insiders are trading, uninformed limit order traders regret trading when their orders execute, and wish that they had traded when their orders do not execute.

Effective restrictions against insider trading make markets more liquid for uninformed traders by removing an important class of informed traders from trading in the markets. This conclusion follows from our understanding of how adverse selection affects markets. It is also a trivial implication of accounting in a zero-sum game. When informed traders make more profits, uninformed traders must lose more. Since uninformed traders are on the wrong side of the market about as often as they are on the right side, their losses on average must be due to transaction costs. Effective restrictions on insider trading therefore reduce uninformed trader transaction costs.

Rebuttal: The Competition to Exploit Insider Information

Whether insider trading makes markets less liquid ultimately depends on how the insiders trade. The argument against insider trading is most compelling when only one trader knows the inside information, and the firm will not release the information soon. This insider will strategically manage his or her trading to obtain maximum value from the information. In practice, the trader probably will trade slowly and unobtrusively to avoid detection. Such a trader—if well capitalized—would impose the greatest costs upon all other traders.

In contrast, suppose that many insiders learn the inside information at the same time. Each insider must trade quickly to profit from the information before another insider does. Those who wait will lose the opportunity to profit as other insiders exhaust the available liquidity and push prices closer to fundamental values. With all insiders trading at once, prices will quickly change as dealers and other liquidity suppliers suspect that news is in the market. In some markets, the resulting order imbalance may cause trading to halt so that prices change on little volume. Competition among many insiders to profit from their informational advantage therefore quickly reveals their inside information. The total profits that insiders consequently obtain will be less than the profits they could obtain if they colluded to trade more slowly.

By making insider trading illegal, we force insiders to trade slowly and unobtrusively to avoid prosecution. The threat of prosecution thus gives insiders strong incentives to collude to avoid detection, and thereby maximize their trading profits. Without restrictions on insider trading, collusive agreements would be extremely hard to enforce because each insider could cheat without threat of prosecution. With restrictions on insider trading, insiders who do not collude increase their probability of being caught.

Rejoinder

In chapter 12, we show that if the rate at which prices adjust to an imbalanced anonymous order flow depends on its composition, bluffers can make money. If, as asserted above, traders can obtain more liquidity when they trade slowly than when they trade quickly, bluffers will trade quickly, as though they were informed traders, and then try to leave the market slowly.

Another Rebuttal: The Effects of Insider Trading on Managerial Compensation

Managers receive direct and indirect compensation for doing their jobs. Their *direct compensation* includes all income and services that their employers give them. This compensation generally includes salaries, bonuses, option grants, retirement benefits, and health benefits. *Indirect compensation* includes all benefits that managers obtain from their jobs and are not explicitly given to them by their employers. These indirect benefits may include the prestige that society grants managers, the satisfaction associated with managing a firm, the satisfaction associated with making decisions that affect other people, and—in some places—the opportunity to trade on insider information. When insiders can trade without restriction, the opportunity to trade on insider information may be their most important indirect employment benefit.

Since the market for managerial talent is highly competitive, indirect compensation can act as a substitute for direct compensation. In particular, the greater the indirect benefits that managers receive from their jobs, the less money their firms must pay them to do their jobs. If all other things are held constant, direct compensation therefore must be higher when insiders cannot trade on inside information.

When managers can trade on inside information, their firms need not pay them as much in direct compensation. With lower managerial compensation, reported corporate earnings will be higher than they would be if insider trading were effectively restricted. Although greater earnings generally increase valuations, this increase would be offset by the illiquidity effects of insider trading. On net, holding all other things constant, permitting insider trading should not affect corporate values.

As a result, if no other problems were associated with insider trading, allowing insider trading merely shifts compensation expense from the firm to the shareholders. Since the shareholders own the firm anyway, they collectively should not care whether the firm pays their managers or whether they pay them through their trading losses. If all shareholders bore these costs equally, and if insiders were able to exploit their positions predictably, insider trading would have no net effect on values.

This conclusion ignores several secondary issues. For example, different tax rates on corporate and personal income, and on ordinary and capital gains income, ensure that shareholders are not indifferent between restricted and unrestricted insider trading. Managerial risk aversion can also affect corporate values because managers tend to prefer compensation schemes that do not force them to bear unpredictable risks.

A switch from direct compensation to compensation through insider trading would benefit long-term investors at the expense of high frequency traders. Traders who trade most frequently generally lose the most to informed traders.

Rejoinder

The result that shareholders as a group should be indifferent between restricted and unrestricted insider-trading regimes assumes that insider

---

▶ **International Comparisons of CEO Compensation**

It is impossible to reasonably compare managerial compensation among countries without considering whether insiders can trade on insider information. In countries where insiders can freely trade on their information, direct compensation will be lower than in countries where the law effectively restricts insider trading.

This observation helps explain why U.S. corporations pay their CEOs higher salaries than do Japanese or German corporations. Insider trading is far more effectively restricted in the United States than in Japan or Germany. ◀

trading does not cause other problems. Below, we discuss many other insider-trading problems.

29.3.1.3 Corporate Control Issues

The least recognized reason why we have insider-trading rules may be the most important reason. Insider-trading rules help ensure that managerial labor markets operate efficiently and that managers do not abuse their positions within their corporations. Insider-trading rules help keep publicly traded firms productive.

Perhaps the most damaging effect of unrestricted insider trading is that it makes insiders reluctant to share information. Managers who freely share information lose their comparative advantage as informed traders. Corporate directors and shareholders therefore know less about the firm than they otherwise would. Consequently, directors find it more difficult to evaluate, and ultimately to control, corporate managers. Shareholders likewise find it more difficult to value their investments.

When insiders can trade on inside information, they may also make managerial decisions that maximize their unique advantage as informed traders. In extreme cases, managers may choose investment projects based on the degree to which projects increase their informational advantage rather than strictly on the net benefits of the projects to the shareholders. Such decisions obviously decrease firm values.

Finally, when managers can trade on inside information, they may front-run trades that their firms make. Firms trade when they repurchase their shares, issue new shares, purchase or sell shares of other firms, take over or merge with other firms, and purchase or sell commodities. Front running such trades spoils the prices that their firms ultimately obtain. Such abuses therefore directly dilute shareholder values.

29.3.2 Why Permit Insider Trading?

The main arguments for unrestricted insider trading involve price efficiency, the costs of enforcement, and incentives for entrepreneurial behavior by managers.

29.3.2.1 Informative Prices

Since insiders are well-informed traders, the price impacts of their orders push prices toward fundamental values. Their trading therefore makes prices more informative.

Effective restrictions on insider trading remove insiders and their information from the market. Insider-trading restrictions therefore make prices less informative. Since informative prices are essential to efficient allocation decisions in market-based economies, insider trading makes production more efficient.

Rebuttal

The value of having informative prices sooner rather than later depends on how much longer it would take prices to adjust to new information if insiders were not allowed to trade. If insiders trade on information that will be common knowledge tomorrow, the incremental value of more informative prices probably is not great. If insiders accelerate the flow of information by months or years, restrictions on insider trading may be quite harmful.

In practice, as noted above, effectively enforcing insider-trading laws is almost impossible when firms do not soon reveal the information on which insiders trade. Therefore, as a practical matter, restrictions on insider trading are effective only against insider trading on information that will soon be made public. Consequently, the increased economic efficiency associated with more informative prices cannot be that great. Moreover, since people usually can reverse or revise recent decisions in response to new information, restrictions on insider trading cannot be very costly if they affect only short-term trading decisions.

Insider trading can make prices more informative only if all information that would be made public with restricted insider trading also would be made public with unrestricted insider trading. As noted above, however, unrestricted insider trading diminishes managerial incentives to share information. Unrestricted insider trading therefore may actually decrease the information in prices.

29.3.2.2 Costs of Enforcement

Insider-trading laws are extremely difficult to enforce because detecting insider trading by confederates is very difficult. Unfortunately, the generally low probability of detection means that no reasonable punishment will deter unethical people from illegal insider trading. Moreover, the costs of effectively enforcing insider-trading restrictions could be a substantial fraction of—if not greater than—the economic value of enforcement.

Many people believe that it is unproductive to have laws we cannot effectively enforce. When laws are routinely broken without consequence, respect for authority often suffers.

Such circumstances often lead to selective enforcement problems. When many people violate the law, but only a few are prosecuted, the authorities who choose whom to prosecute often have tremendous power to selectively prosecute individuals or groups they do not like. Selective prosecution can be highly unfair. If applied to groups based on racial, ethnic, sexual, national, or religious grounds, it can destabilize society.

Rebuttal

A law that is not effectively enforced is very different from no law at all. In societies where people respect the law, most people respect an ineffectively enforced law simply because they are ethical. For most people, the ethical costs of breaking the law are much greater than the expected costs of prosecution. They therefore obey the law much more than we would otherwise expect.

Rejoinder

People respect laws in large part because they are enforced. When enforcement drops and violation rises, respect ultimately falls, as does this argument.

29.3.2.3 Entrepreneurial Incentives

In a famous book and related article, Henry Manne argues that insider trading gives managers incentives to engage in entrepreneurial behavior. In particular, managers who have good ideas can create their own rewards for implementing those ideas by buying stock in their firm before the idea is common knowledge and by selling the stock when its price reflects the value of the new idea. Insider trading allows employees with ideas to buy a piece

▶ **The War on Drugs**

Many people believe that laws against the illegal use of drugs are impossible to enforce effectively. Use remains high despite the large number of people who are in jail for producing, transporting, dealing, possessing, or using illegal drugs.

The illegal drug trade is highly lucrative in large part because it is illegal. The legal restrictions placed on the trade have decreased supply relative to demand, which has caused prices to be much higher than they otherwise would be. The legal restrictions also have allowed dealers to form territorial monopolies because competitors can hardly petition the government for relief under antitrust statutes. The high penalties for drug trafficking also make the penalties for murder committed to protect territorial monopolies relatively less significant.

The high prices of illegal drugs are responsible for much of the burglary, robbery, and prostitution in Western societies. Addicts who need their next fix must get it. The more expensive is the fix, the more crime they must commit. Since criminals often use force to commit these crimes, they expose those who do not use drugs to substantial personal risks.

The high prices of illegal drugs also cause users to become dealers in order to support their habits. These dealers have tremendous incentives to hook new clients. Ironically, because of this factor alone, usage is probably higher than it would be if drug usage and distribution were legal and regulated.

The huge wealth accumulated by drug dealers corrupts society. Criminals use their wealth to corrupt the legal system. Their wealth also corrupts the values of people who see how successful they are. The war on drugs is largely responsible for the extreme social instabilities found in many drug-producing countries.

Although the restriction of insider trading fortunately has not had the same negative effects as the war on drugs, many people believe that the two problems share many essential aspects. ◀

of their firm so that they can realize the benefit of their ideas. It allows them to be entrepreneurs.

Manne argues that this compensation scheme is much more effective than any other compensation scheme that shareholders can construct. Unlike formal compensation schemes that employees must negotiate with their managers or with the shareholders, employees can enter this "entrepreneurial" scheme whenever they want. Although the rewards—insider-trading profits—for implementing a good idea can be quite great, the insider risks losing if the share prices drops. This compensation scheme thus is quite unusual. Shareholders generally cannot create compensation contracts that put their employees at risk of losing substantial wealth.

The risk of loss is the distinguishing characteristic of compensation through insider trading. The only employees who opt for this form of compensation are those who firmly believe that the firm will outperform the market. Shareholders want to retain these employees more than other employees. If employees with good ideas cannot profit from them, they may quit and take them elsewhere. Shareholders cannot compensate everyone who claims to have a good idea because everyone will make such claims. Instead, they must evaluate each claim. Shareholders, however, may be poorly suited for making such evaluations. By allowing compensation that places the employee at substantial risk of loss, shareholders do not have to make these evaluations. Instead, employees self-select their compensation schemes. Only those who are willing to take a position in the firm get the rewards. Insider trading thus encourages entrepreneurial initiative.

Shareholders can give employees stock options to encourage entrepreneurial initiative. They must be careful, however, about to whom they give the options. If they give options to all employees, they give away value without any assurance that the firm will outperform the market. Stock option-based compensation is most effective when employees can choose between taking salary and taking options. In that case, employees are essentially insider traders who use their salaries to buy options.

Rebuttal

Most entrepreneurial ideas take a long time to implement. To provide effective incentives to entrepreneurs within the firm, compensation schemes must benefit insiders when they are successful and penalize them when they are unsuccessful. Insider trading can provide this type of compensation, but it does so only when the insiders establish their positions before they know the outcomes of their initiatives. If insiders can trade after they learn that their initiatives are successful, they will not be penalized if they fail. Because they have little risk of losing, insiders would then have too much incentive to undertake risky projects.

These considerations suggest that regulators should prevent insiders from trading on short-term information which firms will soon release to the public. Such information often is due to surprising financial reports and to significant research advances or failures. The entrepreneurial decisions that led up to these results typically occurred long before the information about the results is available. Regulations should permit insiders to establish their positions before they make these decisions, but not afterward. These considerations suggest that the U.S. restriction on short-term insider-trading profits is sensible.

As discussed above, regulators generally cannot identify insider trading on material information that firms will not soon reveal. Restrictions on insider trading therefore do not effectively preclude the insider trading that can produce proper entrepreneurial incentives. This conclusion, of course, assumes that the law does not prohibit insiders from buying and holding shares for long periods.

Any argument for insider trading based on incentives it creates for corporate insiders to engage in constructive entrepreneurial activity must discriminate between insider trading that produces long positions and that which produces short positions. If insiders can construct net short positions in their firms, they will want to destroy rather than create value. Since destroying value is always much easier than creating value, almost all regulatory authorities prohibit managers from creating short positions in their firms.

29.4 SUMMARY

Regulators try to restrict insider trading in order to remove a class of informed traders from the market place. The assumed purpose of these laws is to make trading more fair, to protect liquidity suppliers from informed traders so that they can supply more liquidity to uninformed traders, and to control corporate managers. These laws narrow bid/ask spreads and make prices less informative in the short run.

The debate on insider trading is quite complex. Although some good arguments suggest that insider-trading laws are not necessary or desirable, these laws are quite popular. Little chance of an early repeal exists. Of greater concern is how much money regulators should spend to enforce insider-trading laws.

29.5 SOME POINTS TO REMEMBER

- Profitable insider trading hurts dealers and uninformed traders.
- Insider trading is hard to detect. Trading on inside information that firms will not soon reveal is especially difficult to detect.
- Insider trading is most profitable when insiders do not compete with each other to profit from their information.
- Profitable insider trading is associated with lower salaries for corporate insiders.
- Insider trading may encourage entrepreneurship among corporate managers.

29.6 QUESTIONS FOR THOUGHT

1. After weighing the arguments for and against insider trading, do you think that insider trading should be restricted? Which arguments do you find most compelling?
2. When can a manager safely trade without worrying about prosecution for insider trading?
3. When can we reasonably assume that insiders are not trading on inside information?
4. Why do people follow reports of insider trades?
5. Suppose a corporation will sell its forecast of its future earnings to anyone for 50,000 dollars. If you buy this information and base your trading decisions upon it, would you be trading on insider information? Would your answer be different if the corporation sells the forecast for the cost of "postage and handling"?
6. Suppose you tell your friend who is a CEO that you intend to sell stock in his firm. He tells you that now would be a very poor time to sell. You therefore decide not to sell. You do not buy, however. Price subsequently rises when another firm offers to buy the company for a substantial premium. You clearly benefited from insider information. How should the law treat this situation?
7. Suppose that a corporation posts material information to its Web site at an unannounced and unscheduled time. By chance, you see the information and trade on it. Are you trading on insider information? Suppose the CEO tells you to look at the Web site. Are you then trading on insider information?
8. A corporate CEO gives a keynote speech at a large trade show in which she describes her expectations for the future prospects of her firm. Her vision surprises many analysts, who revise their valuations of the corporation. If they then trade on this information, will they be trading on insider information? Would the answer be different if

only mutual fund analysts could attend the trade show or if the CEO spoke only in a small session of a large conference?

9. How might a clever insider arrange her trades to minimize the probability of prosecution for insider trading while maximizing her gains from trading on inside information?

10. Should professional securities analysts have better access to information produced by management than do other people? If so, which analysts would qualify for this privilege? What limits, if any, would you place on their trading?

Bibliography

This bibliography provides selected references for further reading. I classified the references using the chapter outline of this book. Since some articles and books cover topics that appear in many of the chapters, the classification is somewhat arbitrary.

The market microstructure literature has grown large very quickly. This bibliography therefore is not comprehensive. I included many works because they provide the first clear presentation of a principle or because they include extensive bibliographies of their topics. I included other works because I especially appreciated what I learned from them or because I found them to be particularly well written.

I undoubtedly failed to include many excellent works simply because I did not remember them. Although I am blessed with an excellent memory for ideas, I regrettably have a poor memory for names. The omission of many excellent works from this bibliography therefore reflects more on me than on them.

General Works

Belonsky, Gail M., and David M. Modest. 1993. Market microstructure: An empirical retrospective. Working paper, Haas School of Business, University of California, Berkeley.

Cohen, Kalman J., Steven F. Maier, Robert A. Schwartz, and David K. Whitcomb. 1986. *The Microstructure of Securities Markets* (Prentice-Hall, Englewood Cliffs, NJ).

Coughenour, Jay, and Kuldeep Shastri. 1999. Symposium on market microstructure: A review of empirical research. *Financial Review* 34(4), 1–28.

Dalton, John M., ed. 1993. *How the Stock Market Works* (New York Institute of Finance, New York).

Downes, John, and Jordan E. Goodman, eds. 1991. *Dictionary of Finance and Investment Terms* (Barron's Educational Series, New York).

Fan, Ming, Sayee Srinivasan, Jan Stallaert, and Andrew B. Whinston. 2002. *Electronic Commerce and the Revolution in Financial Markets* (South-Western, Mason, OH).

Lee, Rubin. 1998. *What Is an Exchange: The Automation, Management and Regulation of Financial Markets* (Oxford University Press, New York).

Lyons, Richard K. 2002. *The Microstructure Approach to Exchange Rates* (MIT Press, Cambridge, MA).

Madhavan, Ananth. 2000. Market microstructure: A survey. *Journal of Financial Markets* 3(3), 205–258.

O'Hara, Maureen. 1995. *Market Microstructure Theory* (Basil Blackwell, Cambridge, MA).

Schwartz, Robert A. 1991. *Reshaping the Equity Markets: A Guide for the 1990s* (Harper Business, New York).

Sharp, Robert. 1989. *The Lore and Legends of Wall Street* (Dow Jones-Irwin, New York).

Stoll, Hans R. 1992. Principles of trading market structure. *Journal of Financial Services Research* 6(1), 75–107.

Teweles, Richard J., Edward S. Bradley, and Ted M. Teweles. 1992. *The Stock Market* (John Wiley & Sons, New York).

Teweles, Richard J., and Frank J. Jones. 1999. *The Futures Game: Who Wins? Who Loses? And Why?* Ben Warwick, ed., 3rd ed. (McGraw-Hill, New York).

Wagner, Wayne, ed. 1989. *The Complete Guide to Securities Transactions: Enhancing Performance and Controlling Costs* (John Wiley & Sons, New York).

Chapter 3: The Trading Industry

Bank for International Settlements. 2001. *Triennial Central Bank Survey of Foreign Exchange and Derivatives Markets Activity* (Bank for International Settlements, Basel, Switzerland).

Garbade, Kenneth D., and William L. Silber. 1978. Technology, communication and the performance of financial markets: 1840–1975. *Journal of Finance* 33(3), 819–832.

Keim, Donald B., and Ananth Madhavan. 2000. The relationship between stock market movements and NYSE seat prices. *Journal of Finance* 55(6), 2817–2840.

Schwert, G. William. 1977. Stock exchange seats as capital assets. *Journal of Financial Economics* 4(1), 51–78.

Securities Industry Association. 2001. *Securities Industry Fact Book* (Securities Industry Association, New York).

U.S. Congress, General Accounting Office. 1986. *Stocks and Futures: How the Markets Developed and How They Are Regulated.* GAO/GGD-86-26 (General Accounting Office, Washington, DC).

U.S. Congress, General Accounting Office. 1991. *Global Financial Markets: International Coordination Can Help Address Automation Risks.* GAO/IMTEC-01-62 (General Accounting Office, Washington, DC).

U.S. Congress, Office of Technology Assessment. 1990a. *Electronic Bulls & Bears: US Security Markets & Information Technology.* OTA-CIT-459 (U.S. Government Printing Office, Washington, DC).

U.S. Congress, Office of Technology Assessment. 1990b. *Trading Around the Clock: Global Securities Markets and Information Technology—Background Paper.* OTA-BP-CIT-66 (U.S. Government Printing Office, Washington, DC).

Chapter 4: Orders and Order Properties

Angel, James J. 1998. Nonstandard-settlement transactions. *Financial Management* 27(1), 31–46.

Copeland, Thomas E., and Dan Galai. 1983. Information effects on the bid-ask spread. *Journal of Finance* 38(5), 1457–1469.

Chapter 5: Market Structures

Amihud, Yakov, and Haim Mendelson. 1987. Trading mechanisms and stock returns: An empirical investigation. *Journal of Finance* 42(3), 533–553.

Amihud, Yakov, Haim Mendelson, and Beni Lauterbach. 1997. Market microstructure and securities values: Evidence from the Tel Aviv Stock Exchange. *Journal of Financial Economics* 45(3), 365–390.

Ball, Clifford A., Walter A. Torous, and Adrian E. Tschoegl. 1985. The degree of price resolution: The case of the gold market. *Journal of Futures Markets* 5(1), 29–43.

Cohen, Kalman J., and Robert A. Schwartz. 1989. An electronic call market: Its design and desirability. In Henry C. Lucas, Jr., and Robert A. Schwartz, eds., *The Challenge of Information Technology for the Securities Markets* (Dow Jones-Irwin, Homewood, IL).

Coval, Joshua D., and Tyler Shumway. 2001. Is sound just noise? *Journal of Finance* 56(5), 1887–1910.

Domowitz, Ian. 1993. A taxonomy of automated trade execution systems. *Journal of International Money and Finance* 12(6), 607–631.

Fishman, Michael J., and Kathleen M. Hagerty. 1995. The mandatory disclosure of trades and market liquidity. *Review of Financial Studies* 8(3), 637–676.

Franks, Julian, and Stephen Schaefer. 1995. Equity market transparency on the London Stock Exchange. *Journal of Applied Corporate Finance* 8(1), 70–77.

Goodhart, Charles, and Ricardo Curcio. 1992. Asset price discovery and price clustering in the foreign exchange market. Working paper, London School of Business.

Grossman, Sanford, and Merton Miller. 1988. Liquidity and market structure. *Journal of Finance* 43(3), 617–633.

Harris, Lawrence. 1991. Stock price clustering and discreteness. *Review of Financial Studies* 4(3), 389–415.

Ho, Thomas S., Robert A. Schwartz, and David K. Whitcomb. 1985. The trading decision and market clearing under transaction price uncertainty. *Journal of Finance* 40(1), 21–42.

Huang, Roger D., and Hans R. Stoll. 1992. The design of trading systems: Lessons from abroad. *Financial Analysts Journal* 48(5), 49–54.

Huang, Roger D., and Hans R. Stoll. 1996. Dealer versus auction markets: A paired comparison of execution costs on NASDAQ and the NYSE. *Journal of Financial Economics* 41(3), 313–357.

Katz, Michael L., and Carl Shapiro. 1985. Network externalities, competition, and compatibility. *American Economic Review* 75(3), 424–440.

Lucas, Henry C., Jr., and Robert A. Schwartz, eds. 1989. *The Challenge of Information Technology for the Securities Markets* (Dow Jones-Irwin, Homewood, IL).

Madhavan, Ananth, David Porter, and Daniel Weaver. 2000. Should securities markets be transparent? Working paper, Marshall School of Business, University of Southern California.

Naik, Narayan Y., Anthony Neuberger, and S. Viswanathan. 1999. Trade disclosure regulation in markets with negotiated trades. *Review of Financial Studies* 12(4), 873–900.

Niederhoffer, Victor. 1965. Clustering of stock prices. *Operations Research* 13(2), 258–265.

Pagano, Marco, and Ailsa Röell. 1992. Auction and dealership markets: What is the difference? *European Economic Review* 36(2/3), 613–623.

Porter, David, and Daniel Weaver. 1998. Post-trade transparency on Nasdaq's national market system. *Journal of Financial Economics* 50(2), 231–252.

Schnitzlein, Charles R. 1996. Call and continuous trading mechanisms under asymmetric information: An experimental investigation. *Journal of Finance* 51(2), 613–636.

Smidt, Seymour. 1979. Continuous vs. intermittent trading on auction markets. *Journal of Financial and Quantitative Analysis* 14(4), 837–886.

Tinic, Seha M., and Richard R. West. 1974. Marketability of common stocks in Canada and the U.S.A.: A comparison of agent versus dealer dominated markets. *Journal of Finance* 29(3), 729–746.

Wagner, Wayne. 1989. Buttonwood II: Considering alternative market structures. In Wayne Wagner, ed., *The Complete Guide to Securities Transactions* (John Wiley & Sons, New York).

Wunsch, Steven. 1989. The single-price auction. In Wayne Wagner, ed., *The Complete Guide to Securities Transactions* (John Wiley & Sons, New York).

Chapter 6: Order-driven Markets

Domowitz, Ian. 1990. The mechanics of automated trade execution systems. *Journal of Financial Intermediation* 1(2), 167–194.

Mendelson, Haim. 1982. Market behavior in a clearing house. *Econometrica* 50(6), 1505–1524.

Chapter 7: Brokers

Brennan, Michael J., and Tarun Chordia. 1993. Brokerage commission schedules, *Journal of Finance* 48(4), 1379–1402.

Chan, Yuk-Shee, and Mark Weinstein. 1993. Reputation, bid-ask spread and market structure. *Financial Analysts Journal* 49(4), 57–62.

Fishman, Michael J., and Francis A. Longstaff. 1992. Dual trading in futures markets. *Journal of Finance* 47(2), 643–672.

Röell, Ailsa. 1990. Dual capacity trading and the quality of the market. *Journal of Financial Intermediation* 1(2), 105–124.

Sofianos, George, and Ingrid Werner. 2000. The trades of NYSE floor brokers. *Journal of Financial Markets* 3(2), 139–176.

Weiss, David M. 1993. *After the Trade Is Made: Processing Security Transactions* (NYFI, New York).

Chapter 8: Why People Trade

Barber, Bard M., and Terrance Odean. 2000. Trading is hazardous to your wealth: The common stock investment performance of individual investors. *Journal of Finance* 55(2), 773–806.

Bernstein, Peter L. 1996. Against the Gods: The Remarkable Story of Risk. (John Wiley & Sons, New York).

DeLong, Bradford J., Andrei Shleifer, Lawrence H. Summers, and Robert J. Waldmann. 1989. The size and incidence of the losses from noise trading. *Journal of Finance* 44(3), 681–696.

DeLong, Bradford J., Andrei Shleifer, Lawrence H. Summers, and Robert J. Waldmann. 1991. The survival of noise traders in financial markets. *Journal of Business* 64(1), 1–20.

Gervais, S., and Terrance Odean. 2001. Learning to be overconfident. *Review of Financial Studies* 14(1), 1–27.

Grinblatt, Mark, and Matti Keloharju. 2001. How distance, language and culture influence stockholdings and trades. *Journal of Finance* 56(3), 1053–1073.

Huberman, Gur. 2001. Familiarity breeds investment. *Review of Financial Studies* 14(3), 659–680.

Karpoff, Jonathan M., and Ralph A. Walkling. 1988. Short-term trading around ex-dividend days: Additional evidence. *Journal of Financial Economics* 21(2), 291–298.

Karpoff, Jonathan M., and Ralph A. Walkling. 1990. Dividend capture in NASDAQ stocks. *Journal of Financial Economics* 28(1/2), 39–66.

Rashes, Michael S. 2001. Massively confused investors making conspicuously ignorant choices (MCI–MCIC). *Journal of Finance* 56(5), 1911–1927.

Reinganum, Marc R. 1986. Is time travel impossible? A financial proof. *Journal of Portfolio Management* 13(1), 10–12.

Sauer, Raymond D. 1998. The economics of wagering markets. *Journal of Economic Literature* 36(4), 2021–2064.

Chapter 9: Good Markets

Amihud, Yakov, and Haim Mendelson. 1986. Asset pricing and the bid-ask spread. *Journal of Financial Economics* 17(2), 223–249.

Amihud, Yakov, and Haim Mendelson. 1991. Liquidity, maturity and the yields on U.S. Treasury securities. *Journal of Finance* 46(4), 1411–1426.

Black, Fischer. 1986. Noise. *Journal of Finance* 41(3), 529–543.

Brennan, Michael J., and Avanidhar Subrahmanyam. 1996. Market microstructure and asset pricing: On the compensation for illiquidity in stock returns. *Journal of Financial Economics* 41(3), 441–464.

Chapter 10: Informed Traders and Market Efficiency

Black, Fischer. 1971. Random walk and portfolio management. *Financial Analysts Journal* 27(2), 16–22.

Chakravarty, Sugato. 2001. Stealth-trading: Which traders' trades move stock prices? *Journal of Financial Economics* 61(2), 289–307.

Fama, Eugene F. 1965. Random walks in stock market prices. *Financial Analysts Journal* 21(5), 55–59; reprinted [1995] in *Financial Analysts Journal* 51(1), 75–80.

Figlewski, Stephen. 1982. Information diversity and market behavior. *Journal of Finance* 37(1), 87–102.

Grossman, Sanford J., and Joseph E. Stiglitz. 1980. On the impossibility of informationally efficient markets. *American Economic Review* 70(3), 393–408.

Hasbrouck, Joel. 1991. Measuring the information content of stock trades. *Journal of Finance* 46(1), 179–208.

Madhavan, Ananth. 1996. Security prices and market transparency. *Journal of Financial Intermediation* 5(3), 255–283.

Malkiel, Burton G. 1973. *A Random Walk Down Wall Street* (Norton, New York).

Pinches, George E. 1970. The random walk and technical analysis. *Financial Analysts Journal* 26(2), 104–109.

Silber, William L. 1994. Technical trading: When it works and when it doesn't. *Journal of Derivatives* 1(3), 39–44.

Treynor, Jack L. 1981. What does it take to win the trading game? *Financial Analysts Journal* 37(1), 55–60.

Treynor, Jack L. 1999. Zero sum. *Financial Analysts Journal* 55(1), 8–12.

Van Horne, James C., and G. G. C. Parker. 1968. Technical trading rules. *Financial Analysts Journal* 24(4), 128–132.

Chapter 11: Order Anticipators

Amihud, Yakov, and Haim Mendelson. 1990. Option market integration: An evaluation. Paper submitted to the U.S. Securities and Exchange Commission.

Angel, James J. 1997. Tick size, share prices, and stock splits. *Journal of Finance* 52(2), 655–681.

Daniel, Kent, David Hirshleifer, and Avanidhar Subrahmanyam. 1998. Investor psychology and security market under- and overreactions. *Journal of Finance* 53(6), 1839–1885.

Harris, Lawrence. 1997. Order exposure and parasitic traders. Working paper, Marshall School of Business, University of Southern California.

Jennings, Robert. 2001. Getting pennied: The effect of decimalization on traders' willingness to lean on the limit order book at the New York Stock Exchange. NYSE Working Paper 2001-01.

Jones, Charles M., and Marc L. Lipson. 2001. Sixteenths: Direct evidence on institutional execution costs. *Journal of Financial Economics* 59(2), 253–278.

Kavajecz, Kenneth A., and Elizabeth R. Odders-White. 2002. Technical analysis and liquidity provision, Working paper, The Wharton School, University of Pennsylvania.

Lo, Andrew W., Harry Mamaysky, and Jiang Wang. 2000. Foundations of technical analysis: Computational algorithms, statistical inference, and empirical implementation. *Journal of Finance* 55(4), 1705–1765.

Schultz, Paul. 2000. Stock splits, tick size, and sponsorship. *Journal of Finance* 55(1), 429–450.

Chapter 12: Bluffers and Market Manipulation

Biais, Bruno, Pierre Hillion, and Chester Spatt. 1999. Price discovery and learning during the preopening period of the Paris Bourse. *Journal of Political Economy* 107(6), 1218–1248.

Jarrow, Robert A. 1992. Market manipulation, bubbles, corners, and short squeezes. *Journal of Financial and Quantitative Analysis* 27(3), 311–336.

Jarrow, Robert A. 1994. Derivative security markets, market manipulation, and option pricing theory. *Journal of Financial and Quantitative Analysis* 29(2), 241–261.

Kumar, Praveen, and Duane J. Seppi. 1992. Futures manipulation with "cash settlement." *Journal of Finance* 47(4), 1485–1502.

Kyle, Albert. 1985. Continuous auctions and insider trading. *Econometrica* 53(6), 1315–1335.

Chapter 13: Dealers

Amihud, Yakov, and Haim Mendelson. 1980. Dealership market: Market making with inventory. *Journal of Financial Economics* 8(1), 31–53.

Amihud, Yakov, and Haim Mendelson. 1989. Liquidity and the cost of capital: Implications for corporate management. *Journal of Applied Corporate Finance* 2(3), 65–73.

Chowdhry, Bhagwan, and Vikram Nanda. 1991. Multimarket trading and market liquidity. *Review of Financial Studies* 4(3), 483–511.

Forster, Margaret M., and Thomas J. George. 1992. Anonymity in securities markets. *Journal of Financial Intermediation* 2(2), 168–206.

Garman, Mark B. 1976. Market microstructure. *Journal of Financial Economics* 3(3), 257–275.

Hansch, Oliver, Narayan Y. Naik, and S. Viswanathan. 1998. Do inventories matter in dealership markets? Evidence from the London Stock Exchange. *Journal of Finance* 53(5), 1623–1656.

Lyons, Richard K. 1997. A simultaneous trade model of the foreign exchange hot potato. *Journal of International Economics* 42(3/4), 275–298.

Madhavan, Ananth, and Seymour Smidt. 1991. A Bayesian model of intraday specialist pricing. *Journal of Financial Economics* 30(1), 99–134.

Madhavan, Ananth, and Seymour Smidt. 1993. An analysis of changes in specialist inventories and quotations. *Journal of Finance* 48(5), 1595–1628.

Manaster, Steven, and Steven C. Mann. 1996. Life in the pits: Competitive market making and inventory control. *Review of Financial Studies* 9(3), 953–975.

Niederhoffer, Victor, and M. F. M. Osborne. 1966. Market making and reversal on the stock exchange. *Journal of the American Statistical Association* 61(316), 897–916.

Sandås, Patrik. 2001. Adverse selection and competitive market making: Empirical evidence from a limit order market. *Review of Financial Studies* 14(3), 705–734.

Silber, William L. 1984. Marketmaker behavior in an auction market: An analysis of scalpers in futures markets. *Journal of Finance* 39(4), 937–953.

Stoll, Hans R. 1976. Dealer inventory behavior: an empirical investigation of NASDAQ stocks. *Journal of Financial and Quantitative Analysis* 11(3), 359–380.

Stoll, Hans R. 1978. The supply of dealer services in securities markets. *Journal of Finance* 33(4), 1133–1151.

Chapter 14: Bid/Ask Spreads

Bagehot, Walter (pseudonym for Jack Treynor). 1971. The only game in town. *Financial Analysts Journal* 27(2), 12–14, 22; reprinted [1995] in *Financial Analysts Journal* 51(1), 81–83.

Benston, George J., and Robert Hagerman. 1974. Determinants of bid-asked spreads in the over-the-counter market. *Journal of Financial Economics* 1(4), 353–364.

Branch, Ben, and Walter Freed. 1977. Bid-asked spreads on the AMEX and the Big Board. *Journal of Finance* 32(1), 159–163.

Cohen, Kalman J., Steven F. Maier, Robert A. Schwartz, and David K. Whitcomb. 1981. Transaction costs, order placement strategy, and existence of bid-ask spread. *Journal of Political Economy* 89(2), 287–305.

Demsetz, Harold. 1968. The cost of transacting. *Quarterly Journal of Economics* 82(1), 33–53.

Dutta, Prajit K., and Ananth Madhavan. 1997. Competition and collusion in dealer markets. *Journal of Finance* 52(1), 245–276.

Glosten, Lawrence R., and Lawrence Harris. 1988. Estimating the components of the bid-ask spread. *Journal of Financial Economics* 14, 123–142.

Glosten, Lawrence R., and Paul Milgrom. 1985. Bid, ask, and transaction prices in a specialist market with heterogeneously informed traders. *Journal of Financial Economics* 14(1), 71–100.

Harris, Lawrence. 1994. Minimum price variations, discrete bid/ask spreads and quotation sizes. *Review of Financial Studies* 7(1), 149–178.

Ho, Thomas S. Y., and Richard G. Macris. 1984. Dealer bid-ask quotes and transaction prices: An empirical study of some AMEX options. *Journal of Finance* 39(1), 23–45.

Ho, Thomas S. Y., and Hans R. Stoll. 1983. The dynamics of dealer markets under competition, *Journal of Finance* 38(4), 1053–1074.

Huang, Roger D., and Hans R. Stoll. 1997. The components of the bid-ask spread: A general approach. *Review of Financial Studies* 10(4), 995–1034.

Neal, Robert, and Simon M. Wheatley. 1998. Adverse selection and bid-ask spreads: Evidence from closed-end funds. *Journal of Financial Markets* 1(1), 121–149.

Stoll, Hans R. 1993. Equity trading costs in-the-large. *Journal of Portfolio Management* 19(4), 41–50.

Subrahmanyam, Avanidhar, and Sheridan Titman. 1999. The going public decision and the development of financial markets. *Journal of Finance* 54(3), 1045–1082.

Tinic, Seha M., and Richard R. West. 1972. Competition and the pricing of dealer service in the over-the-counter stock market. *Journal of Financial and Quantitative Analysis* 7(3), 1707–1727.

Chapter 15: Block Traders

Admati, Anat R., and Paul Pfleiderer. 1991. Sunshine trading and financial market equilibrium. *Review of Financial Studies* 4(3), 443–481.

Angel, James J., Gary L. Gastineau, and Clifford J. Weber. 1997. Reducing the market impact of large stock trades. *Journal of Portfolio Management* 24(1), 69–76.

Barclay, Michael J., and Clifford G. Holderness. 1992. The law and large-block trades. *Journal of Law and Economics* 35(2), 265–294.

Burdett, Ken, and Maureen O'Hara. 1987. Building blocks: An introduction to block trading. *Journal of Banking and Finance* 11(2), 193–212.

Chan, Louis K. C., and Josef Lakonishok. 1993. Institutional trades and intra-day stock price behavior. *Journal of Financial Economics* 33(2), 173–200.

Chan, Louis K. C., and Josef Lakonishok. 1995. The behavior of stock prices around institutional trades. *Journal of Finance* 50(4), 1147–1174.

Easley, David, and Maureen O'Hara. 1987. Price, trade size, and information in securities markets. *Journal of Financial Economics* 19(1), 69–90.

Gemmill, Gordon. 1996. Transparency and liquidity: A study of block trades on the London Stock Exchange under different publication rules. *Journal of Finance* 51(5), 1765–1790.

Grossman, Sanford J. 1992. The informational role of upstairs and downstairs trading. *Journal of Business* 65(4), 509–528.

Holthausen, Robert W., Richard W. Leftwich, and David Mayers. 1987. The effect of large block transactions on security prices: A cross-sectional analysis. *Journal of Financial Economics* 19(2), 237–268.

Holthausen, Robert W., Richard W. Leftwich, and David Mayers. 1990. Large-block transactions, the speed of response, and temporary and permanent stock-price effects. *Journal of Financial Economics* 26(1), 71–96.

Kraus, Alan, and Hans R. Stoll. 1972. Price impacts of block trading on the New York Stock Exchange. *Journal of Finance* 27(3), 569–588.

Madhavan, Ananth, and Mender Cheng. 1997. In search of liquidity: Block trades in the upstairs and downstairs markets. *Review of Financial Studies* 10(1), 175–203.

Saar, Gideon. 2001. Price impact asymmetry of block trades: An institutional trading explanation. *Review of Financial Studies* 14(4), 1153–1182.

Seppi, Duane J. 1990. Equilibrium block trading and asymmetric information. *Journal of Finance* 45(1), 73–94.

Smith, Brian F., D. Alasdair S. Turnbull, and Robert W. White. 2001. Upstairs market for principal and agency trades: Analysis of adverse information and price effects. *Journal of Finance* 56(5), 1723–1746.

Chapter 16: Value Traders

Kagel, John H., and Dan Levin. 1986. The winner's curse and public information in common value auctions. *American Economic Review* 76(5), 894–920.

Thaler, Richard H. 1988. Anomalies: The winner's curse. *Journal of Economic Perspectives* 2(1), 191–202.

Treynor, Jack. 1987. The economics of the dealer function. *Financial Analysts Journal* 43(6), 27–34.

Chapter 17: Arbitrageurs

Brennan, Michael J., and Eduardo S. Schwartz. 1990. Arbitrage in stock index futures. *Journal of Business* 63(1), S7–S32.

Holden, Craig W. 1995. Index arbitrage as cross-sectional market making. *Journal of Futures Markets* 15(4), 423–455.

Shleifer, Andrei, and Robert W. Vishny. 1997. The limits of arbitrage. *Journal of Finance* 52(1), 25–55.

Chapter 18: Buy-side Traders

Bertsimas, Dimitris, and Andrew W. Lo. 1998. Optimal control of execution costs. *Journal of Financial Markets* 1(1), 1–50.

Biais, Bruno, Pierre Hillion, and Chester Spatt. 1995. An empirical analysis of the limit order book and the order flow in the Paris Bourse. *Journal of Finance* 50(5), 1655–1689.

Chakravarty, Sugato, and Craig W. Holden. 1995. An integrated model of market and limit orders. *Journal of Financial Intermediation* 4(3), 213–241.

Handa, Puneet, and Robert A. Schwartz. 1996. Limit order trading. *Journal of Finance* 51(5), 1835–1861.

Harris, Jeffrey H., and Paul H. Schultz. 1998. The trading profits of SOES bandits. *Journal of Financial Economics* 50(1), 39–62.

Harris, Lawrence. 1996. Does a large minimum price variation encourage order display? Working paper, Marshall School of Business, University of Southern California.

Harris, Lawrence. 1998. Optimal dynamic order submission strategies in some stylized trading problems. *Financial Markets, Institutions & Instruments* 7(2), 1–76.

Harris, Lawrence, and Joel Hasbrouck. 1996. Market vs. limit orders: The Superdot evidence on order submission strategy. *Journal of Financial and Quantitative Analysis* 31(2), 213–231.

Keim, Donald B. 1999. An analysis of mutual fund design: The case of investing in small-cap stocks. *Journal of Financial Economics* 51(2), 173–194.

Keim, Donald B., and Ananth Madhavan. 1995. Anatomy of the trading process: Empirical evidence on the motivation for and execution of institutional equity trades. *Journal of Financial Economics* 37(3), 371–398.

Keim, Donald B., and Ananth Madhavan. 1996. The upstairs market for large-block transactions: Analysis and measurement of price effects. *Review of Financial Studies* 9(1), 1–36.

Lo, Andrew W., Craig A. MacKinlay, and June Zhang. 2002. Econometric models of limit-order executions. *Journal of Financial Economics* 65(1).

Chapter 19: Liquidity

Admati, Anat R., and Paul Pfleiderer. 1988. A theory of intraday trading patterns. *Review of Financial Studies* 1(1), 3–40.

Black, Fischer. 1995. Equilibrium exchanges. *Financial Analysts Journal* 51(3), 23–29.

Bloomfield, Robert, and Maureen O'Hara. 1999. Market transparency: Who wins and who loses? *Review of Financial Studies* 2(1), 5–35.

Bloomfield, Robert, and Maureen O'Hara. 2000. Can transparent markets survive? *Journal of Financial Economics* 55(3), 425–459.

Board, John, and Charles Sutcliffe. 2000. The proof of the pudding: The effects of increased trade transparency in the London Stock Exchange. *Journal of Business Finance and Accounting* 27(7/8), 887–909.

Chordia, Tarun, Richard Roll, and Avanidhar Subrahmanyam. 2000. Commonality in liquidity. *Journal of Financial Economics* 56(1), 3–28.

Chordia, Tarun, Richard Roll, and Avandihar Subrahmanyam. 2001. Market liquidity and trading activity. *Journal of Finance* 56(2), 501–503.

Harris, Lawrence. 1990. Liquidity, trading rules and electronic trading systems. *New York University Salomon Center Monograph Series in Finance and Economics* 1990–4.

Hasbrouck, Joel, and Duane J. Seppi. 2001. Common factors in prices, order flow and liquidity. *Journal of Financial Economics* 59(3), 383–411.

Lamoureux, Christopher G., and Charles R. Schnitzlein. 1997. When it's not the only game in town: The effect of bilateral search on the quality of a dealer market. *Journal of Finance* 52(2), 683–712.

Pagano, Marco, and Ailsa Röell. 1996. Transparency and liquidity: A comparison of auction and dealer markets with informed trading. *Journal of Finance* 51(2), 579–611.

Chapter 20: Volatility

Anderson, Torben G., Tim Bollerslev, Francis X. Diebold, and Heiko Ebens. 2001. The distribution of stock return volatility. *Journal of Financial Economics* 61(1), 43–76.

Barclay, Michael J., Robert H. Litzenberger, and Jerold B. Warner. 1990. Private information, trading volume, and stock-return variances. *Review of Financial Studies* 3(2), 233–254.

Barclay, Michael J., and Jerold B. Warner. 1993. Stealth trading and volatility: Which trades move prices? *Journal of Financial Economics* 34(3), 281–306.

Brown, Gregory W., and Jay C. Hartzell. 2001. Market reaction to public information: The atypical case of the Boston Celtics. *Journal of Financial Economics* 60(2–3), 333–370.

French, Kenneth R., and Richard Roll. 1986. Stock return variances: The arrival of information and the reaction of traders. *Journal of Financial Economics* 17(1), 5–26.

Kawai, Masahiro. 1983. Spot and futures prices of nonstorable commodities under rational expectations. *Quarterly Journal of Economics* 98(2), 235–254.

Roll, Richard. 1984. Orange juice and weather. *American Economic Review* 74(5), 861–880.

Schwert, William G. 1989. Why does stock market volatility change over time? *Journal of Finance* 44(5), 1115–1154.

Schwert, William G., and Paul J. Seguin. 1990. Heteroskedasticity in stock returns. *Journal of Finance* 45(4), 1129–1155.

Chapter 21: Liquidity and Transaction Cost Measurement

Beebower, Gilbert. 1989. Evaluating transaction cost. In Wayne Wagner, ed., *The Complete Guide to Securities Transactions* (John Wiley & Sons, New York).

Berkowitz, Stephen A., Dennis E. Logue, and Eugene A. Noser, Jr. 1988. The total cost of transactions on the NYSE. *Journal of Finance* 41(1), 97–112.

Choi, J. Y., Dan Salandro, and Kuldeep Shastri. 1988. On the estimation of bid-ask spreads: Theory and evidence. *Journal of Financial and Quantitative Analysis* 23(2), 219–230.

George, Thomas J., Gautam Kaul, and M. Nimalendran. 1991. Estimation of the bid-ask spread and its components: A new approach. *Review of Financial Studies* 4(4), 623–656.

George, Thomas J., Gautam Kaul, and M. Nimalendran. 1994. Trading volume and transaction costs in specialist markets. *Journal of Finance* 49(4), 1489–1505.

Glosten, Lawrence R. 1987. Components of the bid/ask spread and the statistical properties of transaction prices. *Journal of Finance* 42(5), 1293–1308.

Harris, Lawrence. 1990. Statistical properties of the roll serial covariance bid/ask spread estimator. *Journal of Finance* 45(2), 579–590.

Huang, Roger D., and Hans R. Stoll. 1997. The components of the bid-ask spread: A general approach. *Review of Financial Studies* 10(4), 995–1034.

Keim, Donald B., and Ananth Madhavan. 1997. Transactions costs and investment style: An interexchange analysis of institutional equity trades. *Journal of Financial Economics* 46(3), 265–292.

Keim, Donald B., and Ananth Madhavan. 1998. The cost of institutional equity trades. *Financial Analysts Journal* 54(4), 50–69.

Lee, Charles M. C., and Mark A. Ready. 1991. Inferring trade direction from intraday data. *Journal of Finance* 46(2), 733–746.

Loeb, Thomas F. 1983. Trading cost: The critical link between investment information and results. *Financial Analysts Journal* 39(3), 39–44.

Perold, André. 1988. The implementation shortfall: Paper versus reality. *Journal of Portfolio Management* 14(3), 4–9.

Roll, Richard. 1984. A simple implicit measure of the effective bid-ask spread. *Journal of Finance* 39(4), 1127–1139.

Schultz, Paul. 2001. Corporate bond trading costs: A peek behind the curtain. *Journal of Finance* 56(2), 677–698.

Stoll, Hans R. 1989. Inferring the components of the bid-ask spread: Theory and empirical tests. *Journal of Finance* 44(1), 115–134.

Wagner, Wayne H., and Mark Edwards. 1993. Best execution. *Financial Analysts Journal* 49(1), 65–71.

Chapter 22: Performance Evaluation and Prediction

Ashton, D. J. 1996. The power of tests of fund manager performance. *Journal of Business Finance and Accounting* 23(1), 1–11.

Barber, Brad M., and John D. Lyon. 1997. Detecting long-run abnormal stock returns: The empirical power and specification of test statistics. *Journal of Financial Economics* 43(3), 341–372.

Barber, Brad M., and Terrance Odean. 2000. Too many cooks spoil the profits: Investment club performance. *Financial Analysts Journal* 56(1), 17–25.

Bauman, W. Scott, and Robert E. Miller. 1994. Can managed portfolio performance be predicted? *Journal of Portfolio Management* 20(4), 31–40.

Bierman, Harold, Jr., Lawrence E. Fouraker, and Robert K. Jaedicke. 1961. The use of probability and statistics in performance evaluation. *Accounting Review* 36(3), 409–417.

Brinson, Gary P., L. Randolph Hood, and Gilbert L. Beebower. 1986. Determinants of portfolio performance. *Financial Analysts Journal* 42(4), 39–44.

Brinson, Gary P., Brian D. Singer, and Gilbert L. Beebower. 1991. Determinants of portfolio performance II: An update. *Financial Analysts Journal* 47(3), 40–48.

Brown, Stephen J., William Goetzmann, Roger G. Ibbotson, and Stephen A. Ross. 1992. Survivorship bias in performance studies. *Review of Financial Studies* 5(4), 553–580.

Chen, Zhiwu, and Peter J. Knez. 1996. Portfolio performance measurement: Theory and applications. *Review of Financial Studies* 9(2), 511–555.

Ellis, Charles D. 1975. The loser's game. *Financial Analysts Journal* 31(4), 19–20, 22, 24, 26; reprinted in *Financial Analysts Journal* 51(1), 95–100.

Elton, Edwin J., Martin J. Gruber, and Christopher R. Blake. 1996. Survivorship bias and mutual fund performance. *Review of Financial Studies* 9(4), 1097–1120.

Elton, Edwin J., Martin J. Gruber, and Joel C. Rentzler. 1987. Professionally managed, publicly traded commodity funds. *Journal of Business* 60(2), 175–200.

Elton, Edwin J., Martin J. Gruber, and Joel Rentzler. 1989. New public offerings, information, and investor rationality: The case of publicly offered commodity funds. *Journal of Business* 62(1), 1–16.

French, Dan W., and Glenn V. Henderson, Jr. 1985. How well does performance evaluation perform? *Journal of Portfolio Management* 11(2), 15–18.

Fung, William, and David A. Hsieh. 1997. Survivorship bias investment style in the returns of CTAs. *Journal of Portfolio Management* 24(1), 30–41.

Garcia, C. B., and F. J. Gould. 1993. Survivorship bias. *Journal of Portfolio Management* 19(3), 52–56.

Grinblatt, Mark, and Sheridan Titman. 1989. Portfolio performance evaluation: Old issues and new insights. *Review of Financial Studies* 2(3), 393–422.

Hau, Harald. 2001. Location matters: An examination of trading profits. *Jouranl of Finance* 56(5), 1959–1983.

Murphy, J. Michael. 1980. Why no one can tell who's winning. *Financial Analysts Journal* 36(3), 49–57.

Chapter 23: Index and Portfolio Markets

Atchison, Michael D., Kirt C. Butler, and Richard R. Simonds. 1987. Nonsynchronous security trading and market index autocorrelation. *Journal of Finance* 42(1), 111–118.

Cohen, Kalman J., Steven F. Maier, Robert A. Schwartz, and David K. Whitcomb. 1979. On the existence of serial correlation in an efficient securities market. *TIMS Studies in the Management Sciences* 11(1), 151–168.

Gastineau, Gary L. 2002. *The Exchange-Traded Funds Manual* (John Wiley & Sons, New York).

Harris, Lawrence. 1989. The October 1987 S&P 500 stock-futures basis. *Journal of Finance* 44(1), 77–100.

Harris, Lawrence. 1990. The economics of cash index alternatives. *Journal of Futures Markets* 10(2), 179–194.

Harris, Lawrence, and Eitan Gurel. 1986. Price and volume effects associated with changes in the S&P 500 List: New evidence for the existence of price pressures. *Journal of Finance* 41(4), 815–829.

Harris, Lawrence, George Sofianos, and Jim Shapiro. 1994. Program trading and intraday volatility. *Review of Financial Studies* 7(4), 654–686.

Kawaller, Ira G., Paul D. Koch, and Timothy W. Koch. 1987. The temporal price relationship between S&P 500 futures and the S&P 500 Index. *Journal of Finance* 42(5), 1309–1329.

MacKinlay, Craig A., and Krishna Ramaswamy. 1988. Index-futures arbitrage and the behavior of stock index futures prices. *Review of Financial Studies* 1(2), 137–158.

Renshaw, Edward F., and Paul J. Feldstein. 1960. The case for an unmanaged investment company. *Financial Analysts Journal* 16(1), 43–46; reprinted [1995] in *Financial Analysts Journal* 51(1), 59–62.

Stoll, Hans R. 1988. Portfolio trading. *Journal of Portfolio Management* 14(4), 20–24.

Stoll, Hans R., and Robert E. Whaley. 1988a. Futures and options on stock indexes: Economic purpose, arbitrage, and market structure. *Review of Futures Markets* 7(2), 224–249.

Stoll, Hans R., and Robert E. Whaley. 1988b. Volatility and futures: Message versus messenger. *Journal of Portfolio Management* 14(2), 20–22.

Subrahmanyam, Avanidhar. 1991. A theory of trading in stock index futures. *Review of Financial Studies* 4(1), 17–51.

Treynor, Jack L. 1994. The invisible costs of trading. *Journal of Portfolio Management* 21(1), 71–78.

Wagner, Wayne, and Al Winnikoff. 2001. *Millionaire: The Best Explanation of How an Index Fund Can Turn Your Lunch Money into a Fortune* (Renaissance Books, Los Angeles).

Chapter 24: Specialists

Bacidore, Jeffrey M., and George Sofianos. 2002. Liquidity provision and specialist trading in NYSE-listed non-U.S. stocks. *Journal of Financial Economics* 63(1), 133–158.

Conroy, Robert M., and Robert L. Winkler. 1986. Market structure: The specialist as dealer and broker. *Journal of Banking and Finance* 10(1), 21–36.

Edwards, Amy K. 1999. NYSE specialists competing with limit orders: A source of price improvement. Working paper, U.S. Securities and Exchange Commission.

Glosten, Lawrence R. 1989. Insider trading, liquidity, and the role of the monopolist specialist. *Journal of Business* 62(2), 211–236.

Goldman, M. Barry, and Avraham Beja. 1979. Market prices vs. equilibrium prices: Returns' variance, serial correlation, and the role of the specialist. *Journal of Finance* 34(3), 595–607.

Goldstein, Michael A., and Kenneth A. Kavajecz. 2000. Eighths, sixteenths, and market depth: Changes in tick size and liquidity provision on the NYSE. *Journal of Financial Economics* 56(1), 125–149.

Hakansson, Nils H., Avraham Beja, and Jivendra Kale. 1985. On the feasibility of automated market making by a programmed specialist. *Journal of Finance* 40(1), 1–20.

Harris, Lawrence, and Venkatesh Panchapagesan. 2002. The information content of the limit order book: Evidence from NYSE specialist trading decisions, Working paper, Washington University, St. Louis, MO.

Hasbrouck, Joel, and George Sofianos. 1993. The trades of market makers: An empirical analysis of NYSE specialists. *Journal of Finance* 48(5), 1565–1594.

Kavajecz, Kenneth A. 1999. A specialist's quoted depth and the limit order book. *Journal of Finance* 54(2), 747–771.

Kavajecz, Kenneth A., and Elizabeth Odders-White. 2001. An examination of changes in specialists' posted price schedules. *Review of Financial Studies* 14, 681–704.

Madhavan, Ananth, and George Sofianos. 1998. An empirical analysis of NYSE specialist trading. *Journal of Financial Economics* 48(2), 189–210.

McInish, Thomas H., and Robert A. Wood. 1995. Hidden limit orders on the NYSE. *Journal of Portfolio Management* 21(3), 19–26.

Ready, Mark. 1999. The specialist's discretion: Stopped orders and price improvement. *Review of Financial Studies* 12(5), 1075–1112.

Seppi, Duane J. 1997. Liquidity provision with limit orders and a strategic specialist. *Review of Financial Studies* 10(1), 103–150.

Sofianos, George. 1995. Specialist gross trading revenues at the New York Stock Exchange. Working paper, New York Stock Exchange.

Stoll, Hans R. 1985. The stock exchange specialist system: An economic analysis. *New York University Salomon Center Monograph Series in Finance and Economics* 2.

Chapter 25: Internalization, Preferencing, and Crossing

Battalio, Robert H. 1997. Third market broker-dealers: Cost competitors or cream skimmers? *Journal of Finance* 52(1), 241–252.

Battalio, Robert, and Craig W. Holden. 2001. A simple model of payment for order flow, internalization, and total trading cost. *Journal of Financial Markets* 4(1), 33–71.

Bloomfield, Robert, and Maureen O'Hara. 1998. Does order preferencing matter? *Journal of Financial Economics* 50(1), 3–37.

Chordia, Tarun, and Avanidhar Subrahmanyam. 1995. Market making, the tick size, and payment-for-order flow: Theory and evidence. *Journal of Business* 68(4), 543–575.

Easley, David, Nicholas M. Kiefer, and Maureen O'Hara. 1996. Cream-skimming or profit sharing? The curious role of purchased order flow. *Journal of Finance* 51(3), 811–833.

Hansch, Oliver, Narayan Y. Naik, and S. Viswanathan. 1999. Preferencing, internalization, best execution, and dealer profits. *Journal of Finance* 54(5), 1799–1828.

Harris, Lawrence. 1996. The economics of best execution. Working Paper, Marshall School of Business, University of Southern California.

Kandel, Eugene, and Leslie M. Marx. 1999. Odd-eighth avoidance as a defense against SOES bandits. *Journal of Financial Economics* 51(1), 85–102.

Macy, Jonathan R., and Maureen O'Hara. 1997. The law and economics of best execution. *Journal of Financial Intermediation* 6(3), 188–223.

Securities and Exchange Commission, Division of Market Regulation. 1994. *Market 2000: An Examination of Current Equity Market Developments* (U.S. Government Printing Office, Washington D.C.).

Chapter 26: Competition Within and Among Markets

Biais, Bruno. 1993. Price formation and equilibrium liquidity in fragmented and centralized markets. *Journal of Finance* 48(1), 157–184.

Black, Fischer. 1971. Toward a fully automated exchange. *Financial Analysts Journal* 27(4), 28–35, 44.

Cohen, Kalman J., Steven F. Maier, Robert A. Schwartz, and David K. Whitcomb. 1982. An analysis of the economic justification for consolidation in a secondary security market. *Journal of Banking and Finance* 6(1), 117–136.

Domowitz, Ian. 1995. Electronic derivatives exchanges: Implicit mergers, network externalities, and standardization. *Quarterly Review of Economics and Finance* 35(2), 163–175.

Fabozzi, Frank J., and Christopher K. Ma. 1988. The over-the-counter market and New York Stock Exchange trading halts. *Financial Review* 23(4), 427–438.

Foerster, Stephen, and Andrew G. Karolyi. 1998. Multimarket trading and liquidity: A transaction data analysis of Canada-US interlistings. *Journal of International Financial Markets, Institutions and Money* 8(3–4), 393–412.

Garbade, Kenneth D., and William Silber. 1979. Dominant and satellite markets: A study of dually-traded securities. *Review of Economics and Statistics* 61(3), 455–460.

Hamilton, James L. 1987. Off-board trading of NYSE-listed stocks: The effects of deregulation and the national market system. *Journal of Finance* 42(5), 1331–1345.

Harris, Lawrence. 1993. Consolidation, fragmentation, segmentation and regulation. *Financial Markets, Institutions & Instruments* 2(5), 1–28; reprinted in Robert A. Schwartz, ed., *Global Equity Markets: Technological, Competitive and Regulatory Challenges* (Irwin, Chicago).

Hasbrouck, Joel. 1995. One security, many markets: Determining the contributions to price discovery. *Journal of Finance* 50(4), 1175–1199.

Hendershott, Terrence, and Haim Mendelson. 2000. Crossing networks and dealer markets: Competition and performance. *Journal of Finance* 55(5), 2071–2115.

Lee, Charles M. C. 1993. Market integration and price execution for NYSE-listed securities. *Journal of Finance* 48(3), 1009–1038.

Madhavan, Ananth. 1995. Consolidation, fragmentation, and the disclosure of trading information. *Review of Financial Studies* 8(3), 579–603.

Mendelson, Haim. 1987. Consolidation, fragmentation, and market performance. *Journal of Financial and Quantitative Analysis* 22(2), 189–208.

Miller, Merton H., and Charles W. Upton. 1991. Strategies for capital market structure and regulation. In Alexander Miller, ed., *Financial Innovations and Market Volatility* (Blackwell, Malden, MA).

Chapter 27: Floor Versus Automated Trading Systems

Benveniste, Lawrence M., Alan J. Marcus, and William J. Wilhelm. 1992. What's special about the specialist? *Journal of Financial Economics* 32(1), 61–86.

Glosten, Lawrence R. 1994. Is the electronic open limit order book inevitable? *Journal of Finance* 49(4), 1127–1161.

Mendelson, Morris, and Junius W. Peake. 1979. Which way to a national market system? *Financial Analysts Journal* 35(5), 31–34, 37–42.

Mendelson, Morris, Junius W. Peake, and R. T. Williams. 1979. Toward a modern exchange: The Peake-Mendelson-Williams proposal for an electronically assisted auction market. In Ernest Block and Robert A. Schwartz, eds., *Impending Changes for Securities Markets: What Role for the Exchanges?* (JAI Press, Greenwich, CT).

Peake, Junius W. 1978. The national market system. *Financial Analysts Journal* 34(4), 25–33, 81–84.

Venkataraman, Kumar. 2001. Automated versus floor trading: An analysis of execution costs on the Paris and New York exchanges. *Journal of Finance* 56(4), 1445–1485.

Chapter 28: Bubbles, Crashes, and Circuit Breakers

Brennan, Michael J. 1986. A theory of price limits in futures markets. *Journal of Financial Economics* 16(2), 213–233.

Chance, Don M. 1993. Is federal regulation of stock index futures margins necessary? *Journal of Financial Engineering* 2(1), 1–14.

Coursey, Don L., and Edward A. Dyl. 1990. Price limits, trading suspensions, and the adjustment of prices to new information. *Review of Futures Markets* 9(2), 342–360.

Figlewski, Stephen. 1984. Margins and market integrity: Margin setting for stock index futures and options. *Journal of Futures Markets* 4(3), 385–416.

Friedman, Milton, and Anna Jacobson Schwartz. 1963. *A Monetary History of the United States, 1867–1960* (Princeton University Press, Princeton, NJ).

Greenwald, Bruce C., and Jeremy C. Stein. 1991. Transactional risk, market crashes, and the role of circuit breakers. *Journal of Business* 64(4), 443–462.

Grossman, Sanford. 1988. An analysis of the implications for stock and futures price volatility of program trading and dynamic hedging strategies. *Journal of Business* 51(3), 275–298.

Grundfest, Joseph A., and John B. Shoven. 1991. Adverse implications of a securities transactions excise tax. *Journal of Accounting, Auditing and Finance* 6(4), 409–442.

Hakansson, Nils H. 1978. Welfare aspects of options and supershares. *Journal of Finance* 33(3), 759–776.

Harris, Lawrence. 1989. The dangers of regulatory overreaction to the October 1987 stock market crash. *Cornell Law Review* 74(5), 927–942.

Harris, Lawrence. 1998. Circuit breakers and program trading limits: What have we learned? In R. E. Litan and A. M. Santomero, eds., *Brooking-Wharton Papers on Financial Services* (Brookings Institution, Washington DC).

Hsieh, David A., and Merton H. Miller. 1990. Margin regulation and stock market volatility. *Journal of Finance* 45(1), 3–30.

Katzenbach, Nicholas. 1987. An overview of program trading and its impact on current market practices. NYSE Report, December 21.

Kindleberger, Charles P. 2001. Manias, Panics, and Crashes: A History of Financial Crises, 4th ed. (Wiley Investment Classics, New York.

Kleidon, Allan W. 1992. Arbitrage, nontrading, and stale prices: October 1987. *Journal of Business* 65(4), 483–508.

Kodres, Laura E., and Daniel P. O'Brien. 1994. The existence of Pareto-superior price limits. *American Economic Review* 84(4), 919–932.

Kyle, Albert S. 1988. Trading halts and price limits. *Review of Futures Markets* 7(3), 426–434.

Lee, Charles M. C., Mark J. Ready, and Paul J. Seguin. 1994. Volume, volatility, and New York Stock Exchange trading halts. *Journal of Finance* 49(1), 183–214.

Leland, Hayne E. 1980. Who should buy portfolio insurance. *Journal of Finance* 35(2), 581–594.

New York Stock Exchange, Office of Research and Planning. 1991. The Rule 80A index arbitrage tick test. Report to the U.S. Securities and Exchange Commission, May 31.

Roll, Richard. 1988. The international crash of October 1987. *Financial Analysts Journal* 44(5), 19–35.

Rubinstein, Mark. 1985. Alternative paths to portfolio insurance. *Financial Analysts Journal* 41(4), 42–52.

Rubinstein, Mark, and Hayne Leland. 1981. Replicating options with positions in stock and cash. *Financial Analysts Journal* 37(4), 63–72.

Santoni, Gary J., and Tung Liu. 1993. Circuit breakers and stock market volatility. *Journal of Futures Markets* 13(3), 261–278.

Schwert, William G. 1989. Margin requirements and stock volatility. *Journal of Financial Services Research* 3(2/3), 153–164.

Schwert, William G., and Paul Seguin. 1993. Securities transactions taxes: An overview of costs, benefits and unresolved questions. *Financial Analysts Journal* 49(5), 27–35.

Stiglitz, Joseph E. 1989. Using tax policy to curb speculative short-term trading. *Journal of Financial Services Research* 3(2/3), 101–115.

Subrahmanyam, Avanidhar. 1994. Circuit breakers and market volatility: A theoretical perspective. *Journal of Finance* 49(1), 237–254.

Subrahmanyam, Avanidhar. 1995. On rules versus discretion in procedures to halt trade. *Journal of Economics and Business* 47(1), 1–16.

Subrahmanyam, Avanidhar. 1997. The ex ante effects of trading halting rules on informed trading strategies and market liquidity. *Review of Financial Economics* 6(1), 1–14.

Subrahmanyam, Avanidhar. 1998. Transaction taxes and financial market equilibrium. *Journal of Business* 71(1), 81–118.

Summers, Lawrence H., and Victoria P. Summers. 1989. When financial markets work too well: A cautious case for a securities transactions tax. *Journal of Financial Services Research* 3(2/3), 261–286.

Treynor, Jack L. 1988. Portfolio insurance and market volatility. *Financial Analysts Journal* 44(6), 71–73.

Treynor, Jack. 1998. Bulls, bears, and market bubbles. *Financial Analysts Journal* 54(2), 69–74.

U.S. Securities and Exchange Commission. 1988. *The October 1987 Market Break: A Report by the Division of Market Regulation, U.S. Securities and Exchange Commission* (U.S. Government Printing Office, Washington DC).

Warshawsky, Mark. 1989. The adequacy and consistency of margin requirements: The cash, futures, and options segments of the equity market. *Review of Futures Markets* 8(3), 420–437.

Chapter 29: Insider Trading

Arshadi, Nasser, and Thomas H. Eyssell. 1993. *The Law and Finance of Corporate Insider Trading: Theory and Evidence* (Kluwer Academic Publishers, Boston).

Cornell, Bradford, and Erik R. Sirri. 1992. The reaction of investors and stock prices to insider trading. *Journal of Finance* 47(3), 1031–1060.

DeMarzo, Peter M., Michael J. Fishman, and Kathleen M. Hagerty. 1998. The optimal enforcement of insider trading regulations. *Journal of Political Economy* 106(3), 602–632.

Hagerman, Robert L., and Joanne P. Healy. 1992. The impact of SEC-required disclosure and insider-trading regulations on the bid/ask spreads in the over-the-counter market. *Journal of Accounting and Public Policy* 11(3), 233–243.

Holden, Craig, and Avanidhar Subrahmanyam. 1992. Long-lived private information and imperfect competition. *Journal of Finance* 47(1), 247–270.

Hu, Jie, and Thomas H. Noel. 1997. The insider trading debate. *Federal Reserve Bank of Atlanta Economic Review* 1997(4), 34–45.

Manne, Henry G. 1966a. In defense of insider trading. *Harvard Business Review* 44(6), 113–122.

Manne, Henry G. 1966b. *Insider Trading and the Stock Market* (The Free Press, New York).

Meulbroek, Lisa. 1992. An empirical analysis of illegal insider trading. *Journal of Finance* 47(5), 1661–1700.

Spiegel, Matthew, and Avanidhar Subrahmanyam. 1992. Informed speculation and hedging in a noncompetitive securities market. *Review of Financial Studies* 5(2), 307–330.

Index

Italic page numbers indicate defined terms